Influence of National Culture on IFRS Practice

Münsteraner Schriften zur Internationalen Unternehmensrechnung

Herausgegeben von Peter Kajüter

Band 4

PETER LANG
Frankfurt am Main · Berlin · Bern · Bruxelles · New York · Oxford · Wien

Christian Reisloh

Influence of National Culture on IFRS Practice

An Empirical Study in France, Germany and the United Kingdom

PETER LANG
Internationaler Verlag der Wissenschaften

Bibliographic Information published by the Deutsche Nationalbibliothek
The Deutsche Nationalbibliothek lists this publication in the Deutsche Nationalbibliografie; detailed bibliographic data is available in the internet at http://dnb.d-nb.de.

Zugl.: Münster (Westfalen), Univ., Diss., 2011

D 6
ISSN 1868-7687
ISBN 978-3-631-62052-6

www.peterlang.de

Preface

The adoption of IFRS by the EU in 2005 was an important milestone in the creation of a single capital market in the EU. The IAS regulation required more than 7,000 capital market oriented companies in the EU to prepare their consolidated accounts according to IFRS. On a global level, only a few countries do not require respectively permit the application of IFRS for group accounting. Important capital markets like the US seek convergence with IFRS. Hence, IFRS developed to be the world accounting standard.

The appearance of international accounting harmonization, however, is deceiving. Standardized accounting rules do not imply standardized accounting practice. The same influence factors (e.g. national culture, legal system, tax system) that resulted in the development of different national accounting systems might have an impact on the application of IFRS and, thus, lead to deviating international IFRS practices. The problem of national IFRS practice patterns is further intensified by national enforcement institutions which cannot assure an internationally consistent application of IFRS.

Though being of high practical relevance, the impact of national culture on IFRS practice is largely unexplored. This research gap is addressed by the work of Christian Reisloh. Based on a theory guided conceptual framework he analyzes the association between national culture and IFRS measurement and disclosure practice. Following a content analytical approach the author evaluates 2009 financial statements of 261 French, German and British companies. His study concentrates on the three largest EU capital markets as the sociopolitical context of the EU offers a unique research environment. EU listed companies are required to apply the same set of IFRS as endorsed by the EU. At the same time the EU hosts a great variety of different national cultures that might influence IFRS practice. To investigate the link between culture and IFRS accounting, Christian Reisloh develops various measurement indicators to determine the company's individual degree of measurement conservatism. Disclosure indices on notes subsections like segment reporting are applied to measure the company's individual degree of transparency.

The author describes and analyzes IFRS measurement and disclosure practices from various perspectives. He shows that IFRS measurement practices like the depreciation of plant and machinery or the recognition of intangibles in a purchase price allocation are seldom affected by the national cultural profile of the country. Significant measurement differences are rather attributable to the industry of the company or the degree of internationality. In contrast, differences in IFRS disclosure practice are closely linked to national cultural differences. Additionally, company size is supposed to be of importance when predicting disclosure quantity.

The empirical results of the study contribute greatly to both accounting theory and practice. The field of international comparative accounting research is enriched by innovative IFRS measurement and disclosure indicators. Limitations of prior studies are addressed both conceptually and methodologically. The findings of this study are of high relevance for IFRS interest groups like users of IFRS financial statements, standard setters, regulators or enforcement bodies.

Considering the valuable academic contribution and practical relevance of Christian Reisloh's work, I am sure his thesis will enjoy great popularity among academics and practitioners.

Münster, June 2011 Prof. Dr. Peter Kajüter

Foreword

This study was conducted during my time as a PhD student at the Chair of International Accounting at the University of Münster. The thesis was accepted as a dissertation by the Münster School of Business and Economics in May 2011.

In this foreword I want to thank everyone who supported me in the process of writing this thesis. First of all I would like to thank my supervisor Prof. Dr. Peter Kajüter who accepted me as a PhD student and who enriched my work during the last four years by numerous fruitful discussions and helpful suggestions. He greatly contributed to the success of this study and I deeply appreciate the amount of time and energy he invested in my work. I would also like to thank Prof. Dr. Christoph Watrin who reviewed and evaluated my study as a second referee. My sincere thanks are further given to Prof. Dr. Ulrich van Suntum for being the third referee at my disputation.

I would like to thank Prof. Dr. Stephen A. Zeff for instructive and inspiring discussions at the 2008 EAA Annual Congress in Rotterdam. I received great motivation for my research project from this encounter. I also would like to thank Prof. Dr. Christopher W. Nobes who provided me with a working paper on the determinants of international IFRS practice in the early stages of my work which gave me inspiration and motivation.

My thesis would not have come to a successful end without the support of my dear colleagues and friends at the Chair of International Accounting. They made my time at the chair really worthwhile and with great pleasure I remember the common sailing course, the barbecues at the lake, the encounters at different gastronomic and party locations in Münster, the doctoral seminars, the sailing seminar, the "Jour Fixe" which never was on a fixed day, the Wiwi-Cup, various chair excursions and, of course, the common cooking sessions. Specifically, I would like to thank Daniel Blaesing for discussing and reviewing my work. His constant optimism and humor contributed greatly to the success of my research project. I further would like to thank Matthias Moeschler, who was always available to discuss matters of my research and who supposedly was the only one who seriously read the handouts prior to doctoral seminars. I also would like to thank Kristian Bachert who helped me with statistics and who was my dear co-organizer of two successful sailing seminars. Moreover, I would like to thank Martin Merschdorf who was my contact person for all requests concerning formatting. My sincere thanks are further given to Marcel Baki, who took responsibility for all my IT problems during my time at the chair. Furthermore, I would like to thank Christina Voets for reviewing my study and for being the heart and soul of the chair-team. I also would like to thank Max Saucke for a review of my work. Charlotte Kaiser, Moritz Schröder and Thomas Poplat I would like to thank for moral support and distracting squash sessions during the final stage of my project.

I am grateful to my former colleagues Daniela Barth, Simon Esser and Tobias Dickmann whose helpful comments on my work and the research process in general I always appreciated. Furthermore, I want to give my special thanks to Sonja Heinrich and Leila Prousch who helped with all the administrative barriers associated with the chair work and the PhD program. Last but not least I would like to thank our student research assistants who supported me in literature research and data evaluation.

I owe my deepest gratitude to my girlfriend Kathrin Brost. Her love, understanding and patience helped me through the difficult times of my research project. The fact that we met during my PhD program outweighs the academic achievement of that time by far and with great anticipation I look forward to our common times.

This thesis would not have been possible without my beloved family. Most importantly I would like to thank my parents Susanne and Rainer Reisloh. Their loving support accompanied me during all of my life and they provided me with the freedom to make my own decisions. They always showed great enthusiasm and interest for my projects and I am deeply grateful for their permanent encouragement. To them I dedicate this thesis.

Münster, June 2011 Christian Reisloh

Contents summary

Contents

Index of figures

Index of tables

Index of abbreviations

AA	Allowed Alternative
AACF	Asymmetric Accruals to Cash Flow
AASB	Australian Accounting Standards Board
ADHGB	Allgemeines Deutsches Handelsgesetzbuch
AICPA	American Institute of Certified Public Accountants
AIM	Alternative Investment Market
AISG	Accountant's International Study Group
AktG	Aktiengesetz
Amend.	Amended
ANC	Autorité des Normes Comptables
ANOVA	Analysis of Variance
ARC	Accounting Regulatory Committee
ASB	Accounting Standards Board
ASC	Accounting Standards Committee
ASSC	Accounting Standards Steering Committee
ASCG	Accounting Standards Committee of Germany
AT	Asymmetric Timeliness of Earnings
BaFin	Bundesanstalt für Finanzdienstleistungsaufsicht
B.C.	Before Christ
BFH	Bundesfinanzhof
BGBl.	Bundesgesetzblatt
BilKoG	Bilanzkontrollgesetz
BilMoG	Bilanzrechtsmodernisierungsgesetz
BilReG	Bilanzrechtsreformgesetz
BIS	Department for Business Innovation & Skills
BMJ	Bundesjustizministerium
BT	Benchmark Treatment
BUSINESSEUROPE	European Business Federations
CAC	Cotation Assistée en Continu
CAPM	Capital Asset Pricing Model
CC	Code de Commerce
CCAB	Consultative Committee of Accountancy Bodies
CCAD	Contact Committee on Accounting Directives
CEA	European Insurance and Reinsurance Federation
CESR	Committee of European Securities Regulators
Cf.	Confer
CGU	Cash Generating Unit

CH	Companies House
CNC	Conseil National de la Comptabilité
CNCC	Compagnie Nationale des Commissaires aux Comptes
COB	Commission des Opérations de Bourse
CODM	Chief Operating Decision Maker
CPA	Certified Public Accountant
CRC	Comité de la Réglementation Comptable
DAX	Deutscher Aktienindex
DPR	Deutsche Prüfstelle für Rechnungslegung
DRS	Deutsche Rechnungslegungs Standards
DRSC	Deutsches Rechnungslegungs Standards Committee
DSR	Deutscher Standardisierungsrat
DStR	Deutsches Steuerrecht
EACB	European Association of Co-operative Banks
EADS	European Aeronautic Defence and Space Company
EBF	European Banking Federation
EBIT	Earnings before interests and taxes
EC	European Commission
Ed.	Editor
EDGAR	Electronic Data Gathering, Analysis and Retrieval system
Eds.	Editors
EEA	European Economic Area
EECS	European Enforcers Coordination Session(s)
EFAA	European Federation of Accountants and Auditors
EFRAG	European Financial Reporting Advisory Group
EFTA	European Free Trade Association
E.g.	Exempli Gratia
EMH	Efficient Market Hypothesis
EP	European Parliament
ESBG	European Savings Banks Group
ESMA	European Securities and Markets Authority
EStG	Einkommensteuergesetz
Et al.	Et alii
Etc.	Et cetera
EU	European Union
EUAAF	EU Accounting Advisory Forum
FASB	Financial Accounting Standards Board
FEE	Fédération des Experts Comptables Européens

FIFO	First-in, first-out
FRC	Financial Reporting Council
FREP	Financial Reporting Review Panel
FRRP	Financial Reporting Review Panel
FTSE	Financial Times Stock Exchange
GAAP	Generally Accepted Accounting Principles
GAS	German Accounting Standards
GASB	German Accounting Standards Board
GBP	British Pound Sterling
GDP	Gross Domestic Product
GLOBE	Global Leadership and Organizational Behavior Effectiveness
GoB	Grundsätze ordnungsmäßiger Buchführung
HGB	Handelsgesetzbuch
HMRC	Her Majesty's Revenue and Customs
HR	Hidden Reserves
IAS	International Accounting Standard(s)
IASB	International Accounting Standards Board
IASC	International Accounting Standards Committee
IASCF	International Accounting Standards Committee Foundation
ICAEW	Institute of Chartered Accountants in England and Wales
ICFAR	International comparative financial accounting research
IDV	Individuality Index
I.e.	Id Est
IFRIC	International Financial Reporting Interpretations Committee
IFRS	International Financial Reporting Standard(s)
IOSCO	International Organization of Securities Commissions
IRZ	Zeitschrift für Internationale Rechnungslegung
KapAEG	Kapitalaufnahmeerleichterungsgesetz
KonTraG	Gesetz zur Kontrolle und Transparenz im Unternehmensbereich
KoR	Zeitschrift für internationale und kapitalmarktorientierte Rechnungslegung
KPMG	Klynfeld, Peat, Marwick, Goerdeler
LiFFE	London International Financial Futures and Options Exchange
LIFO	Last-in, first-out
LSE	London Stock Exchange

M	Million
MAS	Masculinity Index
M&A	Mergers and Acquisitions
MDAX	Midcap Deutscher Aktienindex
MTB	Market To Book
NA	Negative Accruals
N/A	Not Applicable
NAICS	North American Industry Classification System
NASDAQ	National Association of Securities Dealers Automated Quotations
No.	Number
N.U.	Name unknown
NYSE	New York Stock Exchange
OECD	Organization for Economic Co-operation and Development
OCI	Other Comprehensive Income
OFR	Operating Financial Review
PAT	Positive Accounting Theory
PCG	Plan Comptable Général
PDI	Power Distance Index
PoC	Percentage of Completion
PPA	Purchase Price Allocation
PPE	Property, Plant and Equipment
PublG	Publizitätsgesetz
PW	Price Waterhouse
PwC	Price Waterhouse Coopers
R&D	Research and Development
ROCE	Return on capital employed
ROE	Return on Equity
ROI	Return on Investment
SAC	Standards Advisory Council
SACCS	Similar And Contrasting Countries Studies
SARG	Standards Advice Review Group
SEC	Securities and Exchange Comission
SFAS	Statement of Financial Accounting Standards
SIC	Standard Industry Code
SPSS	Statistical Package for the Social Sciences

Std.	Standard
StuB	Unternehmenssteuern und Bilanzen
Supp.	Supplement
SWI	Steuer & Wirtschaft International
S&P	Standard and Poor`s
T	Trillion
TecDAX	Technology Deutscher Aktienindex
TEG	Technical Expert Group
UAI	Uncertainty Avoidance Index
UITF	Urgent Issues Task Force
UK	United Kingdom
US	United States
USD	United States Dollar
VIF	Variance Inflation Factor
Vs.	Versus
WFE	World Federation of Exchanges
WPg	Die Wirtschaftsprüfung
ZCG	Zeitschrift für Corporate Governance
ZfbF	Zeitschrift für betriebswirtschaftliche Forschung
ZfCM	Zeitschrift für Controlling & Management

Index of symbols

β	Regression coefficient
DW	Durbin-Watson coefficient
€	Euro
*	Significance level
ε	Error term
F	F-value of the F-Test
i	Item in the company index
j	Item in the industry index
k	Item in the country index
l	Item in the control variable index
m	Item in the disclosure index
n	Absolute value
N	Number of analyzed companies
p	Significance level
r	Spearman correlation coefficient
R^2	Regression coefficient of determination
Σ	Sum
t	t-value of the T-Test

1 Foundation

1.1 Introduction

1.1.1 The international financial accounting language of IFRS

(1) And the whole earth was of one language, and of one speech. (2) And it came to pass, as they journeyed from the east, that they found a plain in the land of Shinar; and they dwelt there. (3) And they said one to another, Go to, let us make brick, and burn them thoroughly. And they had brick for stone, and slime had they for morter. (4) And they said, Go to, let us build us a city and a tower, whose top may reach unto heaven; and let us make us a name, lest we be scattered abroad upon the face of the whole earth. (5) And the LORD came down to see the city and the tower, which the children of men builded. (6) And the LORD said, Behold, the people is one, and they have all one language; and this they begin to do: and now nothing will be restrained from them, which they have imagined to do. (7) Go to, let us go down, and there confound their language, that they may not understand one another's speech. (8) So the LORD scattered them abroad from thence upon the face of all the earth: and they left off to build the city. (9) Therefore is the name of it called Babel[1]; because the LORD did there confound the language of all the earth: and from thence did the LORD scatter them abroad upon the face of all the earth.[2]

The confusion of language was the reason the ancient people had to stop building the Tower of Babel. They had lost their ability to communicate. Building a tower to reach for heavenly spheres is an extremely complex project that requires a huge amount of manpower, organization and coordination. It can only be carried out working as a team. And team work depends essentially on cooperation and communication.

The cited Old Testament psalm may not directly be transferred into today's business world, although the headquarters of some multinational enterprises rise high into the sky. But the fact that the incapability of communication complicates and even prevents cooperation is as true today as it was in biblical times.

Complex organizations that operate in a complex environment depend strongly on efficient and effective communication. **Accounting** in this context is used as the business language to communicate both internally and externally. Management accounting[3] is the language of internal communication, helping the management to understand and react on the complex economic realities the corporation faces. Financial accounting[4] is the language of external communication, providing information for the corporations' sharehold-

---

1 The name of the biblical town Babel etymologically comes from the Hebrew Babhel, which originates from the Akkadian bab-ilu "Gate of God", a translation of the Sumerian Ka-dingir, meaning "confused medley of sounds"; cf. Online Etymology Dictionary 2010.

2 N.U. 1611.

3 The expression management accounting is synonymously used for the German term 'Controlling'.

4 Financial accounting and financial reporting will be used synonymously in the following.

ers and stakeholders. Both internal and external users require accounting information to reach an optimal decision based on that information.

Information providers and information recipients need to speak the same 'language of accounting' as the confusion of languages leads to misunderstandings or misinterpretations; suboptimal management or investment decisions might be the consequence. Focusing on external communication, the investor has to be able to read and fully comprehend the companies' financial statements to reach an optimal investment decision based on the companies' yield and risk potential. Financial accounting as the language of financial statements is the result of a variety of cultural, socio-political, economic and institutional factors and can be referred to as a country's accounting system or Generally Accepted Accounting Principles (GAAP).[5]

Different national environments created different types of national GAAP in the past and cross-border investments were hindered by existing formal and material accounting differences, constituting information barriers to international communication of financial data.[6] This confusion of financial accounting languages on an international level, as well as on a regional (European) level, has negative implications on the comparability of financial statements, the consolidation of foreign accounts, the access to foreign capital markets and the mobility of staff in large public accounting firms. It therewith leads to severe inefficiencies in allocation of resources in an increasingly integrated world economy.[7]

The matter of international financial accounting harmonization was first addressed by *Kraayenhof* in the late 1950s who demanded the reduction of international accounting differences.[8] Since then the process of international financial accounting harmonization[9] has developed constantly. The foundation of the International Accounting Standards Committee (**IASC**) by a group of professional accounting bodies in the year 1973 marks a first important milestone in that process.[10] The establishment of the IASC can be seen as a consequence of the European accounting harmonization process.[11] Before the UK and Ireland entered the European Economic Community[12] in 1973,[13] European accounting harmonization was strongly dominated by Continental European accounting. The IASC was established on the initiative of British accountancy bodies, which feared the loss of Anglo-Saxon influence, "to give a strong signal of Britain's role in what no doubt was perceived as a global accounting community rather than a more narrowly circumscribed Eu-

5 Cf. Evans/Taylor 1982, p. 115; Nobes 1998, p. 163.
6 Cf. Nair/Frank 1981, p. 61.
7 Cf. Doupnik 1987, p. 47.
8 Cf. Kraayenhof 1960, p. 36; Choi/Bavishi 1982, p. 161; Evans/Taylor 1982, p. 116.
9 For a brief overview of the international accounting harmonization process cf. chapter 1.3.2.
10 Cf. Doupnik 1987, p. 47.
11 For a brief overview of the EU accounting harmonization process cf. chapter 1.3.3.
12 The European Economic Community was transferred into the European Union (EU) by the 1992 Treaty of Maastricht, enacted in 1993; cf. European Commission [EC] 2007. The term EU refers to the European Union and all predecessor organizations in the following.
13 Cf. European Commission [EC] 2010b.

ropean one"[14]. Understandably, the expectations associated with the foundation of the IASC, as a first international standard setter, were high.

> *"Provided that the initial enthusiasm and thrust with which the IASC was started is continued, its impact in the years to come will be important. It will take perhaps five to ten years before its full effects are recognized, but after that they will increase each year."*[15]

The 1975 IASC prospect was a little too optimistic, but as a matter of fact the IASC developed a set of International Accounting Standards (IAS) over the next 25 years and in May of 2000 a set of 30 core standards was endorsed by the International Organization of Securities Commissions (IOSCO), recommending the application of IAS to its members.[16] Two years after the promising agreement with the IOSCO the European Parliament (EP) and the Council of the EU issued the so-called IAS Regulation.[17] It states that EU group accounts from companies having their securities admitted to trading on an EU regulated market are to be prepared in accordance with International Financial Reporting Standards[18] (IFRS)[19] for financial years from 2005 on. The EU regulation then affected 28 member countries from the EU and the European Economic Area (EEA), i.e. approximately 7000 European listed companies.[20] Thus, the IFRS project, initiated as a countermovement to the early 1970s EU harmonization efforts, was integrated into the European accounting harmonization process.

In 2007, the most prominent member of the IOSCO, the American Securities Exchange Commission (SEC), finally agreed to accept filings from foreign private issuers[21] in accordance with IFRS without further reconciliations to US-GAAP.[22]

Obviously, the international diversity of financial accounting languages has diminished substantially since the late 1950s. In 2010 there were 91 jurisdictions requiring IFRS for listed companies, five jurisdictions requiring IFRS for some listed companies[23] and 26 jurisdictions permitting IFRS for listed companies (see Table 1-1 and Figure 1-1).

Among the 91 jurisdictions in which IFRS is mandatory for all domestic listed companies there are 30 EAA[24] countries that have adopted IFRS. The single language of accounting

---

14 Hopwood 1994, p. 243.

15 International Accounting Standards Committee [IASC] 1975.

16 Cf. International Organization of Securities Commissions [IOSCO] 2000.

17 Cf. European Commission [EC] 2002.

18 In 2000 the IASC reconstituted to form the IASB; newly issued standards were now called IFRS; cf. Whittington 2005; p. 130ff.

19 The term IFRS refers to both IFRS and IAS in the following.

20 Cf. Hope et al. 2006, p. 1ff.

21 Foreign private issuers, by definition, are US listed companies that do not qualify as US domestic issuers; for the US domestic issuer definition criteria cf. Zülch/Burghardt 2008, p. 98.

22 Cf. Securities and Exchange Commission [SEC]. The release was effective for financial years ending after November 15th of 2007; cf. Erchinger/Melcher 2007, p. 2635ff.

23 Russia and Israel for example excluded banks from IFRS application.

24 The EAA consists of the 27 EU member states and the three European Free Trade Association (EFTA) countries Iceland, Liechtenstein and Norway; cf. European Free Trade Association [EFTA].

used for European group accounts is a big step in the process of European accounting harmonization and a result of the European Internal Market and the European Integration as a whole. Like the introduction of a single European currency in 2002, the Euro, the Europe wide adoption of IFRS in 2005 aims to promote the full integration of the European economy.[25]

IFRS / Listing	Not permitted	Permitted	Required for some	Required for all	No stock exchange	No information
Listed companies	32	26	5	91	19	-
Unlisted companies	38	43	27	25	-	40

Table 1-1: Worldwide IFRS application in 2010 (N = 173)[26]

Figure 1-1: Worldwide IFRS application[27]

Although the EU by adopting IFRS has reached complete *de iure* harmonization of European group accounting for capital market oriented firms, the degree of *de facto* harmonization is questionable. IFRS are designed based on principles instead of rules and deliberately allow for discretion in application to appropriately mirror the economic reality of the individual company.[28] As the EU member states differ considerably with respect to their cultural and institutional environment, it is likely that such differences might affect corporate accounting decisions; i.e., although European listed companies use the same reporting standards, reporting practice could differ systematically across countries.

Subsequent to the above introductory remarks, the following chapter elaborates on the research question and outlines the contribution of this study in more detail.

---

25 Cf. the characteristics of the EU Single Market Mueller 2003, p. 3ff.

26 Cf. Deloitte Touche Tohmatsu 2010.

27 Cf. International Accounting Standards Board [IASB] 2009b.

28 Cf. Watrin/Strohm 2006a, p. 123; Carmona/Trombetta 2008, p. 456ff.

1.1.2 Research questions and contribution

Following the assumption that IFRS financial reporting quality[29] nowadays can compare to US-GAAP, there are several reasons conceivable to reject respectively doubt this assumption. The EU countries have adopted the same set of IFRS as issued by the International Accounting Standards Board (IASB), but financial reporting practice may vary from country to country since reporting standards allow for company individual interpretation of the standards. This room for interpretation may be utilized differently in dependence on the conscious and unconscious intentions and incentives of those preparing the financial statements.[30] As mentioned above, IFRS come from a tradition of **options** and various options like the fair value option have survived the continuous IFRS improvement and US-GAAP convergence process. Moreover, measurement **discretion** provides further opportunities for company specific accounting decisions. Besides overt and covert options and measurement discretion which IFRS explicitly permits, differences in IFRS application might also be related to context factors like **language** or **enforcement** that lie outside the immediate sphere of influence of the IASB. Whereas US-GAAP in the US benefits from a uniform language area, IFRS are issued in English and then translated into each of the European (and other) languages[31] leaving room for wrong or misleading translations.[32] US-GAAP also benefits from a single highly experienced regulatory institution, the SEC, created by the 'Securities Exchange Act of 1934'[33], whereas in Europe there is no such supranational regulatory institution guaranteeing an internationally consistent enforcement of IFRS application.[34]

Apart from imperfect enforcement, misleading translations, overt options, covert options and measurement estimations, *Nobes* lists three more sources that might lead to international differences in IFRS practice: **different versions** of IFRS, **gaps** in IFRS and **transitional or first-time issues** in IFRS.[35] Within this framework of eight possible sources there is plenty of room for IFRS application differences to evolve. In case these differences are randomly distributed, their causal origin is questionable and the impact on international IFRS comparability is difficult to interpret. Nonetheless, if IFRS differences are found to be systematically distributed, a second step could be to determine the context factors associated with these differences to be able to interpret financial statements from different countries accordingly.

As mentioned above, it is conceivable that IFRS financial statements differ systematically, dependent on the external and internal context of the company. Whereas the internal context (e.g. industry) is part of the direct economic reality of the company and, thus, in

---

[29] In accounting literature financial reporting quality is generally referred to as 'decision-usefulness'; cf. Gassen/Sellhorn 2006, p. 4f.

[30] Cf. Gassen/Sellhorn 2006, p. 5.

[31] The EU currently has 23 official languages. Cf. European Commission [EC] 2010a.

[32] Cf. Nobes 2006, p. 237.

[33] Cf. Securities and Exchange Commission [SEC] 2008b.

[34] Especially bank oriented countries like Germany with a long history of credit-based financing just recently started to establish institutionalized enforcement procedures. The German Financial Reporting Enforcement Panel (FREP) was founded in 2005; cf. von Keitz/Stolle 2008, p. 213.

[35] Cf. Nobes 2006, p. 234.

line with the IFRS principle of 'fair presentation', systematic differences due to the external context of the company are unintended and compromise international comparability.[36] However, national financial accounting systems were shaped by "[...] society's ever-changing informational needs and reflect the cultural, legal, social and political conditions [...]"[37]. Consequently, national conditions are likely to continue to have an impact on national IFRS practice, possibly preventing internationally consistent IFRS application.[38]

This study focuses on the possible influence of national cultural conditions. The **research question** to be answered in the course of the study is **if and how national culture affects IFRS application.** Although the focus is on national culture, this study considers other internal and external context factors, as well, to control for possible other influences. Whereas external factors mainly refer to the national institutional environment of the companies, internal factors like size or industry are those the company has a direct influence on. For instance, large multinationals with a long history of high quality accounting standards might exert options differently compared to small or medium sized companies that switched to IFRS when obliged to. Accordingly, this study analyzes inconsistencies in IFRS practice both on a national and an international level and discusses implications for comparability and quality of financial statements.[39]

The **European Union** provides an ideal setting for this study as all EU countries require the same set of IFRS standards as endorsed by the EU. Also, Europe traditionally hosts a wide range of different accounting systems, going from the micro-fair-judgmental, commercially driven, business economics based, extreme judgmental financial accounting system of the Netherlands to the macro-uniform, government-driven, tax-dominated, economic control seeking financial accounting system of Sweden.[40] The different national accounting specifications represent the different cultural and institutional background of European countries; as outlined above, different country characteristics might flow through to IFRS application and lead to IFRS country patterns.

This study's **contribution to accounting research and practice** is manifold. First, cultural accounting research in the past mainly focused on accounting systems. National accounting systems in the EU are not entirely replaced by IFRS and continue to be important for unlisted companies and for tax purposes; nonetheless, accounting research traditionally concentrated on large listed companies. Research on large listed companies bears the advantage of better data availability; furthermore, the listing status of these companies allows for research on capital market reactions. As the accounting system for large listed European companies was standardized by the EU wide adoption of IFRS, future research is likely to focus on accounting practice, i.e. how the new accounting system is applied. As mentioned above, *de iure* harmonization does not imply *de facto* harmonization. This study investigates the association between cultural and other factors on IFRS practice and, thus, contributes to a very current research field.

---

[36] Cf. Kvaal/Nobes 2010, p. 173.
[37] Choi/Meek 2008, p. 35.
[38] Cf. Doupnik/Tsakumis 2004, p. 38ff.
[39] Cf. Nobes 2006, p. 243.
[40] Cf. Nobes/Parker 2008, p. 65; cf. chapter 2.3.2.1.5.

Second, research on market effects of the adoption of IFRS and US-GAAP so far was based on the assumption, that both financial accounting systems were applied consistently.[41] For US-GAAP, this assumption is appropriate in terms of language, enforcement and level of detail. With respect to translation, differing enforcement and more discretion, this assumption might be not as appropriate for IFRS as it is for US-GAAP. IFRS country patterns as a consequence of cultural or institutional differences could result in lower earnings quality. On the premise that lower quality of earnings implies higher costs of capital, this effect could be the reason that so far there was little evidence of IFRS accounting harmonization resulting in lower costs of capital.[42] An analysis of systematic application differences might provide further insight to this issue.

The contribution to financial accounting research consists in evidence on systematically differing IFRS practice in countries that come from distinct cultural and institutional backgrounds. Such evidence would have an impact both on capital market research and comparative international accounting research in general. Moreover, this study is of interest to financial statement users and other interested parties like standard setters or regulators. Financial statement users might be misled by the apparent uniformity promised by adoption of IFRS. **Analysts** and investors might benefit from evidence on the degree of comparability of IFRS reporting practice in Europe; national country or company patterns could be taken into account when analyzing the accordant financial statements; financial figures could be adjusted accordingly.[43]

> *"The International Accounting Standards Committee (IASC) is committed to narrowing these*[44] *differences by seeking to harmonise regulations, accounting standards and procedures relating to the preparation and presentation of financial statements".*[45]

The IASB as **standard setter** might be interested in the progress respectively the status quo of one of the organization's main objectives, viz. the establishment of worldwide financial accounting harmonization and comparability. Based on the *status quo*, the IASB could take action to further improvement and harmonization.

Furthermore, results on IFRS reporting practices might be helpful for **regulatory bodies** in Europe to detect imperfections on national enforcement level and give reason to consider a supranational European regulatory institution.[46] The **SEC** might be particularly interested in a study on the consistency of IFRS application with reference to the recent acceptance of IFRS as equivalent GAAP.[47] A study on that topic might play a role in the current debate on the accreditation of IFRS as an alternative to US-GAAP for listed US

---

41 Cf., e.g., Daske 2006, p. 329ff.; van der Meulen et al. 2007, p. 123ff.; Barth et al. 2008, p. 467ff.

42 Cf. Daske 2006, p. 329.

43 Cf. Kvaal/Nobes 2010, p. 173.

44 'These' refers to international financial accounting differences.

45 Preface to International Financial Reporting Standards.

46 For a discussion on EU enforcement harmonization efforts cf. chapter 1.3.3.2.4; the national enforcement institutions of the countries that are analyzed in this study are briefly described in chapter 1.3.5.3.

47 Cf. Erchinger/Melcher 2008, p. 2292ff.

domestic companies.[48] In February 2010 the SEC published an IFRS work plan[49] "to consider specific areas and factors relevant to a Commission determination in 2011 as to whether, when, and how our [US] current financial reporting system for U.S. issuers should be transitioned to a system incorporating [...] IFRS"[50]. Empirical evidence on international IFRS practice could be of interest with regard to the first work plan area, viz. the sufficient development and application of IFRS for the US capital market.[51] A first IFRS work plan update, published in October 2010, led to no major conclusions; the SEC merely raised concerns over the impact of a shift to IFRS on regulators that rely on US-GAAP and possible funding gaps of the IASB.[52]

The **European Commission** (EC) who implemented the IAS Regulation in 2002 to promote the coalescence of the European capital market might also be interested in the *status quo* of European group accounting harmonization.[53] Especially with respect to the still rudimentary process of European enforcement harmonization, which is the logical next step after having accomplished *de iure* accounting standardization, the results of this study might be useful feedback. Although cultural and institutional country patterns are likely to remain,[54] IFRS accounting comparability would definitely benefit from uniform enforcement institutions.

Before elaborating on the scientific research strategy, the following chapter gives a brief overview of the further outline of this study.

1.1.3 Outline of the study

Based on the above introductory comments on the research problem and the contribution of this study, **chapter one** continues with a description of the scientific research strategy of this study. The research strategy is evaluated from the perspective of the scientific meta discipline philosophy of science. After presenting basic scientific research concepts like critical rationalism and constructivism, the study is positioned with respect to the applied philosophic scientific approach. Subsequently, chapter one deals with international accounting harmonization in the EU context. Introductory remarks on the relationship between accounting diversity and accounting harmonization are succeeded by an overview

---

48 For a discussion of the costs and benefits associated with IFRS adoption in the US and an analysis of the important political factors cf. Hail et al. 2010a, p. 355ff.; Hail et al. 2010b, p. 567ff.

49 The areas addressed in the SEC's IFRS work plan are (1) sufficient development and application of IFRS, (2) the independence of IFRS standard setting, (3) investor understanding and education, (4) examination of the US regulatory environment, (5) the impact on issuers and (6) human capital readiness; cf. Securities and Exchange Commission [SEC] 2010c, p. 1.

50 Securities and Exchange Commission [SEC] 2010c, p. 1. The IFRS work plan is included in the SEC's '2010 Statement'; cf. Securities and Exchange Commission [SEC] 2010a.

51 Cf. Securities and Exchange Commission [SEC] 2010c, p. 1.

52 Cf. American Institute of Certified Public Accountants [AICPA] 2010; Securities and Exchange Commission [SEC] 2010c.

53 Cf. European Commission [EC] 2002.

54 As outlined in more detail in chapter 2.2.4, cultural changes are slow. Although the European integration promotes the harmonization of European institutions, differences are likely to remain in this area as national culture and national institutions are strongly linked.

of the international and, more specifically, the European accounting harmonization process, which culminated in the 2002 issued IAS Regulation. Although the adoption of IFRS in the EU led to substantial harmonization of EU group accounting of capital market oriented companies, there remain reasons and opportunities for differences in IFRS application. After specifying opportunities for differences in IFRS practice in more detail, the regional focus of this study is determined and 'vital' EU countries are selected for further analysis. Following the regional setting of this study, the field of research of international comparative financial accounting is defined; based on an overview of relevant research branches, culture free and culturally grounded IFRS studies are reviewed to identify prior research contributions and limitations.

Having identified the research gap of prior studies, **chapter two** focuses on the theoretical background of this study; the presented theories underline the theoretical association between accounting practice, on the one hand, and national culture and other external and internal context factors, on the other hand. Based on the theoretical perspective, the conceptual framework of this study is developed and refined by specifying external and internal context factors that are assumed to have an impact on IFRS accounting practice. The conceptual framework is the foundation base and sub-hypotheses are built upon. Two groups of hypotheses can be identified. The first group of hypotheses deals with aspects of IFRS measurement and the second group of hypotheses focuses on aspects of IFRS disclosure.

The research design of this study is discussed in **chapter three**. This chapter is split in three subsections. First, the empirical research strategy of the study is defined; accordingly, this study follows a field study approach. Second, the method of data collection is selected; content analysis is used to quantify financial information content. Chapter three ends with a description of the applied methods of data evaluation; descriptive and inferential statistical methods like correlation analysis or regression analysis are introduced with regard to the empirical analysis in chapter four.

The hypotheses that are posited and operationalized in chapter two are tested in **chapter four**. Before going into detail on the hypotheses test results, the company sample is described with respect to different internal context factors like size, industry or profitability. The statistical test results on the particular sub-hypotheses are then presented in order of the tested accounting value. Each accounting value subchapter ends with a robustness test on the cultural model applied in this study.

The empirical results presented in chapter four are briefly summarized in the beginning of **chapter five**. Based on these findings, implications are formulated with regard to IFRS interested parties that are assumed to benefit from insights on international IFRS application (analysts, regulators etc.). The subchapter on limitations segues into the subchapter on the perspectives of the study and some suggestions for future research. The entire outline of the study is displayed in Figure 1-2.

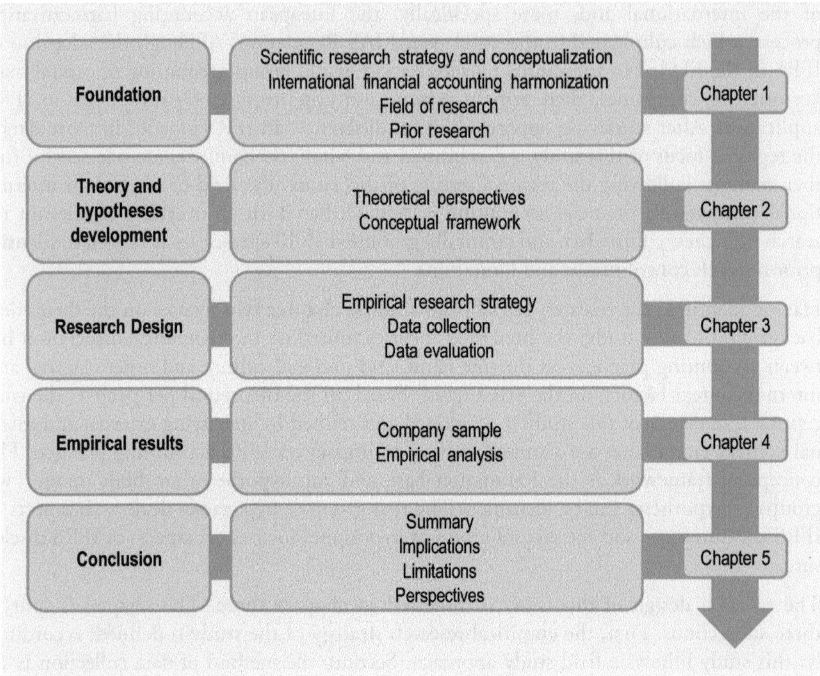

Figure 1-2: Outline of the study

The following chapter elaborates on the research strategy of this study; the research approach is evaluated considering the academic discipline of philosophy of science. The evaluation from a philosophic scientific perspective is a necessary condition precedent to the discussion of prior research; furthermore, the scientific research strategy has implications with respect to the research design and the research methods applied in this study.

1.2 Scientific research strategy and conceptualization

1.2.1 Science and philosophy of science

The term **science** comes from the Latin '*scientia*' meaning knowledge. Knowledge can be defined as rational cognition that differs from intuition or belief by the condition to be justified. Science on the other hand is the entirety of systematically gained, intersubjectively comprehensible knowledge in a context of justification, corresponding to a certain scientific object.[55] The latter definition refers to science as the result of the process of systematically gaining cognition; but science is also the process itself and science can also be seen as an institution, a system consisting of humans and objects that is geared to accumu-

[55] Cf. Fülbier 2004, p. 266.

late cognition.[56] These attempts to circumscribe science show that science is not an analytically definable phenomenon but a social occurrence in a certain sociocultural context.[57]

It is as difficult to define science as it is to define the **philosophy of science**, as everyone can do philosophy. Generally spoken, to philosophize is to think, to understand, to explain the world to oneself. As *Weizsäcker* states, "The philosophy of science asks what enabled the sciences to do so"[58]. Following that statement, the philosophy of science seeks to understand what science is, "it is about that which is required to approach true knowledge [...] to differentiate the meaningful from the meaningless, sense from nonsense, science from non-science"[59]. The philosophy of science, also referred to as the 'science of sciences', originates from general epistemology and deals with the concept, the classification, the principles of cognition, the methodology, the languages, the preconditions, the objectives and the results of particular scientific disciplines such as physics or economics, for example.[60] It is regarded as a scientific meta-discipline and marks a necessary starting point for every scientific project.

Non-metaphysical sciences in general are classified into **formal sciences** (philosophy, logic) and **empirical sciences** (physics, biology, economics).[61] Whereas formal sciences only seek 'logical truth', empirical sciences deal with the description, explanation and application of excerpts of reality and for this reason also seek 'factual truth'.[62] Empirical sciences are not independent from formal sciences. For one thing, the criterion of 'logical truth' is inherent in all sciences. Furthermore, the formal sciences serve as supporting sciences providing the empirical sciences with methodological means and mathematical procedures to solve empirical problems and, as a result, to generate cognition.[63]

Empirical sciences can be further categorized into purely **theoretical sciences** (natural sciences) and **applied sciences** (social sciences).[64] Whether research is done for its own sake without any practical relevance or whether newly gained insights help solving practical problems draws the line between purely theoretical sciences and applied sciences.[65]

Scientific outcome respectively **scientific sub-objectives** can be classified along the dichotomy of theoretical and applied sciences. In an early stage of research it is important to have certain terminological norms, to agree on precise definitions and terms to facilitate and improve scientific communication. Theoretical statements are built on the foundation of the sub-objective 'scientific terminology'. Theoretical statements seek to describe, to explain and to predict and can be further classified into merely descriptive statements, statements that show a tendency and causal statements showing cause-effect relationships.

---

56 Cf. Kornmeier 2007, p. 4f.
57 Cf. Ulrich/Hill 1976a, p. 305.
58 *v.* Weizsäcker 2006, p. 334.
59 Solo 1991, p. 10.
60 Cf. Kornmeier 2007, p. 6.
61 Cf. Raffée 1974, p. 23.
62 Cf. Ulrich/Hill 1976a, p. 305.
63 Cf. Bartel 1990, p. 54.
64 Cf. Ulrich/Hill 1976a, p. 305.
65 Cf. Fülbier 2004, p. 267.

Purely scientific research is limited to these first two scientific sub-objectives 'terminology' and 'theory'. Applied science goes one step further and transfers cause-effect relationships into practical recommendations and solutions. In order to provide 'right' or 'good' recommendations, the pragmatic sub-objective 'scientific technology' must refer to some kind of value system. These 'values' or 'ideologies' are expressed in normative statements originating from 'scientific philosophy', the fourth sub-objective of science in general.[66]

The following subchapters elaborate on the scientific discipline of business economics and business economics research strategies to determine the basic research strategy of this study.

1.2.2 Business economics research strategies

Business economics as well as economics are defined by the same research object, the economic social reality. Whereas business economics concentrates on microeconomic problems related to enterprises, economics focuses on micro- and macroeconomic problems related to the economy. The immanent overlap in microeconomics is resolved by the fact that economics, in contrast to business economics, pay more attention to standardized market-typical companies and the effects on macroeconomic matters.[67] Both scientific disciplines deal with human activity and therefore belong to the social sciences as a sub-discipline of humanities.[68] In reference to the above presented scientific sub-objectives, business economics is generally categorized as an applied science, for business scholars intend to give advice on how to modify and improve business reality taking scientifically gained cognition as a basis for improvement (science as a means to an end).[69]

At the beginning of every research project the researcher has to decide on the research strategy that is best applicable for the research problem to be analyzed. Business economics as an applied science distinguishes between three basic research strategies:

- the conceptual,
- the analytical and
- the empirical research strategy.[70]

The **conceptual** research strategy can be described as a theoretical simulation of reality to identify relationships and to derive practical recommendations from these. This strategy depends on the analytical skills of the researcher. The rationally developed statements are not empirically verified or quantified. In contrast to the conceptual research strategy, the **analytical** research strategy has no intention to describe the entire reality but deals with a concrete real problem. It aims to simplify and abstract the structures of the problem to develop decision-logical methods and models that are applied to that specific problem.

66 Cf. Müller-Böling 1992, p. 1492f.; Fülbier 2004, p. 267.
67 Cf. Bartel 1990, p. 54.
68 Cf. Bartel 1990, p. 54.
69 Cf. Raffée 1974, p. 64; Lingnau 1995, p. 124; Kornmeier 2007, p. 22.
70 Cf. Grochla 1978, p. 71ff.; Al-Laham 1997, p. 9f.

The strong focus on a concrete problem distinguishes the analytical strategy from the conceptual and the empirical research strategy.

The **empirical** research strategy, on the other hand, seeks confrontation with reality and systematically tests statements against reality to support or to confute these statements. The results of an empirical research strategy may be of descriptive nature only or may, in a next step, contain elements of tentative statements respectively assumptions to describe the causal-analytical context of the investigated research problem. As true causality in business economics is difficult to prove, these predictive or explanatory statements usually refer to the statistical association between the analyzed dependent and independent variables.[71]

As aforementioned, this study assesses the influence of national culture on current financial accounting practice; this study, hence, employs an **empirical research strategy**. The following subchapter gives an overview on the empirical research process in general.

1.2.3 The empirical research process

The main goal of empirical research in business economics is to find single case exceeding problem-oriented scientific statements to better understand the business environment and to solve decision problems in business practice, thus, shaping business reality (pragmatic scientific goal).[72] Accordingly, business economics as well as other empirical sciences have to address the research problems of subjectivity (subjective perception, interest related judgements) and communication (precise language, generalizations), inherent in every empirical research process. These problems have to be solved at all three stages of the typical research process, viz.:

- the context of discovery,
- the context of justification and
- the context of application.[73]

The **context of discovery** determines the conditions under which the scholar seeks for cognition. It intends to solve the heuristic problem of how to gain most fruitful cognition and covers aspects like the definition of the scientific object and the exact problem, terms, variables and the development of hypotheses. The core element of the context of discovery is the **conceptual framework.**[74]

The conceptual framework is built on various theories that lead to various assumptions on the relationships between the variables that describe the analyzed research problem;[75] it is an explanatory model to structure and guide the research process.[76] Visualized, the conceptual framework is a system of boxes and lines connecting the boxes. The boxes thereby

---

[71] Cf. Kubicek 1975, p. 31ff.; Grochla 1978, p. 67ff.; Tabachnick/Fidell 2007, p. 122.

[72] Cf. Kubicek 1977, p. 5; Wollnik 1977, p. 39f.; Kajüter 2000, p. 20f.

[73] Cf. Ulrich/Hill 1976a, p. 306.

[74] Cf. Ulrich/Hill 1976a, p. 306f.

[75] Cf. Christensen 2010, p. 287ff.; Macve 2010, p. 303ff.

[76] Cf. Kubicek 1977, p. 16ff.; Wollnik 1977, p. 45.

represent the diverse elements of the particular research problem. One type of boxes stands for the conceptual categories or units of analysis (persons, situations, companies) that are observed and that in reality possess different characteristics. The other type of boxes represents the dimensions to theoretically capture and analyze relevant characteristics of the units of analysis, generally to analyze similarities and dissimilarities (external context factors, e.g. culture, financing system; internal context factors, e.g. size, industrial sector). The lines or arrows connecting the boxes are statements or assumptions of relationships that result from the context of the research problem. If the relationship is deemed not to be clear, the line is marked with a question mark. See Figure 1-3 as an example for a basic model of a conceptual framework.[77]

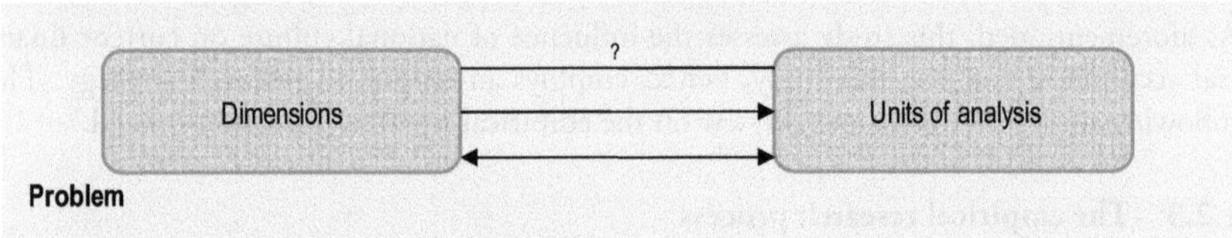

Figure 1-3: The conceptual framework basic model

The conceptual framework, as a whole, is a description of the problem to be analyzed from certain theoretical perspectives. It is a tool to structure the research process, to operationalize the parameters of the problem, to empirically test hypotheses and to possibly find an answer to the formulated research question. Depending on the complexity of the practical problem to be analyzed, the conceptual framework will probably never be able to capture all facets of the research problem. The quality of the conceptual framework in the end is up to its heuristic potential and the type and relevance of its contextual dimensions.[78]

In this study, the context of discovery is accounted for by the conceptual framework which is outlined in detail in chapter 2.3.1. The conceptual framework is based on the theoretical perspective presented in chapter 2.2. On that theoretical grounding, hypotheses are developed and operationalized in chapter 2.3.3 respectively chapter 2.3.4.

The context of discovery, the discovery of relevant unknown problems and problem solving methods, is regarded as not logically verifiable and therefore assigned to the psychology of science (see Figure 1-4).[79] For its lack of logical verifiability, this subarea of the philosophy of science has been rather neglected. Modern philosophers of science mainly concentrate on the **context of justification**, i.e. the task of finding logically derived true statements. The **criterion of truth** is a necessary objective of every science and is emphasized in the context of justification. Truth can be further split up into logical and factual truth. Logically true statements rely only on logical means. In contrast to factual truth, empirical proof is not required.[80] Business economics, as an empirical science, does not

[77] Cf. Kubicek 1977, p. 18.
[78] Cf. Kubicek 1977, p. 16ff.; Wollnik 1977, p. 45.
[79] Cf. Ulrich/Hill 1976a, p. 306.
[80] Cf. Chmielewicz 1994, p. 87ff.

rely on purely logical means, but necessitates reality respectively empirical proof to control for factual truth and valid scientific statements.[81] Consequently, the context of justification focuses on the empirical testing of the conceptual framework (context of discovery) and tries to solve the induction problem of how to conclude from singular to general interrelations and statements. These generalizations have to submit to the criterion of truth (see Figure 1-4).[82]

In this study, the hypotheses that are the result of the theory based conceptual framework are tested empirically in chapter 4.3. The results of the hypotheses tests are summarized and interpreted in chapter 4.4 respectively in chapter 5.

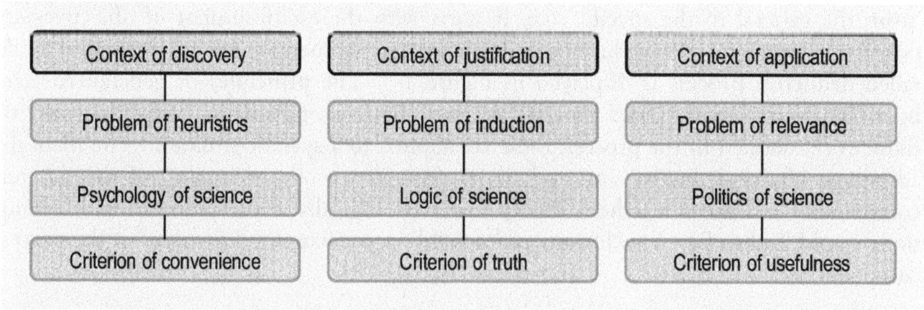

Figure 1-4: Research process of empirical sciences[83]

In a third step, the scholar has to deal with the problem of relevance (see Figure 1-4). The **context of application** is shaped by the criterion of social usefulness and analyses the possible application of scientific outcome.[84] In this study, the context of application, referring to practical relevance and adaptability of the results, is addressed both in the beginning (definition of the problem in chapter 1.1.2) and at the end of this study (implications in chapter 5.2).

According to the above displayed overview, the research process of empirical sciences can be described as the consecutive solution of the three problems of heuristics, induction and relevance (see Figure 1-4).[85] From the perspective of the philosophy of science, different concepts are deployed to meet these problems and criteria along the above described tripartite process of empirical research. The following chapter deals with the most common scientific programs in business economics respectively financial accounting; subsequently, the positioning of this study is described.

---

81 Cf. Kajüter 2000, p. 21.
82 Cf. Ulrich/Hill 1976a, p. 306f.
83 Cf. Ulrich/Hill 1976a, p. 307.
84 Cf. Ulrich/Hill 1976a, p. 306f.
85 Cf. Ulrich/Hill 1976a, p. 306f.

1.2.4 Scientific programs in financial accounting research

1.2.4.1 Basic scientific approaches

Approaches to science can be either normative focusing on 'the way things should be' or positive focusing on 'the way things are'. Whereas normative approaches can be found on both theoretical and technological level of scientific sub-objectives, positive approaches do not exceed theory. The normative approach goes back to the ancient scientific concept of classical rationalism.[86] This scientific concept is based on logical analysis. Knowledge is generated by strictly deductive reasoning.[87] The normative or **deductive** approach goes 'from the general to the specific', i.e. it starts with the establishment of objectives and postulates. From these, conclusions and practical recommendations are derived. The detailed deductive process is displayed in Figure 1-5. The principles or generalized statements of policy are the 'final product' of the objectives, postulates, constraints and the framework, defined in the process; these are applied to a specific situation. The main disadvantage of the deductive approach is its dependence on the quality of the different components and the researcher's ability to reason logically. False premises and assumptions would lead to false conclusions and possibly necessitate modifications of the process' components.[88]

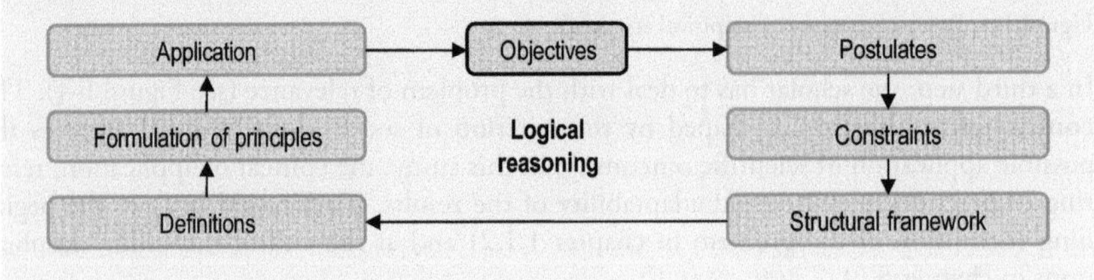

Figure 1-5: Structure of the deductive approach[89]

Classical empiricism, as the origin of positivism and neo-positivism, was a countermovement to rationalism emerging in modern times. According to this concept, knowledge is generated by observation and inductive reasoning based on these observations.[90] Following the positive or **inductive** approach, conclusions are drawn 'from the specific to the general', i.e. observations of a small sample lead to generalizations for "[...] the entire universe or a group of similar situations"[91]. Inductive research cannot be seen isolated from the deductive approach as it requires some initial assumptions and concepts in the first place. Additionally, conclusions inductively drawn from the observations of a small sample are not irrevocable but conceptually falsifiable. The relatively open and flexible ap-

86 Classical rationalism is independent from experience and conclusions are not confronted with reality through empirical testing.
87 Cf. Steinmann/Scherer 2000, p. 1056ff.; Fülbier 2004, p. 268.
88 Cf. Hendriksen 1965, p. 3; Schroeder et al. 2008, p. 112.
89 Cf. Hendriksen 1965, p. 3ff.
90 Cf. Steinmann/Scherer 2000, p. 1056ff.; Fülbier 2004, p. 268.
91 Hendriksen 1965, p. 5.

proach leaves plenty of room for human error, which might have a biasing effect on conclusions and generalizations. It is therefore advisable to subsequently control for human or systematic error by deductive reasoning.[92]

Another, less theoretical, approach that affected especially financial accounting thought in the past is the **pragmatic** or common law approach.[93] Whereas both deductive and inductive approach can be traced back to concepts of scientific thought like rationalism or empiricism, the only theoretical objective of the pragmatic approach is to find a practical solution to an identified problem. It is based on the concept of usefulness.[94] Especially accounting as an applied science, originally driven by the practical needs of merchants, was strongly influenced by the pragmatic approach. As a result of a Darwinist process, only the most useful accounting practices survived over time. With the statutory establishment of corporations in the nineteenth century the information function of accounting gained importance as the owner no longer managed the business himself, but had managers to run the business for him.[95] The appearance of statutory corporations entailed the establishment of statutory accounting rules or principles to satisfy the owner's information needs in an increasingly anonymous principle agent relationship. Standard setters developed first standards without a principle based framework. They rather followed the utilitarian approach by studying common accounting procedures and recommending the accounting practices they regarded as most useful. The advantages of the pragmatic approach are in **simplicity** and the fact that the overall criterion of **usefulness** leads to greater uniformity and consistency. The latter point hints at one of the limitations of the approach, viz. the missing or vague definition of 'usefulness'. Obviously, different accounting user groups have different opinions on what is useful.[96]

The pragmatic approach especially influenced early **accounting thought**, which, consistent with the chosen introductory citation, can be traced back to biblical times. The accounting system documented in the Zenon '*papyri*'[97], discovered in 1915, dates back to the third century B.C. and already knew some type of provisions, written records of all transactions and records of inventory and asset acquisitions/disposals.[98] Although the phenomenon of accounting goes back a long way,[99] the starting point of accounting thought is marked by the publication of the first printed text on that topic, the '*Summa de Arithmetica Geometrica Proportioni et Proportionalita*' by *Pacioli* in 1494.[100] This primarily mathematic work contains a first description of the double-entry bookkeeping system, albeit *Pacioli* did not invent double-entry bookkeeping, an accounting concept originating

92 Cf. Hendriksen 1965, p. 5f.; Schroeder et al. 2008, p. 112.

93 Cf. Hendriksen 1965, p. 6ff.

94 Cf. Schroeder et al. 2008, p. 113.

95 Cf. Schroeder et al. 2008, p. 3f.

96 Cf. Hendriksen 1965, p. 6ff.

97 Papyrus is a thick paper-like material produced from the pith of the papyrus plant (Cyperus papyrus), a wetland sedge that was once abundant in the Nile Delta of Egypt; cf. Buschan 1895, p. 74ff.

98 Cf. Schroeder et al. 2008, p. 2f.

99 Record keeping is known since about 3600 B.C.; first accounting concepts emanate from the early Greek and Roman periods; cf. Hendriksen 1965, p. 16.

100 Cf. Littleton 1962, p. 1; Hendriksen 1965, p. 16; Scott 2006, p. 1; Schroeder et al. 2008, p. 3.

in Italian trading centers in medieval times.[101] Despite these early roots of accounting ideas and methods, accounting is a discipline born out of practical needs, far from philosophical considerations, and "[...] prior to 1930, accounting theory as a well-defined body of logical reasoning did not usually precede accounting practice"[102]. In the beginning of the twentieth century financial accounting thought was further developed and mainly influenced by the **empirical inductive approach**, which is based on elements of the pragmatic and the inductive approach.[103] Observations on accounting problems of practical relevance led to theoretical generalizations. The motivation for this type of research arose from the interest in practical accounting problems. Theory evolved from a "rationalization of practice"[104]. For its practical importance this approach is the oldest and most widespread in financial accounting theory. Being highly relevant to the practical accounting world, it serves at least three purposes. First, it helps to evaluate and improve current practices and standards. Second, it plays an important role in professional accountant's training. And third, it explains and justifies current practice to critics.[105]

Although relevant for early accounting research, the pragmatic approach is not further addressed in this study since scientific programs in modern financial accounting research are mainly characterized by elements of the deductive or inductive approach.

Both approaches are not to be seen as conflicting concepts but rather as complementary concepts.[106] Differing in respect to the source of cognition (ratio vs. observation; deduction vs. induction), both classical rationalism and classical empiricism aim at the ultimate foundation of knowledge assuming that in principle it is possible to obtain true cognition.[107] This epistemological optimism results in the belief that the truth is obvious; it may be hidden and difficult to discover, but once it is unveiled, every critical argument is superfluous and the process of cognition has come to an end.[108]

The concepts of pure deduction respectively pure induction from a contemporary perspective are outdated, but for their epistemological optimism have inspired modern sciences strongly.[109] Modern research concepts in business economics respectively financial accounting research contain elements of both classical concepts. The predominant research programs in modern business economics are critical rationalism, on the one hand, and constructivism, on the other hand.[110]

---

[101] Cf. Hendriksen 1965, p. 16; Scott 2006, p. 1.
[102] Hendriksen 1965, p. 15; cf. also Whittington 1986, p. 381.
[103] Cf. Whittington 1986, p. 6f.
[104] Whittington 1986, p. 6.
[105] Cf. Whittington 1986, p. 8f.
[106] Cf. Whittington 1986, p. 401.
[107] Cf. Kornmeier 2007, p. 38.
[108] Cf. Kern 1979, p. 16.
[109] Cf. Kern 1979, p. 16; Schmid 1996, p. 83.
[110] Cf. Fülbier 2004, p. 268.

1.2.4.2 Critical rationalism

The pursuit of **truth** should be the ultimate goal of every scientist.[111] The problem how truth is found and the question whether there is something like truth at all is subject to the theoretical scientific debate and marks the origin of different theoretical scientific programs. In empiricism, for example, observation is the only source and final instance of truth. Empiricists seek for true cognition by verifying hypotheses empirically throughout the open-minded sensualistic experience of reality and continuous induction.[112]

Critical rationalists, in contrast to empiricists, deny the possibility of verification through perfect induction.[113] As a result, from a critical rationalist's perspective there is no such thing as final truth; only an approximation to truth is deemed possible. The basic idea of critical rationalism is that human knowledge is fallible; knowledge may be assumed to be right for a certain period of time but never true as it can be falsified at any time.[114]

Critical rationalism[115] combines elements of classical rationalism and neo-positivism and is closely connected with *Popper* and a group of theorists called 'falsificationists'.[116] The rationalists' postulation of rational justification is an imminent part of the concept of critical rationalism accepting the constraint that the results of rational deduction are no longer regarded as axiomatic since human ratio in principle is fallible.[117] The gain of critical rationalist cognition can be described as a three step scheme starting with causality in need of explanation respectively an observable problem in reality. Hypotheses are built in a second step to provide proposed solutions to that problem. In a third and last step, these hypotheses are empirically tested and possibly falsified and eliminated.[118]

Whereas empiricists intend to verify hypotheses, critical rationalists try to falsify hypotheses that are built on rational reasoning (**criterion of consistency**). In contrast to a classical rationalist approach, 'falsificationist' hypotheses, as the name implies, have to be falsifiable; i.e. the easier it is to test and possibly falsify a hypothesis empirically, the better it is *per se* (**criterion of falsification**).[119] Knowledge is filtered and advances by means of a trial and error process resulting in qualified or abandoned hypotheses.[120] Qualified in this context refers to the condition that the non-falsified hypotheses fulfill both the criterion of logical truth, for being rationally deducted, and the criterion of factual truth, for being empirically tested. As mentioned earlier, factual truth is to be understood as intersubjectively tested on reality and therefore temporarily right, but not true in an ultimate irrevoc-

---

111 Cf. Popper 1994, p. 225.

112 Cf. Kern 1979, p. 14ff.; Albert 1984, p. 4677.

113 Cf. Ulrich/Hill 1976b, p. 345; Lingnau 1995, p. 124.

114 Cf. Ulrich/Hill 1976b, p. 345; Lingnau 1995, p. 124.

115 The term 'rationalism' emphasizes the importance of rational thought; the term 'critical' expresses the need to challenge hypotheses through falsification; cf. Behrens 1993, p. 4765.

116 Cf. Fülbier 2004, p. 268; Deegan/Unerman 2006, p. 15.

117 Cf. Fülbier 2004, p. 268.

118 Cf. Fülbier 2004, p. 268; Kornmeier 2007, p. 42.

119 Cf. Lingnau 1995, p. 124; Möller/Hüfner 2002, p. 352.

120 Cf. Deegan/Unerman 2006, p. 15.

able sense. According to the school of thought of critical rationalism, a final verification through empirical induction from the specific to the general is not possible.[121]

Denying the possibility of verification of hypotheses, falsificationists deny the idea and development of theories in a narrow sense, i.e. a system of deductively combined, mutually consistent and verified hypotheses. The critical rationalists' concept of theory rather refers to a system of mutually consistent, complementing, non-falsified hypotheses that presumably will not be falsified in the future. These hypotheses in business economics are generally spatiotemporally qualified, valid only for a certain period of time and a certain sociocultural context. Consistent systems of such non-falsified, spatiotemporal qualified hypotheses form so-called quasi-theories.[122] In contrast, nomological hypotheses, very general hypotheses without a certain time or space restraint, are rather unusual in business economics.[123]

The concept of critical rationalism was and still is popular among scholars in business economics respectively financial accounting. Critical rationalist thought lays the foundation for one of the most important financial accounting research streams, which *Whittington* refers to as the **new empiricism based on positivism.**[124] In contrast to normative prescriptive theories, positive theories of accounting seek to explain and predict certain accounting phenomena by empirically testing them. According to the Rochester School of Accounting[125] the term 'positive' originates from economics where it was popularized by *Friedman.*[126] *Christensen* traces *Friedman's* distinction between positive and normative theories back to the nineteenth century to *Keynes*[127] and the philosophical school of positivism.[128] From a philosophical point of view, he recommends to use the term 'empirical' instead of 'positive', as 'positive' refers to "systematized knowledge concerning what is [and] a theory is no such thing [and] science is not solely concerned with what is"[129]. Notwithstanding these philosophical contradictions, 'positive' will be further used in the following as the term is common in financial accounting literature.

Aside from the dominating school of thought of critical rationalism, financial accounting research is also influenced by the scientific program of constructivism.

1.2.4.3 Constructivism

Certain parallels can be identified between critical rationalism and **constructivism.** Constructivists accept the fact that human ratio in principle is fallible, but believe that it is

---

121 Cf. Ulrich/Hill 1976b, p. 345f.

122 Cf. Ulrich/Hill 1976b, p. 346.

123 Cf. Lingnau 1995, p. 125.

124 Cf. Whittington 1986, p. 24ff.

125 Jensen, Watts and Zimmerman, strong supporters of positive research in accounting and originators of positive accounting theory (PAT), form part of the Rochester School of Accounting; cf. Christenson 1983, p. 1.

126 Cf. Friedman 1953, p. 3ff.; Watts/Zimmerman 1986, p. 8; Watts 1995, p. 334.

127 Cf. Keynes 1891.

128 Cf. Tinker et al. 1982, p. 169; Christenson 1983, p. 7.

129 Christenson 1983, p. 7.

possible to come to methodologically correct decisions based on deductive argumentation.[130] Following a purely rational concept of justification, constructivism is a lot closer to classical rationalism. Instead of empirically testing hypotheses, constructivists develop argumentative statements that are the product of strictly deductive reasoning and that can be challenged by different perspectives or different reasoning.[131] Cognition respectively truth in a broader sense is not the result of continuous falsification, elimination and modification of consistent hypotheses but the result of an argumentative process under ideal conditions. In this process experts draw argumentative conclusions that result in tendency statements that, following the idea of a limited fallibilism, are not regarded as axiomatic.[132]

Sharing conceptual elements like methodological rationalism and fallibilism, the scientific programs of critical rationalism and constructivism differ clearly in their concepts of **truth**. Whereas critical rationalists deny the concept of final truth but seek to approximate truth through falsification of rationally gained hypotheses, constructivists refer to a pragmatic model of truth in which truth is defined and decided on in a qualified consensus of experts. This pragmatic model of truth is the basic idea of constructivist justification.[133]

Constructivist thought found its way into another important financial accounting research stream, which *Whittington* labels the **deductive approach**. This purely theoretical approach in financial accounting research was influenced by economic thought and can be classified into, successively, the 'true income' approach, the user needs approach and the information economics approach. The user needs approach and the information economics approach are insofar relevant to this study on financial accounting practice as they entailed a lot of empirical research on what kind of information users of financial information actually need. Especially the information economics approach was influenced by the Chicago School of Economists' "strongly positivist philosophy"[134]. Besides the interest in the actual user's needs and the Chicago School's positivist influence, there was the strong desire among researchers to find empirical evidence for the mostly *a priori* theories that dominated accounting theory up to the 1960s.[135] Consequently, the above described financial accounting research stream of new empiricism based on positivism emerged in the 1960s; large-scale empirical testing of hypotheses was now supported by technological improvements like computers or electronic data bases.[136]

The following subchapter positions this study with respect to research strategy, philosophical scientific orientation and financial accounting research stream.

---

130 Cf. Raffée/Abel 1979, p. 6.
131 Cf. Fülbier 2004, p. 269.
132 Cf. Fülbier 2004, p. 269.
133 Cf. Raffée/Abel 1979, p. 6f.
134 Whittington 1986, p. 25.
135 Cf. Whittington 1986, p. 11ff.
136 Watts/Zimmerman 1986, p. 5.

1.2.5 Positioning of the study

From the perspective of the philosophy of science, this study follows the scientific program of **critical rationalism**. Accordingly, it is to be seen in the tradition of classical rationalism and (neo-) positivism. The rationalist philosophy is expressed in the assumptions respectively hypotheses of the study, which are based on rational deduction. Human ratio, however, is principally fallible and, according to critical rationalist thought, is confronted with reality and possibly falsified. This confrontation with reality is an expression of the positivist philosophy. The interplay of the two scientific philosophies within the scientific program of critical rationalism is displayed by the research design of this study.

As mentioned above, the empirical investigation of this study is based on a theoretical foundation from which falsifiable hypotheses are derived. The theoretical foundation is laid by developing a conceptual framework that integrates various theories in accounting that describe the relationship between accounting practice as the dependent variable and national culture as the independent variable. Although the focus of the critical rationalist approach is on the testing of hypotheses and therewith on the context of justification, the context of discovery is accounted for by the theory-guided development of hypotheses.

Following an empirical research strategy, this study is to be categorized into the above presented financial accounting research stream of **new empiricism based on positivism**, which is based on critical rationalism. The aim of the study is to describe and explain international accounting practice by empirically testing it. Nonetheless, this study's view on positivism (and normativism) is not as narrow-minded as generally in positive accounting research.[137] Using a conceptual framework that bases on the author's theory-guided individual preconception of the research problem, this study does not claim to be entirely value free. According to the concept of critical rationalism, it combines both normativist and positivist elements to allow for a fruitful progress of cognition.

Having exemplified the scientific position and basic research strategy of this study the next chapter deals with international financial accounting harmonization and reasons that might prevent further accounting harmonization.

1.3 International financial accounting harmonization in the EU

This subchapter on international accounting harmonization in the EU starts with the differentiation between harmonization and standardization, followed by an appreciation of arguments in favor and against accounting harmonization in general. A brief description of the commencement of the international accounting harmonization debate segues into a description of accounting harmonization from a European perspective. A chronicle of the legislative milestones of the European harmonization process, which resulted in the adoption of IFRS as endorsed by the EU, is followed by an explication of (1) the institutional prerequisites the EU has established to be involved in the IASB standard setting process, (2) the EU endorsement process and (3) EU enforcement harmonization. The remainder of the chapter discusses reasons and opportunities for potential IFRS differences that re-

[137] For a detailed overview of PAT, as a typical example of positive accounting thought, see chapter 2.2.6.

sult from the application of EU-endorsed IFRS. Moreover, the selection of EU sample countries further specifies the regional focus of the study.

This subchapter is important for the further course of the study in various ways. First, the annotations on international accounting harmonization in general and IFRS in specific are a thematic introduction preceding the review of IFRS related studies in chapter 1.5. Second, reasons for IFRS differences are presented in anticipation of the discussion of external context factors in chapter 2.3.2.1. Third, the analysis of opportunities for IFRS differences lays the foundations for the development and operationalization of hypotheses on differing IFRS practice in chapter 2.3.4. Finally, the selection of sample countries is a necessary prerequisite for the selection of sample companies in chapter 4.2.1.

1.3.1 Accounting diversity versus accounting harmonization

Discussing the concept of harmonization, it is useful to first distinguish between harmonization and standardization. Both terms describe processes. Whereas harmonization describes the process to a state of harmony, standardization describes the process to a state of uniformity. The process of harmonization hereby precedes the process of standardization. Analogously, *Tay/Parker* divide the process from diversity to uniformity into (1) harmonization as the movement away from total diversity to harmony and (2) standardization as the movement towards uniformity (see Figure 1-6).[138] Thus, harmonization is the process between the states of total diversity and harmony and standardization is the process between the states of harmony and uniformity. As the state of harmony, which marks the parting line between harmonization and standardization, is usually difficult to determine, both terms harmonization and standardization are used synonymously in this study.

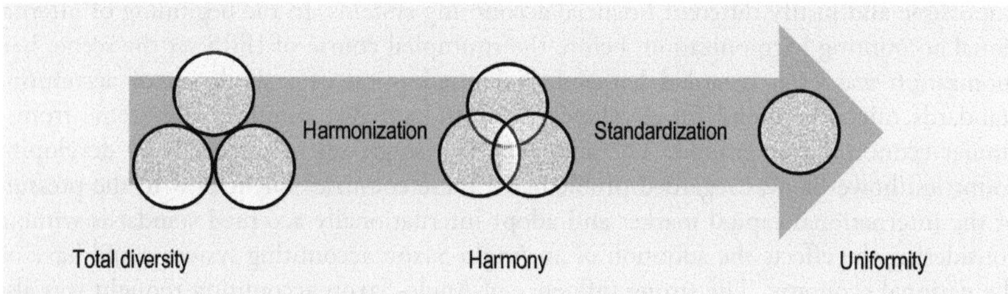

Figure 1-6: The harmonization process[139]

Applying the above described concept of harmonization to international financial accounting research, it is important to further distinguish between harmonization of accounting rules/standards (*de iure* harmonization) and harmonization of accounting practice (*de facto* harmonization).[140] This differentiation is important as the following definitions of harmonization show.

---

[138] Tay/Parker 1990, p. 73.

[139] Adopted from Tay/Parker 1990, p. 73.

[140] Cf. Tay/Parker 1990, p. 73.

> *"Harmonization can be defined as the reduction in differences in accounting practices across countries ultimately resulting in a set of international norms to be followed worldwide."*[141]

> *"Standardization dictates a uniform standard in all countries that participate in the effort. Harmonization, however, implies a reconciliation of different points of view and permits different requirements in individual countries as long as there is no logical conflict."*[142]

The starting and ending point of the process from diversity to uniformity may be states of either *de iure* or *de facto* accounting. A single set of international accounting standards implies *de iure* uniformity but not necessarily *de facto* uniformity. Accordingly, the EU has reached the state of accounting rules uniformity for group accounts of capital market oriented companies; the current state of accounting practice, however, is questionable. Furthermore, it is questionable whether a state of accounting practice uniformity is possible, how such a state is defined and if further accounting harmonization is necessary and reasonable at all.[143]

Opponents to international accounting harmonization argue that harmonization efforts are unnecessary as full harmonization is probably not practical and the pre-IFRS state of the international capital market was sufficient.[144] In fact, the positive development of the pre-IFRS international capital market did not indicate a strong necessity for international accounting harmonization.[145] Harmonization critics further claim that the enormous harmonization efforts by regulators, auditors and companies are not legitimate pursuing a mere illusion of full *de facto* harmonization.[146] Moreover, differences in the economic, political, legal and cultural national environment are assumed to make harmonization impossible and justify different financial accounting systems. In the beginning of international accounting harmonization, before the triumphal course of IFRS set the scene, harmonization was even regarded harmful.[147] The adoption of a single set of accounting standards might be useful for developed Western capitalist countries that come from a similar economic background. The adoption of a single set of standards by developing countries, however, was regarded problematic; these countries might bow to the pressure of the international capital market and adopt internationally accepted standards without considering the effects the adoption of an Anglo-Saxon accounting system could have on the national economy. The strong influence of Anglo-Saxon accounting thought was also criticized by developed Western countries that feared the loss of national accounting identity.[148]

---

141 Doupnik/Salter 1993, p. 41.

142 Meek/Saudagaran 1990, p. 168f.

143 As the accounting rules standardization process is completed in the EU for capital market oriented companies, harmonization and standardization in the following refer to accounting practice.

144 Cf. Goeltz 1991, p. 85ff.; Dargenidou et al. 2006, p. 388ff.; Jeanjean/Stolowy 2008, p. 480ff.

145 Cf. Choi/Levich 1990, p. 140; Ball 2006, p. 5ff.

146 Cf. Cole et al. 2010, p. 22ff.

147 Cf. Samuels/Oliga 1982, p. 69ff.; Hoarau 1995, p. 217ff.

148 Cf. Saudagaran/Meek 1997, p. 137f.

Despite critical opinions on accounting harmonization in general and the adoption of internationally accepted accounting standards like IFRS or US-GAAP in specific, the globalization of the world economy proved supporters of financial accounting harmonization right. As *Choi/Mueller* in 1978 state:

> *"When corporate financial statements were issued and used solely within the confines of a single country, a uninational (ethnocentric) approach to the formulation of accounting standards seemed justified and desirable. In the context of expanded international trade and investment flows, however, ethnocentric approaches to accounting policy formulation are becoming less appropriate."*[149]

From the perspective of an increasingly interlinked and integrated world economy, generally subsumed under the phenomenon of 'globalization', there are mainly three groups which have a strong interest in worldwide harmonized financial accounting: (1) international investors (analysts), (2) international audit firms and (3) international corporations.[150]

The worldwide deregulation of trade and production and the privatization of state-owned companies resulted in an increased demand for capital that could not be entirely met by national capital markets. The resulting globalization of the international capital market led to market inefficiencies as different accounting regimes complicated cross-national comparison of investments.[151] Thus, international **investors** and capital market supervisory organizations like the IOSCO strongly promoted international accounting harmonization. Besides international investors, international **audit firms** had an interest in accounting harmonization; financial statements in accordance with harmonized accounting rules reduce the complexity of international audits and, thus, lead to cost advantages.[152] Another reason for the auditors' support of international accounting harmonization is of political nature. Audit firms especially promoted the development and acceptance of IFRS as the members of the IASC were mainly professional accountancy bodies, which had a considerable influence on the work of the IASC.[153]

As harmonized accounting also reduces the complexity of foreign operations of **international companies**, these companies benefit from cost reductions and competitive advantages, as well. First, harmonized financial accounting rules facilitate reconciliations between internal and external accounting figures.[154] Second, consolidation of group accounts is simplified as similar accounting issues in different countries are accounted for similarly according to harmonized accounting requirements.

Although supporters of international accounting harmonization presented good arguments for an approximation of national accounting systems, the international harmonization process in the beginning only slowly gathered momentum.

---

149 Choi/Mueller 1978, p. 153.

150 Cf. Uhde 1999, p. 29ff.

151 Higher transparency between international financial statements reduces the uncertainty and therewith the risk related to every investment decision. Cf. Kübler 1995, p. 367f.

152 Cf. Doupnik 1987, p. 47.

153 Cf. Ordelheide 1994, p. 30.

154 Cf. Zünd 1992, p. 915.

"Convergence will occur slowly but steadily. There will be short-term 'pain' for just about everyone. Let's hope, however, that this effort promises significant long-term 'gain' in the form of better, less costly and more comparable and consistent financial information."[155]

1.3.2 The international financial accounting harmonization process

As mentioned in the introduction of this study, one of the first who formulated the need for international accounting harmonization was *Kraayenhof* in a key note at the Seventh International Congress of Accountants in 1957. Less than ten years later the first international accounting harmonization organization, the Accountant's International Study Group (AISG), was founded in 1966.[156] The **AISG**, which existed for eleven years, was an association of accountancy bodies from Canada, the UK and the US, which conducted comparative studies on accounting theory and practice in the participating countries.[157] Although the studies on accounting and auditing topics had only little impact on accounting in the AISG member states, the AISG was a first example for the feasibility of accounting harmonization through international cooperation.[158] A next impulse for international respectively regional accounting harmonization came from the **EU**, which began to press ahead its accounting law harmonization efforts in the late 1960s.[159] Although it took the EU more than ten years to reach a consensus on common company law rules,[160] the EU harmonization efforts led to more dynamics in the international accounting harmonization. As mentioned above, the foundation of the **IASC** in 1973 can be interpreted as a reaction to the regional (Continental) European accounting harmonization process. In contrast to the Directives based EU approach, which was time consuming and susceptible to political influence by the EU member states, the IASC was established by private professional accounting organizations from nine different countries.[161] Other international organizations engaged in the international harmonization process, as well. The United Nations (UN) established in 1976 a Group of Experts on International Standards of Accounting and Reporting; the OECD set up a permanent Working Group on Accounting Standards in 1979.[162]

The IASC, succeeded by the IASB in 2001, went a long way until the **SEC** abandoned its policy of accepting foreign companies' financial statements only when reconciled to US-

155 Diaconu 2007, p. 2.
156 Cf. Choi/Bavishi 1982, p. 161.
157 Cf. Mason 1981, p. 156.
158 Cf. Choi/Bavishi 1982, p. 161.
159 Cf. Mueller 2003, p. 10.
160 The rule making process was certainly prolonged by the admittance of the UK, Ireland and Denmark to the EU in 1973 since especially the UK and Ireland came from an accounting background very different to the Continental European accounting model. Cf. European Commission [EC] 2010b.
161 The IASC founding members came from Japan, the UK/Ireland, the US, the Netherlands, Canada, Australia, Mexico, France and Germany, including the three founding members of the AISG. Cf. Zeff 2003, p. 879.
162 Cf. Doupnik 1987, p. 47f.

GAAP. The first formal meeting with the SEC took place in 1984.[163] In the following convergence process with the IASC/IASB the SEC acted mainly throughout the **IOSCO**, being its most important member and representing by far the world's biggest and most advanced capital market.[164] In 1995 the IOSCO and the IASC targeted to complete core standards by 1999 and agreed that, on the condition of successful completion of the core standards project, the IOSCO would consider endorsing IFRS for cross-border offerings.[165] As mentioned above, the core standards project was successful.

Still, the SEC's acceptance of IFRS as an alternative to US-GAAP reconciliations was not in sight. The next step towards further agreement between IASB and SEC was achieved on standard setter level. In 2002 the US standard setter, the Financial Accounting Standards Board (FASB) and the IASB concurred on the 'Norwalk Agreement', pledging "to use their best efforts to (a) make their existing financial reporting standards fully compatible as soon as practicable and (b) to coordinate their future work programs to ensure that once achieved, compatibility is maintained"[166]. Compatibility should be achieved by reducing differences between US-GAAP and IFRS, continuing joint projects[167] and supporting the coordination of their respective interpretative bodies.[168] Shortly after the publication of the 'Norwalk Agreement' the SEC chairman gave hope for a possible schedule for the SEC's acceptance of IFRS:

> *"If, by 2005, there has been sufficient progress in the improvement and short-term convergence of accounting standards, in the development of a process and structure for consistent interpretation and application of IFRS, and in the enhancement of financial reporting infrastructure, then I believe that 2005 could become the target date on which it may be appropriate for the SEC to determine whether foreign private issuers from EU member countries should be required to reconcile from IFRS to U.S. GAAP."*[169]

In fact, in April 2005 the SEC issued a press release envisioning that the era of US-GAAP reconciliations might come to an end for European companies that prepare their annual financial statements in accordance with IFRS by 2009, perhaps as early as 2007.[170] When the SEC in 2007 announced full acceptance of IFRS as issued by the IASB[171] for foreign private issuers, it was a strong signal that IFRS finally was regarded as equivalent or nearly equivalent to US-GAAP.[172] Before that date the SEC was the world's only securities regulatory commission requiring foreign securities issuers to reconcile their national GAAP

---

[163] Cf. International Accounting Standards Board [IASB] 2005.
[164] Cf. Martinez-Diaz 2005, p. 11.
[165] Cf. International Accounting Standards Board [IASB] 2005.
[166] Financial Accounting Standards Board [FASB] 2002, p. 1; cf. Pacter/Colson 2003, p. 67.
[167] Cf., e.g., Watrin/Strohm 2006b, p. 22ff.
[168] Cf. Financial Accounting Standards Board [FASB] 2002, p. 1; Schipper 2005, p. 101f.
[169] Revsine et al. 2005, p. 1018.
[170] Cf. Securities and Exchange Commission [SEC] 2005.
[171] Compliance with IFRS as issued by the IASB has to be stated explicitly in an appropriate note and attested by an independent auditor; cf. Securities and Exchange Commission [SEC], p. 11.
[172] It is suggested that political aspects have played a role as well. For a brief overview of the current debate on the approval of IFRS for US domestic companies see chapter 1.1.2.

financial statements to US-GAAP. The SEC refused to accept non-reconciled national GAAP financial statements to protect investors and to avoid a two-tiered disclosure system that would discriminate domestic against foreign registrants.[173]

Due to the relative maturity and the dominance of the US capital market, US-GAAP for a long time was regarded as the world's only high quality GAAP and therefore used as the dominating benchmark in capital market research.[174] US-GAAP was classified superior to IFRS, which was considered to be less rigorous, less detailed, affording more flexibility and requiring less disclosure.[175]

As mentioned above, IFRS were designed following a principles instead of a rules based approach;[176] the IASC intentionally tried to avoid too detailed regulations that would limit the flexibility necessary "to develop a single set of high quality, understandable, enforceable and globally accepted financial reporting standards based upon clearly articulated principles"[177]. In addition to intentional systematic flexibility, the first versions of IFRS were influenced by a number of political compromises allowing for various national accounting traditions to find way into IFRS and, thus, exposing IFRS to the criticism to be the 'lowest common denominator'.[178] As a result, early IFRS versions contained a lot of options in order to gain as much international acceptance as possible as it was easier for different jurisdictions to identify with IFRS. The first compromise shaped standards were improved substantially during the following years, mainly due to the 'Comparability and Improvements Project' from 1987-1993 and the 'Core Standard Project' from 1995-1998.[179]

The next chapter focuses on the international accounting harmonization process from a European respectively EU perspective.

---

173 Cf. Harris/Muller 1999, p. 286.

174 Cf. Auer 1996, p. 590.

175 Cf. Freisleben/Leibfried 2004, p. 101ff. Capital market research shows mixed results on the question whether financial statements prepared under IFRS are of similar high quality as those prepared under US-GAAP. Whereas *Harris*, as early as 1995, in a detailed case study finds out that accounting measures under IFRS can produce results similar to US-GAAP, *Harris/Muller* in 1999 show that US-GAAP earnings reconciliations from IFRS are value relevant. Although *Harris/Muller* detect that reconciling IFRS to US-GAAP adds value, the results regarding security returns and prices-per-share are mixed. US-GAAP figures are more highly associated with security returns and IFRS figures are more highly associated with prices-per-share. Cf. Harris 1995; Harris/Muller 1999, p. 285ff. In a 1999 study on companies listed on the German 'New Market', *Leuz* examines bid-ask spread and share turnover under IFRS and US-GAAP and concludes that "[...] at least for New Market firms, the choice between IAS and US-GAAP appears to be of little consequence for information asymmetry and market liquidity" Leuz 2003, p. 446. The German 'New Market' was a market segment of the German stock exchange especially for young, technology oriented companies. 'New Market' companies had to publish financial statements in accordance with either IFRS or US-GAAP; cf. 7.3.2 *Regelwerk Neuer Markt* ('New Market' Regulation).

176 Cf. Watrin/Strohm 2006a, p. 123.

177 Cf. International Accounting Standards Board [IASB] 2009b, p. 1.

178 Cf. Harris 1995, p. 1.

179 Cf. International Accounting Standards Board [IASB] 2005.

1.3.3 The EU financial accounting harmonization process

1.3.3.1 EU accounting Directives

The original EU strategy was to harmonize European accounting regulation by EU Directives[180]. According to Article 54(3)(g) of the 1957 Treaty of Rome, the EU member states had concurred to harmonize their company law and to reduce the diversity of European legal and institutional frameworks.[181] As a consequence, the convergence of national accounting regulations via EU Directives was deemed to be the right way to achieve EU wide accounting harmonization. The adoption of an international set of accounting standards then was no option. The first Directive on accounting was developed in the 1970s when the IFRS project was still in its infancy. The EU Directives that had the biggest impact on European accounting were the Fourth and the Seventh Directives.[182]

The **Fourth Directive**[183] was issued in 1978 and concerned the annual accounts of individual companies. *Thorell/Whittington* describe the Fourth Directive as "German regulation modified by the general application of the 'true and fair view' provision"[184]. First considerations on European accounting harmonization that recommended uniform prescriptive accounting as practiced in Germany were supplemented by the British 'true and fair view', when in 1973 Denmark, Ireland and the UK joined the European Community.[185] Besides the overriding principle of the 'true and fair view', which is expressed in standard minimum footnote disclosures, the Fourth Directive contained (1) format rules for balance sheet and profit and loss account, (2) disclosure requirements and (3) comparable valuation principles.[186] Like early IFRS standards, the Fourth Directive can be described as the smallest common denominator as it contained manifold options to meet the needs of differing national accounting characteristics. Nonetheless, two studies[187] of the *Fédération des Experts Comptables Européens* (FEE), which analyzed the degree of accounting harmonization of 1989 and 1991 European annual accounts, documented considerable accounting consistency in the areas the Fourth Directive had addressed. Accounting areas that were not addressed, like pension provisions or deferred taxation, however, still showed significant differences in national accounting practice.[188]

---

[180] EU Directives are legislative acts that oblige EU member states to reach a certain legal result without dictating the exact way to reach that goal.

[181] Cf. Mueller 2003, p. 9.

[182] Cf. Thorell/Whittington 1994, p. 217; Mueller 2003, p. 10.

[183] Cf. European Commission [EC] 1978.

[184] Thorell/Whittington 1994, p. 218.

[185] The origin of the 'true and fair view' concept in European accounting Directives is analyzed in van Hulle 1997, p. 711ff.; for the exemplary implementation of the 'true and fair view' requirements see Aisbitt/Nobes 2001, p. 51ff.

[186] Cf. Simmonds/Azières 1989, p. 7; Mueller 2003, p. 10ff.

[187] Cf. Fédération des Experts Comptables Européens [FEE] 1989; Fédération des Experts Comptables Européens [FEE] 1991 and in more detail Fédération des Experts Comptables Européens [FEE] 1992.

[188] Cf. Thorell/Whittington 1994, p. 217ff.

The **Seventh Directive**[189] was explicitly directed at European group accounts as a reaction to severe legal deficiencies in this accounting area. When the Directive was issued in 1983 only Ireland and the UK comprehensively regulated consolidated accounts.[190] The Seventh Directive essentially served two fundamental purposes. First, it expanded the applicability of the Fourth Directive to group accounts. Second, it dealt with accounting problems inherent only to group accounting like identifying groups or defining the circle of companies to be consolidated. Again, the Seventh Directive, in analogy to its predecessor, was full of options to be exercised by the EU member states, by the firm or by both, which limited the harmonization success of the Directive. One reason for the wide discretion granted to EU member states and companies was the fact that consolidated financial statements were seldom required by national regulation at the time of the conceptual development of the Seventh Directive. The concept of consolidation and disclosure of group accounts was relatively new. Nonetheless, the Seventh Directive was a step into the right direction. Especially the concept of equivalence facilitated European group accounting. According to this concept, company subgroups were released from the preparation of group accounts if their parent's headquarters was situated in an EU country or a non-EU country that had equivalent accounting requirements.[191]

Although the EU accounting Directives[192] led to less accounting diversity in the EU,[193] the instrument of Directives has only **limited potential** to reach full harmonization. The EU Directive process is too inflexible and time consuming[194] to promptly integrate current accounting developments. EU Directives as legislative acts can only lay out the basic accounting requirements. To work out detailed prescriptions and to react on current accounting trends is rather the (national/supranational) standard setters' province. For that reason, after the EU member states had adopted the major EU accounting Directives, the EU harmonization process lost momentum. Apart from general criticism on the legislative instrument of EU Directives, the following main problems were identified as causal for insufficient EU accounting compatibility: First, as mentioned above, the scope of the Directives was incomplete. Certain accounting issues were not covered. Second, the implementation of the Directives was carried out differently by the member states. There was a trend to change the national accounting frameworks and approaches as little as possible and to only do what was necessary. Differing regulations and regulation loopholes were

---

189 Cf. European Commission [EC] 1983.

190 Cf. Petite 1984, p. 82.

191 Cf. Thorell/Whittington 1994, p. 220f.; Mueller 2003, p. 15ff.

192 The Fourth and Seventh Directives are said to have had the main impact on European accounting. Notwithstanding, the EC has issued numerous other more specific Directives such as the Eleventh Directive, e.g., that deals with publishing requirements for industry accounts; cf. European Commission [EC] 1989. Other Directives are directed towards harmonization issues related rather to enforcement; e.g. the Eighth Directive addresses conditions for the approval of auditors; cf. European Commission [EC] 1984; see also Evans/Nobes 1998, p. 125ff.

193 Cf. van der Tas 1992, p. 69ff.; Canibano/Mora 2000, p. 349ff.; Aisbitt 2001, p. 51.

194 It may take countries years to transform EU Directives into national law. By the time this transformation process is completed, the regulations may already be outdated. At the beginning of 1989 the Fourth Directive, which was issued in 1978, was not implemented in Italy, Portugal and Spain; cf. Simmonds/Azières 1989, p. 8.

the result.[195] Third, the EU mutual recognition[196] strategy had not worked out as the SEC rejected such offers. US-GAAP, on the contrary, was generally accepted by the EU capital market. At the same time, large European multinationals called for a set of accounting standards that would allow them to access the international and especially the US capital market.[197] And fourth, most EU members had established national financial accounting standard committees like the British Accounting Standards Board (ASB), which issued national standards and therewith added to a growing variety of different accounting rules.[198]

These structural changes put pressure on the EC to revise its formerly Directive based harmonization strategy. The EC reacted on the described problems with institutional consequences and a reassessment of its strategy. The Contact Committee on Accounting Directives (CCAD) was enacted by the Fourth Directive. The CCAD meets twice a year to coordinate and facilitate the application and interpretation of the Directives. The committee's members are delegates of the responsible national ministries. Its EU wide acceptance is limited, though.[199] The EU Accounting Advisory Forum (EUAAF) was established by the EC subsequent to a 1990 conference on the future of EU accounting harmonization. In contrast to the previous organization, its members are not ministerial bureaucrats but national standard setters and other accounting relevant interest groups. The EUAAF supports the EC in all questions concerning financial accounting via issuing of Advisory Papers. The Forum also assisted the Commission in elaborating new harmonization strategies. Among various options, like the revision of previous accounting Directives or the set up of a supranational European standard setter, the EC decided to cooperate closely with the IASC[200] and the IOSCO to bring European accounting in line with IFRS.[201]

The 1995 EC communication 'Accounting harmonization: a new strategy vis-á-vis international harmonization' admitted that the previous Directive based harmonization efforts did not suffice to meet the challenges of the international capital market and announced the EC's will to participate in the elaboration of international accounting standards via support of and cooperation with the IASC.[202] Moreover, the focus of European accounting harmonization was now laid on group accounts of capital market oriented companies. The shift towards financial statements as a capital market instrument that serves investor information purposes was documented in a 1998 EC communication titled 'Financial services: building a framework for action', in which the EC underlined its objective "to stimulate cross-border investments through more transparency and better comparability

[195] Cf. Goldsmith 1995, p. 12; Haller 2002, p. 159.

[196] Mutual recognition refers to bilateral or multilateral agreements between states to mutually accept the others accounting standards, e.g., for foreign listings; cf. Thorell/Whittington 1994, p. 226.

[197] Cf. European Commission [EC] 1995, p. 2.

[198] Cf. Mueller 2003, p. 26f.

[199] Cf. Contact Committee on Accounting Directives [CCAD] 1990.

[200] According to this new strategy, the CCAD's new task was to cooperate with the IASC in the development of future IAS.

[201] Cf. Mueller 2003, p. 27f.

[202] Cf. European Commission [EC] 1995, p. 2.

of accounts"[203]. This change in strategy was overdue as individual accounting in many European countries like Germany or France traditionally aimed to determine the basis for tax and dividend payments, instead of providing relevant capital market information. The separation of harmonization of individual and group accounting therefore was an important step in the European harmonization process. The CCAD, mainly in charge of all co-operation activities between EC and IASC, in a first conformity project revealed that the EU accounting Directives, when exercised according to IFRS, were generally compatible with IFRS.[204] Two remaining conflicts were solved in later conformity projects. As a consequence of the general compatibility of EU Directives and IFRS and the intensified successful cooperation with the IASC, the 2000 Lisbon Council ended with a milestone in the European accounting harmonization process. Two EC communications in 2000 and 2001 announced the Commission's decision to oblige capital market oriented companies to prepare their group accounts in accordance with IFRS from 2005 on and to establish appropriate endorsement and enforcement processes.[205] The corresponding legislative act, the so-called 'IAS Regulation'[206], was enacted in 2002.[207]

1.3.3.2 The IAS Regulation

1.3.3.2.1 Legal requirements

The EU/EAA fundamental objective to create a single common economic market[208] led to the need to establish a common set of financial accounting standards as a basic requirement for an efficient capital market. Although the EU accounting Directives, as explained above, resulted in higher degrees of EU accounting harmonization, in the long run full harmonization would have been prevented by prevailing national accounting traditions. The adoption of one of the then 15 EU members' existing accounting standards was not considered an option as other EU members feared to be disadvantaged and lose influence. This constellation left the EU basically with two options: (1) to adopt an established set of high quality accounting standards that were internationally accepted and (2) to create its own set of European accounting standards. The first option usually referred to the adoption of US-GAAP and meant the submission to the accounting decisions of the FASB and the SEC, which are designed to meet the requirements of an economy that is not even a member of the EU.[209] The creation of proper EU accounting standards, on the other

[203] European Commission [EC] 1998, p. 10.

[204] Cf. European Commission [EC] 1999, p. 3.

[205] Cf. European Commission [EC] 2000, p. 2; European Commission [EC] 2001.

[206] Contrary to EU Directives, EU regulations are immediately enforceable as law in all member states. EU Directives, as mentioned above, require to be transposed into national law. Cf. the IAS Regulation in European Commission [EC] 2002.

[207] Cf. Haller 2002, p. 164ff.; Mueller 2003, p. 27f.

[208] A single common economic market refers to the free mobility of capital, labor, companies and trade across all EU members' borders. The EU single market was the result of the Single European Act of 1987 and the Treaty of Maastricht of 1992; cf. Mueller 2003, p. 3.

[209] Nonetheless, even after having adopted IFRS as European accounting standards, it is questionable whether the intentioned convergence of US-GAAP and IFRS results in an equal encounter 'in the middle of the Atlantic or rather on Staten Island'; cf. Zeimes/Kühne 2004, p. 20.

hand, would have been accompanied with the creation of a European accounting committee and other supporting institutions and surely would have cost a lot more time and money than the adoption of IFRS. Besides the availability of IFRS as an international joint product,[210] the adoption of IFRS also bore the advantage that it already possessed international credibility through the endorsement by the IOSCO who recommended its adoption to its members. Also, IFRS had already been permitted by some European national jurisdictions as an alternative to national GAAP.[211] Various European listed companies, especially from the Switzerland and Germany, used IFRS for their group account statements.[212]

Nonetheless, compared to the 7,000 companies that were affected by the implementation of the IAS Regulation in 2005/2007, the number of IFRS early adopters was comparably small. The regulation therewith had a major impact on European group accounting for capital market oriented companies. Its content is communicated in eleven articles and 18 recitals. Article 4 of the IAS Regulation determines that after January 1st of 2005 European companies have to prepare their consolidated accounts according to IFRS, if their securities are admitted to trading in the EU.[213] The IAS Regulation accepted two exemptions to this schedule. (1) Companies whose securities were listed in a non-EU state and applied internationally accepted accounting standards (usually US-GAAP) and (2) companies that had only admitted debt securities on a regulated EU market had to apply IFRS for financial years starting from January 1st of 2007 (Article 9 IAS Regulation). The application of IFRS for group accounts of capital market oriented companies is not exclusive. According to Article 5 IAS Regulation, the EU member states further have the possibility to expand IFRS application to annual accounts and/or non capital market oriented companies, an option many member states have exercised.[214]

The release of the IAS Regulation in 2002 was only a milestone, though an important one, on the road determined by the EC's Financial Services Action Plan. Before the enactment of the IAS Regulation, the EC had to create the institutional prerequisites to guarantee the recognition of European interest in the IASB standard development process, the correct transformation of IFRS into European law and European enforcement of IFRS.[215]

---

[210] Among the founder members of the IASC, which later was replaced by the IASB, were accountancy bodies from the EU countries France, the Netherlands, the UK, Ireland and Germany.

[211] Cf. chapter 1.3.5.3.

[212] Cf. Whittington 2005, p. 129; Dumontier/Raffournier 1998, p. 216ff.; Leuz 2003, p. 445ff.

[213] Third country issuers have to prepare their financial statements in accordance with IFRS or 'equivalent' GAAP to be admitted to the EU capital market. The accounting frameworks of Canada, Japan and the US were initially considered 'equivalent'. Cf. van Hulle 2008, p. 76f.

[214] Germany for example processed the option of Article 5 IAS Regulation in the 2004 German Accounting Law Reform Act (BilReG) according to which non capital market oriented companies could opt to prepare their group accounts in compliance with IFRS. Also, IFRS could be applied in individual accounts for informational purposes. See for an overview of how EU member states executed that option European Commission [EC] 2008, p. 1ff.

[215] Another issue mentioned in the preamble of the IAS Regulation is first-time application. The EC considered it necessary that certain provisions were applied when companies changed from local GAAP to IFRS for the first time and that such provisions should be agreed on an international level. The project

1.3.3.2.2 EU institutional prerequisites

Once the decision was taken to harmonize accounting in the EU via IFRS, the EC wanted to make sure that it had a certain voice in the IASC standard setting process. The EC's involvement in the work of the IASC should foreclose the necessity to renegotiate standards on EU level once they had been released by the IASC. Since the IASC, as a private sector body, allowed no state representatives, the EC was granted an observer seat on the board of the IASC and on the Standards Interpretations Committee. When the IASC changed its structure, such an observer position on the board was no longer permitted. Instead, the EC and the International Accounting Standards Committee Foundation (IASCF) agreed on an observer seat on the Standards Advisory Council (SAC)[216] and the International Financial Reporting Interpretations Committee (IFRIC), the successor of the Standards Interpretations Committee.

The constitution of the CCAD was already acknowledged above. Although constituted to coordinate the EU IASB activities, the CCAD is also the mouthpiece of the EU member states since its members are ministerial representatives. To avoid the risk that member state discrepancies constrain the collaboration with the IASB and to create a private sector IASB counterpart on side of the EU, the EC in 2001 founded the European Financial Reporting Advisory Group (EFRAG)[217]. The EFRAG is a European private sector body that was set up by private organizations with an interest in the European capital market, like the European accounting profession, stock exchanges, financial analysts etc.[218] The purpose of the EFRAG is to cooperate with the IASB on eye height, to proactively accompany the IASB standard development process and to deal with all technical accounting aspects.[219] Although the active collaboration with the IASB should render further standard discussion on EU level unnecessary, the EC installed a final barrier to verify the standards' compatibility with EU accounting Directives and EU objectives in general. The EC determined that standards released by the IASB had to pass an endorsement process before they were transferred into EU law.[220]

The EU endorsement process is described in the following subchapter.

---

was added to the IASB work schedule in 2001 and IFRS 1 was issued in 2003, effective for financial years starting on January 1st of 2004. Cf. European Commission [EC] 2002.

216 The SAC is comprised of various accounting related interest groups such as users, preparers, financial analysts, academics, auditors, regulators, professional accounting bodies and investors and is the formal advisory body to the IASB. The SAC was renamed into IFRS Advisory Council. Cf. International Accounting Standards Board [IASB] 2010e.

217 The role of the EFRAG as a European voice in the international standard setting process is analyzed by Enevoldsen/Oversberg 2008, p. 89ff.

218 The European member body organizations are currently: European Business Federations (BUSINESSEUROPE), FEE, European Insurance and Reinsurance Federation (CEA), European Banking Federation (EBF), European Savings Banks Group (ESBG), European Association of Co-operative Banks (EACB) and European Federation of Accountants and Auditors (EFAA); cf. European Financial Reporting Advisory Group [EFRAG] 2010b.

219 Cf. European Financial Reporting Advisory Group [EFRAG] 2010a.

220 Cf. van Hulle 2004, p. 366ff.

1.3.3.2.3 The EU endorsement process

As stated in the IAS Regulation, new or revised IFRS have to be endorsed by the EU before being transferred in European and therewith national law.[221] The EU endorsement process is consistent with the EU comitology approach[222]. In accordance with EU comitology, the EC enacted several committees that form part of the endorsement process and decide if a standard is accepted or not.

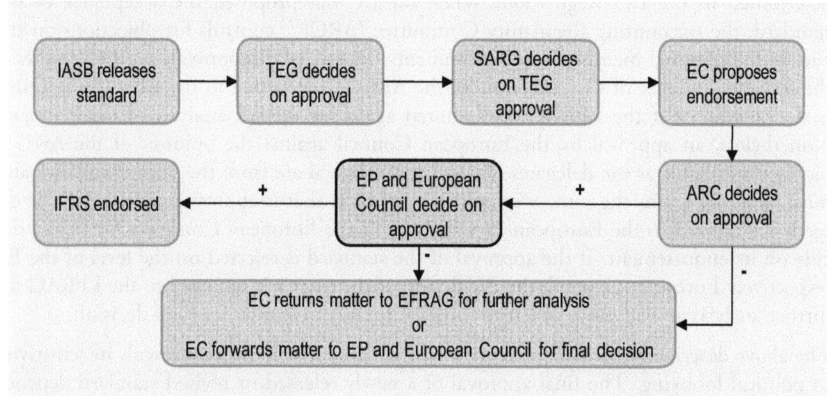

Figure 1-7: The EU endorsement process[223]

In a first step, the Technical Expert Group (TEG), as part of the EFRAG, decides if the IASB standard concurs with EU interests and communicates its approval respectively disapproval to the EC (see Figure 1-7). The conditions a standard has to meet to be endorsed are laid out in Article 3 IAS Regulation. Thus, the standard has to satisfy three basic criteria: (1) to be in line with the 'true and fair view' principle as referred to in the Fourth and Seventh Directive, (2) to be conducive to the European public good and (3) to meet the criteria of understandability, relevance, reliability and comparability. The first criterion does not imply strict conformity with every single provision in the EU accounting Directives.[224] A high degree of conformity is sufficient. If conformity is to be negated but the EC considers the IASB approach to be superior to the Directives' approach, the accounting Directives may be modified accordingly to reflect the IASB approach. The second criterion refers to the recognition of interests of European stakeholders. The case of IAS 39 is a good example for a perceived violation of European interests. The standard was not endorsed as European banks feared to be discriminated by it. Another example for 'public good' violations is presented in the preamble of the IAS Regulation in which the EC postulates convergence of European accounting standards "with international accounting standards that can be used globally, for cross-border transactions or listing any-

[221] Cf. Alexander/Eberhartinger 2010, p. 37.

[222] The EC acts via committees of representatives of EU member states. The large number of committees led to the term 'comitology'; cf. Buchheim et al. 2004, p. 1783ff.; Bergström 2005.

[223] Adopted from Königsgruber 2008, p. 247.

[224] Cf. Wüstemann/Kierzek 2006, p. 17.

where in the world"[225]. Convergence (mainly with US-GAAP) is one of the EC's major objectives to strengthen the competitiveness of the European capital market. The third criterion refers to the general criteria in the IFRS Framework.[226]

Before the Commission on its part suggests the endorsement of the standard, the EC's 'watchdog', the Standards Advice Review Group (SARG), judges whether the TEG's decision is acceptable and balanced. Again, for this decision the SARG consults the criteria as determined in the IAS Regulation. When the EC has proposed the acceptance of the standard, the Accounting Regulatory Committee (ARC)[227] controls for objections on the part of the national member state governments. In case of disapproval, the EC decides if the standard, despite of the objection by the ARC, is forwarded to the EP and the European Council or if the EFRAG is consulted again for further analysis of the problem. Nonetheless, an approval by the European Council against the opinion of the ARC is highly improbable as the delegates of ARC and Council are from the same ministries and most likely represent the same viewpoint. A standard that is approved by the ARC is directly transferred to the European Parliament and the European Council who finally decide on its endorsement. If the approval of the standard is rejected on the level of the EP respectively European Council, the EC decides if the matter is returned to the EFRAG for further analysis and advisory or left to the EP/European Council for final decision.

The above described approval process of the EU endorsement process reveals its sensitivity to political lobbying. The final approval of a newly released or revised standard depends on various parties, each of them following their own political interests. The veto rights of EFRAG representing the private sector, SARG representing the EC, ARC representing the national EU governments and EP complicate the endorsement process.[228] Although EU and IASB, e.g. through the work of the CCAD, proactively try to bring their interests in line, the above exemplified EU endorsement constellation has led to cases of denial in the past, e.g. for IAS 39 or IFRS 9.[229] A deviation between IFRS accounting standards as issued by the IASB and as endorsed by the EU is not in the interest of European global players which are listed or pursue a listing at SEC regulated stock exchanges like the New York Stock Exchange (NYSE), for instance. Even though the SEC now accepts foreign private issuers' financial statements prepared in accordance with IFRS without US-GAAP reconciliation, the financial statements have to comply with IFRS as published by the IASB.[230] This criterion would not be fulfilled in the case of an EU carve out. Also, the development of specific EU-IFRS would oppose the main IASB objective to create a set of worldwide uniform accounting standards. The deviation of IASB- and EU-IFRS lies nei-

[225] European Commission [EC] 2002, preamble, recital No. 5.

[226] Cf. van Hulle 2004, p. 368ff.; Königsgruber 2008, p. 247.

[227] The ARC like the CCAD consists of ministerial delegates of the EU member states and therewith directly represents the national governments in the endorsement process.

[228] A disagreement between ARC and European Council, however, is improbable since both ARC and Council represent the national ministries.

[229] Cf. Buchheim et al. 2008, p. 373; the endorsement of IFRS 9 has been postponed; cf. European Financial Reporting Advisory Group [EFRAG] 2009.

[230] Cf. Securities and Exchange Commission [SEC] 2007.

ther in the interest of the IASB nor in the interest of the EU. An intensified cooperation could prevent future disagreements.[231]

Although the EU has reached *de iure* harmonization for EU group accounting rules,[232] IFRS compliance and, thus, *de facto* harmonization could be prevented by differing enforcement of IFRS. Accordingly, the next chapter addresses the issue of EU enforcement harmonization.

1.3.3.2.4 EU enforcement harmonization

The preamble of the IAS Regulation states that "a proper and rigorous enforcement regime is key to underpinning investors' confidence in financial markets"[233]. To achieve this goal, the EU member states are required to take appropriate measures on national level;[234] the member states' enforcement activities shall be coordinated by the Committee of European Securities Regulators (CESR)[235].[236]

The **ESMA** is an association of the member states' national securities regulators; it was founded by the EC in 2001 (1) to coordinate the work of the national enforcement institutions, (2) to serve as an advisory body to the EC, and (3) to ensure the consistent and timely implementation of EU law in the member states.[237] In contrast to national securities regulators, the ESMA has no sovereign powers; the standards, recommendations and guidelines issued by the ESMA, thus, are not binding for the EU member states.[238] The ESMA basic principles to harmonize European enforcement are outlined in two standards. Standard No. 1 on Financial Information ('enforcement of standards on financial information in Europe') defines enforcement in general and specifically deals with:

- enforcement institutions,
- enforcement methods,
- enforcement sanctions,
- coordination of enforcement and
- enforcement reporting.[239]

Standard No. 2 on Financial Information ('coordination of enforcement activities') further substantiates that European enforcement shall be harmonized via regularly held Eu-

231 Cf. Buchheim et al. 2008, p. 373ff.; Königsgruber 2008, p. 247ff.

232 *De iure* harmonization of EU group accounting refers only to group accounting of companies that have their securities admitted to trading on an EU regulated market.

233 European Commission [EC] 2002, preamble, recital No. 16.

234 The FEE set out nine key features of effective enforcement bodies in a 2002 publication. Cf. Fédération des Experts Comptables Européens [FEE] 2002, p. 4ff.

235 As of January 1st of 2011 the CESR has become the European Securities and Markets Authority (ESMA). In the following the term ESMA also refers to its predecessor organization CESR.

236 Cf. Lamfalussy 2001; European Commission [EC] 2002, preamble, recital No. 16.

237 Cf. Committee of European Securities Regulators [CESR] 2010.

238 Cf. Delger/Committee of European Securities Regulators [CESR] 2008, p. 3; PricewaterhouseCoopers Österreich 2008, p. 13f.; Sanio 2008, p. 524f.; Berger 2009, p. 603.

239 Cf. Committee of European Securities Regulators [CESR] 2003, p. 3ff.

ropean Enforcers Coordination Sessions (**EECS**);[240] these regular meetings may also be attended by non-ESMA members since national enforcement in some EU member states is conducted by private sector institutions like the German Financial Reporting Review Panel (**FREP**)[241].[242] The specific tasks of the EECS are:

- to analyze and discuss the decisions of the national enforcement institutions,
- to identify differing or vague IFRS interpretations and to notify the IASB/IFRIC,
- to exchange experiences with respect to national enforcement practices and
- to provide advice to the ESMA.[243]

Enforcement decisions that are discussed on EECS level are later published in an internal database[244] that is only accessible by ESMA members;[245] some of these cases that are of general importance and that represent the EECS position are anonymized and made public.[246] Although the decisions taken at the EECS are not mandatory for EU enforcement institutions, national enforcers are expected to follow the EECS consensus.[247]

Besides the set-up and development of the EU enforcement database, which is an important tool to harmonize European enforcement, *Berger* lists further advantages of the regular European enforcers meetings.[248] First, EECS decisions are taken jointly; outstanding decisions are discussed at the EECS until the EECS participants have reached a common position that is accepted and applied by all national enforcers; in case of an EECS dissent the IFRIC is sought for advice.[249] Second, the plenary discussions lead to a learning effect of the EECS participants. Third, the monthly EECS form a valuable network of European enforcers that allows for informal consultation and exchange of experience even outside the EECS. And fourth, institutionalized meetings like the EECS serve the purpose to identify common European interests and represent these internationally; the chairperson of the EECS and representatives of the ESMA are in regular contact with the SEC to discuss questions of mutual importance.[250]

Enforcement coordination on the European level is a valuable contribution to the European enforcement and accounting harmonization. Nonetheless, European enforcement is

240 Cf. Ernstberger et al. 2011, p. 7f.

241 The FREP refers to the German *Deutsche Prüfstelle für Rechnungslegung* (DPR). For more information on the FREP cf. chapter 1.3.5.3.2.

242 Cf. Committee of European Securities Regulators [CESR] 2004b, p. 5.

243 Cf. Committee of European Securities Regulators [CESR] 2004a, p. 2.

244 The database is administered by the ESMA. The ESMA decides which enforcement decisions are published in the database and may withdraw decisions from the database, e.g., when these contradict more current interpretations by the IFRIC. Cf. Wüstemann/Kierzek 2006, p. 7.

245 Cf. Committee of European Securities Regulators [CESR] 2004b, p. 4.

246 Cf. Berger 2009, p. 607.

247 Cf. Committee of European Securities Regulators [CESR] 2004b, p. 2; *Heyd/von Keitz* (2007), p. 87; KPMG 2007, p. 32; Berger 2008, p. 507f.

248 Cf. Berger 2009, p. 606f.

249 The chairperson of the IFRIC regularly attends EECS.

250 Cf. Berger 2009, p. 606f.

far from being harmonized since national enforcement practices still differ considerably.[251] A single supranational European enforcement institution should have been the consequence of a common set of European financial accounting standards for capital market oriented companies. However, the unclear legal status of a European enforcement authority with competencies to impose sanctions impeded the timely implementation of such an institution;[252] the establishment of a 'European SEC' would have required a European Treaty and a higher degree of harmonization of EU securities legislation.[253] Also, EU member states' fears to lose control or influence might have played a role in the discussion of a European enforcement body.

1.3.4 Possible differences in IFRS practice

The previous chapters described the process of European accounting harmonization, which culminated in the compulsory implementation of IFRS for group accounts of capital market oriented companies for business years from 2005 respectively 2007 on. One might presume that both European accounting harmonization and European accounting research therewith has come to an end. Nonetheless, as already hinted at in the introductory chapters of this study, there are plenty of opportunities for remaining accounting differences. As long as the European accounting standards allow for some kind of discretion and as long as financial statements are prepared by human beings, there will be possibilities for accounting differences and comparative accounting research. Only the research focus shifts from national GAAP to IFRS, from *de iure* to *de facto* harmonization and therewith from standards to practice.[254]

This chapter is dedicated to one of the central points of this study: possible differences in IFRS practice. It is subdivided into the subchapters (1) reasons for IFRS differences and (2) opportunities for IFRS differences that result from first time adoption, regular application or enforcement of IFRS.

1.3.4.1 Reasons

The reasons for heterogeneous IFRS practice are diverse.[255] *Nobes* suggests that differences in **financing systems**, legal systems and tax systems are the main drivers for international accounting differences.[256] Based on previous research and reasons of conceptual simplicity, he proposes a dualist point of view to describe the dimensions of the different systems. Distinguishing between capital market based and credit based financing systems, he posits that the national accounting system is primarily influenced by a country's financing sys-

[251] Cf. Fédération des Experts Comptables Européens [FEE] 2001, p. 10; Committee of European Securities Regulators [CESR] 2007, p. 2f.; Ernstberger et al. 2011, p. 8.

[252] Cf. Berger 2009, p. 602.

[253] Cf. Fédération des Experts Comptables Européens [FEE] 2002, p. 41.

[254] Cf. Nobes 2006, p. 233ff.

[255] The below mentioned particular reasons are implemented as external context factors in this study and are described in more detail in the conceptualization chapter. Cf. chapter 2.3.2.

[256] Cf. Nobes 2006, p. 234f.

tem.[257] He argues that capital market oriented financing systems imply higher expectations with respect to quantity and quality of public financial information and that regulators and companies adapt to this pressure by stricter and more comprehensive regulations and additional voluntary information. The legal perspective is spanned between the two main **legal systems**: code law versus common law. The different perception of law and its purposes have an impact on the regulation of financial information. Accounting regulation in code law countries is generally provided by the legislative body, whereas common law countries typically have a private sector regulator. There is plenty of empirical evidence that indicates a relationship between a country's legal system and financial accounting practice.[258] Usually, common law countries are associated with higher-quality financial reporting and disclosure.[259]

Tax systems are classified according to the national accounting system's degree of independence from tax regulations.[260] There are countries that traditionally have two separate independent systems for tax and financial accounting (UK) and other countries which have an integrated system for both purposes (Germany). Tax driven accounting choices might have an influence on the companies' group accounts for reasons of convenience or tax conformity. German companies might find it more convenient to adopt tax motivated accounting choices in their individual accounts for their group accounts when IFRS options and discretion allow for this practice. Although there are different accounting systems for different purposes in the UK, tax considerations might play a role for UK companies, as well. As UK companies are allowed to apply IFRS for their individual accounts, tax driven accounting could find a way into group accounting.[261]

Besides institutional factors like the financing, legal or tax system, **national culture** is expected to be associated with national accounting practice patterns.[262] As outlined below (see chapter 2.2.4), cultural and institutional characteristics of a country are closely interlinked and reinforce each other on a mutual basis. Accordingly, these context factors should be taken into account commonly.

Reasons for systematic IFRS accounting differences are only relevant when there is room for inconsistent application. The next section lists opportunities for accounting differences according to IFRS as issued by the IASB and IFRS as endorsed by the EU.

1.3.4.2 Opportunities

According to *Nobes* there are eight sources for possible IFRS accounting differences: (1) different versions, (2) different translations, (3) gaps, (4) overt options, (5) covert options

---

257 Cf. Nobes 1998, p. 166ff.; see also Xiao 2004, p. 193ff.; Tarca et al. 2005, p. 60ff.; Sellhorn/Gornik-Tomaszewski 2006, p. 187ff.

258 Cf., e.g., Ball et al. 2000, p. 1ff.; Jaggi/Low 2000, p. 495ff.; Bushman/Piotroski 2006, p. 107ff.

259 Cf. Ball/Leuz 2001, p. 129.

260 Cf. Nobes/Parker 2008, p. 33ff.

261 Nobes 2006, p. 234f.

262 Cf. Perera/Most 1994, p. 268f.; Hofstede 2001, p. 282f.

and vague criteria, (6) measurement estimations, (7) transitional or first-time adoption issues and (8) imperfect enforcement.[263]

The following subchapters address the issue of opportunities for international accounting differences in more detail.[264] The focus thereby lies on IFRS accounting in Europe.

1.3.4.2.1 Different versions

Systematic accounting differences may occur even before companies decide on concrete IFRS options and IFRS measurement issues. Different versions of IFRS may lead to deviating IFRS practice in different IFRS regions (e.g. EU, Australia) worldwide and even within particular IFRS regions. Although IFRS is intentioned to serve as a worldwide valid international set of accounting standards, IFRS standards first have to be transposed into local law before being legally compulsory for national companies. Deviations from the exact IFRS requirements may lead to international differences. Australia, for example, has adopted IFRS not exactly as suggested by the IASB.[265] Certain Australian IFRS 'carve outs' as the result of lobby work by Australian companies impede international accounting harmonization.[266] The European endorsement process is another example for such conversion difficulties. Established by the EC to convert IFRS into European law, this process was exposed to and influenced by lobbyism in the recent past. Especially European banks had a say when IAS 39 was to be endorsed.[267] The 2005 discussion on the fair value option for all financial assets and liabilities ended in the IASB's amendment of IAS 39, which then was endorsed by the EU. Although the EU seeks to maintain absolute conformity with IFRS as published by the IASB, temporary accounting differences arise when standards are not, late or in a modified way endorsed.[268]

Even if IFRS standards are endorsed exactly as suggested by the IASB, the endorsement process may still lead to accounting differences. The process is rather complex and time consuming and endorsement may take up to more than one year.[269] The length of the endorsement process may result in the unintentional effect that some companies apply the new or modified standard before it is finally endorsed and mandatory for all companies. Companies could tend to early adopt new standards when the accounting issues covered by the new standard fill previous IFRS gaps or to anticipate the EC to rule the retrospective application of particular standards.[270] Besides accounting differences that go back to the duration and complexity of the endorsement process, differences might also result from early adoption of regulations. New IFRS standards usually allow for early adoption

---

263 Cf. Nobes 2006, p. 234.

264 Cf. for another overview on IFRS discretion Tanski 2004, p. 1843ff.

265 Cf. Nobes 2006, p. 236.

266 For instance, according to IAS 31, companies may recognize their interest in a joint venture using proportionate consolidation (IAS 31.30) or, alternatively, the equity method (IAS 31.38). In contrast, Australian companies that apply IFRS are required to use the equity method (AASB 131.38).

267 The endorsement of IFRS 9, the revised standard on financial instruments, also has been postponed by the EU; cf. European Financial Reporting Advisory Group [EFRAG] 2009.

268 Cf. Nobes 2006, p. 236.

269 Cf. Pellens et al. 2007, p. 2503f.; the EU endorsement process is described in chapter 1.3.3.2.3.

270 Cf. Pellens et al. 2007, p. 2505; Pellens et al. 2008, p. 94ff.

so companies can opt to voluntarily apply the new standard before it becomes mandatory. Finally, different versions of IFRS could be a topic for companies whose financial years do not conform to the calendar year.[271]

The European endorsement process and the conceptual IFRS characteristic to allow for early adoption could be the reason for different IFRS versions being applied and, thus, might lead to differences in IFRS practice among European listed companies.

1.3.4.2.2 Different translations

The endorsement process of new or revised standards is not completed with the formal acceptance of the English[272] standard by the EC. In fact, accepted standards need to be published in all official languages[273] of the EU in the Official Journal of the European Communities.[274] Only when translated in all official languages, IFRS standards become European law. The translated standards then become national law in the various European countries. The translation of the English version is usually subcontracted to the IASCF[275]. The IASCF has own personal to translate the English standards into the official European languages and is supported by the Big4 audit firms and translation bureaus. The translations are then transferred to the EC who has to ultimately accept the translations. The EC does not perform a complete review of the translated standards but makes sure that technical terms are in accordance with the European accounting regulations.[276]

Translation always carries the risk that the meaning of the translated information is changed in the process of translation, which may lead to misunderstandings.[277] This problem is exacerbated when translating specific accounting information; accounting standards usually contain a lot of technical terms and are part of a certain 'accounting subculture' that non-members of that culture (e.g. translators) may not fully understand. Accounting as the 'language of business'[278] is another language the translator needs to understand before being able to translate accounting related information. Furthermore, language is closely connected to culture and the way people in different cultures perceive and think.[279] "[...] Language is a cognitive device which provides us with the mental categories in which we think and learn"[280]. Accordingly, an exact translation without loss or distortion of meaning is almost impossible. It is even more difficult when translating technical (accounting) information. Apart from the bare meaning of the words, different accounting

[271] Cf. Nobes 2006, p. 236; Jödicke 2009, p. 64f.

[272] New and revised standards are published by the IASB in English.

[273] The EU currently has 23 official languages. Cf. European Commission [EC] 2010a.

[274] Cf. Article 3, paragraph 4 of the regulation (EC) No 1606/2002; European Commission [EC] 2002.

[275] The IASCF is to become the IFRS Foundation. Cf. International Accounting Standards Board [IASB] 2010g.

[276] Cf. Niehus 2005, p. 2478.

[277] Cf. Parker 2001, p. 315.

[278] Cf. Thorell/Whittington 1994, p. 215.

[279] Cf. Welch/Welch 2008, p. 341f.

[280] Evans 2004, p. 235.

cultures have different accounting concepts and the translated term may unfold a different meaning.[281]

Linguistic accounting research supports this assumption. In three case studies on the translations of accounting concepts such as the German '*Grundsätze ordnungsmäßiger Buchführung*' (GoB; 'principles on orderly accounting'), the German '*Vorsichtsprinzip*' ('prudence principle') and the British concept of 'true and fair view', *Evans* finds substantial differences in meaning.[282] Another study on the translation of the 'prudence principle' in the Fourth Directive suggests an emphasis of the 'prudence principle' in all languages except for the English version.[283] A Canadian study with anglophone and francophone students from Alberta and Québec discovers that the probability numbers the students attached to many equivalent 'uncertainty' expressions are not similarly distributed.[284] This translation effect related to 'uncertainty' expressions is also found in a study by *Doupnik/Richter*.[285]

There are several examples of IFRS translations that are rather inaccurate. IAS 7.07 ('Financial Instruments: Disclosure') e.g. states that "an investment normally qualifies as cash equivalent only when it has a short maturity of, say, three months or less from the date of acquisition". The word 'say' indicates that the period of maturity could also be longer than three months. The Portuguese translation leaves out the word 'say' and limits the period to three months or less, which constitutes a clear deviation from the original English version. Another example concerns the German translation of IAS 31.43. The English version requires Joint Ventures that no longer meet the criteria to be classified as 'held for sale' to "[...] be accounted for using proportionate consolidation or the equity method [...]". The option to also use proportionate consolidated accounting is omitted in the German version of IAS 31.[286]

The above annotations suggest that errors in translations or inaccurate translations in the national IFRS versions may be the cause for *de facto* inconsistent versions of IFRS and therewith result in international accounting differences.

1.3.4.2.3 Gaps

Gaps in IFRS refer to IFRS topics that are not specifically regulated in an IFRS standard or interpretation. For such topics IAS 8.10 indicates that "management shall use its judgement in developing and applying an accounting policy that results in information that is: (a) relevant [...] and (b) reliable [...]". The standard further exemplifies general guidelines applicable in such judgmental processes. According to IAS 8.11, the sources management shall mainly base its judgment on are either (1) standards or interpretations that are concerned with similar accounting problems or, in absence of such guidelines, (2) the general accounting principles of the IFRS Framework. Furthermore, management

281 Cf. Evans 2004, p. 210ff.
282 Cf. Evans 2004, p. 210ff.
283 Cf. Evans/Nobes 1996, p. 361ff.
284 Cf. Davidson/Chrisman 1993, p. 1ff.
285 Cf. Doupnik/Richter 2003, p. 15ff.
286 Cf. Nobes 2006, p. 237; Jödicke 2009, p. 66.

may also consider standards of other standard setting bodies that use a comparable framework, usually understood as a reference to US-GAAP (IAS 8.12).[287] IAS 8.12 further states that accounting literature and common industry practice are also accepted as judgmental guidelines as long as they do not conflict with the criteria defined in IAS 8.11. Following the argumentation of IAS 8.10-12, which refer to the IFRS Framework and other high quality accounting standards (US-GAAP), the possibility of unregulated accounting issues is categorically rejected; IFRS gaps by definition do not exist.[288] Nonetheless, the anchor rule of IAS 8.10-12, which refers to the broadly phrased formulations of the IFRS Framework, leaves plenty of room for management judgment and therewith opportunities for varying accounting practice.

Examples for accounting issues that are not satisfactorily covered by IFRS standards are 'extractive activities' or 'insurance contracts'.[289] The current IASB 'extractive activities' project deals with accounting aspects concerning the search for, finding and extraction of fossil resources like oil or gas and seeks to supersede IFRS 6 ('exploration for and evaluation of mineral resources'). The project focus is on the definition, recognition, measurement and disclosure of reserves and resources.[290] The IASB's 'insurance contracts' project consists of two separate phases. The first phase resulted in the interim standard IFRS 4 ('insurance contracts'). Nonetheless, IFRS 4 only covered the most urgent topics and is currently revised in the second phase of the IASB project.[291]

These two examples of current IFRS projects indicate that there are still some unfinished IASB 'construction sites' that allow for accounting differences. Lacking well-defined IFRS accounting rules, companies could fall back on national GAAP or accepted industry practice. Inconsistent national and international accounting practice would be the result.

1.3.4.2.4 Overt options

As mentioned above, IFRS were a product of compromises in the beginning. The members of the IASC were private sector accountancy bodies from nine different countries from different financial accounting backgrounds. This constellation meant the encounter of different concepts of accounting. The predominance of Anglo-Saxon countries already indicated the broad direction the IASC was heading following its task to develop a single set of internationally accepted accounting standards. Nonetheless, a 75% majority vote was required for IASC decisions and its members tended to represent the interests of their home countries. As a result, the early standards issued by the IASC contained numerous options to meet the members' concerns of an inadequate consideration of their national accounting characteristics. The discrepancy in accounting perspectives and their strong representation at the IASC is understandable to some extent. The intention to create in-

---

[287] Cf. Nobes 2006, p. 237.

[288] Cf. Nobes 2006, p. 236; Pellens et al. 2008, p. 94ff.

[289] Cf. the current IASB work plan: International Accounting Standards Board [IASB] 2010d.

[290] The discussion paper 'extractive activities' was published in April 2010; cf. International Accounting Standards Board [IASB] 2010b.

[291] Currently, comments on the discussion paper 'preliminary views on insurance contracts' are being reviewed by the IASB; cf. International Accounting Standards Board [IASB] 2010f.

ternational accounting standards was principally based on capital market considerations. The development of the particular capital markets of the founder member countries, however, was as heterogeneous as were the national accounting requirements.[292]

The many options of early IFRS led to the legitimate criticism that IFRS was not strict enough and allowed for inconsistent application. Two IFRS improvement projects that ended in 1993 and 2003 removed several of these options. At first the IASC followed the strategy to classify remaining options into 'benchmark treatment' and 'allowed alternative' to indicate the preferred variant.[293] This practice, however, was later abolished and both alternatives are now regarded as equally applicable.[294]

Table 1-2 lists examples of remaining IFRS overt options.[295] Options regarding IFRS 1 ('First time adoption of IFRS') are not included as these are dealt with separately.

Standard	Overt options
IAS 2.25	FIFO or weighted average allowed for cost of inventories
IAS 7.31	Choice of classification for cash flows from interest and dividends
IAS 16.29	Cost and revaluation model allowed for measurement of property, plant and equipment
IAS 19.92-93A	Actuarial gains and losses can be taken (a) immediately in full as OCI, (b) immediately in full as income, (c) in full or in part as income using corridor amortization
IAS 20.24	Asset grants can be shown as a deduction from the asset or as deferred income
IAS 31.30	Choice of proportional consolidation or equity accounting for joint venture entities
IAS 38.72	Cost and revaluation model allowed for measurement of intangible assets
IAS 39.09	Choice of cost or fair value measurement for some financial assets and liabilities
IAS 40.06	Permission to classify a property held under an operating lease as an investment property
IAS 40.30	Choice of cost or fair value as measurement basis for investment property

Table 1-2: Examples of overt option in IFRS; last revised 05.05.2010[296]

The presented overt options allow for different IFRS measurement and disclosure and directly lead to international accounting differences when companies use these options according to national GAAP or industry practice.

292 Cf. Nobes 2006, p. 237.

293 Examples for the distinction into 'benchmark treatment' (BT) and 'allowed alternative' (AA) were: IAS 2.25 permitting for the assignment of cost of inventories the first-in, first-out (FIFO) (BT), the weighted average (BT) and the last-in, first-out (LIFO) (AA) cost formula; IAS 16.35 permitting for the measurement of property, plant and equipment (PPE) the cost model (BT) and the revaluation model (AA); IAS 23.10 permitting borrowing costs to be recognized as an expense as incurred (BT) or capitalized as a 'qualifying' asset (AA); IAS 31.30 permitting the proportionate consolidation (BT) and the equity method (AA) for the consolidation of joint ventures; IAS 38.72 permitting for the measurement of intangible assets the cost model (BT) and the revaluation model (AA).

294 Cf. Nobes 2006, p. 237.

295 See for another extensive overview on overt and covert IFRS options Pöller 2007a, p. 1ff.; Pöller 2007b, p. 172ff.; Pöller 2008, p. 118ff.

296 Adopted from Nobes 2006, p. 238.

1.3.4.2.5 Covert options and vague criteria

In contrast to overt respectively 'true' options, covert options and vague criteria refer to room for discretion offered by various IFRS. Measurement issues that offer room for discretion are treated separately in the consecutive chapter. The discretion of **covert options** often depends on the interpretation of single words like, e.g., 'reliably' or 'probably' (see Table 1-3). In an international context, the interpretations of these terms are subject to both translation effects and culture effects. Above cited linguistic accounting studies on accounting expressions underline the potential for international accounting differences that arise from different linguistic perceptions. Culture studies on probability expressions support this notion. Researchers find significant differences in the intercultural understanding of exactly translated probability expressions (e.g. provisions: 'more likely than not').[297]

The external and internal indicators for the impairment of an asset (IAS 36.12-14) are an example of **vague criteria**. Apart from the sheer number of various external and internal criteria, that, according to IAS 36.13, are not to be regarded as exhaustive, the wording is often inexact and vague. IAS 36.12(a), e.g., assumes an external indicator for impairment when "[...] an asset's market value has declined significantly more than would be expected as a result of the passage of time or normal use", without specifying what is to be understood by 'significantly' or 'normal'. Another vague internal indicator is formulated in IAS 36.12(g), which requires management accounting evidence "[...] that the economic performance of an asset is, or will be, worse than expected". Again, it is left unclear what is meant by 'expected'. Another common example for vague criteria that may have a substantial impact on international accounting distortions is to be seen in the requirements for the capitalization of research and development (R&D) costs. The six criteria in IAS 38.57 like technical feasibility or intention to complete are generally regarded as a factual option to capitalize R&D expenditures.[298] Companies in countries like the UK, in which IFRS is allowed for use in the individual accounts and therewith allowed as a starting point for tax calculations, might be more motivated to interpret the criteria in favor of capitalization than German companies, for example. On the one hand, German accounting traditionally is more conservative and the capitalization of R&D expenditures was introduced to German GAAP just recently by the Accounting Law Modernization Act[299] in 2009. On the other hand, IFRS is only allowed for group accounts which are independent from tax considerations.[300]

Further examples for covert options and vague criteria that are likely to lead to internationally varying IFRS application are shown in Table 1-3.

---

[297] Cf. Doupnik/Richter 2003, p. 15ff.; Doupnik/Riccio 2006, p. 237ff.

[298] Cf. Dawo 2003, p. 205f.; Heyd/Lutz-Ingold 2005, p. 46; Wagenhofer 2005, p. 210.

[299] The Accounting Law Modernization Act refers to the German *Bilanzrechtsmodernisierungsgesetz* (BilMoG).

[300] Cf. Nobes 2006, p. 240; Jödicke 2009, p. 72.

Standard	Covert options and vague criteria
IAS 8.05	The determination of materiality for various purposes
IAS 11.22	Use of PoC method only if the outcome of a contract can be estimated reliably
IAS 12.34	Recognition of deferred tax assets for a loss carryforward only if future taxable profit is probable
IAS 17.08	Lease classification based on 'substantially all the risks and rewards'; no numerical criteria
IAS 21.09-12	Determination of functional currency based on a mixture of criteria
IAS 36.12-14	Identification of an indication of impairment based on a mixture of criteria
IAS 37.14	Recognition of a provision based on probability of outflow of resources
IAS 38.57	Capitalization of development costs when all of various criteria are met
IAS 38.88	Amortization of intangible assets only if useful life is assessed as finite
IAS 41.30	Use of cost basis for a biological asset whose fair value cannot be measured reliably
IFRS 5.08	Treatment of assets as held-for-sale if expected to be sold within one year

Table 1-3: Examples of covert options and vague criteria in IFRS[301]

1.3.4.2.6 Measurement estimations

The IASC *ab initio* followed a consequent investor oriented perspective. IFRS are designed to provide relevant and reliable financial information to the capital market. According to IAS 1.15, "financial statements shall present fairly the financial position, financial performance and cash flows of an entity". The overall principle of fair presentation requires financial information that draw a picture of the financial position and performance of the company as realistic and timely as possible. The principle of prudence, however, conceptually representing a more conservative approach, is only mentioned as one of the sub-criteria of the IFRS qualitative characteristic 'reliability'.[302]

The goal to present information as realistic and timely as possible is articulated in an increasing degree of management judgment. The fair value approach is the outcome of such considerations. The value of an asset or a liability is more realistic when determined by an active market transaction than by cost. When there is no active market, other measurement procedures are applied that require management judgment in estimates. According to IAS 8.33, such estimations are "[...] an essential part of the preparation of financial statements [...]", but also offer room for discretion that management might exploit to follow goals that contradict fair presentation. Estimations are often utilized in cases of earnings management.[303]

Besides earnings management considerations, tax issues and convenience could have an influence on the way companies make use of management judgment in estimates. Asset depreciation, for example, is used in many countries by the fiscal authorities as an instru-

[301] Adopted from Nobes 2006, p. 239.

[302] Cf. F.24-46.

[303] Cf. Healy/Wahlen 1999, p. 367.

ment to generate incentives for corporate investments. Therefore, tax depreciation often differs from the depreciation that best resembles the normal wear of the asset.[304] Depreciation is subject to estimates with regard to useful life and residual value (IAS 16.50/51). Companies that are allowed to use IFRS for their individual accounts (UK) could apply tax minimizing useful life estimates. Also, companies that do not use IFRS for individual accounts could apply the tax minimizing useful life estimates for reasons of convenience. Inconsistent accounting practice would be the result of such behavior.[305]

Further examples of IFRS estimations are listed in Table 1-4.

Standard	Estimations
IAS 2.30/31	Net realizable value of inventories
IAS 11.16	Costs attributable to a contract
IAS 12.51	Tax rate for deferred tax calculations based on the expected manner of settlement or recovery
IAS 16.50-60	Depreciation based on estimates of useful life, residual value, and pattern of consumption
IAS 16.31-34	Fair value when selected as a measurement basis
IAS 19.73	Pension obligations based on estimates of mortality, final salary, etc.
IAS 37.36	Best estimate of provisions based on percentage likelihoods of outflows
IAS 39.48	Fair values for certain financial assets and liabilities
IAS 41	Fair values for biological assets (paragraph 12)
IFRS 2.10	Fair value for equity-settled share-based payment transactions
IFRS 3.16	Identifiable assets and assumed liabilities in a business combination are measured at fair value

Table 1-4: Examples of estimations in IFRS[306]

Management estimations that are influenced by national GAAP, tax optimizing accounting, earnings management or national culture[307] could be the reason for systematical accounting differences.

1.3.4.2.7 Transitional or first-time adoption issues

Transitional or first-time adoption issues refer to opportunities for different accounting patterns related to the process of first-time adoption or adoption of new respectively superseded standards that have a long-term effect on IFRS financial statements. Whereas

[304] Until 2011 it was common in Germany to use the reducing balance method for tax purposes and the minimum useful life time allowed by tax law. When straight line depreciation exceeded reducing balance depreciation, companies changed to straight line depreciation for the remaining years of useful life. As from January 1st of 2011 the reducing balance method is no longer permitted for newly acquired assets; cf. § 7 paragraph 2, sentence 1 EStG.

[305] Cf. Nobes 2006, p. 241.

[306] Adopted from Nobes 2006, p. 241.

[307] For a review of culture studies cf. chapter 1.5.2.

transitional rules for new or superseded standards[308] are outlined in the respective standards, first-time adoption issues are basically clarified in IFRS 1 ('first-time adoption of IFRS'). According to IFRS 1.07, the IFRS accounting policies effective at the end of the first IFRS accounting year are to be applied retrospectively. For reasons of practicability, voluntary and compulsory exemptions to this approach are specified in IFRS 1.13-34B and Appendices B-E. Accounting differences might arise, first, from companies applying voluntary exemptions differently and, second, from different national GAAP practices that survive under IFRS as a result of IFRS exemptions.[309] Appendix C1, for instance, permits companies to choose to not apply IFRS 3 retrospectively for business combinations prior to the IFRS transition date. This exemption allows different national GAAP goodwill practices to continue under IFRS. Whereas IFRS follows an impairment only approach for goodwill acquired in a business combination, national GAAP usually allowed to write off goodwill directly against reserves or to amortize goodwill over a certain number of years.[310] Some countries like France never permitted a write-off against reserves; therefore, French companies supposedly transferred more goodwill to their first-time adoption IFRS balance sheets than other countries that permitted this accounting practice.[311]

Another first-time adoption issue that has a long-term effect on IFRS statements could stem from the transitional revaluation of property, plant and equipment (PPE).[312] IFRS adopting companies can either take the fair value at the date of transition as deemed cost of PPE or the corresponding value according to national GAAP (IFRS 1 Appendix D5-7). Again, national practices may differ with reference to the revaluation of PPE. Some countries required respectively allowed the fair value approach for PPE even before the adoption of IFRS (UK). Other countries only approved the historical cost method (Germany). Companies could find it more convenient to not recognize PPE at its fair value. Accounting differences due to national GAAP deviations would be the result. Such differences from asset revaluation could endure and affect IFRS accounting consistency until the assets are either sold or completely depreciated. Moreover, in the case of assets with an expected infinite useful life, these differences theoretically continue forever. Despite such theoretical considerations, accounting differences from first-time adoption issues are likely to diminish as time passes by; transitional effects associated with the release of new and revised standards, however, are anticipated to disturb consistent IFRS practice from time to time.[313]

---

[308] The option to voluntarily adopt a new standard before it becomes mandatory was already mentioned when dealing with 'different versions' of IFRS.

[309] Cf. Nobes 2006, p. 242.

[310] In Germany it was common to amortize goodwill according to the corresponding tax regulations. § 7 paragraph 1, sentence 3 EStG (German Income Tax Act) defines the useful life of goodwill as a period of 15 years.

[311] Cf. Nobes 2006, p. 242.

[312] Cf. Nobes 2006, p. 242.

[313] Cf. Nobes 2006, p. 242.

Options as part of the transitional regulations in IFRS 1 and other standards are likely to be applied differently by companies from different countries and industries and, thus, may result in dissenting IFRS practice.[314]

1.3.4.2.8 Imperfect enforcement

The previously described opportunities for IFRS accounting differences so far discussed options and scope for discretion that are part of IFRS or the result of international endorsement and translation processes. The last opportunity identified by *Nobes* deals with internationally differing degrees of financial reporting compliance. He posits that the companies' degree of compliance is affected by the quality of the national enforcement system.[315] Some researchers even argue that the enforcement of accounting standards and the prosecution of rule violations are as important as the standards themselves.[316] This implies that high-quality accounting standards could be redundant if the consecutive enforcement of these standards is inadequate.[317]

On the European level, the financial reporting system was standardized for capital market oriented companies by the IAS Regulation. The enforcement mechanisms, however, as an important element in the overall process of providing high quality financial information, are not harmonized; instead, enforcement is independently organized by the national financial supervisory regulations.[318] The centrally coordinated EU wide implementation of standardized national supervisory authorities or a central European enforcement agency should have been the logical consequence of the adoption of IFRS. Unfortunately, as often the case in the European harmonization process, the EU member countries feared to lose further legal autonomy by submitting to a higher-ranking European institution. The concern of low enforcement countries that their national companies could have been disadvantaged in comparison to companies from advanced enforcement countries might have played a role, as well. Additionally, the insufficient harmonization of European securities and stock exchange laws and diverging corporate governance structures among European companies led to the appraisal that the implementation of a central European agency was not feasible.[319] However, the solution of decentralized independent national enforcement bodies whose activities to a certain degree are coordinated and harmonized via participation in monthly EECS[320] and collecting of the results in a public database is surely not appropriate to quickly reach Europe wide similar enforcement and comparable compliance.[321]

---

314 Cf. Nobes 2006, p. 242.
315 Cf. Nobes 2006, p. 242ff.
316 Cf. Sunder 1997, p. 167; Kothari 2000, p. 92.
317 Cf. Nobes 2006, p. 242f.
318 Cf. Fédération des Experts Comptables Européens [FEE] 2000; Securities and Exchange Commission [SEC] 2000.
319 Cf. Wüstemann/Kierzek 2006, p. 18.
320 Cf. Committee of European Securities Regulators [CESR] 2004b; Delger/Committee of European Securities Regulators [CESR] 2008, p. 3.
321 Cf. Jödicke 2009, p. 75ff.

Empirical studies support the assumption that enforcement and compliance differ across European countries; such differences are often associated with the size and extent of the national capital market.[322] *Hope* finds that enforcement differs significantly across a sample of 22 countries and analysts' forecast accuracy is positively associated with national enforcement.[323] Other studies support the notion that strong enforcement systems are related to higher degrees of compliance.[324] These considerations lead to the conclusion that imperfect enforcement respectively internationally varying enforcement could result in different levels of national IFRS compliance and, thus, be the reason for international accounting differences.

The intermediary results of this chapter are further utilized when determining the context factors that are expected to have an influence on IFRS accounting practice (see chapter 2.3.2). Moreover, the described opportunities for deviating accounting practice are the basis for the development of the hypotheses in chapter 2.3.4. Before presenting the field of research of this study and reviewing relevant prior research, the next subchapter substantiates the regional focus of this study.

1.3.5 EU regional focus

The focus of this study is on **EU** member states for the following reasons. First, capital market oriented companies from EU countries have to prepare their group financial statements in accordance with IFRS as endorsed by the EU. Countries outside the EU often implement IFRS in a slightly modified way to account for national particularities. When analyzing the impact of country factors like culture on IFRS practice, such 'minor' modifications could bias the results of the analysis. Second, the EU hosts cultures that differ substantially from one another. To compare, for example, the IFRS countries UK, New Zealand and Australia is not conducive from a cultural perspective. Though all three countries apply IFRS, the cultures of New Zealand and Australia, as former British Colonies, are just too similar to the British culture and accounting differences resulting from cultural differences would be difficult to prove. Third, the availability of an adequately high number of financial statements is another argument for the European capital market. Being the second largest capital market worldwide, the large number of listed companies allows for sufficiently powerful statistical tests.

1.3.5.1 EU country selection

Another issue every scholar has to consider when planning an international accounting research project is the **number of countries** to assess. Influence factors like research strategy, available time and manpower and the availability of data play a role in making this decision. *Wallace/Gernon* distinguish three basic research strategies with respect to the number of countries to be investigated.[325] These strategies cover the whole spectrum from intensive to extensive country studies with one country studies as the intensive extreme

322 Cf. La Porta 1997, p. 1149.

323 Cf. Hope 2003a, p. 235ff.

324 Cf. Street/Bryant 2000, p. 305ff.; Street/Gray 2001; Brown/Tarca 2005, p. 181ff.

325 Cf. Wallace/Gernon 1991, p. 249f.

and all country studies as the extensive extreme. The reasons why countries are selected for a study, generally develop along the two extremes of the intensive/extensive dimension. When selecting only one country, there are usually convincing practical or theoretical reasons for this decision, e.g. the scholar comes from that country or the analyzed matter can only be found in that specific country. Besides a one country research strategy, researchers can also decide to select a few pivotal respectively 'vital' countries. These countries are selected as the scholar expects valuable results from their analysis. The decision to select particular countries for analysis is usually well founded in the research design, financial or personnel restrictions or specific country characteristics that are exceptionally relevant for the test of the hypotheses.[326] The third strategy is to comprise a large number of countries for analysis. Such research strategies are only suited for large financially and personally well resourced research projects. The country selection is random or influenced by country factors that apply to many countries, e.g. state religion.[327]

This study follows the second research strategy of picking a few **'vital' countries**. As financial statements are subjected to an in-depth-analysis of culture relevant content, the expansion of the analysis to more than three countries is inhibited by financial and personnel constraints. The reasons why France, Germany and the UK are regarded as 'vital' for this study are economic vitality, socio-economic similarity and cultural diversity. There are other minor reasons that justify this selection. First, the personal background and the corresponding expertise of the researcher should also be considered in the country decision. It is always easier to include one's own home country in the country sample as language barriers do not exist and the national accounting system is well known. The author's knowledge of languages is another reason for selecting the UK and France. Although it is expected that the listed companies in the sample are large enough to publish their financial statements in English, it may be useful in certain occasions to passably understand the original language. Moreover, international accounting literature is characterized by a predominance of British and US studies. As a result, studies on European countries, except the UK, are seldom. Accordingly, international accounting literature benefits from the recognition of France and Germany as analyzed countries in this study.

Availability of data is another constraint in determining the proper number of countries to be analyzed. Contrary to secondary data that is provided in a standardized database from which it is extracted and further processed electronically and therefore qualifies for multi country analysis, this study mainly follows a **handpicked data** approach. The culture relevant financial information are handpicked from corporate group accounts. Nonetheless, databases are consulted whenever possible to reduce the workload, for example, to gather information on internal context factors like auditor or size of the company.[328]

The motivation to select France, Germany and the UK as sample countries is further substantiated in the following subchapter.

[326] Cf. Franke/Richey 2010, p. 1275ff.
[327] Cf. Wallace/Gernon 1991, p. 249f.
[328] Cf. Wallace/Gernon 1991, p. 249f.

1.3.5.2 Motivation for country selection

The previous subchapter already hinted at the broad variety of criteria that are to be considered when selecting certain countries for a scientific research project. As aforementioned, the selection of countries is limited to the geographic and economic area of the European Union. The 'vital-country' concept, as employed by *Nobes/Parker*,[329] serves as a rationale to further justify the choice of the three EU countries France, Germany and the UK. According to the 'vital-country' concept, international comparative accounting research benefits from the 'vitality', i.e. the economic importance of the respective countries. Economic importance thereby may refer to the gross domestic product (GDP), the size of the capital market, the size of the accounting profession etc.

France, Germany and the UK are to be seen as 'vital' countries according to that definition; the three countries are considered to be **economically important** in a worldwide context and in particular in a European context. Measured by GDP, the UK, France and Germany are the largest EU economies representing more than 50% of the EU-27 zone GDP.[330] Also, the three countries have the **largest and most developed European equity capital markets**. This fact is underlined by the size of the countries' national stock exchanges. Measured by domestic equity market capitalization and total value of share trading in 2008, the French NYSE Euronext (Europe)[331] is the largest European stock exchange, followed by the British LSE and the German *Deutsche Börse*.[332] Traditionally, the LSE was the largest stock exchange in Europe. The French *Paris Bourse* merged into Euronext, a combination of European stock exchanges; the NYSE Euronext (Europe) figures, thus, do not represent the French capital market only. Nonetheless, the *Paris Bourse* was by far the largest stock exchange to form Euronext.

Large equity capital markets also bear the advantage to provide a sufficiently large sample of large or midsize listed domestic companies[333] that publish detailed and comprehensive annual financial statements to be analyzed. The LSE with 2,415 listed domestic companies at year-end 2009 offers the best prerequisites for sample selection; 1,002 domestic companies are listed at the NYSE Euronext (Europe) and 742 domestic companies are listed at the *Deutsche Börse*.[334] The large number of listed companies in France, Germany and the UK assumingly allows for sufficiently large country samples of sufficiently large listed companies.[335] The analysis of financial statements of large companies bears the ad-

---

329 Cf. Nobes 1983, p.1ff.

330 Cf. European Commission [EC] 2009, p. 74.

331 The French stock exchange *Paris Bourse* merged with the Amsterdam and the Brussels Exchange in 2000 to create Euronext. The Lisbon Exchange and the London International Financial Futures and Options Exchange (LiFFE) joined Euronext in 2002. In 2007 Euronext merged with the NYSE. Cf. NYSE Euronext 2010.

332 Cf. World Federation of Exchanges [WFE] 2009, p. 36, 39.

333 As the focus of this study lies on the influence of national culture, only domestic listed companies, i.e. companies that have their headquarters in the particular country, are included in the sample.

334 Cf. World Federation of Exchanges [WFE] 2009, p. 86.

335 The Irish Stock Exchange and the Austrian *Wiener Börse* for example have only 58 respectively 101 domestic companies listed. A sufficiently large country sample of large listed companies would be difficult to obtain. For a description of the company sample of this study cf. chapter 4.2.

vantage that these are generally published in English. For its level of detail and quantity of disclosure, financial statements of large companies are also expected to lead to better research results.[336]

Another indicator that underlines the three countries' vitality with regard to international financial accounting issues is their status as **founding members of the IASC**. Accountancy bodies from France, Germany and the UK were among the nine founding members in 1973.[337]

Apart from their status as 'vital' countries for financial accounting research, the three selected countries are well suited to analyze the effect of **cultural differences**; France, Germany and the UK differ considerably with respect to their national culture. This statement is further substantiated subsequent to the presentation of the culture theoretical concept of this study in chapter 2.2.4.7.2.

Moreover, when studying differences in accounting, it is useful to select similar countries to make sure that the measured differences are actually connected to the tested influence factors and not to another environmental factor that is not controlled for. Being the three leading European economies, France, Germany and the UK are comparable in terms of economic development. Admittedly, Germany has more inhabitants than France and the UK and the GDP is accordingly higher. The GDP *per capita*, however, is similar, the UK ranking slightly higher than France and Germany.[338] Besides economic factors, the selected countries share other similarities. France, Germany and the UK are democratic Western countries engaged in the same political and military alliances. They share the same Christian values and look back on the same Greco-Roman rooted European history.[339]

In the following subchapter France, Germany and the UK are further characterized with respect to their national institutional environment. The country profiles are described based on the external context factors financing system, legal system, tax system, national GAAP system and enforcement system.

1.3.5.3 Country profiles

1.3.5.3.1 France

Although the selected EU countries represent the largest EU equity capital markets, country differences can be observed with respect to the development of the particular capital markets. Compared with the UK, which traditionally relies heavily on equity financing, France and Germany can be considered to have relatively less developed equity capital markets. Following the above presented dichotomy of equity-based financing systems and credit-based systems, France and Germany belong to the latter category. Whereas Germany is a good example for a credit-based financial institution system, the French financing

[336] Cf. Cooke 1989, p. 178f.; Marston/Shrives 1991, p. 205.
[337] Cf. Wallace/Gernon 1991, p. 247f.
[338] Cf. European Commission [EC] 2009, p. 73.
[339] Cf. Schweikart 1985, p. 97; Wallace/Gernon 1991, p. 247.

system is acknowledged to be credit-based governmental. The French government, which traditionally pursues an intervening economic and industrial policy, guided by national interests and macroeconomic plans, tries to distribute the national financial resources according to these plans. When necessary, financial resources are provided by the state; the state therewith acts as an investor.[340]

According to the insider-outsider classification by *Nobes*, France clearly is to be labeled as credit-insider system. Companies tend to be debt financed and the government exerts a considerable influence on national finance practice.[341] Indicators for the development of the financing system, like total market capitalization, total value of stocks traded and total number of companies, support the above classification of the French financing system (see Table 1-5).

	3 year average 2006-2008		
Financing system indicator	France	Germany	UK
Market capitalization of listed companies (in TUSD)	2,231	1,617	3,168
Market capitalization of listed companies (in % of GDP)	89%	50%	121%
Total value of stocks traded (in TUSD)	3,060	2,981	7,017
Total value of stocks traded (in % of GDP)	119%	91%	262%
Total number of listed domestic companies	797	651	2,639

Table 1-5: Financing system indicators for France, Germany and the UK[342]

The **financing system** indicators draw a clear picture of the three sample countries. The UK ranks first, followed by France in second place and Germany ranks third. Measured by market capitalization, the French capital market is ca. 30% smaller than the UK capital market and ca. 30% larger than the German capital market. Furthermore, the total value of stocks traded at the French capital market is only half as high as compared to the British value of stock traded. The number of listed domestic companies emphasizes the previous figures.

As France, in terms of equity capital market development, ranks in between the UK and Germany, the French capital market is assumed to be less investor oriented than its British counterpart, but slightly more investor oriented than the German capital market. Although French companies increasingly rely on equity capital, the French financing system is typically considered to be rather credit-based; capital is traditionally provided by financial institutions and the government.[343] These (large) creditors usually do not rely on public information only, but often have access to insider information.[344]

---

340 Cf. Cable 1985, p. 129f.; Nobes 1998, p. 166; Gernon/Meek 2001, p. 3ff.

341 Cf. Zysman 1983, p. 286; Nobes 1998, p. 167.

342 Cf. World Databank 2010. A three year average is chosen to level the effects of the worldwide economic crisis on financing system indicators.

343 Cf. Zysman 1983, p. 286; Nobes 1998, p. 166.

344 Cf. Nobes 1998, p. 167.

The classification of France as a rather creditor friendly country is supported by the French type of **legal system**. Like most Continental European countries, France is a typical code law country and country of origin of the Napoleonic Code, which had substantial influence on other European legal systems. Code law countries are usually acknowledged to be less investor oriented than common law countries; the accounting rules in these countries are codified by the government, which tends to emphasize the interests of the tax authorities.[345] Nonetheless, the requirements of the international capital market and the corresponding needs of large French multinationals had a considerable influence on French accounting regulation, as the following lines will show.

France has a **financial accounting** tradition going back to the seventeenth century. *Colbert*, a minister of *Louis XIV.*, and *Savary*, a rich influential merchant, constituted the *Code Marchand*, also referred to as the *Code Savary* in 1673; it made accounting books obligatory for merchants using the journal book as accounting evidence.[346] In the eighteenth century, the idea of double-entry bookkeeping was adopted by French accountants and the nineteenth century led to the concept of regarding enterprise and owner as separate entities, therewith introducing the notion of share capital. The twentieth century in French accounting thought was dominated by accounting standardization, which resulted in the establishment of the *Plan Comptable Général* (PCG) in 1947. The PCG was designed to become the French homogeneous national accounting framework; furthermore, it was intended to be a tool in governmental economic planning.[347] It contains the applicable accounting rules, a standardized chart of general ledger accounts and standardized formats for the balance sheet, the profit and loss account and the notes.[348] It was revised in 1957 and made obligatory for all companies taxed on profits in 1965. Moreover, from 1957 on, the PCG was administered by the *Conseil National de la Comptabilité* (CNC), a mixed public and private sector body that was founded for that purpose in 1957.[349] Two more revisions of the PCG followed in 1982 and 1999, mainly as a consequence of the European accounting Directives, which aimed at European accounting harmonization. Besides the PCG, which was codified in 1999, French accounting rules are regulated in the *Code de Commerce* (CC), which sets out a framework of general accounting rules. Whereas the PCG basically deals with rules concerning the presentation and format of financial statements, the CC elaborates upon general accounting rules. According to the CC, the French accounting objectives are reliability, comparability and accuracy of information. Reliability is achieved by the accounting principles of (1) legal compliance, (2) good faith, (3) true and fair view and (4) prudence. These fundamental accounting principles are further detailed in the PCG.[350]

Though French accounting as a consequence of the imposition of a national accounting plan is highly regulated and appears to be highly standardized, French accounting is less uniform as one could expect; especially group accounts used to differ from regulation and

345 Cf. chapter 2.3.2.1.2.
346 Cf. Barth 1953, p. 65f.
347 Cf. Fortin 1996a, p. 67.
348 Cf. Fortin 1996b, p. 4ff.
349 Cf. Nobes/Parker 2008, p. 296.
350 Cf. Gélard 2001, p. 1019ff.

also from one group to another.[351] This diversity in group accounting is partly attributed to the high degree of complexity of French accounting regulation. Additionally, group accounts of French multinationals traditionally deviated from national regulation, where these did not meet the needs of an internationally operating group.[352] When French multinationals started to publish group accounts in the 1960s, they found the rules defined by the PCG inadequate. Consequently, these companies started to use US-GAAP to compete at the international capital market, an approach that in 1980 was legitimized by the French securities supervision authority *Commission des Opérations de Bourse* (COB).[353] Group accounts of foreign listed companies could, thus, be published in accordance with IFRS or standards applied in Anglo-Saxon countries like the US. French groups listed only in France, however, had to comply with French accounting regulation. This confusion of different accounting approaches was improved in 1985, when the transformation of the Seventh EU Directive forced the French legislature to set up a separate body of rules for consolidated accounts. The newly installed dualism of group and individual accounts therewith uncoupled French groups from the rigid tax influenced regulations on individual accounts. Nonetheless, in the 1990s many large listed French companies continued to apply IFRS or US-GAAP in their group accounts, a practice which was generally tolerated by the French legislator.[354] Finally, in 1998 French listed companies were permitted by law to apply IFRS or US-GAAP for their group accounts under certain conditions: these international standards had to be translated into French and were not permitted to oppose the provisions of the European accounting Directives; furthermore, French financial statements in accordance with either IFRS or US-GAAP had to be in line with regulations by the French *Comité de la Réglementation Comptable* (CRC)[355], which for a long time did not take a clear position on that topic.[356] Accordingly, the application of international accounting standards in France was associated with a certain amount of uncertainty.[357]

The implementation of IFRS for capital market oriented EU companies in 2005 finally settled the issue of remaining uncertainty. Although explicitly permitted by the IAS Regulation,[358] the CNC and the CRC[359] decided to not extend IFRS application to French individual accounts. Instead, they chose to seek conversion with IFRS by means of a revision respectively modernization of French GAAP; new regulations concerning, for instance, provisions, depreciation, recognition and measurement of assets or fair value mea-

---

351 Cf. Walton 1992, p. 187; Richard 2001, p. 1135ff.

352 Cf. Scheid/Walton 1992, p. 4ff.

353 Cf. Commission des Opérations de Bourse [COB] 1980, p. 276.

354 Cf. Scheid/Walton 1992, p. 6.07.

355 The CRC was founded in 1998. In analogy to the CNC it is a mixed private and public sector body. Unlike the CNC, the CRC has regulatory power; regulations that are developed by the CNC have to be passed by the CRC; cf. Choi/Meek 2008, p. 61f.; Nobes/Parker 2008, p. 297.

356 Cf. Richard 2001, p. 1135ff.

357 Cf. Richard 2001, p. 1136.

358 Cf. chapter 1.3.3.2.

359 In 2009 the CNC and the CRC were merged into the *Autorité des Normes Comptables* (ANC), the French accounting standard setter; cf. Autorité des Normes Comptables [ANC] 2011, p. 1ff.

surement of financial instruments were issued in line with respectively close to corresponding IFRS rules.[360]

Although tax and accounting law are regulated in different law codes, there is a close link between French individual accounting and **tax accounting.**[361] Various tax related issues find its way into French commercial accounts. Especially when companies make use of tax concessions, these are to be included in the corporate financial statements following the reverse authoritative principle.[362] Nonetheless, it is questionable, in how far tax law exerts an influence on French group accounts. As outlined above, French multinationals early disconnected from French individual accounting and therewith from fiscal influences.[363]

Enforcement in France has a long tradition. The governmental institution COB was founded in 1967 and acts as an independent authority to guarantee the order of the French financial markets.[364] The COB conducts two types of financial statements reviews. First, it reviews all financial statements included in the prospectuses, which have to be approved prior to the issuing of securities. Second, listed companies can submit their financial statements to a voluntary review by the COB. Many French listed companies do so to achieve the trust of the capital market and to facilitate future fund raising. The COB is supported by the *Compagnie Nationale des Commissaires aux Comptes* (CNCC), the national auditors association. The CNCC conducts additional audit quality reviews and reports the results to the COB. The main instrument of enforcement is negative publicity. The COB has the legal power to force companies that do not comply with national accounting requirements to restate their accounts.[365]

1.3.5.3.2 Germany

In analogy to France, the German **financing system** is regarded as rather credit-based.[366] This assumption is supported by the above listed financing system indicators (see Table 1-5); in terms of market capitalization, total values of stocks traded and total number of listed domestic companies, the German equity capital market is the least developed of the three sample countries. In contrast to the French governmentally administered financing system, the German debt capital market is dominated by large financial institutions and insurance companies. Accordingly, the German financing system is also categorized as a credit-insider system, in which financial information is not uniquely distributed by formal public channels. Investor orientation in Germany is considered to be lower than in more developed equity capital markets like the UK.[367]

Comparable to France, the German **legal system** is to be classified as code law system; financial accounting is subject to detailed regulation. Accounting rules and principles are

---

360 Cf. Nobes/Parker 2008, p. 317; see more detailed in Richard 2005.
361 Cf. Eberhartinger 1999, p. 95.
362 Cf. Grünberger 1999, p. 544; Radebaugh et al. 2006, p. 71.
363 Cf. Gélard 2001, p. 1040ff.
364 Cf. Tunc 1982, p. 759.
365 Cf. Gottwald/Paré Valérie 2004, p. 3ff.; Brown/Tarca 2005, p. 189.
366 Cf. Nobes 1998, p. 166.
367 Cf. chapter 2.3.2.1.1.

set out in various Acts, mainly in the German Commercial Code[368]. The statutory accounting rules are supplemented by the principles of proper bookkeeping[369], an expression for generally accepted accounting principles, which the HGB makes reference to. Nonetheless, most of the accounting principles can be traced back to codified rules in the HGB and other Acts.[370]

German **financial accounting** regulation is partly rooted in French accounting thought. The Prussian Civil Code[371], enacted in 1794, was based on the French *Code Savary* and introduced first measurement rules, like the lower of cost or market principle for current assets. The General German Commercial Code[372] of 1861 obliged businesses to draw up an inventory and balance sheet at the close of each year and the Stock Corporation Act[373] of 1870 committed stock companies to publish financial statements, including balance sheet and profit and loss account. Only a few years later, the tax accounts were linked to the commercial accounts by the authoritative principle. The HGB of 1897 introduced accounting rules for all types of businesses and made first reference to the principles of proper bookkeeping (GoB). Aside from minor amendments, the Commercial Code remained in force until 1985.[374]

The economic crisis at the end of the 1920s had an impact on accounting regulation, as well. The Stock Corporations Emergency Decrees[375] introduced the director's report as well as the obligatory audit for stock companies. The Stock Corporation Act was amended twice in 1937 and 1965, the latter amendment including first group accounts requirements; at that time only German companies had to be included in the group accounts.[376] The Disclosure Act[377] of 1969 extended mandatory financial statement publication requirements for stock companies to large companies of any other legal form.[378] The enactment of the Fourth and Seventh Directive led to a comprehensive revision of the Commercial Code in 1985. As mentioned above, both Directives resulted in considerable harmonization of European group accounting.[379] Even so, German GAAP did not meet the needs of German multinationals when these first applied for listing at US stock exchanges in the 1990s. To fulfill the SEC requirements, German companies had to reconcile their financial statements to US-GAAP, a procedure that was costly and time consuming. Additionally, the 1997 founded German NASDAQ pendant *Neuer Markt*, a stock exchange market segment for technology oriented ('New Economy') companies, required financial statements in accordance with IFRS or US-GAAP for listing. As a result of these apparent

---

368 The German commercial code refers to the German *Handelsgesetzbuch* (HGB).

369 The principles of proper bookkeeping refer to the German GoB.

370 Cf. Müller 1988, p. 11f.

371 The Prussion Civil Code refers to the German *Preußisches Allgemeines Landrecht.*

372 The General German Commercial Code refers to the German *Allgemeines Deutsches Handelsgesetzbuch* (ADHGB).

373 The Stock Corporation Act refers to the German *Aktiengesetz* (AktG).

374 Cf. Ballwieser 2001, p. 1223ff.

375 The Stock Corporations Emergency Decrees refers to the German *Aktienrechtsnotverordnung.*

376 Cf. Busse von Colbe 1996, p. 245.

377 The Disclosure Act refers to the German *Publizitätsgesetz* (PublG).

378 Cf. Busse von Colbe 1996, p. 245.

379 Cf. chapter 1.3.3.

accounting internationalization tendencies, the German law makers, analogous to French law makers, in 1998 reacted with an amendment to the HGB;[380] listed firms were now permitted to publish their group accounts in accordance with internationally accepted accounting standards (IFRS/US-GAAP).[381]

German accounting regulation always was detailed and the regulation process used to be exclusively in the hands of the German legislature. When in doubt how to interpret a paragraph the accountant should fall back on (1) deductive reasoning to identify what the legislature had in mind at the time of issuance or (2) consider the interpretations by the German Institute of Certified Public Accountants.[382] Alternatively, accounting issues were discussed in German accounting literature or decided by the Federal Fiscal Court[383]. Codified accounting rules, however, have the disadvantage of being inflexible since the politically influenced legislation process is rather slow; the law cannot be changed promptly to react on new accounting developments. Against the background of an increasingly globalized economy and the momentum gaining European accounting harmonization process in the 1990s, the German legislator reacted via the Commercial Code Reform Act[384] in 1998 and laid the legal foundations for a private sector standard setting body.[385] This body was entitled (1) to develop accounting recommendations for group accounts, (2) to advise the federal Ministry of Justice[386] in accounting regulation and (3) to represent Germany in international standard setting committees.[387] As a consequence of that Act, the Accounting Standards Committee of Germany (ASCG)[388] and the German Accounting Standards Board (GASB)[389] were founded and began their work shortly after foundation.[390]

The GASB members are elected by the ASCG and are responsible for the technical work of developing German Accounting Standards (GAS)[391]; its work is supervised by the ASCG.[392] The ASCG has issued numerous GAS on group accounting that have the legal status of GoB when published by the Federal Ministry of Justice.[393] When the EC issued

---

380 In Commercial Code Reform Act to Facilitate the Raise of Capital (*Kapitalaufnahmeerleichterungsgesetz* (KapAEG)) introduced the possibility for capital market oriented companies to publish their group accounts in accordance with IAS; cf. Pellens et al. 2008, p. 47.

381 Cf. Wendlandt 2008, p. 448ff.

382 Cf. Moxter 1985, p. 20f.; Leffson 1987, p. 29ff.

383 The Federal Fiscal Court refers to the German *Bundesfinanzhof* (BFH).

384 The Commercial Code Reform Act refers to the German *Gesetz zur Kontrolle und Transparenz im Unternehmensbereich* (KonTraG).

385 The KonTraG also required German group accounts to be complemented by segment reporting and cash flow statement.

386 The Federal Ministry of Justice refers to the German *Bundesjustizministerium* (BMJ).

387 Cf. Wendlandt 2008, p. 449.

388 The ASCG refers to the German *Deutsches Rechnungslegungs Standards Committee* (DRSC).

389 The GASB refers to the German *Deutscher Standardisierungsrat* (DSR).

390 Due to unsettled funding issues, the members of the ASCG in June 2010 decided to terminate the contract with the BMJ with effect from January 1st of 2011.

391 The German Accounting Standards refer to the German *Deutsche Rechnungslegungs Standards (DRS).*

392 Cf. Choi/Meek 2008, p. 67.

393 Cf. Ballwieser 2001, p. 1227ff.; Ordelheide 2001, p. 1365ff.; Wendlandt 2008, p. 452ff.; Deutsches Rechnungslegungs Standards Committee [DRSC] 2011b.

the IAS Regulation in 2002, which obliged German capital market oriented companies to publish IFRS group accounts, the GASB in 2003 modified its strategy as a standard setter; according to the new strategy, the GASB explicitly seeks to cooperate with the IASB and other international standard setters to promote the convergence of German group accounting with IFRS.[394]

The 2004 German Accounting Law Reform Act[395] (BilReG) recognized one of the options of the IAS Regulation[396] and permitted non capital market oriented companies to apply IFRS in their consolidated group statements.[397] The EU member state option to allow IFRS for individual accounts (IAS Regulation)[398] was not executed by the German legislator.[399] The government feared that IFRS application in individual accounts could oppose the accounts' purpose as legal basis for dividend distribution and basis for tax calculation.[400] Instead, the HGB was modernized via the 2009 Accounting Law Modernization Act (BilMoG), which led to substantial convergence with IFRS regulations; for instance, the new regulations implemented:

- the option to capitalize self-created intangible assets,
- (limited) fair value measurement of financial instruments,
- a more realistic measurement of provisions[401] and
- internationally unusual accounting options like the recognition of a provision for maintenance expenses were eliminated.[402]

The BilMoG was designed to deregulate and modernize German GAAP to provide especially small and medium sized companies with an economic alternative to IFRS.[403] Moreover, several EU Directives were transformed into national law by the amendments of the BilMoG.[404]

As mentioned above, there is a traditionally strong link between **tax accounts** and commercial accounts in Germany.[405] The Income Tax Act EStG refers to the GoB as basis for tax accounting, if not explicitly indicated otherwise. This so-called authoritative principle was accompanied until 2009 by the reverse authoritative principle, which obliged compa-

---

394 Cf. Deutsches Rechnungslegungs Standards Committee [DRSC] 2011a; Choi/Meek 2008, p. 67.
395 The Accounting Law Reform Act refers to the German *Bilanzrechtsreformgesetz* (BilReG).
396 Cf. chapter 1.3.3.2.
397 Cf. Meyer 2005, p. 41ff.
398 Cf. chapter 1.3.3.2.
399 Cf. Ditting 2005, p. 101ff. Companies may choose, however, to publish individual accounts in accordance with IFRS; cf. Ballwieser 2001, p. 1223ff.
400 Cf. Ernst/Seidler 2008, p. 120f.
401 The measurement of provisions has been made dynamic. Future development of prices, salaries etc. have to be considered; furthermore, provisions (remaining life > one year) are to be discounted. Cf. Wolz/Oldewurtel 2011, p. 41ff.
402 For an overview of the modifications introduced by the BilMoG cf. Bundesministerium der Justiz [BMJ] 2009.
403 Cf. Melcher/Schaier 2009, p. 4ff.
404 Cf. Förschler 2009, p. 38ff.
405 Cf. Eberhartinger 1999, p. 95.

nies to account for certain solely tax motivated issues, like forms of accelerated depreciation or tax exempt investment reserves, in the individual accounts. Also, the prudence principle, an expression of the strongly creditor oriented German accounting approach, governs tax accounting as well as commercial accounting. This is surprising as prudent or conservative accounting contradicts the fiscal political interest to maximize tax yields.[406] The high degree of consistence of tax law and commercial law, institutionalized by the two-sided authoritative principle, led to a majority of German companies having identical statements for tax and commercial purposes.[407] Group accounts of large listed companies, however, have long been uncoupled from individual and tax accounts to meet the information needs of the international capital market. Also, these companies assumingly do not want to communicate their tax profits.[408]

Contrary to France, **enforcement** in Germany is conducted by a private sector body. The German Financial Reporting Review Panel (**FREP**)[409] was institutionalized by the provisions of the *Bilanzkontrollgesetz* (BilKoG) and started its operations in 2005.[410] The German government designed the German enforcement process based on the idea of self-regulation of the capital market; only when self-regulation fails regulatory mechanisms take over. Therefore, the German enforcement system is built as a two-stage system combining the advantages of both private sector system and governmental system.[411] The FREP is a private sector body and directly responsible for the review of annual accounts of listed companies. The FREP selection of annual accounts for review is both random (proactive review) and event driven (reactive review). The companies' cooperation with the FREP is voluntary and the legal power of the FREP limited. When a company is not willing to fully cooperate with the FREP or when the company does not accept the identified misstatement, the German financial market supervisory authority *Bundesanstalt für Finanzdienstleistungsaufsicht* (BaFin)[412] takes over on the second stage. The BaFin is equipped with the legal means to force the company to cooperate. Identified misstatements have to be published by the company itself.[413]

1.3.5.3.3 United Kingdom

The above comparison of **financing system** indicators characterizes the British financing system as strongly equity based (see Table 1-5). Measured by market capitalization, the British equity capital market is 30% larger compared to the French equity capital market; the German capital market is about half as big as the British. The British value of stocks traded of circa seven trillion USD is more than twice as high as the French and the Ger-

406 Cf. Wagner 1990, p. 2334.
407 Cf. Döllerer 1983, p. 159.
408 Cf. Ballwieser 2001, p. 1248ff.
409 The FREP refers to the German *Deutsche Prüfstelle für Rechnungslegung* (DPR).
410 Cf. Müller/Reinke 2010, p. 506.
411 Cf. Choi/Meek 2008, p. 67.
412 The BaFin is comparable to the US SEC.
413 Cf. Hommelhoff 2001, p. 41; Knorr 2004, p. 85; Gelhausen/Hönsch 2005, p. 511; Hommelhoff 2005, p. 57; Zülch 2005a, p. 1ff.; Zülch 2005b, p. 565ff.; Zülch/Burghardt 2007, p. 369; von Keitz/Stolle 2008, p. 213ff.; Meyer 2008, p. 60ff.; Hüttche 2009, p. 325ff.

man values of stocks traded; the latter two each account for approximately three trillion USD. Finally, the number of listed domestic companies in the UK is more than three times the number of French companies and more than four times the number of German companies. These figures suggest that the UK has the most developed equity capital market of the three sample countries. Correspondingly, the UK financing system is usually classified as an equity-outsider system.[414] In contrast to credit-insider financing systems, in which investors and bondholders receive financial information also via private informal information channels, 'outsider' investors rely mainly on public available information. As a consequence, public financial information tends to be more investor oriented.

As mentioned above, the financing system is closely linked to the type of **legal system**. The UK is a typical common law country and has exported this model via the British Empire internationally. Common law is less abstractly codified than code law and in constant development, as the courts administer the law. This flexible, less regulative legal approach of the UK also formed the British **financial accounting** system. Business in the UK traditionally was less regulated and rather characterized by a *laisser-faire* philosophy. Nonetheless, the emergence of the first British multinational companies, related to the expansion of the British Empire in the seventeenth century, expressed the necessity of some type of regulation. The Bubble Act in 1720 determined some first requirements with respect to the formation of new companies; corporations had to be either formed by Royal Charter or by Act of Parliament. Various Companies Acts later, which introduced firm concepts like the limited liability company or the joint stock company, the Companies Act in 1908 came up with the concept of the private company and the requirement for public companies to publish financial statements. The next milestone in British accounting thought was the Consolidation Act in 1947, which introduced the important accounting principle of 'a true and fair view', replacing the 'true and correct view' required before.[415] The 1947 Act also defined measures of the profit and loss account, the balance sheet and group accounts. At about the same time, the Institute of Chartered Accountants in England and Wales (ICAEW) began to issue first recommendations of accounting principles to limit the diversity of accounting practice in those days. These recommendations, however, were not mandatory and therewith of limited use to auditors. The following years were characterized by the consolidation of the British accounting scene. In 1970 the ICAEW founded the Accounting Standards Steering Committee (ASSC), which was soon joined by members of other British accountancy bodies. The successful cooperation under the roof of the ASSC[416] resulted in a provision in the 1989 Companies Act, which required large companies to publish their accounts in accordance

[414] Nobes 1998, p. 167.

[415] As mentioned above, the 'true and fair view' was later adopted by the European Community in the Fourth Directive; for a detailed overview on the 'true and fair view' in British accounting cf. Walton 1993.

[416] The ASSC was renamed in 1976 in Accounting Standards Committee (ASC) and replaced in 1990 by the ASB. The ASB is a private sector standard setter comparable to the US FASB. The ASB's main tasks are to issue accounting standards and to collaborate internationally with standard setters from other countries and the IASB; cf. Accounting Standards Board [ASB] 2011; Alexander/Archer 2000, p. 546.

with the standards issued by the ASC/ASB.[417] Furthermore, the 1989 Companies Act implemented the recommendations of the 1988 Dearing Report[418], which criticized the British standard setting process.[419] As a consequence, the Financial Reporting Council (FRC)[420], the UK's financial accounting regulator, was founded; the FRC sets the general policies of British standard setting and supervises the ASB, the ASB's Urgent Issues Task Force (UITF)[421] and the Financial Reporting Review Panel (FRRP)[422].[423]

Although investment holding companies had existed in the UK from the mid nineteenth century on, the publication of consolidated accounts was rather the exception than the rule until the enactment of the Companies Act in 1947, which required group companies to publish consolidated balance sheets and consolidated profit and loss accounts. In analogy to French and German group accounting, the transformation of the Seventh Directive in 1989 had a major impact on British group accounting.[424] Another milestone in UK group accounting was the 2002 issued IAS Regulation, which require British capital market oriented companies to apply IFRS in their group accounts from 2005 on; companies that have their securities admitted for trading at the Alternative Investment Market (AIM), a market for shares of smaller companies, have to apply IFRS for financial years from 2007 on. In comparison to French or German companies, which come from a creditor oriented Continental European accounting background, British companies are expected to have had the least difficulties switching to IFRS since UK-GAAP and IFRS are conceptually very similar. IFRS originates from Anglo-Saxon accounting thought. Moreover, as aforementioned, the foundation of the IASB was the result of an initiative of British accountancy bodies. Also, five of the nine IASB founding members came from an Anglo-Saxon accounting background.[425] The influence of the investor oriented Anglo-Saxon accounting philosophy on IFRS is accordingly high.[426] Consequently, the degree of convergence between UK-GAAP and IFRS is a lot higher compared to French or German GAAP.[427] Following *Horton/Serafeim*, the main differences between UK-GAAP and IFRS relate to the accounting areas leases, employee benefits, share-based payments, taxation, goodwill and financial instruments.[428] As a consequence of the conceptual proximity, Brit-

[417] Cf. Cooke/Wallace 1995, p. 2633ff.

[418] Cf. Consultative Committee of Accountancy Bodies [CCAB] 1988.

[419] Cf. Roberts et al. 2008, p. 558f.

[420] The FRC is an independent body, which oversees the British standard setting process. Its members come from the industry, commerce and the accounting profession. Cf. Brown/Tarca 2001, p. 272; Financial Reporting Council [FRC] 2011.

[421] The UITF was established by the ASB to address and clarify current accounting issues; the position of the UITF is published in so-called UITF abstracts. Cf. Choi/Meek 2008, p. 80.

[422] For more information on the work of the FRRP see the annotations below.

[423] Cf. Dewing/Russell 2004, p. 112; Choi/Meek 2008, p. 80.

[424] Cf. Walton 1992, p. 186ff.; Küting/Hayn 1995, p. 112f.; Taylor 1995, p. 2809ff.

[425] Cf. chapter 1.3.2. The Dutch accounting system is considered to be closer to Anglo-Saxon than to Continental European accounting; cf. Nobes/Roberts 2000, p. 26.

[426] Cf. Hung/Subramanyam 2007, p. 624; Devalle et al. 2010, p. 89.

[427] Cf. O'Connell/Sullivan 2008, p. 18.

[428] Cf. Horton/Serafeim 2010, p. 729ff. See also Nobes/Parker 2008, p. 325.

ish companies, in contrast to French or German companies, are allowed to apply IFRS in their individual accounts, as well.[429]

The option to issue the individual accounts in accordance with IFRS was introduced by the 2006 Companies Act, which led to further convergence of UK-GAAP and IFRS.[430] The 2006 Companies Act modernized British company law and incorporated EU Directives like the 2003 EU Modernization Directive[431], the EU Transparency Directive and the EU Takeover Directive.[432] Its key policy objectives were to (1) increase stakeholder engagement and promote long-term investments, (2) to modernize and deregulate UK company law and (3) to facilitate the foundation and running of companies.[433] Furthermore, the 2006 Companies Act replaced the two separate company law regimes for Great Britain and Northern Ireland.[434]

In contrast to France and Germany, **tax accounting** in the UK is independent from financial accounting.[435] This autonomy of calculation regimes is mainly founded on the timely difference between tax and commercial accounting regulation. As annotated above, the beginnings of British accounting were rather characterized by a broad diversity of accounting practice and a governmental economic *laissez-faire* policy. Accordingly, the tax authorities had to develop their own consistent set of tax accounting rules of how to recognize and measure taxable profits.[436] Of course, tax and commercial accounting rules were brought into line over time and today base on the same accounting principles. The independence of both spheres, however, has remained. The ASB regards governments and their agencies as one among many secondary users of accounts.[437] Although based on the same accounting principles, tax profits may differ substantially from the companies' earnings as disclosed in the financial statements. First, differences may result from non-taxable income respectively expenditures not allowable for tax. Second, timing differences, which possibly lead to deferred tax assets or liabilities, could lead to different annual results. The reverse authoritative principle, responsible for fiscal influences on French and German individual accounts, does not exist in the UK. Nonetheless, the commercial accounts are the starting point for every tax computation of UK trading profits.[438]

The British national **enforcement** institution is a private sector body. As outlined above, the FRRP was founded as a consequence of the 1989 Companies Act and started its work

---

[429] Cf. Eccles/Holt 2005, p. 377.
[430] Cf. Clark/Knight 2009, p. 261f.
[431] Cf. European Commission [EC] 2003.
[432] Cf. Russel 2008; Clark/Knight 2009, p. 261.
[433] Cf. Department for Business Innovation & Skills [BIS] 2010, p. 3. The Modernization of British company law concerned, inter alia, directors' duties, derivative claims against directors, company meetings and resolutions, enfranchising of indirect shareholders and an enhanced business review for listed companies; cf. Russel 2008.
[434] Cf. Companies House [CH] 2009.
[435] Cf. Eberhartinger 1999, p. 95.
[436] Cf. Lamb 1996, p. 933.
[437] Cf. Accounting Standards Board [ASB] 1999, p. 21.
[438] Cf. Her Majesty's Revenue and Customs [HMRC] 2006.

in 1991.[439] The UK decided to implement a private sector model in accordance to the British standard setting process, which is also organized by a private organization, the ASB. The main purpose of the FRRP is to reveal financial misstatements in annual accounts and interim reports. It possesses the legal power to encourage compliance. When deemed necessary, misstatements are made public by court declaration and the revision of accounts is enforced by court order. The FRRP uses publishing of identified misstatements as an effective instrument to enforce compliance by public pressure. Furthermore, publishing has the educational effect to show other companies how to do it right. The approach followed by the FRRP is not systematical reviewing all annual accounts in a certain order. Instead, the FRRP takes actions when certain matters are brought to its attention. In doing so, between 1992 and 1997 346 annual statements were reviewed by the FRRP; 51% of these reviews resulted in publishing. Since 2004 the scope of the annual accounts reviewed by the FRRP was broadened by implementing an additional random review.[440]

Having substantiated the regional focus of the study, the next chapter presents the field of research this study is attributed to. This chapter lays the foundation for the following review of prior research.

1.4 Field of research

The research area of this study is international financial accounting, which is outlined in more detail in the following subchapter. Based on this general classification, the research area of this study is further specified in the second subchapter on the international financial accounting research subarea international comparative financial accounting research (ICFAR). Furthermore, a research framework for ICFAR is presented and refined to categorize prior research studies reviewed in chapter 1.5.

1.4.1 International financial accounting research

The term 'international accounting' delivers a first description of this field of study. International accounting does not refer to a specific branch of accounting, but covers all branches of accounting embedded in a cross-national or cross-cultural context and therefore can be rather seen as a cross section of accounting.[441]

Weirich et al.'s three-way distinction of **international accounting** from 1971 is a good circumscription of international accounting that coincides largely with more current categorizations of international accounting sub-disciplines.

> *"**World accounting**. In the framework of this concept, international accounting is considered to be a universal system that could be adopted in all countries. A worldwide set of generally accepted accounting principles (GAAP), such as the set maintained in the United States, would be established. Practices and principles*

---

[439] Cf. Dewing/Russell 2004, p. 112; Jupe 1999, p. 312.

[440] Cf. Haller et al. 2001, p. 1673ff.; Brown/Tarca 2005, p. 190; Wüstemann/Kierzek 2006, p. 20; Brown/Tarca 2007, p. 447ff.

[441] Cf. Samuels/Piper 1985, p. 7.

> *would be developed which where applicable to all countries. This concept would be the ultimate goal of an international accounting system.*"[442]
>
> "***International accounting***. *A second major concept of the term international accounting involves a descriptive and informative approach. Under this concept, international accounting includes all varieties of principles, methods and standards of accounting for all countries. This concept includes a set of generally accepted accounting principles established for each country, thereby requiring the accountant to be multiple-principle conscious when studying international accounting. [...] A collection of all principles, methods and standards of all countries would be considered as the international accounting system. These variations result because of differing geographic, social, economic, political and legal influences.*"[443]
>
> "***Accounting for foreign subsidiaries***. *The third major concept that may be applied to international accounting refers to the accounting practices of a parent company and a foreign subsidiary. A reference to a particular country or domicile is needed under the concept for effective international reporting. The accountant is concerned mainly with the translation and adjustment of the subsidiary's financial statement. Different accounting problems arise and different accounting principles are to be followed depending upon which country is used as a reference for translation and adjustment purposes.*"[444]

Using the terms of later approaches to carve out the field of research of international accounting, 'world accounting' can be seen as international accounting harmonization, 'international accounting' can be 'translated' into comparative/descriptive international accounting and 'accounting for foreign subsidiaries' is close to international financial reporting issues related to multinationals.

Gray reviews international accounting research in the UK from 1970 to 1981 and divides his review into the following categories of international accounting:

- comparative international accounting,
- international accounting harmonization,
- international financial reporting issues and
- managerial decision making and financial control in the international context.[445]

The fourth category reveals that *Gray* elects a broader definition, subsuming managerial decision making under international accounting.

In their first 1984 edition of 'International Accounting' *Choi/Mueller* build upon the 1971 definition of *Weirich* et al. adding a fourth category:

- international comparative analysis,

[442] Weirich et al. 1971, p. 97.
[443] Weirich et al. 1971, p. 97.
[444] Weirich et al. 1971, p. 97.
[445] Cf. Gray 1983, p. 18.

- accounting measurement and reporting issues unique to multinational business transactions and the business form of the multinational enterprise,
- accounting needs of international financial markets and
- harmonization of worldwide accounting and financial reporting diversity via political, organizational, professional and standard setting activities.

Samuels/Piper in 1985 perform an extensive literature review and identify three categories concurring with *Weirich et al.*'s classification and add a fourth historical dimension: "the spread of accounting ideas from country to country"[446]. *Meek/Saudagaran* recognize the efforts of various researchers in the 1980s to classify international financial reporting systems by creating a fourth 'classification' category.[447]

This study belongs into the field of **international comparative financial accounting research**; it compares financial reporting practices in an international context. It focuses on nations as context of investigation and does not explicitly respond to problems that are unique to multinational enterprises, although multinationals form part of the sample to be analyzed. The type of financial accounting standards to be examined is IFRS, the product of international financial accounting harmonization. For this reason, the harmonization category is of interest as well. The classification category, introduced by *Meek/Saudagaran*, will not be discussed in detail. Classification studies mainly do not generate new data, but use secondary data from descriptive or comparative studies. While not discussed in detail, classification studies are helpful in determining what countries to select for comparison.[448] Furthermore classification studies indicate which countries the results may be possibly transferred to; a country selected for comparative research should be a representative for other countries of the same cluster so that the findings of the study are transferable.[449]

The following chapter focuses on the international accounting research subdivision international comparative financial accounting research.

1.4.2 International comparative financial accounting research

1.4.2.1 Definition of the field of research

Comparison is a rather simple but useful approach in research to contrast certain characteristics of one research object with the corresponding characteristics of another research object, thereby highlighting the similarities and differences of the studied objects. Studying international accounting, i.e. different accounting systems respectively practices among nations,[450] comparison is a natural approach to gain cognition:

---

[446] Samuels/Piper 1985, p. 3.

[447] Cf. Meek/Saudagaran 1990, p. 154.

[448] Cf. chapter 1.3.5.2.

[449] Cf. Wallace/Gernon 1991, p. 248.

[450] The term 'international' not only names the research object (nation), but also implies a method of research viz. comparison (inter originates from the Latin 'inter', meaning between/among).

"Comparative research undertakes to identify, explain and interpret similarities and differences between phenomena in different locations and cultures."[451]

Nobes was one of the first to publish a textbook on comparative international accounting.[452] The following citation was taken from the tenth edition of 2008.

"Understanding why there have been differences in financial reporting in the past, why they continue in the present, and will not disappear in the future, is one of the main themes of comparative accounting."[453]

Based on this general argument for studying comparative international accounting *Nobes* lists three major reasons why a comparative approach to international accounting is appropriate.

"It serves as a reminder that the US and other Anglo-Saxon countries are not the only contributors to accounting as it is practiced today."[454]

"It allows one to learn from both the achievements and failures of others and to avoid the perils of accounting ethnocentrism."[455]

"It explains why the international harmonization of accounting has been deemed desirable but has proved difficult to achieve."[456]

Especially the second and third aspects are important and closely linked. Without the knowledge about financial reporting practices of other countries and their individual experiences, national improvement and international harmonization is difficult. With respect to the aim of this study, the third aspect surely is most relevant for this study investigating impediments to accounting harmonization in a European context. As the two following citations show, the comparative approach in international financial accounting research is applied to analyze both accounting systems and accounting practice.

"Comparative international accounting is defined to include the description and analysis of accounting systems at the national level, including their historical evolution; comparative analyses of national systems of accounting and financial reporting; and the classification of accounting systems according to patterns of development."[457]

"Comparative accounting is the study of accounting practices in various countries and socioeconomic systems for the purpose of providing explanations for the similarities and differences identified and developing and testing universal accounting theories."[458]

451 Carnegie/Napier 2002, p. 694.

452 The first edition of the homonymous book was published in 1981.

453 Nobes/Parker 2008, p. 4.

454 Nobes/Parker 2008, p. 15ff.

455 Nobes/Parker 2008, p. 15ff.

456 Nobes/Parker 2008, p. 15ff.

457 Gray 1983, p. 19.

458 Wallace/Gernon 1991, p. 210.

Whereas the first definition rather refers to pre-IFRS comparative accounting research, the latter definition encompasses both pre- and post-IFRS research as the focus is on practice instead of systems; accordingly, this definition is better suited to reflect the research problem of this study.

There are two basic approaches in ICFAR, the **culture free** approach, on the one hand, and the **culturally grounded** approach, on the other hand. Whereas the culture free approach to international accounting regards accounting merely as a tool that provides unbiased financial information of an entity, the culturally grounded approach sees accounting as a social phenomenon that cannot be analyzed independently from its organizational, societal and cultural context.[459] As *Choi/Mueller* state:

> *"If we accept the proposition that the environments in which accounting operates are not the same in different countries or even in different organizations, it stands to reason that accounting must necessarily differ from case to case if it is to retain the sharp cutting edge of social utility."*[460]

As introductory outlined, this study assesses the effect of national culture on IFRS practice and, thus, follows the **culturally grounded** approach.

The following section describes the ICFAR field of research in more detail and presents a framework to classify ICFAR studies.

1.4.2.2 ICFAR framework

Wallace/Gernon criticize the absence of a more abstract, theoretical perspective for international accounting in a 1991 article and present a framework for ICFAR that seems to be useful to give an impression of the variety of studies in this field of study and to give structure to the following review of prior research.[461] The framework structures comparative studies in a wider sense covering numerous aspects of international financial accounting research and, hence, lends itself particularly well for structuring relevant studies.

Wallace/Gernon identify three dimensions of ICFAR. While the first dimension (subject matter of research) sets the scene of the study in determining the aspects of accounting to examine, the second dimension (view of accounting) determines whether accounting is seen as a technical, linguistic, economic or sociological phenomenon; the third dimension (function of nation) deals with the function or the role of the nation.[462]

As Figure 1-8 shows, *Wallace/Gernon* span their ICFAR framework inside the third dimension using **nation** as the determining variable.

---

459 Cf. Saudagaran/Diga 1999, p. 57.
460 Choi/Mueller 1978, p. 22.
461 Cf. Wallace/Gernon 1991, p. 209.
462 Cf. Wallace/Gernon 1991, p. 209.

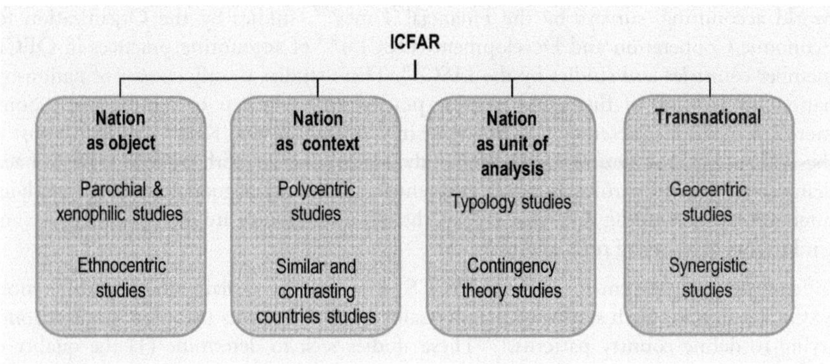

Figure 1-8: ICFAR framework[463]

'Nation as object' studies

The first ICFAR branch 'nation as object' embraces both single country studies that try to identify unique accounting phenomena in the researcher's home country (parochial studies) respectively in a country foreign to him (xenophilic studies) and single country studies that are replications of prior home country studies performed in a foreign country (ethnocentric studies). Single country studies are admitted to the framework as they are seen as a first step or a base for more advanced comparative research.[464] Although single country studies might provide interesting insights with respect to a particular country, these are of little relevance for this study, which seeks to analyze national cultural differences and their effect on financial accounting practice.

'Nation as context' studies

The second ICFAR branch 'nation as context' hosts multi-country studies that use countries as a 'vehicle' to investigate the context in which accounting takes place. 'Nation as context' studies are distinguished into two types of studies, viz. polycentric studies and similar and contrasting countries studies (SACCS).

Polycentric studies are rather descriptive studies that focus on accounting differences and deny universality. Descriptive accounting studies are often carried out by professional accounting firms like Price Waterhouse (PW)[465] or KPMG[466] or by professional accountancy bodies like the American Institute of Certified Public Accountants (AICPA)[467]. Apart from these studies from professional accountants' points of view, there are a series of

463 Adopted from Wallace/Gernon 1991, p. 224.

464 Cf. Wallace/Gernon 1991, p. 223ff.

465 Cf. Price Waterhouse 1973; Price Waterhouse 1976; Price Waterhouse 1979.

466 Cf. *Ordelheide/KPMG* (1995).

467 Cf. American Institute of Certified Public Accountants [AICPA] 1964; American Institute of Certified Public Accountants [AICPA] 1975.

'world accounting' surveys by the Financial Times[468], studies by the Organization for Economic Cooperation and Development (OECD)[469] of accounting practices in OECD member countries and studies by the IASC[470]. These studies mostly consist of nation-by-nation descriptions of financial reporting practices/rules in text or tabular form. Some more recent data is presented by *Ordelheide* in cooperation with KPMG.[471] In contrast to the PW studies, the *Ordelheide/KPMG* study is a product of both professionals and academics and based on rules alone.[472] Polycentric studies are a good start when studying international accounting differences. Nonetheless, these studies are merely descriptive and tend to mix accounting rules and practice.

In contrast to polycentric studies, **SACCS** also seek to explain country differences. SACCS search for both similarities (universality) and differences (country specifications), trying to define country patterns.[473] These studies seek to determine (1) the quality of different national accounting systems, (2) the association between country-specific factors and accounting practice or (3) the value relevance of earnings prepared under different national GAAP.[474]

Especially the investigation of the influence of **country factors** is of interest to this study. *Gray* in a 1980 article develops a conservatism index to measure the correlation of national characteristics with the measurement of company profits; he studies 72 French, German and UK firms in the period from 1972 to 1975 and finds German and French companies to be more conservative than their UK counterparts.[475] *Ali/Hwang* study the association of value relevance[476] of financial accounting data and country factors from 1986 to 1995 and state that value relevance is lower in countries that have (1) a bank oriented financial system, (2) private sector standard setters, (3) a 'Continental' accounting model and (4) tax influenced financial accounting measurements.[477] *Ball et al.* focus on the legal system of countries and reveal that earnings in common law countries (UK, US) are timelier and therefore resolve information asymmetry better than in code law countries (France, Germany).[478] *Guenther/Young* study a similar set of countries over a slightly extended period of time with similar results. Earnings and underlying economic events are

---

[468] Cf. Lafferty et al. 1979; Lafferty/Cairns 1980; Stilling et al. 1984.

[469] Cf. Organisation for Economic Co-operation and Development [OECD] 1980.

[470] Cf. International Accounting Standards Committee [IASC] 1988.

[471] Cf. *Ordelheide/KPMG* (1995).

[472] Cf. Nobes/Parker 2008, p. 68.

[473] Cf. Wallace/Gernon 1991, p. 228ff.

[474] Reconciliation studies on the value relevance of financial accounting information profited from the increasing number of non-US companies listed on US stock exchanges; international accounting researchers intensified their research on US-GAAP reconciliations as these proved to be useful to directly compare earnings figures from different accounting spheres. Cf., e.g., Pope/Rees 1992, p. 190ff.; Cooke 1993, p. 460ff.; Alford 1993, p. 183ff.; Barth/Clinch 1996, p. 135; Rees/Elgers 1997, p. 115ff.; Weetman et al. 1998, p. 189ff.

[475] Cf. Gray 1980, p. 64ff.

[476] The concept of value relevance measures the empirical association between accounting figures and market prices.

[477] Cf. Ali/Hwang 2000, p. 1ff.

[478] Cf. Ball et al. 2000, p. 1ff.

stronger associated in the UK and the US than in Germany or France.[479] *Hung* and *Burgstahler et al.* test the influence of legal systems on earnings management. Whereas *Hung* focuses on shareholder protection laws, *Burgstahler et al.* refer to the legal system as a whole. Both reason that weak legal systems allow for higher levels of earnings management.[480]

'Nation as unit of analysis' studies

The third branch 'nation as unit of analysis' comprises studies that understand nation as a concept by what accounting can be studied. Whereas typology studies ('order the universe') seek to classify nations along certain dimensions, 'contingency theory Studies' ('explain the universe') use nations to develop and to test theories on worldwide accounting systems or the interrelation of accounting systems and their environments.[481]

Typology or classification studies are of little importance for this study. These studies often base on data of polycentric studies and classify countries according to their accounting profile. In analogy to the above mentioned criticism on polycentric studies, typology studies often mix accounting practice and rules and come to deviating results.[482] Also, by classifying accounting systems according to certain defined criteria, typology studies do not exceed mere description.

Contingency theory studies, in contrast, explicitly try to identify universal explanations for national accounting patterns. These studies in principal are relevant for this study since the conceptual framework is grounded on contingency theoretical considerations.[483] Nonetheless, the ICFAR understanding of contingency theory studies differs from this study. The studies *Wallace/Gernon* subsume under contingency theory studies explicitly refer to contingency theory as theoretical framework testing the association between national accounting characteristics and their environment.[484] However, many other studies from other ICFAR subareas like SACCS test the influence of environmental factors like the legal system or the banking system on financial accounting and therewith fall back on elements of contingency theory.[485] The difference between contingency theory studies, according to *Wallace/Gernon*, and contingency theoretical SACCS studies is in their particular understanding of contingency theory. Whereas the former studies seek for universal statements with respect to worldwide accounting, the latter studies generally focus on a few countries and country factors only.[486] As this study focuses on EU member states and

[479] Cf. Guenther/Young 2000, p. 53ff.

[480] Cf. Hung 2000, p. 401ff.; Burgstahler et al. 2006, p. 983ff.

[481] Cf. Wallace/Gernon 1991, p. 241f.

[482] Cf. Nobes/Parker 2008, p. 63.

[483] Cf. chapter 2.2.2.

[484] Cf. Belkaoui 1983, p. 207ff.; Belkaoui 1985; Thomas 1986, p. 253ff.; Cooke/Wallace 1990, p. 79ff.

[485] Cf., e.g., Ali/Hwang 2000, p. 1ff.; Ball et al. 2000, p. 1ff.

[486] When using regression analysis as a statistical tool to investigate the association between accounting characteristics and country factors, the number of recognized country factors is limited by the number of analyzed countries. Analyzing N countries, the number of country factors that are simultaneously considered in the regression analysis is limited to N-1 for reasons of multi collinearity. Accordingly, multi country studies are able to consider more facets of the national environment.

three countries only, it follows a less universal approach compared to the contingency theoretical definition by *Wallace/Gernon*. Consequently, this ICFAR subarea is not further accounted for in the following.

'Transnational' studies

'Transnational' research is divided into geocentric studies and synergistic studies. The former study multinational organizations and test the feasibility of an international set of accounting standards, ignoring cultural differences. The latter explore (1) intercultural reactions in domestic organizations and (2) international accounting harmonization.[487]

Geocentric studies as defined in *Wallace/Gernon's* framework are studies searching for similarities at a global level pursuing the research questions of (1) the functionality of multinational organizations and (2) the feasibility of global accounting standards.[488] Various studies analyzed the above mentioned PW data to test the impact of IFRS on international financial accounting. *Nair/Frank* take all three sets of data for a sample of 37 countries and test the effect IAS 1 to 10 had on accounting practice. Although a direct connection is not shown, they find a significant increase in harmonization of accounting practice during a period of time that coincides with the existence of the IASC.[489] By contrast, *Evans/Taylor* study a 5 country sample from 1975 to 1980 testing for compliance with the IASC and find little impact of the issuance of IFRS on national accounting practices.[490] *Mc Kinnon/Janell* come to similar conclusions. They perform a descriptive analysis of 1979 PW data and state that "[...] the IASC has not succeeded in changing existing standards or setting new standards"[491]. Two later studies support the results of *Nair/Frank*. *Taylor et al.* in a 1986 study survey 'Big 8' firms in 33 IASC countries to analyze the effect of the issuance of five IASC standards. They conclude that comparability and consistency of national and international accounting practice for the five examined standards have improved significantly.[492] *Doupnik* uses the 1975 PW data as a starting point and compares them to handpicked 1983 data of the same set of countries. Again, the author fails to prove a direct linkage between the work of the IASC and harmonization but he shows that differences in financial reporting have decreased and compliance with IFRS has increased.[493]

Synergistic studies see nations as systematically interrelated and try to reveal patterns of universality, e.g. the degree of international accounting harmonization.[494] In a conceptual paper of 1988 *Van der Tas* develops different indices, based on the Herfindahl-Index, to quantify harmonization.[495] He tests one of his indices on a sample of nine European countries over a ten year period from 1978 to 1988 and states that (1) harmony is low

[487] Cf. Wallace/Gernon 1991, p. 234ff.
[488] Cf. Wallace/Gernon 1991, p. 234.
[489] Cf. Nair/Frank 1981, 61ff.
[490] Cf. Evans/Taylor 1982, p. 115ff.
[491] McKinnon/Janell 1984, p. 20.
[492] Cf. Taylor et al. 1986, p. 1ff.
[493] Cf. Doupnik 1987, p. 47ff.
[494] Cf. Wallace/Gernon 1991, p. 236.
[495] Cf. van der Tas 1988, p. 157ff.

both for individual and group accounts and (2) harmony is increasing gradually only for group accounts.[496] *Van der Tas'* indices were adopted by various researchers in the following years. *Herrmann/Thomas* find that fairness oriented countries are more harmonized than legalistic countries.[497] *Archer et al.* and *Emenyonu/Gray* concur with *Van der Tas'* 1992 results and testify little increase in harmonization.[498]

Although 'transnational' studies evaluate international accounting harmonization and the influence of the work of the IASC, these studies do not investigate actual IFRS practice and, thus, are of little relevance for this study.

The above described ICFAR framework by *Wallace/Gernon* is refined in the following subchapter and modified according to the research question of this study.

1.4.2.3 Refinement of the ICFAR framework

This study belongs to the second branch of the above presented ICFAR framework taking **nations as context.** The first branch that takes nations as objects is not relevant for this study since parochial, xenophilic and ethnocentric studies focus on one country only. The third branch 'nation as unit of analysis' encompasses ICFAR studies that follow a slightly different research approach compared to 'nation as context' studies. The former follow a more universal approach; typology and contingency theory studies try to detect universal classification respectively explanation systems. To be able to determine such universalities, the number of analyzed nations has to be accordingly high. In contrast, 'nation as context' studies focus on fewer countries; the focus is not on universal statements but rather on research questions like value relevance or the influence of environmental factors in the context of the analyzed countries. The fourth ICFAR branch is in so far related to this study since 'transnational' studies assess international accounting harmonization and the effect of international accounting standards (IFRS), which are also analyzed in this study. Nonetheless, the focus of this study is different. Instead of investigating the feasibility or the effect of IFRS on national financial accounting, this study assesses the effect of national culture on IFRS practice. Furthermore, geocentric and synergistic studies, as defined by *Wallace/Gernon*, are more detached from the national context; the context of 'transnational' studies is multinational organizations.

Having distinguished 'nation as context' studies from the three other ICFAR branches, the ICFAR framework is refined with respect to the research question of this study. First and in analogy to *Wallace/Gernon*, the following review of prior research differentiates between polycentric studies that only describe and SACCS that also explain accounting phenomena. As outlined above, this study intends to go beyond mere description trying to explain differences in national IFRS practice by means of different national cultural patterns; the focus of the review therewith is on SACCS. Moreover, the above ICFAR scheme is complemented by two further levels of categories to adapt to the two *foci* of this study, viz. national culture and IFRS. The first level distinguishes between **culture** studies

[496] Cf. van der Tas 1992, p. 69ff.

[497] Cf. Herrmann/Thomas 1995, p. 253ff.

[498] Cf. Emenyonu/Gray 1992, p. 49ff.; Archer et al. 1995, p. 67ff.

and non culture studies and therewith accentuates the dichotomy of the culture free and the culturally grounded research approaches. The second level distinguishes between **IFRS** studies and non IFRS studies. Accordingly, the refined ICFAR framework recognizes four different categories of SACCS and two different categories of polycentric studies (see Figure 1-9).

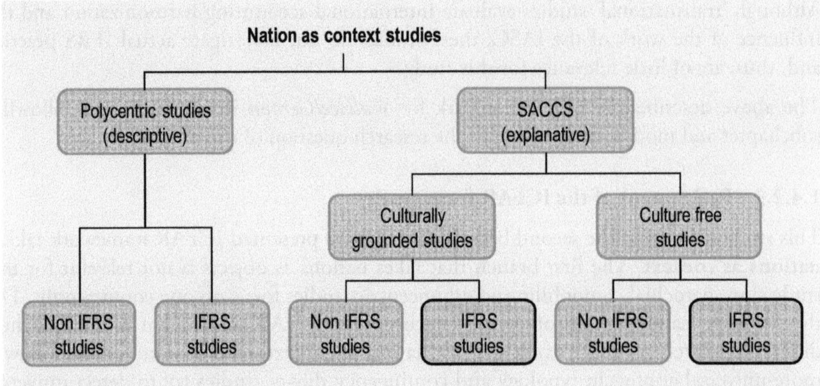

Figure 1-9: Refined ICFAR framework[499]

Only two of the six recognized categories are dealt with in detail in the following review of prior research. As a consequence of the research question of this study, the emphasis of the subsequent review on prior research is on **culturally grounded IFRS studies**. Although ignoring the influence of national culture, IFRS studies that follow the culture free approach are also reviewed in the next subchapter since these studies might provide interesting insights with respect to the application of IFRS and context factors other than national culture. **Culture free IFRS studies** are further split up into (1) studies on the determinants and consequences of IFRS adoption and (2) IFRS practice studies. SACCS that focus neither on the influence of national culture nor on IFRS are considered to be of little relevance for the study. Polycentric studies on IFRS practice are neither included in the following review. First, these studies by definition do not exceed the research level of description and therewith are not compatible with the research approach of this study. Second, IFRS practice studies that only describe without making tentative explanations are seldom;[500] polycentric studies like the 1970s PW studies mainly refer to the rules or practice based description of different national accounting systems; considering the worldwide harmonization of (group) accounting these studies are likely to become less important.

[499] Adopted from Wallace/Gernon 1991, p. 224.
[500] Cf., e.g., Glaum et al. 2007.

1.5 Prior research

This chapter reviews relevant prior research in order to identify the research deficit that this study intends to fill. Prior research is presented structured by the above described refined ICFAR framework distinguishing in a first step between culture free and culturally grounded studies.

1.5.1 Culture free studies

Reviewing culture free IFRS studies, different research streams may be identified. Whereas early IFRS studies mainly focus on the motivation for early adoption and IFRS capital market effects, later IFRS studies often assess the value relevance of the transitional documents (IFRS 1) and differences in IFRS practice. Accordingly, the following review is split in two sections. First, studies on IFRS determinants and consequences are briefly reviewed. These studies investigate firm characteristics of early adopters, reasons for early adoption, IFRS compliance of early adopters and capital market reactions on IFRS figures (value relevance, capital costs). Second and more importantly, **IFRS practice studies** are reviewed. For their conceptual proximity to the research question of this study these studies are discussed in more detail.

1.5.1.1 Studies on IFRS determinants and consequences

Early IFRS studies mainly investigate IFRS financial statements of European companies; as outlined in the presentation of the sample countries' profiles, large listed European companies often chose to voluntarily adopt IFRS since the EU national group accounts regulations in the 1990s did not meet the requirements of the international capital market.[501] Furthermore, some technologically oriented stock exchange segments explicitly required financial statements in accordance with internationally accepted financial reporting standards.[502] Besides an analysis of the motivation for voluntary IFRS adoption and associated company characteristics,[503] early IFRS studies also concentrate on differences in value relevance compared to other accounting systems (mainly US-GAAP) and capital market consequences.[504] Another research area that is covered by early IFRS studies concerns the measurement of IFRS compliance.[505]

Dumontier/Raffournier in 1998 analyze **firm characteristics** of 133 listed companies and find that voluntary IFRS adopters are larger, more diversified on an international level and in ownership structure and less capital intensive.[506] Moreover, *Ashbaugh* finds that voluntary IFRS respectively US-GAAP adopters are likely to be listed at a foreign stock exchange.[507] These results are confirmed by *Tarca* who investigates early adopters from the UK, France, Germany, Japan and Australia in 2004; she finds companies that use

[501] Cf. chapter 1.3.5.3.
[502] Cf. chapter 1.1.2.
[503] Cf. Dumontier/Raffournier 1998, p. 216ff.; El-Gazzar et al. 1999, p. 239ff.
[504] Cf. Harris/Muller 1999, p. 285ff.; Ashbaugh/Pincus 2001, p. 417ff.
[505] Cf. Street et al. 1999, p. 11ff.; Street/Bryant 2000, p. 305ff.
[506] Cf. Dumontier/Raffournier 1998, p. 216ff.
[507] Cf. Ashbaugh 2001, p. 129ff.; Ashbaugh/Pincus 2001, p. 417ff.

IFRS or US-GAAP in addition to local GAAP to be associated with larger size, more foreign revenues and foreign listing.[508] *Cuijpers/Buijink* also suggest that early adopters are associated with an international listing; moreover, these companies are likely to come from a country of lower quality of accounting.[509] The **reasons** why companies choose to early adopt IFRS are assessed by *El-Gazzar et al.*; companies adopt IFRS to increase their exposure to the international capital market and, thus, to attract foreign capital; customer recognition is another argument for early IFRS adoption.[510]

Early studies on the **value relevance** of IFRS figures present mixed results. In a 1985 to 1993 event study on 35 listed non-financial companies *Auer* reveals that IFRS provide more value relevant information compared to local GAAP, but less value relevant information in comparison to earnings announcements in accordance with the EC accounting Directives.[511] A multinational 1992/1993 case study in Australia, Sweden, France, Germany, Italy, New Zealand and Switzerland shows that IFRS accounting measure can be comparable to US-GAAP.[512] In contrast, a 1992 to 1996 US-GAAP reconciliation study testifies that US-GAAP earnings reconciliations are value relevant compared to IFRS.[513] Later studies on IFRS value relevance analyze the transitory documents of companies that (mainly in 2005) switched to IFRS. Transitory IFRS studies are comparable to US-GAAP reconciliation studies. As IFRS 1: 'First-time adoption of IFRS' requests substantial reconciliations to IFRS, researchers use regression analysis to test reconciliation figures on value relevance. *Horton/Serafeim* examine a sample of 605 companies from Spain, France, Italy and the UK and find that IFRS earnings adjustments explain share prices in France, Italy and the UK and stock returns in France and the UK. IFRS equity adjustments explain neither share prices nor stock returns.[514] A second study by *Horton/Serafeim* reveals that investors react mainly on negative earnings adjustments and regard share based payments, goodwill amortization, financial instruments and deferred taxes as value relevant.[515] *Christensen et al.* study a slightly larger sample of 187 listed firms and show that the stock market reacts significantly only on early released reconciliations.[516]

With respect to an expected positive effect on corporate capital costs, *Daske* investigates financial statements in accordance with IFRS respectively US-GAAP for a 1993 to 2002 company sample; he finds the change from local to international GAAP to be associated with rather higher **costs of capital**.[517] In contrast, *Leuz/Verrecchia* attest companies that switch from local to international GAAP lower cost of capital;[518] furthermore, *Leuz* suggests that the choice between IFRS and US-GAAP is of little consequence with regard to

---

508 Cf. Tarca 2004, p. 60ff.
509 Cf. Cuijpers/Buijink 2005, p. 487ff.
510 Cf. El-Gazzar et al. 1999, p. 239ff.
511 Cf. Auer 1996, p. 587ff.
512 Cf. Harris 1995.
513 Cf. Harris/Muller 1999, p. 285ff.
514 Cf. Horton/Serafeim 2007, p. 206ff.
515 Cf. Horton/Serafeim 2010, p. 725ff.
516 Cf. Christensen et al. 2007.
517 Cf. Daske 2006, p. 329ff.
518 Cf. Leuz/Verrecchia 2000, p. 91.

information asymmetry and market liquidity.[519] A positive market reaction is also measured by *Armstrong* who analyzes capital market reactions for European companies that adopted IFRS in the period from 2002 to 2005; the capital market especially appreciates the IFRS adoption from companies that come from 'poor' information environments.[520] These results suggest that the capital market reacts heterogeneously on IFRS figures by early adopters. This reaction may also be associated with different degrees of **compliance** with IFRS. *Street et al.* find very mixed and selective results on compliance, although compliance with IFRS is confirmed by the auditor.[521] Moreover, *Street/Bryant* attest early adopters higher degrees of compliance if these are US listed.[522]

Having substantiated the determinants and consequences of IFRS adoption, the following subchapter presents studies that investigate IFRS practice.

1.5.1.2 IFRS practice studies

The reviewed studies mainly analyze financial statements from 2005, the first year of mandatory IFRS application in the EU, and later years. In contrast to pre-2005 studies, which primarily focus on voluntary early adoption, mandatory IFRS studies have the advantage of greater and more diversified company samples. In accordance with the comparative research approach of this study, the following review of IFRS practice studies concentrates on multi country studies. IFRS practice studies that focus on one country only ('nation as object' studies) are not discussed.[523]

The Big4 auditor *Ernst & Young* reviews 2005 financial statements of 65 European and Australian companies to assess the degree of consistency and comparability of IFRS financial statements; the companies are selected based on highest market capitalization. In contrast to other studies, which focus on a differentiation by nation, *Ernst & Young* analyze IFRS financial statements according to industry. Nonetheless, they attest the presentation of IFRS financial statements to be strongly influenced by national practice and attribute this finding to the absence of a specific presentation standard. Furthermore, they find consistency and comparability to be restricted by the wide discretion granted by IFRS; measurement estimates are often not sufficiently explained with respect to key judgments and parameter sensitivity. Most importantly, *Ernst & Young* find the companies' capital market communication to substantially rely on non IFRS measures; companies seem to mistrust IFRS financial information to suffice capital market expectations.[524]

Apart from an industry based analysis of IFRS practice, *Ernst & Young* conduct a topic based analysis. They focus on the accounting topics (1) business combinations, (2) corporate financial instruments, (3) employee benefits, (4) impairment of assets, (5) income

[519] Cf. Leuz 2003, p. 445.
[520] Cf. Armstrong et al. 2008.
[521] Cf. Street et al. 1999, p. 11ff.
[522] Cf. Street/Bryant 2000, p. 305.
[523] Cf., e.g., Carlin et al. 2007; Demaria/Dufour 2007; Aledo et al. 2009; Haller 2010, p. 681ff.; Meyer/Weiss 2010, p. 848ff.
[524] Cf. Ernst & Young 2006, p. 2f.

taxes and (6) share-based payments.[525] The study by *Ernst & Young* is expandable in various ways. First, the study is mainly descriptive. The interpretation of the results does not exceed some tentative conclusions with regard to industrial and national patterns. As the focus lies on industry and not on country, no country factors are tested for a possible influence; in fact, no statistical tests are performed at all. Second, the assessed sample consists of 65 companies only. Selected based on market capitalization instead of country, the tested companies per country are few; the number of analyzed financial statements per country certainly allows for no representative results. Finally, the study is not based on a theory-guided conceptual framework; the study is a mere snapshot of accounting topics *Ernst & Young* considers as important and practically relevant.

A study of *von Keitz* in cooperation with *KPMG* analyses 2005 group account data from a ten country sample[526] to assess whether IFRS adoption has led to global consistency and whether companies' accounting practice is influenced rather by national or industrial accounting practice.[527] The final sample of 199 companies is not statistically representative as it contains the largest 20 'blue chip' companies of each country plus a selection of companies from the Standard & Poor's (S&P) S&P Europe 350 Index that *KPMG* "felt should be included in this survey"[528]. The financial statements had to be available publicly on May 31st of 2006, in English, prepared under IFRS or IFRS 'equivalents'[529] and the company had to agree to participate in the study. Financial statements of 'blue chip' companies that did not meet these criteria were replaced by the next company in the index.[530]

The study analyses 26 explicit options taken from 13 standards. *Keitz/KPMG* find that practice choices are influenced rather by national than by industrial accounting practice. Only financial institutions show cross-border accounting patterns. In analogy to the *Ernst & Young* study, the *Keitz/KPMG* study is rather descriptive; the purpose of the study is to assist IFRS users in the preparation of their financial statements.[531] The samples per country do not exceed 20 companies; thus, the results are difficult to transfer to other companies. The described accounting issues are selected intuitively; no theoretical framework is applied.

Another study by *Keitz* investigates national GAAP related country differences with respect to IAS 38. *Keitz* analyzes financial statements of 77 companies from France, Sweden, Spain, Germany and the Netherlands; the focus is on the recognition, measurement and disclosure of intangible assets. She finds IAS 38 accounting quality to differ across countries and attributes these country differences to IFRS complexity and discretion and possibly to different national enforcement institutions.[532]

[525] Cf. Ernst & Young 2006, p. 16ff.
[526] Including seven EU countries, Hong Kong, South Africa and Switzerland.
[527] Cf. KPMG/von Keitz 2006a.
[528] KPMG/von Keitz 2006a, p. 1.
[529] IFRS as adopted by the EU and Hong Kong Financial Reporting Standards were accepted as being equivalent.
[530] Cf. KPMG/von Keitz 2006a, p. 1.
[531] Cf. KPMG/von Keitz 2006b, p. 3.
[532] Cf. von Keitz 2007, p. 340ff.

The interpretations of the results, however, are merely tentative statements that are not statistically verified. Furthermore, the relatively small country samples allow for no conclusions on the total population of the companies in the respective countries. The largest country sample is the German sample which consists of 17 companies.[533]

Kvaal/Nobes analyze a sample of 232 companies from five different countries[534] where IFRS is mandatory. The countries are chosen for possessing the five largest stock markets. The companies chosen were listed in the corresponding 'blue chip' indices. Foreign companies, i.e. companies not legally registered in that country, and companies not using IFRS are excluded from the sample.[535] *Kvall/Nobes* select 16 explicit IFRS options to test the null hypothesis that IFRS practices are the same in all countries. Therefore they formulate alternative hypotheses based on the behavior of 'inertia'. 'Inertia' in this context refers to companies trying to exercise IFRS accounting options the way they used to under national GAAP, if that is possible. All 16 options are tested by alternative hypotheses like "H_1: Spanish companies are more inclined than others to use the by-nature format of the income statement"[536].

The results show that explicit IFRS options are not exercised consistently on an international level. Furthermore, *Kvaal/Nobes* detect national country patterns; these are tested on the hypothesis that deviations from the patterns are explained by the company's attention to global investors' needs. Global investor orientation is approximated by the companies' market value and SEC listing. Controlling for auditor, industry sector and country, *Kvaal/Nobes* find that deviations from country patterns are explained by capital market orientation only within the UK.[537]

The study by *Kvaal/Nobes* is limited in several ways. Although *Kvaal/Nobes* test more companies per country in comparison to the above described IFRS practice studies, only the UK sample, which consists of 98 companies, is considered to be sufficiently large to allow for robust statistical results; the German sample, for instance, consists of only 23 companies.[538] Moreover, the study lacks a conceptual framework; the hypotheses are developed based on the intuitive assumption that companies tend to apply IFRS according to pre-IFRS practice. Also, *Kvaal/Nobes* do not directly test for the influence of country factors. Instead, they test for influence factors related to deviations from pre-IFRS practice. National culture, as a potential external context factor, is not considered.

The following chapter reviews SACCS that explicitly recognize national culture as a financial accounting influence factor.

[533] Cf. von Keitz 2007, p. 340.
[534] Including Australia, France, Germany, Spain and the UK.
[535] Cf. Kvaal/Nobes 2010, p. 173ff.
[536] Kvaal/Nobes 2008, p. 13ff.
[537] Cf. Kvaal/Nobes 2008, p. 29ff.
[538] Kvaal/Nobes 2010, p. 176.

1.5.2 Culturally grounded studies

The below discussed culture studies employ the *Hofstede-Gray* framework. This framework formulates assumptions on the relationship between national culture respectively predetermined national cultural dimensions and financial accounting respectively predetermined accounting values.[539] In analogy to the previous chapter on IFRS studies, this chapter on culture studies is split in two sections. The first section gives an introduction to culture studies that apply the original *Hofstede-Gray* framework focusing on financial accounting systems. Later culture studies often apply the refined *Hofstede-Gray* framework focusing on financial accounting practice. Correspondingly, the second section reviews culture studies that explicitly investigate the association between **national culture** and **IFRS practice.**

1.5.2.1 Culture studies applying the Hofstede-Gray framework

Gray's accounting value framework respectively the *Hofstede-Gray* framework, as often referred to in the accounting literature, has been tested in various empirical studies. *Salter/Niswander*, for example, attest the framework particularly strong explanatory power with regard to different financial reporting practices. As far as professional and regulatory accounting structures are concerned, however, they suggest the integration of further context factors into the model, like the development of the national capital market or the influence of the taxation system.[540]

Chanchani/MacGregor in 1999 provide an extensive review of studies that deal with the relationship between culture and financial reporting.[541] They classify these studies into (1) pre-*Gray* literature, (2) *Gray's* 1988 paper and (3) post-*Gray* literature. Their review, however, focuses rather on conceptual issues than empirical results. A more recent review that focuses on empirical results was published by *Doupnik/Tsakumis* in 2004.[542] They review culture studies, published between 1990 and 2003, that apply the *Hofstede-Gray* framework. All reviewed studies commonly take the *Hofstede* cultural dimensions as independent variables. Some studies additionally include further institutional variables like market capitalization and marginal tax rate[543] or market capitalization and legal system[544] to add explanatory power. Other studies add further internal control variables like firm size, debt ratio and internationality.[545] One of the studies tests the *Hofstede-Gray* framework for one country only,[546] the other studies follow a multi-country approach including between six and 39 countries in the investigation.[547]

---

539 The *Hofstede-Gray* framework is described in detail in chapter 2.2.4.
540 Cf. Salter/Niswander 1995, p. 390.
541 Cf. Chanchani/MacGregor 1999, p. 1ff.
542 Cf. Doupnik/Tsakumis 2004, p. 1ff.
543 Cf. Salter/Niswander 1995, p. 379ff.
544 Cf. Jaggi/Low 2000, p. 495ff.
545 Cf. Zarzeski 1996, p. 18ff.
546 Cf. Sudarwan/Fogarty 1996, p. 463ff.
547 For an extensive overview of culturally grounded studies applying the *Hofstede-Gray* framework cf. Jödicke 2009, p. 236ff.

The empirical results of the reviewed studies generally support the supposition that national culture has an influence on financial accounting systems, although the results are not entirely consistent with respect to particular cultural dimensions. Whereas *Eddie* and *Gray/Vint* find full support for all of *Gray's* predicted relationships, *Sudarwan/Fogarty* only support four of the 13 hypothesized relationships, the latter possibly a result of the unilateral research design.[548] The data is gathered in different ways. *MacArthur* analyzes comments by corporate managers and accounting bodies from 23 countries on draft E32: 'comparability of financial statements as issued by the IASC'.[549] *Roberts/Salter* ask partners of Big6 accounting firms in 23 countries to fill out a questionnaire and comment on the desirability of uniform accounting rules.[550]

It is noted as a résumé of the reviewed studies on the *Hofstede-Gray* framework that the cultural dimensions that best predict accounting values are associated with financial accounting practice. The accounting values less predicted by cultural values are rather attributed to financial accounting systems. Considering in particular the Europe-wide implementation of IFRS, *Doupnik/Tsakumis* suggest for future research on *Gray's* hypotheses to rather focus on financial accounting **practice.**[551]

1.5.2.2 Culture studies on IFRS practice

This section discusses only studies that apply the refined *Hofstede-Gray* framework and, thus, focus on the relationship between national culture and financial accounting practice. In consideration of the research question of this study the following review includes only culture studies that explicitly investigate **IFRS practice.**

Schultz/Lopez conduct an experiment with accountants from France, Germany and the US.[552] Given the same economic facts and similar IFRS related accounting standards, the participants had to decide on the amount of warranty estimates. The authors suggest a relationship between the accountants' decision and the country's legal system, its financing system and its national culture. They find national culture to have a significant influence on warranty estimates. As expected, the accountants from France and Germany by trend resolve higher warranty estimates than accountants from the US. These results have to be interpreted carefully as the authors neither control for current national accounting practice nor for effects implied by national tax regulations.[553]

Another experiment was conducted by *Doupnik/Richter* who assess the effect culture has on the interpretation of probability expressions as used in various IFRS standards (e.g. provisions: 'more likely than not').[554] Again, the candidates were given the same economic facts and similar accounting standards. Based on the refined *Hofstede-Gray* framework, *Doupnik/Richter* suggest that accountants from the US assign higher numerical probability

[548] Cf. Eddie 1990, p. 22ff.; Gray/Vint 1995, p. 33ff.; Sudarwan/Fogarty 1996, p. 463ff.

[549] Cf. MacArthur 1996, p. 213ff.

[550] Cf. Roberts/Salter 1999, p. 121ff.

[551] Cf. Doupnik/Tsakumis 2004, p. 34ff.

[552] Cf. Schultz/Lopez 2001, p. 271ff.

[553] Cf. Schultz/Lopez 2001, p. 271ff.

[554] Cf. Doupnik/Richter 2004, p. 1ff.

to verbal probability expressions compared to accountants from Germany. Although they find some support for the posited relationship between national culture and IFRS practice, *Doupnik/Richter* do not control for institutional factors that might have an influence on the accountants' judgments.[555]

Doupnik/Riccio also investigate the impact of culture on the national perception of verbal probability expressions.[556] They had Brazilian and US auditors decide on the numerical probability of different IFRS probability expressions. The refined *Hofstede-Gray* framework is tested by assessing probability expressions that determine the threshold for recognition of items that either increase or decrease net income. Additionally, probability expressions are analyzed that determine the threshold for the disclosure of information in the notes. In both cases they expect Brazilian auditors to follow a more cautious approach than their US counterparts, which results in lower net income and fewer notes items. In concordance with *Doupnik/Richter*, the empirical results support the associations posited by the refined *Hofstede-Gray* framework. Nevertheless, the study shows similar limitations, controlling only for the influence of Big4 affiliation, but disregarding the influence of other institutional context factors. Also, neither US nor Brazilian auditors possess sufficient IFRS experience; probability expressions in Brazilian respectively US-GAAP might therefore have a biasing effect on the results.[557]

Tsakumis conducted an experiment with US and Greek auditors to investigate the refined *Hofstede-Gray* framework.[558] He confronted the participants with two different IFRS scenarios involving the recognition and disclosure of (1) a contingent asset and (2) a contingent liability. He posits that Greek auditors are more (less) likely to recognize contingent liabilities (assets) and less likely to disclose the existence of contingent liabilities/assets than US auditors. *Tsakumis* finds only support with regard to IFRS disclosure. The results for asset/liability recognition, however, show no significant differences between Greek and US auditors. The limitations of the above described studies also apply for the work of *Tsakumis*. Institutional influences are blanked out and the IFRS experience of the participants at the time of the study was low. Moreover, the auditors had an IFRS workshop prior to the experiment that might have had an impact on the results.[559]

Jödicke follows an approach different from the experiments presented above. He evaluates annual financial statements from French, German and British listed companies to draw conclusions from the way companies form and release provisions to cultural reasons. Following the refined *Hofstede-Gray* framework, he posits that companies from more conservative countries like Germany or France by trend overestimate 'other provisions' and in the following years have to release more 'other provisions' than companies from less conservative countries like the UK. Controlling for company size, industry, profitability and provision specific characteristics like materiality and maturity of 'other provisions', he finds support for a provisions-release-quote country-order according to their national cul-

---

555 Cf. Doupnik/Richter 2004, p. 1ff.
556 Cf. Doupnik/Riccio 2006, p. 237ff.
557 Cf. Doupnik/Riccio 2006, p. 237ff.
558 Cf. Tsakumis 2007, p. 27ff.
559 Cf. Tsakumis 2007, p. 27.

tural characteristics. French countries release more 'other provisions' than German companies and German companies release more than UK companies.[560] *Jödicke* tries to control for national tax effects by excluding tax provisions from the analysis. Nevertheless, tax regulations and tax minimizing accounting behavior might have effects on provisions other than tax provisions. Also, institutional context factors are not taken into account.[561]

The following chapter summarizes the above review of prior research by pointing out its contributions and limitations. Subsequently, the research gap is highlighted.

1.5.3 Prior research contributions, limitations and research gap

Before addressing prior research limitations, prior research **contributions** are presented with respect to the conceptualization and research design of this study. The briefly discussed studies on the determinants and consequences of IFRS adoption indicate that early adoption of IFRS is associated with internal context factors like firm size, cross-listing or foreign operations. These context factors might also have an influence on IFRS practice and will be considered in the conceptual framework of this study. Furthermore, studies on the reaction of the capital market (cost of capital studies, value relevance studies) suggest the existence of country differences; capital market effects are rather measured for companies that come from an accounting environment that is considered to be of lower quality compared to Anglo-Saxon accounting standards (US-GAAP, UK-GAAP). These country differences might be linked to different cultural or institutional country settings and might lead to differences in IFRS practice. Studies on IFRS compliance support the assumption of IFRS country differences; moreover, differences in IFRS compliance are found to be associated to an US-listing. Accordingly, the influence of an US-listing will be recognized in this study.

The systematic influence of country context factors is supported by prior studies that specifically investigate IFRS practice in several countries. Without further analyzing cultural or institutional country factors, these studies link differences in IFRS practice to different national local GAAP regulations. Furthermore, these studies also assess the influence of internal context factors like industry, auditor or internationality, which might be influential with respect to IFRS practice. The limited degree of consistency of IFRS financial statements is attributed to the wide discretion granted by IFRS measurement rules. IFRS measurement practice, thus, might be a potentially fruitful area to investigate differences in IFRS practice. Finally, these studies list further IFRS accounting areas like covert or overt options that might be susceptible to nationally differing IFRS application.

The culturally grounded studies that base on the *Hofstede-Gray* framework and that do not analyze IFRS contribute insofar to this study as these studies indicate a stronger cultural influence on accounting values related to IFRS practice. Following the refined *Hofstede-Gray* framework, which focuses primarily on accounting practice, the research approach of this study is affirmed. The reviewed culturally grounded IFRS studies directly concern the research question of this study. These studies are mainly supportive with re-

[560] Cf. Jödicke 2009, p. 227ff.
[561] Cf. Jödicke 2009.

spect to cultural influences. Furthermore, these studies introduce further internal context factors that are assumed to have an effect on IFRS practice like auditor, size, industry or profitability. Also, external context factors like the legal system or the financing system are controlled for a possible influence on IFRS practice. The internal and external context factors are integrated into the conceptual framework of this study.

The reviewed studies also contribute with respect to the **research design** of this study. Most of the culture free IFRS studies are based on a content analysis of financial statements. Content analysis is a common research method to investigate actual corporate accounting practice. In contrast to the experimental research design of the culturally grounded IFRS studies, content analytical empirical results are better suited to formulate generalized statements.

The above review of prior research also reveals certain **limitations**; the presented culture free and culturally grounded studies are expandable in various ways. Most of the **culture free studies** that investigate IFRS practice in an international context are of rather descriptive nature and seldom reach beyond tentative interpretations. As referred to above, *Kvaal/Nobes* control for various internal context factors like capital market orientation or auditor; **country factors**, nonetheless, are only accounted for by an unspecific country variable.[562] Especially national culture, the main topic of this study, is not accounted for. Furthermore, *Kvaal/Nobes* focus on deviations from national accounting patterns instead of country differences as a result of the cultural or institutional environment.[563] Apart from a different conceptual focus, culture free IFRS studies are also expandable with respect to the type of IFRS **accounting choices**. Prior research studies mainly focus on overt options and disregard accounting areas like covert options and measurement estimations, which allow for considerably more discretion; accordingly, these areas are expected to be even more susceptible to external influence factors like national culture. Furthermore, IFRS disclosure is only rudimentarily investigated on a multi country basis and, thus, offers plenty of research opportunities. Another limitation of the discussed IFRS studies is the **small number** of analyzed financial statements per country. Advanced statistical tests like regression analysis often require higher sample numbers per country. Furthermore, the presented studies are based on **no conceptual framework**. The selection of context factors and the interpretation of results are mostly intuitive.

The review of **culturally grounded studies** shows that this field of research is still young and offers plenty of research opportunities. The presented studies reveal certain limitations that are addressed by this study. First, only one study analyzes IFRS practice by means of actual corporate financial statements. The other culture related IFRS practice studies are **experiments**. As mentioned above, the investigation of IFRS practice under laboratory conditions might bias the empirical results; statistical associations determined by experimental analysis might be not transferable to financial accounting reality. Second, the experimental culture studies might be biased as one or both sample countries are countries in which the application of IFRS is not required respectively allowed.[564] Thus,

---

[562] Cf. Kvaal/Nobes 2010, p. 173ff.
[563] Cf. Kvaal/Nobes 2010, p. 173ff.
[564] IFRS were introduced in Brazil in 2010; cf. KPMG 2010.

the Brazilian and US participants' **IFRS experience** is considered to be rather low and the experimental accounting choices might be strongly influenced by national GAAP. Third, most of the reviewed culturally grounded studies do not control for other **institutional country factors** like the financing system or the tax system. Country influences on accounting decisions could be rashly attributed to national culture although other country factors are possibly more relevant. Fourth, the **conceptual framework** of the discussed studies is limited to theoretical consideration of the *Hofstede-Gray* framework. Additional theories, e.g. to predict the influence of internal context factors on accounting practice, are not considered. And fifth, the reviewed studies do not integrate **different cultural concepts** (e.g. GLOBE study) to test the robustness of the empirical results.

Based on the above outlined limitations of prior culture free and culturally grounded IFRS practice studies, the identified **research gap** is defined as follows:

- Analysis of IFRS accounting choices is limited to overt options.
- Limited multi country analysis of IFRS disclosure.
- Limited recognition of institutional context factors.
- Limited recognition of internal context factors.
- Rudimentary conceptual framework.
- Deficient sample country selection (US, Brazil).
- The number of analyzed companies per country is limited.
- Interpretations are often tentative statements without statistical proof.

These limitations are addressed in the further course of this study on the influence of national culture on IFRS practice. The selection of the sample countries was substantiated and described in chapter 1.3.5. The theory based conceptual framework is outlined in chapter 2.3. Various external and internal context factors are integrated into the conceptual framework in chapter 2.3.2. The selection of analyzed measurement and disclosure related IFRS accounting choices is presented in chapter 2.3.4. The size of the respective country samples is determined in chapter 4.2, and the elaborate statistical analysis of the empirical data is performed in chapter 4.3.

The following chapter summarizes the intermediary results of the 'foundation' chapter leading over to the theoretical perspectives of this study.

1.6 Summary

The first chapter of this study is basically split in four. First, the research question of this study is substantiated. Second, scientific research strategies are discussed with respect to conceptual applicability to the research question. Third, financial accounting harmonization and possible barriers to further harmonization are described from an EU perspective. And fourth, previous studies are reviewed and the contributions and limitations are evaluated with regard to the research question of this study.

This study is a tentative answer to the research question whether differences in national culture are associated with systematic differences in IFRS practice. These differences are assessed in the geo-political context of the EU, which requires European capital market oriented companies to publish their group accounts in accordance with IFRS. The research question is analyzed applying an **empirical research strategy** that is to be seen in the tradition of **critical rationalism**; falsifiable hypotheses are developed based on a theory-guided conceptual framework and tested empirically on actual corporate financial statements. Accordingly, this study follows a positivist research approach. Previously hypothesized relationships between national culture and IFRS practice are tested empirically to make explanatory and predictive statements on IFRS practice; this study therewith belongs to the financial accounting research stream of **new empiricism based on positivism.**

The subchapter on **international accounting harmonization** begins with a confrontation of critical and supportive opinions on international accounting harmonization. Critics argue that *de facto* accounting harmonization is an illusion and unnecessary with regard to international capital market requirements. Supporters of international accounting harmonization are mainly international investors, international audit firms and international companies that anticipate capital market and operational cost efficiencies from worldwide harmonized financial accounting.

Before the adoption of IFRS, European accounting harmonization was mainly promoted by means of the Fourth and Seventh Directive. Whereas the **Fourth Directive** harmonized individual accounting, the **Seventh Directive** harmonized group accounting in EU member states. The EC abandoned its Directive based strategy to accounting harmonization in the 1990s and decided to cooperate closely with the IASC and the IOSCO to harmonize European accounting via IFRS. Various conformity and improvement projects later, the **IAS Regulation**, which required capital market oriented European companies to adopt IFRS from 2005 on, was enacted in 2002. Besides the formal introduction of IFRS into European legislation, the IAS Regulation also contained provisions to create the institutional prerequisites (1) to assure the recognition of EU interests in the IFRS standard setting process, (2) to guarantee harmonized enforcement of IFRS accounting rules and (3) to transform IFRS as issued by the IASB into EU law (endorsement).

The presented country factors identified as reasons for IFRS country differences are **national culture** and other institutional factors like the national financing, legal or tax system. Subsequently, eight potential opportunities for a systematically differing IFRS application in the EU are discussed. First, different versions of IFRS may result from the duration and complexity of the EU endorsement process or IFRS early adoption regulations. Second, cross national misunderstandings of IFRS could be a consequence of the translation into the official EU languages. Third, gaps in IFRS that are filled by applying the general accounting principles of the IFRS Framework or comparable frameworks might lead to inconsistent IFRS application. Fourth, overt options like the cost or revaluation model allowed for measurement of PPE are another source for differences. Fifth, covert options and vague criteria as expressed by the R&D capitalization criteria catalogue or vague terms like 'probably' might lead to inconsistencies in IFRS practice. Sixth, measurement estimations, e.g. for the fair value model, allow for corporate discretion. Seventh, transitional or first-time adoption issues are related to various exemptions permitted by standard that allow for corporate accounting choices. Last, imperfect enforcement as a consequence of different national financial supervisory authorities is another possible opportunity for systematically differing IFRS practice in the EU.

Subsequently the regional focus of the study is concretized. The countries to be analyzed are **France**, **Germany** and the **UK**. These EU countries are selected based on the 'vital' country concept, i.e. based on economic importance and relative cultural differences. Whereas both France and Germany are characterized as 'insider' code law countries with a closely linked individual and tax accounting system, the UK is classified as an 'outsider' common law country with a tax independent individual accounting system.

The remainder of chapter one deals with relevant **prior research**. After determining the field of research of this study, a framework is developed to classify and review ICFAR studies. Based on the research question of the study, IFRS practice studies and culture related IFRS practice studies are reviewed and discussed in more detail. Based on the review of prior studies, limitations are identified. Accordingly, prior studies are limited with respect to the internal and external context controlled for in these studies. The number of analyzed companies per country is limited and the interpretation of the results is often not substantiated by statistical analysis. Furthermore, prior research mainly focuses on selected accounting issues like overt options in IFRS. Also, prior research lacks theoretical foundation; research design and interpretation are of rather intuitive nature. This study contributes to reduce the described research deficit. Apart from the scientific contribution to the academic field of ICFAR, this study provides valuable insights for users of IFRS financial statements like investors, analysts and other IFRS interested parties like regulators, standard setters, auditors or enforcement institutions.

In the following chapter on theory and hypotheses development the theoretical perspectives of the study are described. The theoretical perspectives constitute the conceptual framework of this study from which hypotheses are derived.

2 Theory and hypotheses development

2.1 Overview

Based on the scientific program and the research strategy outlined in chapter one, chapter two discusses relevant theories that underline the assumed relationship between national culture and IFRS accounting practice. The discussed theories also link other internal and external context factors that serve as control variables to IFRS practice. Based on the presented theories the conceptual framework of this study is developed.

The first section of this chapter deals with theoretical perspectives. This study employs more than one theory in the conceptual framework to analyze the research problem comprehensively from different angles. Introductory, **system theory** and contingency theory are discussed. **Contingency theory** originally emanates from general system theory and serves as basic foundation for the conceptual research framework of this study.

To enhance the explanatory potential of the conceptual framework, further accounting theories are implemented. The first two theories establish the theoretical connection between national culture and other external context factors and the dependent variable IFRS practice. Whereas the **societal effects approach** is applied to theoretically specify the influence of institutional factors like legal system or tax system, **culture theory** by *Hofstede* and culture theoretical considerations by *Gray* connect cultural dimensions to accounting dimensions. **Institutional economics** and **positive accounting theory** (PAT) theoretically found the relationship between internal context factors like size or industry and IFRS practice.

The identifiable constant characteristic for three of the four applied theories (1) societal effects approach, (2) culture theory and (3) institutional economics is **institutions**[565]. Institutions are the core element of the societal effects approach and institutional economics. Institutions are an important element of culture theory, as well, as *Hofstede* acknowledges the reinforcing effect of institutional consequences; he attributes the temporal stability of his model of culture in part to the influence of institutions.[566]

The different theoretical concepts are integrated in the **conceptual framework** of this study, which can be interpreted as the theoretical 'transformation' of the research question (context of discovery). The conceptual framework is then refined with respect to the external and internal **context** of the organization. Based on the proposed theoretical link between context and financial accounting and the concrete specification of that context, falsifiable **hypotheses** are developed and operationalized (context of justification).

---

565 The term 'institution' refers to organizations and organizational structures but also comprises institutions like the market, money, marriage, language, human rights, social norms, the constitution, contracts, property etc. Cf. Picot 1991, p. 144; Göbel 2002, p. 1.

566 Cf. chapter 2.2.4.

2.2 Theoretical perspectives

As mentioned above, this study follows the culturally grounded approach.[567] The aim of the study is to assess the influence of national culture on financial reporting practice under IFRS. The next sections address eligible theories to describe and explain this relationship. Contingency theory as an outcome respectively further development of system theory is used to theoretically found the basic conceptual framework. Further theories are then presented to theoretically link external and internal context factors to financial accounting outcome as a basis for hypotheses development.

2.2.1 System theory

System theory is one of the major all-round theoretical concepts employed in various scientific disciplines.[568] It is intentionally formulated abstractly to fit well for all kinds of systems: natural, biological, mechanical or social.[569] The explanatory **contribution** made by system theory to this study is its understanding of organizations as social systems that are embedded in the suprasystem environment; it, thus, serves as a basic theoretical framework to describe organizations and organizational context. Furthermore, both contingency theory and the societal effects approach are based on system theoretical thought.

A system can be defined as "an organized, unitary whole composed of two or more interdependent parts, components, or subsystems and delineated by identifiable boundaries from its environmental suprasystem"[570].

To substantiate this general definition, *Wolf* identifies five core features of systems:[571]

- Systems contain elements with system specific characteristics allowing for delineation from other systems.
- System elements follow a hierarchical order divided into elements, subsystems, super-systems etc.
- System components (elements, subsystems etc.) are in manifold relationships with each other interchanging energy, material, information etc.
- System components and relationships define the state and behavior of the system redefining its characteristics and allowing for system change.
- System components and relationships built the structure of the system providing order and continuity of the system.

These features not only apply to closed deterministic systems apparent in the natural sciences but also to open systems, characteristic for the social sciences. For that reason, system theory from the 1950s on was adopted by business economics, first by organiza-

---

[567] Cf. chapter 1.4.2.
[568] Cf. Wolf 2005, p. 126.
[569] Cf. Kast/Rosenzweig 1973, p. 11.
[570] Kast/Rosenzweig 1973, p. 10.
[571] Cf. Wolf 2005, p. 127f.

tion and management theory. The system approach promised to be useful in understanding the growing complexities of organizations.[572]

The two mainstreams of modern system theory are general systems theory and cybernetics, cybernetics being more mathematical and application-oriented. In contrast to former system theoretical views, **general systems theory** explicitly focuses on open systems and the relationship between the system (inner system) and its environment (outer system). *Kast/Rosenzweig* present a brief overview of widely accepted key concepts of general systems theory, elaborating the difference between closed and open systems (see Table 2-1). This overview underlines the suitability of general systems theory to describe and analyze the functionality of vivid organizations. Social organizations are open systems embedded in a larger supra-system, the environment, to which they maintain various input-output-relationships, permitted by permeable system boundaries. The key concept of negative entropy accentuates the dependence on the outer system. Without the inner-outer-system-relationships the organization could not survive. Multiple goal seeking, the organization not only pursues the economic goal of maximizing profit but also ecological, ethical, political and technological goals to survive and to best adapt to the environment.[573]

Key concept	Interpretation
Components view	A system is composed of interrelated parts or elements
Holism, Synergism	The whole is more than the sum of the individual parts
Open systems view	Open system exchange information, energy or material with their environments
Transformation	Systems transform received inputs in some way and export outputs
Boundaries	Permeable boundaries separate open systems from its environment
Negative entropy	Transforming resources the system avoids the decay process of closed systems
Dynamic equilibrium	Open system may maintain a dynamic equilibrium through the inflow of resources
Feedback	Information on output or process are fed back to the system leading to change
Hierarchy	There is a hierarchical order of the components of the system (sub-, supra-system)
Internal elaboration	Open systems are greater differentiated with a higher level of organization
Multiple goal seeking	Open systems have multiple goals or purposes
Equifinality	Certain results may be achieved with different initial conditions and in different ways

Table 2-1: Key concepts of general system theory[574]

General system theorists explicitly recognize the interrelationship between social systems respectively business entities and their environment and the various influences the particular environment exerts on these. Furthermore, general system theory is generally applicable to all kind of intra- and extra-organizational systems, including the corporate financial

[572] Cf. Carlisle 1973, p. 48f.; Wolf 2005, p. 131.
[573] Cf. Wolf 2005, p. 131f.
[574] Adopted from Kast/Rosenzweig 1973, p. 40f.

accounting system.[575] Hence, general system theory might provide a solid theoretical foundation to the conceptual framework and the corresponding hypotheses to be developed. The organization respectively the persons responsible for the corporate accounting system might consciously or unconsciously conform to environmental (cultural) requirements to achieve the organizational optimum and to guarantee the survival of the social system.

Nevertheless, general system theory in its original form is not directly applied in this study as it is not consistent with the ultimate objective of this study, viz. to determine the general interrelation between national culture and corporate IFRS accounting practice. General system theory denies the possibility of such universal single-case exceeding relationships. Instead, system theorists advocate system-specific contingencies that for reasons of the system-specific decision-making process cannot be transferred to other systems. Spatiotemporal relationships are deemed highly improbable, which is why general system theory is not applicable as a conceptual framework in this study. This system theoretical deficiency marks one of the major distinctions to contingency theory[576], a theoretical concept that originates from system theory.[577]

The next section elaborates on contingency theory, one of the most popular and controversial theories in the social sciences.

2.2.2 Contingency theory

2.2.2.1 The basic model of contingency theory

Contingency theoretical thought can be well summarized by the Solomonian answer appropriate to almost every research question, viz.: 'it all depends [...]'.[578] In fact, a certain situational outcome depends on the situation and the particular circumstances of the situation. Contingency theory as a scientific concept in business economics emerged in the late 1950s as an answer respectively reaction to the purely universalistic research approaches that dominated the first half of the nineteenth century.[579] Inspired by linear programming and other mathematical models, scholars tried to find universal first-best solutions of how to organize and manage an enterprise until the late 1940s.[580] However, the ever-growing complexities of modern industrial organizations were not satisfactorily explicable applying the conventional universalistic management and organization theories.[581]

---

[575] The corporate financial accounting system refers to financial accounting practice.

[576] The denominations contingency theory/approach and situation theory/approach are mainly used synonymously in literature. Cf. Ulrich 1993, p. 123. In this study the Anglophone term contingency theory/approach will be used.

[577] Cf. Wolf 2005, p. 134.

[578] Cf. Schreyögg 1980, p. 306.

[579] Cf. Donaldson 1996, p. 58.

[580] Cf. Hellriegel/Slocum 1976, p. 5; Wolf 2005, p. 153.

[581] Cf. Donaldson 2001, p. 3.

The contingency theoretical perspective mainly goes back to early works of *Woodward*[582], *Udy*[583], *Stinchcombe*[584] or *Burns/Stalker*[585].[586] These authors analyzed the association between organizational characteristics like hierarchy levels or the degree of bureaucracy and organizational conditions like industry or technology.[587] Furthermore, the organizational characteristics were linked to levels of corporate success; *Woodward*, for example, found more successful companies to have a certain span of control on the first hierarchy level.[588] These early contingency theoretical studies showed that organizational structures depend on the contingencies the organization is confronted with;[589] the results of these studies strongly indicated that, in contrast to prior universalist thought:

> *"There is no one best way to manage an organization."*[590]

As aforementioned, this cognition first led to the development of (general) system theory, the conceptually close antecessor concept. The main difference between the two similar concepts was the fact that system theorists proclaimed single-case solutions applicable only to the one assessed entity and not transferable to other entities.[591] Nevertheless, system theoretical thought inspired the notion of enterprises as **open systems** being in manifold transaction interrelationships with and therefore depend on their particular environment.[592] Hence, contingency theory can be seen as a blend of the two extreme positions: (1) the universalistic approach, framing rules valid independently from the situation the organization is confronted with and (2) the single case approach, issuing statements that are applicable to one organization and one situation only (see Figure 2-1).[593]

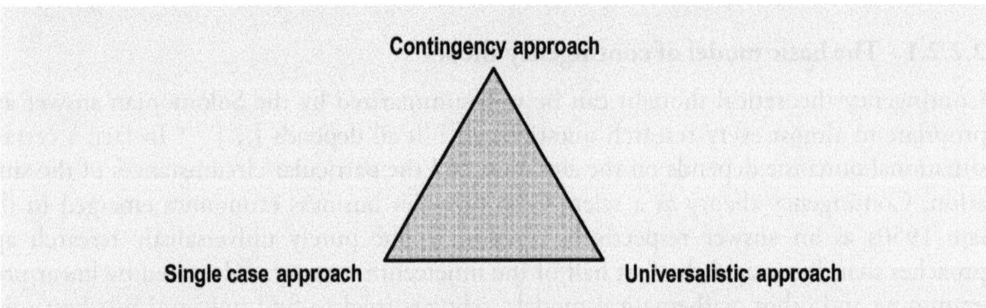

Figure 2-1: Contingency theory as a blend of different research approaches[594]

582 Cf. Woodward 1958; Woodward 1965.
583 Cf. Udy, JR. 1959.
584 Cf. Stinchcombe 1959.
585 Cf. Burns/Stalker 1961.
586 Cf. Otley 1980, p. 461; Wolf 2005, p. 149f.
587 Cf. Woodward 1958, p. 16ff.; Stinchcombe 1959, p. 168.
588 Cf. Woodward 1958, p. 21.
589 Cf. Lawrence/Lorsch 1969, p. 1.
590 Drazin/*de* van Ven 1985, p. 514.
591 Cf. Hellriegel/Slocum 1976, p. 5f.
592 Cf. Lawrence/Lorsch 1969, p. 6ff.
593 Cf. Brose 1984, p. 231; Jenner 2001, p. 79.
594 Adopted from Hellriegel/Slocum 1976, p. 6.

> *"In this way, contingency research brings some of the abstractions and generalizations of system theory down to specific relationships with practical managerial implications."*[595]

First applied in organization theory and then adopted by other business economics disciplines, contingency theory is one of the fundamental paradigms and meta-theories of business economics and the social sciences as a whole.[596] Denying the universality of organizational behavior and organizational configuration, proponents of this view assume universality of the interrelation between the environmental situation and organizational behavior/configuration.[597] Contingency theory in the beginning profited from the technological advances in context-analytical statistical techniques as researchers were not only able to posit contingency hypotheses, but also to statistically test them; for that reason, contingency theory always was and still is popular among critical rationalists who empirically test and possibly falsify their hypotheses.[598]

From an organization theoretical perspective, the central research questions of contingency theory can be defined as follows:

- Which context factors determine the organizational configuration?
- How can context and organizational configuration be operationalized?
- Which implications have particular configurations on the organizational success?[599]

Following these research questions, the contingency concept provides the scholar with the theoretical means to conceptually structure the research process and to identify and test alternative configurations in a particular situation that have proved to be successful in the past; research results may then be transferred to other research objects in a comparable situation to give situation-adequate recommendations (see also Figure 2-2).[600]

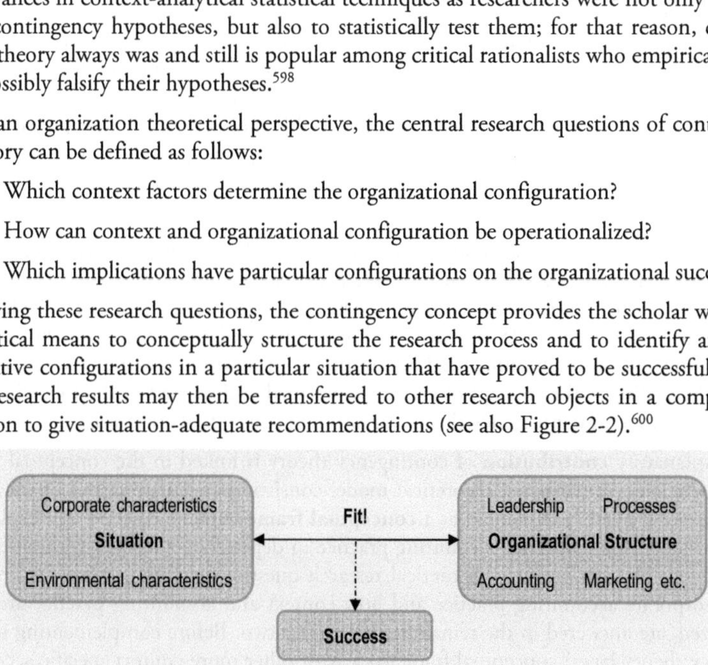

Figure 2-2: The basic model of the contingency approach in organization theory[601]

---

[595] Brown/Moberg 1980, p. 15.

[596] Cf. Otley 1980, p. 413f.; Raffée 1993, p. 37ff.

[597] Cf. Lawrence/Lorsch 1969, p. 14ff.

[598] Cf. Otley 1980, p. 413f.; Raffée 1993, p. 37ff.; Jenner 2001, p. 80; Wolf 2005, p. 151ff.

[599] Cf. Kieser/Kubicek 1978, p. 112ff.

[600] Cf. Jenner 2001, p. 79.

[601] Adopted from Wolf 2005, p. 156.

The inclusion of success respectively performance into the contingency theory basic concept is characteristic for organization theory.[602] The original contingency concept consisting of situation/context, research object/organization and the interrelationship between both variables has been expanded in various studies by the additional component of organizational success/performance.[603] Being able to reliably allocate certain situation-organizational-structure combinations to certain levels of efficiency and economic success would mean to advance from a merely descriptive-explicative to a prescriptive-normative organization theory, an idea attractive to both scientists and practitioners; as attractive as this idea is, the concept of success is afflicted with various conceptual difficulties.[604] First of all, it often remains unclear how the phenomenon of success is defined: is success related to effective or rather efficient organizational activity? Second, whose success is to be measured (stockholder, manager, employee)? Third, what are the correct indicators to measure success, how many indicators are to be taken into account and how are these indicators correctly measured? Other problems in integrating the concept of success into contingency theoretical studies are related to possible multi-causality, the applied temporal perspective (future- or past-orientation), the appropriate period of time, the aspired level of success (satisfying vs. optimizing) or the theoretical relevance of the utilized measurement methods.[605]

The contingency theoretical model that is applied in this study contains no elements of organizational success. Aside from conceptual deficiencies implied by the integration of success, the focus of this study is different. The aim of this study is to assess the influence of national culture on IFRS practice. Action recommendations based on the economic implications of culturally influenced accounting choices are not within the scope of this study. Accordingly, the concept of success is not further discussed in the following annotations on different contingency theory variants and conceptual criticism.

The explanatory **contribution** of contingency theory is linked to the conceptual basis of this study. The contingency theoretical model consisting of situation and organizational structure is applied in this study as a **conceptual framework** to describe and explain single-case exceeding corporate accounting practice in dependence on the organizational environment. The contingency theoretical research questions, which context factors determine corporate accounting practice and how context and accounting practice are operationalized, are answered in the remainder of chapter two. Before complementing the contingency theory based conceptual framework with other more context specific accounting theories, the above displayed basic model of the contingency approach is adjusted to fit to the research question of this study.

2.2.2.2 Contingency theoretical variants

This section presents alternative conceptual forms contingency theoretical models can assume. From these alternatives a contingency theoretical basic research model is devel-

[602] Cf. Meyer/Rowan 1977, p. 352.
[603] Cf. Ginsberg/Venkatraman 1985, p. 424; Ruekert et al. 1985, p. 13ff.; Donaldson 1987, p. 3.
[604] Cf. Wolf 2005, p. 164ff.
[605] Cf. Wolf 2005, p. 164ff.

oped that incorporates the peculiarities of the research question of this study. The above presented basic concept of contingency theory from an organization theoretical perspective is modified as follows.

Transposing the above described concept of contingency theory to the research question of this study, the organizational structure, which represents the 'system' organization, is replaced by the relevant subsystem to be analyzed, which is the corporate accounting system respectively corporate **accounting practice** as the observable and analyzable accounting system's outcome.[606] The different internal and external context factors that form the 'situation' are not part of the present discussion; these are dealt with in detail in chapter 2.3.2. The above modifications result in the following contingency theoretical basic model (see Figure 2-3).

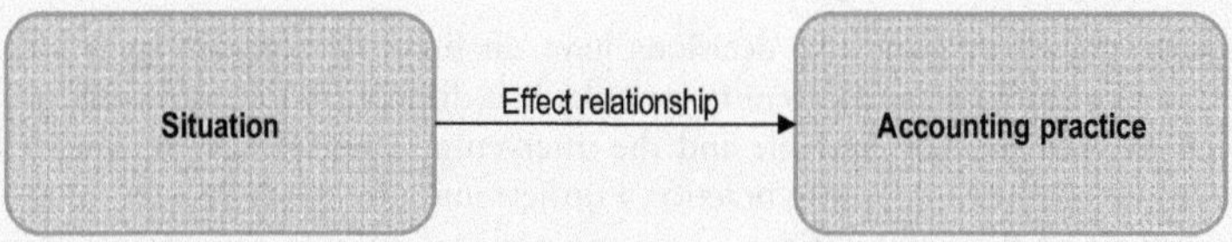

Figure 2-3: The contingency theoretical basic model[607]

This basic model illustrates the simple effect relationship between situation and accounting practice; it is the 'starting point' for the conceptual remarks to come. The careful choice of the appropriate contingency theoretical alternatives is important since the conceptual quality of the investigation depends on it.[608]

Context deterministic vs. context open

The perception of the context is one of the central issues to set up a contingency model. Context determinism is based on the assumption of a "quasi-mechanical relationship"[609] between situation and organization. This notion of contingency theory belongs to a research stream anteceding the context open variant and established the term 'contingency'. The context in this case is understood as a fixed construct that the organization and its decision-makers have no influence on. The organization is other-directed by the deterministic context and its decision-makers are mere transformers of the situational circumstances trying to find the one 'best-fit' reaction to the situation.

In contrast to the deterministic variant, the **context open** or voluntaristic variant posits that the organization is able to influence the situation and to choose among options defined by the open context. The decision-makers possess a certain amount of discretion. This perspective presents a more realistic view on organizational activity as today's com-

---

606 Cf. Roberts/Scapens 1985, p. 443ff.; Thomas 1986, p. 255; Thomas 1991, p. 41.

607 Adopted from Ulrich 1993, p. 126.

608 Cf. for the following sections on contingency theoretical variants Wolf 2005, p. 156ff.

609 Ulrich 1993, p. 130.

plex environments usually offer various choices of action and the exertion of influence on the institutional environment, for instance through lobbying, is common practice.[610]

This view is also more accurate with regard to the research question of this study. Assessing corporate financial accounting practice, as the result of culturally influenced accounting decisions, explicitly allows for the possibility of organizational choice and discretion. Accounting choice and discretion is always subject to a certain degree of subjectivity as the decisions are taken by the members of the organization and every member has individual experiences, preferences and beliefs. The personalistic open context model meets these concerns and integrates a subjective component into the effect relationship between independent and dependent variable. These personalistic influences can be accommodated for by an intervening variable 'decision processes' or 'subjective discretion', interposed between situation and accounting practice.[611]

Recognizing the effect subjective decisions have on financial accounting, it will not be included in this study as an intervening variable. It is difficult if not impossible to separate the effects the independent variable and the intervening variable have on the dependent variable, the corporate accounting practice. Furthermore, this study focuses on the cultural environment of the organization. The same national culture, the organization is embedded in, has an influence on the members of the organization as well and affects their accounting decisions. Corporate decision processes are affected by both objective reasoning and subjectively exercised discretion. For that reason, subjective discretion is seen as an organizational component in interrelationship with corporate accounting practice.

Mono causal vs. multi causal

Mono causal studies examine the relationship between only one (important) context factor and the target factor. These studies generally fail to satisfactorily explain complex situations. Multi causal studies, on the other hand, include all variables deemed relevant to explain the target factor. Multivariate context factors can be examined successively or simultaneously. Successive testing is generally inferior to parallel testing as the successive order of testing is often random and complex interdependencies are not appropriately reflected. This study employs multivariate testing.[612]

Point in time oriented vs. period of time oriented

Period of time oriented studies capture much more of the complex reality than the snapshots of point in time oriented studies and therefore principally are to be preferred. Nevertheless, longitudinal section studies are related to considerably more work and therefore are more seldom in business economics than cross section studies.[613]

---

610 Cf. Mazey/Richardson 1993; Austen-Smith/Wright 1996, p. 543ff.

611 Cf. Ulrich 1993, p. 159ff.

612 Cf. Wolf 2005, p. 158.

613 Cf. Wolf 2005, p. 158ff.

This study follows a point in time oriented approach. It analyzes the association between national culture and other context factors and accounting practice at a certain point of time; the development of the analyzed associations is not in the scope of the study.

Having outlined the basic parameters of the contingency model applied in this study as a conceptual framework, the following chapter ends the contingency theoretical subchapter with a critical discussion.

2.2.2.3 Critical appraisal of contingency theory

The academic popularity of contingency theory is a result of its conceptual plausibility.[614] The general system view and the understanding of organizations as open systems that operate in environments they have to adapt to are intuitively comprehensible. The contingency approach cured system theoretical deficiencies and was a conceptual compromise between universalistic and single-case research streams. In times of increasing individualization and complexity, contingency theory offers a concept to describe and to interpret social, technical, legal, economic and ecologic diversity.[615]

Despite of or due to its great popularity and widespread application in various scientific disciplines, contingency theory is subject to critical argument.[616] The most important critical matters are discussed in the following, differentiating between conceptual and methodological problems. Subsequently, the concept is appraised with regard to applicability in this study.

2.2.2.3.1 Conceptual criticism

As introductory stated, contingency theoretical assumptions follow the scheme: 'it all depends [...]'. This phrase symbolizes both the advantage and the disadvantage of the concept. Being applicable to a number of different problems of various scientific branches, this concept could be suspected to be too loose or too inexact regarding its conceptualization and theoretical implications. In fact, contingency theory is criticized to be no 'real' theory at all but rather a formal-analytical framework or conceptual guideline to structure empirical research processes. It only posits to analyze the relationship between context and structure variables but delivers no theoretical hints which context variables to have a look at and how to model the relationship.[617] The lack of theoretical performance is widely attested and the criticism legitimate. Contingency theory in this study is therefore merely used as a theoretical foundation for the conceptual framework outlined in chapter 2.3. The lack of content-theoretical explanatory power is resolved in this study by consulting other material theories (see the following subchapters) to derive hypotheses from.

Conceptual contingency theory criticism is often concerned with the ability to deliver concrete recommendations of how to act in a certain situation. A **holistic approach** as contingency theory tries to capture the entire reality of a situation and not just a snap-shot

614 Cf. Auerbach 2009, p. 119.
615 Cf. Wolf 2005, p. 168.
616 Cf. Staehle/Conrad 2009, p. 52ff.; Kieser et al. 2010, p. 40ff.
617 Cf. Ulrich 1993, p. 123; Wolf 2005, p. 169.

of it. The more complex the situation, the more context factors exist, often leading to differing action-recommendations. This problem is often met by building typologies of different situation-classes. This procedure unfortunately leads to a loss of information; furthermore, a growing number of variable combinations conditions larger sample sizes per situation-class which results in additional empirical effort. The momentum of accounting choice is an important element of this study. Differing choices resulting in differing action-recommendations do not undermine the conceptual validity of this study.[618]

Another issue related to conceptual criticism concerns **environmental determinism**. Contingency theory is accused to be too deterministic for taking the environment as given and pursuing the first-best structural solution to a certain situation. This critical matter has already been addressed in the previous subchapter and is related to the context deterministic vs. context open debate; as mentioned above, this study follows an open context approach accepting (1) different structural solutions leading to identical results and (2) the interdependence of accounting and its environment.[619]

The conceptual criticism in most instances does not affect this study. Most of it is related to organization thought, which implies concrete action-recommendations and a measurable success component; as outlined above, the aim of this story is to describe and to explain and not to give action-recommendations. The content-theoretical handicap is 'cured' by application of additional theories.

2.2.2.3.2 Methodological criticism

Methodological criticism does not pertain to contingency theory as a conceptual guideline to fruitful research but to the empirical statistical application and interpretation of it. The following list exemplifies critical issues:[620]

- inadequate consideration of prior research context factors, assumptions, results,
- superficial/abstract capture of reality; results are not exploitable/understandable,
- interdependence of context variables,
- assumption of linear statistical relationships,
- deficient operationalization of variables,
- situation change unconsidered (mainly cross-sectional studies),
- past oriented perspective.

These methodological problems are not contingency theory specific but generally inherent in empirical research work, most of them part of the process of statistical analysis. If accounted for carefully and correctly, research results should not be affected. The above listed problems are addressed in different chapters of this study. Chapter 1.5 contains an extensive analysis of prior research. The explicit application of contingency theory on fi-

618 Cf. Jenner 2001, p. 82f.
619 Cf. Thomas 1986, p. 254ff.
620 Cf. Wolf 2005, p. 169ff.

nancial accounting research is rather unusual[621] and the impact of the context factor culture on IFRS practice, as well, is rather unexplored. Nevertheless, the existing studies and findings are adequately integrated into the research program of this study. Multi collinearity on the other hand is a serious issue and may influence the results of multivariate statistical models. Accordingly, the interaction of the context variables is assessed in chapter 4.3. Relevant context variables are selected based on prior research results and the theoretical framework of this study.

Research problems like the neglect of situational change and the focus on the analysis of past data are closely connected with the here utilized method of data collection, i.e. the content analysis of annual financial statements. Notwithstanding, this method is favored in this study since the aim of this study is to analyze real world financial reporting practice.[622] Also, financial statements are selected for reasons of data availability. These advantages clearly compensate for the expounded problem of unidimensionality. Additionally, analyzing past data does not hinder the possibility of making tentative future-oriented statements.

After presenting, evaluating and selecting contingency theory as a basic theoretical guideline respectively conceptual framework for this study, the next subchapters outline further material theories integrated into the framework as a basis for hypotheses development.

2.2.3 The societal effects approach

Contingency theoretical considerations serve well as a broad research framework in the tradition of critical rationalism. Nonetheless, its theoretical use is limited in explaining the association between national culture and accounting practice. Contingency theory rather concentrates on a few contingencies in the close task environment of the organization such as scale, production technology etc.; these context factors develop a certain rationale irrespective of variables of the wider social, political and economic environment. National culture, which this study seeks to investigate, is not taken into account as an environmental context factor. Furthermore, contingency theory is criticized to be too deterministic focusing on a limited number of constant relationships between contingencies and aspects of the organization structure. The organizational structure is described by aspects like specialization, formalization or centralization. The organization members' attitudes or behavior, important for the assessment of the influence of culture on accounting choice, however, are not predicted. The focus is on organizational structures, neglecting human behavior and interaction. Cultural influences are ignored as contingency theorists argue that

---

[621] Researchers often assess the influence of certain context variables like the financing system on financial accounting and therewith implicitly follow a contingency theoretical approach without explicitly referring to contingency theory as a conceptual framework; cf., e.g., La Porta 1997, p. 1131ff.; Ali/Hwang 2000, p. 1ff.; Jaggi/Low 2000, p. 495ff.

[622] Alternatively, financial accounting practice could be analyzed by means of an experiment; cf., e.g., Schultz/Lopez 2001, p. 271ff.; Doupnik/Richter 2004, p. 1ff. It is difficult, however, to transfer the empirical results gained under laboratory conditions to the real world and actual financial accounting practice.

cultural effects are superimposed by contingencies.[623] This negligence of cultural influences contradicts the culturally grounded approach of this study.[624]

As annotated above, the original contingency approach that deals with one or a few strict contingencies in a context deterministic relationship certainly is not directly applicable to the research context of this study. The **societal effects approach**, on the other hand, heals some of the conceptual deficiencies of contingency theory and integrates conceptual considerations like the **open context** perspective or a more **personalistic** view. These were already addressed above when describing more recent contingency theoretical perspectives. Again, this underlines the conceptual flexibility of contingency theory.

The societal effects approach[625], in contrast to the original contingency approach, acknowledges both the influence of the human factor and the dependence on the national institutional environment.[626] Organizational structures and practices are presumed to be affected by the relatively permanent, systematic features of a society.[627] Advocates of this approach see "[...] the business organization as socially constituted and thus reflecting national distinctiveness in institutional arrangements"[628]. The organization as an institution itself within a social environment reflects the institutional parameters of that environment; the boundaries between organization and society are regarded as permeable. Furthermore, the relationship between the institutional setting and the organizational forms and practices is not deterministic and unidirectional.[629] According to the societal effects approach, institutions have an effect on the values and dispositions of the organizational members who in return may have an influence on the institutions through their actions. Such interdependencies in the case of financial accounting may refer to certain accounting best practice patterns that are later turned into standards respectively standard interpretations. Alternatively, companies could participate in the IASB due process or engage in political lobbyism. *Bhimani* situates the societal effects approach in the middle between the unidirectional determinism of contingency theory and total constructivism. Organizational choices are the product of objective constraints determined by the institutional surroundings of the organization and the subjectivism of autonomous human behavior and interaction.[630]

The phenomenon of culture is not excluded from the societal effects perspective but manifested in societal institutions that are defined as "[...] patterns of habitualized reciprocal social action"[631]. **Culture** is rather accepted to have a "mediating influence"[632]. Both cultural and institutional approach are rather seen as complementary approaches that in em-

---

[623] Cf. Maurice et al. 1980, p. 59f.; Lane 1989, p. 22ff.
[624] Cf. chapter 1.4.2.
[625] Cf. Maurice et al. 1980, p. 59ff.; Sorge/Warner 1986; Sorge/Maurice 1993, p. 57ff.
[626] Cf. Maurice et al. 1980, p. 61.
[627] Cf. Bhimani 2005, p. 254.
[628] Lane 1989, p. 31.
[629] Cf. Liouville/Schmidt 1996, p. 259.
[630] Cf. Lane 1995, p. 10; Bhimani 1999, p. 421ff.
[631] Lane 1989, p. 35.
[632] Maurice 1979, p. 46.

pirical research practice are often combined.[633] Different to the culturalist perspective of *Hofstede*, who also incorporates institutions and the interrelationship between culture and institutions in his culture model,[634] culture from the societal effects perspective is not accounted for as a separate context factor to be distinguished from other institutional factors.[635]

Despite apparent differences between contingency and societal effects approach, both approaches share some similarities. Both approaches can be categorized as being **situational**. The organization is influenced by the situation it is in; it is the product of the situational paths it has followed in the past. In analogy to one of the key assumptions of the contingency approach, the societal effects approach posits that the main organizational goals do not differ across countries; the way these goals are reached is shaped by societal institutions. Other elements, characteristic for the universalist contingency approach, are necessary to successfully assess societal effects from an empirical perspective. In the process of cross national sample selection it has to be made sure that contingency theoretical important context factors like size are controlled for. Otherwise, these effects could bias the results for cultural respectively societal factors. As mentioned above, other universalist assumptions of the contingency approach are incorporated into the theoretical foundation of this study, as well.[636]

The societal effects approach complements the contingency theoretical framework of this study and fits well to the research question of this study. The accounting practice of a company is the result of both institutional constraints like the accounting system or the tax system and the accountant's individual choice. The accountant is not entirely free in his accounting decisions but has to remain within the general limits of the law. Within these limits there are legal accounting options and room for discretion the accountant may choose from and come to an individual decision. The explanatory **contribution** of the societal effects approach, thus, is related to the conceptualization of the organizational context. This study employs a combination of the cultural approach by *Hofstede* and the societal effects approach as theoretical foundation for the relationship between external context factors and accounting practice as an outcome of the organizational and individual adaption to the social environment. Both theories predict the influence of institutional variables on the organization and its members. Focusing primarily on the context factor culture, culture theory by *Hofstede* is applied to treat culture as the central influence factor.

The following chapters depict the **culture grounded perspective** of this study and the theoretical connection to accounting practice. The definition and understanding of national culture and the notion, how it affects society, societal institutions and social interaction is important to answer the research question of this study whether and how national culture exerts influence on the use of the business language of IFRS. Furthermore, the presentation and discussion of national cultural dimensions is necessary to describe and

[633] Cf. Lane 1989, p. 31ff.
[634] Cf. chapter 2.2.4.
[635] Cf. Lane 1989, p. 31ff.
[636] Cf. Lane 1989, p. 37f.

explain national cultural differences. Based on an understanding of cultural differences, the theoretical link is established to financial reporting values to analyze the association between differences in culture and differences in IFRS practice.[637] Before elaborating on culture theory according to *Hofstede* in more detail, different cultural approaches are presented to outline similarities and differences compared to the *Hofstede* approach; one of these alternative approaches is used to test the empirical results of this study, which base on the *Hofstede* framework, for robustness.[638]

2.2.4 Culture theory

2.2.4.1 Concepts of culture

2.2.4.1.1 Definition of culture

The word culture etymologically comes from the Latin noun '*cultura*' which is derived from the Latin verb '*colere*' which means 'to build', 'to plant', 'to care for' or 'to cultivate'.[639] Culture first referred to the cultivation of things like the acre ('*agri cultura*') or the garden ('*horti cultura*') but was later metaphorically transferred to human cultivation of the body ('*cultura corporis*') and more importantly the mind ('*cultura animi*'). Culture in this context originally had two meanings, one active, describing the process, and one passive, describing the state. The 'culture one does' relates to the refinement of something/someone that/who has the potential to be refined, but is not able to reach that state of higher cultivation without the help from outside. The result of this process of cultivation is a higher state of culture, 'the culture one has'. The term of culture, originally attributed to the degree of sophistication of things and individuals, came to its modern more abstract meaning when transferred from individuals to groups of people and societies, representing their traditions, institutions and ways of living.[640]

The concept of culture is highly abstract and the term culture is used in various contexts. Speaking of culture we may refer to national culture, local culture, organizational culture, family culture, soccer culture, cultural artefacts, the arts and many other phenomena that are labeled as some kind of culture. All these phenomena have in common that a group of humans shares the same values, beliefs, behaviors and other distinct conceptual attributes that are characteristic for 'their own' culture. Culture is something made and shared by humans.

In the following, when not complemented with an additional attribute, the term culture is synonymously used for **national culture.**

The phenomenon culture, often oversimplified used as a synonym for 'nation', has long been neglected in business economics research and treated as a residual factor for non-explainable national variations. In absence of a satisfactory theoretical framework, culture

[637] Cf. chapter 2.2.4.5.
[638] Cf. chapter 4.3.1.7 and 4.3.2.4.
[639] Cf. Online Etymology Dictionary 2011.
[640] Cf. Busche 2000, p. 69ff.; Dahl 2004, p. 1.

was regarded too problematic. *Child* in a 1981 paper summarizes the scientific culture problem as follows: (1) culture has rarely been defined, (2) the boundaries of a cultural unit are difficult to define, (3) the identification of cultural variables is problematic, (4) there is little specification of organizational subcomponents of culture and (5) the measurement of cultural attributes is difficult.[641]

Stating that culture has rarely been defined, *Child* refers to the fact, that there is no single, across all academic branches generally accepted, definition of culture. *Kroeber/Kluckhohn* in a 1952 monograph list a total of 164 different definitions of culture.[642] Culture is a highly abstract concept and cannot be attributed to a single academic discipline. From an anthropological point of view the phenomenon of culture is defined as follows:

> *"Culture consists in patterned ways of thinking, feeling and reacting, acquired and transmitted mainly by symbols, constituting the distinctive achievements of human groups, including their embodiments in artifacts; the essential core of culture consists of traditional (i.e. historically derived and selected) ideas and especially their attached values."*[643]

To put it in a nutshell, *Child* defines culture from a holistic anthropological perspective as "a complex system which is all-embracing of a society's 'folkways'"[644].

2.2.4.1.2 Conceptual alternatives

The following review of concepts of culture presents six regularly cited national cultural approaches in chronological order to better categorize the cultural dimensions according to *Hofstede* and to display similarities and differences to his approach.[645] All concepts commonly approximate national culture by means of cultural dimensions. Whereas the first two approaches by *Kluckhohn/Strodtbeck* and *Hall* are based on theoretical considerations only, the latter four approaches by *Hofstede*, *Trompenaars*, *Schwartz* and *House et al.* are tested empirically to quantify national cultural differences.

The cultural approach by *Kluckhohn/Strodtbeck*[646] is based on dimensions of basic human assumptions. These are (1) the character of human nature, (2) the relationship between humans and nature, (3) the relationship between humans, (4) human time orientation and (5) human activity orientation. The first dimension refers to the basic question whether humans are good or evil or a mixture of both. If humans comply with nature, live in harmony with nature or subordinate nature, is part of the second dimension. The human to human dimension distinguishes between individualistic and collectivistic cultures.

---

[641] Cf. Child 1981, p. 304ff.

[642] Cf. Kroeber et al. 1952, p. 125ff. The work of *Kroeber/Kluckhohn* refers to societies and the common ground members of a society share; cf. McGrath et al. 1992, p. 117. Accordingly, the listed definitions do not necessarily refer to national culture. The assumption that a society coincides with the nation is a simplification of the complexities of human social life; cf. Hofstede 2001, p. 13ff.

[643] Kluckhohn 1951, p. 86.

[644] Child 1981, p. 323.

[645] The following short summary is mainly based on Dahl 2004; Kutschker/Schmid 2011, p. 702ff.; Kirca et al. 2009, p. 113f.

[646] Cf. Kluckhohn/Strodtbeck 1961.

The fourth dimension is characterized by the two poles past and future oriented, the center being present oriented. The last dimension describes the level of human activity and varies between the extremes of 'being' and 'doing', the intermediate form labeled as 'being-in-becoming'.

Based on his experience in the Foreign Service, the anthropologist *Hall*[647] identified four cultural dimensions: (1) context orientation, (2) space orientation, (3) time orientation and (4) information speed. The first and most commonly known dimension differentiates between high and low context cultures. High context (e.g. China, Japan) implies that only a small part of the inter-personal transferred information is explicitly expressed; the larger part is implicitly existent in the interacting persons. Space orientation is determined by the interculturally varying perception of 'private sphere' and 'territory'. *Hall's* third dimension captures how cultures structure their time. Different from *Kluckhohn/Strodtbeck,* he distinguishes between monochronic and polychronic cultures, the first referring to a linear concept of time and the latter to a circular concept of time, in which past, present and future intermingle. The speed of encoding and decoding information in communication situations is the idea of the last criterion.

Whereas the two above described concepts are merely theoretical considerations which lack empirical prove, *Hofstede*[648] operationalized and measured national cultural differences. Analyzing 116,000 questionnaires of an IBM international employee attitude survey, *Hofstede* identified five cultural dimensions[649] he labeled: (1) power distance,(2) uncertainty avoidance, (3) individualism versus collectivism, (4) masculinity versus femininity and (5) long-term versus short-term orientation.[650]

By far not reaching the scope of the *Hofstede* survey, *Trompenaars*[651] in the early 1990ies gathered information from approximately 30,000 respondents from 57 countries. His concept is based on the following seven dimensions: (1) universalism vs. particularism, (2) individualism vs. collectivism, (3) affectivity vs. neutrality, (4) specificity vs. diffusivity, (5) status attribution vs. status achievement, (6) time orientation and (7) the human environment relationship. The first dimension relates to rules conformity. Universalists stick to general rules, whereas particularists evaluate each specific situation. The second dimension closely resembles the *Kluckhohn/Strodtbeck* human to human dimension. The degree of inter-personal affection or emotion is covered by the third dimension. Specificity vs. diffusivity refers to the level of social engagement of individuals. In diffuse cultures the

---

647 Cf. in particular for the space dimension Hall 1966; for the context dimension cf. in particular Hall/Hall 1976; for the time dimension cf. in particular Hall 1983; for the information speed dimension cf. in particular Hall/Hall 1990.

648 Cf. Hofstede 1980a.

649 Cf. Hofstede 2001, p. 29. For a detailed description of the *Hofstede* dimensions cf. chapter 2.2.4.3.

650 The first data analysis resulted in only four dimensions. The fifth dimension long-term vs. short-term orientation was added later improving the explanation capacity of the model especially for Asian countries. This dimension is neglected in the following since this study focuses on cultural differences in Europe and for European countries some values of the fifth dimension are missing. Also, long-term orientation is negatively correlated with individualism. Cf. Yeh/Lawrence 1995, p. 655ff.; Archambault/Archambault 2003, p. 177.

651 Cf. Trompenaars 1993.

areas of life of individuals are not clearly separated but merge smoothly. Dimension five relates to the question whether status in a society is gained by birth, religion, age or by achievement. The time dimension is a combination of the two above mentioned time concepts of *Kluckhohn/Strodtbeck* and *Hall*. The last dimension is also found within the concept of *Kluckhohn/Strodtbeck*, representing the relationship between humans and nature.

Another large empirical investigation of cultural values was conducted by *Schwartz*[652] in the early 1990s. He asked more than 60,000 participants from 63 countries to assess the importance of 57 values presented to them in form of the 'Schwartz Value Inventory'. Other than *Hofstede* and *Trompenaars*, he explicitly distinguishes between the individual and the culture-level analysis of data. At the individual-level *Schwartz* identifies ten distinct value types: (1) power, (2) achievement, (3) hedonism, (4) stimulation, (5) self-direction, (6) universalism, (7) benevolence, (8) tradition, (9) conformity and (10) security; these are merged into two bipolar conceptual dimensions, viz. openness to change ((3)-(5)) vs. conservation ((8)-(10)) and self-enhancement ((1)-(3)) vs. self-transcendence ((6)+(7)). At the culture-level, the level both *Hofstede* and *Trompenaars* claim to analyze, *Schwartz* derives seven value types that form three cultural value dimensions which show a certain intersection with the dimensions presented above. The first dimension resembles the individualism/collectivism dimension as (1) conservatism/embeddedness is opposed by autonomy which is further split into (2) intellectual autonomy and (3) affective autonomy. The second dimension deals with the relationship between humans and their (social) environment; (4) harmony is opposed by (5) mastery. The last dimension is span between the two poles (6) hierarchy, which stands for unequal status and power distribution, and (7) egalitarianism, which is inspired by equal distribution of status, power and other resources.

One of the largest and the most recent cross-cultural studies is the GLOBE (Global Leadership and Organizational Behavior Effectiveness) study. *House et al.*[653] adopt the *Hofstede* dimensional approach for culture and identify nine cultural dimensions: (1) uncertainty avoidance, (2) power distance, (3) institutional collectivism, (4) in-group collectivism, (5) gender egalitarianism, (6) assertiveness, (7) future orientation, (8) human orientation and (9) performance orientation.

Two of the above presented cultural concepts are described in more detail in the following. As outlined above, this study employs the cultural concept of *Hofstede*. It is by far the largest empirical investigation in this field of study and the validity of *Hofstede's* cultural dimensions has been demonstrated in numerous studies. Before addressing culture theory according to *Hofstede* and describing the *Hofstede-Gray* framework, the GLOBE study is discussed. Although the GLOBE study is not as comprehensive as the *Hofstede* study, it is the most current[654] large scale cross-cultural study. Its cultural dimensions are used in the

[652] Cf. Schwartz 1994, p. 85ff.

[653] Cf. House et al. 2004.

[654] The *Hofstede* survey data were gathered between 1967 and 1973; cf. Hofstede 2001, p. 41.

course of the study to test the robustness[655] of the empirical results on the relationship between cultural factors and IFRS practice.

2.2.4.1.3 GLOBE study

An international team of researchers collected culture relevant data in 62 countries in the period from 1994 to 1997.[656] *House et al.* analyzed circa 17,000 questionnaires on culture and leadership; these were filled out by managers from 951 local organizations from the food processing, financial services and telecommunication services industries.[657] The aim of the GLOBE study was not primarily to assess cultural dimensions, but to analyze interdependencies between cultural dimensions and leadership, i.e. which leadership style is most effective when operating in a certain cultural environment.[658]

The GLOBE dimensions originally base on the *Hofstede* dimensions; two dimensions are split in two and two further dimensions are identified. The *Hofstede* individualism-collectivism dimension is split into (1) institutional collectivism, which measures the degree to which institutions support the collective distribution of resources respectively collective behavior, and (2) in-group collectivism, which measures the degree of group members' solidarity (family, organization). The *Hofstede* masculinity-femininity dimension is split into (1) assertiveness, which measures the degree to which members of a society show dominant, assertive, confronting and aggressive behavior, and (2) gender egalitarianism, which measures the degree to which societies enforce equal treatment of genders. Furthermore, human orientation measures the degree, to which societies provide incentives for fair, generous, compassionate and altruistic behavior. Additionally, performance orientation measures the degree to which societies provide incentives for performance improvement respectively excellent performance. Future orientation is another label for the fifth *Hofstede* dimension long-term versus short-term orientation.[659] Although labeled identically, the two first dimensions uncertainty avoidance and power distance do not exactly mean the same as defined by *Hofstede*.[660]

The nine GLOBE dimensions were determined for both societal practices ('as is') and societal values ('should be').[661] Accordingly, the authors designed their questionnaires "[...] to capture both the tangible attributes of culture [practices] and the intangible attributes [values]"[662].

---

655 For the robustness tests cf. chapter 4.3.1.7 and chapter 4.3.2.4.

656 Cf. House et al. 2004 in the following, when referring to the GLOBE study.

657 Cf. Cieslewicz 2010, p. 17.

658 Cf. Schmid/Kotulla 2010, p. 61.

659 Cf. Hofstede 2006, p. 883.

660 For a comparison of the *Hofstede* and the *House et al.* concepts of uncertainty avoidance cf. Venaik/Brewer 2010, p. 1294ff.

661 Cf. Venaik/Brewer 2010, p. 1296.

662 Brewer/Venaik 2010, p. 1317.

2.2.4.1.4 Critical appraisal of the GLOBE study

To allow for a meaningful comparison of the GLOBE study and the *Hofstede* study, basic differences and similarities have to be taken into account.[663] First, the GLOBE data (1994-1997), as mentioned above, is more current than the *Hofstede* data (1967-1973). Both countries choose an industrial setting. Whereas *Hofstede* analyzes one company (IBM) only, *House et al.* analyze 951 companies from three different industries. From the perspective of actuality and industrial diversification, the GLOBE study is clearly to be preferred. Second, the GLOBE study is performed by a team of researchers, whereas the *Hofstede* study is mainly conducted by himself. Third, *House et al.* question mainly managers;[664] *Hofstede* questions mainly non-managerial employees. Fourth, *House et al.* follow a theory driven approach in their study, whereas *Hofstede* assesses data that is gathered for IBM management purposes. Fifth, the GLOBE study is characterized by a central US inspired research design; the *Hofstede* questionnaire, on the other hand, is developed in cooperation with local researchers who conducted the pilot interviews. Sixth, the GLOBE study aims to assess both organizational and societal culture; *Hofstede* focuses on societal values only.

The above listed differences and similarities of the two studies present a mixed picture with regard to an assessment of the quality of the two research designs.[665] Most of the described characteristics can be interpreted both as possible advantages and disadvantages, dependent on the perspective of the judge. The GLOBE study is surely more current and the questionnaire is designed for a specific purpose; *Hofstede*, on the contrary, uses the IBM questionnaire, which is tailored to the needs of the IBM employees. On the other hand, the GLOBE study leaves the impression of trying to capture too much information. The GLOBE questionnaire is designed to assess culture on a societal and organizational level. Furthermore, it contains questions on practices and values and, additionally, dimensions of leadership are investigated.[666]

Despite differences in research design, research focus and research purpose, *Hofstede* finds the GLOBE study's results to be more similar to his own results than expected.[667] He performs two factors analyses on (1) the country scores of the GLOBE cultural dimensions and (2) the GLOBE questionnaire items. The first factor analysis, in contrast to the nine GLOBE dimensions, results in five meta-dimensions that are significantly associated with the five *Hofstede* dimensions. The second factor analysis on questionnaire item level confirms the former results. Numerous items are significantly correlated with the *Hofstede* dimensions.[668]

---

[663] Cf. Hofstede 2006, p. 883ff.

[664] For a critical discussion of the questioning of managers cf. Den Hartog et al. 1999, p. 242; Euwema et al. 2007, p. 1040; Hoppe/Bhagat 2009, p. 529.

[665] Cf. Hofstede 2006, p. 883ff.

[666] Cf. Christopher Earley 2006, p. 924.

[667] Cf. Hofstede 2006, p. 893.

[668] Cf. Hofstede 2006, p. 889ff.

The factor analysis results by *Hofstede* show that the gathered data of both studies do not differ as much as suggested by the different country scores.[669] Although the labels of the cultural dimensions of both studies imply similar dimensions, the meanings of the dimensions are different and therefore difficult to compare. *Hofstede's* work is criticized to describe the multi facet phenomenon culture by a few dimensions only and consecutive culture studies try to compensate for this 'deficiency' by integrating more cultural dimensions into their models. Nonetheless, the integration of additional dimensions is only advisable when the statistical data allow for independent dimensions. *Hofstede*, for example, first identifies independent factors that describe cultural differences and then interprets the meaning of these factors based on the content of the questionnaire items.

In contrast, *House et al.* take the *Hofstede* dimensions as a basis and then split up two dimensions and add two more for conceptual considerations. The cultural part of the questionnaire is developed based on the above described nine dimensions.[670] At first glance, the capture of additional dimensions is to be regarded as positive; culture is likely to have more facets than assumed by the four respectively five dimensions of *Hofstede*. However, the results on the nine practices and values dimensions show that seven of the nine practices dimensions are, surprisingly, negatively correlated with the corresponding values dimensions.[671] Furthermore, most dimensions are also strongly correlated with other dimensions and, thus, not independent from one another.[672] Accordingly, the GLOBE questions, designed from the start to capture nine dimensions, might have induced conceptual interferences into the GLOBE cultural dimensions. In fact, a factor analysis performed by *Hofstede* shows that the cultural differences, measured by the cultural questions of the nine categories, can be aggregated to five factors only, which partly resemble the five factor model of *Hofstede*. As mentioned before, *Hofstede's* cultural dimensions are not developed to describe national culture *per se* but try to approximate cultural **differences** between societies. The respondents' answers to the questions and therewith the questions limit the range of cultural differences covered with the particular questionnaire; the challenge then is to determine what exactly the aggregated factors measure and how to label them.[673]

Apart from a disputable determination and interpretation of the GLOBE cultural dimensions, *Peterson/Castro* attest the GLOBE measures conceptual difficulties with respect to aggregation of data; they find "ambiguities and apparent inconsistencies in the description of GLOBE's measure development process"[674]. Although *House et al.* accentuate that they follow a theory-driven instead of an empirically derived (*Hofstede*) approach, the GLOBE study does not provide a coherent theoretical framework to link individual assessments to general assessments on macro level.[675] *Earley* states that "as a values study the GLOBE

[669] Cf. the GLOBE country scores House et al. 2004, p. 365ff.; cf. the *Hofstede* country scores of the four original dimensions Hofstede 2001, p. 87, 151, 215, 286.

[670] Cf. Hofstede 2006, p. 883.

[671] Cf. Taras et al. 2010, p. 1331.

[672] Cf. Hofstede 2010, p. 1340.

[673] For a more detailed critical discussion of the *Hofstede* study cf. chapter 2.2.4.4.

[674] Peterson/Castro 2006, p. 507.

[675] Cf. Christopher Earley 2006, p. 928.

work is one of many"[676]. Moreover, the results of the GLOBE study are criticized to be affected by a Western respectively US-centric research approach.[677]

The critical comparison of the GLOBE study and the *Hofstede* study indicates conceptual differences between both studies, but also shows similarities with respect to statistical data on cultural country differences.[678] Although the GLOBE study contains more current data, this study applies the *Hofstede* concept for the following reasons. First, the *Hofstede* framework still is the most applied cultural framework in intercultural research;[679] its application in numerous recent studies supports this notion.[680] Second, as outlined in more detail in the succeeding chapter, culture is expected to change only slowly over time and cultural patterns that have developed over hundreds of years are supposedly not much affected by a period of thirty years.[681] Third, the *Hofstede* study explicitly focuses on cultural country differences, whereas the GLOBE study rather pursues a more comprehensive description of national cultures, which is resembled by additional cultural dimensions. Since this study wants to measure the association between cultural differences and differences in IFRS practice, the *Hofstede* approach seems to be more qualified with respect to the research question. And fourth, the *Hofstede* study (116,000 participants)[682] is far more extensive than the GLOBE study (17,000 participants). Nonetheless, the data of the GLOBE study is used for a robustness test to incorporate current developments in intercultural research.[683]

The following chapters describe and appraise culture theory according to *Hofstede* in more detail.

2.2.4.2 Culture theory according to Hofstede

In concordance with *Hofstede*, this study understands culture as "the collective programming of the mind that distinguishes the members of one group or category of people from another"[684]. Everyone is run by this "software of the mind"[685]; it is developed at the early stage of everyone's life, makes human behavior to a certain degree predictable and therewith social systems possible. *Hofstede* identifies three broad levels of mental programming: (1) universal, (2) collective and (3) individual programming.

---

676 Christopher Earley 2006, p. 928.

677 Cf. Hofstede 2006, p. 884; Hoppe/Bhagat 2009, p. 529.

678 For a detailed comparison of the *Hofstede* and the GLOBE study cf. Christopher Earley 2006, p. 922ff.

679 Cf. Sivakumar/Nakata 2001, p. 555ff.; Kirkman et al. 2006, p. 285ff.; Chakrabarti et al. 2008, p. 219;

680 Cf. Doupnik/Richter 2004, p. 1ff.; HassabElnaby/Mosebach 2005, p. 19ff.; Arnold et al. 2007, p. 327ff.; Clements et al. 2008; Hope et al. 2008, p. 357ff.; Huerta/Salter 2008; Fidrmuc/Jacob 2009; Jödicke 2009.

681 Various more current *Hofstede* replication studies confirm this assumption; cf. chapter 2.2.4.4.

682 Cf. chapter 2.2.4.2.

683 Cf. chapter 4.3.1.7 and 4.3.2.4.

684 Hofstede 2001, p. 9; for culture theory according to Hofstede cf. Hofstede 1980a; Hofstede 1980b; Hofstede 1982; Hofstede 1983, p. 75ff.; Hofstede 1993. The following annotations on Hofstede's culture theory are based on his revised 2001 publication Hofstede 2001.

685 Hofstede 2001, p. 1.

The bottom most basic **universal** level refers to the biological programming of all humans and includes basic expressive human behavior like laughing, for instance. Contrary to universal programming, the top level **individual** programming contains the individual personality, unique to every individual. Both levels are part of the human genetic heritage, the universal level completely and the individual level at least in parts. The level between the two poles universal and individual contains **collective** programming, i.e. mental programs that are shared only by a certain group of people and that can be described as **human culture.** In contrast to the other two levels, this part contains only little genetically inherited programming; it is mostly learned. Collective respectively cultural programming is shared by people who are genetically different but who went through the same or similar learning processes in the family, at school and other social institutions.

Culture as the collective programming of the mind consists of invisible elements like values, the core element of every culture, but also of visible elements like symbols, heroes or rituals. *Hofstede* displays the invisible and visible components of culture in an 'onion diagram', with values being the invisible core of every culture and rituals, heroes and symbols (practices) being the visible outer layers of culture.

The outer most superficial layer contains the **symbols** of a culture, i.e. words, gestures or objects that have a certain meaning only to the members of that culture and that may not be understood or misinterpreted by members of a different culture. Symbols are easily exchanged and often have only a short life span. Therefore symbols are represented by the outer layer.

The second outer layer is occupied by **heroes**, real or imaginative persons, alive or dead, who serve as role models in cultures. The inner layer is **rituals.** Rituals are actions or behaviors that are technically unnecessary but have a certain meaning to a human collectivity (e.g. greeting, thanking, baptism, business lunch etc.) that is only or best understood by members of that collectivity.

"Culture is to a human collectivity what personality is to an individual."[686]

Culture is not to be confounded to equal the obvious signs of a collectivity, the superficial practices, represented by the outer layers of the 'onion diagram'. The core elements of every culture are **values.** *Hofstede* defines a value as "a broad tendency to prefer certain states of affairs over others"[687]. Values are non rational feelings including a tendency of preference to make decisions or to have opinions of the kind: evil vs. good, ugly vs. beautiful or moral vs. immoral. Values respectively systems of mutually interdependent sometimes conflicting values form the center of *Hofstede's* culture model as displayed in Figure 2-4.

His culture model is a way to explain the operating mechanisms in a society that grant the stability of the cultural heritage, i.e. the maintenance of collectively shared value systems across generations. In the center are the societal norms, the value systems of major groups of the population. These originate in ecological factors like the geographic, economic or demographic situation a society is embedded in respectively confronted with. The institu-

686 Hofstede 2001, p. 10.
687 Hofstede 2001, p. 5.

tional settings of a society, including institutional structures and institutional ways of functioning, are the consequence of a certain societal value system. Social institutions refer to family patterns, socialization, education, religion etc; as outlined in Figure 2-4, institutions, as 'culture's consequences', reinforce both the ecological factors and the societal norms they are a product of. According to *Hofstede,* relatively closed societies remain stable and unchanged even if institutions are changed.[688] The constant in the center of the model, the societal norms, are not easily affected by institutional changes and with time lead to an adjustment respectively correction of the changed institutions.[689]

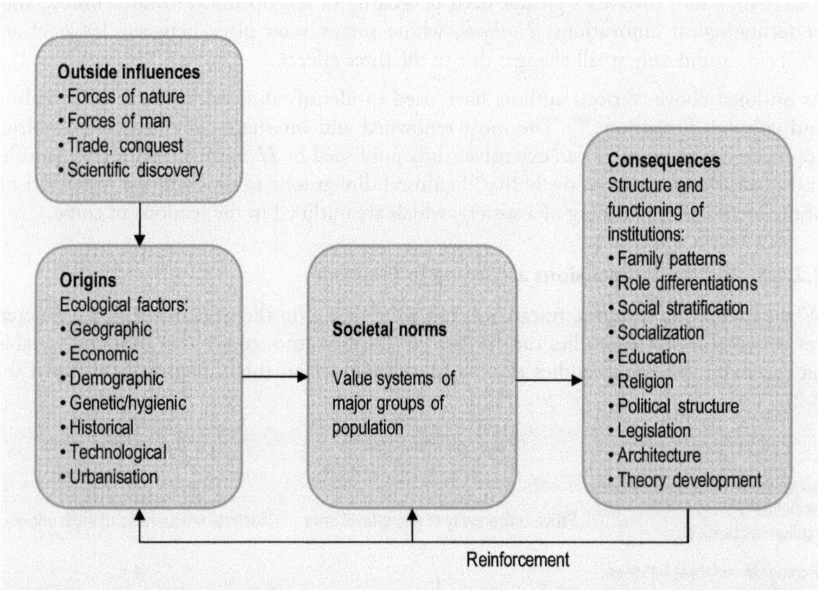

Figure 2-4: Hofstede's culture model[690]

The relatively closed mutually reinforcing circular system of origins, value systems and institutions is mainly changed by outside influences, by forces of nature (climate change, diseases, earthquakes) and by forces of man (trade, conquest, political and economic domination, technological breakthroughs).[691] Changes from the outside generally have only little impact on the societal norms unless changes are so grave (military conquest) that the impact on the ecological factors and therewith indirectly on the societal norm is not absorbed by the self-regulating abilities of the system. Nevertheless, the homeostatic quasi-equilibrium of the system has helped human collectivities (e.g. Sinti and Romanies) to preserve cultural identity even when facing severe outside influences.

688 Cf. Hofstede 2001, p. 11.
689 Cf. Hofstede 2001, p. 11ff.
690 Adopted from Hofstede 2001, p. 12.
691 Cf. Hofstede 2001, p. 12.

Due to the reinforcement mechanism national cultures are extremely stable.[692] Still, shifts in value may occur as a result of the phenomena (1) age, (2) generation and (3) zeitgeist. **Age** effects correspond to shifts in values as a result of growing older (e.g. elder people have greater security needs). **Generation** effects refer to values that are picked up at young age and carried along for the rest of the life. **Zeitgeist** effects, at last, are the result of grave culture wide changes independent from age. The three effects do not change the self-regulating cultural system itself, but may have a certain influence; for example, when the demographic or the medical development leads to an older society, the values of the whole society may shift towards a greater need of security or less openness towards immigration or technological innovations. *Hofstede*, whose survey took place between 1967-69 and 1971-73, found only small changes due to the three effects.

As outlined above, various authors have tried to identify dimensions to describe culture and cultural dimensions.[693] The most renowned and internationally accepted empirical approach was the result of an extensive study published by *Hofstede* in 1980. He identified and quantified four respectively five[694] cultural dimensions to describe the characteristics of the mental programming of a society, which are outlined in the sections to come.

2.2.4.3 Cultural dimensions according to Hofstede

When comparing societies, researchers can either focus on the similarities or the differences between societies. Studies can further be classified into studies that examine variables on the micro-level and studies that examine variables on the ecological level (see Table 2-2).

	Focus on similarities	Focus on differences
Micro-level variables within societies (culture as black box)	1 Prove universality of micro-level laws	2 Illustrate uniqueness of each society
Ecological variables between societies (culture specific)	3 Determine types or subsets of societies	**4** **Determine dimensions of societies and macro-level laws**

Table 2-2: Research strategies for comparative multisociety studies[695]

According to *Hofstede's* culture model, his study focuses on ecological variables between societies. Culture is not treated as a black box but analyzed and fit into four cultural dimensions that explain 49% of the total variance between the countries. His study therewith is to be categorized into the fourth cell.

The data of the study was collected between 1967 and 1973 as a part of the IBM international employee attitude survey. In two survey cycles a total of 116,000 questionnaires

[692] Cf. Hofstede 2001, p. 13.

[693] Cf. Kluckhohn/Strodtbeck 1961; Hall 1966; Hall/Hall 1976; Hall 1983; Trompenaars 1993; Schwartz 1994, p. 85ff.; Inglehart et al. 1998; Smith et al. 2002, p. 188ff.; Inglehart 2004.

[694] Cf. chapter 2.2.4.1.

[695] Adopted from Hofstede 2001, p. 27.

from 72 countries in 20 languages were evaluated focusing on country differences in employee values. Using correlation and factor analysis, the four cultural dimensions (1) power distance, (2) uncertainty avoidance, (3) individualism vs. collectivism and (4) masculinity vs. femininity were identified and statistically quantified to explain country differences. The first two dimensions were identified through an eclectic analysis of data incorporating theoretical reasoning and correlation analysis. The latter two dimensions are the product of a country-level factor analysis of scores on work goal importance. For each cultural dimension *Hofstede* calculates an index that shows relative differences between countries.

The four cultural dimensions are presented in more detail in the following subchapters to create a deeper understanding of what the particular dimensions stand for. The notion on the accounting relevant explanatory potential of each dimension is necessary to establish the conceptual link to the accounting values that are outlined in chapter 2.2.4.6. Each of the cultural dimension subchapters contains (1) the 'one-line' definition according to *Hofstede*, (2) a general description of the particular dimension, (3) reference to the questions the dimension index was calculated on and (4) the societal norm of the dimension as a comparison of the two index poles.

2.2.4.3.1 Power distance

Hofstede defines power distance as a dimension of national culture as:

> *"[...] the extent to which the less powerful members of institutions and organizations within a country expect and accept that power is distributed unequally."*[696]

As part of their universal mental programming humans show dominance behavior, i.e. they establish certain hierarchies everyone has to subordinate to. Dominance behavior inevitably creates inequalities. How these inequalities are dealt with is subject to the collective level of mental programming and represented by the cultural dimension of power distance. Power distance, thus, describes how different societies handle inequality (e.g. in prestige, wealth, power, status etc.). The level of inequality in a society is determined by the power struggle between two social forces. One force, regularly exercised by those who are ranked higher in terms of wealth, status etc., tries to maintain the *status quo* and even to enlarge existing inequalities. The counterforce, regularly exercised by those who are ranked lower in terms of wealth, status etc., seeks to eliminate such imparities. The struggle between the two extreme positions is disarmed by so-called 'crisscross' structures, members of society who cannot be allocated to neither elite nor underclass and who form to the social middleclass. The size of the middleclass distinguishes pluralist from elitist societies.

Organizations like IBM are based on the concept of unequal power distribution and generally possess extensive hierarchies to organize and most efficiently deal with complex task sharing in order to build a product or perform a service. How the imparity of the boss-subordinate relationship is handled by both boss and subordinate depends on their particular value systems. As people do not carry different value systems for work time and lei-

[696] Hofstede 2001, p. 98.

sure time, conclusions may be drawn from the values revealed in work situations to the value system in general.

The power distance index (PDI) was calculated based on three questions from the IBM questionnaire.[697] The first question asks if subordinates are afraid to disagree with their boss, the two other questions ask the subordinate how he perceives his boss and what kind of boss he prefers, given certain earlier described manager types ((1) autocratic, (2) persuasive/paternalistic, (3) consultative, (4) democratic[698]). Whereas the first two questions rather indicate the employees' perception, the third question (preferred manager) directly expresses a value. The PDI is calculated on the country mean scores measuring (1) the fear of disagreement, (2) the perception of the boss as either autocratic or persuasive/paternalistic and (3) the manager preference of anything but consultative.

Remarkably, the PDI scores show that all Latin countries (European as well as American), in comparison to all Germanic countries (including the English), rank relatively higher. *Hofstede* attributes this incident to the influence the Roman Empire had on the European and accordingly on the American Latin countries. The Rome dominated Latin countries very early had to adopt the highly hierarchical political, economic and military system the Roman Empire was built on. The highest leader of all Latin countries was the Roman Emperor who had absolute power. Such a concentration of power then was completely unknown to the Germanic tribes who followed local leaders. This broad historically founded differentiation between Germanic and Latin countries also affects institutional aspects like the legal system, for instance.[699] In concordance with these general annotations, Mexico (PDI: 81; rank: 5/6) and Italy (PDI: 50; rank: 34), e.g., score considerably higher than the Netherlands (PDI: 38; rank: 40) and Germany (PDI: 35; rank: 42/44).[700]

The PDI societal norm, as part of the center of the *Hofstede* culture model, is brought together intuitively by *Hofstede* and is based on previous research from various scientific disciplines. The PDI norm contrasts the two extreme positions low and high PDI countries to illustrate the characteristics of this dimension. It basically deals with the opposing notions of interdependence, inequality and hierarchy in society.[701] It has to be kept in mind that countries can be anywhere in between the two extremes pictured; not all characteristics apply in all countries and naturally individuals may deviate from the norm.

2.2.4.3.2 Uncertainty avoidance

How cultures deal with uncertainty[702] about the future is an essential part of the cultural heritage; the ways a culture handles uncertainty is expressed in the culture's technology (all human artifacts), law (all formal and informal rules) and religion (all knowledge of the unknown). These ways of dealing with uncertainties of nature (technology), other humans

---

697 For a tabular overview of all PDI country scores cf. Hofstede 2001, p. 87.

698 The fourth manager type in the second survey round was changed to participative (consensus) style.

699 Cf. chapter 2.3.2.1.2.

700 Cf. Hofstede 2001, p. 87.

701 For a more detailed overview on low and high PDI characteristics cf. Hofstede 2001, p. 98.

702 Uncertainty avoidance is not to be confounded with risk avoidance as it includes no statement of probability (anything could happen in an uncertain situation).

(law) and the unknown (religion) are culture specific and reinforced through social institutions like family, school and state; some cultures accept uncertainty more easily than others and therefore require less human made sources of security respectively predictability. Based on prior research, *Hofstede* describes the necessity of security/predictability as a culture's **intolerance of ambiguity**; high levels of intolerance are expressed in "tendencies toward prejudice, rigidity and dogmatism, intolerance of different opinions, traditionalism, superstition, racism, and ethnocentrism"[703].

Hofstede defines uncertainty avoidance as a dimension of national culture as:

> *"[...] the extent to which the members of a culture feel threatened by uncertain or unknown situations."*[704]

Organizations have to cope with uncertainty, as well. They ideally deal with an uncertain environment by imposing short-run oriented decision schemes that promise short-run feedback to react promptly and measurements (plans, budgets, long-term supplier/buyer contracts, labor agreements etc.) that create a more predictable 'quasi negotiated' environment. The organizational equivalents to a society's technology, law and religion are technology, rules and rituals. Whereas technology improves the predictability of short-run outcomes, rules seek to make the organizations' stakeholders' behavior more predictable. Organizational rituals can be both social (business meetings) and uncertainty avoiding (control systems, budgeting, reporting). Again, people at work do not behave differently than at home and uncertainty avoiding behavior expressed in an organization can be transferred to the cultural environment the organization is embedded in.[705]

The three questions selected from the IBM questionnaire to picture uncertainty avoidance refer to rule orientation, employment stability and stress. The first question inquires whether company rules should not be broken, the second question asks, how long the employee expects to work for IBM and the third question asks, how often the employee feels tense or nervous at work. The first two questions are directly connected to uncertainty avoiding behavior. Stress, however, is a highly subjective emotion. Humans have different stress thresholds; the same situation might result in the feeling of being stressed for one person, whereas another person remains totally calm. Still, stress, as a reaction of employees to comparable work situations at IBM, is a good indicator for the perceived amount of uncertainty in that situation and allows inferences to be made about the general level of perceived uncertainty in that society.

The uncertainty avoidance index (UAI) is calculated based on the country mean scores for the three questions described above.[706] Greece (UAI: 112; rank: 1) and Portugal (UAI: 104; rank: 2) have the two highest UAI scores. Countries like Austria (UAI: 70; rank: 24/25) and Germany (UAI: 65; rank: 29) are found in the center span and Sweden (UAI: 29; rank: 49/50) and Denmark (UAI: 23; rank: 51) rather at the end of the investigated countries.

[703] Hofstede 2001, p. 146.
[704] Hofstede 2001, p. 161.
[705] Cf. Hofstede 2001, p. 146ff.
[706] For a tabular overview of all UAI country scores cf. Hofstede 2001, p. 151.

The UAI associated mental programming forms the UAI societal norm, which is shared by majority in a society. The UAI norm basically represents the perceived level of uncertainty about the future and human countermeasures to make the future more predictable. People in low UAI countries are more relaxed when it comes to facing change, diversity and all types of different/foreign behavior; they are rather curious than afraid. People in high UAI countries, on the contrary, fear everything that is different from what they know and react with conservatism, traditionalism and strict rules.[707]

2.2.4.3.3 Individualism versus collectivism

Hofstede defines individualism versus collectivism as a dimension of national culture as follows:

> *"Individualism stands for a society in which the ties between individuals are loose: Everyone is expected to look after him/herself and her/his immediate family only. Collectivism stands for a society in which people from birth onwards are integrated into strong, cohesive in-groups, which throughout people's lifetime continue to protect them in exchange for unquestioning loyalty."*[708]

The biological (universal) programming makes humans – like wolves – belong to the gregarious species. The level of gregariousness respectively collectivism in a society, however, is influenced by the collective mental programming, i.e. by cultural patterns omnipresent in that society. Borrowed from the German language, the distinction between high and low individualist societies is best described by *Gesellschaft* (high individualism index (IDV)) vs. *Gemeinschaft* (low IDV).[709]

This dimension is strongly connected to the economic development of a country. 78% of IDV variance is predicted by national wealth and geographic latitude.[710] Looking at the transformation process from traditional to modern societies, the relationship between the complexity of the smallest social unit, the family, and the complexity of the society as a whole, interestingly, follows a curvilinear function. The nuclear families in a hunting-gathering society develop into extended families, clans or tribes in more complex agricultural societies and redevelop into nuclear families in urban-industrialized societies. The development of the smallest social unit is transferred and reinforced by other institutions, educational, religious or political. Collectivism is closely connected to the need for security. In economically developed countries the individuals are not forced to be part of a collectivity in order to guarantee their personal survival, but are free to focus on their own. According to *Hofstede*, the cultural key element is the self-concept, i.e. the individual way of self-perception.[711] Whereas Western cultures strongly emphasize personality and therewith the individual as an entity separate from society, in the traditional Chinese culture there is no such concept. In their opinion the individual is best attended when the collec-

[707] For a more detailed overview on low and high UAI characteristics cf. Hofstede 2001, p. 161.

[708] Hofstede 2001, p. 225.

[709] Cf. Hofstede 2001, p. 211.

[710] Cf. Hofstede 2001, p. 209.

[711] Cf. Hofstede 2001, p. 210.

tivity is best attended. The well-being of the individual is inseparably connected to the well-being of the collectivity.

Hofstede also distinguishes between 'guilt cultures' (individualist societies) and 'shame cultures' (collectivist societies). The first is associated with one's own picture. To feel guilty, there is no need for others. The concept of shame, however, requires an audience, actual or imagined; shame is closely linked to the objectively justified or subjectively perceived opinion of others. Another distinctive criterion is the way societies communicate. Individualist societies tend to use low-context communication (everything is made explicit); collectivist societies are used to high-context communication (little has to be said); most of the information, although unsaid, is already implicitly existent.

Organizations as social institutions mirror the degree of individualism in a society. Collectivist cultures demand emotional dependence of the organization's members; employees are morally involved and their well-being is linked to the success of the organization. By contrast, employees in individualist cultures are much more independent; their involvement in the organization is based on rational calculation and not moral considerations. In return, the organization grants them greater responsibility.

Both the individualism index (IDV) and the masculinity index (MAS; see the following subchapter) were calculated on the country mean scores of 14 work goal questions of the type: 'How important is to you to (have an opportunity for high earnings?)'. The IDV and the MAS represent the two main factors that explain country differences. The work goals the IDV was derived from are personal time (+), freedom (+), challenge (+), use of skills (-), physical conditions (-) and training (-). The first three goals with a positive correlation coefficient stand for the employee's independence from the organization; the latter refer to benefits received from the organization and represent dependence on the organization and greater involvement.

The country mean scores on the six work goal questions result in high IDV scores for Anglo-Saxon countries like the US (IDV: 91; rank: 1) or Australia (IDV: 90; rank: 2). Except for Portugal (IDV: 27; rank: 33/35), all EU countries in the *Hofstede* sample rank among the first 20 countries. The lowest IDV scores are achieved by Central respectively South American countries like Colombia (IDV: 13; rank: 49) or Guatemala (IDV: 6; rank: 53).[712]

The IDV societal norm[713], as a commonly shared value system, is marked by the two poles individualist vs. collectivist cultures. The family, a mirror of society, is the first milestone on the way into an either individualist or collectivist society. Societies with a low IDV value see the family as the smallest unit of society. Children are born into a group that grants them a certain degree of security and to which one belongs for life. A strong 'We' consciousness leads to the establishment of in-groups and out-groups one belongs to or does not; it also entails the horizontal and vertical integration (extended families) of people of the same group. Individualist societies, in contrast, understand the individual as the smallest unit of society ('I' consciousness). Parents of nuclear families want their child-

[712] For a tabular overview of all IDV country scores cf. Hofstede 2001, p. 215.

[713] For a more detailed overview on low and high IDV characteristics cf. Hofstede 2001, p. 227.

ren to think for themselves and, when the time has come, to go their own ways in life. The horizontal and vertical integration is low.[714]

2.2.4.3.4 Masculinity versus femininity

The fourth dimension is not a result of the biological (universal) programming of humans, but a result of the basic biological differences between genders or, rather, how societies perceive and deal with these differences. Their physical and mental (universal programming) characteristics made men and women adopt different roles in families and societies. These roles survived when societies transformed from hunting-gathering to agricultural to urban-industrialized societies and were not considerably dissolved until the 20th century; in the 20th century the biological constraint of hard physical labor was lifted by the labor market of the postindustrial service oriented society, which led to more gender equality. Still, different gender roles prevail in the human collective programming, subsumed by *Hofstede* under the dimension masculinity vs. femininity.[715]

Hofstede defines masculinity and femininity as a dimension of national culture as follows:

> *"Masculinity stands for a society in which social gender roles are clearly distinct: Men are supposed to be assertive, tough, and focused on material success; women are supposed to me more modest, tender, and concerned with the quality of life. Femininity stands for a society in which social gender roles overlap: Both men and women are supposed to be modest, tender, and concerned with the quality of life."*[716]

Transferred to the working environment in an organization like IBM, the gender specific roles are expressed in feminine and masculine work goals; women generally pursue the 'social' goals like relationships and supporting others and men put more emphasis on the 'ego' goals like career and remuneration. As mentioned in the preceding subchapter, the IDV and the MAS scores were the outcome of a factor analysis on 14 work goal questions in the IBM questionnaire. According to the respective work goals, the remaining two factors that explained country differences were labeled 'intrinsic/extrinsic' (IDV) and 'social/ego' (MAS). The 'social/ego' factor was a product of the work goals inter-personal relation manager (+), cooperation (+), desirable area (+), employment security (+), challenge (-), advancement (-), recognition (-) and earnings (-); the first four work goals with a positive correlation coefficient represent feminine work goals ('social'), the latter four stand for masculine work goals ('ego'). The country mean scores of these 8 work goal questions form the basis for the MAS as an indicator for the gap between masculine and feminine values on country level.[717]

The MAS country score is relatively high for the Germanic countries like Austria (MAS: 9; rank: 2) or Germany (MAS: 66; rank: 9/10), which rank among the top ten

[714] Cf. Hofstede 2001, p. 225ff.
[715] Cf. Hofstede 2001, p. 279ff.
[716] Hofstede 2001, p. 297.
[717] Cf. Hofstede 2001, p. 281ff.

MAS countries and considerably low for Scandinavian countries like Norway (MAS: 8; rank: 52) or Sweden (MAS: 5; rank: 53).[718]

The roles, which males and females adapt early in life, are mostly determined by gender role socialization in the family; roles are defined by the male and female biological prerequisites only to a small degree. Children adapt to the role models they see in their families. Later in life or when adequate role models are missing, as the case for single parents, children look for role models in their wider familiar and social environment or in the media to identify with and to copy their behavior. The gender-related values, as a part of a society's value system and shared by a majority, are summarized by *Hofstede* in the masculinity societal norm.[719]

2.2.4.4 Critical appraisal of Hofstede's culture theory

The work of *Hofstede* has been acknowledged and criticized widely. As mentioned above, the study benefits from its pioneer work in the field of intercultural research and the great number of participants, which supports the representativeness of the results obtained. However, the study has been subject to substantial criticism. *Hofstede* regards his study as a paradigm shift in intercultural research and, as such, criticism is part of the scientific maturation process.[720] The following section exemplarily discusses the main criticism as mentioned in the relevant literature.[721]

The cooperation with a multinational corporation like IBM holds various advantages, both technically and financially, in terms of organization, data collection and availability of willing participants in many countries. Nevertheless, the cooperation with IBM is also seen critical. First, the IBM questionnaire was not designed to measure cultural differences, but to help IBM better run and coordinate its international operations, improve business processes, enhance employee satisfaction etc.[722] Moreover, the questionnaire was designed from the perspective of an American global player and is most likely influenced by Western culture.[723] The questions relevant to Americans might be irrelevant or misinterpreted by other cultural areas. Second, it is arguable whether IBM employees truly represent their national cultures. Whereas IBM employees in developed countries belonged to the social middle-class, their colleagues from undeveloped countries at the time of the survey most probably belonged to their nation's upper class as IBM demanded a certain technological and educational background.[724] Moreover, the strong organizational culture of IBM might bias the results.[725]

---

[718] For a tabular overview of all MAS country scores cf. Hofstede 2001, p. 286.

[719] Cf. Hofstede 2001, p. 299.

[720] Cf. Kuhn et al. 1970, p. 89ff.

[721] Cf. in the following Goodstein 1981, p. 51ff.; Dorfman et al. 1988, p. 127ff.; Yeh 1989, p. 149ff.; Cray/Mallory 1998, p. 49ff.; McSweeney 2002, p. 89ff.; Kutschker/Schmid 2011, p. 731ff.

[722] Cf. Williamson 2002, p. 1377.

[723] Cf. Kutschker/Schmid 2011, p. 732ff.

[724] Cf. Hofstede 2001, p. 42.

[725] Cf. McSweeney 2002, p. 95.

Apart from the sheer size of *Hofstede's* study, its scientific popularity is also grounded in its intuitive comprehensibility describing cultural differences via four bipolar cultural dimensions and the favorable statistical applicability of the four culture scales. Still, critics doubt that a complex phenomenon like culture can be fully captured by only four dimensions.[726] Furthermore, the sample size varies significantly from country to country. Only six countries (Belgium, France, UK, Germany, Japan and Sweden) provide more than 1,000 respondents. 15 countries are represented by a sample smaller than 200.[727] Other objections are directed towards *Hofstede's* simplifying decision to take the nation as unit of analysis. Some nations like Belgium or Switzerland can hardly be regarded as culturally homogenous.[728] Last, critics complain that the *Hofstede* data is more than thirty years old and has not been updated so far.[729] It is therefore questionable whether the data is still valid. Major political or economic changes may have had an impact on the national cultural heritage, especially on cultural dimensions like individualism vs. collectivism that are closely related to the economic development of the country.

Some of the critical aspects are disarmed by the country selection of this study.[730] All three countries are Western countries and provide robust samples with more than 1,000 respondents for each IBM survey round. The countries are among the most developed countries in the world; employees of IBM, thus, should resemble the average social class. Additionally, the analyzed countries have not suffered major political or economic changes ever since the *Hofstede* study was conducted.[731]

Other criticism is addressed by *Hofstede* in the second edition of 'culture's consequences'. He points out that his study is not designed to fully capture the entire cultural spectrum but to carve out **differences** between national cultures.[732] The IBM employees therefore are as good a sample as any other group of the national population. *Hofstede* is aware that nations are not the best unit of analysis assuming that there is one mainstream national culture, which in most cases there is not; but for reasons of practicability there is no alternative when studying cultures on a worldwide level. Concerning the number of different cultural dimensions, he comments that additional cultural dimensions should be added when conceptually and statistically independent from the existent dimensions. *Hofstede*

[726] Cf. Westwood/Everett 1987, p. 194; Williamson 2002, p. 1381; Jones 2007, p. 5.

[727] Cf. Hofstede 2001, p. 475ff.

[728] Cf. Baskerville 2003, p. 6ff.

[729] Cf. Johnson/Lenartowicz 1998, p. 351; Baskerville-Morley 2005, p. 389f.; Jones 2007, p. 5.

[730] Cf. chapter 1.3.5.

[731] This statement is true except for the fall of the Berlin Wall and the reunification of Germany. Still, it is most improbable that 40 years of communism completely changed the Eastern German culture. Additionally, as only 18 Million East Germans were absorbed by more than 60 Million West Germans and ever since there was constant fluctuation between Eastern and Western Germany, complemented by social and economic assimilation programs; as per today, the effect of this German epoch should not be a major concern when studying German culture; cf. Boehnke et al. 1994, p. 191ff.; Szabo et al. 2002, p. 55ff.

[732] Cf. Hofstede 2001, p. 73.

refuses the argument of outdated data. He argues that cultural values that were developed in centuries hardly change in a comparably short time period of three to four decades.[733]

Moreover, various replication studies have shown that the *Hofstede* scores are still valid.[734] As IBM removed the values and beliefs questions from their questionnaire, there has been no IBM update since 1973, except for one local survey for IBM Australia in 1985 and another for IBM UK and IBM Hong Kong. Both surveys resulted in only small index shifts. Many other non-IBM studies replicated the *Hofstede* work, disarming the arguments of organization specific bias and of being outdated.[735] *Sondergaard* in 1994 reviewed 61 published and unpublished replication studies and basically confirmed the dimensions of *Hofstede*.[736]

Hostede's work certainly marks a milestone in intercultural research[737] and, until today, is the most comprehensive work that quantifies national cultural patterns.[738] Most of the mentioned points of criticism are mitigated by the country selection of this study or various replication studies. Accordingly, the conceptual framework of this study incorporates the ***Hofstede* cultural approach.**

Based on the preceding annotations on culture theory and cultural dimensions according to *Hofstede*, the following chapter establishes the theoretical link between national culture and financial accounting. This interlink is necessary to develop the hypotheses on the association between culture and IFRS practice in chapter 2.3.3.

2.2.4.5 Accounting values as part of the societal value system

It is unquestionable that accounting could be independent from cultural influences.[739] Speaking in terms of visible elements of culture (symbols, heroes, rituals), accounting as the 'language of business' is the carrier of business symbols that only or mainly in business have a particular meaning. It can also be considered as a type of business ritual to reduce chaos and uncertainty in the highly complex and dynamic organizational environment. As accounting is not an entirely technical activity, but an activity that is guided by human made rules and that depends on human judgment, it is most probable that accounting rules and accounting practice vary along national cultural patterns.[740]

Culture had long been neglected as an environmental factor that has an influence on accounting systems and practice. Other context factors like the legal system or the financial system deemed more important; this assumption might be grounded in the abstractness

---

733 Cf. Hofstede 2001, p. 73.

734 Cf., e.g., Hall 1989; Hoppe 1990; Lowe 1996, p. 101ff.; Helmreich/Merritt 1998; Mouritzen/Svara 2002; van Nimwegen 2002.

735 Cf. Hofstede/McCrae 2004, p. 53.

736 Cf. Sondergaard 1994, p. 447ff.; Hofstede 2001, p. 66f.; Radebaugh et al. 2006, p. 43.

737 Cf. Tung/Verbeke 2010, p. 1259.

738 The *Hofstede* study had 116,000 respondents fill out the questionnaire, whereas *Schwartz* had 60,000 respondents, *Trompenaars* had 30,000 respondents and *House et al.* had 17,000 respondents fill out the respective questionnaires.

739 As outlined above, this study follow the culturally grounded approach; cf. chapter 1.4.2.

740 Cf. Perera/Most 1994, p. 268f.; Hofstede 2001, p. 282f.

and the difficult handling of the phenomenon culture. When *Hofstede's* pioneering work made cultural patterns more accessible and statistically analyzable, researchers began to incorporate culture as a context factor to explain accounting differences.[741]

Gray was the first to identify and connect four accounting values, which were derived from both accounting literature and accounting practice, to the cultural values by *Hofstede*.[742]

The accounting dimensions set into relationship with the cultural dimensions were:

- professionalism vs. statutory control,
- uniformity vs. flexibility,
- conservatism vs. optimism and
- secrecy vs. transparency.[743]

To illustrate the assumed mechanisms between *Hofstede's* cultural respectively societal values and *Gray's* accounting values, he extends *Hofstede's* culture model by the components 'accounting values' and 'accounting systems' (see Figure 2-5).

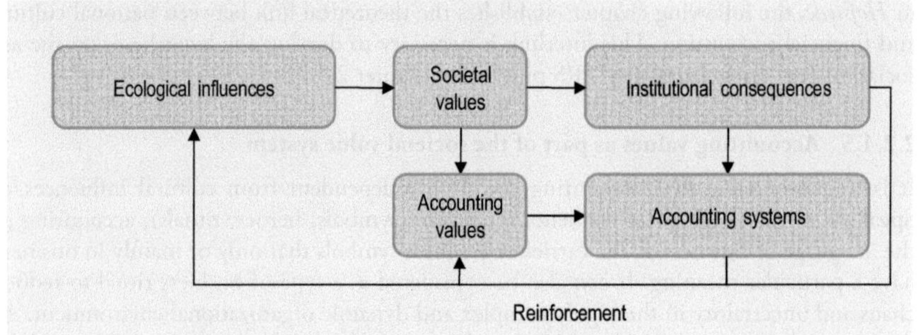

Figure 2-5: Culture, societal values and the accounting sub-culture[744]

Gray in his modified culture model highlights the accounting sub-culture that in *Hofstede's* original culture model was integrated in societal values and institutional consequences. According to *Gray*, the accounting system is influenced in two ways.[745] On the one hand, the accounting system is directly influenced by the accounting values, which are influenced by the societal values, the general value systems of major groups of the population. On the other hand, the accounting system is indirectly predisposed by societal values through institutional arrangements like the legal system or the tax system etc. Again, the reinforcing effects of institutions and accounting system on value system and ecology lead to the stability of the model and the manifestation of the values.

[741] Cf. Harrison/McKinnon 1986, p. 233ff.

[742] Cf. the following annotations on Gray's accounting values primarily Gray 1988, p. 1ff. and Radebaugh et al. 2006, p. 41ff.

[743] Cf. Gray 1988, p. 8.

[744] Adopted from Gray 1988, p. 7.

[745] Cf. Gray 1988, p. 5.

Before integrating *Gray's* considerations into the conceptual framework of this study, his accounting dimensions are briefly presented in the following subchapter.

2.2.4.6 Accounting values according to Gray

2.2.4.6.1 Professionalism vs. Statutory Control

The professionalism dimension specifies the level of public accounting regulation, varying between the two extreme positions professional self-regulation and public regulation.[746] Code law countries like Germany or France generally tend to have very detailed and prescriptive legal requirements. This system is based on the Roman *ius civile* and its ideas of justice and morality; codified rules are applicable to as many situations as possible. This high degree of regulation also affects commercial law and accounting regulation. Although things are changing due to the adoption of international Anglo-Saxon rooted accounting standards, most code law countries impose statuary control on national accounting. Common law countries like the UK or the US, on the contrary, only to a limited extent rely on codified law but mainly on the interpretation of the courts. Naturally, as accounting was not sufficiently regulated by law, the accounting profession in these countries had to implement mechanisms of self-regulation to guarantee the true presentation of corporate financial results.[747]

Gray links the professionalism dimension with *Hofstede's* dimensions of individualism, uncertainty avoidance and to a smaller degree to power distance.[748] He argues that individualist societies value individual and also professional independence higher than statutory control and prefer self-regulation to public regulation. Moreover, he suggests that cultures with a low level of uncertainty avoidance do not feel the necessity of strict detailed rules. Extensive sets of rules are an instrument to enhance security and predictability and therefore are rather attributed to societies that highly avoid uncertainty. Last, *Gray* sees a loose connection between professionalism and power distance. He posits that low power distance cultures, in which the individual enjoys more freedom, more equally distributed rights and more trustworthiness, by trend favor professional regulation over regulation imposed by the government. Based on these theoretical remarks *Gray* hypothesizes that:

> *"The higher a country ranks in terms of individualism and the lower it ranks in terms of uncertainty avoidance and power distance then the more likely it is to rank highly in terms of professionalism."*[749]

2.2.4.6.2 Uniformity vs. Flexibility

The second accounting dimension *Gray* regards as significant refers to an issue already addressed when describing the international accounting harmonization process. When the IFRS were first conceptualized, the standards were the product of various compromises

---

[746] Gray 1988, p. 8ff.
[747] Cf. chapter 1.3.5.3.3.
[748] Gray 1988, p. 9.
[749] Gray 1988, p. 9.

and only the high degree of flexibility granted the support of all national IASC members. Over the years and with growing international support of the idea of a single set of international accounting standards, IFRS options were removed and the overall uniformity level increased.

Accounting uniformity seeks to achieve the highest inter-company and inter-temporal comparability possible, whereas accounting flexibility stands for accounting practices that best suit the circumstances of the individual company.[750] *Gray's* second dimension spans between these two poles, allocating France and Germany among the more uniform countries and the UK and the US among the more flexible countries. Countries, which pursue a rather uniform accounting approach, often use the same accounting system with minor adjustments for tax purposes; national fiscal planning issues and macroeconomic goals play a decisive role in accounting designs.

Again, *Gray* assumes a connection between uniformity and the cultural dimensions of uncertainty avoidance, individualism and power distance.[751] He argues that high uncertainty in a society is accompanied by the need for strict written rules and conformity, leaving little room for interpretation and flexibility. Accounting options and discretion imply necessary decisions the accountant has to take. Decisions are further linked to the insecurity, which decision to take; this insecurity can be avoided in designing accounting standards more uniformly. Furthermore, accounting uniformity is characteristic for rather collectivist societies with a strong belief in conformity, group norms, equal treatment and strict organization from above. Higher flexibility, on the contrary, is more associated with individualistic cultures which value the freedom granted by little and flexible rules. Last, *Gray* sees a weak relation between uniformity and large power distance, large PDI societies accepting the imposition of strict uniform rules more willingly. *Gray* summarizes these considerations in his second hypothesis stating that:

> *"The higher a country ranks in terms of uncertainty avoidance and power distance and the lower it ranks in terms of individualism then the more likely it is to rank highly in terms of uniformity."*[752]

2.2.4.6.3 Conservatism vs. Optimism

The conservatism dimension undoubtedly is one of the most important dimensions in accounting and has been the research object in numerous studies.[753] The conservatism or prudence principle is an accounting principle imminent in accounting standards worldwide. The level of prudence, however, varies from country to country. Whereas in Germany, for example, the prudence principle marks one of the major guidelines in national accounting, in UK or US-GAAP and also in IFRS the principle is only one of the minor principles subordinate to the all exceeding principle of 'true and fair view' respectively 'fair presentation'. Various empirical studies have investigated the varying levels of conservat-

750 Gray 1988, p. 9.
751 Gray 1988, p. 9ff.
752 Gray 1988, p. 10.
753 Cf., e.g., Pourjali/Meek 1995, p. 3ff.; Amat et al. 1999; Schultz/Lopez 2001, p. 271ff.; Lainez/Gasca 2006, p. 68ff.; Noravesh et al. 2007, p. 254ff.

ism internationally and the supposed context factors as, e.g., the development of the capital market or the influence of tax laws.[754]

The most intuitive connection between culture and conservatism is via the cultural dimension of uncertainty avoidance. A conservative or cautious approach in accounting, as expressed by prudent measurement practices (later revenue recognition; earlier realization of losses), is closely related to the uncertainty of future events and therewith uncertainty avoidance.[755] Apart from this rather obvious relation between culture and accounting, *Gray* further assumes that individualism and masculinity might have a certain impact on the level of conservatism. High levels of individualism and masculinity are associated with the social recognition of excellent individual achievement and performance. Strong achievement orientation, in turn, might result in increased pressure to succeed and hence to a less conservative accounting approach. Power distance, however, is assumed to have no direct influence on conservatism. *Gray* follows from his analysis that:

> *"The higher a country ranks in terms of uncertainty avoidance and the lower it ranks in terms of individualism and masculinity then the more likely it is to rank highly in terms of conservatism."*[756]

2.2.4.6.4 Secrecy vs. Transparency

Secrecy is an important dimension as accounting relates closely to the question how much information to publish and, thus, to deliver to outsiders of the company.[757] This dimension is closely related to the previous dimension. Both secrecy and conservatism can be subsumed under a **cautious accounting approach**. The two dimensions differ insofar that conservatism is the measurement dimension, whereas secrecy is the disclosure dimension, referring explicitly to the quantity of published information. Conservatism, in contrast, deals with the decision of publishing information in a more conservative or more optimistic way.

Disclosure studies that assess the amount and quality of statutory and voluntary information are another popular branch of international accounting research. Results indicate that country differences relate, e.g., to the development of the capital market and company ownership.[758] Countries like the UK or the US that traditionally have well development capital markets and a high percentage of shareholder owned companies show higher levels of transparency than countries like Germany or France that traditionally rely more on debt financing and privately owned companies.

From the cultural perspective, *Gray* assumes a strong linkage between secrecy and the cultural dimension of uncertainty avoidance, power distance and individualism and a less stronger linkage to masculinity.[759] The disclosure of financial information bears the risk

---

[754] Cf., e.g., Doupnik/Salter 1995, p. 189ff.; Salter/Niswander 1995, p. 379ff.; Amat et al. 1999, p. 1ff.
[755] Cf. Gray 1988, p. 10.
[756] Gray 1988, p. 10.
[757] Cf. Gray 1988, p. 11.
[758] Cf. Healy/Palepu 2001, p. 405ff.; Fan/Wong 2002, p. 401ff.
[759] Cf. Gray 1988, p. 11.

that this data in the hands of a competitor or a financial analyst might have a negative impact on the company. Risk-averse, uncertainty avoiding accountants therefore prefer to disclose as little information as possible. Risk neutral or optimistic accountants, on the contrary, might see the positive effect of surplus voluntary information on the purchase decisions of financial investors and the share price of the company and opt for more transparency. *Gray* further remarks that secretiveness is more common in societies with large power distance as a way to manifest these power inequalities.[760] Information is power and information available to anyone inhibits power to accumulate unequally. Finally, *Gray* posits that high levels of individualism and masculinity entail high levels of transparency.[761] Individualist societies are rather open-minded and express their individualism openly, opposed to collectivist societies, in which the major concern is the benefit of the collective respectively the company; information to outsiders are restricted as far as possible. Feminine cultures that attach special importance to emotional values, social relationships and communication supposedly prefer transparency to secrecy. These conceptual considerations lead *Gray* to his fourth hypothesis that states:

> *"The higher a country ranks in terms of uncertainty avoidance and power distance and the lower it ranks in terms of individualism and masculinity then the more likely it is to rank highly in terms of secrecy."*[762]

2.2.4.7 The Hofstede-Gray framework

Altogether, *Gray* hypothesizes 13 relationships between *Hofstede's* cultural values and the accounting values professionalism, uniformity, conservatism and secrecy. According to *Gray*, masculinity assumingly has no influence on professionalism or uniformity and power distance has no effect on conservatism (see Table 2-3).

	Accounting value			
Cultural Dimension	Professionalism	Uniformity	Conservatism	Secrecy
Individualism	+	-	-	-
Power Distance	-	+	n/a	+
Uncertainty Avoidance	-	+	+	+
Masculinity	n/a	n/a	-	-
+/-	Positive/negative relationship hypothesized between cultural dimension and accounting value			
n/a	No relationship hypothesized			

Table 2-3: Relationships between accounting values and cultural dimensions[763]

From *Gray's* hypotheses follows, that the most important cultural dimensions with respect to the national accounting system are uncertainty avoidance and individualism. While

760 Cf. Gray 1988, p. 11.
761 Cf. Gray 1988, p. 11.
762 Gray 1988, p. 11.
763 Adopted from Doupnik/Tsakumis 2004, p. 13.

power distance supposedly has some influence on all accounting values except for conservatism, masculinity seems to be of less importance.

Gray further specifies the relationship between accounting values and accounting systems by dividing the accounting system into the two components statutory/professional authority and enforcement, on the one hand, and measurement and disclosure characteristics, on the other hand. He attributes the accounting dimensions professionalism and uniformity to the accounting system characteristics authority and enforcement and conservatism and secrecy to the accounting practice oriented accounting values measurement and disclosure (see Figure 2-6).[764] This basic distinction by *Gray* into (1) accounting systems and (2) accounting practice related accounting values is picked up by other researchers, who refine the *Hofstede-Gray* framework and apply it primarily to accounting practice related research questions.[765]

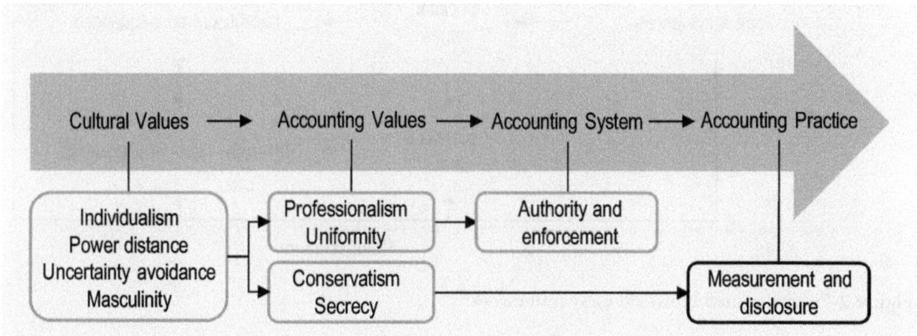

Figure 2-6: From cultural values to the application of financial reporting standards[766]

2.2.4.7.1 Refinement of the Hofstede-Gray framework

Gray originally designed his framework to describe the relationship between cultural values and accounting systems via accounting values. He then classified national accounting systems using *Hofstede's* country scores according to the dimensions authority /enforcement and measurement/disclosure.[767] As described in chapter 1.5.2.1, various studies tested the culture-accounting relationships assumed in the *Hofstede-Gray* framework; these studies generally support the secrecy hypothesis, but show mixed results with respect to the conservatism hypothesis. The mixed results may be partly ascribed to conceptual difficulties in developing country measures for accounting system characteristics like enforcement or conservatism.[768] The second culture related research stream presented in chapter 1.5.2.2 concentrates on tests of the *Hofstede-Gray* framework with regard to accounting practice, thus, avoiding above mentioned conceptual difficulties. The results suggest wide consistency with the *Hofstede-Gray* framework and indicate that cultural val-

---

764 Cf. Gray 1988, p. 12.
765 Cf. Doupnik/Tsakumis 2004, p. 40.
766 Adopted from Deegan/Unerman 2006, p. 96.
767 Cf. Gray 1988, p. 12f.
768 Cf. Tsakumis 2007, p. 31.

ues via accounting values have an influence on accounting practice decisions. As expressed in studies by *Schultz/Lopez, Doupnik/Richter* or *Tsakumi*, the *Hofstede-Gray* framework can be refined by replacing accounting systems with **accounting practice** (see Figure 2-7).[769] Whereas the original framework suggests that national cultural values have an influence via accounting values and institutional consequences on accounting systems, the refined framework posits that national cultural values also have an influence on the accountant's financial reporting decisions and therewith on the accountant's judgment.[770] The understanding of the refined cultural framework is in concordance with *Hofstede* who states that, the more human judgment is involved in accounting decision processes, the more these processes are ruled by cultural values and influenced by cultural differences.[771]

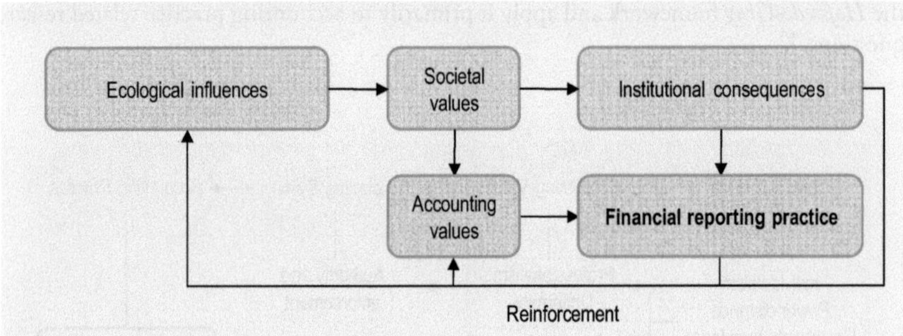

Figure 2-7: The refined Hofstede-Gray framework[772]

This study investigates the association between national culture and IFRS practice and, thus, applies the **refined *Hofstede-Gray* framework.**

Before providing an overview of selected aspects of institutional economics and PAT as a theoretical basis to explain the relationship between internal context factors and accounting practice, the following subchapter applies the *Hofstede-Gray* framework to the sample countries of this study.

2.2.4.7.2 Application of the Hofstede-Gray framework

As outlined in chapter 1.3.5.2, cultural diversity of the sample countries is a necessary prerequisite to allow for robust test results on the posited relationship between national cultural differences and differences in IFRS practice. Prior literature suggests that stronger findings may be achieved, if companies are chosen from countries that show substantial differences with regard to *Hofstede's* cultural index scores.[773]

Despite the socio-economic similarities of France, Germany and the UK, the *Hofstede* study supports the notion that the sample countries differ considerably with regard to na-

---

[769] Cf. Schultz/Lopez 2001, p. 273; Doupnik/Richter 2004, p. 6f.; Tsakumis 2007, p. 31f.
[770] Cf. Doupnik/Tsakumis 2004, p. 40.
[771] Cf. Hofstede 2001, p. 383.
[772] Adopted from Doupnik/Tsakumis 2004, p. 41.
[773] Cf. Gernon 1993, p. 105f.; Sivakumar/Nakata 2001, p. 560; Doupnik/Tsakumis 2004, p. 42.

tional cultural values. Following the *Hofstede-Gray* framework, the accounting practice relevant accounting values of conservatism and secrecy are posited to be mainly related to the cultural dimension of uncertainty avoidance. *Gray* expects power distance to have no influence respectively only a minimum influence. Individualism and masculinity are assumed to have a small negatively correlated influence on both conservatism and secrecy. The following table shows that the selected countries differ considerably with respect to the accounting relevant cultural dimension uncertainty avoidance (see Table 2-4).

	EU country			Accounting value	
Cultural dimension	France	Germany	UK	Conservatism	Secrecy
Uncertainty avoidance	86 (10-15)	65 (29)	35 (47-48)	+	+
Masculinity	43 (35-36)	66 (9-10)	66 (9-10)	-	-
Individualism	71 (10-11)	67 (15)	89 (3)	-	-
Power distance	58 (10-11)	35 (42-44)	35 (42-44)	n/a	+
+/-	Positive/negative relationship hypothesized between cultural dimension and accounting value				
n/a	No relationship hypothesized				

Table 2-4: Hofstede scores and ranks for France, Germany and the UK[774]

The national level of uncertainty avoidance permits a clear country ranking with respect to the **degree of cautious accounting**; cautious or prudent accounting in the following summarizes both conservative and secretive accounting since both accounting values show the same relationships with *Hofstede's* cultural values.[775] According to the UAI ranking, accounting in France is more cautious than in Germany and German accounting is more cautious than British accounting. This ranking is supported by the MAS ranking, according to which France scores lower than Germany and the UK. However, masculinity indicates no difference between German and British accounting. The above ranking is only partly supported by the individualism ranking. Although the UK has the highest IDV score and, as a consequence, is expected to be the least cautious accounting country, France scores slightly higher than Germany, what contradicts the above UAI based ranking.

Despite this inconsistency, the UAI based ranking is regarded to be dominant. First, the connection between uncertainty avoidance and caution is expected to be the strongest, a connection that is supported by empirical evidence.[776] Second, empirical tests of the *Gray* hypotheses indicate that individualism plays a rather minor role in determining the accounting values of conservatism and secrecy.[777]

---

[774] The country rank is displayed in brackets.

[775] Power distance is an exemption as *Gray* posits no relationship between conservatism and power distance.

[776] Cf., e.g., Eddie 1990, p. 22ff.; Doupnik/Salter 1995, p. 189ff.; Salter/Niswander 1995, p. 379ff.; Amat et al. 1999; Hope 2003b, p. 218ff.; Lainez/Gasca 2006, p. 68ff.

[777] Cf. the empirical research on the *Hofstede-Gray* framework in chapter 1.5.2.

The dominant UAI ranking of France being more cautious than Germany and Germany being more cautious than the UK is an indicator for the cultural diversity of the three countries and, thus, their suitability as research objects for this study.[778] The cultural diversity of France, Germany and the UK is underlined by a scoring model of the individual cultural dimension country ranks.

The **country caution scoring model** recognizes the country ranks of the three cultural dimensions that *Gray* expects to be most influential with respect to accounting practice according to the posited association with conservatism respectively secrecy.[779] Since *Gray* expects masculinity and individualism to be negatively associated with both conservatism and secrecy, masculinity and individualism country ranks are reversed by subtracting the country rank from the lowest country rank[780] possible plus one; the highest masculinity country score, which indicates a low level of cautious accounting practice, thus, scores one. The formula of the country caution scoring model is displayed in Formula 2.1.

Formula 2.1 $$CC_i = RUAI_i + (LCR + 1 - RMAS_i) + (LCR + 1 - RIDV_i)$$

where

CC_i	=	*Country caution score*
$RUAI_i$	=	*Country uncertainty avoidance rank*
$RMAS_i$	=	*Country masculinity rank*
$RIDV_i$	=	*Country individualism rank*
LCR	=	*Lowest country rank*
i	=	*1,2,3 (country index)*

The scoring model employs country ranks instead of index values as the latter are not mathematically standardized[781] and only represent relative country differences. The *Hofstede* cultural dimension country ranks of 53 countries and regions are the basis for the calculation (LCR = 53);[782] accordingly, country caution scores lie between 3 (UAI rank: 1; MAS rank: 53; IDV rank: 53) and 159 (UAI rank: 53; MAS rank: 1; IDV rank: 1).[783] A **lower** score stands for higher levels of caution and therewith higher levels of conservatism and secrecy.

The following table illustrates the calculation of the caution country scores (see Table 2-5). Although empiricism supports the notion that conservatism and secrecy mainly result from uncertainty avoidance, all cultural dimensions enter the below calculation as equally weighted by one.[784]

778 National culture related influences on accounting practice are assumed to be stronger if the countries differ more with respect to the particular cultural dimensions.

779 Power distance is not recognized in the scoring model as the assumed influence on the accounting values of conservatism and secrecy is little.

780 The lowest country rank (LCR) equals the total number of analyzed countries.

781 Cf. Müller/Gelbrich 2004, p. 110f.

782 Cf. Hofstede 2001, p. 87, 151, 215, 286.

783 The highest caution for instance is calculated as follows: 53 + (53 + 1 - 1) + (53 + 1 – 1) = 159.

784 Cf. Jödicke 2009, p. 141f.

	EU country			Accounting Value	
Cultural Dimension	France	Germany	UK	Conservatism	Secrecy
UAI rank	12,5	29	47,5	+	+
MAS rank	35,5	9,5	9,5	-	-
IDV rank	10,5	15	3	-	-
Country caution score	74,5	112,5	143		
+/-	Positive/negative relationship hypothesized between cultural dimension and accounting value				

Table 2-5: Caution scoring model based on equally weighted cultural dimensions[785]

Even though equally weighted, the country caution scoring model indicates that France, Germany and the UK differ considerably with respect to the accounting practice relevant cultural dimensions. In analogy to the above discussed UAI ranking, France is expected to be the most cautious and, thus, the most conservative and secretive country of the three; in contrast, the UK is assumed to be the least cautious country. Germany ranks in between the two other countries. From the perspective of cultural diversity, France, Germany and the UK seem to be well suited to assess culture related differences in IFRS practice.

The thesis of cultural diversity for the sample countries France, Germany and the UK is supported by *Hofstede* who places these countries in different national cultural clusters. According to the *Hofstede* clusters, France is clustered with Belgium only. Germany is clustered with Italy, Switzerland and South Africa. The UK is member of an Anglo-Saxon cluster, together with Australia, the US, Canada, Ireland and New Zealand.[786]

Having substantiated the characterization of France, Germany and the UK as culturally different sample countries, the elaboration of the conceptual framework is continued in the following subchapters. These provide an overview of selected aspects of institutional economics and PAT as a theoretical basis to explain the relationship between internal context factors and accounting practice.

2.2.5 Institutional economics

Institutional economics, also referred to as information economics, originates from the neoclassical school of thought.[787] In contrast to neoclassical economics, institutional economics denies the neoclassical basic assumption of perfect markets, unlimited individual information processing ability and perfect contracts. According to institutional economics, the emergence and form of institutions are a result of and can be described and explained by these market deficiencies. The focus thereby lies on the efficiency of institutions, understood as alternative solutions to market imperfections, and institutional arrangements. The basic assumptions of institutional economics are:

- scarcity of resources (neoclassical economics),

[785] Adopted from Jödicke 2009, p. 142.
[786] Cf. Hofstede 2001, p. 62.
[787] Cf. Lewis et al. 1995, p. 17.

- methodological individualism (neoclassical economics),
- individual utility maximization (neoclassical economics),
- stable individual preferences (neoclassical economics),
- uneven distribution of information, knowledge and ability,
- transaction costs as a result of business activity,
- various interdependencies between the corporative actors,
- system of rules to structure and define transactions (contracts),
- institutions as contract bound objects of analysis and
- information asymmetries as a reason for coordination problems.[788]

Institutional economics as a theoretical family includes different research streams. The most important are property rights theory, transaction cost theory and agency theory, assigned to the institutional economics subcategory '**new institutional economics**'.[789] These institutional economics research streams focus on the relationship between different situations and complex meta-concepts systems and, hence, are well suited as theoretical additives to supplement contingency theory in the process of hypotheses development.[790]

The next subchapter deals with **agency theory** as a subcategory of new institutional economics. The explanatory **contribution** of agency theory to the conceptual framework of this study is determined by its theoretical understanding of the association between internal context factors like firm size or profitability and corporate financial accounting practice.

2.2.5.1 Agency theoretical basic assumptions

There are two main streams in agency theoretical literature that can be categorized along the dichotomy of normativism and positivism, viz. 'normative principal agent literature', the normative mathematical branch of agency theory, and 'positive agency literature', the more empirical approach, focusing on the description and analysis of complex institutions.[791] This study follows a positive research approach. The following annotations on agency theory therefore concentrate on positive agency theory only.[792]

Agency theory regards the institution as a "nexus of [incomplete] contracts"[793], leaving the various actors room for discretion and choice; agency theory is a theory of delegation.[794]

---

788 Cf. Wolf 2005, p. 258f.

789 The term new institutional economics was shaped by *Williamson* who originally conceived it only for transaction cost theory. Cf. Richter/Bindseil 1995, p. 134.

790 Cf. Wolf 2005, p. 281.

791 Cf. Wenger 1988, p. 506f.; Richter et al. 2003, p. 176.

792 The term agency theory refers to positive agency theory in the following.

793 Fama/Jensen 1983, p. 302.

794 Cf. Spremann 1987, p. 9; Kiener 1990, p. 19; Hartmann-Wendels 1992, p. 72f.; Wolf 2005, p. 276.

"We define an agency relationship as a contract under which one or more persons (the principal(s)) engage another person (the agent) to perform some service on their behalf which involves delegating some decision making authority to the agent"[795]

Agency theory describes and analyzes all institutional cooperative actions as **principal agent relationships** in which the principal entrusts the agent with an assignment the agent gets compensated for.[796] The principal is assumed to be able to evaluate the outcome of that assignment. However, the outcome depends both on the performance of the agent and exogenous risks the agent has no influence on. The bottom line is: the principal is not able to directly conclude from the outcome of the deal to the agent's efforts.[797] Typical principal agent relationships are between owner and manager, employer and employee, supervisory board and executive board, state and citizen, patient and doctor etc.[798] The almost universally applicable basic principal agent relationship is mostly assessed for the case of owner and manager, symbolizing the typical separation of ownership and control.[799]

Principal agent relationships are assumed to have the following characteristics:

- The agent's actions can influence the well-being of both agent and principal,
- principal and agent have differing objectives (hidden characteristics),
- the agent is better informed than the principal (information asymmetries),
- the rationality of both principal and agent is limited and
- both actors have temporally stable and individually consistent preferences.[800]

This constellation of situational characteristics may lead to opportunistic behavior by the agent, mainly caused by asymmetric information. The consequence is a reduced principal's welfare. These phenomena are referred to as adverse selection and moral hazard.

2.2.5.2 Principal agent conflicts

The asymmetric information problem **adverse selection**[801] (opportunism *ex ante* conclusion of contract) occurs when the principal is able to observe the agent but cannot judge the agent's qualities respectively behavior adequately; he cannot be sure if the agent's behavior leads to maximized benefits from the perspective of the principal. The agent, instead, might only seek to maximize his own benefits.[802] The most common example for

[795] Jensen/Meckling 1976, p. 308.
[796] Cf. Rahman et al. 2010, p. 4.
[797] Cf. Spremann 1991, p. 572; Pfaff/Zweifel 1998, p. 184f.
[798] Cf. Ross 1973, p. 134; Picot 1991, p. 150.
[799] Cf. Fama/Jensen 1983, p. 301; Kiener 1990, p. 20.
[800] Cf. Wolf 2005, p. 277.
[801] The problem of adverse selection was originally attributed to insurances, the insurance company being unable to assess the health risk of an individual ex ante. Insurances thus were preferably purchased by high-risk individuals leading to an inefficient allocation of risk. Cf. Arrow 1991, p. 40.
[802] Cf. Breid 1995, p. 824; Subramaniam 2006, p. 59.

adverse selection is the often cited 'market for lemons'.[803] In this case, the used car market is a market of imperfect information; the buyer is not able to judge the quality of used cars adequately. This leads to an average price for good cars and bad cars ('lemons' in American English) with the result that high quality car owners prefer to not sale the car at this relatively low price and leave the market. The bad cars, on the other hand, remain on the market as the average price is relatively high, leading in the end to a market for 'lemons' only.[804]

Moral hazard (opportunism *ex post* conclusion of contract) is the result of information asymmetries and differing targets of agent and principal. The principal cannot observe the performance of the agent directly but has to focus his assessment of the agent's performance on the outcome of the relationship. Additionally, the agent might acquire an informative advantage in the process of performance, the principal is not aware of. This leads to problems of hidden action and hidden information, leaving the agent room to opportunistically maximize his personal well-being by abusing the given freedom (shirking, hold-up, consumption on the job).[805]

Both agent and principal may contribute to mitigate the problems of adverse selection and moral hazard; the principal can take measures to make the agent act in the principal's interest (incentives) and the agent can choose to change his behavior. The application of counteractive governance measures respectively the adjusted behavior of the agent implies pecuniary and non-pecuniary costs, so-called **agency costs** (see Figure 2-8).[806]

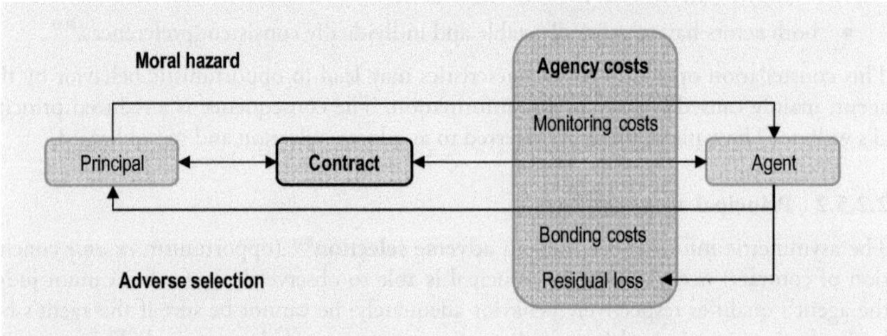

Figure 2-8: The principal agent basic model[807]

Agency costs, as a deviation from the economic efficiency optimum of the principal agent relationship, are tripartite, incurred by the principal or the agent, plus a residual term of all other welfare loss. Costs defrayed by the principal are referred to as **monitoring costs.** These costs are associated with all actions of the principal to make the agent act in the

803 Cf. Akerlof 1970, p. 489.
804 Cf. Spremann 1991, p. 574; Erlei et al. 2007, p. 148ff.
805 Cf. Hartmann-Wendels 1989, p. 714f.; Richter et al. 2003, p. 174; Subramaniam 2006, p. 59.
806 Cf. Kräkel 2007, p. 24.
807 Adopted from Jensen/Meckling 1976, p. 308.

principal's own interest and may result from the surveillance of the agent, the establishment of appropriate incentives or the modification of disadvantageous contracts.

Even in case of optimal monitoring and bonding activities by both the principal and the agent, there is always a remaining difference between the made decisions and the welfare maximizing optimum from the perspective of the principal. This difference is referred to as **residual loss.**[808]

2.2.5.3 Principal agent information strategies

In order to mitigate the above listed principal agent conflict, resulting from information asymmetries, differing objectives and opportunistic behavior, principal and agent can adapt their behavior *ex ante* and *ex post* contract conclusion to lower information asymmetries, to harmonize objectives and to build confidence (see Table 2-6).[809]

	Lower information asymmetries		Harmonization of objectives		Confidence building	
	Principal	Agent	Principal	Agent	Principal	Agent
Ex ante	Screening	Signaling	Contractual preselection	Self-selection Reputation	Screening of trustworthiness	Signaling of reputation
Ex post	Monitoring	Reporting	Incentives	Bonding Reputation	Leap of faith, extrapolation of good experiences	Building up social capital

Table 2-6: Solutions for agency problems[810]

This study analyzes financial statements and the information provided to investors, analysts and other stakeholders. Accordingly, the principal agent sub-problem that is most relevant to this study is **information asymmetries.**

To lower information asymmetries, principal and agent may follow different information strategies. The principal's instruments to gather relevant information are 'screening' and 'monitoring'. **Screening** refers to the selection process previous to contractual agreements. Before delegating decision competences, the principal screens various agents to judge their aptitude. Agents, the principal expects to not act in his own best interest, shall be identified and assorted via the 'screening' process. **Monitoring**, on the other hand, refers to the control process after the agent has been selected and contracted. The principal intends to reassess the appropriateness of his decision to contract the agent and to find out, if the agent really behaves according to the principal's goals.[811]

The agent's instruments to lower information asymmetries are **signaling** and reporting. In the selection process *ex ante* contract conclusion the agent tries to signal the principal that he possesses the required characteristics. In the case of the employer-employee-

[808] Cf. Jensen/Meckling 1976, p. 308; Göbel 2002, p. 125ff.

[809] Cf. Göbel 2002, p. 110.

[810] Adopted from Göbel 2002, p. 110.

[811] Cf. Stiglitz 1975, p. 238ff.; Arrow 1991, p. 45f.; Jost 2001, p. 28f.; Göbel 2002, p. 110ff.

relationship, the job applicant tries to convince the employer of his qualities by means of an academic degree, professional experience, social involvement etc. Once a contractual agreement is achieved, the agent has to affirm the principal's decision by making his actions and the results of these actions transparent to the principal (**reporting**).[812]

Transferred to the principal agent relationship between investor and manager, **financial reporting** is used by the manager *ex ante* (signaling) and *ex post* (reporting) contract conclusion to disarm the agency theoretic conflict caused by information asymmetries and, thus, to mitigate the 'lemons problem'. In analogy to the above cited 'lemons problem', there are good and bad investment opportunities the investor *per se* is not able to distinguish. *Ex ante* contract conclusion, i.e. before the investor buys the company's shares and becomes a principal, the company's manager utilizes the annual financial statements to signal that the company has nothing to hide and is trustworthy, e.g. via high compliance, additional voluntary information or the acceptance and application of corporate governance rules. *Ex post* contract conclusion, the manager informs the shareholder about the development and prospect of their investment in the company. Still, reporting does not necessarily lead to a realistic picture of the economic potential of a company. Instead, managers might abuse financial reporting to send wrong, misleading signals to stimulate investments. There are several solutions to limit and avoid the misuse of financial reporting and to convince the agent (manager) to publish as much private information as possible, leading to a most realistic public picture of the company. One solution consists in optimal contracts between investor and manager that give incentives for full disclosure of private information. Another solution is regulation of financial reporting practice to limit discretion the manager might abuse to maximize his own welfare. Compliance with regulated standards is supervised by auditors and enforced by enforcement institutions. Finally, there are information and financial intermediaries, financial analysts and rating agencies, on the one hand, and financial institutions, on the other hand, which analyze and evaluate financial information and which try to uncover managers' private information.[813]

Before integrating agency theory into the conceptual framework, the following subchapter presents the theoretical concept of PAT. Analogous to agency theory, the explanatory **contribution** of PAT is linked to the conceptualization of the internal organizational context. Containing several agency theoretical elements, PAT is described subsequent to agency theory.

2.2.6 Positive Accounting Theory

One of the most popular and most controversially discussed theories of positive accounting research is the so-called 'positive accounting theory' (PAT) by *Watts/Zimmerman* (and others).[814] PAT was primarily developed in two 1978 and 1979 papers by *Watts/Zimmerman*[815]. In 1986 they published an extensive work on that topic, entitled

[812] Cf. Spence 1973, p. 355ff.; Breid 1995, p. 824; Spence 2002, p. 434ff.
[813] Cf. Healy/Palepu 2001, p. 407ff.
[814] Cf. Whittington 1987, p. 327.
[815] Cf. Watts/Zimmerman 1978, p. 112ff. and Watts/Zimmerman 1979, p. 273ff.

'positive accounting theory'[816]. Being the most prominent example of positive accounting research, PAT is presented and discussed shortly to theoretically ground the association between internal context factors like, e.g., size and industry and accounting practice.

2.2.6.1 PAT basic assumptions

While the scientific disciplines of economics and accounting developed independently during the nineteenth and the beginning of the twentieth century, accountants began borrowing from economic theory ever since the 1930s.[817] This transfer of economic theory and methodology was essential to the development of positive accounting research. *Watts/Zimmerman* identify the beginnings of modern positive accounting research in studies by *Ball/Brown*[818], *Beaver*[819] and others in the 1960s when empirical methods originating from finance respectively economic analysis were adopted in accounting.[820] The theories and concepts of PAT resort to both finance and economics. The early positive accounting studies by *Ball/Brown* and others make use of financial concepts like the efficient market hypothesis (EMH), the capital asset pricing model (CAPM) and the market model to show and to analyze the relationship between accounting numbers and securities prices. Based on these results, *Watts/Zimmerman* apply economic concepts like agency theory and the principle of rationality to develop PAT.

Relying upon the **EMH,**[821] *Watts/Zimmerman* suggest that the capital market would react on new or unexpected information and share prices would adjust to form a new zero profits equilibrium.[822] They suggest that accounting earnings announcements that result in a share price reaction can be useful.[823] To distinguish normal or expected rate of returns on securities from abnormal or unexpected rate of returns and thereby determining if the market reaction is actually a result of the earnings announcement, *Watts/Zimmerman* and other positive accounting researchers employ the **CAPM** and the market model to calculate or model expected rates of return.[824]

Although accounting research based on the EMH was able to demonstrate the relationship between accounting numbers and share prices, it could neither explain nor predict accounting choices as it regularly assumed zero information and contracting costs.[825] An efficient market would 'see through' management's accounting changes and, provided that these changes do not affect taxes, there are no cash flow consequences and the effect on firm value and share price is zero.[826] Thus, without observable market reactions it is

---

816 Cf. Watts/Zimmerman 1986.

817 Cf. Hendriksen 1965, p. 45ff.

818 Cf. Ball/Brown 1968, p. 159ff.

819 Cf. Beaver 1968, p. 67ff.

820 Cf. Watts/Zimmerman 1990, p. 131ff.

821 According to the EMH, an efficient market allows for no trading profits on the given set of information, cf. Finnerty 1976, p. 1141.

822 Cf. Watts/Zimmerman 1986, p. 16ff.

823 Cf. Watts/Zimmerman 1986, p. 35.

824 Cf. Watts/Zimmerman 1986, p. 21ff.; Deegan/Unerman 2006, p. 211.

825 Cf. Watts/Zimmerman 1990, p. 132f.

826 Cf. Deegan/Unerman 2006, p. 212.

impossible to explain accounting behavior. To create observable firm value effects, *Watts/Zimmerman* introduced **agency theory** to PAT.[827] They assumed that all individuals merely act in self-interest trying to maximize their own welfare.[828] This general agency theory based assumption requires mechanisms respectively contracts so that all parties accommodate individual goals, driven by self-interest, with the higher goal of maximizing firm value and thereby the welfare of the shareholders.[829] The contracts necessary to solve agency theoretic conflicts result in contracting costs. *Watts/Zimmerman* use agency, information and other contracting costs to formulate hypotheses to explain and predict accounting choice. In a 1990 review paper on ten years of PAT research *Watts/Zimmerman* identify the following three most popular and most frequently tested PAT hypotheses.[830]

The **bonus plan hypothesis** predicts that managers exercise accounting options according to their personal compensation plans. These compensation plans might include bonuses in form of cash, stocks or stock options. As *Watts/Zimmerman* state, this hypothesis does not necessarily imply that managers always choose accounting methods that lead to an increase in earnings and therefore management's bonuses. Managers might also have incentives to choose accounting methods that have a negative effect on earnings, for example when compensation plans define certain minimum income levels. Managers could in a bad year prefer to further reduce income and take an 'earnings bath' to increase income and to be able to cross the bonus threshold in future years. Also, compensation plans that reward a good performance with stock options could be the reason for income reducing accounting methods in years stock options are granted.[831]

The **debt/equity hypothesis** predicts that managers of firms with a high debt/equity ratio have strong incentives to choose accounting methods that increase earnings to avoid debt covenant violations and costly penalties for breach of contract. The **political cost hypothesis** uses firm size as a proxy variable for political attention and predicts that larger firms rather than smaller firms make use of accounting discretion to lower earnings in order to avoid public speculations on the legitimacy of these earnings.[832]

2.2.6.2 The concept of political costs

Political costs, as expressed in the PAT political cost hypothesis, are costs that arise from too much **political attention**. The reasons for an increased public and therewith political attention are manifold. According to PAT, public attention may be attracted by high profitability, for instance.[833] The energy sector is an example for a profitable industry that is negatively associated by the public for continuously rising energy prices, intransparent cost structures and oligopoly rents. Another example for negative publicity is the profitable oil industry, which is criticized by the public for polluting the environment. Also, the

[827] Cf. Watts/Zimmerman 1979, p. 275ff.
[828] Cf. Watts/Zimmerman 1978, p. 113.
[829] Cf. Deegan/Unerman 2006, p. 215.
[830] Cf. Watts/Zimmerman 1990, p. 138f.
[831] Cf. Watts/Zimmerman 1978, p. 116; Watts/Zimmerman 1990, p. 138f.
[832] Cf. Watts/Zimmerman 1990, p. 139.
[833] Cf. Watts/Zimmerman 1990, p. 139.

banking sector attracts negative public attention; being responsible for the international economic crisis, banks and rating agencies nowadays have to cope with an extremely negative public image. The public outrage often brings politicians to act and do something against the perceived injustice. Stricter regulations, corporate break-ups or even expropriations could be the result. Besides costs that are related to regulative consequences, political costs could also be connected to higher labor agreements. High profits are usually successfully employed in labor union negotiations to argue in favor of a substantial pay rise.[834]

To avoid the (political) costs that stem from such adverse political actions, companies try to improve their public image by public campaigns in the media and influence legislative processes by lobbying etc. As suggested in the political cost hypothesis, firms are even assumed to adjust their accounting figures and try to appear less profitable to escape political repression. The political cost hypothesis further says that companies tend to reduce political costs dependent on firm size. Several empirical studies support this notion.[835] As the above described examples of the energy, oil and banking industry indicate, industry might be another context factor associated with higher amounts of political costs.[836]

2.2.6.3 PAT conceptual criticism

According to *Watts/Zimmerman's* review of PAT research, the empirical results, with some limitations, are generally consistent with the above cited PAT hypotheses.[837] Nevertheless, PAT research is controversially discussed and widely criticized for a number of reasons.[838] Apart from methodological and conceptual issues, which will not be dealt with at this point, *Watts/Zimmerman* are criticized for their view of accounting theory, the "single minded way in which they present their own view of the subject, dismissing the *a priori* theories of the 1960s as 'excuses'"[839]. In their view, which "is also the view of theory in science"[840], the sole objective of accounting theory lies in explanation and prediction of accounting practice.[841] Normative prescriptive research, in contrast, is to be understood as 'unscientific' and, being grounded on objectives and objective functions defined by the researcher himself, is influenced by individual value concepts and susceptible to subjectivity.[842] Their claim of theoretical superiority of fact-based positive accounting research is subject to extensive criticism.

The emergence of positive accounting research can be seen as a change of paradigm in accounting from purely normative to positive empirical research; thus, it is not surprising that PAT is criticized with respect to its view on normativism. Critics argue that PAT is

---

834 Cf. Watts/Zimmerman 1978, p. 115.
835 Cf. Siegfried 1975, p. 559ff.
836 Cf. Watts/Zimmerman 1978, p. 115.
837 Cf. Watts/Zimmerman 1990, p. 138ff.
838 For an overview of PAT criticism cf. Watts/Zimmerman 1990, p. 140ff., or Deegan/Unerman 2006, p. 247ff. See also Christenson 1983, p. 1ff.; Lowe et al. 1983, p. 19ff.; Sterling 1990, p. 97ff.; Mouck 1992, p. 35ff.; Laughlin 2007, p. 271ff.
839 Whittington 1987, p. 327.
840 Watts/Zimmerman 1986, p. 2.
841 Cf. Watts/Zimmerman 1986, p. 2.
842 Cf. Tinker et al. 1982, p. 170; Watts/Zimmerman 1986, p. 7; Sterling 1990, p. 99.

not to be regarded as value-free as both the decision of what to do research on and the decision of what theory to take as a basis go back to value judgments.[843] The assumption of the economic principle of rationality, too, is an expression of value judgment.[844] Also, adopting the view that, whatever accounting practice is like, is right, has normative implications.[845] It is further reasoned that research has to go beyond explanation of the *status quo* and to prescribe and implicitly improve accounting practice.[846]

The debate on the supremacy of either of the competing concepts is fairly dispensable as both concepts are complementary components of the process of empirical research as "any empirical observation [...] implies selectivity and categorization which imply a theoretical standpoint"[847]. This judgment is underlined by prior annotations on the scientific philosophical classification of this study (see chapter 1.2).

The subsequent chapter presents the conceptual framework of this study incorporating the above depicted theories to build a solid theoretical foundation for the development of the hypotheses.

2.3 Conceptual framework

2.3.1 Development of the conceptual framework

The basic conceptual framework is based on **contingency theory**. According to the above described multivariate open context contingency model, financial accounting practice respectively IFRS practice depends on the situation of the company; the situation is determined by internal and external context factors. This basic framework is refined by material theories to adapt the basic conceptual framework to the specific research question of this study, viz. to analyze the influence of national culture on IFRS practice, and to control for effects other than national culture.

The research question of this study is theoretically captured by the above outlined *Hofstede-Gray* framework. **Culture theory** by *Hofstede* is integrated into the conceptual framework to theoretically describe the effect national culture respectively societal values have on IFRS practice. The link between *Hofstede's* cultural dimensions and IFRS practice is established by means of the *Hofstede-Gray* framework. *Gray* identifies four accounting values he assumes to be associated with national culture. The two accounting values that are most relevant to this study are **conservatism** and **secrecy**; both values are directly linked to financial accounting practice in general and IFRS practice in specific. Whereas conservatism is expected to affect IFRS **measurement** practice, secrecy is assumed to have an influence on IFRS **disclosure** practice. In addition to the direct link between national culture and IFRS practice, *Hofstede* assumes national culture to have an indirect effect on IFRS practice via national institutions. According to *Hofstede's* culture model, the societal

843 Cf. Deegan/Unerman 2006, p. 248.
844 Cf. Haller 1994, p. 604.
845 Cf. Whittington 1986, p. 401.
846 Cf. Deegan/Unerman 2006, p. 247.
847 Whittington 1986, p. 401.

value system forms national institutions ('institutional consequences'), which reinforce national societal values and which are expected to have an influence on financial accounting respectively IFRS practice (e.g. legal system).

The influence of national culture on the national institutional setting is also acknowledged by the **societal effects approach**. According to the societal effects approach, national culture is expected to have only a mediating influence on institutions; the organizational setting and (financial accounting) practices are influenced primarily by the institutional surroundings of the organization. Thus, financial accounting relevant institutional context factors are assumed to have an impact on financial accounting practice. Consequently, the societal effects approach is incorporated into the conceptual framework to theoretically underline the assumed association between external context factors like the financing system or the legal system and IFRS practice.

Besides the influence of national culture and national institutions, IFRS practice may also be determined by context factors internal to the organization. As outlined above, **agency theory** and **PAT** serve as a theoretical basis in this study to underline the relationship between internal context factors and IFRS practice. Especially the concepts of **agency costs** and **political costs** and the cost avoidance strategies **signaling** and **reporting** are useful to theoretically explain the relationships between corporate context factors and management's financial accounting decisions. For example, as outlined in the previous chapter, political costs are expected to play a role when considering the impact of size or industry on accounting choice. As pointed out above, larger firms are more likely to attain negative public attention than smaller firms. Also, certain industries are more likely to be confronted with negative publicity and react by means of financial reporting strategies, e.g. by reporting more private information. Signaling strategies could be applied when the company decides to be audited by a Big4 auditor. Financial statements audited by an auditor of high reputation signal the capital market higher compliance and build confidence.[848]

Hence, the conceptual framework of this study is tripartite. The three types of context factor groups (1) national culture, (2) national institutions and (3) corporate factors and their influence on IFRS practice are theoretically displayed by the theories of culture, societal effects, agency and positive accounting (see Figure 2-9).

The main influence factor of this study on IFRS practice is **national culture.** The external and internal context factors displayed in Figure 2-9 are integrated in the conceptual framework to control for systematical effects on IFRS practice other than national culture. These are further substantiated in the following subchapter.

[848] Cf. Dumontier/Raffournier 1998, p. 225. The theoretical background of the internal context is described in more detail in chapter 2.3.2.2.

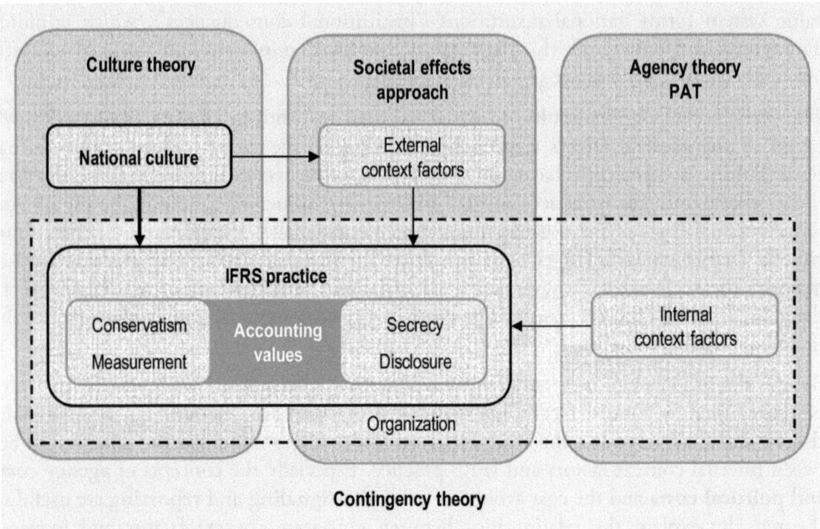

Figure 2-9: Conceptual framework

2.3.2 Refinement of the conceptual framework

The above presented culture studies revealed limitations in the area of additional institutional context factors.[849] To respond to these limitations, this section provides an overview of different external and internal context factors that might have an impact on IFRS practice.

According to the **societal effects approach**, the particular organization and the organizational decisions are influenced by the specific situation the organization is in; i.e. both the organization, as a system, and the organization's accounting system, as an organizational subsystem, are the result of the organizational environment and the situation paths it has followed in the past. Transposed to the refined *Hofstede-Gray* framework, IFRS practice, as the result of the organizational decision process, is influenced by the organizational environment respectively **external context factors.** Besides these external factors which the organization has no influence on, there are **internal context factors** that may have a systematic influence on the accounting decisions of the company. **Agency theory** and **PAT** provide the theoretical basis to explain the effect of factors internal to the organization.

2.3.2.1 External context factors

International accounting literature names several external context factors that are assumed to have an influence on national accounting practice.[850] *Radebaugh et al.* provide an exten-

[849] Cf. chapter 1.5.2.

[850] Cf. Radebaugh 1975, p. 41.

sive overview of various environmental constraints: finance and capital markets, taxation, the accounting profession, accounting education and research, the political system, the social climate, economic growth and development, inflation, the legal system, accounting regulation, culture, international factors, enterprise ownership and enterprise activities.[851] *Deegan/Unerman* additionally assume religion and 'accidents in history' (e.g. colonial influence) to play a role in the national accounting practice.[852]

Among this comprehensive collection of external context factors, various context factors most probably play only a minor role when analyzing three large Western European countries like France, Germany and the UK. The political system and social climate in the three countries are very similar. Other context factors like economic growth and development and inflation may once have been of more importance but lost relevance in the process of European economic integration. Moreover, all three countries are Christian countries, so religion seems not to be a significant context factor either. Colonial influence appears to be of great importance when investigating countries with a colonial heritage. A popular example for such influences is the former British Empire. Countries like Australia or New Zealand entirely adopted the British accounting system.[853] In central Europe, however, such influences are small. Certainly, during the French occupation of Germany under Napoleon or the German occupation of France in World War II or the Allies occupation after World War II also ideas of accounting were transported across national borders.[854] Still, such effects may surely be neglected when analyzing IFRS practice in these countries. Other influential factors like enterprise activity are controlled for by the integration of internal context factors into the conceptual framework of this study.

Culture, legal system, financing system and tax system are the determinants accounting literature expects to have most impact on national accounting practice.[855] Another context factor deemed significant to actual accounting practice is enforcement on the national level.[856] Furthermore, *Kvaal/Nobes* suggest that national GAAP might have an impact on IFRS practice since companies might choose to exert options the way they did under national GAAP.[857]

The possible impact of the financing system, the legal system, the tax system, the enforcement system and national GAAP on IFRS practice is discussed in the following subchapters.

2.3.2.1.1 Financing system

The context factor financing system basically refers to the companies' sources of finance. Naturally, all companies depend strongly on internally generated sources, i.e. company profit. With respect to external sources, companies have mainly two alternatives that also

[851] Cf. Radebaugh et al. 2006, p. 16.
[852] Cf. Deegan/Unerman 2006, p. 99ff.
[853] Cf. Gernon/Meek 2001, p. 5.
[854] Cf. Roberts et al. 2008, p. 220f.
[855] Cf. Deegan/Unerman 2006, p. 88ff.; Nobes/Parker 2008, p. 26ff.; Roberts et al. 2008, p. 200ff.
[856] Cf. Rahman et al. 2002, p. 56.
[857] Cf. Kvaal/Nobes 2010, p. 173.

display two different types of financing systems. External sources can be either provided by private investors, implying a rather **equity-based** financing system, or provided by banks and other financial institutions, implying a rather **credit-based** financing system.[858] The accounting literature further distinguishes between credit based systems that are governmentally administered and credit based systems in which the government tries not to interfere with the capital market and financial institutions.[859] Typically, the US and the UK are considered to be countries in which companies rely mainly on private shareholders' capital. Continental European countries like France and Germany, on the contrary, have comparably less developed capital markets; capital traditionally used to be provided by banks and other financial institutions like insurance companies.[860]

	Strong credit-based	Strong equity-based
Insider dominated	1 Credit-insider system	2 Equity-insider system
Outsider dominated	3 Credit-outsider system	4 Equity-outsider system

Table 2-7: Financing systems[861]

Based on the general distinction between equity and debt-based financing systems, *Nobes* integrates the finance concepts of 'insiders' and 'outsiders' to classify financing systems along a four field matrix that consists of the dimensions equity vs. debt and 'insider' vs. 'outsider' financiers (see Table 2-7).[862] He suggests '**insiders**', such as governments, banks, families and large institutional investors, to have a close relationship to the company, which enables them to gain timely and frequent 'insider' information. This close relationship is established, e.g., by the right to name members of the board of directors or other privileged relationships. '**Outsiders**', i.e. private individual shareholders or well diversified institutional investors, however, depend on the information that is provided via public channels like annual financial statements or *ad hoc* announcements. *Nobes* no further distinguishes between governmentally administered and financial institutionally dominated credit-based financing systems; both systems are 'insider' systems. Government investors perceive the same private information as large institutional investors. Eventually, his four field matrix can be reduced to only two relevant categories of financing systems: (1) credit-insider systems and (2) equity-outsider systems (fields one and four in Table 2-7).[863]

The type of financing system has a significant effect on the type of published financial information.[864] Financial information in an equity-outsider financing system serves other purposes compared to a credit-insider financing system. The former requires future

[858] Cf. Levine 2002, p. 398ff.
[859] Cf. Zysman 1983, p. 286.
[860] Cf. Cable 1985, p. 129ff.; Nobes 1998, p. 166; Gernon/Meek 2001, p. 3f.
[861] Adopted from Nobes 1998, p. 166.
[862] Cf. Nobes 1998, p. 166; Schleicher et al. 2010, p. 143ff.
[863] Japan is an example for an equity-based / 'insider' financing system. The credit-based / 'outsider' category is rather uncommon. Cf. Nobes 1998, p. 167; Franks/Mayer 2001, p. 943f.
[864] Cf. Choi 1973, p. 170ff.; Busse von Colbe/Pohlmann 1981, p. 177f.; Nobes 1995.

oriented realistic information that support investors in their decision-making processes. The latter has a foreground interest in creditor protection and favors a more conservative approach. Of course, there are elements of both categories in most countries. Still, it can be posited that both rule-makers and preparers adapt to the dominant informational demand in their country, be it 'outsider' investor friendly or 'insider' creditor friendly information. Different informational purposes result in differing accounting practice.[865]

The financing system seems to be a potentially useful context factor in explaining differing financial reporting practices and is included in the conceptual framework of this study as a control variable. The type of financing system is approximated in this study by the degree of development of the national equity capital market, which, in turn, is approximated by total national market capitalization divided by GDP.[866] This ratio is regularly applied in the accounting literature to determine the type of national financing system.[867]

2.3.2.1.2 Legal system

Legal systems are another important variable that is assumed to have an influence on accounting practice.[868] Literature distinguishes broadly between two types of legal systems: code law and common law.[869] Continental European countries employ various forms of Romano-Germanic respectively **code law**; code law often contains elements of the French Napoleonic codes that were spread across Europe during the French occupation in the beginning of the nineteenth century. As the name implies, code law generally codifies respectively prescripts morally and ethically preferable behavior. In sharp contrast to this first notion of law, **common law** prohibits unwanted behavior, instead of prescribing wanted behavior. Common law was developed in the UK and later promulgated in the British Empire, which is why countries like Australia or the US also rely on common law legal systems. Common law statutes are less specific and more flexible than code law statutes; common law is continuously developed at the courts and therefore also referred to as case law.[870]

The conceptual differences in code and common law countries also apply for commercial law and accounting regulation.[871] Hence, in code law countries like France or Germany accounting rules are specified in detail in the commercial code. The accounting code, as part of the commercial code, originally was not designed to explicitly serve investors' needs, but principally to ensure orderly business conduct. Furthermore, as the commercial code usually was written by the legislative body of the particular country, the needs of the tax authorities, one of the main users of financial information, found their way into the

---

[865] Cf. Nobes 1998, p. 167.

[866] For an overview of the development of the respective equity capital markets in France, Germany and the UK cf. chapter 1.3.5.3.1.

[867] Cf. Levine/Zervos 1996, p. 324; García/Liu 1999, p. 30; Perotti/van Oijen 2001, p. 58f.; Claessens et al. 2006, p. 319; Armour et al. 2009, p. 344.

[868] Cf., e.g., Jaggi/Low 2000, p. 495ff.; Bushman/Piotroski 2006, p. 107ff.

[869] Cf. Beck et al. 2003, p. 653ff.; Bartov et al. 2010, p. 3f.

[870] Cf. Roberts/Salter 1999, p. 124; Roberts et al. 2008, p. 205f.

[871] Cf. Radebaugh et al. 2006, p. 17; Bartov et al. 2010, p. 3f.

code and strongly influenced its development.[872] Besides prescriptive detailed disclosure rules, the accounting code in code law countries also contains principles of measurement and general bookkeeping. In common law countries like the UK, there is no such thing as a comprehensive code of accounting. Instead, the Companies Acts basically contain disclosure requirements and general accounting principles. The overriding principle states that financial statements in the UK must reflect a 'true and fair view' of the economic situation of the company. This principal accounting requirement was interpreted by the British courts, stating that companies had to present their financial statements in accordance to the standards issued by the private sector body, the ASB.[873] As part of the common law system, the standards set by the ASB are case decisions; each standard deals with a single accounting issue. In the US, the influence of the legislative body on accounting is even less. The authority for financial accounting, instead, was delegated to the SEC and by the SEC further delegated to the FASB. The overriding principles of 'true and fair view' (UK) or 'fair presentation' (US) suggest that the common law approach to accounting is strongly investor oriented. The impact of statutory considerations that are influenced by the tax authorities is rather low.[874]

The preceding annotations on code law and common law legal systems indicate that the type of legal system affected the development of different accounting systems. Nonetheless, it is questionable whether the legal system has an influence on the application of international financial reporting standards, i.e. on the accountants' decisions. To control for effects related to a country's legal system, this context factor is controlled for by a dummy variable[875] that is one for code law countries and zero for common law countries. As mentioned above, the legal system has a strong influence on both tax system and national accounting system. Both context factors are discussed in the following subchapters.

2.3.2.1.3 Tax system

Taxation in some countries has a major impact on financial accounting. *Roberts et al.* identify three main types of tax systems that can be characterized as follows: (1) tax system and accounting system are largely independent from each other, (2) in a common system financial reporting rules are also used for tax purposes and (3) in a common system tax rules are also used for financial reporting purposes.[876] The UK belongs to the first type of system and France and Germany belong to the second type of system; accordingly, only these two systems are discussed in the following.

In the UK, tax system and financial reporting system are two separate systems set by different bodies.[877] Companies, thus, present two types of financial statements: one

[872] For the same reason, the regulations for financial statements of individual companies were generally more detailed than the regulations for consolidated statements; cf. chapter 1.3.5.3.

[873] See also the British country profile in chapter 1.3.5.3.3.

[874] Cf. Busse von Colbe/Pohlmann 1981, p. 176f.; Roberts et al. 2008, p. 207f.

[875] A dummy variable is a dichotomous variable that represents two dichotomous characteristics of an originally qualitative variable; cf. Hardy 2007, p. V.

[876] Cf. Roberts et al. 2008, p. 208ff.

[877] Cf. Roberts et al. 2008, p. 208.

represents the 'true and fair view' of company's assets, liabilities and profits and the other incorporates the tax specific rules that have an impact on areas like depreciation, provisions etc. The influence of tax rules on UK accountants' financial reporting decisions is presumably low. In France and Germany, however, both tax accounting and financial reporting are strongly interlinked. In Germany, for example, the relationship between tax and financial reporting traditionally was shaped by (1) the **authoritative principle**[878], meaning that tax accounting should be based on financial accounting, and (2) the reverse authoritative principle[879], meaning that specific tax allowances can only be recognized in the tax accounts of the company when these are also recognized in the individual accounts.[880] Especially small companies that obligatorily had to publish annual financial statements, but had no interest in fund-raising at the capital market, often decided to issue one set of financial statements only to avoid the extra effort of two types of financial statements. Naturally, tax rules have a skewing effect on financial statements. Tax depreciation, e.g., generally does not resemble the real loss of value of an asset but is guided by economic and fiscal policies designed to provide incentives for corporate investments.[881]

It is questionable whether tax rules also have an impact on financial accounting of large capital market oriented companies. It may be assumed that the effect of tax rules on financial reporting practices of large listed French and German companies can be rather neglected; these large companies generally have two types of financial accounts, one for tax purposes and another for capital market purposes. Accordingly, group accounts can be expected to be rather free of tax related influences.[882] Current studies confirm this notion. *Gee et al.* analyze the tax influence on IFRS in Germany and the UK and conclude that "[...] German IFRS practice is likely to be mostly free of tax influence, especially for large groups [...]"[883]. The independence of IFRS practice of large German groups *Gee et al.* attribute to IFRS requirements that differ substantially from German tax rules.[884] This conclusion is in line with *Nobes/Schwencke* who suggest a strong influence of tax accounting on financial accounting as long as tax computation is the only purpose of accounting; however, the influence of tax accounting diminishes and financial accounting practice is disconnected from tax accounting practice when investor-related purposes come into play.[885]

Nonetheless, the tax system is considered as a possible influence factor in this study. The type of tax system is considered by a dummy variable that is one for the authoritative principle countries Germany and France and zero for the UK. This variable indicates that

[878] The authoritative principle refers to the German *Maßgeblichkeitsprinzip*.

[879] The reverse authoritative principle refers to the German *umgekehrtes Maßgeblichkeitsprinzip*.

[880] The reverse authoritative principle was recently abolished via the German Accounting Law Modernization Act (BilMoG) which came into effect in 2009; cf. Herzig/Briesemeister 2009, p. 926ff.; Utz/Hoheisel 2010, p. 322.

[881] Cf. Haller 1992, p. 310ff.; Hoogendoorn 1996, p. 783ff.; Lamb et al. 1998, p. 173ff.; Roberts et al. 2008, p. 208ff.

[882] Cf. Eberhartinger 1999, p. 94.

[883] Gee et al. 2010, p. 114.

[884] Cf. Gee et al. 2010, p. 114.

[885] Cf. Nobes/Schwenke 2006, p. 69.

the tax system in Germany and France, in contrast to the UK, is not independent from the national financial reporting system. This procedure is in line with prior studies that recognize the influence of the national tax system. *Alford et al.* approximate the national tax system by the degree of alignment of financial and tax accounting, distinguishing between low and high level alignment.[886] In analogy to the above authoritative principle classification, France and Germany are considered to have a high level of financial and tax accounting alignment, whereas the UK is classified as low level alignment country.[887] Since the tax system and legal system dummy variables have the same country distribution (France/Germany vs. UK), both context factors are covered by the same dummy variable. This approach is supported by the conceptual proximity of the two context factors; code law accounting regulations are often influenced by the needs of the tax authorities and therefore closer to tax regulations.[888]

2.3.2.1.4 Enforcement system

Imperfect enforcement of accounting rules has already been addressed as a possible reason for differences in IFRS application.[889] *Nobes*, among others, assumes that the quality of the national enforcement system and, as a consequence, the compliance with national accounting rules varies internationally; stronger enforcement is usually associated with higher degrees of compliance.[890] Enforcement is an important context factor when comparing accounting practices in the European context. IFRS was adopted in the EU to improve the quality and comparability of European financial statements and, thus, to support the goal of a single European capital market. The mere adoption of IFRS and the statutory requirement to apply IFRS does not necessarily lead to correct and consistent IFRS practice. The rules have to be supervised and enforced by an institution that possesses the legal and disciplinary means to do so.[891]

According to *Brown/Tarca*, three elements of the enforcement process can be distinguished.[892] First, accounting rules are enforced internally by the **management** of the particular company. On the company level, enforcement is supported by the **internal control system** of the company and, if existent, the department of **internal audit**. Nonetheless, full compliance with accounting rules is likely to be not entirely achieved for various reasons. Some accounting issues may be too complex[893] and the company lacks the professional competence to correctly display them in the financial statements. Time constraints may also play a role in accounting processes that are driven by the need to report financial

---

886 Cf. Alford 1993, p. 187. See also Lamb et al. 1998, p. 186; Ali/Hwang 2000, p. 6.

887 Cf. Alford 1993, p. 188ff.

888 Cf. Roberts et al. 2008, p. 207.

889 Cf. chapter 1.3.4.2.8.

890 Cf. Hope 2003a, p. 265; Nobes 2006, p. 242.

891 The key elements of functioning enforcement systems are (1) prevention and (2) sanction. The element of prevention, implied by the mere threat of an enforcement review, motivates companies *ex ante* review to comply with IFRS. In case of deficient compliance the element of sanction makes companies correct identified misstatements *ex post* review. Cf. Berger 2009, p. 599f.

892 Cf. Brown/Tarca 2005, p. 183.

893 Cf. Meyer 2010, p. 157f.

figures as soon as possible (fast close). Besides constraints of time and professionalism, capital market expectations exert constant pressure on the companies' management to report results as positive as possible and to potentially depart from full compliance accounting. Share-based payment plans could be another more personal motive to do so. In the light of these considerations, the other two elements of the enforcement process come into play. Independent **auditors** who audit and testify the compliance of the financial statements with the corresponding set of rules are the second stage in the triple-stage enforcement process. The last element is an additional oversight mechanism in form of an independent **supervisory body** that has sufficient legal power to monitor the companies' financial reporting and to enforce regulations.[894]

Systematic differences are likely to arise mainly from the elements auditors' expertise and enforcement institution. Regarding these two elements, the influence of the auditor is expected to be of minor relevance with respect to systematic differences. When assessing the accounting practice of large European listed companies, it is likely that the majority of these companies are audited by a **Big 4** auditor. Global audit firms like Pricewaterhouse-Coopers or Ernst & Young usually follow an internationally standardized audit approach; their employees are consistently trained and international assignments are common. For this reason the employment of a Big 4 auditor might rather lead to standardized IFRS practice than to accounting differences. To verify this assumption, the companies' auditor is incorporated as an internal context factor to this study.[895]

Apart from the companies' type of auditor, the different organization of the **national oversight institutions** could be a cause for differences in international accounting practice.[896] These institutions basically have a tripartite spectrum of tasks to fulfill. First, the mere possibility of an audit by such an organization should proactively improve compliance and accounting quality. Second, they are the official contact point for complaints regarding published financial statements. Third and most importantly, they inform the capital market of incorrect annual accounts, which might lead to adverse publicity and negative share price reactions.[897]

Although the national enforcement activities of EU member states are coordinated and supervised by the ESMA,[898] differences between national enforcement systems are likely to remain.[899] It may be doubted that the German enforcement institution FREP is as experienced as the British FRRP which began operations in the beginning of the 1990s, when the German capital market, in comparison to the British capital market, was a lot less de-

[894] Cf. Brown/Tarca 2005, p. 182.

[895] The internal context factor auditor is outlined in chapter 2.3.2.2.3.

[896] For a comprehensive comparison of the enforcement systems of France, Germany and the UK plus Austria and Italy cf. *Löffler/Rohatschek* (2007); for a review of the enforcement systems of France, Germany and the UK cf. Eiselt/Pleitner 2010, p. 302ff.; see also Berger 2010, p. 15ff.

[897] Cf. Zimmermann 2003, p. 354; von Keitz/Stolle 2008, p. 213.

[898] Cf. chapter 1.3.3.2.4.

[899] Cf. Fédération des Experts Comptables Européens [FEE] 2001, p. 10; Committee of European Securities Regulators [CESR] 2007, p. 2f.; Ernstberger et al. 2011, p. 8.; Meyer/Naumann 2009, p. 808.

veloped.[900] Also, the perception of such an institution by the national companies and therewith the pressure that emanates from it surely differs depending on the different mechanisms employed by the national enforcement institutions and their disciplinary powers; the threat of a random review has more potential in terms of pressure to comply than a voluntary review that is based on the companies' decision to submit to such a review.[901] Instruments, like the type of publication of financial misstatements, fines for insufficient cooperation, the right to interview the companies' auditors or the right to inspect the records of supervisory board meetings, might have an influence on the enforcement effectiveness as well.[902]

Following the above argumentation, enforcement can be considered as an important external context factor when analyzing financial accounting practice. Nevertheless, the enforcement system will not be treated separately in this study. On the one hand, the quality of enforcement is difficult to measure. The age of the enforcement institution, for example, is assumed to be an improper indicator for its effectiveness. The French COB is a lot older than the British FRRP. Still, the British capital market is a lot more developed than the French capital market and the British random and event driven review system supposedly is more effective than the French voluntary review system. It is also questionable whether the measures, implemented in Germany and mainly derived from Anglo-American enforcement systems have the same effect in Germany and lead to comparable compliance.[903]

On the other hand, the development of the enforcement system is strongly related to the development of the financing system. The context factor financing system stands for the development of the capital market and it can be posited that the development of the capital market is a good proxy for the development and effectiveness of the corresponding enforcement system.

2.3.2.1.5 National GAAP

The national accounting system could be a relevant context factor when analyzing IFRS issues that are dealt with in a specific way under national GAAP. This study analyzes IFRS differences that, *inter alia*, result from IFRS overt and covert options; the way these options were exerted under national GAAP could have an influence on the way they are exerted under IFRS; companies could choose to opt consistently for group and individual accounts when possible. *Kvaal/Nobes* assume that companies tend to follow pre-IFRS practice for reasons of inertia respectively continuity.[904]

Both labels basically describe the same behavior, viz. applying IFRS the way it was done under national GAAP. Inertia describes the phenomenon from a rather negative perspec-

[900] In 1990 the UK had a capital market capitalization of listed companies in % of GDP of 84%. Germany had a ratio of 21%; cf. World Databank 2010.

[901] Cf. Eiselt/Pleitner 2010, p. 308.

[902] Cf. Berger 2009, p. 617f. The differing characteristics of the national enforcement bodies of France, Germany and the UK are briefly discussed in chapter 1.3.5.3.

[903] Cf. Naumann 2000, p. 669f.; Ernstberger et al. 2008, p. 31.

[904] Cf. Kvaal/Nobes 2010, p. 173; see also chapter 1.5.1.2.

tive. Inertial behavior refers to companies' choices that are motivated by considerations of simplicity and convenience.[905] Companies might fear to leave their accounting routine for lacking experience with international accounting standards or lacking the professional competence to judge the consequences of their actions. Continuity, however, describes the phenomenon from a more positive view. It stands for the intentional decision to provide the shareholder with financial information that changes as little as possible compared to pre-IFRS figures. Additionally, one might argue that continuous behavior is cost minimizing as the implementation of new accounting rules implies certain set-up costs that result from training, coaching etc.

In a 2008 study *Kvaal/Nobes* find empirical evidence for such a behavior.[906] Analyzing IFRS choices of blue chip companies from UK, Spain, France, Australia and Germany, they test whether differences in IFRS practice are random or follow certain country patterns that resemble pre-IFRS practice. The results suggest that national GAAP find its way into IFRS practice. When possible, companies favor options according to pre-IFRS practice. *Kvaal/Nobes* further investigate why companies deviate from their national country profile. They discover that deviations can be explained by the companies' international capital market orientation and the companies' auditor.[907] However, *Kvaal/Nobes* do not control for other cultural and institutional country factors that might explain the country patterns. Furthermore, they only investigate overt options.[908]

It is questionable whether large listed companies' accounting choices are affected by considerations of inertia respectively continuity. These companies surely possess the resources and accounting know-how to implement IFRS without paying too much attention to national accounting patterns. Also, these companies can expect their shareholders to be well versed in international accounting standards; the intention of a continuous application of accounting rules is unlikely to have a measurable effect either. Furthermore, for some areas of IFRS discretion it might be difficult to determine what national accounting practice looked like before the adoption of IFRS.[909] Certainly, some accounting issues, like the capitalization of development costs, were not allowed by national (German) GAAP in 2005 and supposed country patterns are easily determined. Nonetheless, national patterns could be distracted by IFRS early adopters or US-GAAP users.

The three **sample countries** differ considerably with respect to national GAAP classification studies. Classification of national accounting systems[910] has a long tradition in accounting research. The 1967 study by *Mueller* is regarded as a pioneer work in this area.[911] He sees the national accounting system as a result of national environmental factors and identifies four groups of national accounting systems: (1) accounting within a macroeconomic framework (Sweden), (2) the microeconomic approach (Netherlands), (3) account-

[905] Cf. Kvaal/Nobes 2008, p. 9f.
[906] Cf. Kvaal/Nobes 2008, p. 29ff.
[907] Cf. Kvaal/Nobes 2008, p. 29ff.
[908] Cf. chapter 1.5.1.2.
[909] National practice regarding overt options are ascertainable; cf. Kvaal/Nobes 2010, p. 178ff.
[910] As outlined in the following, the label national accounting system may refer to both accounting rules and accounting practice.
[911] Cf. Nobes/Parker 2008, p. 55f.

ing as an independent discipline (UK) and (4) uniform accounting (France).[912] This early approach to national accounting system classification belongs to the early **extrinsic** classification studies, which are based on external country factors like culture, regulatory surroundings or auditors' competence. **Intrinsic** classification studies, which were more popular from the 1970s on, in contrast, measure accounting practice directly by evaluating secondary data by Price Waterhouse[913] or the AICPA[914] or by generating own primary data.

The primary data was mainly provided by large accountancy bodies or large accounting firms and was then interpreted by individual researchers or teams of researchers using cluster analysis. An early cluster analysis of 1973 measurement practices results in four categories allocating UK in the British Commonwealth model and France and Germany in the Continental Europe model.[915] These early intrinsic classification studies are susceptible to criticism, mainly due to vagueness of what to be classified, lack of model, lack of hierarchy and inappropriate discriminating features.[916] *Nobes* tries to respond to the criticism by classifying only developed Western countries according to accounting practices of public companies, focusing only on measurement and valuation.[917] This more focused, sophisticated hierarchic classification of public companies in 14 developed Western countries evaluates nine factors for differentiation, like the importance of tax rules in measurement, conservatism or consolidation practices.[918] The *Nobes* national accounting system classification is displayed in Figure 2-10.

Again, Germany and France, on the one hand, and the UK, on the other hand, are categorized separately, expressing the basic dissimilarity of their national accounting systems. Although the two Continental European national accounting systems of France and Germany are classified similarly, both being macro-uniform, government-driven and tax-dominated, both countries are still grouped separately, an indicator for differing national accounting families.

912 Cf. Mueller 1967.

913 Cf. Price Waterhouse 1973; Price Waterhouse 1976; Price Waterhouse 1979.

914 Cf. American Institute of Certified Public Accountants [AICPA] 1964; American Institute of Certified Public Accountants [AICPA] 1975.

915 Cf. Nair/Frank 1980, p. 429.

916 Cf. Nobes/Parker 2008, p. 63.

917 Cf. Nobes 1983, p. 1ff.

918 Cf. Nobes/Parker 2008, p. 63ff.

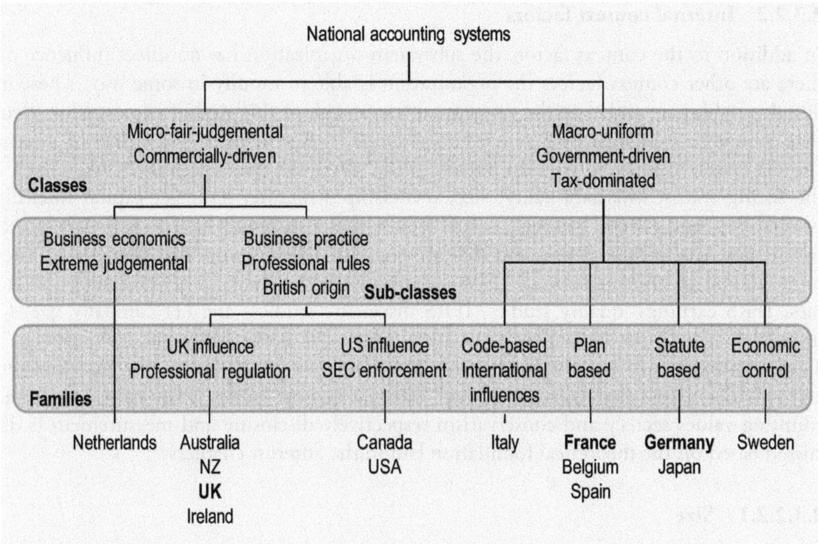

Figure 2-10: Classification of national accounting systems[919]

Contrary to *Nobes*, who clearly focuses on accounting practice, a more recent intrinsic classification concentrates on the classification of countries according to accounting rules.[920] *D'Arcy* applies cluster analysis on the *Ordelheide/KPMG* data[921] to classify national accounting systems according to financial reporting requirements.[922] She finds the British accounting system to be more capital market oriented than the French and the German accounting system. Furthermore, the three countries differ with respect to the degree of national accounting determinism. The French accounting system is characterized by more prohibitions and requirements than the German accounting system, which is more deterministic than the British accounting system.[923]

The above presented classification studies present a rather dichotomous picture of the three sample countries that is characterized by the macro-uniform accounting systems of France and Germany, on the one hand, and the micro-fair-judgmental accounting system of the UK, on the other hand. Consequently, the dualism of national GAAP systems is accounted for by the above introduced dummy variable that expresses the dichotomy between Anglo-Saxon case law countries and Continental European code law countries.

[919] Adopted from Nobes/Parker 2008, p. 65.

[920] The term accounting system is used for both national accounting practices and rules.

[921] Cf. *Ordelheide/KPMG* (1995).

[922] Cf. D'Arcy 2001, p. 343ff.

[923] Cf. D'Arcy 2001, p. 343ff.

2.3.2.2 Internal context factors

In addition to the context factors the subsystem organization has no direct influence on, there are other context factors the organization is able to modify in some way. These internal variables are added to the conceptual framework of this study to control for effects that cannot be explained by external factors alone.[924] Again, there is a variety of internal context factors that could have an impact on the decisions the organization takes, such as the listing status, internationality, size, ownership structure, leverage, capital intensity, profitability, auditor etc. Internal context factors that assumingly have an influence on the companies' accounting choices and that are regularly used in empirical studies that assess international accounting choices (IFRS compliance studies, voluntary IFRS adoption studies, IFRS earnings' quality studies, IFRS disclosure studies) are: (1) company size, (2) industrial sector, (3) auditor, (4) internationality, (5) profitability and (6) leverage.[925] These context factors are discussed briefly in the following sections. Following some general remarks on the characteristics of each internal context factor, its influence on the accounting values secrecy and conservatism respectively disclosure and measurement is discussed based on the theoretical foundation laid in the anterior chapters.

2.3.2.2.1 Size

The size variable is a prominent variable in empirical accounting research. Empirical studies show that the size of the reporting company is positively associated with more **disclosure** and higher degrees of compliance and accounting quality.[926] The reasons for this relationship are manifold. Large companies ordinarily have more resources and better trained staff. Contrary to small companies, larger companies often possess sophisticated internal control systems. They also tend to have larger and technologically better equipped management accounting and financial accounting departments; professional training processes are often institutionalized, leading to better educated employees. Also, the size-effect leads to relatively decreasing information costs for larger companies as these costs are allocated on more produced units. Furthermore, larger firms have more reputation to loose and are exposed to more pressure by the capital market and the public in general. From the PAT perspective, the relationship between size and capital market information is supported by the concepts of agency costs and political costs.[927] Larger companies are more complex and often have a broader diversified ownership structure from which higher agency costs result.[928] Higher political costs arise from the stronger perception of larger companies by the national regulatory institutions. Confronted with higher agency and

---

[924] Cf. Jaafar/McLeay 2007, p. 185.

[925] Cf., e.g., Dumontier/Raffournier 1998, p. 216ff.; El-Gazzar et al. 1999, p. 239ff.; Street/Bryant 2000, p. 305ff.; Ashbaugh 2001, p. 129ff.; Cuijpers/Buijink 2005, p. 487ff.; Tarca et al. 2005; van Tendeloo/Vanstraelen 2005, p. 155ff.; Gassen/Sellhorn 2006, p. 365ff.; Fischer/Kloepfer 2008, p. 623ff.; Francis et al. 2008, p. 331ff.; Hope et al. 2008, p. 357ff.; Kvaal/Nobes 2010, p. 173ff.

[926] Cf., e.g., Wallace et al. 1994, p. 41ff.; Wallace/Naser 1995, p. 311ff.; Zarzeski 1996, p. 18ff.; Dumontier/Raffournier 1998, p. 216ff.; Jaggi/Low 2000, p. 495ff.; Ashbaugh 2001, p. 129ff.

[927] Cf. Hossain et al. 1994, p. 335ff.; see also chapter 2.2.6.

[928] Cf. Hagerman/Zmijewski 1979, p. 142f.

political costs, companies try to reduce these costs by compensating existing information asymmetries by means of more financial information.[929]

From the perspective of political costs, size could also have an impact on accounting **measurement** and therewith accounting conservatism. Larger firms attract more public attention by their size and the public may associate large firms with monopolies and monopoly rents. To avoid such associations, which could result in political consequences like increased regulation or higher taxation, larger companies could tend to conservative accounting and reduce earnings.[930]

Financial accounting literature presents a variety of different company figures as **proxies** for size, such as capital market value, total assets, turnover, number of employees, number of shareholders or annual profit.[931] Some of these company figures are rather problematic when comparing companies from different sectors, e.g. when comparing the balance sheet total of companies from the financial and the industrial sector. Other context factors may be very unstable over time and, thus, not representative for the true size of the company, as for example the annual profit. This study employs the logarithmized capital market value of the company, which is a commonly used proxy for company size.[932] Since the capital market value is not entirely free of temporal variations either, the number of employees and the logarithmized total assets are additionally tested for a size related influence on the dependent variables.[933]

2.3.2.2.2 Industry

The industrial sector might affect accounting practice for a number of reasons. It is supposable that certain industries develop accounting competences that are rather undeveloped in other industries. For example, R&D intensive industries like the chemical industry are more often concerned with intangible assets than other less R&D intensive industries like the textile industry. Also, the chemical industry specific accounting know-how is likely to be more sophisticated when it comes to issues concerning IAS 38 ('intangible assets'). Another example could be the building and construction industry which probably possesses higher professional competence with respect to IAS 11 ('Construction contracts') than other industrial sectors like the consumer goods industry. Other context factors, not directly associated with an industry's business operations but with general industry constraints, could have an impact on accounting practice, as well. Industries like the pharmaceutical industry are probably more exposed to litigation risks than other industries. This might result in higher provisions and higher levels of prudent accounting.

Industry is expected to have an influence on companies' **disclosure** practices. Institutional economic theory presumes the industry factor to have an influence on proprietary costs or

[929] Cf. Hagerman/Zmijewski 1979, p. 142f.; Meek et al. 1995, p. 556.

[930] Cf. Watts/Zimmerman 1978, p. 121; Kim/Jung 2007, p. 20.

[931] Cf., e.g., Roberts 1992, p. 600; Craig/Diga 1998, p. 258; Holland 1998, p. 271; Core/Guay 2001, p. 257.

[932] Cf., e.g., DeAngelo 1988, p. 10; Dempsey 1989, p. 751; Frankel/Lee 1998, p. 291.

[933] Alternative size proxies are especially applied to control for bias on the companies' capital market values as a consequence of the worldwide economic crisis.

political costs.[934] Highly competitive industries like the computer industry or the chemical industry are probably more sensitive when publishing information on their products or R&D projects than less competitive industries. Companies from such industries assumingly modify financial information accordingly to minimize respectively avoid proprietary costs that result from possible competitive disadvantages.[935] Similar cost considerations might lead to industry specific accounting behavior in politically sensitive industries, as well.[936] Political costs might be higher in industries that attract more interest by the responsible regulative institutions and the public in general. The military industry and the energy industry are examples for such industries. Industries that are in the public and/or political focus could try to reduce political costs by signaling.[937] More transparent financial information could convince the public, for instance, that profits are not realized by means of the oligopoly structure of the industry (energy sector) or profits are not achieved in countries that have the reputation of a 'rogue state' (military sector).

In analogy to the internal context factor size, political cost considerations regarding disclosure are transferable to **measurement** issues. Especially in highly regulated industries high profitability is likely to be answered by political action from which political costs arise. As a consequence, managers have an incentive to engage in more conservative accounting and avoid high profits.[938] Also, accounting practice could be affected by industry specific best practice patterns. Such industry characteristic accounting practices are developed over time, for instance, when the accounting practices of typically large representatives of an industry serve as an example for smaller companies of that same industry. Reasons for this type of 'herding behavior' could be the lack of professional competence, cost considerations or simply convenience.[939]

The industry of the sample companies is determined by the internationally consistent Standard Industry Classification (SIC) system.[940] Industry is integrated as an independent variable into the statistical analysis in two ways. When comparing significant mean differences by industry, the study refers to a ten-industry-grouping that is based on the SIC classification.[941] When using industry as a proxy in the multiple regression analysis, the single categories of the ten-industry-grouping are included by means of nine dummy va-

934 Cf. Meek et al. 1995, p. 555ff.

935 Cf. Verrecchia 1983, p. 182; Cohen 2002, p. 6.

936 Cf. Watts/Zimmerman 1978, p. 121.

937 Cf. Inchausti 1997, p. 56.

938 Cf. Lara et al. 2009a, p. 343.

939 Cf. Cooke 1991, p. 177; Dye/Sridhar 1995, p. 158.

940 The SIC code was developed by the US government to categorize companies according to their industry. It was replaced in 1997 by the North American Industry Classification System (NAICS) but is still widely applied, as, for example, by the SEC. The SEC Electronic Data Gathering, Analysis and Retrieval system (EDGAR) filings still require the companies' SIC code. Cf. Securities and Exchange Commission [SEC] 2010b. For a complete list of the primary code cf. Securities and Exchange Commission [SEC] 2008a. The SIC code data availability in commercial databases like Osiris or Compustat underlines its remaining importance.

941 Cf. chapter 4.2.3.

riables that score one if the company belongs to a particular industry and zero otherwise.[942]

2.3.2.2.3 Auditor

The type of auditor is another variable often employed in relevant accounting literature to explain accounting practice.[943] The distinction between large (Big4)[944] and small (non Big4) auditors is based on the assumption that auditors have an influence on the quality of their clients' financial statements. Big4 auditors are generally associated with higher levels of accounting quality since large audit firms are expected to have better professional resources than smaller competitors. They have a worldwide network of subsidiaries which proves to be useful in cross-national audits and specialized departments for accounting issues like accruals for pensions or structured financial products that are too complex to be handled by the local audit team. Training processes are coordinated nationally or internationally and integrated in the employees' working routine. Also, the high degree of standardization of the audit approach of Big4 companies and an institutionalized quality management is likely to lead to higher quality audit results. Furthermore, the Big4 have a high reputation to lose, a reputation that is mainly based on their perceived independence.[945] To underline their independence, they have to make sure that their clients comply with international and national accounting regulations.[946] Also, large auditors are better targets for shareholder class-action lawsuits; their financial resources offer better possibilities for compensation.[947] Size is another argument when discussing reputation. Large audit firms assumingly are not as dependent on single clients as smaller audit firms. The latter might be more willing to make concessions to the client when threatened of possibly losing him.[948] The loss of a major client for a small or medium large audit firm could result in severe financial consequences.[949]

Companies choose to be audited by a Big4 auditor for different reasons. Obviously, for large multinational companies with subsidiaries in numerous countries it is more convenient to be audited by a firm that is also present in these countries. Following the general assumption that large audit firms possess a higher reputation in terms of audit quality, companies also choose Big4 auditors to add more credibility to their financial state-

[942] The tenth industry is implicitly covered by the nine other dummy variables.

[943] Cf., e.g., Francis 2004, p. 352ff.; Chen/Cheng 2007, p. 287; Boone et al. 2010, p. 336.

[944] The label Big4 includes the largest four audit firms, which are in order of 2009 revenues: PricewaterhouseCoopers, Deloitte Touche Tohmatsu, Ernst & Young and KPMG; cf. PricewaterhouseCoopers 2009; Deloitte Touche Tohmatsu 2009; Ernst & Young 2009; KPMG 2009. Accounting studies before 2002 usually refer to the Big5, Big6 or Big8 audit firms. The largest audit firms were called Big8 until 1989. Various mergers and acquisitions in the 1990s led to the remaining Big5 audit firms. The Enron accounting scandal and the involvement of Arthur Andersen resulted in the sale of the Arthur Andersen subsidiaries to the other now Big4 companies; cf. Khurana/Raman 2004, p. 474.

[945] The Arthur Andersen / Enron case showed what a loss in reputation may lead to.

[946] Cf. Dumontier/Raffournier 1998, p. 225.

[947] Cf. Simunic/Stein 1996, p. 120.

[948] Cf. Alsaeed 2005, p. 315.

[949] Cf. Malone et al. 1993, p. 254.

ments.[950] This assumption is in line with agency theoretical suppositions. Firms seek financial statement credibility to increase investors' trust and, thus, reduce information asymmetries implied agency costs that result from the contractual relationship between the company and the owner.[951] Companies use the reputation of the auditor to signal the capital market the trustworthiness of the company's financial statements. The results of empirical studies that implement the type of auditor as a context factor are mixed but generally support the assumption that Big4 audit firms are associated with higher degrees of **disclosure.**[952] Some studies identify a positive but insignificant relationship between audit firm size and extent of disclosure.[953] Few studies, in contrast, come to the result of a significantly negative relationship.[954] Following the above arguments, this study expects Big4 auditors to have a positive influence on disclosure.

The size of the audit firm is also assumed to have an effect on **measurement**; Big4 audit firms are generally associated with higher degrees of conservatism. As mentioned above, Big4 auditors have more reputation to lose and a more solid financial background and, consequently, are more likely to be involved in shareholder class-action lawsuits. The risk of conviction in such a lawsuit and the imposition of fines are assumed to be higher, if the clients' assets/revenues are found to be overstated respectively, if the clients' liabilities/expenses are understated.[955] Hence, to mitigate the risk of lawsuits and corresponding penalties, Big4 auditors have an increased interest in their clients to report conservative accounting figures.[956] From the perspective of signaling theory, Big4 audited companies could seek to benefit from this reputation of more conservative accounting to signal the market the credibility of their financial figures.

This study controls for the internal context factor auditor by a dichotomous variable that is one if the company is audited by a Big4 auditor and that is zero otherwise.

2.3.2.2.4 Internationality

Internationality respectively international capital market orientation is expected to have an influence on financial accounting choices, especially when it comes to international accounting standards. The degree of international capital market orientation is approximated in this study via three internationality indicators:[957] (1) foreign listing, (2) SEC listing and (3) international operations.

---

[950] Cf. Dumontier/Raffournier 1998, p. 225.

[951] Cf. Watts/Zimmerman 1983, p. 613ff.

[952] Cf. Singhvi/Desai 1971, p. 129ff.; Craswell/Taylor 1992, p. 295ff.; Raffournier 1995, p. 261ff.; Camfferman/Cooke 2002, p. 3ff.; Glaum/Street 2003, p. 64ff.

[953] Cf. Forker 1992, p. 111ff.; Wallace et al. 1994, p. 41ff.

[954] Cf. Wallace/Naser 1995, p. 311ff.

[955] Cf. St. Pierre/Anderson 1984, p. 242.

[956] Cf. DeFond/Subramanyam 1998, p. 35. The empirical results on the influence of the type of auditor are not consistent. *Piot et al.*, e.g., find auditors to be associated with more optimistic earnings figures; cf. Piot et al. 2010.

[957] The indicators foreign listing and SEC listing are not entirely independent from one another since SEC registered companies are also listed abroad.

Companies that are listed at a stock exchange, different from the one in their home country, face additional regulations and capital market pressure. This statement is further emphasized, when companies, whose home capital market is rather undeveloped (Germany, France), opt for a listing at one of the highly developed capital markets (UK, US). A listing at the US capital market in the past meant that these companies had to reconcile their national GAAP financial statements to US-GAAP.[958] Naturally, only companies that possessed the means to fulfill the strict disclosure requirements of the SEC chose to take this step.[959] Although this barrier has been removed with the SEC's acceptance of foreign private issuers' financial statements in accordance with IFRS, the adoption of US-GAAP surely has/had an influence on the accounting practice of SEC registered companies.

Empirical studies suggest a positive relationship between the number of foreign stock exchange listings and the level of **disclosure.**[960] Other studies report a relationship between foreign listings and the probability of using non-local GAAP.[961] *Kvaal/Nobes* find foreign listings to be related to companies that deviate from national accounting profiles.[962] The results of these studies are in line with agency theoretical assumptions. Companies try to reduce information asymmetries and agency costs that result from international listings by increasing the level of disclosure.[963] The listing at a foreign stock exchange and especially the listing at a SEC regulated stock exchange can be interpreted as the consequence of a signaling strategy. Companies hereby indicate that their financial reporting system fulfills the higher requirements of international reporting standards, viz. US-GAAP. Furthermore, the provided financial information are also likely to be more relevant for international investors.

International operations could also be an indicator for internationality. Companies that are not listed in a foreign country, but that are internationally oriented, having international shareholders, suppliers or generating substantial parts of their turnover abroad, have a motivation to provide financial information according to internationally accepted accounting standards. Empirical evidence supports this assumption.[964]

Internationality could also be related to aspects of conservatism and IFRS **measurement** practice. Companies from high conservatism countries like France or Germany that are listed at higher developed capital markets like the US market could tend to follow a less conservative accounting approach; adapting to US-GAAP, these companies seek to be able to compete with domestic US companies.[965] *Gray* supports this notion and attributes the effect to the different needs of financial statement users.[966] Companies could be influ-

[958] Cf. Amir et al. 1993, p. 230; Barth/Clinch 1996, p. 135f.; Rees/Elgers 1997, p. 115.
[959] Cf. Saudagaran/Biddle 1992, p. 106.
[960] Cf. Cooke 1992, p. 229ff.; Meek et al. 1995, p. 555ff.
[961] Cf. El-Gazzar et al. 1999, p. 293ff.; Murphy 1999, p. 121ff.; Ashbaugh 2001, p. 129ff.
[962] Cf. Kvaal/Nobes 2008, p. 30.
[963] Cf. Inchausti 1997, p. 54.
[964] Cf. Dumontier/Raffournier 1998, p. 216ff.; El-Gazzar et al. 1999, p. 239ff.; Murphy 1999, p. 121ff.
[965] Cf. Radebaugh et al. 1995, p. 170ff.
[966] Cf. Gray 1980, p. 74.

enced by the different equity driven demand of US investors and decide to adjust to the US accounting philosophy.[967]

Three proxies are applied to control for the degree of internationality in this study. First, foreign stock exchange listing is integrated by means of a dummy variable. Second, the listing at a stock exchange that is regulated by the SEC is analyzed separately by another dummy variable. Third, the internationality of the companies' business operations is accounted for by the percentage of foreign sales to total sales.

2.3.2.2.5 Profitability

Profitability may also affect the company's measurement and **disclosure** decisions. Following the argumentation of the above described 'lemon problem' by *Akerlof*, profitable 'good lemon' companies have an interest to distinguish themselves from unprofitable 'bad lemon' companies and, consequently, communicate their profitability to the capital market.[968] As a result, profitable companies are assumed to disclose more voluntary information than their non-profitable counterparts.[969] This signaling theoretical assumption is supported by agency theoretical considerations. According to the information asymmetries concepts, the principal is only restrictedly able to judge the agent's performance. A well performing agent therefore has an interest to assure the principal of his performance by disclosing additional financial information, thus, underlining his claim for higher compensation.[970] Besides claims for higher compensation, managers of profitable companies could just be proud of their achievements and disclose more information to inform the public on their achievements and improve their reputation. Information provided by profitable companies could also tend to be more detailed and more precise when such information help investors to smooth earnings across periods.[971] Other researchers argue inversely that especially unprofitable companies have an interest to disclose more voluntary information to enhance credibility on the capital market and to reduce litigation risk.[972] Nonetheless, it is generally assumed that low profitability or losses might rather be associated with less disclosure as these companies may feel threatened by a negative capital market reaction and decide to obscure unfavorable results.[973] Although the latter argumentation is intuitively more convincing, empirical results on the relationship between the performance of a company and the quantity of disclosure are mixed.[974]

Firm performance may also have an effect on the companies' **measurement** decisions. Following political cost theory, highly profitable companies may be affected by adverse political actions like expropriation, break-up, regulation or wealth transfer via taxation.[975] As the public associates high profits with monopoly rents, politics seek to correct these

[967] Cf. Biddle/Saudagaran 1989, p. 61.
[968] Cf. Akerlof 1970, p. 489; cf. chapter 2.2.5.1.
[969] Cf. Foster 1986, p. 32.
[970] Cf. Singhvi/Desai 1971, p. 133f.; Naser et al. 1993, p. 131.
[971] Cf. Imhoff 1992, p. 108ff.; Newman/Sansing 1993, p. 93ff.
[972] Cf. Lang/Lundholm 1993, 251f.
[973] Cf. Wang et al. 2008, p. 18.
[974] Cf. Lang/Lundholm 1993, p. 246ff.; Wallace et al. 1994, p. 41ff.; Camfferman/Cooke 2002, p. 3ff.
[975] Cf. Stigler 1971, p. 3; Peltzman 1976, p. 213ff.

market inefficiencies by regulation or obtaining a share of these rents by wealth transfer via taxes. All costs of regulation, which include legal costs of opposing the political actions and wealth transfers, can be subsumed under political costs. Political costs also refer to the extra labor costs that result from inflated wage agreements in the context of high firm profitability. To avoid the public attention raised by high profits and therewith to avoid political costs, companies could opt to follow a more conservative accounting approach and reduce profits.[976]

To control for firm profitability, absolute profit figures like net income are usually deflated by balance sheet parameters like total assets or income statement parameters like total sales.[977] This study employs both balance sheet and income statement based figures; firm profitability is approximated by means of return on investment (ROI)[978] and profit margin[979].

2.3.2.2.6 Leverage

Prior research demonstrates that financial leverage is an important variable in explaining corporate accounting practice.[980] The financial leverage indicator reflects the company's capital structure. As interest payments, in contrast to dividends, are tax deductible, higher leverage reduces the companies' capital costs. Nonetheless, higher leverage might also be an indicator for a precarious financing situation of the company. Dependent on the relative amount of debt to equity and the debt structure (short-term vs. long-term), high leverage could also lead to liquidity problems.

From an agency theoretical perspective, high debt to equity ratios are associated with more (voluntary) **disclosure.**[981] To reduce information asymmetries between outside creditors and management, companies could be motivated to disclose more financial information and therewith reduce monitoring costs.[982] Also, debt covenants could explicitly require additional information to inform the financial institution in detail about the companies' business activities and, thus, to ensure repayment.[983] The reduction of information asymmetries as a consequence of additional financial information could also lead to a reduction of cost of capital; the interest rate risk premium related to financial uncertainty is lower.[984] Such a reduction of cost of debt is more attractive for highly leveraged companies as the positive effect on interest payments is comparably larger. Empirical studies show mixed results with respect to the relationship between disclosure and cost of capital,

[976] Cf. Watts/Zimmerman 1978, p. 115; Watts 2003a, p. 210; Watts 2003b, p. 299; Guay/Verrecchia 2006, p. 156.
[977] Cf. Liebowitz 1982, p. 239; Gallo et al. 1996, p. 1780; Lehn/Makhija 1997, p. 92; Boubakri/Cosset 1998, p. 1087.
[978] The ROI is defined by net income divided by total assets.
[979] Profit margin is defined by net income divided by total sales.
[980] Cf. Zmijewski/Hagerman 1981, p. 129; Bartov/Bodnar 1996, p. 398.
[981] Cf. Chow/Wong-Boren 1987, p. 539.
[982] Cf. Raffournier 1995, p. 265.
[983] Cf. Myers 1977, p. 164ff.; Schipper 1981, p. 86; Wallace et al. 1994, p. 44.
[984] Cf. Wang et al. 2008, p. 18f.

but mainly support the suggested relationship.[985] *Leuz* attributes the lack of consistent empirical evidence to the fact that many studies are US-GAAP studies; he argues that the posited cost of capital effect is difficult to show in the 'rich' US-GAAP disclosure environment.[986] He finds support for a disclosure related reduction of cost of capital for German companies that come from a 'poor' disclosure environment and switch to IFRS respectively US-GAAP.[987]

With respect to **measurement** practice, highly leveraged companies are suggested to follow a less conservative approach. Debt may be responsible for agency conflicts between debt holders and shareholders since shareholders benefit from wealth transfers from bondholders via overpayment of dividends; overpaying dividends, the companies' assets, available to fulfill the debt holder's claims, are reduced and the default risk increased.[988] In the simplified case of the owner-managed company, the owner may promise to opt for the less risky investment program, then issue debt at lower interest rates and finally decide to take the more risky investment program. Information asymmetries between management and debt holder allow for such constellations. The owner-manager therewith passes on more risk to the debt holder than previously agreed on in the debt contract.[989] The debt holder's stake in chances and risks is asymmetric. He does not participate in the higher chances associated with a more risky investment via higher interest rates, but runs the risk of losing his entire money in the case of bankruptcy as a result of a failed investment. Besides opportunistic wealth loss caused by debt influenced investment decisions, *Jensen/Meckling* identify further agency costs associated with debt like monitoring and bonding costs and costs related to bankruptcy and restructuring.[990]

Debt covenants may serve to mitigate agency costs that result from contractual relationships between debt holders and share holders respectively debt holders and management.[991] Such debt covenants could hinder the company to take more risky investments than previously agreed on or oblige the company to provide more information to the debt holders to reduce information asymmetries. Financial measures like earnings ratios or debt to equity ratios can be used to exercise a certain control on the companies' investment decisions and prevent opportunistic behavior.[992] Nonetheless, due to remaining information asymmetries, debt holders are not able to ultimately control the correctness of the financial measures agreed on in debt covenants; the preparation of these figures is the responsibility of the company. According to the debt/equity hypothesis of PAT, companies with a high debt to equity ratio may have strong incentives to choose accounting methods that increase earnings to avoid debt covenant violations and costly penalties for breach of

---

985 Cf., e.g., Diamond/Verrecchia 1991, p. 1325; Leland 1992, p. 859; Wang 1993, p. 249; O'Hara 2003, p. 1335; Botosan et al. 2004, p. 233; Easley/O'Hara 2004, p. 1553; Lambert et al. 2008, p. 2.
986 Cf. Leuz/Verrecchia 2000, p. 91.
987 Cf. Leuz/Verrecchia 2000, p. 91.
988 Cf. Ahmed et al. 2002, p. 870.
989 Cf. Hirshleifer/Thakor 1992, p. 438ff.
990 Cf. Jensen/Meckling 1976, p. 333ff.
991 Cf. Nikolaev 2010, p. 138.
992 Cf. Ball et al. 2008, p. 169.

contract.[993] Consequently, higher leveraged companies are assumed to be less conservative than less leveraged companies.

In the next subchapter the above described internal and external context factors that are assumed to have an influence on IFRS practice are integrated into the conceptual framework of this study.

2.3.2.3 Integration of external and internal context factors

In this study the **external** context of the organization is described via five institutional context factors. The context factor financing system distinguishes between financing systems that rely mainly on equity financing and financing systems that rely mainly on debt financing. The degree of equity financing is approximated in this study by the degree of equity capital market development as measured by total market capitalization divided by GDP. As outlined above, the context factors legal and tax system are closely associated. Whereas legal systems can be grouped into common and code law legal systems, the latter context factor distinguishes between tax systems that are closely connected to the national accounting system and tax systems that are mostly independent from national GAAP. Since code law countries are usually characterized by strong interdependencies between tax and commercial accounting, both context factors are approximated by the same dummy variable. Furthermore, this dummy variable also distinguishes between the Continental European accounting systems of France and Germany, on the one hand, and the Anglo-Saxon accounting system of the UK, on the other hand. Consequently, the institutional environment of the three sample countries is basically bipolar. The context factor enforcement system is presumed to be closely related to the type of financing system and, analogously, is approximated by the degree of capital market development.

The **internal** context of the organization is represented by firm size, industry, auditor, internationality, profitability and leverage. Firm size is measured by logarithmized total assets, logarithmized market capitalization and number of employees. The industrial setting of this study is described by the supranational SIC industry-grouping, which distinguishes between ten different industries. The type of auditor is approximated by a dummy variable that is one for companies that are audited by a Big4 auditor and that is zero for companies that are audited by other auditors. In analogy to firm size, the degree of internationality is also measured by three different proxies. Whereas SEC listing and foreign listing are covered by two dummy variables, the degree of foreign operations is measured by the percentage of foreign sales to total sales. Two proxies control for the influence of the context factor profitability; profit margin is an entirely profit and loss accounts related indicator and return on investment is a combined profit and loss accounts / balance sheet indicator. Finally, the degree of corporate leverage is controlled for by the company individual debt to equity ratio.

Following the above presentation and discussion of external and internal context factors, the conceptual framework is refined with respect to the organizational context (see Figure 2-11).

---

[993] Cf. Duke/Hunt III 1990, p. 47; Zhang 2008, p. 35; see also chapter 2.2.6.

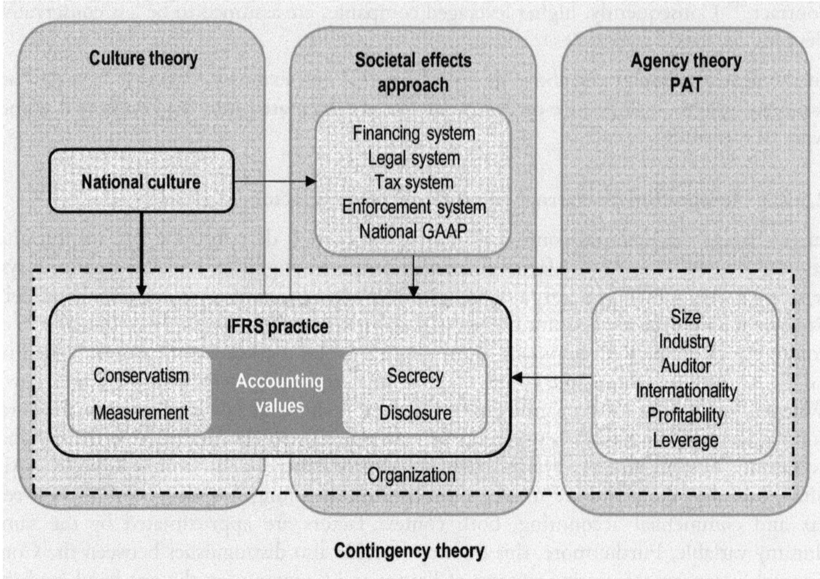

Figure 2-11: Refined conceptual framework

Based on the refined conceptual framework, the base hypotheses of this study are developed in the subsequent chapter.

2.3.3 Development of the base hypotheses

As displayed in Figure 2-11, the *Hofstede-Gray* framework forms the central part of the conceptual framework. Since the focus of this study is on **IFRS practice**, the only accounting values to be tested are **conservatism**, the accounting dimension of measurement, and **secrecy**, the accounting dimension of disclosure. The accounting values of professionalism and uniformity are parameters more characteristic for the national accounting system than for national accounting practice. Such systematical context factors rather belong to the institutional consequences of culture, which are integrated into the analysis via explanatory control variables.

Prior research supports this approach; empirical results suggest the strongest association between *Hofstede's* cultural dimensions and the accounting values of conservatism and secrecy.[994] The empirical studies, which test the *Hofstede-Gray* framework on the associations between culture and the accounting values of conservatism and secrecy, identify the cultural dimension of uncertainty avoidance to be most influential.[995] Besides uncertainty avoidance, individualism, masculinity and power distance are also included in the test design of this study to control for possible cultural effects. According to *Gray*, **power dis-**

[994] Cf. Baydoun/Willett 1995, p. 83f.

[995] Cf. Jödicke 2009, p. 238f.

tance is assumed to have a minor effect on secrecy only. However, power distance is also tested for a possible influence on conservatism since various previous studies indicate a power distance effect comparable to uncertainty avoidance.[996] Consequently, power distance is assumed to be positively associated with conservatism in this study and, thus, is expected to have the same effect on conservatism and secrecy, which both resemble a rather cautious accounting approach.[997] The influence of uncertainty avoidance, individualism and masculinity on IFRS measurement and disclosure practice is posited in accordance with *Gray*.[998]

Based on the preceding considerations, the **conservatism** base hypotheses are posited as follows:

H_1: Companies from countries that rank higher in terms of uncertainty avoidance follow a more conservative measurement approach under IFRS.

H_2: Companies from countries that rank higher in terms of individualism follow a less conservative measurement approach under IFRS.

H_3: Companies from countries that rank higher in terms of masculinity follow a less conservative measurement approach under IFRS.

H_4: Companies from countries that rank higher in terms of power distance follow a more conservative measurement approach under IFRS.

Analogous, the **secrecy** base hypotheses are posited as follows:

H_5: Companies from countries that rank higher in terms of uncertainty avoidance follow a more secretive disclosure approach under IFRS.

H_6: Companies from countries that rank higher in terms of individualism follow a less secretive disclosure approach under IFRS.

H_7: Companies from countries that rank higher in terms of masculinity follow a less secretive disclosure approach under IFRS.

H_8: Companies from countries that rank higher in terms of power distance follow a more secretive disclosure approach under IFRS.

In the next subchapter the above posited base hypotheses are transformed into operationalizable sub-hypotheses.

2.3.4 Development of the sub-hypotheses

Based on the conceptual framework, the following sub-hypotheses further specify the relationship between national culture and the accounting phenomena of conservatism and secrecy. Both accounting dimensions represent accounting practice and stand for a **cautious accounting** approach, the first for cautious measurement and the latter for cautious

---

[996] Cf., e.g., Chow et al. 1995, p. 29ff.; Pourjali/Meek 1995, p. 3ff.; Sudarwan/Fogarty 1996, p. 463ff.

[997] Cf. Gray 1988, p. 8.

[998] Cf. Chapter 2.2.4.6.

disclosure.[999] Accordingly, the sub-hypotheses employ various indirect and direct conservatism and secrecy indicators to measure the assumed degree of measurement conservatism respectively disclosure secrecy; whereas the **indirect indicators** analyze the particular accounting value from a more global perspective, the **direct indicators** cover specific IFRS measurement and disclosure issues. The conservatism and secrecy indicators are tested for a statistical association with national cultural dimensions. Based on the test result, the sub-hypotheses are confirmed respectively denied; the sub-hypotheses results then allow for conclusions on the base hypotheses of this study.

This chapter also deals with the **operationalization** of the tested indicators. Operationalization generally refers to the measurability of hypothesized relationships and therewith to the measurability of dependent and independent variables. Measurable in this context means statistically analyzable. Accordingly, the particular variables are attributed numerical values of different scale to be able to test statistical relationships. This chapter only recognizes the operationalization of the dependent variables. The external and internal control variables were operationalized in chapter 2.3.2.

To begin with, the next chapter deals with the development and operationalization of the **conservatism** sub-hypotheses.

2.3.4.1 Development of the conservatism sub-hypotheses

As previously mentioned, conservatism respectively prudence is an accounting principle commonly used to distinguish between national accounting systems and practice. According to *Sterling*, conservatism is "the most ancient and probably the most pervasive principle of accounting valuation"[1000]. Generally speaking, a conservative approach to accounting is characterized by a preference for the lowest possible values for assets and revenues and the highest possible values for liabilities and expenses.[1001] In analogy to this notion, accounting literature distinguishes between two variants of conservatism, viz. **conditional** or income statement conservatism, on the one hand, and **unconditional** or balance sheet conservatism, on the other hand.[1002] The two variants differ with regard to their dependency on (good or bad) news. Conditional conservatism is expressed by an asymmetrically timely recognition of gains and losses; earnings show bad news earlier than good news. In contrast, unconditional conservatism is independent from the type of news. Conservatism in this context refers to a preference for low book values of net assets as a result of expense acceleration or income deferral.[1003] Following the above conservatism definition, this study employs an **unconditional** approach to conservatism.

The above posited conservatism base hypotheses are tested in two ways. First, these hypotheses are tested on a global level using **indirect** conservatism indicators that approximate conservative accounting in general, instead of focusing on particular accounting choices.

---

999 Cf. Gray 1988, p. 8.

1000 Sterling 1967, p. 110.

1001 Cf. Belkaoui 1985, p. 239; Noravesh et al. 2007, p. 261.

1002 Cf. Basu 1997, p. 8; Beaver/Ryan 2005, p. 269ff.; Qiang 2007, p. 759ff.; Fülbier et al. 2008, p. 1317; Pellens et al. 2008, p. 170; Lara et al. 2009a, p. 336ff.

1003 Cf. Pellens et al. 2008, p. 170.

Second, the conservatism base hypotheses are tested via **direct** conservatism indicators by applying the above described understanding of unconditional conservative accounting to the above depicted opportunities for IFRS differences, in particular to options and measurement estimates. The focus therewith lies on accounting decisions that can be directly observed in the companies' financial statements.

The following two subchapters develop and operationalize **conservatism** sub-hypotheses based on indirect and direct conservatism indicators to test the statistical association between cultural dimensions and the accounting value of conservatism.

2.3.4.1.1 Indirect conservatism indicators

In contrast to direct conservatism indicators that deal with particular directly observable accounting choices,[1004] indirect conservatism indicators also account for non-observable conservative accounting choices like accruals, for instance.[1005] Conservatism, as one of the most important accounting values, has been subject to investigation in various studies; manifold conservatism measures have been developed. *Wang et al.* identify five key concepts of accounting conservatism that are dealt with in empirical conservatism literature.[1006] These concepts of conservatism can be categorized according to the above twofold conservatism definition.

The first two concepts focus on (good/bad) news and the assumption that bad news is recognized faster than good news. Whereas *Basu*[1007] expects conservatism to be expressed by (1) an asymmetric timeliness of earnings (**AT**), *Ball/Shivakumar*[1008] expect (2) the asymmetric timeliness of accruals to cash flows (**AACF**) to indicate conservatism. Accordingly, both concepts analyze the degree of conditional or news-dependent conservatism, assuming higher degrees of conservatism for higher degrees of asymmetric timeliness. Conservatism is measured via cross-sectional regression analysis explaining (1) earnings per share by stock market returns (AT) respectively (2) accruals by cash-flows from operating activities (AACF).[1009] Although both concepts are frequently applied in accounting literature, this study applies unconditional conservatism concepts, which offer the possibility to determine firm-specific conservatism indicators.[1010]

1004 Cf. chapter 1.3.4.2.4 to chapter 1.3.4.2.6.

1005 Cf. Ahmed et al. 2002, p. 873f.

1006 Cf. Wang et al. 2009, p. 165ff.

1007 Cf. Basu 1997, p. 3ff.

1008 Cf. Ball/Shivakumar 2005, p. 83ff.

1009 Stock market returns and accordingly cash flows from operating activities are used as proxies for news (good news are represented by positive values; bad news are represented by negative values); a dummy variable distinguishes between good and bad news. The corresponding β-coefficients measure the degree of conservatism. Cf. Basu 1997, p. 3ff.; Ball/Shivakumar 2005, p. 83ff.

1010 Cf. Wang et al. 2009, p. 1ff.

The most commonly tested high-level concepts of unconditional or news-independent conservatism suggest conservatism to be indicated by (3) hidden reserves (HR)[1011], (4) understated book values (**MTB**)[1012] and (5) negative accruals (**NA**)[1013].

This study only employs the latter two indicators to measure unconditional conservatism. The concept of *Penman/Zhang*, which estimates hidden inventory, R&D and advertising reserves, is not applied in this study. First, the LIFO inventory cost formula is not permitted under IFRS. Second, advertising expenditures are often not reported separately in the financial statements. And third, R&D capitalization is already accounted for as a direct conservatism indicator.[1014]

The first two sets of conservatism sub-hypotheses that are based on the indirect conservatism indicators MTB and NA are developed in the next two subchapters.

2.3.4.1.1.1 Market to book value

The **MTB** concept is an outcome of the discounted residual income valuation model;[1015] conservatism in this context is regarded as a tendency to report lower net book values compared to the economic value of the company, which is approximated by its market value. In analogy to the above described HR concept, conservatism is approximated by hidden reserves. In comparison to *Penman/Zhang* who estimate hidden reserves mainly by the economic potential of R&D respectively advertising investments, *Beaver/Ryan* suggest the capital market to better estimate the amount of hidden reserves. Accordingly, the market based hidden reserves concept is far more comprehensive compared to the HR concept of hidden reserves.[1016] Furthermore, the corresponding data on market and book values is directly accessible via financial accounting databases.

Hidden reserves as a result of understated book values are determined by comparing the company's market value to the corresponding book value. The market to book ratio is a common financial ratio used by investors or analysts to identify undervalued or overvalued securities. *Beaver/Ryan* further decompose this measure into a bias and a lag component[1017] regressing the actual MTB ratio on a series of lagged stock returns. Although sta-

---

[1011] The HR concept by *Penman/Zhang* uses hidden reserves as a proxy for conservatism. As hidden reserves are not directly observable in the financial statements, the authors suggest to estimate hidden reserves. Hidden reserves in this context refer to three types of reserves: (1) inventory reserves (LIFO reserve as reported in the notes), (2) R&D reserves (capitalized R&D expenditures amortized by industry specific coefficients) and (3) advertising reserve (capitalized advertising expenditures amortized using sum-of-the-years-digit depreciation over two years). Cf. Penman/Zhang 2002, p. 237ff.

[1012] Cf., e.g., Beaver/Ryan 2000, p. 127ff.; Ahmed et al. 2002, p. 867ff.; Ahmed/Duellman 2007, 411ff.; Lara et al. 2009b, p. 161ff.

[1013] Cf. Givoly/Hayn 2000, p. 287ff.

[1014] Cf. chapter 2.3.4.1.2.

[1015] Cf. Feltham 1995, p. 689ff.; Beaver/Ryan 2000, p. 127ff.; Zhang 2000, p. 125ff.

[1016] Hidden reserves could also be the result of an accelerated depreciation policy that exceeds the economic usage of an asset; alternatively, companies might choose the historical cost method instead of the fair value method. Increasing asset market prices would then lead to hidden reserves.

[1017] The bias component refers to continuously higher (lower) book values compared to market values and measures the degree of conservatism. The lag component, in contrast, refers to the deferred recognition of unexpected economic gains (losses) in companies' book values. Cf. Beaver/Ryan 2000, p. 128.

tistically more sophisticated, the application of the *Beaver/Ryan* bias component leads to very similar results compared to the simple MTB ratio.[1018] As a consequence, this study employs the simple MTB ratio as a proxy for firm-specific accounting conservatism.[1019]

Apart from aspects of practicability, the strengths of the MTB ratio lie in its theoretical founding and firm-specificity. A weakness of the approach is that the MTB ratio may overstate the true degree of conservatism since growth opportunities are usually not included in the book value.[1020] Market values might be biased by inflated capital markets expectations as a result of large sales growth.[1021] To avoid bias caused by expected growth opportunities, sales growth is controlled for in this study in addition to other firm performance indicators like profit margin or ROI.[1022]

In analogy to the above presented conservatism base hypotheses, the MTB related conservatism sub-hypotheses are posited as follows:

H_{1a}: Companies from countries that rank higher in terms of uncertainty avoidance are likely to have higher market to book ratios.

H_{2a}: Companies from countries that rank higher in terms of individualism are likely to have lower market to book ratios.

H_{3a}: Companies from countries that rank higher in terms of masculinity are likely to have lower market to book ratios.

H_{4a}: Companies from countries that rank higher in terms of power distance are likely to have higher market to book ratios.

2.3.4.1.1.2 Negative accruals value

Besides the above market-value based conservatism proxy, the study also uses an accrual-based conservatism proxy, following the **NA** concept by *Givoly/Hayn*.[1023] The basic idea of accrual accounting is to measure the performance of a company by recognizing economic events instead of cash transactions (cash accounting).[1024] Accordingly, accruals of one period are reversed in the following periods; conservative accounting in one period may lead to non-conservative accounting in the next period. Following that logic and assuming that in the long run accrual accounting results equal cash accounting results, *Givoly/Hayn* take negative accumulated accruals as a proxy for conservative accounting. Analogous to the MTB ratio, the NA concept allows for the calculation of firm-specific conservatism values. Additionally, the NA concept is not market based and therewith free of biased market expectations. Nevertheless, negative accruals are not independent from growth; sales

---

[1018] Cf. Ahmed/Duellman 2007, p. 418.

[1019] The data on company MTB ratios were taken from the commercial database Osiris.

[1020] Cf. Ahmed/Duellman 2007, p. 418.

[1021] Cf. Ahmed et al. 2002, p. 873; Wang et al. 2009, p. 11ff.

[1022] Cf. chapter 2.3.2.2.5.

[1023] Cf. Givoly/Hayn 2000, p. 287ff.

[1024] Cf. Ohlson/Zhang 1998, p. 85ff.; Reichelstein 2000, p. 243ff.

growth affects accruals such as inventory or receivables.[1025] As a consequence, sales growth is controlled for, as well.

The NA based conservatism sub-hypotheses are posited as follows:

H_{1b}: Companies from countries that rank higher in terms of uncertainty avoidance are likely to have lower negative accruals values.

H_{2b}: Companies from countries that rank higher in terms of individualism are likely to have higher negative accruals values.

H_{3b}: Companies from countries that rank higher in terms of masculinity are likely to have higher negative accruals values.

H_{4b}: Companies from countries that rank higher in terms of power distance are likely to have lower negative accruals values.

Assuming that in the long run net income equals cash flows, *Givoly/Hayn* expect conservative companies to use accruals as an instrument to lower earnings and to have negative accumulated accruals (net income < cash flows) in the short respectively medium term.[1026] In analogy to *Givoly/Hayn*, this study determines the NA value by subtracting cash flows from operating activities[1027] from net income[1028] before extraordinary items[1029] and depreciation and amortization[1030] (see Table 2-8).

	Modified net income		Net income
		+/-	Extraordinary items
		+	Depreciation and amortization
-	Operating cash flows	=	Modified net income
=	**Negative accruals (NA)**		

Table 2-8: Calculation of the NA value

Givoly/Hayn add back depreciation and amortization to make net income and cash flows from operating activities comparable.[1031] As depreciation and amortization reverse the positive accrual (net income > cash flows) that was recognized when the asset was acquired and that was not reported under cash flows from operating activities, these are eliminated from the calculation of NA.[1032] According to this correction, depreciation and amortization accruals are not recognized by NA. This limitation, however, is of minor concern

1025 Cf. Ahmed/Duellman 2007, p. 420; Wang et al. 2009, p. 14f.

1026 Cf. Givoly/Hayn 2000, p. 292.

1027 The cash flows from operating activities values were taken from the companies' cash flow statements. Operating activities are defined in IAS 7.13-15.

1028 The net income values were taken from the companies' income statements.

1029 The extraordinary items values were taken from the companies' income statements.

1030 The depreciation and amortization values were taken from the companies' statement of fixed assets.

1031 Cf. Givoly/Hayn 2000, p. 292; Ahmed et al. 2002, p. 873; Wang et al. 2009, p. 15.

1032 Cf. Ahmed et al. 2002, p. 873.

since conservatism, as expressed in different depreciation practices,[1033] is accounted for in separate conservatism sub-hypotheses.[1034]

Subtracting operating cash flows, which is net income corrected for accruals like provisions, accounts receivables/payables, inventories etc., from net income, the result equals changes in operating accruals as listed in the cash flow statement; only the sign of the corresponding accrual values is reversed. Consequently, accruals that increase cash flows (e.g. lower accounts receivables) lead to lower accrual values. Having calculated the annual corporate accrual values before depreciation and amortization, these are deflated by total assets and averaged using a three year estimation period ending in 2009.[1035]

Following the two sets of conservatism sub-hypotheses based on indirect conservatism indicators, the next subchapter elaborates on direct conservatism indicators.

2.3.4.1.2 Direct conservatism indicators

The identified accounting areas that, on the one hand, are directly observable in financial statements and, on the other hand, might represent different degrees of conservatism, as defined above, are (1) capitalization of development costs, (2) recognition of intangible assets in a purchase price allocation, (3) asset depreciation and (4) fair value measurement. The following sections dwell on the accounting conservatism relationship in more detail.

2.3.4.1.2.1 Capitalization of development costs

A covert option that has a significant influence on a company's assets is linked to the requirement to capitalize development costs when the criteria in IAS 38.57 are met. As explained above, the vague **capitalization** criteria offer the company broad discretion in deciding on the fulfillment of the criteria, which turns the obligation to capitalize development costs in a factual option. In concordance with the preceding conservatism definition, the decision not to capitalize development costs but to expense these costs is regarded to be characteristic for a more conservative accounting approach. Thus, the third set of conservatism sub-hypotheses is posited as follows.

H_{1c}: Companies from countries that rank higher in terms of uncertainty avoidance are likely to capitalize less development costs.

H_{2c}: Companies from countries that rank higher in terms of individualism are likely to capitalize more development costs.

H_{3c}: Companies from countries that rank higher in terms of masculinity are likely to capitalize more development costs.

H_{4c}: Companies from countries that rank higher in terms of power distance are likely to capitalize less development costs.

The third set of conservatism sub-hypotheses $H_{1\text{-}4c}$ refers to the relationship between culture and capitalized development costs. However, the absolute figure of capitalized devel-

---

[1033] Depreciation practices are analyzed with respect to tangible assets only.

[1034] Cf. chapter 2.3.4.1.2.3.

[1035] Cf. Givoly/Hayn 2000, p. 292; Ahmed et al. 2002, p. 873.

opment costs is not representative for the company's level of conservatism since larger firms naturally spend more on R&D and, thus, capitalize more development costs than smaller firms. Accordingly, the ratio of capitalized development costs divided by total R&D costs is used as an indicator to measure the degree of accounting conservatism in this matter.

The decision to capitalize development costs may also depend on the companies' industry. Development costs of certain industries might be less qualified to fulfill the IFRS criteria catalogue than others, for example, when the admission to the market and therewith the future economic success of an active pharmaceutical ingredient depends on complex uncertain clinical tests and uncertain official approbation procedures. Industries like the pharmaceutical industry could prefer to avoid the extra effort of preparation and documentation of asset capitalization. Other highly competitive high-technology industries might tend not to capitalize development costs for reasons of secrecy. Consequently, both size and industry, among other internal context factors, are controlled for in the test of the hypotheses.

2.3.4.1.2.2 Purchase price allocation

The accounting process of purchase price allocation (**PPA**) in the course of a business combination may also be influenced by conservatism. The 2004 published and 2008 revised IFRS 3 deals with financial reporting of transactions "[...] in which an acquirer obtains control of one or more businesses" (IFRS 3.A). The 2008 revision of IFRS 3 was aimed to promote international accounting convergence[1036] and to improve the existing standard with regard to relevance, reliability and comparability.[1037] The revised standard includes several improvements, such as the obligatory application of the acquisition method or the impairment-only-approach for goodwill. To further promote transparency in business combinations, the recognition of intangible assets was simplified to diminish the share of the goodwill as a residual of the PPA.[1038]

An intangible asset has to be identifiable to be separately recognized, i.e. the asset has either to be separable or based on contractual or legal rights (IAS 38.11/12).[1039] Apart from meeting the definition criteria of being identifiable, an intangible asset also has to meet the concrete recognition criteria in IAS 38.21-24 to be recognized. Thus, IAS 38.21 requires that expected future economic benefits attributable to the asset are probable and its costs can be measured reliably.[1040] As an outcome of the 2008 revision of IFRS 3, the concrete recognition criteria of an intangible asset are assumingly fulfilled when transferred via a business combination (IAS 38.33/35).[1041] Accordingly, the possibilities to recognize intangible assets in a business combination were considerably increased. All the same, the

---

1036 This statement refers to convergence mainly with US-GAAP.
1037 Cf. Watrin/Strohm 2006b, p. 22; Watrin et al. 2009, recital No. 5.
1038 Cf. Arbeitskreis "Immaterielle Werte im Rechnungswesen" der Schmalenbach-Gesellschaft für Betriebswirtschaft e.V. 2009, p. 5.
1039 Cf. Schüle 2006, p. 25; Wulf 2008, p. 31.
1040 Cf. Stolowy et al. 2001, p. 348f.
1041 Cf. Schultze et al. 2008, p. 1350; Braun 2009, p. 49f.

nature and the specific characteristics of intangible assets still entail a certain amount of discretion; companies often can decide whether to recognize an intangible asset or not.

This decision is linked to conservatism. The residual of the PPA, the goodwill, has the potential to defer expenses. Although IFRS require a yearly impairment test, the preconditions for impairments are rather vague and interpretable according to the needs of the company. Also, when testing for impairment at the level of cash generating units (CGU), the loss of purchased goodwill may be compensated by internally created goodwill. A distinction between the two is difficult and companies are likely to take advantage of that discretion when necessary.[1042] The separate recognition of intangibles, however, leads to the amortization of the assets over their useful lifetimes.[1043] Therefore, higher recognition of intangibles results in higher expenses in the income statements in the following years, which, according to the above definition, is an expression of a more conservative accounting approach. Thus, the fourth set of conservatism sub-hypotheses is:

H_{1d}: Companies from countries that rank higher in terms of uncertainty avoidance are likely to recognize more intangible assets in a PPA.

H_{2d}: Companies from countries that rank higher in terms of individualism are likely to recognize less intangible assets in a PPA.

H_{3d}: Companies from countries that rank higher in terms of masculinity are likely to recognize less intangible assets in a PPA.

H_{4d}: Companies from countries that rank higher in terms of power distance are likely to recognize more intangible assets in a PPA.

The absolute figures of **intangibles** recognized in a PPA are not meaningful as the size of the business combination might affect the amount of capitalized intangibles. As a consequence, this study employs the ratio of recognized intangibles[1044] divided by the total assets[1045] of the acquired company. Higher ratios imply higher degrees of conservatism. Again, industry is an important internal context factor that has to be controlled for. Business combinations in R&D intensive industries like software or pharmaceuticals certainly show higher percentages of first-time recognized intangible assets.

2.3.4.1.2.3 Tangible assets depreciation

Depreciation of assets is related to considerations of conservatism not only when deciding whether to depreciate an asset or not.[1046] Companies further have an influence on the amount of yearly depreciation and therewith on the level of expenses, when determining the depreciation method and the useful life of assets. According to IAS 16.60-62, the depreciation method shall resemble "the expected pattern of consumption of the future economic benefits embodied in the asset" (IAS 16.61); IAS 16.62 exemplarily lists the most

---

1042 Cf. Wasserhess 2006, p. 92; Fischer/Schneider 2007, p. 86; Kuhner 2008, p. 21.

1043 This statement is true, if the useful lifetime is not regarded as indefinite.

1044 Recognized intangible assets refer to in the PPA newly recognized intangibles, i.e. fair value adjustments of intangible assets.

1045 Total assets refer to the acquired company's total assets book value.

1046 This is the case, e.g., for intangible assets that are assumed to have an indefinite useful life.

common depreciation methods: the straight-line method, the diminishing balance method and the units of production method.[1047] Whereas the straight-line method assumes constant consumption of future economic benefits, the diminishing balance method as an accelerated depreciation method assumes higher consumption at the beginning of the useful lifetime of an asset. Accelerated depreciation methods are associated with relatively higher depreciation rates in the first years and, according to the above definition, represent the more conservative accounting approach of the two methods. Apart from the method of depreciation, the expected useful life of an asset is another parameter the company can modify to accelerate or defer expenses. Comparably shorter useful lives in this context represent higher levels of conservatism. Based on these remarks on depreciation, the fifth set of conservatism sub-hypotheses is posited as follows.

H_{1e}: Companies from countries that rank higher in terms of uncertainty avoidance are likely to depreciate assets faster.

H_{2e}: Companies from countries that rank higher in terms of individualism are likely to depreciate assets slower.

H_{3e}: Companies from countries that rank higher in terms of masculinity are likely to depreciate assets slower.

H_{4e}: Companies from countries that rank higher in terms of power distance are likely to depreciate assets faster.

This study operationalizes conservatism in asset **depreciation** in two ways. First, the depreciation method is captured via a dummy variable which is one for accelerated depreciation and zero for straight-line depreciation. Second, the average useful life per asset group is calculated as a conservatism indicator, shorter average useful lives expressing higher degrees of conservatism. The average useful life of an asset group is calculated by historical costs at the beginning of the year divided by annual depreciation[1048].

This ratio is subject to certain limitations. The calculated useful life figures of an asset group are likely to differ from the real values since annual depreciation figures as published in the statement of fixed assets might be affected by:

- asset impairments that are not reported separately,
- the application of the diminishing balance method or
- asset acquisitions during the year.

In the above cases annual asset depreciation would differ from scheduled straight-line depreciation and lead to biased calculated useful life figures. These effects, however, have to be accepted for reasons of practicability since (1) some companies do not distinguish be-

[1047] The straight-line and the diminishing balance methods are the most common depreciation methods. The units of production method is not examined with respect to conservative accounting as the depreciation does not depend on the management's decision but on the output of the company.

[1048] Annual depreciation figures exclude asset impairments when reported separately; see discussion below.

tween scheduled and non scheduled depreciation[1049] and (2) financial statements usually contain no information when an asset was acquired and operational. The few companies that apply the diminishing balance method are excluded from the tested sample.

The biasing effect of newly acquired assets is accepted in this study mainly for two reasons. First, assets are often capitalized in the last quarter of the year and the *pro rata* yearly depreciation is generally low.[1050] This disproportionate last quarter capitalization is mainly related to budget considerations and year-end start-of-operations-notifications. Second, taking historical costs at the end of the year and, thus, including asset acquisition would also lead to biased useful life figures since first-time depreciation usually deviates from the beginning of the financial year. Moreover, depreciation ratios might also be biased by historical costs values that include fully depreciated assets that have not been disposed yet.

To control for bias that results from the above outlined limitations in calculating PPE useful life figures from the statement of fixed assets, these figures are complemented by a second set of depreciation indicators. These indicators are calculated based on the lowest and highest useful life values per asset group that are reported in the 'accounting policies' section in the notes of the financial statements. Again, the average useful life values published in the notes are only an approximation to the real values. Depending on the particular PPE age structure of the company, the real values might differ from the 'official' average values.

Also, depreciation periods might be affected by tax accounting depreciation periods, which are often guided by economic and fiscal policies designed to provide incentives for corporate investments. Although tax accounting is expected to have little influence on the financial statements of large listed companies, which usually have two types of accounts, tax depreciation periods might flow through to the commercial accounts, especially in countries that are characterized by the authoritative principle (France, Germany).[1051] Accordingly, the influence of the tax system is controlled for by a dummy variable that distinguishes between countries that apply the authoritative principle and countries that do not apply the authoritative principle.

The average useful life indicators are only calculated for groups of PPE. Intangible assets regularly consist to a large extent of goodwill, which is not amortized but (at least) yearly tested for impairment. The remaining intangibles are usually of minor importance in relation to total assets. Additionally, intangible assets are often too specific to be compared on an intercompany basis and some companies fail to report intangibles with an indefinite useful life separately; calculated average useful life figures would, thus, be biased.

In analogy to the previously presented conservatism indicators, industry is controlled for (among other internal context factors) since industry specific depreciation practice is likely to have a biasing effect.

[1049] In case impairments are not reported separately, it is difficult to determine whether there are no impairments or whether impairments are included in the annual depreciation figures and bias the useful life indicators.

[1050] Cf. Sivitanides et al. 2001, p. 32.

[1051] For a discussion of the context factor tax system cf. chapter 2.3.2.1.3.

2.3.4.1.2.4 Fair value measurement

A common overt option that reflects the level of conservatism is the **fair value** measurement option. Fair value measurement is certainly one of the most controversially discussed concepts of IFRS.[1052] The FREP identified accounting complexity as one of the main causes of IFRS accounting errors and fair value measurement as one of the main drivers of IFRS accounting complexity; 70% of the 2008 respectively 61% of the 2009 accounting errors determined by the FREP are related to fair value issues.[1053] Accordingly, this overt option lends itself particularly well for fruitful empirical analysis.

The fair value measurement option is part of various IFRS standards. After initial recognition, companies may choose between the cost and the revaluation model for **PPE** and **intangibles** (IAS 16.29; IAS 38.72). According to IAS 39.45, **financial assets** are classified into four categories (IAS 39.09) of which some (e.g. financial assets at fair value through profit and loss) require fair value measurement. Companies possess discretion in classifying financial assets; for instance, companies may designate hybrid contracts that contain one or more embedded derivatives as financial assets (liabilities) at fair value through profit and loss (IAS 39.11A). Furthermore, according to IAS 40.30, companies may choose between the cost and the fair value model for **investment property**. Another factual option for fair value measurement is formulated in IAS 40.12. A **biological asset**, which shall be measured at its fair value, may be measured at cost, if the fair value of the asset cannot be measured reliably (IAS 40.12; IAS 40.30).

An asset's fair value is based on an arm's length transaction between knowledgeable willing parties (IAS 38.08). This definition ideally refers to the asset's **market value**. If the criteria of an active market (IAS 38.08) are not met, the company may fall back to comparable transactions at an active market; if there are neither active markets nor comparable transactions, the fair value is determined using a generally acknowledged evaluation method like the discounted cash flow method (IAS 39.48A).[1054] As active markets seldom exist for assets like, e.g., intangibles, companies regularly apply measurement methods that typically offer plenty of discretion with respect to the utilized parameters.[1055]

Fair value measurement is associated with both advantages and disadvantages. The use of the fair value method offers the opportunity to realize an asset's hidden reserves and to report the asset at a value that exceeds its historical costs. The fair value concept therewith is in line with the overall IFRS principle of 'fair presentation'.[1056] Nonetheless, the concept may lead to increased volatility in the company's balance sheet and income statement when the asset's value is linked to a volatile market. Also, the use of non-standardized

---

[1052] The IFRS regulations on fair value measurement are currently revised by the IASB. In May 2009 the IASB published an exposure draft on fair value measurement for public comment; cf. International Accounting Standards Board [IASB] 2009a. In June 2010 the IASB published further enhancements to a disclosure proposal on Level 3 fair value measurements; cf. International Accounting Standards Board [IASB] 2010a.

[1053] Cf. Meyer 2010, p. 18ff.

[1054] Cf. Baetge 2009, p. 15.

[1055] Cf. Bieg et al. 2008, p. 2549; Obermaier 2009, p. 547.

[1056] Cf. Küting 2009, p. 829.

measurement methods makes asset valuation susceptible to earnings increasing manipulation. Therefore, the fair value concept is regarded as the less conservative measurement practice.

In this study, **investment property** is the only asset class to be tested with respect to fair value application. Other studies on fair value application have shown that this option is rarely applied for PPE or intangibles.[1057] The fair value method is not tested for financial assets since financial asset measurement decisions are less unambiguous and inter-company comparability is assumed to be limited. This study analyzes the application of the companies' fair value measurement in order to conclude on the level of conservatism. The complex four category system of IAS 39, which allows for voluntary designation of certain financial assets and liabilities to be measured at their fair value (fair value option), assumingly allows for no consistent evidence on the companies' degree of conservatism.

Following the above argumentation on the association between conservatism and the use of fair value measurement, the set of conservatism sub-hypotheses is posited as follows:

H_{1f}: Companies from countries that rank higher in terms of uncertainty avoidance are less likely to choose fair value measurement for investment property.

H_{2f}: Companies from countries that rank higher in terms of individualism are more likely to choose fair value measurement for investment property.

H_{3f}: Companies from countries that rank higher in terms of masculinity are more likely to choose fair value measurement for investment property.

H_{4f}: Companies from countries that rank higher in terms of power distance are less likely to choose fair value measurement for investment property.

Among the internal context factors that assumingly have an influence on fair value measurement, especially industry is to be highlighted; previous research indicates that the fair value method for investment property is rather common in the real estate industry.[1058] As outlined above, other internal context factors like size or profitability may have an effect on fair value accounting and the degree of conservatism, as well, and are controlled for.

The Fair Value hypotheses $H_{1\text{-}4f}$ are operationalized by means of a dummy variable that is one when the company uses the fair value method to measure investment property and zero otherwise. This information is extracted directly from the financial statements' notes.

The posited sub-hypotheses so far only affected the accounting value of conservatism. The next section is designated to the development and operationalization of sub-hypotheses related to the accounting value of **secrecy**.

2.3.4.2 Development of the secrecy sub-hypotheses

Gray defines the accounting value of secrecy as "a preference for confidentiality and the restriction of disclosure of information about the business"[1059]. From this definition fol-

[1057] Cf. von Keitz 2005; Küting et al. 2007; Christensen/Nikolaev 2010.
[1058] Cf. Bachert/Kajüter 2010.
[1059] Gray 1988, p. 8.

lows that companies from countries that rank higher in terms of secrecy tend to disclose less financial information to outsiders of the company. *Gray* explicitly refers to the quantity, i.e. the scope and detail of information.[1060] The quality respectively value relevance of information is not directly addressed, although the quality of disclosure may be related to the quantity of disclosure. The quantity of information is not only measured by pages, sentences or words but in particular in content. An analysis of the content of a piece of financial information concentrates, besides the sheer length of the text, especially on the different parts of information that are requested by a standard or disclosed voluntarily.[1061] Thus, a short text, that contains all requested information, scores higher in terms of information quantity and lower in terms of secrecy than a longer text that contains mainly voluntary irrelevant information.

Apart from the financial figures in the balance sheet, the income statement, the statement of changes in equity and the statement of cash flows, investors and other users of financial statements receive corporate financial information basically from the management report and the notes. This study focuses on disclosure in the **notes**. The management report respectively management commentary has yet not been institutionalized in a standard by the IASB.[1062] Therefore, companies usually report management information like corporate objectives, strategies, prospects or risks according to national management reporting requirements, which differ internationally.[1063] Also, management reporting regulations are often less precise and detailed than IFRS standards that require additional information in the notes. This makes management reports less comparable on an international level. The notes, however, are part of the financial statements and obligatory for all companies that prepare these in accordance with IFRS. Furthermore, the analysis of notes disclosure is of high practical relevance; as outlined in the 2005-2009 enforcement report of the FREP, accounting errors related to notes disclosure are among the top three types of error.[1064]

Analogous to the above posited conservatism sub-hypotheses, the secrecy sub-hypotheses employ both indirect and direct secrecy indicators which are described in the following two chapters.

2.3.4.2.1 Indirect secrecy indicators

As the notes make up the largest part of the financial statements, it is difficult to analyze the entire notes in detail. Thus, the analysis and comparison of corporate disclosure practice is split in two separate parts. First, the overall quantity of notes information is determined at a more global level for the company sample investigated in this study. Second,

---

[1060] Cf. Gray 1988, p. 11.

[1061] In the following, disclosure or content quality refers to the quantity of decision-useful information. Disclosure quality in the sense of true information that appropriately represents the economic reality of the company is not covered by that definition.

[1062] Cf. Kajüter et al. 2010, p. 184. In December 2010 the IASB published the IFRS Practice Statement on Management Commentary, a broad framework that provides guidance for corporate management commentary. Nonetheless, the Practice Statement has not the status of an IFRS and compliance is not required; cf. International Accounting Standards Board [IASB] 2010c.

[1063] Cf. Dietsche/Fink 2008, p. 261; Buchheim 2009, p. 1685; Kajüter/Guttmeier 2009, p. 2333.

[1064] Cf. Meyer 2010, p. 17.

selected notes subareas are analyzed in more detail to determine the content quantity of the disclosed information. Whereas the indirect secrecy indicator measures general information quantity, i.e. pages, sentences or words without considering the content of the information, the direct secrecy indicators measure content quantity, i.e. information parts that have a specific meaning like revenues or R&D costs, for instance.

Integrating the above posited relationships between *Hofstede's* cultural values and the accounting value of secrecy, the first secrecy sub-hypotheses related to notes general information quantity are stated as follows:

H_{5a}: Companies from countries that rank higher in terms of uncertainty avoidance are likely to disclose less information in the notes.

H_{6a}: Companies from countries that rank higher in terms of individualism are likely to disclose more information in the notes.

H_{7a}: Companies from countries that rank higher in terms of masculinity are likely to disclose more information in the notes.

H_{8a}: Companies from countries that rank higher in terms of power distance are likely to disclose less information in the notes.

Disregarding the company specific content of the notes, the **number of words** contained in the notes is used as an indicator for information quantity.[1065] To avoid bias that results from different languages, the English version of the notes is consulted for word count.

The number of words is determined electronically by (1) copying the notes content into a WORD document and using the word count function in WORD and (2) using an add-on program for the Adobe Acrobat Reader to count words directly in the PDF document. The count results of the PDF tool differ by 2-4% from the lower results of WORD count. These differences, however, are systematic and apply for all companies of the sample; thus, the relative differences remain constant independent from the method of counting.

The count results employed in the statistical analysis originate from the PDF word count; the word count in WORD missed some company results as the PDF content could not be extracted to WORD. The notes word count included the entire notes section of the group accounts. The auditor's statement typically marked the endpoint of the analysis; it was not included in the word count. Also, some companies described their accounting procedures just before the 'official' notes' section. As such information pertains to the notes, this information was considered in the word count, too.

As mentioned above, high information quantity does not necessarily imply high content quantity. The following section therefore elaborates content specific secrecy indicators.

[1065] Words are the smallest meaningful unit of measurement and word count is more precise than counting pages or sentences; cf. Wilmshurst/Frost 2000, p. 7; Krippendorff 2004, p. 100. Word count is assumed to provide maximum robustness in determining the quantity of disclosure; cf. Zeghal/Ahmed 1990, p. 42.

2.3.4.2.2 Direct secrecy indicators

The notes subareas that are analyzed in more detail with respect to content specific information are selected mainly based on two reasons. First, to guarantee a sufficiently large sample, the notes subarea should be **relevant for all companies** of the three country samples, i.e. all companies should be principally obliged to report information on that topic. For instance, past studies have demonstrated that the disclosure of M&A activities varies strongly from company to company.[1066] A 2005 investigation of *Glaum* in cooperation with PricewaterhouseCoopers shows significant deficiencies with respect to M&A disclosure.[1067] At the same time, this accounting area is of major relevance for investors and financial analysts. Nonetheless, not every company had a business combination in 2009. Although the country samples consist of large listed companies only, 2009 M&A activities were influenced by the worldwide economic crisis and only half of the analyzed companies had a business combination to report. Especially the French company sample is characterized by few business combinations; only 38 French companies report one or more business combinations in 2009.[1068] A French disclosure sample of only 43% of the original country sample would limit the statistical power of the hypotheses test results. Accordingly, disclosure on business combination, although potentially interesting, is not selected for a more detailed content analysis.

Second, the analyzed notes subareas should be of **practical relevance**; prior research or regulators' evidence should indicate that the notes sections to be analyzed prove to be problematic, i.e. susceptible to differences in accounting application. And third, the selected notes subarea should be related to information the company perceives as potentially **sensitive**; the degree of secrecy is assumed to be higher for sensitive information.

The notes sections selected for further analysis, which fulfill the above defined criteria of reporting requirement and practical relevance,[1069] are (1) segment reporting and (2) income tax reporting.

2.3.4.2.2.1 Segment reporting

According to IFRS 8.2, all capital market oriented companies have to disclose segment information in their individual and group accounts; i.e. all sample companies are required to extend their notes with a section on segment reporting. As the result of the short-term convergence project of the IASB and the FASB, IFRS 8 was issued in 2006 and replaced IAS 14, which, until then, regulated IFRS segment reporting; companies that publish their financial statements in accordance with IFRS are required to apply IFRS 8 for financial years starting on or after January 1st of 2009 (IFRS 8 IN9).[1070] By issuing IFRS 8, the IASB widely adopted US-GAAP segment reporting rules, codified in SFAS 131, and the-

---

[1066] Cf., e.g., Lee 1974, p. 1ff.; Aisbitt 2003, p. 4ff.; Shalev 2009, p. 239ff.; Ballas/Tzovas 2010, p. 40ff.

[1067] Cf. Glaum et al. 2007.

[1068] 49 German companies report one or more business combinations; 48 British companies report one or more business combinations.

[1069] Previous studies identified deficiencies with respect to notes disclosure on corporate segments and income taxes; cf. Loitz/Weber 2008, p. 2149ff.; Meyer 2010, p. 153ff.

[1070] Cf. Kajüter/Barth 2007, p. 428ff.

rewith replaced the 'risk and reward approach' of IAS 14 by the 'management approach' of SFAS 131.[1071] Following the 'management approach', companies shall present segment information "through the eyes of management" (IFRS 8.BC6). Segment information shall be based on internal reporting structures to provide financial statement users with unaltered internal management accounting data.[1072]

As companies are required to publish possibly sensitive management accounting data, which, e.g., competitors might be interested in, the subarea of segment reporting is supposed to be well suited to analyze secretive accounting behavior. Furthermore, the requirements of IFRS 8 offer scope for discretion management might use for earnings management purposes.[1073] Especially with respect to disclosure requirements, IFRS 8 contains only few mandatory requirements; in accordance with the 'management approach' and to relieve companies from extra disclosure effort, most of the reportable segment information is only to be published, when the company regularly reports that information to the chief operating decision maker (CODM) (IFRS 8.23/24).[1074] Consequently, companies might abuse this regulation and, for instance, modify internal reporting structures to be not obliged to publish certain pieces of information.

Besides the above outlined potential for differences in accounting practice, an analysis of 2009 segment reporting practice might reveal some interesting insights from an accounting research perspective; 2009 is the first year of obligatory IFRS 8 application.[1075] Moreover, segment reporting content analysis is of high practical relevance since the German enforcement institution FREP put segment reporting into the focus of FREP audits in 2010.[1076] Besides accounting issues like the designation and definition of segments or reconciliations of segment figures, especially the completeness of the segment information was analyzed by the FREP in past audits.[1077]

Also, empirical results on segment reporting quantity are of interest to financial statement users. Analysts and investors benefit from the increased quantity of information and the higher reliability of 'management approach' based segment information.[1078] The high decision usefulness of segment reporting emphasizes the importance and practical relevance of the notes subsection on segment reporting.

Based on the above argumentation, the quantity of segment information in the notes is analyzed with respect to an association with the *Hofstede* cultural dimensions; in analogy to the above depicted *Hofstede-Gray* framework, the relationships between cultural dimen-

[1071] Cf. Fink/Ulbrich 2006, p. 233f.; Kirsch 2007, p. 61.
[1072] Cf. Grottke/Krammer 2008, p. 671.
[1073] Cf. Rogler 2009a, p. 500ff.; Rogler 2009b, p. 576ff.
[1074] Cf. Kajüter/Barth 2007, p. 432.
[1075] As some of the analyzed financial statements belong to the annual period 2008/2009 some companies were permitted to report segment information in accordance with IAS 14. Nonetheless, most of these companies made use of the right of early adoption of IFRS 8. Two segment reports in accordance with IAS 14 were excluded from the content analysis.
[1076] Cf. Meyer 2010, p. 158.
[1077] Cf. Meyer 2010, p. 153ff.
[1078] Cf. Kajüter/Barth 2007, p. 432f.

sions and the accounting value of secrecy as measured by segment information quantity in the notes are hypothesized as follows:

H_{5b}: Companies from countries that rank higher in terms of uncertainty avoidance are likely to disclose less segment information in the notes.

H_{6b}: Companies from countries that rank higher in terms of individualism are likely to disclose more segment information in the notes.

H_{7b}: Companies from countries that rank higher in terms of masculinity are likely to disclose more segment information in the notes.

H_{8b}: Companies from countries that rank higher in terms of power distance are likely to disclose less segment information in the notes.

To operationalize the segment information hypotheses, a disclosure index[1079] is built on the disclosure requirements as defined in IFRS 8.20-24. Additionally, a second segment reporting disclosure index also captures voluntary information that is not required respectively recommended by the standard.[1080] The following section presents the second direct secrecy indicator.

2.3.4.2.2.2 Income tax reporting

Another accounting area the FREP identified as problematic with respect to IFRS compliance is deferred taxes; in the 2005-2009 ranking of the most frequent accounting errors determined in a FREP audit, accounting errors related to deferred taxes are in the fourth place, in front of accounting issues like financial instruments, cash flow statements or consolidation.[1081]

Income tax information may contain possibly sensitive information the company could prefer to hide from financial statements users. Similar to segment information, income tax information in the notes may be partly based on internal management accounting data. For instance, unused tax losses may be capitalized only "[...] to the extent that it is probable that future taxable profit will be available against which the unused tax losses and unused tax credits can be utilized" (IAS 12.34). The probability of future taxable profits is determined by means of internal budget figures. Competitors or the fiscal authorities might be interested in information on the company's unused tax losses, which allow for conclusions on the company's internal earnings forecasts. The fiscal authorities might also have an interest in information on foreign taxes, which possibly allow for conclusions on foreign profits and transfer prices. Following the above argumentation, companies that come from a more secretive cultural environment might tend to disclose as little information on income taxes as possible. As a consequence, income tax reporting is assumed to be suited to observe secretive accounting practice.

Furthermore, income tax reporting is selected for analysis to have a sufficiently large company sample; all sample companies have to report income tax information in accordance

---

1079 Cf. chapter 3.3.3.

1080 The development of the segment reporting disclosure index is further substantiated in chapter 3.3.3.3.

1081 Cf. Meyer 2010, p. 17.

with IAS 12.[1082] Furthermore, the standard requires comprehensive disclosures on current and deferred income taxes in the notes (IAS 12.79ff.). The relatively wide spectrum of different tax information allows for country respectively company patterns to develop.

Analogous to the previous segment reporting sub-hypotheses, the secrecy sub-hypotheses on income tax reporting are posited as follows:

H_{5c}: Companies from countries that rank higher in terms of uncertainty avoidance are likely to disclose less income tax information in the notes.

H_{6c}: Companies from countries that rank higher in terms of individualism are likely to disclose more income tax information in the notes.

H_{7c}: Companies from countries that rank higher in terms of masculinity are likely to disclose more income tax information in the notes.

H_{8c}: Companies from countries that rank higher in terms of power distance are likely to disclose less income tax information in the notes.

To operationalize the income tax information hypotheses, a disclosure index[1083] is built on the disclosure requirements as defined in IAS 12.79-88. In analogy to the segment reporting disclosure index, a second income tax reporting disclosure index also captures voluntary information that is not required by the standard.[1084]

Having developed and operationalized the various conservatism and secrecy sub-hypotheses, the next chapter summarizes chapter two.

2.4 Summary

Chapter two presents the theoretical perspectives of this study. Introductory, (general) **systems theory** is discussed; systems theory and the concept of organizations as open systems that stand in manifold relationships with the environment inspired organizational theory and found its way into other theoretical concepts like contingency theory or the societal effects approach.

The meta-concept of **contingency theory** assumes that the organization as a system and organizational subsystems are the result of the external and internal contingencies the organization is confronted with. The situational approach of contingency theory serves as a basic conceptual framework to theoretically capture the research question of this study, i.e. if and how national culture is associated with IFRS practice. The contingency theoretical approach applied in this study is characterized as (1) context open, (2) personalistic, (3) multi causal and (4) point in time oriented. Accordingly, organizations are assumed to be affected by various context factors in an open context they adapt to by choosing among different, possibly equivalent, situational options considering elements of subjectivity.

[1082] IAS 12 is to be applied for annual periods starting on or after January 1st of 1998; cf. IAS 12.89.

[1083] Cf. chapter 3.3.3.

[1084] The development of the income tax reporting disclosure index in further substantiated in chapter 3.3.3.3.

The conceptual framework based on contingency theory is further substantiated by additional material theories like the **societal effects approach**. The societal effects approach is less deterministic compared to the typical contingency theoretical approach and explicitly recognizes the influence of national institutions like the legal or financing system; the organization, an institutions itself, reflects the institutional parameters of its environment. According to the societal effects approach, national culture is only implicitly accounted for as manifested in societal institutions. As a consequence, the societal effects approach is complemented by integrating **culture theory** by *Hofstede* into the conceptual framework of the study. *Hofstede* determines four cultural dimensions to explain culture related country differences. The cultural dimension of (1) **power distance** describes the extent to which different cultures accept inequalities in power and status. The culture individual perception of insecurity associated with the unknown is expressed by the cultural dimension of (2) **uncertainty avoidance**. The cultural dimension of (3) **individualism** vs. collectivism distinguishes between 'I' and 'we' consciousness cultures. The cultural predominance of masculine values like toughness or feminine values like tenderness marks the poles of the (4) **masculinity** vs. femininity dimension.

The cultural dimensions by *Hofstede* are linked to accounting by the accounting dimensions of *Gray*. The **accounting values** specifically associated with accounting practice are conservatism vs. optimism and secrecy vs. transparency. Both accounting values represent a cautious accounting approach. Whereas **conservatism** relates to cautious, i.e. prudent, measurement practice, **secrecy** relates to cautious, i.e. restrictive, disclosure practice. *Gray* expects uncertainty avoidance to be positively associated with conservatism and secrecy. The cultural dimensions of individualism and masculinity, however, he posits to be negatively associated with both accounting values; accordingly, companies from highly individualistic respectively masculine countries tend to be less conservative and secretive. *Gray* expects power distance to be positively associated with the accounting value of secrecy only. Nonetheless, in analogy with empirical results of prior studies, this study expects power distance to also have a positive effect on conservatism.

The societal effects approach and the *Hofstede-Gray* framework complement the contingency theoretical framework of this study with respect to the cultural and institutional external context factors. The theoretical foundation of the internal context factors, on the other hand, is mainly derived from institutional economics and PAT. **Institutional economics** introduces concepts like information asymmetries, individual opportunism and contracts to reduce the costs that result from opportunistic behavior. The institutional economics sub-discipline **agency theory** describes contracting processes in the relationship between principal and agent, which is characterized by the delegation of decision making power to the agent and information asymmetries. The principal agent relationship leads to the information problems of adverse selection and moral hazard; principal and agent face these agency problems by means of *ex ante* (principal: screening; agent: signaling) respectively *ex post* (principal: monitoring; agent: reporting) information strategies to lower information strategies. Information strategies like signaling are applied by companies, for instance, when employing a Big4 auditor to signal the capital market a high degree of compliance. Furthermore, the concept of agency costs theoretically explains the association between larger and more internationally oriented companies and secrecy.

Companies seek to reduce agency costs, which depend on the degree of complexity of contractual relationships between principal and agent, by increased disclosure. According to **PAT** by *Watts/Zimmerman*, highly leveraged companies apply optimistic accounting measures to avoid debt covenant violations. Furthermore, *Watts/Zimmerman* suggest in their political costs hypothesis that larger companies are likely to apply more conservative accounting measures to avoid public attention and reduce political costs that, e.g., result from higher regulation.

The **conceptual framework** of this study is based on the foundation of contingency theory and built on the theoretical pillars of the societal effects approach, culture theory by *Hofstede*, agency theory and PAT. The conceptual framework is supplemented by concrete external and internal **context factors** to control for accounting influences other than culture. The external context factors supposed to be most influential are the financing system, legal system, tax system, enforcement system and national GAAP. The internal context factors controlled for are company size, industrial sector, type of auditor, internationality, profitability and leverage.

Based on the theoretically founded conceptual framework, the **hypotheses** on the cultural influence on the accounting values of conservatism and secrecy are developed. The conservatism and secrecy base hypotheses are posited in accordance with the *Hofstede-Gray* framework and further developed in accounting value specific sub-hypotheses. Conservatism is investigated by means of the indirect conservatism indicators (1) market to book value and (2) negative accruals value; direct conservatism indicators are (3) capitalization of development costs, (4) capitalization of intangibles in a PPA, (5) depreciation of tangible assets and (6) investment property fair value measurement. The degree of secrecy is determined via (1) total notes disclosure, (2) segment and (3) income tax information quantity.

3 Research design

3.1 Overview

The chapter on research design is split in three separate sections on:

- empirical research strategies,
- methods of data collection and
- methods of data evaluation.

The first subchapter presents different empirical research strategies like the case study, the field study or the experiment. The second subchapter links the specific research strategy of this study with the applied method of data collection. This study collects data by means of content analysis; the content analytical instrument disclosure index is applied to quantify notes information on operating segments and income tax. The third subchapter deals with the statistical evaluation of the collected data. Following some statistical basic information on significance levels, outliers etc., the statistical procedures of descriptive and inferential statistics are presented. Apart from univariate statistical tests like the T-Test or the Analysis of Variance (ANOVA), this study applies correlation and regression analysis to investigate the statistical association between internal and external context factors and accounting practice.

3.2 Empirical research strategy

As outlined in chapter one, this study follows an empirical research approach. Theoretically rationalized hypotheses are tested empirically to confirm respectively falsify the posited relationships. The quality of the hypotheses test results depends essentially on the research design, which is developed in consideration of the research question of the study. Before selecting the appropriate method of data collection, the researcher has to decide on the general research strategy of the study; empirical data may be generated via different scientific strategies like the case study, the field study or the experiment.[1085] These are briefly described in the following; subsequently, the research strategy of this study is defined.

Case studies belong to the branch of qualitative empirical research; the scientific case study is a conceptually open and flexible research approach, which is defined as "[...] an empirical inquiry that investigates a contemporary phenomenon within its real-life context, especially when the boundaries between phenomenon and context are not clearly evident"[1086]. Case studies in the social sciences are usually guided by a previously developed theoretical framework and may be complemented by quantitative data collection; the focus of a case study may be explorative, descriptive and/or explanative.[1087] Case studies are often employed in comparatively new and complex research areas to get a first impression, to identify the fundamentals, to abstract and to trace back the new to the

1085 Cf. Kubicek 1975, p. 35ff.
1086 Yin 2009, p. 13.
1087 Cf. Borchardt/Göthlich 2009, p. 34f.

known.[1088] In contrast to large scale quantitative studies, case studies offer the advantage of a more comprehensive and detailed description of reality; however, case study data usually does not allow for a statistical conclusion on the population.[1089]

Field studies refer to large scale empirical investigations of real-life situations.[1090] In contrast to case studies, field studies are less detailed but analyze more cases and therefore allow for more generalized statements.[1091] The large number of cases implies that field studies generally follow a quantitative research approach; quantitative data is easier to process and evaluate statistically.[1092] Large sale empirical field studies are closely connected to the above presented research program of critical rationalism; the theoretically deducted hypotheses are confronted with reality by testing them empirically on a sufficiently large number of cases.[1093] However, the complexity of reality and the impossibility to control for all other influence variables limit the explanatory potential of field studies with respect to cause-and-effect relations.

The **experiment** is expected to be the most stringent form of hypotheses testing.[1094] Experiments analyze prior hypothesized associations in a highly controlled (social) environment. The test subjects respectively test objects are placed in specifically designed and permanently controlled[1095] situations; modifying particular independent variables while controlling for all other relevant variables, experimental research designs may reveal cause-and-effect relations.[1096] Experiments may be further distinguished into field and laboratory experiments. Whereas field experiments are assumed to lead to higher external validity since the test person/object is investigated in its 'natural' environment, laboratory experiments are generally characterized by higher internal validity since laboratory conditions allow for a better control of confounding variables.[1097]

As outlined above, this study is to be seen in the tradition of critical rationalism. Accordingly, the field study approach is preferred to the case study approach; a large scale quantitative field study allows for a generalization of results and, thus, the confirmation respectively denial of the posited hypotheses. The explorative investigation of the comparably mature research area of international comparative financial accounting is not deemed necessary. The review of relevant prior research revealed that the experimental research design is quite common for IFRS related culture studies. Nonetheless, this study seeks to analyze actual corporate IFRS practice under real-life conditions; a laboratory experiment would cast doubt on the external validity of the empirical data and, thus, on its transferability to business reality. Furthermore, it promises to be interesting, if the experimental

---

1088 Cf. Stickel-Wolf/Wolf 2005, p. 189f.
1089 Cf. Borchardt/Göthlich 2009, p. 36.
1090 Cf. Kajüter 2000, p. 65.
1091 Cf. Kubicek 1975, p. 63.
1092 Cf. Riesenhuber 2009, p. 7.
1093 Cf. Riesenhuber 2009, p. 1ff.
1094 Cf. Atteslander 2008, p. 166.
1095 The conditions of the experiment are controlled for by means of control techniques like elimination, stabilization, matching or randomization; cf. Schnell et al. 2005, p. 224.
1096 Cf. Atteslander 2008, p. 166.
1097 Cf. Schnell et al. 2005, p. 225f.

research results are confirmed by a field study. Based on the previous consideration, this study follows a **field study** approach to analyze the association between national culture and IFRS accounting practice.

Following the preferred empirical research strategy of the field study, the research design is further developed by determining the concrete method of data collection (see Figure 3-1).

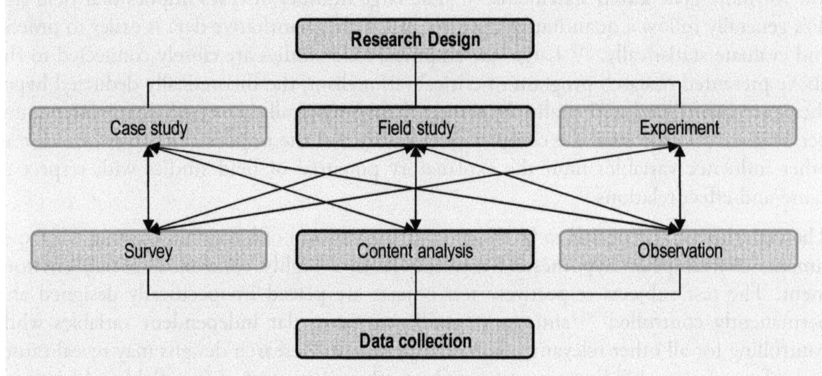

Figure 3-1: Research design and data collection[1098]

The next subchapter elaborates on the most basic methods of data collection: survey, content analysis and observation.[1099]

3.3 Data collection

3.3.1 Methods of data collection

Every empirical research project is based on data that provides information on the research subject/object; data collection in this context refers to the systematic and targeted gathering of that information.[1100] Three basic methods of collecting data are presented in the following to select the method that is assumed to be most appropriate with respect to the research question of this study.

The **survey** is the most popular method of collecting data in the social sciences;[1101] survey participants are confronted with certain verbal, written or other stimuli to receive their personal statements with respect to the analyzed research object.[1102] Types of surveys may be distinguished into verbal, written and online surveys. Whereas verbal surveys usually refer to the personal or telephone interview, written surveys are conducted via standardized questionnaires; participants in online surveys, which became rather popular in the

1098 Adopted from Esser 2010, p. 151.
1099 Cf. Schnell et al. 2005, p. 319.
1100 Cf. Hammann/Erichson 2000, p. 81.
1101 Cf. Diekmann 2007, p. 371.
1102 Cf. Böhler 2004, p. 85.

last years,[1103] fill out online questionnaires.[1104] The latter instrument has the advantage that the data are gathered electronically and, thus, are directly analyzable. Surveys offer the advantage of great flexibility; the questions in interviews or questionnaires may be designed according to researcher's information needs; furthermore, the gathered data is unique and difficult to replicate. However, survey data could be biased by the person of the interviewer and/or misleading question design.[1105]

Content analysis is an empirical method of collecting data to measure the communication content of texts and other communication media like photos, movies or paintings.[1106] In financial accounting research, content analysis usually refers to the analysis of financial statements, proceedings of meetings, business letters, company directives, ad-hoc disclosures, newspaper articles etc. In contrast to the above described research method of the survey, content analysis is non reactive and therewith not susceptible to bias associated with the type of analysis (e.g. interviewer).[1107] However, content analytical data is not necessarily more objective than survey data; as outlined in more detail in the following subchapters, the information content of documents is generally measured by means of information categories respectively category systems; these categories are developed by the researcher and therewith vulnerable to subjectivity and error.[1108]

Generally speaking, all empirical methods of data collecting are based on **observation**, defined as the visual, acoustic or haptic sensation of events.[1109] Accordingly, the results of a telephone interview or the categorization of financial statement information, for example, are also determined by observation. Uncoupled from the mere sensation of events, scientific observation specifically refers to the planned and systematic, research problem oriented recording, control and interpretation of visual/acoustic data.[1110] In analogy to content analysis, the researcher has to develop an observation system to be able to select, classify and encode observations.[1111] Correspondingly, the development of category respectively rating systems that are designed to capture excerpts of reality implies a certain degree of subjectivity.

Although observation is the most direct form of collecting data, this method is not applied in this study. First, the high degree of subjectivity is likely to have a biasing effect on the empirical data. Second, it would prove difficult to observe accounting practice in a sufficiently large number of companies. Furthermore, the final product of the corporate financial accounting process, the financial statements, is published by the companies and therewith made available to the researcher. Although financial statements do not mirror the entire financial accounting decision process, a lot of accounting choices are directly evaluable by the researcher. Information on IFRS practice might also be collected by means of

---

1103 Cf. Batanic et al. 2002, p. 7.
1104 Cf. Kaya 2009, p. 51.
1105 Cf. Kaya 2009, p. 52ff.
1106 Cf. Atteslander 2008, p. 179.
1107 Cf. Schnell et al. 2005, p. 407f.
1108 Cf. Atteslander 2008, p. 189ff.
1109 Cf. Diekmann 2007, p. 456.
1110 Cf. Bortz/Döring 2006, p. 240; Atteslander 2008, p. 67.
1111 Cf. Cranach/Frenz 1969, p. 393.

a survey. Nonetheless, the results of that survey could be biased by the interviewer or the questionnaire design and, thus, differ from real-life IFRS practice. Considering the research question of this study, i.e. the analysis of actual IFRS practice, the method of **content analysis** of financial statements is assumed to provide the most realistic and least biased empirical data on corporate accounting practice. Content analysis in general and content analytical instruments are presented and discussed in the following sections.

3.3.2 Content analytical foundation

> *"Content analysis is a research technique for the objective, systematic, and quantitative description of the manifest content of communication."*[1112]

The above definition of content analysis identifies objectivity, systematization and quantification as basic distinguishing characteristics of content analysis. A content analysis has to be based on explicitly formulated precise rules and procedures to guarantee results that are independent from the respective analyst (objectivity). The rules of analysis have to be applied consistently and be relevant to the scientific problem (systematization). The criterion of quantification distinguishes content analysis from mere critical reading. The analyst's judgments are quantified and therewith measurable.[1113] In contrast to quantitative content analysis, in qualitative content analysis text parts are not counted but interpreted.[1114] As this study employs a **quantitative content analysis**, the following annotations focus on this instrument only.

Content analysis is based on the inter-personal communication model in which a sender transmits information to a receptor. The sender codes the information in form of a message which is then decoded by the receiver.[1115] The processes of codification and decodification are influenced by the situation and the contingencies of the situation of sender and receptor (see Figure 3-2).[1116] Transferred to the context of this study, the organization is the sender, which codes financial information in form of the corporate financial statements to transmit it to shareholders, analysts and other receptors of that information.

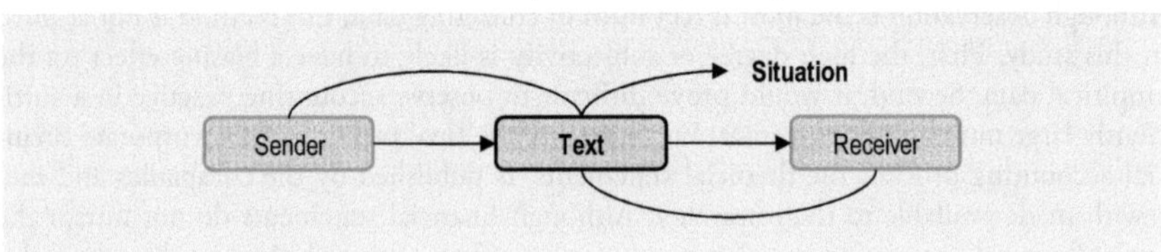

Figure 3-2: The communication model[1117]

Content analysis focuses on the **message** to retrieve information about the sender, the receptor or the situation they are in. Translated to the research question of this study,

[1112] Berelson 1971, p. 18.
[1113] Cf. Kassarjian 1977, p. 9f.
[1114] Cf. Bortz/Döring 2006, p. 149.
[1115] Cf. Müller-Böling 1992, p. 1501.
[1116] Cf. Atteslander 2008, p. 182.
[1117] Adopted from Merten 1995, p. 16.

content analysis focuses on companies' financial statements to conclude on the organization and its situation. In contrast to other scientific data evaluation methods, like the observation or the interview, content analysis bears the advantage to be non-reactive, i.e. the object of analysis is not influenced by the type of analysis and is time stable.[1118]

The process of content analysis can be divided into six different steps. First, **hypotheses** are developed that shall be tested by means of content analysis. Second, the basic **population** is determined. These first two steps are not content analysis specific but inherent to empirical research processes in general. The first content analysis specific action is to determine the **object of analysis**, i.e. the document or text that shall be evaluated with respect to its content.[1119] The documents to be analyzed in this study are the financial statement notes in general and the notes information on corporate segments and current and deferred taxes in specific. According to *Kromrey*, these documents have to meet the demands of (1) being relevant regarding the research question and purpose of the study, (2) existence and (3) availability.[1120] Investigating the impact of culture on financial accounting practice and therewith financial statements, the criterion of relevance is met by notes information. After determining the type of document to be analyzed, these documents have to be obtained for the entire population.[1121] The companies' notes were downloaded from the investor relations section on their respective homepages; all sample companies offered English versions of their financial statements.

In the fourth step the content analytical **category system** is developed. The category system is a system of transformational rules that transfers the content of the analyzed document into numerical information. This process of transformation is also referred to as the process of codification, which is recorded in a code book to guarantee the consistent application of codes. The numerical codification is required to statistically interpret and utilize the content analytical data. The category system is then applied to all documents to be analyzed. The codified results of the content analysis are processed electronically for further statistical analysis. In a last step, the results of the content analysis are published respectively presented.[1122]

The category system is the core element of content analysis.[1123] *Berelson* who is often cited in this context states: "content analysis stands or falls by its categories"[1124]. This study employs a **disclosure index** to define content analytical categories and to measure disclosure quantity.

3.3.3 Disclosure index

Two different approaches can be distinguished in the content analysis of financial statements: (1) subjective and (2) semi-objective. The disclosure index approach is among the

[1118] Cf. Müller-Böling 1992, p. 1501.
[1119] Cf. Unerman 2000, p. 669.
[1120] Cf. Kromrey 2006, p. 173.
[1121] Cf. Atteslander 2008, p. 197; Diekmann 2007, p. 595.
[1122] Cf. Atteslander 2008, p. 197; Diekmann 2007, p. 595.
[1123] Cf. Kromrey 2006, p. 326.
[1124] Berelson 1952, p. 147.

semi-objective approaches. Although more objective than subjective analyst ratings, the identification of keywords and assignment of words and phrases to disclosure index categories implies a certain element of subjectivity.[1125] In contrast to other content analytical approaches, which encompass all of the text, like thematic content analysis or readability studies, disclosure index studies *ex ante* specify a list of relevant items (categories) and categorize the text to be analyzed accordingly. Text passages that do not relate to the categories are ignored.[1126]

When developing a disclosure index, the researcher has to decide (1) which items and (2) how many items to include in the index, (3) how to measure the items (binary / ordinal), (4) if and how to group items in hierarchical order (nested / unnested) and (5) if and how to weight items.[1127] The following chapters elaborate further on disclosure index characteristics. Subsequently, the quality criteria of reliability and validity are described and evaluated with respect to this study.

3.3.3.1 Selection of disclosure index items

The researcher, in principle, is free in his decision which items and how many items to include in the disclosure index. Nonetheless, to guarantee the validity[1128] of the research instrument, accounting literature provides various means to assist the researcher in the selection of disclosure index items. The consideration of the **purpose of the study** is an elementary requirement for item selection. Multi country studies naturally have different requirements with respect to the selection of items than single country studies.[1129] Whereas in a single country[1130] study items may be selected according to the personal experience of the researcher, in a multi country study this approach is not recommendable for lack of sufficient experience. Also, items that may be relevant in one country may be negligible in the context of another country. Another popular approach to assist in the development of a disclosure index is the **user oriented** approach. According to this intuitively comprehendible approach, the researcher selects items users of that information attach most importance to. This approach is associated with a number of problems.[1131] First, the researcher has to decide which the relevant user groups are. Financial statements, as the unit of analysis of this study, have multiple user groups, like shareholders, employees or suppliers, with different information needs. Second, once the researcher has decided in favor of a user group, influence factors like perception-stability and group-homogeneity could play a role in identifying the 'true' user needs. Assuming that the user group and its information needs are homogeneous, the users still had to be asked, in person or by questionnaire, what their information needs are; such opinion surveys require substantial extra effort by the particular researcher. Relevant accounting **literature** presents another source that may assist the researcher in item selection. He can adopt a disclosure index that is

[1125] Cf. Smith/Taffler 2000, p. 638.
[1126] Cf. Beattie et al. 2004, p. 208.
[1127] Cf. Beattie et al. 2004, p. 209f.
[1128] See chapter 3.3.4.2 for more detailed annotations on validity.
[1129] Cf. Marston/Shrives 1991, p. 202.
[1130] The single country is often the home country of the researcher.
[1131] Cf. Courtis 1992, p. 32.

successfully applied in a comparable study if it appears to be appropriate; or he may adopt only parts of indices to develop a newly constituted index that fits better the research question. Nevertheless, the reutilization of indices or parts of indices may lead to unintentional measurement results and often, especially for not or little assessed research questions, there are no comparable indices to borrow from. Still, a review of relevant literature and other sources, like legal requirements or interpretations and recommendations by the standard setter, is essential previous to disclosure index development. Especially for financial statements, which are based on legal requirements, the corresponding accounting standards provide valuable information with respect to the selection of disclosure items.[1132]

This study follows the latter approach and takes **legal requirements** as a basis for the development of the disclosure indices. As the legal requirements provided by IFRS are equally applicable in the three analyzed countries, this approach also meets the distinctive characteristics of a multi country study. Segment and income tax reporting quantity are each measured by two separate indices; one represents only statutory information[1133]; the other one also includes voluntary information. The voluntary information categories are the result of the content analysis pretest[1134] in which additional information was identified and classified. To avoid national differences, the pretest was conducted using random samples from all three countries. The user oriented approach is not applied for the above mentioned limitations. Instead of focusing on a certain user group,[1135] this study recognizes the information needs of all financial statement user groups by focusing on legal requirements and voluntary information, which the individual company decided to publish. The decision to develop user group independent disclosure indices is closely associated with the decision on the weight of the single items in relation to the index as a whole. User groups often not only decide which items are important to them, but also which items are more important than others.

3.3.3.2 Weighting of disclosure index items

Following the selection of research question relevant items, the researcher has to decide on the weighting of the individual items and therewith on their relative importance in reference to the index they are part of. The weightings can be determined by the researcher himself, based on the experience of the researcher and a literature review. This procedure, however, is open to substantial influences of subjectivity. Alternatively, as mentioned above, the items' weight may be determined by surveying relevant **user groups**. Again, different user groups may have different information preferences leading to inconsistent and mistakable disclosure indices. Researchers, who use disclosure indices based on the

---

[1132] Cf. Marston/Shrives 1991, p. 201ff.

[1133] Statutory information also refers to recommended information. Especially IFRS 8 recommends the publication of segment information like, e.g., segment liabilities that is only obligatory when reported regularly to the chief operating decision maker; cf. IFRS 8.23.

[1134] A pretest was conducted to check the reliability of the coding process; cf. Anderson/Gerbing 1991, p. 732ff.; Kolbe/Burnett 1991, p. 245. See also chapter 3.3.4 on content analysis quality factors.

[1135] Studies that analyze the content of financial statements and follow a user oriented approach generally conduct interviews with financial analysts to identify user relevant items.

weight users have attributed to the indices' items, make certain assumptions with regard to the users' preferences. First, they assume that users are capable of self-reflection with respect to their own information preferences and needs. Second, users attribute weights to items independent of what other items are available to them. Third, the relative importance users attribute to disclosure index items remains constant over time.[1136]

If these assumptions apply to information users like financial analysts in general, is questionable. Research on human information processing indicates that even user experts show little insight in the way they process information. *Slovic et al.* show on a sample of stockbrokers and students that stockbrokers have less insight in the use of financial information than their student counterparts. Also, more experienced stockbrokers are less accurate in assigning relative importance to items.[1137] The second assumption is even more questionable. Especially in financial accounting it is not likely that the absence or addition of one piece of information leaves the relative importance of the other items unchanged. Financial analysts, for instance, utilize financial ratios like return on capital employed (ROCE) or profit margin. When one of the components is missing, the relative importance of the other component is lower since the ratio is not calculable. Relative importance of financial data is also influenced by the general economic conditions the company is in. An unfavorable debt to equity ratio is surely more concerning in the situation of an economic crisis than in a quickly recovering economy with promising sales increases. Consequently, the assumption of constant relative importance of financial disclosure items may be valid only for certain types of information.[1138]

Even when following a **non-user** oriented approach, the researcher may decide to weight items according to type of information presented. For instance, qualitative information scores one and quantitative information scores two. This scale may be further broken down in (1) little qualitative information, (2) detailed qualitative information and (3) quantitative information. This approach is surely more objective than having analysts rate the importance of items on a one to five scale. Nonetheless, there is still room for elements of subjectivity, e.g. drawing the line between detailed and non-detailed qualitative information or judging the relative importance of quantitative information in per cent or absolute figures. Also, weighted indices often show similar results compared to unweighted indices, i.e. index score company rankings differ only slightly.[1139] It is suggested that companies that disclose more important items also disclose more unimportant items.[1140] When using a weighted index, it is therefore advisable to compare the results with the results of an unweighted index to check for plausibility.[1141]

For the above criticism associated with weighted indices, this study employs an **unweighted disclosure index** in which every disclosure item is weighted by one.[1142] According-

1136 Cf. Dhaliwal 1981, p. 386.
1137 Cf. Slovic et al. 1972, p. 297ff.
1138 Cf. Dhaliwal 1981, p. 386ff.
1139 Cf., e.g., Firth 1980, p. 105; Chow/Wong-Boren 1987, p. 536.
1140 Cf. Gray et al. 1995, p. 54.
1141 Cf. Marston/Shrives 1991, p. 203.
1142 Unweighted indices are considered to be an appropriate research instrument for user group independent disclosure studies. Cf. Cooke 1989, p. 182; Hossain et al. 1995, p. 77.

ing to this principle of equally importance, an item scores one when it is mentioned and zero when it is missing.[1143] There is one quasi exemption to this rule. In the disclosure index on current and deferred taxes there are items like deferred tax assets or deferred tax liabilities which score one, if they are mentioned in total, and another one, if the information is further substantiated, split by corresponding balance sheet item. The detailed information by balance sheet item is counted as an extra piece of information and scores accordingly extra. There are other items like unrecognized deferred tax assets for which the standard explicitly requires the declaration of an amount. In such cases, the mere annotation that there are unrecognized deferred tax assets, without specifying the amount, yields no point. Also, even unweighted disclosure indices are subject to an implicit weighting of categories; categories that contain more items than other categories possess a stronger weight on category level, although all category items are weighted by one.[1144]

The last two chapters have dealt with the selection and weighting of disclosure items in general. The next chapter discusses the development of the disclosure indices employed in this study to measure corporate notes disclosure in more detail.

3.3.3.3 Development of the disclosure indices

This study employs **four different disclosure indices.** Segment reporting and income tax reporting are each analyzed by means of two disclosure indices; one index measures **statutory** information only and a second index measures both **statutory and voluntary** information. The indices are developed based on legal requirements[1145] and relevant accounting literature. The statutory requirements were taken from the corresponding IFRS standards, IFRS 8 for notes information on reportable segments and IAS 12 for notes information on income taxes.[1146] When necessary, cumulated information requirements were split up into single disclosure items; for example, a common requirement for current and deferred tax was split up into two separate items. The items taken from the statutory requirements constitute the statutory disclosure indices. The additional voluntary information items were identified by a literature review of segment and income tax disclosure studies[1147] and the pretest, conducted prior to the actual field study.

The **segment reporting** disclosure indices consist of 43 (combined) respectively 23 (statutory) items that are divided into three main categories and one category 'other' (see Table

1143 Cf. Cooke 1989, p. 182.

1144 Cf. Singleton/Globerman 2002, p. 99; Coy/Dixon 2004, p. 84.

1145 Especially IFRS 8 contains various information requirements that are obligatory "[...] if the specified amounts are [...] reviewed by the chief operating decision maker or are otherwise regularly provided to the chief operating decision maker [...]" (IFRS 8.24). If not regularly reported to the CODM, the disclosure of the particular items is voluntary. However, since these items are specified by the respective standards, they are included in the statutory indices.

1146 The reportable segment disclosure requirements are described in IFRS 8.20-24. The income tax disclosure requirements are described in IAS 12.79-88.

1147 Cf., e.g., Meek/Gray 1989, p. 315ff.; McKinnon/Dalimunthe 1993, p. 33ff.; Botosan/Harris 2000, p. 329ff.; Feldkämper 2000, p. 1459ff.; Hacker/Dobler 2000, p. 811ff.; Alvarez/Fink 2003, p. 275ff.; Hope 2003a, p. 235ff.; Botosan/Stanford 2005, p. 751ff.; Kwok/Sharp 2005, p. 74ff.; Meyer et al. 2006, p. 83ff.; Kajüter/Barth 2007, p. 428ff.; Richter 2010, p. 511ff.

3-1). The first category contains general information like a description of the segments, whether key performance indicators have been named or whether the CODM has been defined. Information on the segmental profit and loss situation like segment revenues, other revenues or expenses is gathered in the second category.

Segment reporting disclosure index		All items	Statutory items
1. General segment information		13	5
2. Segment profit and loss information		**18**	**13**
Thereof	2a. Segment profit and loss	2	1
Thereof	2b. Segment revenues	9	6
Thereof	2c. Segment expenses	7	6
3. Segment balance sheet information		**10**	**4**
Thereof	3a. Segment assets	6	3
Thereof	3b. Segment liabilities	4	1
4. Other segment information		2	1
Σ		**43**	**23**

Table 3-1: Composition of the segment reporting disclosure index

The third category refers to balance sheet information like segment assets, capital expenditure or segment liabilities. The last category subsumes 'other' information like segment cash flows and number of employees per segment.[1148]

The **income tax reporting** disclosure indices consist of 52 (combined) respectively 29 (statutory) items that are divided into three main categories (see Table 3-2). In analogy to the index on segment information, the first category is composed of general tax information like the nominal local corporate tax rate, the tax effect of changes in accounting policy or the explanation of tax rate changes. The second category contains information on current tax like the actual current tax expense, current tax adjustments with respect to prior years or the aggregated current tax effect on equity. Deferred tax information forms the third category, which is further divided into five subcategories. The first subcategory includes general information as, for example, the effect tax rate changes or business combinations have on deferred taxes. Information on deferred tax assets and liabilities, like the amount, the profit and loss impact and the expiry date, are gathered in the following three categories, two subcategories for each assets and liabilities and one extra category for netted information.[1149] The fifth subcategory encompasses information on unrecognized deferred tax assets and liabilities.[1150]

[1148] For a detailed overview of the segment reporting disclosure index items according to item category see Appendix A, Table A 2.

[1149] To avoid double counts of information, companies can either score for items of the separate categories or score for items of the netted category.

[1150] For a detailed overview of the income tax reporting disclosure index items according to item category see Appendix A, Table A 3.

Income tax reporting disclosure index		All items	Statutory items
1. General tax information		7	3
2. Current tax information		9	8
3. Deferred tax information		**36**	**18**
Thereof	3a. General information	10	8
Thereof	3b. Deferred tax assets	6	2
Thereof	3c. Deferred tax liabilities	6	2
Thereof	3d. Deferred tax assets/liabilities netted	9	3
Thereof	3e. Unrecognized deferred tax assets/liabilities	5	3
Σ		**52**	**29**

Table 3-2: Composition of the income tax reporting disclosure index

The disclosure indices on segment reporting and income tax are both binary indices. Existing items score one and missing items score zero. When an item is missing, the researcher cannot be sure, if the company consciously decided not to disclose that item or if the items is just not relevant for the company. There are several possible solutions to this problem. The most obvious solution is to select only items that are relevant for all sample companies.[1151] If the relevance of the items cannot be determined, the researcher can use relative index scores, dividing the company score by the maximum score possible for that company.[1152] To find out if a non-disclosed item is relevant for a company, *Cooke* suggests to read the entire annual report and then decide if the item is relevant or not.[1153] To avoid the problem of judging, if an item is relevant or not for a company, the items selected for the disclosure indices in this study are principally relevant to all sample companies. Also, as previously mentioned, banks, insurance companies and financial institutions are excluded from the sample since their business model is different from the business model of industrial companies and notes disclosure might correspondingly differ substantially. The statutory items were predetermined by IFRS disclosure requirements and are therewith basically applicable to all IFRS applying companies. With respect to voluntary disclosure items, the approach of this study is to only select items for the indices composition that theoretically could be disclosed by every company, e.g., number of employees or effective corporate tax rate. Non-results,[1154] like the remark that companies do not disclose certain items since these were not reported to the CODM[1155] or do not disclose items since these

[1151] Cf. Buzby 1974, p. 430.

[1152] Cf. Buzby 1975, p. 27.

[1153] Cf. Cooke 1989, p. 189.

[1154] Non-results in this case refer to justified negative announcements; i.e. the company declares that the item is not disclosed for a certain reason.

[1155] Cf., e.g., IFRS 8.23; IFRS 8.24.

are not relevant for the company,[1156] are counted as if the item had been disclosed properly and score one.

According to the binary coding structure, the corporate index score equals the sum of items disclosed by the company (see Formula 3.1 and Formula 3.2). The maximum sum of the disclosure indices depends on the type of index; the higher items sum represents the combined index and the lower items sum represents the statutory index.

Formula 3.1 $$DI_{SE} = \sum_{m=1}^{43/23} d_m$$

Formula 3.2 $$DI_{IT} = \sum_{m=1}^{52/29} d_m$$

where

DI_{SE}	=	*Segment reporting disclosure index*
DI_{IT}	=	*Income tax reporting disclosure index*
d_m	=	*1 if item m is disclosed and 0 otherwise*

3.3.4 Content analysis quality factors

The main objective of systematic categorization is a reduction of information and therewith a reduction of complexity. Subsuming the information to be analyzed under a category system, the researcher no longer has to deal with a lot of pieces of unstructured information, but with a few sorted categories only. To allow for such a reduction of information complexity, the category system has to fulfill certain requirements. First and most importantly, it has to be built on the understanding of the **research question** to be examined. Accordingly, the category system has to be exhaustive, i.e. all research question relevant information has to be attributable to a specific category. Furthermore, all categories have to be unique. The assignment of information to categories should be free of doubt. To allow for statistical data analysis, the categories have to be independent from one another, i.e. the allocation to one category has no influence on the codification of the rest of the text. Finally, the researcher has to decide how many categories to implement. Again, the number of categories should be determined with respect to the research question and the requirement of full coverage of relevant information. Nonetheless, practicability implies certain limits with respect to the maximum number of categories, which, thus, is often a tradeoff between capture of complexity and practicability. This tradeoff is well described by the controversial relationship of the research quality factors of validity and reliability.[1157]

[1156] E.g., companies do not disclose "[...] the amount of investment in associates and joint ventures accounted for by the equity method [...]" (IFRS 8.24) as they have neither associates nor joint ventures.

[1157] Cf. Lisch/Kriz 1978, p. 70f.

The overall quality of empirical research instruments like the disclosure index is usually determined by their validity and reliability. Whereas **validity** assures that research is based on fact and the research process reproduces the real world truthfully, **reliability** assures that the research process leads to data that is duplicable and therewith independent from the external conditions of the research process. The relationship between validity and reliability is controversial. Validity requires reliability. But high reliability does not guarantee validity. A research instrument that measures data reliably may produce invalid data as the perspective of the researcher is different from the perspective of anybody else. The data is measured reliably, but is objectively wrong.[1158]

Regarding the researcher's decision on the appropriate number of categories, the category system's validity by tendency is improved by a growing number of relevant categories; more categories capture more linguistic complexity. Nevertheless, the relationship between number of categories and validity is not a straight-line relationship and certainly not true, if the category system is already exhaustive. Reliability, on the other hand, is improved, if the number of categories is reduced. The item allocation decision is easier for only a few categories; moreover, the possibility of forgetting a category and, as a consequence, allocating a piece of information into the wrong category is lower.[1159]

The relationship between validity and reliability becomes clearer in the following paragraphs which depict the two concepts in more detail. Also, the relationship to this study is established.

3.3.4.1 Reliability

It is of utmost importance that the process of content analysis is free of biases and distortions, intentional or accidental. Possible biases may be of inter-temporal, inter-personal or inter-instrumental kind. The researcher has to make sure that the results of the data analysis remain constant, no matter how and by whom the data is generated. These general considerations are subsumed under the scientific concept of reliability.

> *"The importance of reliability rests on the assurance it provides that data are obtained independent of the measuring event, instrument or person. Reliable data, by definition, are data that remain constant throughout variations in the measuring process."*[1160]

In contrast to most aspects of validity, reliability can be tested. The data analysis is replicated under different conditions and the results are compared. Equal results indicate a reliable research design. There are three types of reliability, permitting reliability tests with an increasing level of reliability (see Figure 3-3).

[1158] Cf. Krippendorff 2004, p. 212f.
[1159] Cf. Lisch/Kriz 1978, p. 71.
[1160] Kaplan/Goldsen 1965, p. 83f.

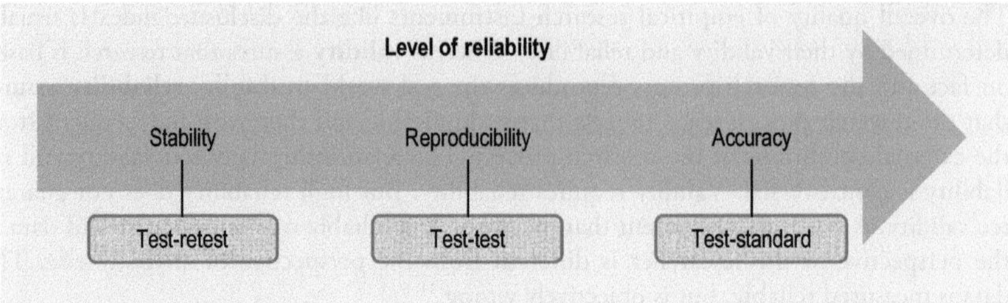

Figure 3-3: Types of reliability[1161]

The first degree of reliability is **stability**. Stability measures intra-observer inconsistencies over time. A content analysis performed by the same researcher, using the same data and following the same procedures at two points of time, that leads to the same results is regarded as stable. Differing, i.e. unstable test results document poor reliability. Such individual disagreements can be caused by distraction, carelessness or learning through practice patterns. Intra-observer inconsistencies may also result from a deficient documentation of the research procedures. If there is no codebook or the wording of the codebook is ambivalent, the researcher will experience difficulties in obtaining the same results at different points of time. Stability is the weakest form of reliability and easily controlled for by a retest. The researcher replicates the data analysis of an early data set and checks for inconsistencies. It is convenient to perform retests at different stages of the research process to identify inconsistencies as early as possible and to be able to correct the procedures accordingly.[1162]

The second level of empirical reliability is **reproducibility**. Whereas stability only controls for intra-observer inconsistencies, reproducibility also controls for inter-observer inconsistencies. When more than one researcher is involved in the analysis of the same data, following the same research process, the data reliability might also be affected by different individual perception. Applying the same codebook, different encoders might interpret the instructions differently or perceive the same text passage to be analyzed slightly or completely different. The results of such an analysis would differ and limit its reproducibility. Inter-observer inconsistencies can be tested by comparison of data sets analyzed by different researchers. The number of inconsistently analyzed data categories in relation to the total number of categories is a proper indicator for the degree of reproducibility.[1163]

The strongest measure of reliability is **accuracy**. The performance of the data analysis is not compared inter-temporally or inter-personally but with reference to the correct standard procedure. Given that such a standard procedure exists, the degree of accuracy is measured by deviations from that standard. Standard in this context does not necessarily mean ultimate truth but may also refer to standards on which researchers have agreed.

[1161] Adopted from Krippendorff 2004, p. 215.
[1162] Cf. Kolbe/Burnett 1991, p. 245ff.; Merten 1995, p. 303.
[1163] Cf. Milne/Adler 1999, p. 239ff.; Mayring 2003, p. 113.

The test-standard design is often used taking experienced encoders as a standard and comparing their results to the results of inexperienced encoders.[1164]

The different aspects of reliability are incorporated into the research design of this study as follows. To avoid inter-observer inconsistencies, the content analysis was performed by **one person**, the author, only. Accordingly, encoder and author of the codebook were the same person. Thus, misinterpretations of the codebook were minimized. Also, the content analysis of the notes information on segment and income tax reporting was carried through separately to concentrate on **one topic** only at a time. Moreover, time lags in the course of the data analysis were minimized to reduce possible distractions. The content analysis was further improved with respect to intra-observer reliability by an initiatory **pretest**, an intermediary retest and a final **retest**. The original codebook was tested by means of the pretest, evaluating five data sets per country and later integrating the findings[1165] into the final **codebook** version. Using the same final category system, these 15 initially pretested data sets were retested twice in the middle and at the end of the segment reporting and income tax reporting content analysis, to control for inconsistencies as a result of learning through practice etc. The results of the retests show only minimal inconsistencies and suggest a correspondingly high degree of reliability.[1166]

3.3.4.2 Validity

The quality factor of validity specifies, if the research instrument, the disclosure index, really measures what it is supposed to measure.[1167] Validity depends on the precision of the category system, how exact the categories are determined and if the operationalization is plausible ('face validity').[1168] Besides 'face validity', which refers to 'obvious' respectively logical relations, *Krippendorff* further distinguishes between social validity and empirical validity in his typology of validation efforts in content analysis.[1169] Whereas **social validity** concerns the social relevance of the research, i.e. how research contributes to the public discussion of important social topics, **empirical validity** indicates "the degree to which available evidence and established theory support intermediate stages of a research process and its results"[1170]. To validate the empirical evidence and therewith to verify the valid functionality of the disclosure index, the following validity test criteria can be employed: (1) analysis validity, (2) content validity, (3) criterion validity and (4) inference validity.[1171]

1164 Cf. Milne/Adler 1999, p. 239ff.; Mayring 2003, p. 115.

1165 Findings mainly refer to wording imprecision and additional voluntary information that was not yet part of the original codebook which based on the statutory IFRS requirements.

1166 Since no standard procedure exists for segment reporting respectively income tax reporting content analysis, the degree of accuracy could not be determined.

1167 Cf. Früh 2001, p. 183.

1168 Cf. Früh 2001, p. 171f.

1169 Cf. Krippendorff 2004, p. 319.

1170 Krippendorff 2004, p. 319.

1171 Cf. Rössler 2005, p. 193ff.

Discrepancy in meaning between researcher and encoder (analyst) and, thus, discrepancy in content analytical judgment signals poor **analysis validity.**[1172] This criterion is comparable to the inter-observer reliability criterion mentioned above. Both criteria refer to a different perception of the same real phenomenon. Whereas the latter reliability criterion is limited to inconsistencies in the field work, analysis validity measures how well the encoder implements the researcher's category system with respect to the researcher's original intentions. To be able to utilize the collected data to test the researcher's hypotheses, the data gathering process has to follow the same logic the hypotheses are based on. Accordingly, the understanding of the researcher in this context is set as 'standard understanding', which then has to be met by the encoder's understanding. One way to test analysis validity is to have the researcher participate in the field work of data analysis and to measure differences between encoder's and researcher's codifications. To avoid differences in the process of analysis and to approximate the researcher's and the encoder's understanding, the encoder should be thoroughly trained by the researcher and participate in pretests.[1173]

Analysis validity is of no concern in this study since researcher and encoder are the same person. To preclude inter-personal inconsistencies, both on the conceptual and the field work level, hypotheses development, hypotheses operationalization (development of the category system), data collection and hypotheses testing are performed by the author.

The second criterion, **content validity**, is closely connected to the content analysis category system.[1174] Content validity is the extent to which the content analytical instrument captures all the features of the construct that is to be tested. To include all relevant aspects that define the tested concept (e.g. segment and income tax notes disclosure) into the category system, researchers should consult external sources like prior research results or conduct expert interviews previously to the field work. A previous 'scan' of the documents to be analyzed and the analysis of the pretest may also bring valid findings to incorporate into the category system. Regularly used open categories ('others') might indicate that certain aspects have been left out so far. Also, the codebook can be used to judge the content validity of the analysis.[1175]

The concern on content validity was met in this study by means of a revision of prior literature. As the notes content to be analyzed is mainly determined by statutory IFRS requirements, the respective standards on segment reporting and income tax reporting formed the basis of the two category systems. The pretest resulted in further categories of voluntary information that companies published in addition to the information required by the respective standard. The category system of this study contains no open categories for information items that do not fit into other categories; instead, voluntary information was gathered in information specific categories.

In contrast to analysis and content validity criteria, which particularly play a role in the design and realization of the content analysis, the two remaining validity criteria are rather

[1172] Cf. Krippendorff 2004, p. 313ff.; Rössler 2005, p. 193ff.
[1173] Cf. Krippendorff 2004, p. 313ff.; Rössler 2005, p. 193ff.
[1174] Cf. Holsti 1969, p. 143; Rössler 2005, p. 193ff.
[1175] Cf. Holsti 1969, p. 143; Rössler 2005, p. 193ff.

suited for an *ex post* verification of the content analysis' results.[1176] Both criteria use external data, mainly other studies on the same or a similar topic, to test for validity. **Criterion validity** is given, when the study's results are supported or unexpected results and differences are plausibly explained by topic relevant prior content analyses. This direct or indirect confirmation process is not limited to quantitative studies. Qualitative studies may also prove to contain valuable insights since these generally assess a few exemplary cases in greater detail. The criterion of **inference validity** is also based on the comparison with external data and focuses on the conclusions that can be drawn from the content analysis with respect to the sender, the receptor and the situation of the analyzed piece of information. In contrast to criterion validity, this criterion emphasizes studies from a different methodological background (e.g. interview) to compare these with the content analytical conclusions. Due to the generally high degree of specificity that is characteristic for empirical studies and the various parameters to take into account (context factors, sample, year etc.), it proves difficult to find comparable studies and draw meaningful conclusions.[1177]

Having specified the method of data collection, the following subchapter deals with the statistical evaluation of the collected data.

3.4 Data evaluation

The data obtained by means of disclosure indices, word count and other types of content analytical procedures is difficult to interpret at a first glance. To be able to make verifiable statements on the collected data and to decide whether the posited hypotheses are rather supported or refused, the data has to be evaluated statistically. Statistics in this context refer to all methods or procedures that help to capture, to refine, to analyze, to display, to model and to predict measurable and systematically observable mass data that describe real phenomena.[1178] The following chapters deal with statistical methods that are applied in this study to draw conclusions on the analyzed research question.

3.4.1 Statistical foundation

Before presenting the applied statistical methods in detail, this introductory section comments on statistical fundamentals like the significance level or the scale level.

Statistical test results are usually accompanied by a certain **significance level**, which is an indicator for the error probability of the test results.[1179] Commonly used significance levels are 5% or 1%.[1180] A test performed at a significance level of 5% is generally accepted to lead to significant results; tests performed at 1% are highly significant.[1181] The significance

[1176] Cf. Holsti 1969, p. 144f.; Mayring 2003, p. 112; Rössler 2005, p. 193ff.
[1177] Cf. Holsti 1969, p. 144f.; Mayring 2003, p. 112; Rössler 2005, p. 193ff.
[1178] Cf. Eckstein 2008, p. 10.
[1179] Cf. Sterling 1959, p. 30.
[1180] Cf. Hope 1968, p. 589.
[1181] Significant results are marked by one star (*). Highly significant results are marked by two stars (**). Cf. Saville 1990, p. 177.

level in statistical tests is generally expressed by the p-value. A significant p-value of 5% refers to a 95% probability that the null hypothesis is false.[1182]

Furthermore, statistical tests often require the tested data to have a certain **scale level.** Four scales of measurement are commonly distinguished: (1) nominal or classificatory scale, (2) ordinal or ranking scale, (3) interval scale and (4) ratio scale.[1183] Whereas nominal scaled data are classified in categories without implying a specific rank of the categories (e.g. gender), ordinal scaled data can be ranked in a certain order (e.g. school grades).[1184] In contrast to interval scaled data (e.g. date), the rank of ordinal data has no implications with respect to relative size or degree of difference; for interval scaled data, however, the distance between two interval scale classes is known numerically. Ratio scale is the highest scale level and, contrary to interval scale, is characterized by an absolute zero point (e.g. weight); the ratio of two points is independent of the unit of measurement (e.g. kilogram, gram).[1185]

In this context, especially the **scale level of the disclosure indices** in this study is debatable. Disclosure indices are usually supposed to reach the level of ordinal measurement, i.e. companies that have an index score twice as high as other companies are only supposed to rank higher than these other companies, but not twice as high. There is a debate whether disclosure indices can reach the level of interval measurement.[1186] In the case of unweighted indices, interval scale level would request that one disclosed item is exactly as important as another disclosed item. Accordingly, researchers conduct user group surveys *ex ante* disclosure index development to put a weight to the index items and, thus, achieve interval scale level. It is questionable, however, whether the assumption of equal items in unweighted indices or previously conducted user ratings to built weighted indices achieve the level of measurement of interval scale.[1187] The assumption that disclosure indices provide only ordinal data makes the calculation of mean values impossible since the central tendency of ordinal data is the median. Parametric tests like the T-Test had to be replaced by non-parametric tests. Nonetheless, the requirement of metric data is controversial. Some researchers argue that parametric tests like the T-Test are robust against the violation of the metric data criterion, as long as the criteria of normal distribution and variance homogeneity are fulfilled.[1188] Various disclosure index studies assume the disclosure index scores to be interval scaled and the application of parametric tests statistically acceptable, often complemented by non-parametric tests to test for the robustness of results.[1189] Accordingly, when performing parametric tests in this study, these are safeguarded by **non-parametric tests.**[1190]

1182 Cf. Eckstein 2008, p. 237ff.
1183 Cf. Stevens 1946, p. 677ff.; Siegel 1956, p. 21ff.
1184 Cf. Velleman/Leland Wilkinson 1993, p. 66.
1185 Cf. Siegel 1957, p. 15.
1186 Cf. Marston/Shrives 1991, p. 199ff.; Coy/Dixon 2004, p. 82ff.
1187 Cf. Marston/Shrives 1991, p. 199.
1188 Cf. Gregoire/Driver 1987, p. 159ff.; Davison/Sharma 1990, p. 137ff.
1189 Cf. Firth 1979, p. 277ff.
1190 Cf. Barth 2009, p. 131f.

Univariate and multivariate statistical tests bear the risk that the results of the analysis are biased by **outliers**; outliers are extreme values that differ considerably with respect to the mean value of the analyzed variable.[1191] To improve the robustness of the performed statistical tests, outliers are eliminated from the data samples. For this purpose outliers are defined as cases that lie more than three standard deviations from the data sample's mean.[1192] Outliers are only eliminated for the univariate (e.g. T-Test) and multivariate (correlation analysis; regression analysis) statistical tests; the descriptive analyses contain all sample values to describe the sample as it is.[1193]

The statistical program used to perform the following statistical tests is **SPSS**[1194]. SPSS is a Windows based user-friendly package of statistical programs to analyze data of all scale levels.[1195] Following an introduction on descriptive statistics, the next three subchapters successively deal with univariate, bivariate and multiple statistical analyses.

3.4.2 Descriptive statistics and univariate analysis

Descriptive statistics are performed in the beginning of every statistical data analysis to receive a first impression and to assess the quality of the data. The main features of variables or combinations of variables are described quantitatively; this first assessment is often supported by graphical analysis. In contrast to inferential statistics[1196], which seek to draw conclusions from a collection of data, descriptive statistics present the mere facts of variables, like the frequency distribution, the mean value etc., without employing probabilistic formulation.[1197] These basic variable characteristics, like the scale level or the distribution, have an influence on the type of statistical tests that may be performed on the data, e.g., to infer on significant differences in the population. Measures used to describe the distribution of a variable are measures of central tendency, like mean or median, and measures of dispersion, like standard deviation, percentiles or range.[1198]

This study employs mean and median as measures of central tendency and standard deviation, 5%/95% percentile, minimum and maximum as measures of dispersion. Descriptive statistics are presented (1) for the entire sample and (2) on a country by country level to demonstrate national differences. Different means of the three country samples do not necessarily mean that the countries differ with respect to that variable; the different mean values could be due to chance. To eliminate the possibility of difference by chance with a certain security level, emphasis is put on the significance level of the performed test.[1199] As

1191 Cf. Schendera 2007, p. 163ff.

1192 Cf., e.g., Chaloner/Brant 1988, p. 651; Knorr/Ng 1997, p. 220; Wiggins 2000, p. 3. Three standard deviations is the SPSS default value.

1193 One extreme outlier is eliminated from the MTB sample prior to descriptive analysis; cf. chapter 4.3.1.1.1.

1194 The abbreviation SPSS originally stood for Statistical Package for Social Sciences. Today SPSS stands for Superior Performing Software System. Cf. Eckstein 2008, p. 2.

1195 Cf. Eckstein 2008, p. 2.

1196 For a more detailed description of inferential statistics cf. Bankhofer/Vogel 2008, p. 91ff.

1197 Cf. Mosler/Schmid 2006, p. 4f.

1198 Cf. Toutenburg et al. 2006, p. 17ff.

1199 Cf. Bankhofer/Vogel 2008, p. 125ff.

outlined above, a test of significance indicates whether the previously defined null hypothesis can be rejected. Comparing, e.g., the depreciation period means of plant and machinery of French and UK companies, the null hypothesis to be rejected would be: the means of depreciation periods of plant and machinery of French and UK companies are equal.

The following **univariate tests** are applied in this study to test for statistical significance of group differences.

T-Tests refer to a group of statistical hypotheses tests in which the test statistic follows a Student's t distribution. The T-Test generally refers to (1) the independent one-sample T-Test, which tests the null hypothesis that the population mean equals a prior specified value μ_0, and (2) the independent two sample T-Test, which tests the null hypothesis that the mean value of sample one equals the mean value of sample two. The T-Test is a widely accepted test for mean value comparison. Nonetheless, it is limited to the comparison of only two sample groups at a time. The following statistical hypotheses test is also used for mean comparison. In contrast to the T-Test, it bears the advantage to be able to test more than two samples at a time.[1200]

ANOVA is a statistical procedure which compares different estimates of variance.[1201] Differences of variance within each group are compared to differences of variance between the groups. From substantial differences between the two variance estimates, the researcher concludes that the analyzed groups come from different sampling distribution of means and the null hypothesis of equal means is rejected. Small differences suggest that the observed differences of means are due to random error and therewith not significant.[1202] The result of the ANOVA test is reflected by the F-value, which indicates, at a predetermined significance level, if the null hypothesis of equal group mean values can be rejected.[1203] However, the ANOVA results only show whether differences in group mean values exist without indicating which of the tested groups differ significantly with respect to their mean values. Accordingly, when the ANOVA suggests significantly different mean values, it is complemented by the **Scheffé-Test**; the Scheffé-Test is a rather conservative multiple comparison test to analyze pair wise group differences in mean values.[1204]

To use **parametric tests** like the T-Test or ANOVA on a variable, the analyzed variable has to fulfill certain conditions with regard to scale level and distribution. First, the variable needs to be at least **interval scaled**; nominal and ordinal data do not allow for meaningful mean calculation. Second, the variable should also be **normally distributed**.[1205] This precondition can be tested both graphically and statistically.[1206] A histogram of the frequency distribution of the variable is a good first indicator to check for normal distribution. Also, possible outliers may be identified, which may distort the image of a normal

[1200] Cf. Brosius 2004, p. 475ff.
[1201] Cf. Westfall 1986, p. 1572ff.
[1202] Cf. Tabachnick/Fidell 2007, p. 38.
[1203] Cf. Eckey et al. 2002, p. 93ff.
[1204] Cf. Brosius 2004, p. 513f.
[1205] Cf. Brosius 2004, p. 475ff.
[1206] Cf. Paul/Zhang 2010, p. 1101ff.

distribution. The result of the graphical analysis can be verified by parametric and non-parametric[1207] statistical tests of normal distribution.[1208] The third criterion is **homogeneity of variance** in the different test groups.[1209]

If the requirements of normal distribution or homogeneity of variance[1210] are not fulfilled, the results of the T-Test may still be useful; the T-Test reacts robustly on a violation of these criteria.[1211] Nonetheless, when applied in this study, both T-Test and ANOVA are supported by **non-parametric tests** to safeguard the rejection of the accordant null hypothesis.[1212]

So far the different variables are only described and checked for mean value differences on a standalone basis. The existence of differences is determined by rejecting the corresponding null hypothesis that there are no differences. Nonetheless, so far it is not clear which context factors are responsible for these difference. The following two chapters present statistical methods to measure the statistical relationship between two and more variables.

3.4.3 Bivariate correlation analysis

The association between the dependent conservatism and secrecy variables and the various internal and external context factors, in a first step, is analyzed using bivariate correlation analysis. Bivariate correlation analysis measures the degree of association between two variables without implying a particular relationship. Whereas in multiple regression analysis the researcher distinguishes between dependent and independent variables, in correlation analysis this prior distinction is not necessary. The correlation coefficients are displayed in the correlation matrix, which lists the bivariate dependencies of all variables. The **correlation coefficient** is an indicator that measures the strength and the direction of the bivariate relationships.[1213] The sign of the coefficient marks the direction of the association. A positive correlation coefficient between segment reporting and company size, for instance, suggests that larger companies tend to disclose more information on segment reporting. The amount of the correlation coefficient varies between -1 and +1. Values close to -1

1207 Parametric tests offer the advantage of stronger test results. Nonetheless, these tests are based on the assumption of certain parameter characteristics. When these parameter assumptions are not fulfilled, non-parametric tests are applied. Cf. Gravetter/Wallnau 2008, p. 472ff.

1208 The Shapiro-Wilk-Test and the Kolmogorv-Smirnov-Test are parametric normal distribution tests. The Mann-Whitney-U-Test or the Kruskal-Wallis-Test may be applied as non-parametric tests. Cf. Brosius 2004, p. 404, 844f.; Eckstein 2008, p. 253ff.

1209 The *Levene*-test is a standard test included in statistical programs like SPSS that controls for intergroup homogeneity of variance. Cf. Brosius 2004, p. 475ff.

1210 The SPSS T-Test statistics always present the T-Test results for the assumption of variance homogeneity and non-homogeneity. To be on the safe side, the researcher should use the T-Test results for assumed non-homogeneity.

1211 Cf. Heeren/D'Agostino 1987, p. 79ff.; Brosius 2004, p. 475ff.

1212 This study employs the Kruskal-Wallis-Test as a non parametric test to safeguard the ANOVA results; cf. Smith 2011, p. 74ff.; the Mann-Whitney-U-Test is used to safeguard the T-Test results; cf. Deluc-chi/Bostrom 2004, p. 1162.

1213 Cf. Anderson 2009, p. 114ff.

respectively +1 stand for strongly negative respectively positive associations.[1214] No association is measured for correlation coefficients of 0.[1215] The significance level attributed to each correlation coefficient indicates the error probability of mistakenly rejecting the null hypothesis, which assumes no linear association between the two tested variables. However, a strongly significant correlation coefficient is no proof for a causal relationship between the two variables.[1216] As bivariate correlation analysis is limited to the association between two variables, it ignores the effect of third variables on the association between the two tested variables. The effect of third variables can be tested via multiple regression analysis.[1217] Comparable to statistical test procedures on group differences, correlation analysis also distinguishes between parametric and non-parametric correlation coefficients. This study employs the non-parametric rank correlation coefficient by *Spearman* as it does not require the tested variables to be metric and normally distributed.[1218] The precondition of normal distribution is only restrictedly met by the variables tested in this study.

Correlation analysis is applied to identify possibly important context factors. When testing different variables for the same context factor,[1219] correlation analysis may give a first hint, which variable has the strongest influence on the dependent variable. Also, when two predictor variables are highly correlated, the inclusion of both variables adds only little explanatory power to the regression analysis. In such a case the individually less influential variable can be excluded from further analysis. Summarized, correlation analysis is a good start to gain a feeling for the analyzed data. Nonetheless, the results of the correlation analysis have to be interpreted with caution; the measured correlation does not account for the influence of third variables and correlation does not imply causality.[1220]

3.4.4 Multiple regression analysis

3.4.4.1 The multiple regression model

Including more than one independent variable in the regression model, multiple regression analysis is able to assess the effect third variables have on the association between independent and dependent variable.[1221] Causality, however, can neither be demonstrated

---

1214 Different degrees of correlation may be interpreted as follows: (1) r = 0; no correlation, (2) r = 0 - 0,2; very weak correlation, (3) r = 0,2 – 0,4 = weak correlation, (4) r = 0,4 – 0,6; medium correlation, (5) r = 0,6 – 0,8; strong correlation, (6) r = 0,8 – 1; very strong correlation and (7) r = 1; perfect correlation. Cf. Brosius 2004, p. 525.

1215 Cf. Salvatore/Reagle 2002, p. 158f.

1216 Cf. Backhaus et al. 2011, p. 21; Tabachnick/Fidell 2007, p. 3.

1217 See the following chapter for a review on multiple regression analysis.

1218 The parametric Pearson coefficient requires at least interval scale level and normal distribution. Cf. Backhaus et al. 2011, p. 486; Eckey et al. 2008, p. 178ff.

1219 For example, the internal context factor size is measured by the variables total assets, market capitalization and number of employees; 'internationality' is measured by the variables foreign listing, SEC listing and share of foreign sales.

1220 Cf. Granger 1988, p. 204; Silverstein et al. 2000, p. 165.

1221 Multiple regression analysis only assesses the effect of third variables that are integrated in the analysis. The effect of missing variables on the hypothesized relationship is not evaluated and is mirrored in the regression analysis error term; cf. Zellner 1975, p. 138.

by regression analysis as this is "[...] a logical and experimental, rather than statistical problem"[1222].

Multiple regression analysis is used in this study to model the relationship between two or more variables.[1223] In contrast to correlation analysis, regression analysis is applied when the direction of the association between the variables is known or assumed by the researcher. Linear regression analysis assumes a linear association between dependent and independent variable and estimates the missing parameters based on linear functions. Single factor regression analysis assesses the relationship between one dependent and one independent variable. Multiple regression analysis describes the relationship between one dependent and two or more independent variables. Multivariate regression analysis, which is not applied in this study, investigates the relationships between several dependent and independent variables.[1224]

Multiple regression models are generally described by the following formula:[1225]

Formula 3.3 $$y_i = \beta_1 x_1 + \cdots + \beta_p x_p + \varepsilon_i$$

where

y_i	=	*dependent variable*
x_i	=	*independent variable*
β	=	*regression coefficient*
ε	=	*error term*
i	=	*1,...,n*

The dependent variable (regressand) is explained by the independent variables (regressor) according to the corresponding regression coefficients. Analogous to correlation coefficients, regression coefficients vary between -1 and +1.[1226] Values closer to -1/+1 imply higher negative/positive associations. No association is assumed for regression coefficients of 0.[1227] The error term ε captures all influence factors that have an impact on the regressand other than the regressors.[1228]

3.4.4.2 Multiple regression assumptions

Linear regression analysis underlies certain **assumptions.** As mentioned above, regression analysis assumes a linear relationship between dependent and independent variables to estimate missing parameters. In a non-linear relationship, the variables have to be trans-

[1222] Tabachnick/Fidell 2007, p. 122.

[1223] Cf. Williams 1959, p. 396; Cohen 2009, p. 64ff.

[1224] Cf. Litz 2000, p. 16ff.

[1225] Cf. Kinney 1986, p. 341.

[1226] The regression coefficients may be interpreted as follows: (1) r = 0; no association, (2) r = 0 - 0,2; very weak association, (3) r = 0,2 – 0,4 = weak association, (4) r = 0,4 – 0,6; medium association, (5) r = 0,6 – 0,8; strong association, (6) r = 0,8 – 1; very strong association and (7) r = 1; perfect association. Cf. Brosius 2004, p. 525.

[1227] Cf. Cohen 2009, p. 261f.

[1228] Cf. Bauer et al. 2009, p. 179ff.

formed first to fit the condition of linearity. SPSS automatically controls in a T-Test for linearity between regressand and regressor. The T-value indicates if the null hypothesis of missing linearity can be rejected. The corresponding significance level mirrors the error probability of that test. Variables that are analyzed via regression analysis have to be at least interval scaled.[1229] This basic requirement results from the way the regression parameters are estimated. To determine the line that best describes the linear relationship between the analyzed variables, the least square method is applied.[1230] According to this method, the squares of the distances between the individual data points and the possible regression line are added and minimized. The line of 'least squares' then represents the regression's best estimate. There is one exception to the condition of metric scale level. So-called dummy or 0/1 variables are allowed to be integrated into the regression model.[1231] Such dummies may be utilized to distinguish between Big4 and non-Big4 companies, for instance.

Furthermore, the independent variables have to be controlled for **multi collinearity,** i.e. for correlation between two or more variables. Highly correlated regressors may have a biasing effect on the regression results. The regression coefficients of the correlated variables may be understated respectively overstated. To detect multi collinearity, SPSS calculates specific multi collinearity measures like 'tolerance' or 'variance inflation factor' (VIF).[1232] The tolerance value of a regression coefficient measures the degree of how much an independent variable is explained by other independent variables. Tolerance values below 0.1 raise suspicion that there might be a case of multi collinearity.[1233] Values below 0.01 strongly indicate multi collinearity.[1234] The VIF value is the reciprocal value of the tolerance value. Accordingly, high VIF values above 10 suggest cases of multi collinearity.

Moreover, the error terms or **residuals** of a regression analysis have to fulfill certain requirements. Representing the difference between the actual values of the dependent variable and the regression's estimates, residuals are used to calculate the **coefficient of determination R-squared**, a measure of how well a regression approximates real data points.[1235] To evaluate the quality of a regression model, the residuals have to be randomly distributed. A systematic distribution of the error terms (autocorrelation) would imply that relevant context factors that explain the dependent variable had been omitted. Regression residuals should not only be randomly distributed, but also normally distributed; again, normal distribution of residuals may be verified using graphical analysis. To rule out a systematic distribution, residuals should be tested for autocorrelation. The *Durbin-Watson* coefficient measures the residuals' first order correlation.[1236] The coefficient varies

[1229] Cf. Gelderman 2000, p. 6ff.
[1230] Cf. Wolberg 2006, p. 31ff.
[1231] Cf. Kleinbaum 2008, p. 217ff.; Bauer et al. 2009, p. 184ff.
[1232] Cf. Henseler et al. 2009, p. 302.
[1233] Cf. Chen/Feng 2001, p. 337.
[1234] Cf. Bauer et al. 2009, p. 184ff.
[1235] Cf. Fahrmeir/Brachinger 1996, p. 108ff.
[1236] Cf. Assenmacher 2002, p. 169ff.

between 0 and 4. A test value around 2 implies little autocorrelation. Test values outside the 1-3 interval indicate strong autocorrelation.[1237]

The above assumptions have to be met to be able to draw unbiased conclusions from the regression analysis. The main indicators to pay attention to are the regression coefficients (see above) and the coefficient of determination. As aforementioned, the latter reflects the regression's quality level, i.e. how well the regressand is explained by the function obtained from the regression analysis. R-squared assumes values between 0 and 1; higher values represent higher values of explanation.[1238] A comparatively high R-squared value of 0.5 means that 50% of the dependent variable's variance is explained by the included independent variables. R-squared is not independent from the number of independent variables; additional variables may increase R-squared without adding explanatory power. For this reason, an **adjusted R-squared** is applied in this study, which compensates such effects.[1239] The **F-value** is another important indicator that is calculated to reject the null hypothesis that sample and population are not related. The significance level of the F-value determines if the regression results on the sample are transferable to the population.[1240]

3.4.4.3 Multiple regression analysis proceeding

As outlined above, various external and internal independent variables are integrated in the regression model of this study to explain the dependent conservatism and secrecy variables. Nonetheless, not all independent variables have an influence on the particular conservatism/secrecy indicator. Some variables only predict the indicator in combination with other variables; some variables even disturb the prediction quality of the regression model. Furthermore, the number of **country variables**[1241] included in the regression analysis is limited by the number of tested countries minus one. Accordingly, when including all country variables in the model, only the two best predictor variables are taken into consideration. The other five are excluded by SPSS for reasons of perfect multi collinearity. The same is true for the **industry variables.** SPSS automatically excludes one of the ten industry variables for multi collinearity as the tenth variable is explained perfectly by the other nine variables.

Except for these cases of perfect multi collinearity of country and industry variables, all other variables are included in the respective regression models, although some variables may disturb and downgrade the estimation quality of the analysis. As a consequence, this study additionally uses **forward and backward stepwise regression analysis**[1242] to filter

1237 Cf. Brosius 2004, p. 580ff.

1238 Cf. Fahrmeir/Brachinger 1996, p. 108ff.

1239 Cf. Wooldridge 2009, p. 200f.

1240 Cf. Litz 2000, p. 104ff.

1241 Country variables refer to the cultural and the institutional variables.

1242 Forward selection starts with no variables and adds variables one by one according to highest additional explanatory power until no significant variables are left. The significance level for additional variables is usually 5%. Backward selection, on the contrary, starts with all variables and eliminates the variables one by one according to lowest explanatory power. Whereas forward regression analysis only includes

out the variable combination that best explains the variance of the dependent variable and, thus, achieves the highest adjusted R-squared value. Accordingly, the number of external and internal variables that are included in the respective regression model varies depending on the particular conservatism/secrecy indicator. The **included variables** are pointed out at the beginning of each regression analysis subchapter. The discussion of the regression analysis results, thus, is limited to the 'first-best' regression model only.

Variable groups that approximate the same context factor (e.g. size) may show increased levels of **multi collinearity**. When more than one variable of the same variable group are included in the regression model of highest explanatory power, multi collinearity is controlled for by the quality factors tolerance and VIF.[1243]

The parametric linear regression analysis is safeguarded by a non-parametric **rank regression analysis** in this study.[1244] In a rank regression analysis the variables are transformed to ordinal scale level and ranked according to value. A non-parametric test like the rank regression analysis bears the advantage that the relationship between regressand and regressor is not required to be linear. Neither do residuals have to be normally distributed, nor does autocorrelation bias results.[1245]

3.5 Summary

Chapter three covers various issues related to the **research design** of the study. The decisions on the empirical research strategy, the method of data collection and the method of data evaluation lay the methodological groundwork for the empirical analysis in chapter four. Considering the research question and the philosophic scientific approach of this study, the **field study** is chosen as the appropriate empirical research strategy to explain and predict the association between national culture and IFRS practice. Data on corporate IFRS practice is gathered evaluating financial statements by means of **content analysis**. The content analytical instrument **disclosure index** is employed to systematically determine segment and income tax information quantity. This study employs a total of four disclosure indices as content analytical category systems, two for each segment and income tax information. These indices are developed mainly based on regulatory requirements and satisfy the content analytical quality factors of **reliability** and **validity**.

The final section on data evaluation presents descriptive and inferential statistical methods to analyze the hypothesized relationships between dependent and independent variables. **Descriptive statistics**, like the calculation of mean or standard deviation, are used for a first quantitative and graphical analysis of the empirical data. **Correlation** and **regression analysis** determine the existence, direction and strength of potential statistical associations between two and more variables. The assumptions of parametric tests, like the T-Test, ANOVA or multiple regression analysis, are discussed and alternative non-parametric tests are introduced. The following chapter presents the empirical test results.

---

significant variables backward regression analysis may also contain non-significant variables; cf. Brosius 2004, p. 590.

[1243] See the preceding subchapter.

[1244] Cf., e.g., Lang/Lundholm 1993, p. 246ff.

[1245] Cf. Cooke 1998, p. 209ff.; Ryan 2009, p. 95ff.

4 Empirical results

4.1 Overview

In chapter four the previously theoretically posited and operationalized hypotheses are tested empirically. The content of this chapter is split in two sections. First, the analyzed industry sample is presented. The selection of the companies is described and the companies are briefly characterized according to the internal context factors size, industry, auditor, internationality, profitability and leverage. The second part of the chapter is assigned to the statistical analysis of the gathered empirical data. Conservatism and secrecy indicators are analyzed to investigate the possible influence of national culture. Each indicator subchapter ends with a critical discussion of the empirical results.

4.2 Company sample

4.2.1 Sample selection

As aforementioned, this study analyzes financial statements of listed companies in the EU. The regional focus is on the **EU** since all capital market oriented companies are required to apply IFRS as endorsed by the EU; the EU setting, thus, guarantees sufficiently large sample numbers. Furthermore, the analysis of financial statements of **listed** companies bears the advantage of publicly available financial data. Investigating listed companies, the researcher may further decide between the analyses of large, medium or small listed companies. On the one hand, small or medium companies might be more suited to assess the association between national culture and IFRS practice as these companies are assumed to be less experienced with respect to international accounting standards. Large companies, in contrast, often adapted IFRS or US-GAAP before 2005 to access the international capital market; these companies might have adapted their corporate accounting practices to international accounting practices and therefore are less susceptible to cultural influences. On the other hand, large listed companies are of higher economic importance (vitality) for the national/international capital market;[1246] financial statement users like analysts or investors are likely to be more interested in empirical evidence on the IFRS practice of large listed companies. Moreover, large companies may be preferred over small or medium companies for reasons of better availability of electronic data and English versions of the companies' financial statements. Following the arguments of economic importance and data availability, this study analyzes financial statements of **large** listed EU companies. The largest listed companies of the French, German and British equity capital markets are selected based on national stock indices as of December 31st of 2009.

The German companies are selected with reference to the *Deutsche Börse* **HDAX**. The HDAX contains all shares included in the selection indices DAX, MDAX and TecDAX. Covering all industrial sectors, the HDAX lists the **110 largest companies** listed in the German Prime Standard. The **DAX** is the German blue chip index based on the 30 largest and top-selling stock companies trading on the Frankfurt Stock Exchange. The

[1246] See for the 'vital' country concept chapter 1.3.5.2.

MDAX, the German Midcap index, comprises the 50 largest (market capitalization/order book volume) Prime Standard shares, following the DAX 30 selection and excluding companies from the technological sector. The 30 largest (market capitalization/order book volume) technological companies, except for those included in the DAX, are gathered in the **TecDAX**.

The 110 largest listed French companies are selected from the CAC 40, the CAC Next 20 and the CAC Mid 100 at the reference date. The **CAC 40** is the French blue chip index. Of the 100 largest listed companies that had the highest free float market capitalization and share turnover during the last twelve months, the CAC 40 contains the companies that are "[…] a relevant benchmark for portfolio management [and] a suitable underlying asset for derivatives products"[1247]. The **CAC Next 20** is calculated based on the 20 largest listed companies ranked after the CAC 40. The French Midcap index is the **CAC Mid 100** containing the 100 largest listed companies following the CAC 40 and the CAC Next 20. Only the largest 50 markets caps were selected from the CAC Mid 100 to have a French sample that is comparable to the German HDAX sample.

The UK sample consists of the 100 companies that are part of the FTSE 100 plus the ten largest companies that are part of the FTSE 250 at the end of 2009. The **FTSE 100** contains 100 LSE listed companies with the highest market capitalization. Its composition is determined quarterly. Companies are replaced when FTSE 250 companies, according to their market capitalization, would rank among the top 90 companies of the FTSE 100. The **FTSE 250** is also a market value weighted index comprising the 250 largest listed companies after the FTSE 100. Both indices form the FTSE 350.

The basic sample consists of 330 German, French and UK companies. Banks, financial service companies and insurance companies are eliminated from the sample as the business model of companies from the financial sector is not comparable to the business model of industrial corporations.[1248] The different business model is underlined by sector specific accounting rules like IFRS 4 (Insurance Contracts). The exclusion of financial institutions is common practice in empirical accounting studies.[1249]

The industry of the sample companies is determined by the internationally consistent **SIC** system[1250]. The national stock exchanges LSE, *Deutsche Börse* and NYSE Euronext each have their own industry classification system. These systems might differ substantially with respect to denomination of and allocation to the particular industrial categories. To allow for international comparability, the four digit primary SIC code is used to classify the sample's companies accordingly. The company SIC codes are taken from the commercial database Osiris. **Financial institutions** whose SIC code begins with the number six are excluded from the sample.

1247 NYSE Euronext 2009, p. 2.

1248 Cf. Ernst & Young 2006, p. 4.

1249 Cf., e.g., Maher et al. 1992, p. 201; Loughran/Ritter 1997, p. 1825; Carcello/Nagy 2004, p. 61; Maury/Pajuste 2005, p. 1819; Faulkender/Petersen 2006, p. 51.

1250 See chapter 4.2.3.

The original sample contains a few companies that are considered to be **foreign** with regard to the national stock exchanges they are listed at. To guarantee that the companies listed at LSE, *Deutsche Börse* and NYSE Euronext are shaped by the national culture of the particular country, companies that do not have their headquarters in the respective country are excluded from the sample. EADS for example, listed at the NYSE Euronext and the Frankfurt stock exchange, is a Pan-European company with headquarters in the Netherlands. EADS therefore was excluded from both the French and the German sample. Royal Dutch Shell was excluded from the UK sample; its headquarters are also situated in the Netherlands. Finally, companies that did not publish 2008/2009 financial statements are eliminated from the sample. This is the case for only one company. The British company Cadbury became part of Kraft Foods in February of 2010 and, as a consequence, was delisted. No financial statements were published for 2009.

The following Table 4-1 shows the country-by-country transition from basic to adjusted population, taking into account company eliminations regarding financial institutions, foreign companies and missing financial statements.

	Germany	France	UK	Σ
Basic sample	110	110	110	330
Financial institutions	- 12	- 15	- 20	- 37
Foreign companies	- 5	- 7	- 9	- 21
No Financial statements	0	0	- 1	- 1
Adjusted sample	**93**	**88**	**80**	**261**

Table 4-1: Adjusted company sample

The following chapters present descriptive data to characterize the 261 companies of the adjusted sample. The criteria used to characterize the adjusted sample are context factors that are also employed as internal control variables in the regression analysis to control for effects other than culture. The sample companies are described according to size, industry, auditor, internationality, profitability, and financial leverage.

4.2.2 Size

Size is an indicator for the company's degree of complexity, which, according to agency theory, is one of the main drivers of agency costs. Complex companies engage more in internal control systems and corporate disclosure to handle the complexity of corporate processes and to diminish equity costs. Company size is measured and controlled for by means of market capitalization, total assets and number of employees; total assets are described to allow for comparison with market capitalization.[1251]

[1251] German and French financial statement figures are almost exclusively presented in Euro. UK financial statements, however, are published in British Pound Sterling (GBP), US-Dollar (USD) or Euro. To compare corporate characteristics on a transnational level, financial figures in currencies other than Euro (GBP, USD) are translated into Euro using the corresponding exchange rate at the companies' closing date.

The size of the companies according to **market capitalization** varies significantly between € 129 million (Medigene, a German biotechnology company) and € 141 billion (BP)[1252] with a median of € 3,290 million and a mean of € 9,578 million. The sample of German companies contains smaller companies than the French or the British samples. 32 German companies have a market capitalization smaller than one billion € compared to four French and no British companies. The French sample contains most companies in the ranges from one to five and five to 20 billion € and the UK sample contains most companies that have a market capitalization larger than € 20 billion. The following Table 4-2 lists further statistical measures and displays an aggregated country by country diagram.

Criterion (M€)	Market capitalization
Minimum	129
5% quantile	398
1. quartile	1,537
Median	3,290
Mean	9,578
3. quartile	7,896
95% quantile	45,255
Maximum	141,008
Standard deviation	17,279

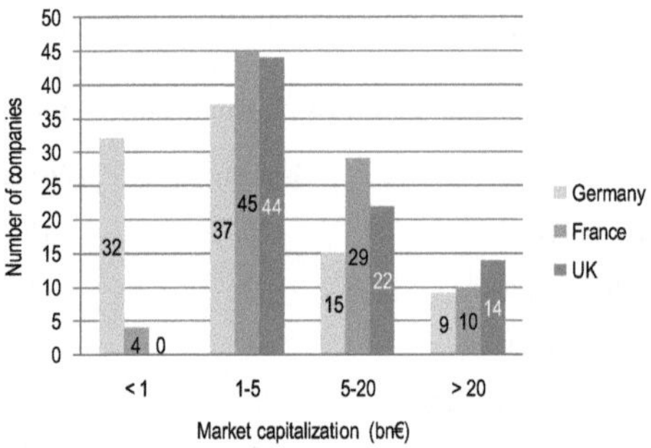

Table 4-2: Sample characteristics according to the size criterion market capitalization

Another variable that measures corporate size independent from the capital market is **total assets.** In analogy to the companies' market capitalization, total assets vary substantially between the minimum of € 66 million (Medigene) and the maximum of € 117 billion (Volkswagen) with a median of € 5,512 million and a mean of € 16,849 million. The total assets figures by country show a similar picture as compared to market capitalization. The German sample comprises a lot more smaller companies with a total asset value of less than one billion €. German companies also dominate the total asset range between one and five billion. Whereas UK companies dominate the total asset range between five and 20 billion €, French companies outnumber German and UK companies in the range larger than € 20 billion. Table 4-3 provides a more detailed overview of the statistical total asset measures.

This study also incorporates the **number of employees** as a corporate size variable that does not base on book or market values. As a relatively small number of employees can manage a relatively large amount of corporate assets, total assets or market capitalization might be misleading with respect to the complexity of such a company. For that reason, size of the company is also measured by number of employees.

[1252] The market capitalization reference date is December 31st of 2009 and therewith long before the Gulf of Mexico oil spill.

Criterion (M€)	Total assets
Minimum	66
5% quantile	541
1. quartile	2,029
Median	5,212
Mean	16,849
3. quartile	17,337
95% quantile	67,497
Maximum	117,178
Standard deviation	30,217

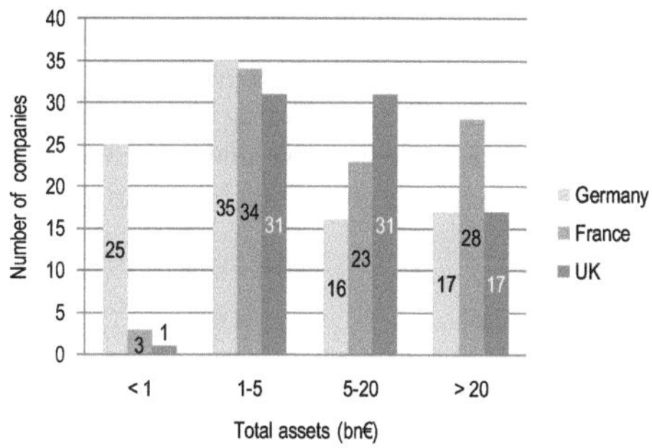

Table 4-3: Sample characteristics according to the size criterion total assets

The number of employees varies between the French real estate company Mercialys which employs only 63 employees and the UK security company G4S which employs 592,964 employees. The sample companies of this study have an average workforce of 51,857. German companies are predominant in the two lowest classes up to 20,000 employees. UK firms dominate the mid segment from 20,000 to 100,000 employees and French firms dominate the top segment of companies that have workforces larger than 100,000. Detailed figures and a graphical country by country overview are presented in Table 4-4.

Criterion	Number of employees
Minimum	63
5% quantile	380
1. quartile	4,520
Median	18,381
Mean	51,857
3. quartile	64,643
95% quantile	198,713
Maximum	592,964
Standard deviation	87,285

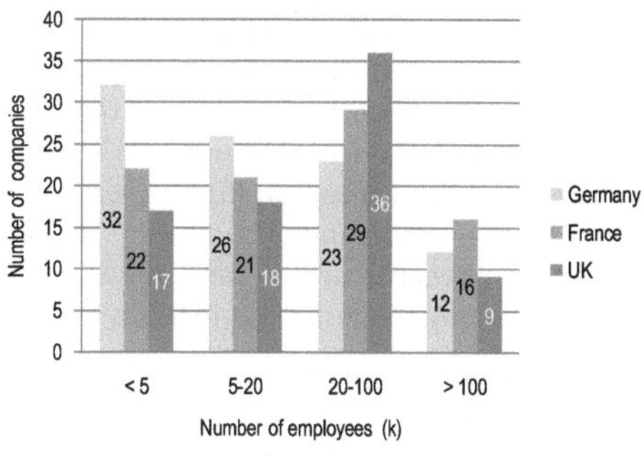

Table 4-4: Sample characteristics according to the size criterion number of employees

The presented figures show that the sample companies are not uniformly distributed among the three countries with respect to corporate size. This effect is controlled for by integrating the size variables into the analysis of the study.

Approximating the same internal context factor, the three size variables market capitalization, total assets and number of employees correlate strongly (see Table 4-5). Nonetheless, all three variables are employed to control for size effects since the particular variables cover different aspects of size. For instance, size as measured by market capitalization is assumed to be a lot more volatile than size as measured by number of employees; the latter size variable, in contrast, may be a deficient proxy for size respectively complexity when comparably few employees are responsible for comparably large amounts of total assets (e.g. real estate). When including more than one size variable into the particular regression analysis that best predicts the analyzed conservatism/secrecy indicator, **multi collinearity** of the size variables is controlled by means of the quality factors tolerance and VIF.

	Market capitalization	Total assets	Number of employees
Market capitalization	1.000	0.812**	0.580**
Total assets	0.812**	1.000	0.704**
Number of employees	0.580**	0.704**	1.000

** represents significance at the 1% level

Table 4-5: Size correlation matrix

4.2.3 Industry

The research design of the hypotheses requires industry to be controlled for since industry is expected to be an influential internal context factor.[1253] The industrial sector of a company might be influential, for instance, with regard to investment property fair value measurement or R&D capitalization behavior. The industry of the company is also to be taken into account when excluding certain problematic companies like banks or insurance companies from the sample. As aforementioned, the US SIC code is applied to consistently classify the sample companies according to their particular industry. The four digit SIC primary code list is rather detailed and has to be aggregated to give an impression of the companies' industrial distribution. Thus, the companies are grouped according to the *French/Fama* grouping.[1254] *French/Fama* classify the **SIC** categories into a ten class industry portfolio and distinguish between (1) consumer non-durables, (2) consumer durables, (3) manufacturing, (4) energy, (5) high technology, (6) telecommunication, (7) shops, (8) healthcare, (9) utilities and (10) other.[1255] 'Other' contains all industry classes that do not fit into the categories one to nine, for example mines, construction or transport. The country by country industry classification is illustrated in Figure 4-1.

The German sample is rather technology driven and clearly dominated by companies from the industrial sectors manufacturing, business equipment and consumer durables (automotive). The 'other' segment is comparably small. French and UK companies, on the contrary, to a large percentage belong to the 'other' segment. Apart from this 'collection' category, French companies also show a clear industrial focus with 28 companies belonging to industrial sectors. British companies have the lowest percentage of industrial companies. The predominant categories are consumer non-durables and shops. Also, the

[1253] Cf. chapter 2.3.2.2.2.

[1254] Cf. French/Fama 2010.

[1255] See for the *French/Fama* SIC code industry mapping Appendix A, Table A 1.

UK sample contains the most companies from the oil, gas and coal extraction and products segment.

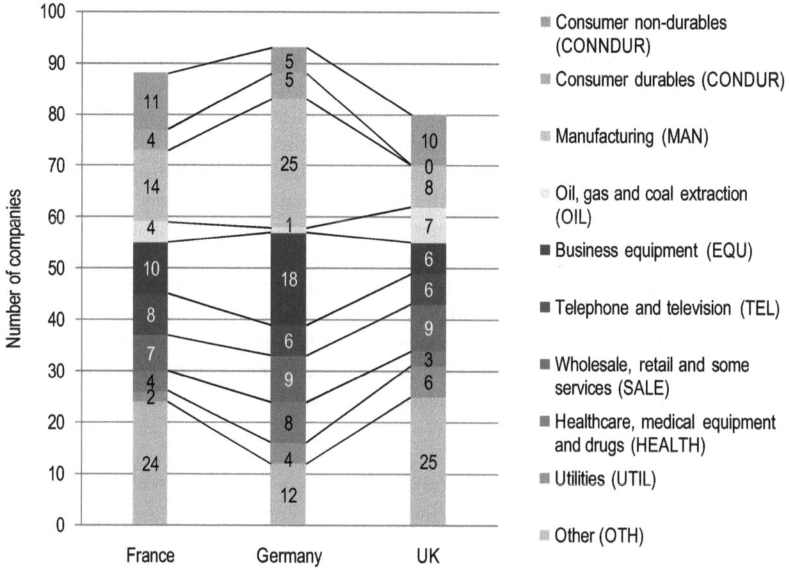

Figure 4-1: Sample industry classification

4.2.4 Auditor

As the company sample consists of the largest listed companies in France, Germany and the UK, most of the companies are audited by large Big4 auditors. Only 16 (6%) of the sample companies are audited by a non-Big4 auditor. The percentage of companies audited by a non-Big4 auditor is highest in Germany (12%) compared to France (5%) and the UK (1%); only one British company (Randgold Resources) is audited by a non-Big4 auditor (see Table 4-6).

	France		Germany		UK		Σ	
	No.	%	No.	%	No.	%	No.	%
Big4 auditor	84	95	82	88	79	99	245	94
Non-Big4 auditor	4	5	11	12	1	1	16	6

Table 4-6: Sample characteristics according to the criterion auditor

The following section describes the company sample with respect to the internal context factor internationality.

4.2.5 Internationality

As mentioned above, internationality is measured by three separate variables. The first variable is **foreign listing**. Companies that access the international capital market are assumed to be more internationally oriented. Almost all French companies (99%) are listed at a stock exchange outside their home country.[1256] Whereas 78 (84%) German companies are listed abroad, only 52 (65%) British companies access a foreign capital market. The low percentage of foreign listed British companies is likely to be associated to the strength of the British capital market; British companies obtain sufficient capital at their home capital market. The second internationality variable is **SEC listing**. Listings at a US stock exchange that is supervised by the SEC are analyzed separately as the US capital market is the most advanced capital market in the world; a SEC listing therefore is assumed to be an even stronger indicator for internationality. Furthermore, until recently the SEC required foreign private issuers to reconcile their financial statements to US-GAAP; accordingly, IFRS practice of SEC registered companies could be influenced by US-GAAP. Although the UK sample shows the smallest percentage of foreign listed companies compared to the French or German sample, British companies (20%) are more often listed at a stock exchange that is regulated by the SEC than French (7%) or German (4%) companies (see Table 4-7).

	France		Germany		UK		Σ	
	No.	%	No.	%	No.	%	No.	%
Foreign listing	87	99	78	84	52	65	217	83
SEC listing	6	7	4	4	16	20	26	10

Table 4-7: Sample characteristics according to the criteria foreign and SEC listing

The third internationality variable is independent from the sample companies' listings and measures internationality by foreign sales divided by total sales. The **foreign sales** proxy is an indicator for the degree of internationality of the companies' operations; companies that have a high percentage of foreign sales are expected to have a more complex business model than companies that only operate in their home country. The comparison of foreign sales percentages of the country samples indicates that especially the British company sample is characterized by heterogeneous foreign sales ratios. British companies dominate the company classes of very low internationality (0%-20% foreign sales) and very high internationality (80%-100% foreign sales); almost half of the British sample companies have a foreign sales percentage of 80% and more. The foreign sales percentages of French and German companies are comparable. Whereas the French sample contains more companies that are characterized by high internationality (60%-80% foreign sales), the German sample dominates the company class of very high internationality (80%-100% foreign sales). The company classes of low (20%-40% foreign sales) and medium (40%-60% foreign sales) internationality indicate comparable company number considering the total sample sizes of the three sample countries (see Table 4-8).

[1256] This high percentage is likely to be associated with the companies' NYSE Euronext listing since the NYSE Euronext also encompasses the Amsterdam, the Brussels and the Lisbon stock exchanges.

Criterion (%)	Foreign sales
Minimum	0.00
5% quantile	0.00
1. quartile	0.48
Median	0.72
Mean	0.62
3. quartile	0.85
95% quantile	0.97
Maximum	1.00
Standard deviation	0.30

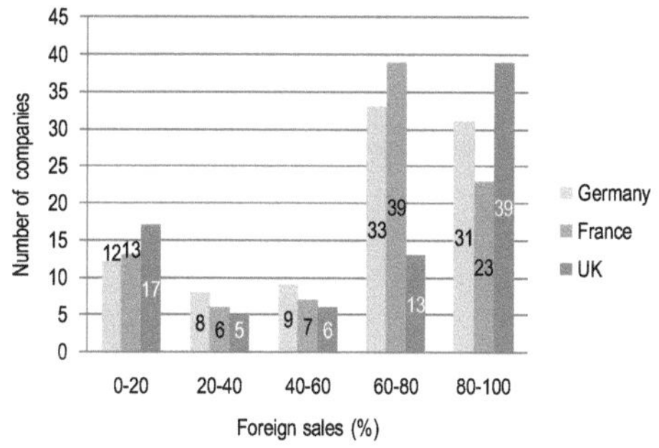

Table 4-8: Sample characteristics according to the criterion foreign sales

4.2.6 Profitability

As outlined above, the profitability situation of a company may affect the way companies make use of accounting discretion and options. Companies could use a bad year to get rid of accounting legacy debts and make it a worse year ('big bath accounting').[1257] Or companies could interpret accounting rules optimistically to reach the profit zone when running the risk of slightly missing it. Alternatively, companies that want to justify extraordinarily positive results to the employees, labor unions or the public in general could tend to augment disclosure to clarify the reasons for such results. Generally speaking, a company's profitability could influence both tested accounting values of conservatism and secrecy.[1258]

This study employs an income figure before interest and taxes, putting EBIT in relation to total revenues and total assets. The first performance indicator refers to the companies' profit margin[1259], the latter to the companies' return on investment (ROI)[1260]. The following figure displays the sample companies' **profit margin** and **ROI** distribution by country for 2009 (see Figure 4-2).

Figure 4-2 shows that the sample companies are mainly distributed in a similar area. Also, the number of profitable companies outweighs the number of unprofitable companies. The linear graphs that resemble the companies' distribution by country indicate that French and UK companies follow a similar distribution. According to these graphs, French and UK companies are characterized by a more extremely positive respectively negative profit margin values and German companies by more extremely positive respectively negative ROI values. This difference in distribution may result from larger amounts of total assets of French and UK companies.[1261]

[1257] Cf. Walsh et al. 1991, p. 173ff.
[1258] See also chapter 2.3.2.2.5.
[1259] Cf. Brigham/Ehrhardt 2008, p. 133.
[1260] Cf. Laux 2006, p. 285ff.
[1261] Cf. the anterior chapter.

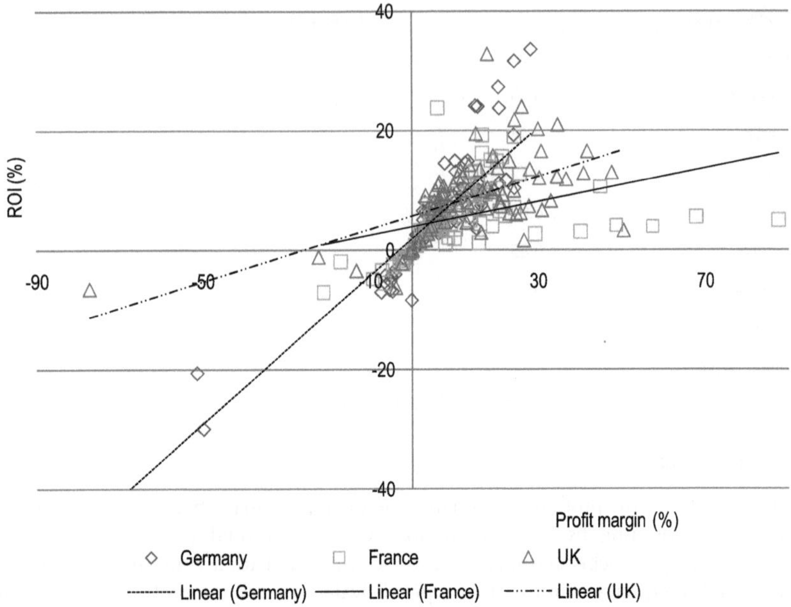

Figure 4-2: Sample characteristics according to ROI and profit margin after taxes[1262]

Considering the remaining negative outliers in Figure 4-2, French and UK companies tend to have strongly negative profit margins combined with comparably slightly negative ROIs. German negative outliers, on the contrary, are accompanied by also strongly negative ROIs. The picture looks different with respect to positive outliers. The extremely positive outliers are mainly French and German companies. French companies tend to be allocated closer to the X-axis, which indicates a stronger profit margin influence. Influenced by comparably higher ROI values, German companies tend to be closer to the Y-axis of the coordinate system. British positive outliers are mainly found in between.

The table below, which lists further profitability characteristics of the three country samples, shows that British companies, measured by ROI and profit margin, are generally more profitable than French and German companies and French companies are generally more profitable than German companies (see Table 4-9). With respect to the latter country combination, the profitability results measured by profit margin are more explicit than the ROI results, which show a rather mixed picture.

[1262] Four outliers have been removed from the company sample for better graphical display.

Criterion (%)	ROI				Profit margin			
	Total	France	Germany	UK	Total	France	Germany	UK
Minimum	-65.75	-7.08	-65.75	-34.39	-92.75	-21.06	-92.75	-77.19
5% quantile	-5.48	-2.74	-7.56	-2.16	-6.46	-5.86	-6.86	-2.59
1. quartile	2.78	2.83	1.18	5.66	3.13	3.66	1.01	5.72
Median	6.20	4.95	5.26	8.26	8.20	10.06	6.27	13.10
Mean	6.13	6.20	4.25	8.24	10.27	12.50	3.78	15.34
3. quartile	10.02	9.34	8.23	12.16	16.63	16.98	11.95	24.26
95% quantile	19.53	15.97	23.85	20.34	34.85	43.92	21.39	40.90
Maximum	60.36	60.36	33.54	32.82	132.69	87.56	28.20	132.69
Standard deviation	9.86	8.13	12.19	8.10	18.99	16.26	17.48	21.44

Table 4-9: Sample characteristics according to ROI and profit margin

4.2.7 Leverage

Financial leverage is measured by the **debt to equity ratio.**[1263] Different degrees of leverage may be interpreted in a number of ways. For instance, high financial leverage values may be the result of an external growth strategy of the company that was mainly financed externally. In this case, high leverage could be interpreted as an indicator for high potential regarding future economic success. Nonetheless, high values of leverage may also result from the constantly poor sales situation of a company and therewith rather represent low potential for future economic success. Moreover, as interest payments are tax deductible, higher leverage to a certain degree also implies lower cost of capital.[1264] Besides economic factors, the leverage figure may also be industry influenced; certain capital-intensive industries like auto manufacturing traditionally have higher debt to equity ratios than other less capital-intensive industries.[1265] The following table lists information on the statistical attributes of the sample's debt to equity ratios. Furthermore, the companies' ratios are displayed, divided into five debt to equity classes on a country by country basis, in the adjacent graphic (see Table 4-10).

Table 4-10 shows that German and French companies are mainly found in the lower debt to equity ratio classes. British companies, in contrast, dominate the class of ratios larger than 400%. Four companies have negative debt to equity ratios indicating negative equity. Two of these companies are French; the other two are from the UK.

1263 Cf. Gibson 2007, p. 260f.

1264 This statement is true until a certain point is reached at which the risk of bankruptcy overweighs the benefits of tax deductibility. Cf. Moosa 2002, p. 192.

1265 Cf. van Horne/Wachowicz 2005, p. 137f.

Criterion (%)	Leverage
Minimum	-72.39
5% quantile	0.27
1. quartile	1.03
Median	1.66
Mean	2.75
3. quartile	3.01
95% quantile	5.76
Maximum	205.15
Standard deviation	13.65

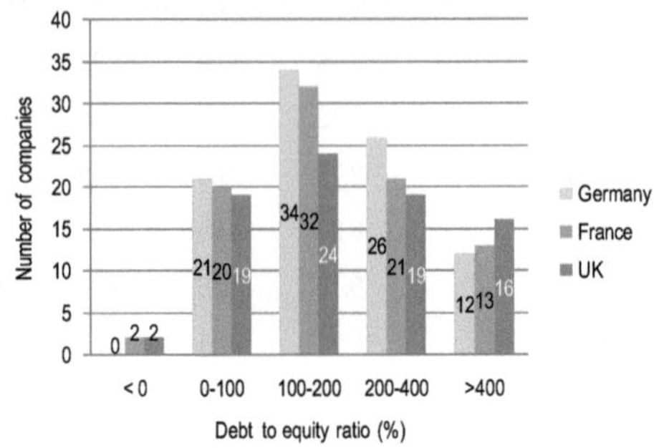

Table 4-10: Sample characteristics according to the criterion leverage

Following the above remarks on the company sample's basic characteristics, the next chapter presents the test results of the various conservatism and secrecy hypotheses that are analyzed in this study.

4.3 Empirical analysis

4.3.1 Conservatism

In chapter 2.3 two sets of hypotheses on conservatism were derived. The first two hypotheses to be tested employ conservatism indicators of a more general nature, viz. the market to book value and the negative accruals measure. The other conservatism hypotheses deal with specific accounting areas that are assumed to be affected by varying degrees of conservatism. These concern measurement issues like (1) the capitalization of development costs, (2) the capitalization of intangibles in a PPA, (3) depreciation periods of tangible assets and (4) fair value measurement of investment property. As posited above, the cultural dimensions of uncertainty avoidance and power distance are hypothesized to be positively associated and masculinity and individualism are hypothesized to be negatively associated with conservative IFRS practice.

In accordance with the above chapter on statistical fundamentals,[1266] the statistical analysis of the particular hypotheses is split in three separate parts. First, the dependent variable is described statistically to give a first impression on the data. The description is followed by a correlation analysis of the relationship between dependent and independent variables. The correlation analysis, which measures only bivariate relationships, is complemented by multiple regression analysis to control for multivariate influences. Each indicator subchapter concludes with a critical analysis of the obtained results and the denial respectively confirmation of the tested sub-hypotheses.

[1266] Cf. chapter 3.4.1.

4.3.1.1 Market to book value

The market to book value (MTB) is one of the two more global conservatism indicators. In comparison to the direct indicators, which approximate conservatism in a specific accounting area, MTB indicates conservatism as a result of various observable and non-observable accounting choices. Following the above definition of conservatism, characterized by understated assets/revenues and overstated liabilities/expenses, higher MTB values stand for higher degrees of conservatism. Besides the relative understatement of book values, however, high MTB values could also mirror the capital market's expectation with regard to the future growth potential of the company. Accordingly, various performance and growth measures are controlled for.

Before such effects are analyzed, the following chapter begins with a descriptive country by country analysis of the MTB distribution.

4.3.1.1.1 Descriptive analysis

The market to book value is determined for all 261 companies of the sample. However, the sample to be analyzed in the following consists of 260 values only. One negative value of -128.53 was identified as an extreme outlier and eliminated from the UK sample prior to any statistical analysis for the extremely biasing effect on the sample as a whole. Before going into detail on mean value comparison test results, some basic statistical data on the MTB distribution is provided. The following table presents statistical characteristics like minimum, maximum, standard deviation and different quantiles of the three country samples and the total sample (see Table 4-11).

Value (%)	Total	France	Germany	UK
N	260	88	93	79
Minimum	-13.16	-1.73	0.36	-13.16
5% quantile	0.64	0.54	0.60	0.69
1. quartile	1.16	1.06	1.31	1.25
Median	1.82	1.54	1.72	2.37
Mean	2.46	1.82	2.15	3.52
3. quartile	2.78	2.13	2.48	3.44
95% quantile	6.04	4.33	4.62	7.45
Maximum	42.65	8.07	7.94	42.65
Standard deviation	3.57	1.37	1.38	6.01

Table 4-11: MTB descriptive statistics

The above table shows that the three country samples can be grouped in two, France and Germany, on the one side, and the UK, on the other side. The two Continental European company samples show a much more similar distribution than the UK sample. Both countries have a standard deviation that is considerably lower than the UK standard deviation. The clear difference in measure of variation is supported by the extreme values of the three samples. Although the extreme negative outlier of the UK sample is eliminated from the sample, the total sample minimum still forms part of the British sample. The positive end of the MTB scale supports the impression of greater variation from the negative end of the scale. The total sample maximum value also is part of the UK sample. The quantile analysis indicates that the UK sample especially varies from French and German samples with respect to higher quantiles. Whereas the lower 5% quantile and the first quartile values are comparable to the French and German sample, higher quantiles differ substantially. This variation at the upper end of the MTB distribution is underlined by the following boxplot[1267] diagram of the three country samples (see Figure 4-3).

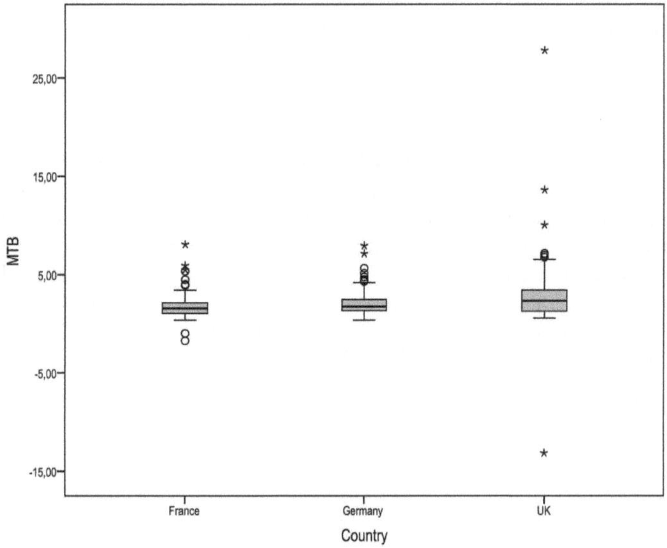

Figure 4-3: MTB boxplot diagram by country

Despite the elimination of one extreme negative outlier from the UK sample, the UK sample includes one more negative and three positive outliers. The German sample contains only positive outliers and the French sample is characterized by both positive and negative outliers; German and French outliers are not as extreme as the British outliers; thus, both samples are considered to be more homogeneous than the British sample.

[1267] The boxplot or Box-Whisker plot offers a graphical description of the distribution of statistical data. The central line of the box marks the median of the distribution; the outer lines of the box mark the upper and lower quartiles. The ends of the two whiskers outside the box mark the lowest value still within the 1.5 interquartile range (IQR) of the lower quartile and the highest value still within 1.5 IQR of the upper quartile. The interquartile range is the difference between first and third quartile. Outliers between 1.5 and 3 IQR are marked by a circle and extreme outliers larger than 3 IQR are marked by an asterisk.

As outlined in chapter 3.4.1, the following univariate and multivariate statistical tests are performed on MTB data that is adjusted for outliers that lie more than three standard deviations from the mean.

When comparing the mean values of the three country samples, the German sample scores slightly higher than the French sample. The UK sample has by far the highest mean value of the three, which may, however, be a consequence of the extreme positive outliers shown above. ANOVA supports the notion that the **country** mean values differ significantly ($F = 4.854$; $p = 0.009$**). The non-parametric Kruskal-Wallis-Test encourages the result ($p = 0.002$**). A multiple comparison (Scheffé-Test) of the three groups shows that the significant differences in country mean values are between Germany and the UK ($p = 0.041$*) and between France and the UK ($p = 0.008$**). The mean value difference between France and Germany is not significant ($p = 0.814$). These results therewith underline the first impression of the descriptive statistical analysis above. These first findings indicate that the MTB value might be affected by country factors, at least between France and Germany, on the one hand, and the UK, on the other hand. If and which country factors have an effect on MTB, is further analyzed in the following chapters on correlation and regression analysis.

Another mean value comparison test is performed on **industry** level. ANOVA indicates weakly significant country differences ($F = 1.800$; $p = 0.069$). The weakly result, however, may be related to further outliers of the sample as the non-parametric Kruskal-Wallis-Test rejects the null hypothesis of equal distribution of MTB across industries at the significance level of $p = 0.002$**. Correlation and regression analysis will show which industries in specific are associated with a possible influence on the dependent variable MTB.

A last mean value comparison test is conducted for the type of auditor, distinguishing between **Big4** auditors and other auditors. However, the T-Test leads to no significant results ($t = -0.413$; $p = 0.683$)[1268]. This result is backed up by the non-parametric Mann-Whithney-U-Test which retains the null hypothesis of equal distribution of MTB across the two auditor categories ($p = 0.248$). The choice of auditor, thus, is not expected to have an influence on the distribution of MTB.

Mean value comparison leads to some interesting insights indicating country and industry as potentially influential context factors. The following chapter assesses, which country factors in specific have an influence on MTB. Additionally, other control variables like leverage or size are tested for a potential influence.

4.3.1.1.2 Correlation analysis

This study employs a two-tailed non-parametric Spearman's correlation coefficient to measure the pair wise association between dependent and independent variables. Although *ex ante* posited, the assumed direction of the relationship between the variables is not important in two-tailed correlation analysis. Correlation analysis is generally performed before regression analysis to receive a first idea of the association of certain variables.

[1268] Equal variances not assumed.

Three of the four **cultural** variables are significantly correlated with MTB. Uncertainty avoidance (r = -0.224; p = 0.000**) and power distance (r = -0.191; p = 0.002**) are significantly negatively and masculinity is significantly positively (r = 0.191; p = 0.002**) related to MTB. However, all relationships are contrary to the expected. Whereas uncertainty avoidance and power distance are assumed to correlate positively with conservatism, masculinity is expected to correlate negatively with conservatism and therewith higher values of MTB. These unexpected results with respect to cultural factors are indicated by the above descriptive statistical analysis; the UK sample is characterized by higher MTB values compared to its Continental European counterparts. Given that MTB is a proxy for conservatism, the British companies, thus, are labeled the most conservative as measured by MTB. Regression analysis will show if these surprising results proof to be stable when integrating more possible context factors into the model to be tested.

With respect to **institutional** country factors, legal system and tax system are expected to have an influence on MTB. LEGTAX, which distinguishes between code law and common law legal systems and dependant and independent tax systems, is significantly negatively correlated to MTB (r = -0.193; p = 0.002**). In this dummy variable France and Germany are represented by one. Accordingly, France and Germany are associated with rather low MTB values; this finding underlines the results of the above descriptive statistical analysis.

Apart from country factor related influences, the above comparison of mean values also indicates an **industry** related influence. Accordingly, correlation analysis identifies the three industries business equipment (r = 0.182; p = 0.004**), wholesale/retail (r = -0.143; p = 0.022*) and other (r = -0.138; p = 0.028*) to correlate significantly with MTB. The former industry is related to higher MTB values and the latter two industries are related to lower MTB values.

Size also seems to play a role with respect to different MTB values, although the results are mixed. Whereas size measured by logarithmized market capitalization (r = 0.168; p = 0.007**) is significantly positively associated with MTB, size measured by number of employees (r = -0.157; p = 0.012*) and logarithmized total assets (r = -0.255; p = 0.000**) is significantly negatively correlated. The correlation analysis of the context factors that approximate the companies' degree of **internationality** shows consistent results. Companies that are listed at a stock exchange under the mandate of the SEC (r = 0.126; p = 0.043*) and companies that have high percentages of foreign sales (r = 0.194; p = 0.002**) are significantly positively correlated with higher MTB values. These internationality factors indicate an association between higher internationality and higher MTB values, i.e. higher conservatism. This result is unexpected since internationality is rather associated with less conservatism.

The above mixed results challenge the assumption that MTB is an adequate proxy for conservatism. As aforementioned, a companies' high MTB could also be the result of market expectations as a consequence of high company profitability respectively growth. The correlation between MTB and the tested profitability and growth indicators encourage this posit. The **profitability** indicators profit margin (r = 0.334; p = 0.000**) and

ROI ($r = 0.497$; $p = 0.000$**) and the **growth** measure sales growth ($r = 0.320$; $p = 0.000$**) are significantly positively correlated with MTB.[1269]

The following chapter on regression analysis will show if the tentative results of the descriptive and correlation analysis are affirmed, when (1) the variables are classified in dependent and independent variables and (2) the multiple influence of various variables is tested simultaneously.

4.3.1.1.3 Regression analysis

The regression model that tests the influence of internal and external context factors on the conservatism indicator MTB includes four cultural factors and two further institutional country factors to test for country specific influences. Furthermore, the model controls for industry, size, internationality, Big4 auditor, profitability and sales growth. The size measure market capitalization and the leverage measure debt to equity ratio are not recognized in the MTB regression analysis since both measures are mathematically linked to MTB and interpretations would be accordingly difficult.[1270] The MTB regression model is displayed in Formula 4.1.

Formula 4.1

$$\begin{aligned} MTB_i = {} & \beta_1 UAI_k + \beta_2 MAS_k + \beta_3 IDV_k + \beta_4 PDI_k + \beta_5 LEGTAX_k \\ & + \beta_6 FINMCAP_k + \sum_{j=1}^{9} \beta_{j7} IND_{ij} + \beta_8 EMP_i \\ & + \beta_9 LTASS_i + \beta_{10} FORLIST_i + \beta_{11} SECLIST_i \\ & + \beta_{12} FORSALES_i + \beta_{13} BIG4_i + \beta_{14} PROFIT_i \\ & + \beta_{15} ROI_i + \beta_{16} SALGRO_i + \varepsilon_i \end{aligned}$$

where

MTB_i	=	*market to book value*
UAI_k	=	*uncertainty avoidance index*
MAS_k	=	*masculinity index*
IDV_k	=	*individualism index*
PDI_k	=	*power distance index*
$LEGTAX_k$	=	*legal / tax system index*
$FINMCAP_k$	=	*financing system index*
IND_{ij}	=	*the companies' industry*
EMP_i	=	*the companies' number of employees*
$LTASS_i$	=	*the companies' logarithmized total assets*

[1269] The MTB correlation coefficients are listed in Appendix A, Table A 4.

[1270] Market capitalization is the numerator of the MTB ratio; furthermore, MTB and debt to equity ratio have the same denominator. The integration of the two variables into the MTB regression model results in exceptionally large adjusted R^2 values > 80%.

$FORLIST_i$ = *dummy variable for the companies' foreign listing*
$SECLIST_i$ = *dummy variable for the companies' SEC listing*
$FORSALES_i$ = *the companies' foreign sales to total sales ratio*
$BIG4_i$ = *dummy variable for the companies' auditor*
$PROFIT_i$ = *the companies' profit margin*
ROI_i = *the companies' return on investment*
$SALGRO_i$ = *the companies' sales growth*
$\beta_{1\text{-}16}$ = *regression coefficients*
ε_i = *the companies' error term*
i = *1,…,n (company index)*
j = *1,…,9 (industry index)*
k = *1,2,3 (country index)*

The variable combination that has the highest explanatory potential with respect to MTB is identified by forward regression analysis; the variables uncertainty avoidance, telecommunication industry, SEC listing, total assets, foreign listing and return on investment explain 13.8%[1271] of the MTB variance (see Table 4-12). Backward regression analysis leads to no higher values of adjusted R-squared.

R	R^2		Adjusted R^2	Std. error of the estimate			Durbin-Watson	
0.398	0.158		0.138	2.741			2.100	
	Sum of squares		df	Mean square		F	Sig.	
Regression	351.585		6	58.598				
Residuals	1,870.307		249	7.511		7.801	0.000	
Total	2,221.892		255					
Variables	Beta (rank)	B	Std. error	Beta	t	Sig.	Tolerance	VIF
(Constant)		7.166	1.885		3.802	0.000		
UAI	-0.099	-0.015	0.009	-0.101	-1.603	0.110	0.845	1.184
TEL	-0.003	1.971	0.663	0.175	2.974	0.003	0.973	1.028
LTASS	-0.232**	-0.544	0.268	-0.124	-2.030	0.043	0.908	1.101
FORLIST	-0.066	-1.000	0.505	-0.123	-1.979	0.049	0.872	1.146
SECLIST	0.116	2.157	0.625	0.217	3.454	0.001	0.853	1.172
ROI	0.424**	0.046	0.018	0.154	2.590	0.010	0.957	1.045

Table 4-12: MTB regression analysis results

The examination of the regression model premises reveals no major deficiencies with respect to transferability of results, distribution and autocorrelation of residuals and multi collinearity of independent variables. The F-value of 7.801** implies that the regression

[1271] This figure refers to the adjusted R^2.

results of the tested sample are transferable to the population. Although not perfectly normal distributed, graphical analysis of the MTB residuals distribution indicates nearly normal distribution. Furthermore, the Durbin-Watson coefficient implies a low level of residuals autocorrelation (DW = 2.100). The multi collinearity indicators tolerance and VIF reveal acceptably low levels of multi collinearity (see Table 4-12).

The regression analysis provides some interesting insights in comparison to the correlation analysis above. None of the **cultural** and **institutional** variables that significantly correlate with MTB are affirmed to have a possible influence on market to book value when other more influential variables are taken into consideration. Although uncertainty avoidance adds explanatory power to the MTB regression model, the variable is not significantly associated to MTB (β = -0.101; p = 0.110). Furthermore, the sign of the regression coefficient is contrary to the hypothesized relationship between uncertainty avoidance and conservatism. The MTB regression results neither confirm the influence of the industries that significantly correlate with MTB; instead, companies from the telecommunication **industry** are significantly associated with higher MTB ratios (β = 0.175; p = 0.003**). The significance of that industry, however, is not confirmed by the non parametric rank regression analysis (see Table 4-13).

Adjusted R^2	Variables	Beta	Sig.	Variables	Beta	Sig.
0.301	RUAI	-0.099	0.085	RFORLIST	-0.066	0.236
	RTEL	-0.003	0.955	RSECLIST	0.116	0.039
	RLTASS	-0.232	0.000	RROI	0.424	0.000

Table 4-13: MTB rank regression analysis results

The influence of the context factor **size** is supported by the significant result for total assets (β = -0.124; p = 0.043*); large companies tend to have lower market to book values. The significant non parametric test result supports the influence of the context factor size. The correlation results of the **internationality** variables are only partly supported by regression analysis. Companies that are listed abroad are significantly associated with lower MTB values (β = -0.123; p = 0.049*). In contrast, companies that are listed at a stock exchange that is regulated by the SEC are related to higher MTB ratios (β = 0.217; p = 0.001**). Since only the latter regression result is supported by rank regression analysis, internationality is expected to have a positive influence on MTB. Only one of the two **profitability** variables, which significantly correlate with MTB, is affirmed by regression analysis. Whereas correlation analysis indicates a significant influence of both profit margin and ROI, only ROI is confirmed by regression analysis to be significantly associated with MTB (β = 0.154; p = 0.010**). Furthermore, the ROI variable is characterized by the strongest measured rank regression result (see Table 4-13).

The following chapter will analyze the results of the regression analysis in more detail and present first tentative interpretations.

4.3.1.1.4 Implications

Although ANOVA mean value comparison indicates a country related influence on MTB, none of the analyzed **cultural** and institutional country factors adequately approximates the difference in country MTB. Even after eliminating the internal variables that show the strongest association to MTB, none of the tested country factors proves to be significantly associated with MTB; internal context factors associated to capital market expectations assumingly are better proxies to explain the MTB distribution. However, the comparably low adjusted R-squared of 13.8% indicates that the included variables explain only a small percentage of the MTB variance; accordingly, other not tested country factors might be better proxies to describe the MTB distribution.

With respect to the integrated cultural variables, all MTB related conservatism hypotheses are denied (see Figure 4-4).

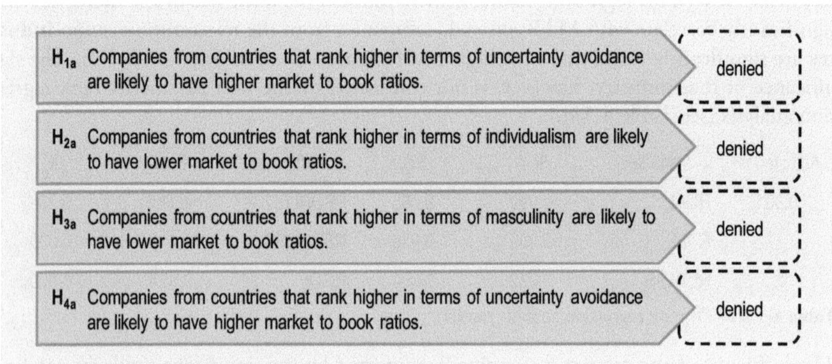

Figure 4-4: MTB hypotheses test results

The results of the above regression analysis suggest that the internal context factors size, internationality and profitability might serve as predictors for MTB. Whereas size is associated with lower MTB values and lower conservatism accordingly, profitability is related to higher degrees of conservatism as measured by MTB. The results for internationality are mixed. Companies that are listed abroad are related to lower MTB values. In contrast, US listed companies are related to higher MTB values. Nonetheless, only the latter result is confirmed by rank regression analysis, thus, contradicting the previously posited relationship between internationality and conservatism. As outlined above, **internationality** is assumed to be related to lower degrees of conservatism. More specifically, companies from conservative countries like France or Germany that are listed at a SEC regulated stock exchange are expected to adapt to the less conservative US-GAAP accounting sphere in order to compete with US domestic companies. A possible explanation for the unexpected MTB regression results might be linked to the characteristics of the company sample. As demonstrated in the above description of the company sample, most of the US listed companies are British and therewith come from a traditionally rather optimistic accounting background. Furthermore, US-GAAP is generally considered the more conservative accounting regime in comparison to UK-GAAP.[1272] US listed British companies might be influenced by US-GAAP and, accordingly, adopt a more conservative accounting approach resulting in higher MTB values.

In analogy to the internationality variable SECLIST, the negative relationship between **size** and MTB also contradicts prior theory based assumptions. The association between larger companies and lower conservatism is unexpected from the perspective of political cost theory; large companies receive more public attention and are, thus, expected to be more conservative to raise no suspicion of oligopoly rents respectively exceptionally high profitability. A highly tentative explanation for the unexpected association between size and MTB could be that larger companies have comparably higher equity book values, which result in lower market to book ratios.

Similar to large companies, profitable companies are also expected to follow a more conservative accounting approach to lower public attention and to mitigate the risk of political costs. The significantly positive MTB regression result therewith confirms the posited association between **profitability** and accounting conservatism. This association, however, may not entirely be attributable to considerations of conservatism, but to capital market expectations. Profitable companies are expected by the capital market to perform positively in the future; profitability is also connected to the expectation of higher dividends distributed by the company, having the shareholders participate in the economic success of the company. The positive expectations of the capital market increase the demand of profitable companies' shares and, as a consequence, increase the market value of these companies. Higher MTB values may, thus, be also related to higher market expectations.

Finally, the MTB regression analysis suggests an association between conservatism and **industry**. Accordingly, telecommunication companies are characterized by higher MTB values and, thus, tend to be more conservative than other companies. This finding is in line with agency theoretical considerations; companies in the telecommunication sector are usually quite profitable.[1273] Furthermore, this industry is likely to be more in the public eye than other industries since a lot of people are directly affected via (high) monthly telephone bills. To lower such negative public attention and to avoid possible political costs, telecommunication companies could try to be more conservative and lower earnings. This suggestion is very tentative, however, as the result is not confirmed by the non-parametric test.

The following chapter presents the empirical results of the conservatism indicator negative accruals values.

4.3.1.2 Negative accruals value

The negative accruals value (NA) is the second global conservatism indicator tested in this study. In contrast to the market-value based MTB proxy, NA measures conservatism by opposing accrual accounting to cash accounting. Cash flows from operating activities that exceed net income before depreciation and amortization lead to negative NA values,

[1272] Cf., e.g., Weetman/Gray 1990, p. 111; Huijgen/Lubberink 2005, p. 1275.
[1273] Cf. Littlechild et al. 2008, p. 357ff.

which represent conservative accounting.[1274] Positive NA values, in contrast, stand for optimistic accounting. In analogy to the MTB proxy, sales growth is controlled for as an additional firm performance indicator as "[...] sales growth is likely to affect accruals such as changes in receivables and inventory [...]"[1275]. The effect of the inclusion of sales growth is analyzed via correlation and regression analysis. Before going into inferential statistical analysis, basic descriptive statistics of the dependent variable NA are presented.

4.3.1.2.1 Descriptive analysis

The negative accruals value is determined for all 261 companies of the sample. All values are included in the following analysis; no extreme outliers are excluded from the sample. The following table presents the NA distribution's basic statistical characteristics (see Table 4-14).

Value (%)	Total	France	Germany	UK
N	261	88	93	80
Minimum	-96.78	-21.09	-96.78	-52.94
5% quantile	-25.84	-12.82	-31.22	-34.63
1. quartile	-6.80	-7.07	-6.70	-6.43
Median	-1.70	-2.73	-1.53	-1.32
Mean	-1.95	-1.68	-2.89	-1.17
3. quartile	3.16	1.43	4.07	3.47
95% quantile	17.44	12.22	19.44	24.41
Maximum	75.57	40.26	48.94	75.57
Standard deviation	15.23	9.26	17.38	17.77

Table 4-14: NA descriptive statistics

The above table suggests a different country grouping compared to the MTB distribution. German and UK sample are both characterized by extreme negative and extreme positive outliers and a standard deviation that is almost twice as high as the standard deviation of the French sample. The picture drawn by the different quantiles is difficult to interpret. Whereas British companies dominate the lower and upper 5% quantiles of the NA distribution, having both the lowest 5% quantile value and the highest 95% quantile, French companies have the lowest first quartile value and German companies have the highest third quartile value. The median ranks France first in terms of negative accrual accounting, followed by Germany ranking second and the UK. This statistical snapshot mirrors the expected country sequence with regard to the cultural factor of uncertainty avoidance; high uncertainty is associated with high conservatism and high conservatism implies low negative accrual values. Nonetheless, the mean value comparison of the three country

[1274] For a more detailed description of the NA value cf. chapter 2.3.4.1.1.2.
[1275] Ahmed et al. 2002, p. 877.

samples shows a different picture. The lowest NA value is attributed to the German sample; the highest value belongs to the British sample. This constellation, however, may well be influenced by outlier data points since the German sample has the two lowest outliers and the British sample has the two highest outliers (see Figure 4-5).

The boxplot diagram, as displayed in Figure 4-5, supports the notion that outliers may have an effect on mean value calculation. The edges of the box, which mark the first and third quartiles, and the whiskers of the three country samples, which mark the 1.5 IQR range, appear to be comparable at first glance. A significant mean value difference on a country by country basis is therefore questionable.[1276]

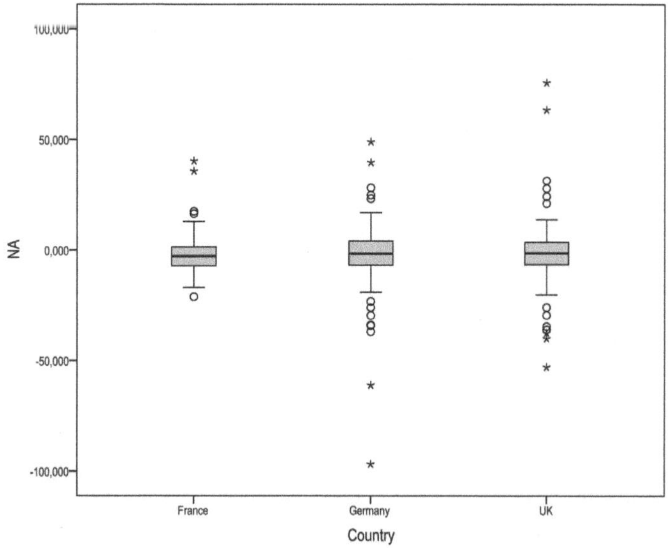

Figure 4-5: NA boxplot diagram by country

ANOVA supports the first impression of the above NA distribution boxplot. The mean value difference by **country** is not significant (F = 0.055; p = 0.947). This result is supported by the non-parametric Kruskal-Wallis-Test, which leads to retaining the null hypothesis of equal distribution of NA across countries (p = 0.428). The country samples are not regarded as independent samples. From the ANOVA results follows that NA is probably not influenced by country factors. Correlation and regression analysis will further investigate this question.

Another ANOVA is performed to test mean value differences across industries. The test results suggest that **industry** is not an important context factor with respect to NA

[1276] As outlined above, outliers that lie more than three standard deviations from the sample's mean are eliminated from the sample for the following univariate and multivariate statistical tests. Cf. chapter 3.4.1.

(F = 1.021; p = 0.424); the non-parametric test comes to the same result (p = 0.235). Analogously, the type of auditor, distinguishing between **Big4** and other auditors, assumingly has no effect on NA. The results of a corresponding T-Test are non-ambiguous (t = -1.354; p = 0.196)[1277] and supported by the non-parametric Mann-Whitney-U-Test (p = 0.229).

Mean value comparison indicates that NA is neither affected by country, nor by industry, nor by type of auditor. The following two chapters analyze in detail, which other context factors may be good predictors for NA.

4.3.1.2.2 Correlation analysis

As already suggested by ANOVA in the previous chapter, country factors assumingly have no influence on the companies' negative accrual values. The correlation coefficients of both **cultural** and **institutional** factors are not significant. **Industry** factors, however, which ANOVA indicates as not relevant for NA, yield one significant result. The affiliation to the healthcare industry assumingly has a very weak influence on accrual accounting (r = 0.139; p = 0.027*). The regression analysis will show whether the influence of this indicator endures when more variables are included in the model.

The main influential context factors are **leverage** and profitability. The companies' debt to equity ratio is negatively correlated with NA (r = -0.202; p = 0.001**); higher indebted companies are related to lower NA values and therewith higher degrees of conservatism. This result is in contrast with the expected effect of leverage on conservatism. According to PAT, highly indebted companies are rather associated with accounting optimism since these companies assumingly try not to violate debt covenants.

The significantly positively correlated **profitability** variable return on investment (r = 0.145; p = 0.021**) hints at an association between NA and profitability. Consequently, profitable firms are assumed to be related to higher NA values and, for the negative sign of this conservatism indicator, to less conservatism. Again, this finding contradicts the political cost theoretical assumption that profitable companies make use of conservatism to diminish public attention. However, disregarding the theoretical perspective of the profitability indicators, the positive association between NA and profitability is plausible; lower NA values (e.g. caused by higher provisions), *ceteris paribus*, also lead to lower EBIT values and, accordingly, lower profitability variables. The positive relationship between NA and profitability, thus, is to be interpreted carefully. Finally, the **growth** factor sales growth (r = 0.158; p = 0.012*) is significantly positively associated with NA. This finding is consistent with high sales growth resulting in higher accounts receivables and/or higher inventories and, thus, leading to higher NA values.[1278]

4.3.1.2.3 Regression analysis

The following regression analysis tests if the associations identified in correlation analysis are affirmed when the assumed NA influence factors are recognized simultaneously. The

[1277] Equal variances not assumed.

[1278] The NA correlation coefficients are listed in Appendix A, Table A 4.

right hand side of the regression model is similar to Formula 4.1; NA is tested for the influence of the four cultural factors that are supposed to be related to levels of conservatism and the above listed external and internal control variables. In contrast to the MTB regression model, the NA regression model also controls for the size variable logarithmized market capitalization and leverage (see Formula 4.2).

Formula 4.2

$$\begin{aligned} NA_i = {} & \beta_1 UAI_k + \beta_2 MAS_k + \beta_3 IDV_k + \beta_4 PDI_k + \beta_5 LEGTAX_k \\ & + \beta_6 FINMCAP_k + \sum_{j=1}^{9} \beta_{j7} IND_{ij} + \beta_8 LMCAP_i \\ & + \beta_9 EMP_i + \beta_{10} LTASS_i + \beta_{11} FORLIST_i \\ & + \beta_{12} SECLIST_i + \beta_{13} FORSALES_i + \beta_{14} BIG4_i \\ & + \beta_{15} LEV_i + \beta_{16} PROFIT_i + \beta_{17} ROI_i + \beta_{18} SALGRO_i \\ & + \varepsilon_i \end{aligned}$$

NA_i	=	*negative accruals value*
UAI_k	=	*uncertainty avoidance index*
MAS_k	=	*masculinity index*
IDV_k	=	*individualism index*
PDI_k	=	*power distance index*
$LEGTAX_k$	=	*legal / tax system index*
$FINMCAP_k$	=	*financing system index*
IND_{ij}	=	*the companies' industry*
$LMCAP_i$	=	*the companies' logarithmized market capitalization*
EMP_i	=	*the companies' number of employees*
$LTASS_i$	=	*the companies' logarithmized total assets*
$FORLIST_i$	=	*dummy variable for the companies' foreign listing*
$SECLIST_i$	=	*dummy variable for the companies' SEC listing*
$FORSALES_i$	=	*the companies' foreign sales to total sales ratio*
$BIG4_i$	=	*dummy variable for the companies' auditor*
LEV_i	=	*the companies' leverage*
$PROFIT_i$	=	*the companies' profit margin*
ROI_i	=	*the companies' return on investment*
$SALGRO_i$	=	*the companies' sales growth*
$\beta_{1\text{-}18}$	=	*regression coefficients*
ε_i	=	*the companies' error term*
i	=	*1,…,n (company index)*
j	=	*1,…,9 (industry index)*
k	=	*1,2,3 (country index)*

Forward regression analysis identifies three significant variables from the influence spheres of size, internationality and profitability as significant predictors. Although neither total assets, nor foreign sales, nor profit margin lead to significant correlation results, these variables prove to be influential when tested in combination with other variables and explain 6.1%[1279] of NA variance. Backward regression analysis identifies further variables that increase the predictive power of the tested NA regression model. Besides another size variable (number of employees) and another internationality variable (foreign listing), the industries consumer durables, business equipment, healthcare and utilities are integrated as additional predictors leading to a slightly increased adjusted R-squared of 9.3% (see Table 4-15).

R	R^2	Adjusted R^2	Std. error of the estimate			Durbin-Watson	
0.354	0.126	0.093	10.471			1.926	
	Sum of squares	df	Mean square		F	Sig.	
Regression	3,844.492	9	427.166				
Residuals	26,754.828	244	109.651		3.896	0.000	
Total	30,599.320	253					
Variables	B	Std. error	Beta	t	Sig.	Tolerance	VIF
(Constant)	18.644	8.365		2.229	0.027		
CONDUR	6.559	3.620	0.110	1.812	0.071	0.964	1.037
EQU	-2.611	2.097	-0.079	-1.245	0.214	0.891	1.122
HEALTH	4.997	2.747	0.111	1.819	0.070	0.969	1.032
UTIL	5.141	3.314	0.099	1.551	0.122	0.873	1.145
EMP	0.000	0.000	0.082	1.150	0.251	0.700	1.428
LTASS	-3.481	1.247	-0.210	-2.792	0.006	0.631	1.584
FORLIST	-2.774	1.843	-0.095	-1.505	0.134	0.904	1.106
FORSALES	5.927	2.295	0.159	2.582	0.010	0.943	1.061
PROFIT	0.057	0.018	0.197	3.249	0.001	0.979	1.022

Table 4-15: NA regression analysis results

The examination of the regression model premises reveals no major deficiencies with respect to transferability of results, distribution and autocorrelation of residuals and multi collinearity of independent variables. The F-value of 3.896** signifies that the regression results of the tested sample are transferable to the population. Although not perfectly normal distributed, graphical analysis of the NA residuals distribution indicates nearly normal distribution. Furthermore, the Durbin-Watson coefficient implies a low level of

[1279] This figure refers to the adjusted R^2.

residuals autocorrelation (DW = 1.926). The multi collinearity indicators tolerance and VIF reveal acceptably low levels of multi collinearity (see Table 4-15).

Only one of the two **size** variables is significantly associated with NA. Companies that are characterized by higher amounts of total assets are related to lower NA values and therewith higher degrees of conservatism (β = -0.201; p = 0.006**). Furthermore, as indicated by forward regression analysis, the **internationality** variable foreign sales is significantly associated with NA; larger percentages of foreign sales imply higher NA values (β = 0.159; p = 0.010**). Finally, the **profitability** measure profit margin (β = 0.197; p = 0.001**) is assumed to have a positive influence on NA. Only foreign sales is confirmed by rank regression analysis (see Table 4-16).

Adjusted R^2	Variables	Beta	Sig.	Variables	Beta	Sig.
0.028	RCONDUR	0.042	0.499	RLTASS	-0.146	0.128
	REQU	-0.005	0.935	RFORLIST	-0.062	0.335
	RHEALTH	0.119	0.059	RFORSALES	0.135	0.031
	RUTIL	0.092	0.164	RPROFIT	0.064	0.344
	REMP	0.040	0.672			

Table 4-16: NA rank regression analysis results

4.3.1.2.4 Implications

With respect to the influence of country and, specifically, **cultural** factors, the empirical results are clear. Neither ANOVA nor correlation nor regression analysis indicate an influence of culture. In accordance with the other global conservatism indicator MTB, the NA related conservatism hypotheses are to be denied (see Figure 4-6).

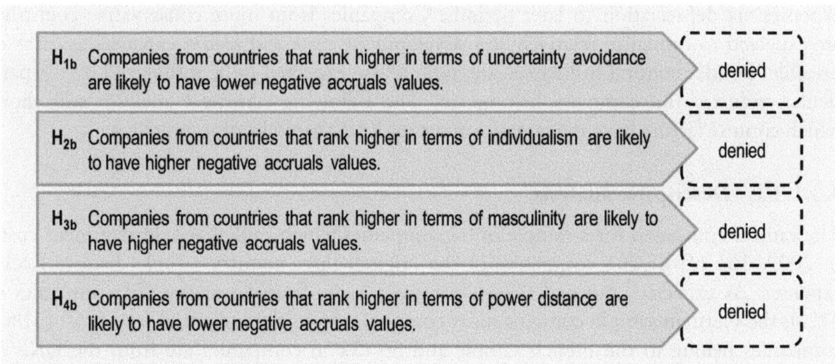

Figure 4-6: NA hypotheses test results

The internal context factors that are significantly associated with negative accruals are size, internationality and profitability. Firm **size** is assumed to have a negative and internationality and profitability are assumed to have a positive influence on NA. Since lower NA values represent higher levels of conservatism larger companies are suggested to be more conservative than smaller companies. This finding is in line with agency theoretical assumptions: larger companies follow a more conservative accounting approach to lower public attention. Nonetheless, the influence of the size variable total assets is not supported by the non parametric test and might only be random.

In analogy to the context factor size, the association between NA and the **internationality** variable FORSALES confirms prior assumptions. Companies that rely to a high percentage on international operations are likely to have adapted to internationally accepted accounting procedures (mainly US-GAAP), which are in the case of French or German companies certainly less conservative than domestic GAAP.

Only the association between profit margin and NA is supported by the result of the rank regression analysis. Companies that are characterized by higher **profitability** are related to lower degrees of conservatism. As mentioned in the MTB implications section, this result opposes the assumption of political cost theory. A possible explanation for this relationship could stem from the relationship between NA and earnings. Since negative accruals (e.g. higher provisions) have a negative effect on earnings figures like the EBIT, lower NA values (more negative accruals) are likely to be associated with lower profit margins. Prior studies confirm this association.[1280]

The last two chapters on empirical results related to global conservatism indicators suggest that IFRS measurement practice is free of cultural influences. The following chapters deal with conservatism indicators that measure conservatism in specific accounting areas.

4.3.1.3 Capitalization of development costs

The ratio of capitalized development costs per total R&D costs measures conservatism by means of lower ratios since the capitalization of R&D costs postpones the realization of expenses via depreciation to later periods. Companies from more conservative countries are expected to capitalize relatively less development costs and realize expenses as early as possible. Besides cultural influences, the ratio is also expected to be influenced by the particular industry the company belongs to. The following statistical analyses will show which context factors have the largest impact on R&D capitalization practices.

4.3.1.3.1 Descriptive analysis

The ratio is computed for a sample of 82 companies which capitalized development costs in 2009. 161 of the 261 companies in the original three country sample disclose R&D expenses. As expected, most of these companies come from Germany (75 companies = 47%); the German sample contains most companies from the industrial sector. 50 (31%) companies belong to the French sample and 36 (22%) companies are from the UK.[1281] With respect to the 82 companies that disclose capitalized development costs, the country by country distribution is even more unbalanced. 47 (57%) companies come from Ger-

[1280] Cf., e.g., Givoly/Hayn 2000, p. 295ff.; Ahmed et al. 2002, p. 885.

[1281] The percentages in brackets are calculated on the basis of 161 companies.

many, 22 (27%) companies are French and 13 (16%) companies are British.[1282] When setting the latter figures in relation to the country figures of companies that report R&D expenditures, German companies (63%) capitalize development costs relatively more often than French companies (44%) and British companies (36%). This first indicator draws a picture different from the expected conservatism country ranking. Nonetheless, these figures are probably strongly influenced by the industrial characteristics of the companies. The following annotations concentrate on the 82 companies that capitalize development costs (see Table 4-17).

Value (%)	Total	France	Germany	UK
N	82	22	47	13
Minimum	0.00	0.00	0.00	0.01
5% quantile	0.02	0.02	0.02	0.05
1. quartile	0.09	0.18	0.07	0.11
Median	0.19	0.25	0.16	0.20
Mean	0.22	0.26	0.20	0.23
3. quartile	0.31	0.35	0.30	0.25
95% quantile	0.54	0.47	0.57	0.61
Maximum	0.87	0.49	0.63	0.87
Standard deviation	0.17	0.14	0.17	0.22

Table 4-17: CAPRD descriptive statistics

The above table shows minimum values for France and Germany of 0.00. As only companies that capitalize development costs are included in the above compilation, the minimum value is not zero but considerably smaller than 0.01 (1%). The negative extreme of the capitalization ratio distribution is dominated by French and German companies. Companies from these countries represent the minimum value and have the lowest 5% quantile values. The positive extreme, however, is controlled by British companies, which represent the maximum value and have the highest 95% quantile value. The section in between the extreme edges of the total distribution is mainly dominated by French companies, which score highest with respect to first quartile, median and third quartile. British companies score higher than German companies for first quartile and median, but lower for the third quartile. The mean value suggests a country ranking of France followed by the UK and Germany. The UK mean value, however, might be influenced by an UK extreme outlier of 87% (see Figure 4-7). This extreme value surely has an influence on the UK standard deviation, as well, which is higher than the standard deviation of France and Germany. This assumption is supported by the below whiskers of the three country samples; the upper whisker of the German boxplot reaches further compared to

[1282] The percentages in brackets are calculated on the basis of 82 companies.

the British pendant. Except for the British outlier, no more outliers are recognized (see Figure 4-7).[1283]

The interpretation of the distributions of the three country samples, described quantitatively and graphically in Table 4-17 and Figure 4-7, suggests existing country sample differences; the country sample distributions deviate substantially from one another. Further statistical analysis will show whether these observed differences can be attributed to 'real' country differences or rather to differences in the industrial distribution of the three country samples.[1284] Indeed, ANOVA based mean value comparison suggests that **country** *per se* leads to no significant sample differences (F = 0.795; p = 0.455). This result is affirmed by the non-parametric Kruskal-Wallis-Test, which retains the corresponding null hypothesis (p = 0.174).

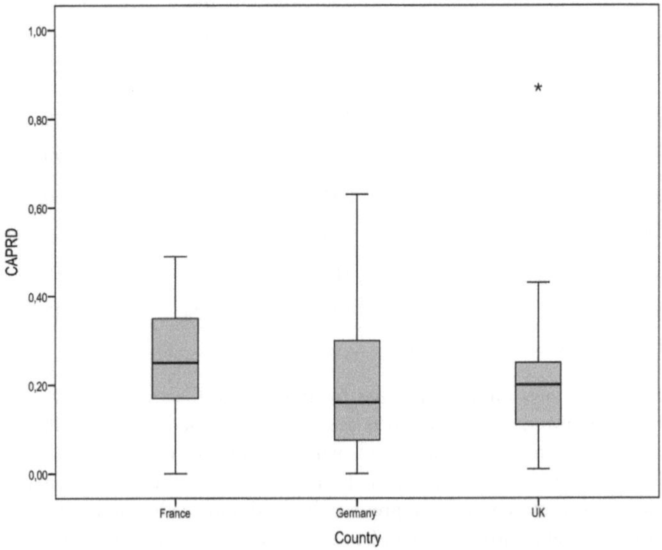

Figure 4-7: CAPRD boxplot diagram by country

Consequently, the observed differences between the country samples may be random or affected by **industry**. In fact, ANOVA mean value comparison by industry indicates significant industry differences (F = 2.894; p = 0.006**), which are confirmed by the non-parametric test (p = 0.026*). As shown above, industries are not equally distributed across the three analyzed countries and, thus, industry might lead to differences between country samples that are not conditional upon country. Correlation and regression analysis will provide further insights which industries are associated with R&D capitalization practice. A T-Test on the dummy variable **Big4** auditor leads to no significant mean value differ-

[1283] The following statistical tests are performed on data that is adjusted for outliers. Cf. chapter 3.4.1.
[1284] Cf. chapter 4.2.3.

ences ($t = -1.304$; $p = 0.243$)[1285]. This result is confirmed by the Mann-Whitney-U-Test ($p = 0.111$).

The above tests show that only industry is expected to have an influence on CAPRD. The following chapter on correlation analysis will further specify which industries are the most influential and how much CAPRD is affected by accounting industry practice.

4.3.1.3.2 Correlation analysis

As suggested by the above country based ANOVA, the analyzed **cultural** country factors are not significantly correlated to CAPRD. Whether the integration of further influential variables enhances or diminishes the potential of cultural country factors as CAPRD predictors is analyzed in the next section on regression analysis. The **institutional** country factors, which approximate the legal, the financing and the tax system of the respective country, are not significantly correlated to CAPRD either. With respect to country factors, the ANOVA test results of the previous section are confirmed.

In concordance with the above ANOVA test results, correlation analysis affirms that **industry** could have an influence on CAPRD. The industrial sector that is assumed to have the strongest effect on CAPRD is manufacturing ($r = -0.306$; $p = 0.005^{**}$). Companies that belong to the manufacturing industry are associated with lower R&D capitalization rates. Another industry that is significantly correlated with CAPRD is utilities ($r = 0.255$; $p = 0.021^{*}$). Companies from that sector tend to have comparably higher CAPRD scores. Another weakly significant industry to be mentioned is business equipment ($r = -0.212$; $p = 0.055$); this industry is also negatively correlated with CAPRD.

Furthermore, **internationality** seems to play a role in R&D capitalization practice. Foreign sales ($r = -0.243$; $p = 0.028^{*}$) is significantly negatively correlated with CAPRD. Accordingly, companies that have higher percentages of foreign sales to total sales are assumed to have lower CAPRD rates and, thus, to be more conservative. This result is surprising since internationality is expected to be associated with lower degrees of conservatism. The next chapter on regression analysis tests the robustness of the correlation analysis results when more than one influence factor is taken into consideration.[1286]

4.3.1.3.3 Regression analysis

The tested CAPRD regression model integrates the four *Hofstede* variables plus the control variables listed in detail in Formula 4.2. The external and internal control variables are subsumed under CONVAR[1287]. Except for sales growth, which is only included as a control variable for the two global conservatism indicators, all control variables remain the same as in Formula 4.2; the control variables cover the possibly influential context areas industry, size, internationality, auditor, leverage and profitability as well as national institutions (see Formula 4.3).

[1285] Equal variances not assumed.

[1286] The CAPRD correlation coefficients are listed in Appendix A, Table A 4.

[1287] CONVAR refers to the external and internal control variables: LEGTAX, FINMCAP, IND, LMCAP, EMP, LTASS, FORLIST, SECLIST, FORSALES, BIG4, LEV, PROFIT and ROI.

Formula 4.3

$$CAPRD_i = \beta_1 UAI_k + \beta_2 MAS_k + \beta_3 IDV_k + \beta_4 PDI_k + \beta_l CONVAR_{i/k} + \varepsilon_i$$

where

$CAPRD_i$	=	*percentage of capitalized development costs to total R&D costs*
UAI_k	=	*uncertainty avoidance index*
MAS_k	=	*masculinity index*
IDV_k	=	*individualism index*
PDI_k	=	*power distance index*
$CONVAR_{i/k}$	=	*country and company control variables*
β_{1-l}	=	*regression coefficients*
ε_i	=	*the companies' error term*
i	=	*1,...,n (company index)*
k	=	*1,2,3 (country index)*
l	=	*5,...,17 (control variable index)*[1288]

The regression model that scores highest in terms of CAPRD explanatory power consists of internal context factors only. As indicated by ANOVA and correlation analysis, cultural or institutional variables are of little relevance with respect to CAPRD. Four variables stem from the set of industrial variables: consumer non-durables, oil and gas, telecommunication and utilities. Furthermore, the size variable number of employees is included in the 'first-best' CAPRD regression model. Also, internationality variables are recognized, viz. SEC listing and foreign sales. Finally, the auditor variable Big4 is considered. These variables explain CAPRD by 29.3%[1289] (see Table 4-18).

The examination of the regression model premises reveals no major deficiencies with respect to transferability of results, distribution and autocorrelation of residuals and multi collinearity of independent variables. The F-value of 5.193** signifies that the regression results of the tested sample are transferable to the population. Although not perfectly normal distributed, graphical analysis of the CAPRD residuals distribution indicates nearly normal distribution. Furthermore, the Durbin-Watson coefficient implies a low level of residuals autocorrelation (DW = 2.110). The multi collinearity indicators tolerance and VIF reveal acceptably low levels of multi collinearity (see Table 4-18).

Six of the eight included control variables were identified by regression analysis to be significantly associated with CAPRD. Accordingly, CAPRD is assumed to be best explained by the variables industry, size, internationality and auditor. The two significant **industries** are oil and gas (β = 0.307; p = 0.008**) and utilities (β = 0.363; p = 0.001**). These findings indicate that companies from these two industries are associated with higher percentages of capitalized development costs.

1288 Sales growth was only included in the regression model for the two global conservatism indicators. In the following sales growth is not considered as an independent variable. The control variable index therefore contains only 13 elements.

1289 This figure refers to the adjusted R^2.

R	R^2	Adjusted R^2	Std. error of the estimate			Durbin-Watson	
0.602	0.363	0.293	0.144			2.110	
	Sum of squares	df	Mean square		F	Sig.	
Regression	0.859	8	0.107				
Residuals	1.510	73	0.021		5.193	0.000	
Total	2.369	81					
Variables	B	Std. error	Beta	t	Sig.	Tolerance	VIF
(Constant)	0.465	0.091		5.088	0.000		
CONNDUR	0.080	0.059	0.132	1.369	0.175	0.940	1.063
OIL	0.338	0.124	0.307	2.724	0.008	0.689	1.452
TEL	0.161	0.082	0.204	1.957	0.054	0.802	1.246
UTIL	0.237	0.067	0.363	3.522	0.001	0.822	1.216
EMP	0.000	0.000	0.279	2.766	0.007	0.857	1.167
SECLIST	-0.152	0.071	-0.265	-2.140	0.036	0.571	1.750
FORSALES	-0.186	0.087	-0.223	-2.138	0.036	0.804	1.243
BIG4	-0.178	0.063	-0.273	-2.822	0.006	0.936	1.069

Table 4-18: CAPRD regression analysis results

The positive association between industry and CAPRD is underlined by the significant rank regression test results; although not as strongly significant as in normal regression analysis, the rank regression coefficients of the oil and gas and the utilities industries indicate a significantly positive relation to CAPRD (see Table 4-19).

Adjusted R^2	Variables	Beta	Sig.	Variables	Beta	Sig.
0.145	RCONNDUR	0.118	0.264	REMP	0.124	0.278
	ROIL	0.269	0.032	RSECLIST	-0.212	0.118
	RTEL	0.182	0.117	RFORSALES	-0.200	0.071
	RUTIL	0.267	0.017	RBIG4	-0.271	0.014

Table 4-19: CAPRD rank regression analysis results

Besides industry, the **size** of the company seems to play a role as well. Size as measured by number of employees ($\beta = 0.279$; $p = 0.007$**) is another significant predictor for CAPRD; the significantly positive relationship suggests that larger companies tend to capitalize more R&D in comparison to smaller companies. This result, however, is not affirmed by rank regression analysis which finds the number of employees not to be significant. The significant **internationality** factors show a homogeneous picture. Both SEC listing ($\beta = -0.265$; $p = 0.036$*) and foreign sales ($\beta = -0.223$; $p = 0.036$*) are negatively associated with CAPRD. The degree of internationality therewith seems to be related to lower CAPRD rates and, thus, more conservatism. Notwithstanding, this association is not confirmed by rank regression analysis for either of the two variables. A significantly negative relationship to CAPRD, which is also confirmed by the non-parametric test (see Table 4-19), is measured for the **auditor** variable ($\beta = -0.273$; $p = 0.006^{**}$). The latter result indicates that companies, which are audited by one of the four 'high-quality' audit firms, tend to capitalize less development costs.

The next chapter discusses the above findings with respect to the *ex ante* posited hypotheses (culture factors) and theoretically founded assumptions (institutional and company factors).

4.3.1.3.4 Implications

None of the above performed statistical tests indicates a country factor related influence on CAPRD. In analogy to the previously tested global conservatism indicators, the **culture** related hypotheses, thus, are denied (see Figure 4-8).

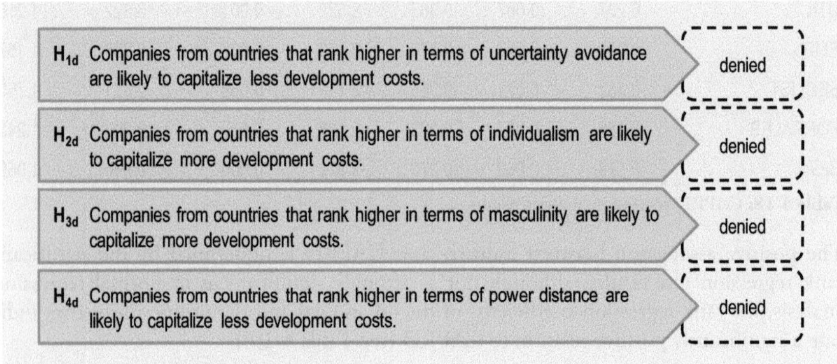

Figure 4-8: CAPRD hypotheses test results

The two influential CAPRD predictors identified by regression analysis and confirmed by rank regression analysis are industry and auditor. The **industrial** influence on CAPRD is intuitively comprehendible. Some industries are characterized by more R&D activities than others and some products in development are more qualified to meet the IAS 38 criteria for capitalization than others. The two industries that show the strongest industry patterns are oil and gas and utilities. Both industries are characterized by large infrastructure investments in oil and gas exploration respectively energy generation and transportation facilities. These capital and time intensive investments are usually long-term projects and, thus, capitalized as development costs. The significantly positive association between the described industrial membership and CAPRD is plausible.

Besides industrial influences, the type of **auditor** is another significant CAPRD predictor. According to the significantly negative correlation coefficient, Big4 audited companies are connected to lower CAPRD rates and, thus, more conservative accounting. This association is surprising since the performed T-Test shows no auditor inducted mean value differences. The result, however, is not unexpected; Big4 audited companies are expected to be associated with higher degrees of accounting conservatism.[1290] As Big4 companies tend to have a more solid financial background, these companies are more attractive as litigation targets. Also, Big4 audit firms receive more public attention and have more reputation to lose. Consequently these firms have an interest in their clients to follow a conservative accounting approach; conservative accounting lowers the risk of financial misstatements that may result in shareholder class-action lawsuits.

The regression results on the two internationality indicators suggest a negative association between **internationality** and CAPRD. As lower CAPRD rates are assumingly connected to higher degrees of conservatism, this result, although debilitated by rank regression analysis, is unexpected. A higher degree of internationality is expected to lead to less conservatism since internationally oriented companies are assumed to be more experienced with respect to internationally accepted financial reporting standards like US-GAAP, which are traditionally less conservative than Continental European accounting standards. In the case of development cost capitalization, a proximity to US-GAAP, however, might have a different effect. As US-GAAP capitalization requirements are generally stricter than IFRS requirements, US-GAAP influenced capitalization practice may be interpreted as more conservative.[1291] Following this argumentation, the unexpected negative relationship between the two internationality factors and CAPRD is allegeable.

The last significant association is determined for the **size** variable number of employees. As mentioned above, large companies are rather associated with higher degrees of conservatism. The unexpected positive sign of the size variable's regression coefficient could be explained to the companies' manpower. The assessment whether the capitalization criteria are fulfilled and its documentation require a substantial effort by the company's accounting department. Small companies could tend to capitalize less development costs as they do not have the human resources and they rank the corresponding effort too high. Also, smaller companies could lack adequate cost accounting and project management systems to reliably determine the stage of the development process and the related expenses. This argumentation, however, is to be interpreted carefully; the 261 largest national stock companies that are analyzed in this study all possess a certain size. Also, the unexpected size result is not confirmed by rank regression analysis, which raises further doubt on its reliability.

4.3.1.4 Purchase price allocation

The amount of intangible assets that are recognized in a PPA divided by total assets (**INT**) is another indicator for the degree of corporate conservatism. The capitalization criteria for intangible assets in a PPA grant the companies substantial discretion in deciding how much of the purchase price to allocate to the acquired intangible assets, which are then amortized over their useful lifetimes. In contrast, the goodwill as the residual of the PPA is impaired and, thus, only leads to expenses if the yearly performed impairment test indi-

[1290] Cf. chapter 2.3.2.2.3.

[1291] Cf. Ashbaugh/Olsson 2002, p. 111ff.; Ampofo/Sellani 2005, p. 225f.; van der Meulen et al. 2007, p. 127.

cates the need for a write-off. Again, the criteria for impairment allow for corporate discretion and impairments could be influenced respectively managed by the company. Consequently, companies might decide to recognize less intangible assets to defer amortization expenses to later periods. In analogy to the above conservatism definition, higher INT values are therefore suggested to indicate higher degrees of conservatism.

Besides accounting discretion that might be affected by national cultural patterns, the amount of goodwill might also be influenced by **industry** practice. Business combinations in the software or pharmaceutical industry, for instance, are supposedly better qualified for the potential capitalization of intangible assets than other less intangibles oriented industries. The following sections will analyze possible influence factors in more detail.

4.3.1.4.1 Descriptive analysis

135 companies report at least one business combination for 2009; this means that more than half of the 261 analyzed financial statements contain information regarding PPA. When a company has more than one business combination, the ratio of recognized intangibles to total assets is calculated based on the total amounts of all business combinations. In relation to country sample size, the UK sample with 48 (60%) companies contains relatively more companies that engage in the acquisition of another company than the German sample with 49 (53%) companies and the French sample with only 38 companies (43%).

	France	Germany	UK	Σ
Number of companies that have a business combination	38	49	48	135
- Thereof: companies that disclose information on intangibles[1292]	12 (32%)	40 (82%)	36 (75%)	88
- Thereof: companies that disclose information on total assets[1293]	6 (16%)	34 (69%)	33 (69%)	73

Table 4-20: Use of the fair value method by country

As outlined in Table 4-20, only six French, 34 German and 33 British companies provide sufficient information to calculate the above presented intangibles ratio. Especially French companies disclose no or little information on the PPA and corresponding value adjustments. Thus, to allow for statistically robust results, only German and British companies are considered in the following analyses.

As outlined in Table 4-21, the minimum value belongs to the British sample. This value results from a negative intangible assets value adjustment. Both British and German companies show comparable low 5% quantile values. Except for the median, all other calculated quantiles are dominated by the German sample. Accordingly, mean value comparison suggests a country ranking of Germany ranking before the UK (see Table 4-21). As higher INT values are assumingly connected to higher degrees of conservatism, a country ranking led by Germany, which, based on its cultural profile, is expected to be more conservative than the UK, confirms the suitability of INT as a conservatism indicator. How-

[1292] Intangibles refer to PPA related fair value adjustments of intangible assets.

[1293] Total assets refer to the total asset book values of the acquired company.

ever, the German sample is also characterized by a much higher standard deviation, which might be an indicator for outliers.

Value (%)	Total	Germany	UK
N	67	34	33
Minimum	-0,02	-0,01	-0,02
5% quantile	0,00	0,00	0,00
1. quartile	0,11	0,14	0,07
Median	0,40	0,32	0,50
Mean	1,23	1,57	0,88
3. quartile	1,05	1,06	1,00
95% quantile	6,25	7,31	1,55
Maximum	13,30	13,30	11,27
Standard deviation	2,50	2,93	1,93

Table 4-21: INT descriptive statistics

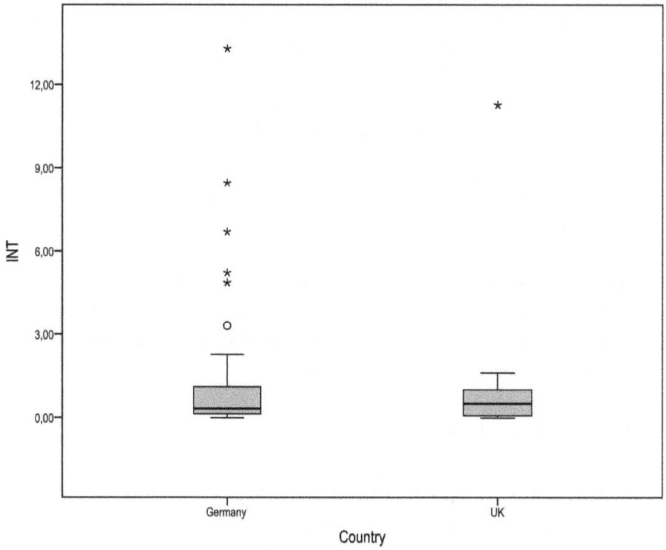

Figure 4-9: INT boxplot diagram by country

Although the descriptive statistics suggest possible country differences between Germany and the UK, the boxplot diagrams of the two countries show a rather comparable picture;

as suggested by Figure 4-9, the higher quantile values of the German sample might be related to the higher number of positive outliers.[1294]

The T-Test confirms this assumption; it identifies no significant **country** differences (F = 1.382; p = 0.175). This result is confirmed by the Kruskal-Wallis-Test (p = 0.979). ANOVA of **industry** grouped mean values shows similar results (F = 0.871; p = 0.535). The non-parametric test supports the ANOVA result (p = 0.503). The above suggested influence of industry on PPA practice therewith is not confirmed. A last T-Test is performed to test the influence of the type of **auditor** on PPA accounting practice. In contrast to the above country and industry based mean value comparison tests, the T-Test identifies a significant mean value difference for the variable Big4 (t = 3.744, p = 0.001**)[1295]. However, this results in not affirmed by the independent samples Mann-Whitney-U-Test (p = 0.215).

The performed tests indicate no influence of the context factors country and industry; only a weak influence of Big4 is suggested. The following section on correlation analysis will provide further insight regarding the possible influence of other internal context factors on INT.

4.3.1.4.2 Correlation analysis

Correlation analysis confirms the results of the above T-Test with respect to possible country differences. Neither **cultural** nor **institutional** variables produce significant correlation results. Analogously, the above results on **industry** and **Big4** auditor are mainly confirmed; only the business equipment industry is significantly correlated with INT (r = 0.300; p = 0.016*). Two more significant INT correlations are determined for the context factors internationality and leverage. The **internationality** factor SEC listing is significantly positively correlated with INT (r = 0.331; p = 0.008**). Furthermore, companies that are characterized by higher **leverage** are significantly correlated with higher INT values (r = 0.301; p = 0.016*).[1296]

Correlation analysis demonstrates that the single influence of the tested context factors *per se* is rather weak. Only three indicators prove to be significantly correlated with INT. The following chapter on regression analysis assesses whether the combination of various indicators leads to a higher degree of explanatory power.

4.3.1.4.3 Regression analysis

The INT regression model remains unchanged in comparison to the previously tested dependent variable. The standard regression model (see Formula 4.4), which integrates all tested variables, is backed up by forward and backward regression analysis to find the best predicting regression model. The eight variables that best explain INT (adjusted R^2 = 0.161) are uncertainty avoidance, the industrial variables business equipment, tele-

[1294] The following statistical tests are performed on data that is adjusted for outliers. Cf. chapter 3.4.1.
[1295] Equal variances not assumed.
[1296] The INT correlation coefficients are listed in Appendix A, Table A 4.

communication and utilities, the size variable logarithmized market capitalization, the internationality factor SEC listing, auditor and ROI.

Formula 4.4
$$INT_i = \beta_1 UAI_k + \beta_2 MAS_k + \beta_3 IDV_k + \beta_4 PDI_k + \beta_l CONVAR_{i/k} + \varepsilon_i$$

where

INT_i	=	*percentage of newly recognized intangible assets to total assets*
UAI_k	=	*uncertainty avoidance index*
MAS_k	=	*masculinity index*
IDV_k	=	*individualism index*
PDI_k	=	*power distance index*
$CONVAR_{i/k}$	=	*country and company control variables*
$\beta_{1\text{-}l}$	=	*regression coefficients*
ε_i	=	*the companies' error term*
i	=	*1,…,n (company index)*
k	=	*1,2,3 (country index)*
l	=	*5,…,17 (control variable index)*

The examination of the regression model premises reveals no major deficiencies with respect to transferability of results, distribution and autocorrelation of residuals and multi collinearity of independent variables. The F-value of 2.506* signifies that the regression results of the tested sample are transferable to the population. Although not perfectly normal distributed, graphical analysis of the INT residuals distribution indicates nearly normal distribution. Furthermore, the Durbin-Watson coefficient implies a low level of residuals autocorrelation (DW = 2.054). The multi collinearity indicators tolerance and VIF reveal acceptably low levels of multi collinearity (see Table 4-23).

Only two of the eight included variables are determined as significant INT predictors. First, the **cultural** factor of uncertainty avoidance has a certain predictive potential. The regression coefficient is significantly positively related to INT (β = 0.281; p = 0.033*). Companies from high UAI countries are, thus, related to higher INT values and, thus, higher conservatism. The predictive potential of uncertainty avoidance is unexpected with reference to the above T-Test and correlation analysis results. Correspondingly, the significant UAI result is not affirmed by rank regression analysis (see Table 4-22).

Adjusted R^2	Variables	Beta	Sig.	Variables	Beta	Sig.
0.105	RUAI	0.026	0.858	RLMCAP	-0.054	0.722
	REQU	0.293	0.051	RSECLIST	0.336	0.018
	RTEL	-0.020	0.873	RBIG4	0.154	0.274
	RUTIL	0.007	0.954	RROI	-0.075	0.648

Table 4-22: INT rank regression analysis results

R	R^2	Adjusted R^2	Std. error of the estimate			Durbin-Watson	
0.517	0.267	0.161	1.147			2.054	
	Sum of squares	df	Mean square		F	Sig.	
Regression	26.357	8	3.295				
Residuals	72.303	55	1.315		2.506	0.021	
Total	98.660	63					
Variables	B	Std. error	Beta	t	Sig.	Tolerance	VIF
(Constant)	0.768	2.098		0.366	0.716		
UAI	0.023	0.011	0.281	2.185	0.033	0.805	1.242
EQU	0.523	0.405	0.164	1.290	0.202	0.821	1.218
TEL	0.537	0.508	0.135	1.057	0.295	0.816	1.226
UTIL	1.050	0.640	0.205	1.639	0.107	0.855	1.169
LMCAP	-0.465	0.310	-0.225	-1.498	0.140	0.589	1.698
SECLIST	1.325	0.541	0.333	2.448	0.018	0.721	1.388
BIG4	1.504	0.762	0.256	1.975	0.053	0.793	1.261
ROI	0.021	0.014	0.220	1.556	0.125	0.668	1.497

Table 4-23: INT regression analysis results

Second and as indicated by correlation analysis, **internationality** seems to be influential with respect to INT ($\beta = 0.333$; $p = 0.018$*). Companies that are listed at a stock exchange that is regulated by the SEC are associated with higher values of INT and therewith a rather conservative accounting approach. This result, in contrast to uncertainty avoidance, is confirmed by the non-parametric test (see Table 4-22). Finally, regression analysis detects a weakly significantly positive relationship between INT and type of **auditor** ($\beta = 0.256$; $p = 0.053$). As suggested by the weakly significant regression result, this finding is not supported by the non-parametric robustness test.

4.3.1.4.4 Implications

The only significant **cultural** factor is uncertainty avoidance. In concordance with the posited conservatism hypothesis, regression analysis suggests companies from high uncertainty avoidance countries to have higher INT values and therewith show more conservatism. This tentative assumption of an UAI related cultural influence is challenged by the above rank regression analysis result which indicates no significant relationship; furthermore, country-based mean value comparison clearly contradicts any influence of country factors. As mentioned above, the influence of UAI, which even on a bivariate correlation basis is to be considered as highly improbable, is likely to be associated with the German sample's remaining number of outliers.[1297]

As a consequence, the posited INT hypotheses are denied (see Figure 4-10).

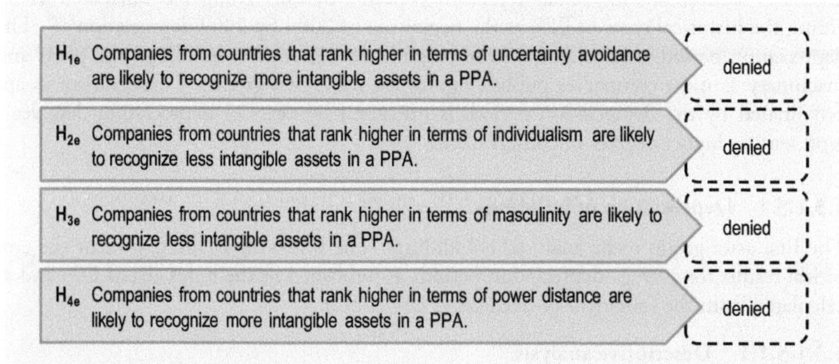

Figure 4-10: INT hypotheses test results

The **internationality** variable SEC listing predicts a positive relationship between companies that are listed in the US and INT. As mentioned above, this finding contradicts the assumption that internationality cultivates rather optimistic accounting practices. In analogy to the argumentation in chapter 4.3.1.1.4 (MTB), this unexpected regression results might be linked to the high percentage of British SEC registered companies. Following the assumption that US-GAAP accounting is more conservative than UK-GAAP accounting,[1298] SEC registered British companies might have adapted to the comparably more conservative US-GAAP accounting approach resulting in higher INT values. This interpretation, however, is of highly tentative nature.

The next chapter presents another conservatism indicator that approximates conservatism via asset depreciation periods. The chapter is split in two sections analyzing corporate depreciation of (1) buildings and (2) plant and machinery.

4.3.1.5 Tangible assets depreciation

Two aspects of tangible asset depreciation were considered as conservatism indicators. The results on the first indicator **depreciation method**, however, do not allow for robust statistical analysis. Only three sample companies used accelerated depreciation, considered to represent the more conservative depreciation approach, in their 2009 group accounts. Accordingly, conservatism as determined by the type of depreciation method is not further discussed in the following.

[1297] Cf. chapter 4.3.1.4.1. The remaining outliers lie less than three standard deviations from the INT mean.

[1298] Cf., e.g., Weetman/Gray 1990, p. 111; Huijgen/Lubberink 2005, p. 1275.

The data on the second conservatism indicator, **depreciation period**, is collected in two ways. First, the depreciation period was determined by taking the 'official' corporate depreciation span by asset area as published in the notes and calculating the average number of years. Additionally, the actual depreciation period by asset group was calculated by dividing the historical costs of PPE at the beginning of 2009 by 2009 depreciation[1299]. The depreciation period is calculated for the tangible asset groups of buildings and plant and machinery as most companies publish figures for these two groups. Conservatism as approximated by the depreciation period, is measured by years of depreciation, less years representing higher degrees of conservatism.

4.3.1.5.1 Depreciation of buildings

The first asset group to be analyzed is buildings. The following chapters present the empirical results for average depreciation periods as published in the notes (BUILD1) and as calculated from the statement of fixed assets (BUILD2).

4.3.1.5.1.1 Descriptive analysis

The **BUILD1** sample consists of 237 companies, which disclose information on the depreciation periods of buildings in the notes. The sample companies' minimum and maximum depreciation period values belong to the French company sample. With respect to the other calculated quantiles the British company sample scores highest (see Table 4-24).

	BUILD1				BUILD2			
Value (years)	Total	France	Germany	UK	Total	France	Germany	UK
N	237	82	85	70	226	71	88	67
Minimum	10.00	10.00	16.50	11.50	6.70	8.96	6.70	6.70
5% quantile	20.00	20.00	19.70	25.00	11.27	11.63	11.78	11.54
1. quartile	25.00	25.00	25.00	25.00	20.77	19.96	21.44	20.91
Median	30.00	27.50	30.00	35.00	25.60	23.21	27.22	26.96
Mean	31.57	29.99	29.82	35.55	28.86	27.24	28.06	31.61
3. quartile	35.00	34.38	33.50	44.38	32.38	28.40	32.69	34.34
95% quantile	50.00	45.00	39.50	50.00	61.61	66.47	45.37	73.93
Maximum	76.00	76.00	50.00	75.00	104.38	104.38	73.15	102.84
Standard deviation	9.71	10.21	6.46	11.26	15.58	16.44	11.23	19.06

Table 4-24: BUILD1 and BUILD2 descriptive statistics

Until reaching the median, the French and German samples show comparable quantile values. In the upper quartile and the 95% quantile, however, French companies score considerably higher than German companies. The highest standard deviation is noted for

[1299] Depreciation refers to scheduled depreciation only. For a discussion of limitations of this indicator see chapter 2.3.4.1.2.3.

the British sample, which is followed closely by the French sample. The German standard deviation is much lower than the British and the French. Mean value comparison suggests a country ranking of the UK ranking first, followed by France and Germany, which have almost the same mean value. According to this first country ranking, Germany and France appear to be more conservative than the UK since shorter depreciation periods are associated with higher yearly depreciation expenses. This first impression, however, is only speculative and has to be confirmed by country based ANOVA.

The BUILD2 sample consists of only 226 companies; some of the (mainly French) companies did not publish 2009 depreciation figures on an asset group basis. Accordingly, the French share of companies is much smaller. Apart from a different company distribution by country, the BUILD2 depreciation figures differ substantially from the BUILD1 figures. The minimum of BUILD1 is 10.00 years compared to 6.70 years for BUILD2. The maximum of BUILD1 is 76.00 years compared to 104.38 years for BUILD2. The boxplot diagrams for BUILD1 and BUILD2 as displayed in Figure 4-11 and Figure 4-12 show that the latter distribution is far more affected by outliers than the BUILD1 distribution. Especially the upper end of the BUILD2 distribution contains various outliers in all three country samples. The mean values of the total samples of BUILD1 ($\mu = 31.57$) and BUILD2 ($\mu = 28.86$), however, are quite comparable. Whereas the outer edges of the two samples differ substantially, the inner quantiles are similar and mostly dominated by BUILD1 values. The BUILD2 standard deviation ($s = 15.58$), on the other hand, as a consequence of manifold outliers, is much higher than the BUILD1 standard deviation ($s = 9.71$).

Both the German and the British sample comprise companies that depreciate buildings according to the **BUILD2** minimum value of 6.70 years. The maximum of 104.38 years is contributed by a French company. The lower country quantiles, including the median, are dominated by companies from the German sample; the upper quantiles are dominated by British companies. Except for the outer 5% and 95% quantiles, French companies have the lowest quantile values. The French mean value of 27.24 years is excelled by the German mean value of 28.06 years and the British mean value of 31.61 years. Similar to BUILD1, this first mean value comparison indicates a country ranking in analogy to the uncertainty avoidance ranking of the three countries.

The country ranking of the BUILD2 standard deviations is comparable to BUILD1. The British sample has the highest standard deviation followed by France; the German sample has the lowest standard deviation. The different standard deviations and distribution characteristics of the BUILD1 and BUILD2 country samples are illustrated in the following boxplot diagrams (see Figure 4-11 and Figure 4-12).[1300]

[1300] The following statistical tests are performed on data that is adjusted for outliers. Cf. chapter 3.4.1.

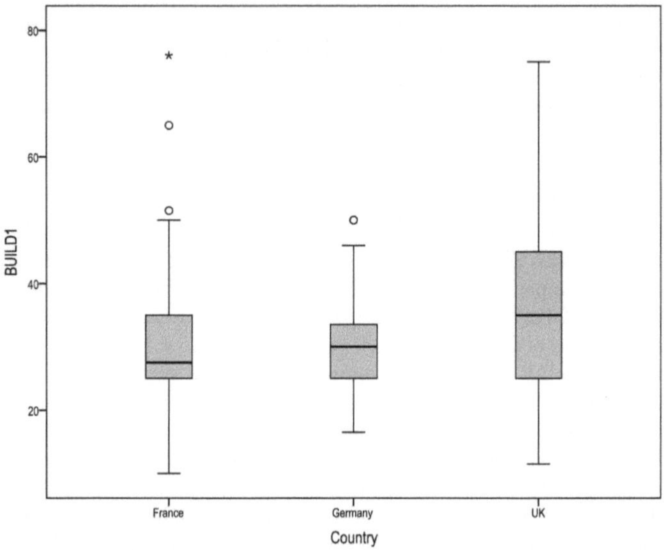

Figure 4-11: BUILD1 boxplot diagram by country

The **BUILD1** boxplot diagram suggests different **country** samples; the country distributions' characteristics differ with respect to median, box and whiskers. ANOVA confirms this assessment indicating significantly differing country mean values between at least two of the three sample countries (F = 11.299; p = 0,000**). The Kruskal-Wallis-Test rejects the null hypothesis of equal distribution across country samples at the significance level of p = 0.001**. The above BUILD1 mean value comparison suggests a country difference between Germany and France, on the one hand, and the UK, on the other hand. In fact, multiple comparison (Scheffé-Test) of the three groups indicates that the country combinations France/UK (p = 0.002**) and Germany/UK (p = 0.001**) differ significantly from one another. Germany and France, on the contrary, do not differ significantly (p = 0.993). As outlined above,[1301] the significant differentiation between Germany and France, on the one hand, and the UK, on the other hand, might be related to the tax systems of the three countries; both Germany and France are characterized by the authoritative principle and depreciation periods might be affected by tax accounting.

Besides country influences, BUILD1 is assumed to be strongly affected by the particular **industry** the company belongs to. According to the products and services of the various industries, different types of buildings are possibly necessitated, which have different depreciation periods. Again, the ANOVA result supports the intuitive assumption of industrial depreciation patterns (F = 2.747; p = 0.005**). The non-parametric test comes to the same result (p = 0.042*).

[1301] Cf. chapter 2.3.4.1.2.3.

Auditor seems to be of no influence; neither the parametric T-Test (t = 0.854; p = 0.409)[1302] nor the non-parametric Mann-Whitney-U-Test show significant differences across the two categories of type of auditor (p = 0.630).

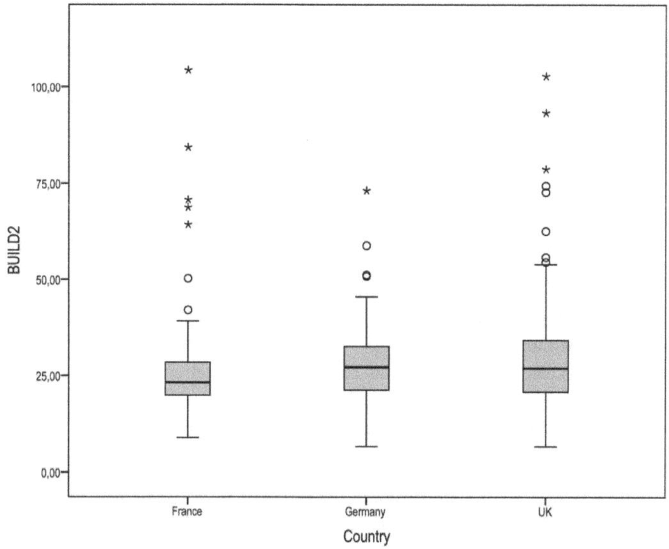

Figure 4-12: BUILD2 boxplot diagram by country

The **BUILD2 country** boxplots look different from the BUILD1 boxplots. All three country samples, especially the French and the British samples, have (extreme) outliers. Nonetheless, the BUILD2 boxes and whiskers do not differ as much as measured for BUILD1. According to country based ANOVA, no significant country differences are detected for BUILD2 (F = 1.140; p = 0.322). However, this result is not confirmed by the non-parametric test. The Kruskal-Wallis-Test rejects the null hypothesis of equal distribution at the significance level of p = 0.049*. This result suggests a significant country related influence, which is possibly biased by the remaining outliers[1303] of the BUILD2 distribution.

The influence of **industry** is not as strongly significant as measured for BUILD1 (F = 2.434; p = 0.012*). Again, this result might be associated with the distribution's remaining outliers; the non-parametric test reject the null hypothesis at the significance level of p = 0.005**. Correlation and regression analysis will cast further light on this issue. Analogous to BUILD1, the effect of **auditor** is not significant (t = 1.807, p = 0.090)[1304]; the non-parametric test supports this finding (p = 0.118).

[1302] Equal variances not assumed.

[1303] The remaining outliers lie less than three standard deviations from the BUILD2 mean.

[1304] Equal variances not assumed.

4.3.1.5.1.2 Correlation analysis

As indicated by the above ANOVAs, **BUILD1** is mainly correlated with the indicators country and industry. In fact, five of the six country factors are significantly correlated with BUILD1. The **cultural** factor that has the strongest significant correlation coefficient is uncertainty avoidance (r = -0.240; p = 0.000**). Companies from high UAI countries are assumingly associated with shorter depreciation periods and, thus, higher degrees of conservatism. Both masculinity (r = 0.181; p = 0.005**) and individualism (r = 0.150; p = 0.022*) are significantly positively related to BUILD1. Both relationships comply with the posited hypotheses on the influence of masculinity and individualism on conservatism respectively depreciation periods. The posited association between BUILD1 and power distance, which is expected to be positively associated with conservatism, is also confirmed by correlation analysis. Companies from high PDI countries are related to shorter depreciation periods and, thus, higher conservatism (r = -0.181; p = 0.005**).

The **institutional** factor that has the strongest correlation with BUILD1 is the combined legal and tax system factor (r = -0.232; p = 0.000**). Consequently, companies from code law countries respectively countries that recognize the authoritative principle tend to be associated with shorter depreciation periods and higher conservatism. Taking into consideration the above posited relationships between the legal/tax system and conservatism, the correlation follows the previously posited direction.

The two **industries** that are significantly correlated with BUILD1 are manufacturing (r = -0.176; p = 0.007**) and wholesale and retail (r = 0.142; p = 0.030*). Companies from the manufacturing sector are associated with shorter depreciation periods and companies from the wholesale/retail sector are associated with longer depreciation periods.

Except for country and industry factors, the internal context factors internationality, leverage and profitability prove to be influential. The **internationality** measure, which is significantly correlated with BUILD1, is foreign listing (r = -0.151; p = 0.021*). Foreign listed companies tend to have lower BUILD1 depreciation periods. In contrast, highly **leveraged** companies are associated with higher BUILD1 values (r = 0.144; p = 0.027*). Finally, high **profitability** as measured by profit margin (r = 0.186; p = 0.004**) is also correlated with higher BUILD1 values respectively lower conservatism.

Although similar indicator groups seem to be relevant, the correlation results for **BUILD2** are different from BUILD1. Only three of the four **cultural** factors show (weakly) significant correlations with BUILD2. Uncertainty avoidance (r = -0.128; p = 0.057) and power distance (r = -0.163; p = 0.015*) are negatively correlated with BUILD2 and therewith associated with shorter depreciation periods. Masculinity, on the other hand, is significantly positively correlated with calculated depreciation periods (r = 0.163; p = 0.015*). The signs of the three significant correlations are the same as determined for BUILD1 and, thus, in accordance with the above posited hypotheses. Contrary to BUILD1, which is significantly associated with the type of national legal/tax system, no **institutional** factor leads to significant correlation results with respect to BUILD2.

The only significant **industry** factors are consumer durables (r = 0.133; p = 0.047*) and telecommunication (r = -0.247; p = 0.000**). Whereas companies from the former industry tend to apply longer BUILD2 depreciation periods, companies from the latter industry are associated with lower BUILD2 values. The industries determined for BUILD1 seem to be not relevant for BUILD2. Furthermore, correlation analysis shows that the **internationality** variable foreign sales is significantly associated with BUILD2 (r = -0.131; p = 0.050*).[1305]

The following chapter on regression analysis assesses, which of the described possibly relevant influence factors has the highest explanatory potential with respect to BUILD1 and BUILD2.

4.3.1.5.1.3 Regression analysis

The right hand side of the applied BUILD1 and BUILD2 regression model equals the regression models tested before (see Formula 4.5).

Formula 4.5
$$BUILD1_i(BUILD2_i) = \beta_1 UAI_k + \beta_2 MAS_k + \beta_3 IDV_k + \beta_4 PDI_k + \beta_l CONVAR_{i/k} + \varepsilon_i$$

where

$BUILD1_i$	=	*average depreciation period of buildings (corporate accounting policies)*
$BUILD2_i$	=	*calculated depreciation period of buildings (statement of fixed assets)*
UAI_k	=	*uncertainty avoidance index*
MAS_k	=	*masculinity index*
IDV_k	=	*individualism index*
PDI_k	=	*power distance index*
$CONVAR_{i/k}$	=	*country and company control variables*
β_{1-l}	=	*regression coefficients*
ε_i	=	*the companies' error term*
i	=	*1,…,n (company index)*
k	=	*1,2,3 (country index)*
l	=	*5,…,17 (control variable index)*

Again, the **BUILD1** factor combination with highest explanatory power was identified via forward and backward stepwise regression analysis. The included variables of that combination are the cultural factor uncertainty avoidance, the industries consumer non-durables, manufacturing, oil and gas, business equipment, telecommunication and healthcare, the size measure number of employees, the internationality factors foreign listing and foreign sales, leverage and the profitability measure profit margin; these variables explain BUILD1 by 18.6% (see Table 4-25).

The examination of the **BUILD1** and **BUILD2** regression models' premises reveals no major deficiencies with respect to transferability of results, distribution and autocorrelation of residuals and multi collinearity of independent variables. The F-values of 5.431** (BUILD1) respectively 4.919** (BUILD2) signify that the regression results of the tested

[1305] The BUILD1 and BUILD2 correlation coefficients are listed in Appendix A, Table A 4.

samples are transferable to the populations. Although not perfectly normal distributed, graphical analysis of the BUILD1 and BUILD2 residuals distributions indicates nearly normal distribution. Furthermore, the Durbin-Watson coefficients imply low levels of residuals autocorrelation (BUILD1: DW = 1.931; BUILD2: DW = 1.899). The multi collinearity indicators tolerance and VIF reveal acceptably low levels of multi collinearity (see Table 4-25 and Table 4-27).

R	R^2	Adjusted R^2	Std. error of the estimate			Durbin-Watson		
0.477	0.228	0.186	7.760			1.931		
	Sum of squares	df	Mean square		F	Sig.		
Regression	3,924.591	12	327.049		5.431	0.000		
Residuals	13,308.777	221	60.221					
Total	17,233.368	233						
Variables	B	Std. error	Beta	t	Sig.	Tolerance	VIF	
(Constant)	42.531	2.183		19.486	0.000			
UAI	-0.100	0.027	-0.236	-3.707	0.000	0.859	1.164	
CONNDUR	-2.352	1.808	-0.086	-1.301	0.195	0.797	1.254	
MAN	-3.185	1.503	-0.147	-2.119	0.035	0.721	1.386	
OIL	-5.921	2.679	-0.140	-2.210	0.028	0.876	1.141	
EQU	-1.972	1.759	-0.072	-1.121	0.263	0.842	1.188	
TEL	-4.955	2.081	-0.150	-2.381	0.018	0.882	1.134	
HEALTH	-3.537	2.199	-0.101	-1.608	0.109	0.887	1.127	
EMP	0.000	0.000	0.110	1.769	0.078	0.898	1.113	
FORLIST	-2.218	1.511	-0.096	-1.467	0.144	0.811	1.233	
FORSALES	-4.089	1.913	-0.139	-2.137	0.034	0.830	1.205	
LEV	0.033	0.036	0.055	0.907	0.365	0.941	1.063	
PROFIT	0.061	0.023	0.162	2.686	0.008	0.960	1.042	

Table 4-25: BUILD1 regression analysis results

The **BUILD1** regression results confirm the systematic influence of country variables. In concordance to the strongly significant correlation analysis results, the **cultural** factor that is most influential with respect to BUILD1 is uncertainty avoidance ($\beta = -0.236$; $p = 0.000^{**}$). As hypothesized above, companies from countries that are characterized by high uncertainty avoidance are associated with shorter depreciation periods and, thus, higher degrees of conservatism. This finding is supported by the non-parametric rank regression analysis (see Table 4-26). The other cultural or institutional country factors lead to no significant regression results when tested in combination with uncertainty avoidance.

Adjusted R^2	Variables	Beta	Sig.	Variables	Beta	Sig.
0.136	RUAI	-0.191	0.004	RHEALTH	-0.121	0.066
	RCONNDUR	-0.105	0.120	REMP	0.032	0.644
	RMAN	-0.210	0.003	RFORLIST	-0.031	0.647
	ROIL	-0.111	0.088	RFORSALES	-0.082	0.219
	REQU	-0.123	0.064	RLEV	0.084	0.229
	RTEL	-0.147	0.022	RPROFIT	0.222	0.001

Table 4-26: BUILD1 rank regression analysis results

Besides cultural influences, the internal context factor **industry** is suggested to possess certain explanatory potential. Three of the six industry variables included in the model are significantly associated with BUILD1. These industries are manufacturing (β = -0.147; p = 0.035*), oil and gas (β = -0.140; p = 0.028*) and telecommunication (β = -0.150; p = 0.018*). All three industries are related to shorter depreciation periods. Two of the industries are confirmed by rank regression analysis. The non-parametric test indicates that both manufacturing and telecommunication are significantly negatively associated with BUILD1 (see Table 4-26). Also, an **internationality** factor seems to play a role in explaining BUILD1; foreign sales is significantly negatively associated with BUILD1 (β = -0.139; p = 0.034*). Finally, **profitability** as measured by profit margin is determined as potentially influential. Profitable companies are significantly associated with longer depreciation periods (β = 0.162; p = 0.008**). Rank regression analysis affirms only the influence of profitability; the association between internationality as measured by foreign sales and BUILD1 is not supported (see Table 4-26).

The variables included in the **BUILD2** regression model are similar to those included for BUILD1. Besides the cultural factor uncertainty avoidance, the control variables stem mainly from the context factor groups of industry, size and internationality. The industrial factors are consumer non-durables, consumer durables, telecommunication, wholesale and retail and utilities. Two size measures are included, viz. number of employees and total assets. Furthermore, the internationality measures SEC listing and foreign sales are suggested to have explanatory potential. Contrary to BUILD1, auditor is recognized as a BUILD2 control variable. These measures explain 16.3% of the BUILD2 variance; only five variables are significantly associated with BUILD2 (see Table 4-27).

R	R^2	Adjusted R^2	Std. error of the estimate			Durbin-Watson	
0.452	0.204	0.163	12.143			1.899	
	Sum of squares	df	Mean square		F	Sig.	
Regression	7,979.076	11	725.371				
Residuals	31,112.167	211	147.451		4.919	0.000	
Total	39,091.243	222					
Variables	B	Std. error	Beta	t	Sig.	Tolerance	VIF
(Constant)	4.856	10.483		0.463	0.644		
UAI	-0.104	0.043	-0.156	-2.400	0.017	0.894	1.119
CONNDUR	4.309	2.678	0.103	1.609	0.109	0.926	1.080
CONDUR	11.916	4.610	0.167	2.585	0.010	0.900	1.111
TEL	-11.590	3.206	-0.238	-3.615	0.000	0.867	1.153
SALE	5.354	2.972	0.118	1.801	0.073	0.877	1.140
UTIL	-6.896	4.090	-0.113	-1.686	0.093	0.843	1.186
EMP	0.000	0.000	-0.148	-1.923	0.056	0.638	1.567
LTASS	5.193	1.617	0.258	3.210	0.002	0.583	1.716
SECLIST	-5.546	2.905	-0.130	-1.909	0.058	0.816	1.226
FORSALES	-11.587	3.193	-0.246	-3.629	0.000	0.823	1.214
BIG4	3.701	3.591	0.068	1.030	0.304	0.871	1.148

Table 4-27: BUILD2 regression analysis results

In analogy to the BUILD1 regression model, **BUILD2** is best explained by the **cultural** factor uncertainty avoidance (β = -0.156; p = 0.017*). The sign of the regression coefficients is as posited above. The significance of the UAI result is confirmed by rank regression analysis (see Table 4-28).

Adjusted R^2	Variables	Beta	Sig.	Variables	Beta	Sig.
0.147	RUAI	-0.202	0.002	REMP	-0.170	0.068
	RCONNDUR	0.079	0.215	RLTASS	0.254	0.008
	RCONDUR	0.134	0.037	RSECLIST	-0.100	0.144
	RTEL	-0.267	0.000	RFORSALES	-0.224	0.001
	RSALE	0.026	0.695	RBIG4	0.080	0.223
	RUTIL	-0.086	0.201			

Table 4-28: BUILD2 rank regression analysis results

The significant **industrial** factors determined for BUILD2 are consumer durables ($\beta = 0.167$; $p = 0.010$**) and telecommunication ($\beta = -0.238$; $p = 0.000$**). Both industries are affirmed by the non-parametric test to have a significant impact. Only one of the two **size** variables, viz. total assets, is significantly associated with BUILD2 ($\beta = 0.258$; $p = 0.002$**); accordingly, larger companies are associated with longer depreciation periods. Rank regression supports the significant total assets result (see Table 4-28).

The influence of the **internationality** factor foreign sales, which was indicated by correlation analysis, is confirmed as significant by both regression ($\beta = -0.246$; $p = 0.000$**) and rank regression analysis. Accordingly, internationally oriented companies tend to depreciate buildings over a shorter period of time. The described regression analysis results are discussed in the following chapter with respect to the *ex ante* assumed relationships between independent and dependent variables.

4.3.1.5.1.4 Implications

The regression analyses for BUILD1 and BUILD2 present similar results. Except for the influence of profitability (BUILD1) and size (BUILD2), both conservatism indicators are best explained by the cultural factor uncertainty avoidance, industry and internationality. BUILD1 is assumed to be the better proxy for corporate depreciation practice as its distribution is less disturbed by outliers. Of course, the application of average depreciation periods does not necessarily lead to the true number of years of depreciation; still BUILD1 is less biased by corporate investment cycles. Companies that invested only little in the last periods and did not engage in adequate asset retirements might show an overstated historical cost basis in comparison to yearly depreciation; in case the statement of fixed assets contains a lot of fully depreciated assets, yearly depreciation, taken as basis for calculation, does not truly represent *de facto* average depreciation. Furthermore, high investments at the beginning of the year could result in misleading interpretations of average depreciation periods since these investments are not recognized in the historical costs at the beginning of the year. The described constellations might be responsible for unusually low respectively high calculated BUILD2 depreciation periods.[1306]

The **cultural** factor that is supposed to be most influential with respect to building depreciation is uncertainty avoidance. Uncertainty avoidance is significantly associated with both BUILD1 and BUILD2 and shorter depreciation periods. The previously posited positive relationship between uncertainty avoidance and conservatism, as expressed by lower depreciations periods, is supported by regression and rank regression analysis. Accordingly, the uncertainty avoidance related conservatism hypothesis is confirmed; the other cultural value based hypotheses have to be denied with respect to depreciation of buildings (see Figure 4-13).

[1306] For a more detailed discussion of the depreciation indicators cf. chapter 2.3.4.1.2.3.

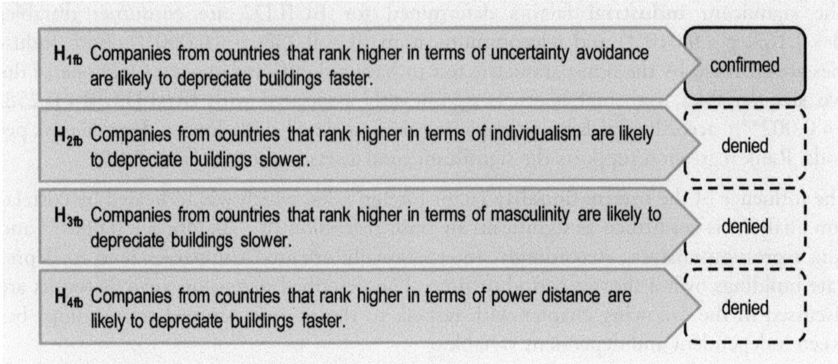

Figure 4-13: BUILD1 and BUILD2 hypotheses test results

Although correlation analysis indicates a significant association between BUILD1 and the combined legal/tax system indicator, this result is not affirmed by regression analysis. As outlined above, the significant correlation with the legal/tax system dummy variable might be related to an influence of the countries' tax system and France and Germany applying the authoritative principle. However, when tested in combination with other country factors, uncertainty avoidance proves to be more influential compared to LEG-TAX.[1307] Accordingly, **institutional** factors are assumed to have only limited explanatory potential with respect to depreciation of buildings.

As outlined above, **industry** is an important predictor for both BUILD1 and BUILD2. With respect to the explanatory power of the particular **industries**, however, the regression results are mixed. Only telecommunication is identified as a significant predictor for both BUILD1 and BUILD2. BUILD1 is also predicted by the industries manufacturing and oil and gas. BUILD2 is also explained by consumer durables. Except for the consumer durables industries, all industry factors are significantly negatively associated with depreciation of buildings and therewith shorter depreciation periods; only the influence of the oil and gas industry on BUILD1 is not confirmed by non-parametric testing.

A tentative explanation for shorter depreciation periods in telecommunication and manufacturing could be frequent technological change in plant and machinery as well as in buildings equipment. When advances in technology require new plants and equipment, firms might decide to build new and better equipped factory buildings, instead of renovating the old buildings. Shorter depreciation periods could also result from industry practice, which was determined by large companies of that industry and then adopted by smaller companies. The consumer durables industry, which encompasses the automotive or furniture industry, is characterized by longer depreciation periods for buildings. Longer depreciation could be related to longer product life cycles of these industries. Especially in the automotive industry the production and assembly lines are usually used for several consecutive car type series; since buildings are commonly renewed when production lines

[1307] National tax depreciation regulations for buildings are too diverse to directly investigate the association between tax depreciation periods and commercial depreciation periods.

are renewed, longer depreciation periods of buildings might be a consequence. Nonetheless, buildings are not as closely connected to the industries' products and services as plant and machinery; conclusions from an industry's product to industrial depreciation patterns of buildings, thus, have to be interpreted carefully.

Another influence factor that leads to significant regression results for both BUILD1 and BUILD2 is the internationality variable foreign sales. In analogy to the previously discussed conservatism indicator CAPRD, **internationality** is positively associated with conservatism. As mentioned before, the sign of this relationship is rather unexpected; a plausible explanation with regard to depreciation of buildings is not apparent. The foreign sales finding is confirmed by rank regression analysis for BUILD2 only and, assuming that BUILD1 is the more valid indicator, might be only random.

The last two significant influence factors on depreciation of buildings are size and profitability. Whereas size as measured by total assets is determined as significant for BUILD2, profitability as measured by profit margin is suggested to be significantly associated with BUILD1. According to the BUILD2 **size** finding, large companies are related to comparably longer depreciation periods and, thus, less conservatism. This result is unexpected but in accordance with the previously determined associations between size and conservatism (MTB). Furthermore, companies that are characterized by higher profit margins are related to longer BUILD1 depreciation periods and lower conservatism. Analogous to the NA regression results, the negative association between **profitability** and conservatism contradicts the political cost theory based assumption. A tentative intuitive interpretation of the measured association could be that longer depreciation periods lead to higher earnings and, thus, higher profitability.

The following chapter on depreciation of plant and machinery will show if the associations assessed for the conservatism indicators BUILD1 and BUILD2 are confirmed.

4.3.1.5.2 Depreciation of plant and machinery

The second set of depreciation related conservatism indicators analyzes depreciation of plant and machinery; this indicator is suggested to be even more influenced by industrial practice than the preceding indicator on depreciation of buildings. In analogy to the preceding indicator, the depreciation periods of plant and machinery are determined (1) by means of the published average depreciation figures in the notes (PLANT1) and (2) by calculation based on the figures in the statement of fixed assets (PLANT2). The following sections present the empirical results and analyze the two variable distributions.

4.3.1.5.2.1 Descriptive analysis

Data on PLANT1 is collected on a sample of 222 companies, 75 French companies, 83 German companies and 64 British companies. Only 210 companies provide adequate data to calculate PLANT2 as some (mostly French) companies do not publish yearly depreciation figures per asset group. The **PLANT1** distribution ranges between a minimum of 2.50 years (UK) to a maximum of 52.50 years (France) (see Table 4-29). The British country sample scores highest in all quantile categories except for the 5% quantile; the French sample contributes the highest 5% quantile value. With regard to the German and

French sample, the lower quantile results are mixed and both country samples have identical median values; in the upper quantiles French companies score higher than German companies. Mean value comparison predicts a country ranking equal to the BUILD1 country ranking of UK ranking first, followed by France and Germany. Also, the German country sample has a considerably lower standard deviation compared to the French and British samples.

The **PLANT1** and **PLANT2** distributions appear to be more similar in comparison to the BUILD1 and BUILD2 distributions. The minimum values of both indicator samples differ only by 0.10 years. The quantile values of both indicators differ between 0.96 (5% quantile) and 3.26 years (median). Only the PLANT2 maximum of 83.00 years varies substantially from the PLANT1 maximum of 52.50 years. The standard deviation of PLANT2 exceeds the standard deviation of PLANT1 by 1.26 years; this difference assumingly can be (at least partly) attributed to the difference in maximums.

	PLANT1				PLANT2			
Value (years)	Total	France	Germany	UK	Total	France	Germany	UK
N	222	75	83	64	210	67	82	61
Minimum	2.50	5.00	4.00	2.50	2.40	2.40	3.05	2.60
5% quantile	5.03	5.50	5.05	4.08	5.99	6.21	5.16	6.29
1. quartile	7.50	6.94	7.50	7.50	9.50	11.15	8.83	9.36
Median	10.00	10.00	10.00	11.00	13.26	13.50	13.91	12.50
Mean	12.20	12.29	11.17	13.43	15.00	16.55	14.30	14.23
3. quartile	15.00	15.00	13.00	16.13	17.44	18.64	17.44	15.66
95% quantile	27.38	22.50	18.00	30.00	29.05	29.96	27.53	27.84
Maximum	52.50	52.50	37.50	42.50	83.00	83.00	36.99	37.83
Standard deviation	7.74	8.64	5.61	8.32	9.00	11.85	7.27	7.21

Table 4-29: PLANT1 and PLANT2 descriptive statistics

Although the two samples at first glance appear to be quite similar, differences can be observed with respect to the distributions of the three country samples. Whereas PLANT1 is dominated by the British sample, **PLANT2** is mainly dominated by the French sample, which scores highest in all quantile categories except for the 5% quantile. Comparing only the German and British sample, the 5% and 25% quantiles are led by the British sample; regarding median and third quartile, German companies score higher. The upper edge of both distributions, again, is dominated by British companies. The standard deviations of the three country samples may be grouped in two; German and British standard deviations are comparable; the French standard deviation is much higher. PLANT2 mean value comparison suggests a country ranking different from the PLANT1 distributions. France ranks first, followed by Germany and the UK. The German and British sample differ only slightly.

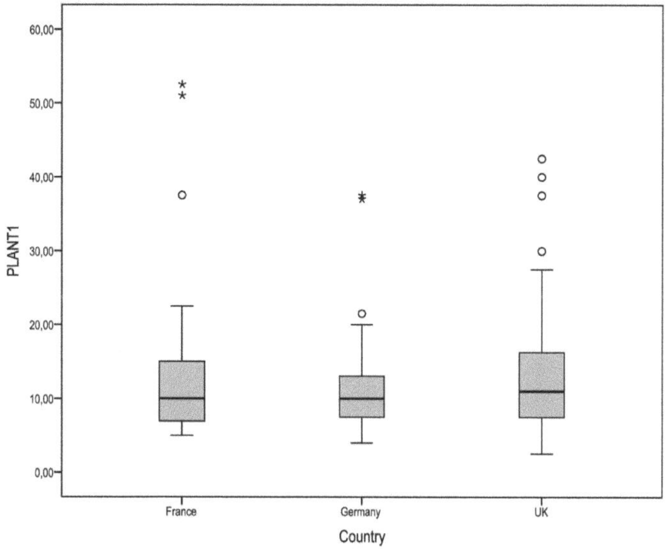

Figure 4-14: PLANT1 boxplot diagram by country

The above **PLANT1** boxplot diagram attests the French and British country samples to be more similar with respect to box and whiskers (see Figure 4-14). The box of the German sample is considerably smaller; especially the upper edge of the box lies closer to the median. All three country samples have outliers; French and German samples each have two extreme outliers. Despite partially differing distribution characteristics, the PLANT1 country distributions seem to be a lot more similar compared to the BUILD1 and BUILD2 country distributions.[1308]

Even though the above mean value comparison by **country** indicates differences in mean values, ANOVA suggests that these country differences are not significant ($F = 2.418$; $p = 0.092$). The parametric result is confirmed by the Kruskal-Wallis-Test ($p = 0.521$). **Industry**, on the other hand, is identified as a significant influence factor by ANOVA ($F = 18.614$; $p = 0.000$**) and the non-parametric robustness test ($p = 0.000$**). Moreover, the ANOVA test result confirms a much stronger industrial influence compared to depreciation of buildings (BUILD1: $F = 2.747$; BUILD2: $F = 2.434$). The T-Test on different categories of **auditor** yields no significant results ($t = 0.553$; $p = 0.593$)[1309]; also, the null hypothesis of equal distribution of the two auditor categories is retained by the independent samples Mann-Whitney-U-Test ($p = 0.741$).

1308 The following statistical tests are performed on data that is adjusted for outliers. Cf. chapter 3.4.1.

1309 Equal variances not assumed.

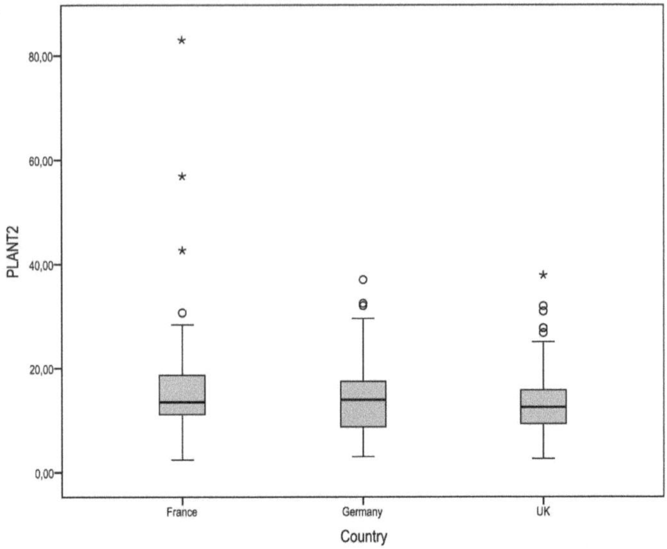

Figure 4-15: PLANT2 boxplot diagram by country

The **PLANT2** country distributions as displayed in Figure 4-15 also present a rather homogeneous picture. All country samples contain outliers; the French sample is characterized by three extreme outliers, which assumingly have an influence on the French distribution characteristics as a whole. The French outliers are also likely to be responsible for the comparably high French mean value. The impression of similar **country** distributions is confirmed by the ANOVA test (F = 0.021; p = 0.979) and the Kruskal-Wallis-Test (p = 0.748); the above measured mean value difference between France, Germany and the UK is not significant. The ANOVA result for **industry**, however, is strongly significant (F = 5.285; p = 0.000**), though not as clear as measured for PLANT1; the non-parametric test confirms this finding at the significance level of p = 0.003**. As outlined above, the calculated depreciation indicator BUILD2 might be affected by differing corporate investment policies, which might have a biasing effect on the BUILD2 industry result accordingly. In contrast, mean value comparison across categories of **auditor** lead to significant differences (t = 2.800, p = 0.019*)[1310], which, however, are not confirmed by the non-parametric test (p = 0.088).

The following two chapters on correlation and regression analysis provide further insight whether national culture, in combination with other variables, has a significant effect on PLANT1 and PLANT2 and which other control variables might serve as explanatory variables.

[1310] Equal variances not assumed.

4.3.1.5.2.2 Correlation analysis

As suggested by ANOVA, none of the six country variables are correlated with **PLANT1**. The significant correlations rather relate to the context factors of industry and size; internationality and profitability are also identified as possibly relevant context factors. The **industries** that are significantly correlated with PLANT1 are (1) oil and gas (r = 0.174; p = 0.010**), (2) business equipment (r = -0.229; p = 0.001**), (3) wholesale and retail (r = -0.218; p = 0.001**) and (4) utilities (r = 0.309; p = 0.000**). Whereas companies from the oil and gas and utilities industries are associated with longer depreciation periods, companies from the business equipment and wholesale and retail industries are associated with shorter depreciation periods.

In contrast to the correlation results on BUILD1 and BUILT2, **size** seems to be a relevant context factor when it comes to explain different depreciation periods of plant and machinery. Both logarithmized market capitalization (r = 0.166; p = 0.014*) and logarithmized total assets (r = 0.221; p = 0.001**) are significantly positively correlated with PLANT1; number of employees, on the other hand, indicates no significant association. Another significant correlation is determined for **internationality** as measured by SEC listing. SEC registered companies are significantly correlated with higher PLANT1 values (r = 0.139; p = 0.040*). Finally, **profitability** as measured by profit margin is significantly positively correlated with depreciation of plant and machinery as published in the notes (r = 0.172; p = 0.011*).

The correlation results of **PLANT2** differ slightly from the results of PLANT1. The important context factors are industry, size and leverage. As outlined above, the ANOVA **industry** results indicate a strong industry based influence for PLANT2. This result is confirmed by correlation analysis. The industries manufacturing (r = 0.141; p = 0.043*), wholesale and retail (r = -0.171; p = 0.014*) and utilities (r = 0.229; p = 0.001**) are significantly correlated with PLANT2; manufacturing and utilities are related to longer depreciation periods and wholesale and retail to shorter depreciation periods.

Besides industry, **size** assumingly has substantial predictive power with regard to PLANT2. In addition to logarithmized market capitalization (r = 0.220; p = 0.001**) and logarithmized total assets (r = 0.341; p = 0.000**), the third size variable number of employees (r = 0.155; p = 0.026*) is significantly correlated with PLANT2, as well. All size variables are positively associated with longer depreciation periods. The same positive association is determined for highly leveraged companies (r = 0.144; p = 0.039*). PLANT2 is not significantly correlated with **profitability**.[1311]

4.3.1.5.2.3 Regression analysis

The PLANT1 and PLANT2 basic regression model, which is based on the four cultural values plus external and internal control variables, is described in Formula 4.6.

Formula 4.6

$$PLANT1_i(PLANT2_i) = \beta_1 UAI_k + \beta_2 MAS_k + \beta_3 IDV_k + \beta_4 PDI_k + \beta_l CONVAR_{i/k} + \varepsilon_i$$

[1311] The PLANT1 and PLANT2 correlation coefficients are listed in Appendix A, Table A 4.

where

$PLANT1_i$	=	*average depreciation period of plant and machinery (corporate accounting policies)*
$PLANT2_i$	=	*calculated depreciation period of plant and machinery (statement of fixed assets)*
UAI_k	=	*uncertainty avoidance index*
MAS_k	=	*masculinity index*
IDV_k	=	*individualism index*
PDI_k	=	*power distance index*
$CONVAR_{i/k}$	=	*country and company control variables*
$\beta_{1\text{-}l}$	=	*regression coefficients*
ε_i	=	*the companies' error term*
i	=	*1,...,n (company index)*
k	=	*1,2,3 (country index)*
l	=	*5,...,17 (control variable index)*

The **PLANT1** regression model with most explanatory power contains no cultural factor. The only institutional country factor recognized is financing system; PLANT1 influence factors are rather found across categories of control variables. Except for auditor, all other internal context factor categories, even though not in any case significant, are incorporated. Almost all industry factors are included in the model. These variables are consumer non-durables, oil and gas, business equipment, telecommunication, wholesale/retail, healthcare and utilities. Furthermore, the size variables number of employees and total assets assumingly play a role in explaining PLANT1. The included internationality factors are SEC listing and foreign sales. The remaining explanatory factors are leverage and the size measure profit margin (see Table 4-30).

The examination of the **PLANT1** and **PLANT2** regression models' premises reveals no major deficiencies with respect to transferability of results, distribution and autocorrelation of residuals and multi collinearity of independent variables. The F-values of 15.312** (PLANT1) respectively 9.286** (PLANT2) signify that the regression results of the tested samples are transferable to the populations. Although not perfectly normal distributed, graphical analysis of the PLANT1 and PLANT2 residuals distributions indicates nearly normal distribution. Furthermore, the Durbin-Watson coefficients imply low levels of residuals autocorrelation (PLANT1: DW = 2.122; PLANT2: DW = 2.211). The multi collinearity indicators tolerance and VIF reveal acceptably low levels of multi collinearity. Only the size variables number of employees and total assets (PLANT1) respectively number of employees and market capitalization (PLANT2) are characterized by tolerably higher levels of multi collinearity (see Table 4-30 and Table 4-32). Despite slightly higher levels multi collinearity, the size variables are included in the PLANT1 and PLANT2 regression models for their explanatory contribution. The elimination of one of the size variables from the respective regression models results in a considerable loss of explanatory power.

R	R^2	Adjusted R^2	Std. error of the estimate			Durbin-Watson	
0.716	0.512	0.479	4.898			2.122	
	Sum of squares	df	Mean square		F	Sig.	
Regression	5,142.713	14	367.337				
Residuals	4,894.135	204	23.991		15.312	0.000	
Total	10,036.847	218					
Variables	B	Std. error	Beta	t	Sig.	Tolerance	VIF
(Constant)	-2.470	4.715		-0.524	0.601		
FINMCAP	-1.090	0.861	-0.065	-1.266	0.207	0.908	1.102
CONNDUR	-1.834	1.133	-0.086	-1.619	0.107	0.844	1.185
OIL	2.158	1.731	0.067	1.247	0.214	0.839	1.192
EQU	-3.527	1.199	-0.157	-2.941	0.004	0.843	1.186
TEL	-3.270	1.387	-0.126	-2.358	0.019	0.841	1.189
SALE	-2.424	1.294	-0.103	-1.873	0.062	0.788	1.268
HEALTH	-3.071	1.378	-0.115	-2.229	0.027	0.905	1.105
UTIL	15.480	1.632	0.499	9.483	0.000	0.862	1.160
EMP	0.000	0.000	-0.219	-3.260	0.001	0.530	1.886
LTASS	2.501	0.708	0.240	3.534	0.001	0.517	1.932
SECLIST	2.241	1.254	0.101	1.787	0.075	0.741	1.349
FORSALES	-1.762	1.288	-0.073	-1.368	0.173	0.844	1.185
LEV	0.045	0.025	0.092	1.763	0.079	0.878	1.140
PROFIT	0.017	0.014	0.058	1.161	0.247	0.952	1.051

Table 4-30: PLANT1 regression analysis results

The above described **PLANT1** regression model explains 47.9%[1312] of PLANT1 variance. Six of the 14 included variables are determined as significant, four industry variables and two size variables (see Table 4-30). The significant **industry** variables are business equipment (β = -0.157; p = 0.004**), telecommunication (β = -0.126; p = 0.019*), healthcare (β = -0.115; p = 0.027*) and utilities (β = 0.499; p = 0.000**); whereas companies from the former three business sectors are associated with shorter depreciation periods, companies from the utilities sector are associated with longer depreciation periods. The strongly significant regression analysis result of utilities, however, is not confirmed by rank regression analysis (see Table 4-31).

1312 This figure refers to the adjusted R^2.

Adjusted R^2	Variables	Beta	Sig.	Variables	Beta	Sig.
0.231	RFINMCAP	-0.071	0.281	RUTIL	0.120	0.065
	RCONNDUR	-0.110	0.090	REMP	-0.223	0.026
	ROIL	0.071	0.279	RLTASS	0.227	0.021
	REQU	-0.252	0.000	RSECLIST	0.110	0.111
	RTEL	-0.188	0.003	RFORSALES	0.022	0.729
	RSALE	-0.205	0.001	RLEV	0.129	0.065
	RHEALTH	-0.138	0.032	RPROFIT	0.118	0.102

Table 4-31: PLANT1 rank regression analysis results

The regression results of the **size** variables are contradictory. Whereas number of employees (β = -0.219; p = 0.001**) is significantly negatively related to PLANT1, logarithmized total assets (β = 0.240; p = 0.001**) is significantly positively related to PLANT1. Both results are confirmed by rank regression analysis (see Table 4-31).

R	R^2	Adjusted R^2	Std. error of the estimate			Durbin-Watson	
0.523	0.274	0.244	5.957			2.211	
	Sum of squares	df	Mean square		F	Sig.	
Regression	2,635.997	8	329.500		9.286	0.000	
Residuals	6,989.886	197	35.482				
Total	9,625.883	205					
Variables	B	Std. error	Beta	t	Sig.	Tolerance	VIF
(Constant)	-2.999	6.226		-0.482	0.631		
IDV	-0.063	0.047	-0.086	-1.321	0.188	0.875	1.143
OIL	4.000	2.121	0.120	1.886	0.061	0.916	1.092
SALE	-2.124	1.545	-0.090	-1.375	0.171	0.862	1.160
UTIL	9.796	1.926	0.322	5.087	0.000	0.919	1.088
LMCAP	-2.720	1.364	-0.242	-1.995	0.047	0.250	3.999
EMP	0.000	0.000	-0.165	-2.014	0.045	0.552	1.813
LTASS	5.513	1.325	0.530	4.162	0.000	0.228	4.393
BIG4	2.743	2.107	0.082	1.302	0.195	0.928	1.077

Table 4-32: PLANT2 regression analysis results

In contrast to the above PLANT1 regression model, the **PLANT2** regression model incorporates only eight variables of which four show significant results (see Table 4-32). Individualism is included as the only country factor; the IDV regression coefficient, however, is not significant. The remaining variables stem from the variables categories industry, size and auditor. The industries oil and gas, wholesale and retail and utilities are included as industry factors and market capitalization, number of employees and total assets are included as size measures. These variables explain 24.4%[1313] of the PLANT2 variance.

The significant variables very much resemble the PLANT1 regression analysis results. In contrast to PLANT1, which is significantly associated with four different **industries**, PLANT2 is only associated with utilities (β = 0.322; p = 0.000**). In analogy to PLANT1, the utilities sector is related to longer depreciation periods; the PLANT2 utilities result is affirmed by the non-parametric test (see Table 4-33).

Adjusted R^2	Variables	Beta	Sig.	Variables	Beta	Sig.
0.168	RIND	-0.089	0.187	RLMCAP	-0.235	0.048
	ROIL	0.093	0.158	REMP	-0.087	0.376
	RSALE	-0.158	0.017	RLTASS	0.567	0.000
	RUTIL	0.162	0.014	RBIG4	0.024	0.716

Table 4-33: PLANT2 rank regression analysis results

The results for the internal context factor **size**, again, present an ambiguous picture. Concordant to the PLANT1 regression results, number of employees (β = -0.165; p = 0.045*) is significantly negatively and total assets (β = 0.530; p = 0.000**) is significantly positively related to PLANT2. Furthermore, PLANT2 is also significantly negatively associated with the third size variable market capitalization (β = -0.242; p = 0.047*). Unlike the PLANT1 rank regression analysis results, number of employees does not pass the non-parametric robustness test (see Table 4-33). As mentioned above, the size variables total assets and market capitalization show increased levels of multi collinearity. Nonetheless, tolerance value and VIF indicate that the levels of multi collinearity are acceptable; the significant size results are not to be rejected (see Table 4-32).

The mostly homogeneous regression results for PLANT1 and PLANT2 are briefly discussed in the following chapter.

4.3.1.5.2.4 Implications

The effect of country and, more specifically, **cultural** factors on depreciation periods of plant and machinery is minimal. Although individualism is included in the PLANT2 regression model, the IDV regression coefficient is not significant. In contrast to the BUILD1/BUILD2 hypotheses test results, which confirm the systematic influence of uncertainty avoidance, the four culture based hypotheses for PLANT1 and PLANT2 are denied (see Figure 4-16).

[1313] This figure refers to the adjusted R^2.

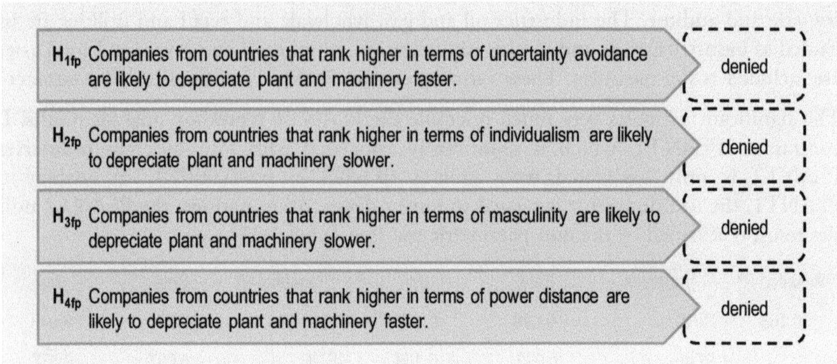

Figure 4-16: PLANT1 and PLANT2 hypotheses test results

Although *per se* quite homogeneous, the PLANT1/PLANT2 results differ substantially from the BUILD1/BUILD2 results. Only the telecommunication sector was determined as a significant industrial sector for three of the four tested depreciation indicators (BUILD1, BUILD2 and PLANT1). Apart from telecommunication, three more **industries** are identified as relevant predictor variables: business equipments, healthcare and utilities. Whereas the telecommunication (PLANT1), the business equipment (PLANT1) and the healthcare (PLANT1) sectors are related to shorter depreciation periods, the utilities (PLANT2) industry is associated with longer depreciation periods.

These findings could be connected to technological change. The former three high-tech industries refer to computers, software and electronic equipment and are typically affected by shorter cycles of technological change and, accordingly, shorter cycles for plant and machinery. In contrast, the utilities industry is rather characterized by longer plant and machinery cycles. Power plants are not as easily affected by technological change as computer chips or software. The significantly positive association between PLANT2 and utilities supports this argumentation.

The regression results on the **size** variables number of employees and total assets for PLANT1 and PLANT2 allow for different interpretations; whereas number of employees and market capitalization (only PLANT2) are negatively associated with depreciation periods of plant and machinery, total assets are positively associated with both dependent variables. Notwithstanding, the positive association between size and depreciation, though unexpected with regard to conservatism considerations, is deemed more probable. First, the significant association between number of employees and PLANT2 is not confirmed by rank regression analysis. Second, the PLANT2 total assets result is a lot stronger compared to the number of employees result. And third, the finding of size, being positively associated with depreciation periods, equals the significant finding for BUILD2. Again, the positive relationship between size and PLANT1/PLANT2 contradicts the political cost related assumption of larger companies being more conservative. A tentative interpretation could be that larger companies attach relatively more importance to higher earnings figures, achieved by less conservative accounting, than to political costs; the pressure of the capital market seems to be more influential than public pressure. Effective lobbying could be another reason for companies disregarding the risk of political intervention.

The following chapter presents the empirical results on the last tested specific accounting area. Conservatism is approximated by fair value measurement of investment property.

4.3.1.6 Fair value measurement

The fair value measurement hypotheses posit a relationship between cultural factors and fair value measurement of investment property. Companies from countries that, according to their cultural profile, are assumed to be less conservative are expected to use fair value measurement more often to measure investment property. The financial statement analysis showed that only 68 of the total 261 companies (26%) present investment property in their balance sheets. Of these companies only 15 (22%) chose the fair value method over historical cost accounting (see Table 4-34). This sample is far too small to allow for a robust statistical analysis. The results of the financial statement analysis, nonetheless, allow for some tentative interpretations.

	France	Germany	UK	Σ
Country caution score[1314]	105.5	161.0	199.5	
1. Number of companies that have investment properties	19	34	15	68
2. Number of companies that use the fair value method (2/1)	4 (21%)	4 (12%)	7 (47%)	15
3. Thereof: number of real estate companies	3	0	5	8
4. Total number of real estate companies	8	0	5	13
5. Non-real-estate companies that use the fair value method (5/1)	1 (5%)	4 (12%)	2 (13%)	7

Table 4-34: Use of the fair value method by country

The cultural profile of the three analyzed countries suggests a conservatism ranking of France, being the most conservative country, followed by Germany and the UK, as the least conservative country.[1315] Consequently, the French sample is expected to contain relatively less companies that use fair value measurement than the German sample and German companies are expected to use less fair value measurement than British companies. The results in Table 4-34 show that the number of British companies that use fair value measurement for investment property is almost twice as high as compared to the corresponding number of French and German companies. In relation to the number of companies that report investment property, almost half of the investment property relevant British companies choose the fair value method. French (21%) and German (12%) companies make relatively less use of the fair value method. These basic statistics are in line with the culture based assumption that British companies make more use of the fair value method. Nonetheless, the type of industry could also play a role in the decision of

[1314] A lower caution score indicates a higher caution level. From a higher caution level follows the assumption of higher conservatism and higher secrecy. Cf. chapter 2.2.4.7.2.

[1315] Cf. chapter 2.2.4.7.2.

how to measure investment property. Real estate companies usually choose the fair value method for valuation purposes as these companies possess the most valuation know-how with respect to real estate property.[1316] With respect to the sample of this study, the above assumption is true for British and French companies. Five of seven British and three of four French companies that use the fair value method are from the real estate sector. Therewith all British and 37.5% of the French real estate companies evaluate investment property according to the fair value method. The German sample contains no real estate companies.

Only seven non-real-estate companies use the fair value method for investment property. In relation to the number of companies that have investment property, the British sample contains most non-real-estate companies (13%), closely followed by Germany (12%) and France (5%).

These figures are not qualified to make robust statements of fair value country practice. Nevertheless, British companies by tendency use the fair value method more often than German and French companies. Taken into consideration that three of the four French fair value companies are real estate companies, it may be posited that German companies in general apply fair value measurement more often than their French counterparts. This posit is supported by the fact that only three of eight French real estate companies use the fair value method, although these companies are supposed to be able to reliably determine investment property fair values.

The above comments on national fair value application are to be understood as mere tendency statements. The limited number of cases makes the statistically robust falsification/approval of the above posited hypotheses impossible (see Figure 4-17). Consequently, no further empirical tests have been performed on the issue of fair value measurement of investment property.

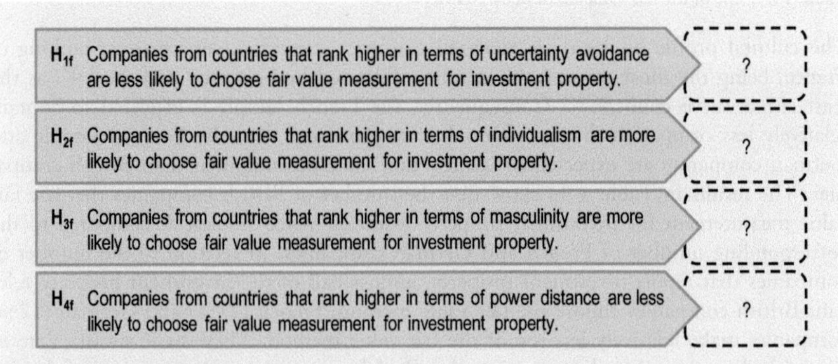

Figure 4-17: Fair value hypotheses test results

[1316] Cf. Christensen/Nikolaev 2010, p. 3.

In the following chapter the culture related empirical results on the above conservatism indicators are tested for robustness by means of the cultural dimensions of the GLOBE study.

4.3.1.7 Conservatism robustness test

The national cultural dimensions employed to approximate cultural patterns stem from the above described *Hofstede* IBM study. As mentioned before, the results of this study have been successfully applied in numerous accounting studies; nonetheless, the wide academic attention the *Hofstede* study has achieved also led to criticism. Although culture is expected to change very slowly over time and more recent replication studies confirm the *Hofstede* results, his study is often criticized to be **outdated.**[1317] Consequently, in the following robustness test the *Hofstede* dimensions are replaced by the more current cultural dimensions identified by *House et al.* in the above presented GLOBE study.[1318]

Whereas *Hofstede* describes national cultural differences by means of four respectively five cultural dimensions, *House et al.* determine two times nine value and practice related cultural dimensions. As outlined above, these dimensions are inspired by the *Hofstede* dimensions. Accordingly, *House et al.* recognize the dimensions uncertainty avoidance and power distance. Institutional collectivism and in-group collectivism resemble the *Hofstede* dimension of individualism, gender egalitarianism and assertiveness can be linked to the *Hofstede* dimension of masculinity and future orientation is similar to the *Hofstede* dimension of long-term versus short-term orientation. Additionally, *House et al.* determine the dimensions human orientation and performance orientation.[1319]

In contrast to *Hofstede,* who explicitly measures cultural values, *House et al.* measure both cultural values ('should be') and cultural practices ('as is'), distinguishing between 'should be' questions, starting with the words 'I believe that [...]' and 'as is' questions, starting with the words 'In this society [...]'. *Hofstede* criticizes this operationalization of cultural values and practices as naive:[1320]

> *"Asking 'as is' questions basically assumed that these people were in a position to compare their society with other societies. This assumption, I believe, is naïve – it takes international experience plus an unusually open mind to produce anything like a credible comparison between one's own society and others."*[1321]

Indeed, the GLOBE study's differentiation between values and practices is subject to considerable criticism; surprisingly, seven of the nine value dimensions are significantly negatively correlated with the corresponding practices dimensions.[1322] *Maseland/Hoorn* argue

---

[1317] Cf. Johnson/Lenartowicz 1998, p. 351; Baskerville-Morley 2005, p. 389f.; Jones 2007, p. 5.

[1318] Cf. chapter 2.2.4.1.3 and chapter 2.2.4.1.4; see House et al. 2004 for more detailed information on the GLOBE study.

[1319] Cf. chapter 2.2.4.1.3.

[1320] For a critical discussion of the GLOBE study's distinction between societal values and societal practices cf. Maseland/van Hoorn 2010, p. 1325ff.; Brewer/Venaik 2010, p. 1316ff.

[1321] Hofstede 2006, p. 886.

[1322] Cf. Brewer/Venaik 2010, p. 1316. For a detailed discussion on the scientific debate see Taras et al. 2010, p. 1330ff.

that, instead of measuring cultural values, *House et al.* rather measure marginal preferences and attribute this assumption to the limitations of the GLOBE self-report questionnaires.[1323] *Hofstede* suggests that the participants of the GLOBE study rather demonstrated their 'should be' values ideology when answering 'as is' questions.[1324] Consequently, the GLOBE study's cultural practices are comparable to *Hofstede's* understanding of cultural values. In his definition of cultural values, *Hofstede* clearly distinguishes between 'values as the desired' and 'values as the desirable'. Whereas *Hofstede's* cultural values capture the desired, i.e. what people actually desire, the GLOBE study's cultural values capture the desirable, i.e. what people think they should desire.[1325]

To allow for comparability with respect to the *Hofstede* results, the robustness tests are performed using the GLOBE study's cultural **practices scores**. Furthermore, only the GLOBE dimensions that are conceptually close to the tested *Hofstede* dimensions are tested in the following to allow for comparable results based on the *Hofstede-Gray* framework. The regression model that is used to test the associations between the six financial accounting relevant GLOBE dimensions and the direct and indirect conservatism indicators is displayed in Formula 4.7.

Formula 4.7
$$CONS_i = \beta_1 UA_k + \beta_2 GEQ_k + \beta_3 ASS_k + \beta_4 ICOL_k + \beta_5 GCOL_k + \beta_6 PD_k + \beta_l CONVAR_{i/k} + \varepsilon_i$$

where

$CONS_i$	=	*conservatism indicators*[1326]
UA_k	=	*uncertainty avoidance index*
GEQ_k	=	*gender egalitarianism index*
ASS_k	=	*assertiveness index*
$ICOL_k$	=	*institutional collectivism index*
$GCOL_k$	=	*in-group collectivism index*
PD_k	=	*power distance index*
$CONVAR_{i/k}$	=	*country and company control variables*
$\beta_{1\text{-}l}$	=	*regression coefficients*
ε_i	=	*the companies' error term*
i	=	*1,…,n (company index)*
k	=	*1,2,3 (country index)*
l	=	*7,…,20 (control variable index)*

As indicated by the conservatism indicators' ANOVAs and as confirmed by the respective regression analyses, country effects are only observable for the conservatism indicators **BUILD1** and **BUILD2**. In contrast to the *Hofstede* regression analyses, which finds the

[1323] Cf. Maseland/van Hoorn 2010, p. 1325ff.

[1324] Cf. Hofstede 2006, p. 885ff.

[1325] Cf. Hofstede 2006, p. 885ff.

[1326] CONS refers to the conservatism indicators: MTB, NA, CAPRD, INT, BUILD1, BUILD2, PLANT1 and PLANT2.

cultural factor uncertainty avoidance to be most influential with respect to BUILD1 and BUILD2, the GLOBE regression analyses identify power distance (BUILD1: $\beta = -0.269$; $p = 0.000$**; BUILD2: $\beta = -0.141$; $p = 0.037$*), as defined by *House et al.,* to be significantly associated with depreciation periods of buildings. The sign of the PD regression coefficient is as posited above. Companies from countries that are characterized by higher power distance are associated with shorter depreciation periods and more conservatism accordingly (see Table 4-35).

Hofstede			*House et al.*		
Adj. R^2	Sig. variables	β	Adj. R^2	Sig. variables	B
BUILD1					
0.186	UAI	-0.236**	0.194	PD	-0.269**
BUILD2					
0.163	UAI	-0.156*	0.165	PD	-0.141*
* (**) represents significance at the 5% (1%) level					

Table 4-35: Conservatism robustness test results

Although the above presented GLOBE results differ with respect to the relevant cultural dimension, they confirm the (strongly) significant influence of national culture. Since uncertainty avoidance and power distance are both assumed to be negatively associated with conservatism both dimensions are conceptually close and stand for a cautious financial accounting approach. The deviating results with respect to depreciation periods of buildings are likely to be associated with **conceptual differences** between the *Hofstede* and the GLOBE dimensions. As mentioned above, the *House et al.* dimensions of uncertainty avoidance and power distance do not exactly coincide with the equally labeled *Hofstede* dimensions.[1327] Alternatively, the differing results might be associated to **changed cultural values.** Nonetheless, as previously pointed out, national culture is assumed to change only slowly;[1328] furthermore, the *Hofstede* dimensions have been confirmed by more current replication studies.[1329]

Following the results of GLOBE study robustness test, the BUILD1 and BUILD2 hypotheses test results are generally supported with respect to an influence of national culture. However, the GLOBE results differ with respect to the particular cultural dimension. As these differences are likely to be associated with different conceptual approaches of the two culture studies, the *Hofstede* hypotheses test results are not rejected. Furthermore, the focus of this study is the assessment of the influence of national culture on IFRS practice in general. The interpretation of cultural differences might be affected by the view of the researcher and, thus, subjectivity.

[1327] Cf. Hofstede 2006, p. 883.

[1328] Cf. Hofstede 2001, p. 73.

[1329] Cf., e.g., Hall 1989; Hoppe 1990; Helmreich/Merritt 1998; Mouritzen/Svara 2002; van Nimwegen 2002.

The following chapters present the empirical results on the second group of culture related hypotheses. The hereby tested accounting value is secrecy.

4.3.2 Secrecy

Gray suggests an influence of national culture on financial accounting practice in particular for the accounting values of conservatism and secrecy. According to *Gray*, secrecy is assumed to be affected by all four cultural values defined by *Hofstede*. Uncertainty avoidance and power distance are posited to be positively associated with secrecy and individualism and masculinity are posited to be negatively associated with secrecy.

The degree of secrecy in financial accounting is typically approximated by the quantity of corporate disclosure; companies, which choose to not disclose required financial information and/or report little or no voluntary information, are labeled more secretive. The quantity of information and therewith the degree of secrecy is measured in this study in two ways. First, the total content of the companies' notes is counted by word to determine a global measure for disclosure quantity. Second, two areas of financial information included in the notes are analyzed in more detail by means of disclosure indices. The areas selected for further analysis are segment reporting and income tax reporting. Before describing the empirical results on corporate segments and income tax, the following chapter addresses the issue of total notes disclosure.

4.3.2.1 Total notes disclosure

The corporate specific total notes disclosure values were determined by means of electronic word count. Although more words do not necessarily imply more information content, the number of words is a first global indicator to measure corporate notes disclosure. The limitations of this indicator are recognized in the interpretation of the results.

The following subsections present the results of the descriptive and inferential statistical analysis.

4.3.2.1.1 Descriptive analysis

The word count relevant sample consists of 258 companies. Three French financial statements were not countable, neither in WORD nor in PDF format. The descriptive analysis of the notes word count (NOTES) draws a clear but unexpected picture. Comparing country quantile values, except for the 5% quantile, all quantiles are dominated by French companies. The French sample also contributes the total sample's maximum of 89.416 words. The minimum, on the contrary, belongs to the German sample; moreover, the German sample scores higher than the British sample in all quantile categories. Mean value comparison of the three country samples underlines the impression of the analyzed distribution characteristics; French companies have a higher mean value than German companies and German companies have a higher mean value than British companies (see Table 4-36).

Value (words)	Total	France	Germany	UK
N	258	85	93	80
Minimum	5.783	9.892	5.783	9.907
5% quantile	13.913	14.030	14.284	14.152
1. quartile	20.815	22.071	20.824	19.175
Median	25.610	27.814	25.870	23.401
Mean	27.812	30.223	27.698	25.383
3. quartile	31.551	33.948	31.499	29.307
95% quantile	47.160	58.280	46.772	45.180
Maximum	89.416	89.416	57.944	58.746
Standard deviation	11.214	13.349	10.038	9.488

Table 4-36: NOTES descriptive statistics

The country mean value ranking equals the country standard deviation ranking. Moreover, all country samples have outliers; the French country sample is characterized by an extreme outlier, which is also the maximum of the total sample (see Figure 4-18). Except for the French extreme outlier, the graphical comparison of the country samples' boxplot diagrams suggests comparability with respect to box and whisker size. The French box appears to be slightly larger than its German and British counterparts; the British sample is characterized by shorter whiskers.[1330]

ANOVA finds the company sample to differ significantly with respect to **country** mean values (F = 4.103; p = 0.018*); this result is confirmed by the non-parametric Kruskal-Wallis-Test, which rejects the null hypothesis of equal distribution across countries at the significance level of p = 0.020*. Multiple mean value comparison (Scheffé-Test) detects that the significant difference in mean values only concerns the French and the British company sample (p = 0.021). The respective mean value differences between German and French sample and German and British sample are not significant.

Besides the influence of country, ANOVA suggests that NOTES is also affected by the **industry** of the company (F = 2.146; p = 0.026*). The Kruskal-Wallis-Test rejects the correspondent null hypothesis at a weak significance level of p = 0.096. Although not significant at the p = 0.050 level, the results of the parametric and non-parametric tests suggest that industry is to be considered as influential when explaining NOTES distribution. The T-Test on type of **auditor** adds the Big4 variable to the group of potentially influential context factors for notes word count (t = 3.529; p = 0.002**)[1331]; the influence of auditor is confirmed by the Mann-Whitney-U-Test at the significance level of p = 0.023*.

[1330] The following statistical tests are performed on data that is adjusted for outliers. Cf. chapter 3.4.1.
[1331] Equal variances not assumed.

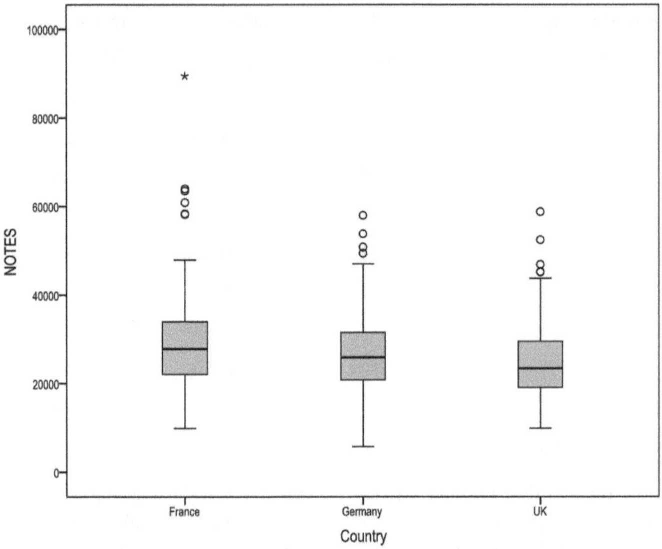

Figure 4-18: NOTES boxplot diagram by country

Country, industry and auditor are identified as potential NOTES context factors. The following chapter on correlation analysis will show whether and how these context factors are correlated with the secrecy indicator NOTES.

4.3.2.1.2 Correlation analysis

As suggested by ANOVA, country factors are significantly correlated with the dependent variable NOTES. Three of the four **cultural** factors, viz. uncertainty avoidance (r = 0.172; p = 0.006**), masculinity (r = -0.132; p = 0.035*) and power distance (r = 0.132; p = 0.035*) show a significant correlation with NOTES. Whereas uncertainty avoidance and power distance are positively correlated with NOTES, masculinity is negatively correlated with NOTES. The signs of the measured correlations are not as posited in the sub hypotheses: uncertainty avoidance and power distance are expected to be associated with higher degrees of secrecy and, thus, less notes disclosure. However, the positive correlation coefficients of both variables suggest otherwise. Also, masculinity is posited to have a negative influence on secrecy; the result of the correlation analysis suggests a negative influence on notes quantity and therewith more secrecy. Furthermore, correlation analysis suggests an influence of the **institutional** factor legal/tax system. Companies from code law countries respectively countries, which recognize the authoritative principle, are associated with more notes disclosure (r = 0.164; p = 0.009**). Similar to the correlation results on cultural factors, the correlation result for this institutional variable is surprising since code law countries that are also characterized by an influential tax system are expected to be associated with comparably less notes information. Regression analysis will show whether these unexpected relationships remain when considering the influences of more than one context factor at a time.

Although ANOVA indicates that **industry** is a significant influential factor, correlation analysis on the various industry dummy variables leads to no significant results. The applied **size** measures, on the other hand, draw an entirely different picture. All three size variables are strongly significantly correlated with NOTES; market capitalization ($r = 0.384$; $p = 0.000^{**}$), number of employees ($r = 0.380$; $p = 0.000^{**}$) and total assets ($r = 0.518$; $p = 0.000^{**}$) are associated with higher quantities of notes disclosure and less secretive accounting accordingly.

Another set of control variables that is related to higher degrees of disclosure is **internationality**. Companies that are listed abroad ($r = 0.157$; $p = 0.012^{*}$) and companies that are registered by the SEC ($r = 0.212$; $p = 0.001^{**}$) are significantly positively correlated with NOTES. The same positive association is determined for the variable type of **auditor** ($r = 0.142$; $p = 0.023^{*}$). Big4 audited companies are suggested to disclose more extensive notes than companies audited by other auditors. Highly leveraged companies are associated with higher degrees of notes disclosure, as well ($r = 0.289$; $p = 0.000^{**}$). **Profitability**, in contrast, seems to have no significant effect on NOTES.[1332]

4.3.2.1.3 Regression analysis

Eleven of the 17 tested cultural and control variables (see Formula 4.8) are included in the regression model that best explains NOTES. The cultural factors individualism, the industry factors consumer non-durables, telecommunication and utilities, the size factors number of employees and total assets, the internationality factors foreign listing, SEC listing and foreign sales, leverage and the profitability measure profit margin explain a total of 42.3%[1333] of NOTES' variance.

Formula 4.8

$$NOTES_i = \beta_1 UAI_k + \beta_2 MAS_k + \beta_3 IDV_k + \beta_4 PDI_k + \beta_l CONVAR_{i/k} + \varepsilon_i$$

where

$NOTES_i$	=	*notes word count*
UAI_k	=	*uncertainty avoidance index*
MAS_k	=	*masculinity index*
IDV_k	=	*individualism index*
PDI_k	=	*power distance index*
$CONVAR_{i/k}$	=	*country and company control variables*
β_{1-l}	=	*regression coefficients*
ε_i	=	*the companies' error term*
i	=	*1,...,n (company index)*

[1332] The NOTES correlation coefficients are listed in Appendix A, Table A 4.

[1333] This figure refers to the adjusted R^2.

k	=	*1,2,3 (country index)*
l	=	*5,…,17 (control variable index)*

The examination of the regression model premises reveals no major deficiencies with respect to transferability of results, distribution and autocorrelation of residuals and multi collinearity of independent variables. The F-value of 17.905** signifies that the regression results of the tested sample are transferable to the population. Although not perfectly normal distributed, graphical analysis of the NOTES residuals distribution indicates nearly normal distribution. Furthermore, the Durbin-Watson coefficient implies a low level of residuals autocorrelation (DW = 1.911). The multi collinearity indicators tolerance and VIF reveal acceptably low levels of multi collinearity (see Table 4-37).

R	R^2	Adjusted R^2	Std. error of the estimate			Durbin-Watson	
0.669	0.448	0.423	7,809.936			1.911	
	Sum of squares	df	Mean square		F	Sig.	
Regression	12,013,135,439.403	11	1,092,103,221.764		17.905	0.000	
Residuals	14,821,810,367.868	243	60,995,104.395				
Total	26,834,945,807.271	254					
Variables	B	Std. error	Beta	t	Sig.	Tolerance	VIF
(Constant)	-6,697.985	7,072.739		-0.947	0.345		
IDV	-251.391	56.163	-0.231	-4.476	0.000	0.851	1.174
CONNDUR	-2,803.375	1,664.144	-0.083	-1.685	0.093	0.943	1.060
TEL	5,058.723	1,902.116	0.133	2.660	0.008	0.915	1.093
UTIL	6,638.357	2,564.764	0.131	2.588	0.010	0.881	1.135
EMP	0.010	0.007	0.084	1.483	0.139	0.707	1.415
LTASS	6,975.126	917.797	0.452	7.600	0.000	0.642	1.558
FORLIST	2,409.688	1,431.273	0.088	1.684	0.094	0.833	1.201
SECLIST	7,273.012	1,818.302	0.211	4.000	0.000	0.818	1.222
FORSALES	4,056.112	1,709.360	0.120	2.373	0.018	0.884	1.131
LEV	-65.015	37.083	-0.087	-1.753	0.081	0.916	1.092
PROFIT	-14.458	12.798	-0.055	-1.130	0.260	0.975	1.026

Table 4-37: NOTES regression analysis results

The above described NOTES regression model identifies four significant context factors: national culture, industry, size and internationality (see Table 4-37). The only significant **cultural** factor is individualism (β = -0.231; p = 0.000**). Although not significantly correlated with NOTES, individualism proves to be influential when tested in combination with other context factors. Surprisingly, the regression analysis suggests that companies from countries that are characterized by high individualism are associated with less notes disclosure and, thus, higher levels of secrecy. According to the above posited secrecy hypotheses, individualism is expected to be associated with lower levels of secrecy, However, the result is confirmed by the strongly significant rank regression analysis result (see Table 4-38). Although identified by correlation analysis as potentially influential, the **institutional** variable legal/tax system leads to no significant NOTES regression results when tested in combination with individualism.

Adjusted R^2	Variables	Beta	Sig.	Variables	Beta	Sig.
0.359	RIND	-0.212	0.000	RFORLIST	0.124	0.021
	RCONNDUR	-0.090	0.083	RSECLIST	0.125	0.024
	RTEL	0.084	0.105	RFORSALES	0.114	0.033
	RUTIL	0.090	0.103	RLEV	0.111	0.061
	REMP	-0.042	0.587	RPROFIT	-0.047	0.417
	RLTASS	0.503	0.000			

Table 4-38: NOTES rank regression analysis results

The other three variables that contribute to the explanatory power of the NOTES regression model have already been identified by correlation analysis as possibly important influence factors. The weakly significant correlation result for the **industry** factor utilities is supported by regression analysis. Companies from the utilities industry are related to significantly higher NOTES values ($\beta = 0.131$; $p = 0.010$**). Furthermore, the telecommunication industry is significantly positively associated with NOTES ($\beta = 0.133$; $p = 0.008$**). Notwithstanding, the rank regression analysis results of the two industries are not significant (see Table 4-38).

The **size** variable logarithmized total assets, characterized by the highest measured correlation coefficient, is the only significant size variable in the tested regression model. Total assets are strongly significantly associated with NOTES ($\beta = 0.454$; $p = 0.000$**). The sign of the relationship remains unchanged in comparison to correlation analysis; larger companies are assumed to disclose more information as measured by words in the notes. The non parametric test confirms this finding. Two of the three recognized **internationality** factors are significantly associated with NOTES. Companies that are listed at a stock exchange regulated by the SEC ($\beta = 0.211$; $p = 0.000$**) respectively companies that are strongly engaged in foreign sales ($\beta = 0.120$; $p = 0.018$*) are significantly related to higher NOTES values. Moreover, the third internationality indicator foreign listing is weakly significantly associated with higher NOTES values ($\beta = 0.088$; $p = 0.094$). The significantly positive influence of the three internationality indicators is affirmed by the non-parametric rank regression analysis (see Table 4-38). The other internal context factors show no significant influence.

The following chapter discusses the above described regression analysis results.

4.3.2.1.4 Implications

Although correlation analysis indicates a significant association between NOTES and the three **cultural** variables uncertainty avoidance, masculinity and power distance, the only significant cultural factor identified by regression and rank regression analysis is individualism. When tested in combination with other variables, individualism is suggested to have the highest predictive potential of the tested country factors. Nonetheless, the individualism regression result is contrary to expected. As hypothesized above, individualism is assumed to be negatively associated with secrecy and, thus, positively with disclosure quantity as measured by NOTES. The regression results, however, confirm the findings of the descriptive analysis: companies from the UK, which is considered to be more individualistic than France and Germany, disclose less information in the notes. This result is surprising since the UK is also characterized by the most developed equity capital market of the three sample countries and more developed capital markets are usually associated with lower degrees of secrecy.[1334]

A tentative explanation for this unexpected finding could be that notes word count is an inappropriate secrecy indicator. In comparison to the management report for example, the notes of the financial statements are much more regulated by accounting standards and leave less room for voluntary information. The limited room for voluntary information could result in secrecy to be less detectable. Also, simple word count of notes information does not allow for conclusions on the quantity of relevant company information. Some companies tend to copy substantial parts of the relevant standards into the notes, instead of providing only the relevant information that concern the company. Such behavior could result from missing IFRS experience and could be an indicator for uncertainty. British companies, which report comparably less notes information as counted in words, might leave out such unimportant **'boilerplate' accounting** information since they are more experienced with international accounting standards than French or German companies. Also, German and French companies, which are regarded to be less experienced with reference to international accounting standards, could seek to convince the international capital market otherwise by publishing relatively more notes information. Such accounting practice could be interpreted as a corporate **signaling strategy**.

The appropriateness of word count as an indicator for accounting secrecy is further discussed when comparing the NOTES results with the disclosure results on segment and income tax reporting. Contrary to NOTES, which approximates information quantity by number of words, the segment and income tax secrecy indicators measure information quantity by means of disclosure indices. These indices on statutory and voluntary segment and income tax information count information items instead of words and therefore are suggested to be better proxies for corporate financial reporting quantity.

[1334] As outlined in chapter 2.3.2.1.1, financing systems that are characterized by highly developed equity capital markets are classified as 'outsider' system. Information is primarily provided via public information channels like financial statements; accordingly, public financial information quantity is assumed to be higher.

With respect to the NOTES variable, the prior posited hypotheses on the relationship between cultural factors and total notes information as measured by number of words are denied (see Figure 4-19).

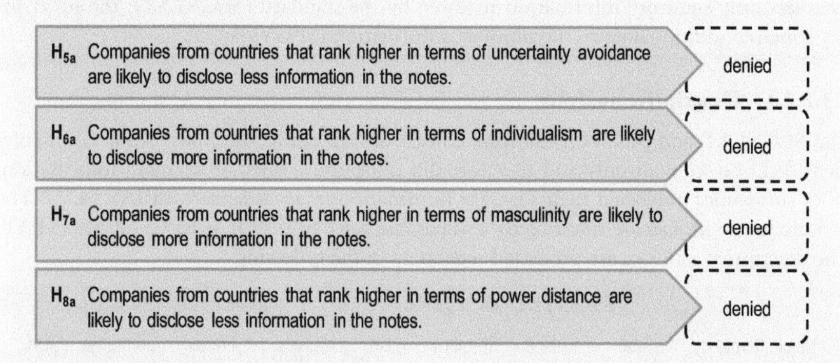

Figure 4-19: NOTES hypotheses test results

Besides the cultural factor individualism, industry, size and internationality are determined as significant NOTES predictors. Companies from the utilities sector are suggested to disclose more information than other industries. As the utilities **industry** is often associated with monopolistic rents, increased notes information could be interpreted as a signaling strategy to reduce political costs. Notwithstanding, the significant utilities result is not confirmed by rank regression analysis. Political cost theory could also explain the determined positive relationship between **size** and NOTES. Large companies tend to raise more public attention, which leads to higher political costs. Also, large companies are more complex than smaller companies and therefore face higher agency costs. Large companies try to reduce political and agency costs that mainly result from information asymmetries by disclosing more information. Agency costs might also be the reason for the positive association between the **internationality** factor SEC listing and secrecy. International companies are more complex than nationally operating companies and also have higher agency costs that result from information asymmetries. Again, increased notes information could be interpreted as a corporate strategy to solve respectively mitigate such agency conflicts.

4.3.2.2 Segment reporting

The above notes word count led to unexpected results with regard to cultural influences, although previous empirical studies found the accounting value of secrecy most susceptible to cultural influences in accordance with *Hofstede-Gray* framework.[1335] To verify the above NOTES results, two more secrecy indicators are employed in this study; these indicators apply disclosure indices to measure information quantity in a more sophisticated way compared to word count. The accounting areas selected for analysis are segment re-

[1335] Cf., e.g., Hope 2003a, p. 235ff.; Lainez/Gasca 2006, p. 68ff.; Noravesh et al. 2007, p. 254ff.

porting and income tax reporting. Both issues are obligatory for companies that apply IFRS. The following subchapters present the empirical results on segment reporting. Two disclosure indices are developed to measure segment information content;[1336] one index measures only statutory information required by the standard (SEGSTAT); the other index contains additional items of voluntary information (SEGVOL).[1337]

4.3.2.2.1 Descriptive analysis

The SEGSTAT and SEGVOL samples consist of 252 companies only; some companies identified one segment only and therefore did not publish separate segment information; other companies published their segment information in accordance with IAS 14.[1338] The two disclosure indices are not directly comparable since SEGVOL is based on SEGSTAT. The descriptive statistics are presented separately in the following.

	Statutory segment reporting				Voluntary segment reporting			
Value (items)	Total	France	Germany	UK	Total	France	Germany	UK
N	252	84	90	78	252	84	90	78
Minimum	1.00	1.00	5.00	4.00	4.00	4.00	9.00	7.00
5% quantile	6.00	5.00	7.45	7.00	9.00	7.15	13.00	11.00
1. quartile	9.00	8.00	11.00	10.00	14.00	12.00	16.25	14.00
Median	11.00	10.00	13.00	11.00	17.00	16.00	19.00	17.00
Mean	11.30	10.24	12.51	11.05	17.12	15.05	19.03	17.14
3. quartile	13.00	12.25	14.00	12.00	20.00	18.00	22.00	19.00
95% quantile	16.00	15.00	16.55	15.00	24.00	22.85	24.55	24.00
Maximum	19.00	18.00	18.00	19.00	29.00	25.00	29.00	27.00
Standard deviation	3.07	3.43	2.75	2.50	4.53	4.54	4.03	4.13

Table 4-39: SEGSTAT and SEGVOL descriptive statistics

The **SEGSTAT** sample is clearly dominated by German companies; the German sample scores highest in all above listed quantiles (see Table 4-39). Only the maximum value is contributed by the British sample. The minimum value, on the other hand, belongs to the French sample which, except for the third quantile, has the lowest quantile values of the three country samples. However, the French sample is characterized by the highest standard deviation followed by Germany and the UK, which both have quite similar standard deviations. Mean value comparison indicates a country ranking of Germany in first place, the UK in second place and France in third place. This ranking is not exactly as expected with reference to the cultural profile of the countries. The expected ranking from least to

[1336] Cf. chapter 3.3.3.3.

[1337] For the single items of the segment reporting disclosure indices cf. Appendix A, Table A 2.

[1338] Two companies chose to report segment information in accordance with IAS 14 since their financial statements belonged to the annual period 2008/2009.

most secretive (UK→Germany→France) is only in part supported. Even though France ranks last with respect to SEGSTAT, the British SEGSTAT mean value is outnumbered by the German sample. ANOVA will demonstrate if the measured mean value differences are significant.

The inclusion of voluntary information in the **SEGVOL** index only amplifies the characteristics of the SEGSTAT index. German companies score highest in all quantiles and even contribute the total sample's maximum value. The French sample, on the contrary, is described by the lowest values in all listed quantiles and contribute the total sample's minimum value. Again, the standard deviations of the German and the British sample are comparable; the French sample has the highest standard deviation of the three. Mean value comparison supports the SEGSTAT result; the distances between the three countries have increased, though. Accordingly, the SEGVOL index is expected to display possible country differences even better as compared to the SEGSTAT index.[1339]

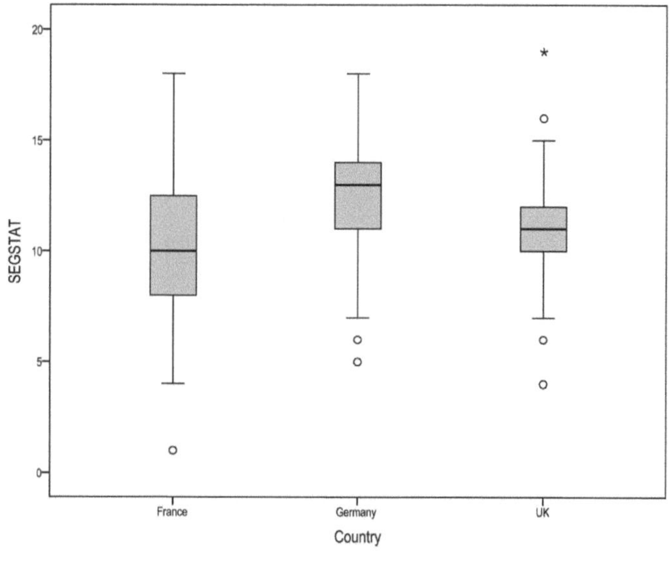

Figure 4-20: SEGSTAT boxplot diagram by country

The above **SEGSTAT** boxplot diagram by country sample underlines the assumption of possible country differences (see Figure 4-20). The UK box is considerably smaller than the German box, which is considerably smaller than the French box. Also, the British whiskers are shorter than German whiskers, which are shorter than French whiskers. Only the UK sample is characterized by an extreme (positive) outlier; all country samples contain negative outliers. ANOVA confirms the existence of significant SEGSTAT **country** differences (F = 13.550; p = 0.000**); the independent samples Kruskal-Wallis-Test re-

[1339] The following statistical tests are performed on data that is adjusted for outliers. Cf. chapter 3.4.1.

jects the null hypothesis of equal distribution across country samples at the significance level of p = 0.000**. As significant ANOVA results do not imply significant country differences between all country pairs included, the country pairs are tested separately for country differences using the multiple comparison Scheffé-Test. According to the Scheffé-Test, only the country differences between France and Germany (p = 0.000**) and France and the UK (p = 0.006**) are found to be significant.

In contrast to the external context factor country, the internal context factor **industry** is suggested to have no significant influence on segment reporting practice. Neither parametric nor non-parametric (p = 0.329) mean value comparison across categories of industry lead to significant results (F = 1.378; p = 0.198). T-Test mean value comparison by type of **auditor** comes to the same result. SEGSTAT mean values of Big4 audited companies do not differ significantly from SEGSTAT mean values of companies audited by other auditors (t = -0.183, p = 0.857)[1340]; this finding is supported by the Mann-Whitney-U-Test (p = 0.979).

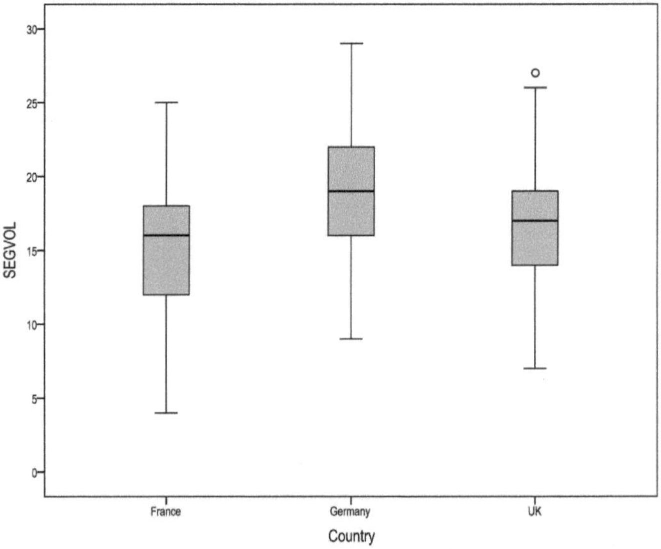

Figure 4-21: SEGVOL boxplot diagram by country

The above **SEGVOL** boxplots of the three country samples appear to be more similar with respect to box and whisker size (see Figure 4-21). The horizontal position of the three boxes, however, still differs substantially and might indicate possible country differences. In fact, ANOVA confirms strongly significant **country** differences (F = 19.242; p = 0.000**). The ANOVA result is supported by the non-parametric test at the significance level of p = 0.000**. Furthermore, the significant country differences do not only

[1340] Equal variances not assumed.

concern the country combinations France/Germany and France/UK but all country combinations. Accordingly, the Scheffé-Test indicates significant country differences between France and Germany (p = 0.000**), France and the UK (p = 0.017*) and Germany and the UK (p = 0.008**). The ANOVA **industry** result (F = 1.622; p = 0.109) and the T-Test **auditor** results (t = 0.767, p = 0.453)[1341] are similar to the respective SEGSTAT results. No significant influence is found. The parametric results for industry (p = 0.185) and auditor (p = 0.369) are confirmed by the respective non-parametric tests.

The following section on correlation analysis provides further insight, which of the tested country factors are responsible for the above measured mean value country differences of SEGSTAT and SEGVOL.

4.3.2.2.2 Correlation analysis

The results of the **SEGSTAT** correlation analysis suggest mainly two variable groups to be significantly correlated with statutory segment reporting. First, three of the four **cultural** factors are significantly correlated with SEGSTAT. Whereas masculinity is positively correlated with SEGSTAT (r = 0.230; p = 0.000**), individualism (r = -0.233; p = 0.000**) and power distance (r = -0.230; p = 0.000**) are negatively correlated with SEGSTAT. The signs of the correlation coefficients of masculinity and power distance are as posited above; higher SEGSTAT values imply lower degrees of secrecy. Only the individualism result is not as expected; individualism is expected to be negatively associated with secrecy as indicated by lower SEGSTAT values. Second, both **profitability** indicators are significantly correlated with statutory segment reporting. Profit margin (r = -0.186; p = 0.003**) and return on investment (r = -0.155; p = 0.014**) are significantly associated with lower SEGSTAT values and, thus, higher degrees of secrecy. Besides these variables, only one more measure from the **industrial** set of variables shows a significant result. Companies from the wholesale/retail sector are significantly negatively correlated with SEGSTAT (r = -0.126; p = 0.046*).

The **SEGVOL** correlation analysis leads to similar results and suggests a strong influence of country and profitability. All **cultural** factors are significantly correlated with SEGVOL. Uncertainty avoidance (r = -0.176; p = 0.005**), individualism (r = -0.203; p = 0.001**) and power distance (r = -0.309; p = 0.000**) are strongly significantly correlated with lower SEGVOL values. Masculinity (r = 0.309; p = 0.000**), on the other hand, is strongly significantly correlated with more extensive statutory and voluntary segment reporting. In analogy to the SEGSTAT correlation analysis, individualism is the only cultural factor that shows an association different from the posited one. Also, **institutional** context factors are not significantly associated with segment reporting quantity.

Although questioned by ANOVA, **industry** appears to have a certain influence on SEGVOL, as well. In contrast to SEGSTAT, which is significantly negatively correlated with the wholesale/retail sector, SEGVOL is significantly positively correlated with the manufacturing industry (r = 0.127; p = 0.044*). Regression analysis will demonstrate if the weak influence remains when integrating more context factors into the model. The **prof-**

[1341] Equal variances not assumed.

itability measures that significantly correlate with SEGSTAT also significantly correlate with SEGVOL. Companies with higher profit margin (r = -0.207; p = 0.001**) respectively higher return on investment (r = -0.137; p = 0.030*) significantly correlate with lower SEGVOL values. In contrast to the SEGSTAT correlation results, the **size** measures number of employees (r = 0.141; p = 0.025*) and total assets (r = 0.138; p = 0.029*) are significantly associated with SEGVOL. Accordingly, larger companies are related to more voluntary segment information and, thus, lower degrees of secrecy. Finally, companies that are characterized by higher **leverage** (r = 0.185; p = 0.003**) are significantly correlated with higher SEGVOL values.[1342]

The next chapter analyzes the explanatory potential of the considered cultural and control variables by means of regression analysis.

4.3.2.2.3 Regression analysis

The two SEGSTAT and SEGVOL regression models are described in Formula 4.9. The variables that provide most explanatory power with respect to **SEGSTAT** are power distance, legal/tax system, oil and gas industry, wholesale/retail industry, healthcare industry, market capitalization and total assets.[1343] These measures explain 16.0%[1344] of the total SEGSTAT variance (see Table 4-40). The **SEGVOL** regression model consists basically of the same context factors; only the size variable market capitalization is replaced by the internationality variable foreign sales and leverage. Although both variables are not significantly associated with SEGVOL, the SEGVOL regression model has more explanatory potential compared to the SEGSTAT regression model; SEGVOL variance is explained by 21.6%[1345] (see Table 4-42).

Formula 4.9

$$SEGSTAT_i\ (SEGVOL_i) = \beta_1 UAI_k + \beta_2 MAS_k + \beta_3 IDV_k + \beta_4 PDI_k + \beta_l CONVAR_{i/k} + \varepsilon_i$$

where

$SEGSTAT_i$	=	*statutory segment reporting disclosure index*
$SEGVOL_i$	=	*voluntary segment reporting disclosure index*
UAI_k	=	*uncertainty avoidance index*
MAS_k	=	*masculinity index*
IDV_k	=	*individualism index*
PDI_k	=	*power distance index*
$CONVAR_{i/k}$	=	*country and company control variables*
β_{1-l}	=	*regression coefficients*
ε_i	=	*the companies' error term*

[1342] The SEGSTAT and SEGVOL correlation coefficients are listed in Appendix A, Table A 4.

[1343] The number of operating segments, which might be associated to segment reporting quantity, was also tested for a possible influence. However, such an influence could not be confirmed.

[1344] This figure refers to the adjusted R^2.

[1345] This figure refers to the adjusted R^2.

i	=	*1,…,n (company index)*
k	=	*1,2,3 (country index)*
l	=	*5,…,17 (control variable index)*

The examination of the **SEGSTAT** and **SEGVOL** regression models' premises reveals no major deficiencies with respect to transferability of results, distribution and autocorrelation of residuals and multi collinearity of independent variables. The F-values of 7.836** (SEGSTAT) respectively 9.660** (SEGVOL) signify that the regression results of the tested samples are transferable to the populations. Although not perfectly normal distributed, graphical analysis of the SEGSTAT and SEGVOL residuals distributions indicates nearly normal distribution. Furthermore, the Durbin-Watson coefficients imply low levels of residuals autocorrelation (SEGSTAT: DW = 1.902; SEGVOL: DW = 1.931). The multi collinearity indicators tolerance and VIF reveal acceptably low levels of multi collinearity; only the two size variables market capitalization and total assets show increased but still acceptable multi collinearity for SEGSTAT (see Table 4-40 and Table 4-42).

R	R^2	Adjusted R^2	Std. error of the estimate			Durbin-Watson	
0.428	0.184	0.160	2.810			1.902	
	Sum of squares	df	Mean square		F	Sig.	
Regression	432.969	7	61.853				
Residuals	1,926.110	244	7.894		7.836	0.000	
Total	2,359.079	251					
Variables	B	Std. error	Beta	t	Sig.	Tolerance	VIF
(Constant)	11.516	2.145		5.368	0.000		
PDI	-0.118	0.019	-0.416	-6.087	0.000	0.715	1.399
LEGTAX	1.733	0.463	0.262	3.741	0.000	0.683	1.464
OIL	1.884	0.858	0.131	2.196	0.029	0.938	1.066
SALE	-1.661	0.613	-0.159	-2.710	0.007	0.968	1.034
HEALTH	-1.163	0.790	-0.087	-1.472	0.142	0.956	1.046
LMCAP	-1.052	0.595	-0.202	-1.769	0.078	0.256	3.905
LTASS	1.574	0.509	0.343	3.096	0.002	0.272	3.671

Table 4-40: SEGSTAT regression analysis results

Five of the seven variables included in the **SEGSTAT** regression model have significant regression coefficients. The only **cultural** factor, which is significantly associated with SEGSTAT, is power distance (β = -0.416; p = 0.000**). Companies from high power distance countries like France are related to less statutory segment information. The strong influence of country factors is underlined by the **institutional** factor LEGTAX, which suggests a positive connection between code law countries respectively countries that have the authoritative principle and SEGSTAT (β = 0.262; p = 0.000**). Both country factor results are confirmed to be strongly significant by the non-parametric rank regression analysis (see Table 4-41).

Adjusted R^2	Variables	Beta	Sig.	Variables	Beta	Sig.
0.150	RPDI	-0.410	0.000	RHEALTH	-0.065	0.269
	RLEGTAX	0.296	0.000	RLMCAP	-0.134	0.202
	ROIL	0.137	0.022	RLTASS	0.275	0.008
	RSALE	-0.146	0.014			

Table 4-41: SEGSTAT rank regression analysis results

Besides country differences, SEGSTAT is assumingly affected by the context factors industry and size. The influence of the wholesale/retail **industry**, the only industry that correlates significantly with SEGSTAT, is affirmed by regression analysis. Coherent with the correlation analysis results, companies from the wholesale/retail industry are significantly negatively associated with SEGSTAT (β = -0.159; p = 0.007**). Additionally, companies from the oil and gas sectors are suggested to be positively associated with SEGVOL (β = 0.131; p = 0.029*). Both regression results are supported by the non-parametric test. Although correlation analysis indicates that **size** only significantly correlates with SEGVOL, the context factor also seems to be relevant for SEGSTAT when tested in combination with other context factors. The size factor total assets is significantly positively associated with SEGSTAT (β = 0.343; p = 0.002**). Moreover, the result passes the rank regression robustness test (see Table 4-41). This significant result is constrained in explanatory power only by slightly higher levels of multi collinearity in combination with the size variable market capitalization. However, tolerance value and VIF are still acceptable; accordingly, the significant total assets result is not to be rejected (see Table 4-40).

The results of the **SEGVOL** regression analysis are comparable to the just described SEGSTAT results. Except for the influence of the oil and gas industry, the influential context factors are the same (see Table 4-42). Moreover, the attributed signs of the respective regression coefficients are the same, as well. Accordingly, the **cultural** factor power distance (β = -0.504; p = 0.000**) is significantly negatively associated with SEGVOL; also, the institutional factor LEGTAX is related to higher SEGVOL scores (β = 0.283; p = 0.000**). Especially power distance is characterized by a comparably strongly negative regression coefficient. The inclusion of voluntary information in SEGVOL appears to emphasize the importance of the cultural effect even more. Both country factor results are confirmed by rank regression analysis (see Table 4-43).

The only **industry** that is significantly related to SEGVOL is the wholesale/retail industry. In analogy to SEGSTAT, companies from that industry are assumed to disclose less segment information (β = -0.123; p = 0.030*). Rank regression analysis confirms the significant association (see Table 4-43). The predictive power of **size** measured by total assets is affirmed by both regression and rank regression analysis. Again, total assets are significantly positively associated with information quantity of segment reporting (β = 0.244; p = 0.000**).

R	R^2	Adjusted R^2	Std. error of the estimate			Durbin-Watson	
0.491	0.241	0.216	4.012			1.931	
	Sum of squares	df	Mean square		F	Sig.	
Regression	1,244.237	8	155.530				
Residuals	3,912.191	243	16.100		9.660	0.000	
Total	5,156.429	251					
Variables	B	Std. error	Beta	t	Sig.	Tolerance	VIF
(Constant)	12.362	2.708		4.566	0.000		
PDI	-0.210	0.028	-0.504	-7.633	0.000	0.715	1.398
LEGTAX	2.766	0.645	0.283	4.287	0.000	0.718	1.392
OIL	1.986	1.226	0.093	1.620	0.106	0.938	1.066
SALE	-1.894	0.870	-0.123	-2.176	0.030	0.979	1.022
HEALTH	-2.050	1.117	-0.104	-1.835	0.068	0.975	1.025
LTASS	1.656	0.400	0.244	4.144	0.000	0.900	1.111
FORSALES	1.149	0.903	0.073	1.273	0.204	0.937	1.067
LEV	0.025	0.020	0.073	1.279	0.202	0.961	1.040

Table 4-42: SEGVOL regression analysis results

Adjusted R^2	Variables	Beta	Sig.	Variables	Beta	Sig.
0.206	RPDI	-0.484	0.000	RHEALTH	-0.087	0.132
	RLEGTAX	0.288	0.000	RLTASS	0.203	0.002
	ROIL	0.120	0.043	RFORSALES	0.022	0.706
	RSALE	-0.112	0.050	RLEV	0.120	0.065

Table 4-43: SEGVOL rank regression analysis results

The regression analyses of the two secrecy indicators SEGSTAT and SEGVOL lead to considerably consistent results with respect to potential influence factors. Summarized, SEGSTAT and SEGVOL are mainly explained by the cultural factor power distance, the external control variable legal/tax system and the internal control variables industry and size. The following section discusses the regression analysis results with respect to the prior posited sub-hypotheses.

4.3.2.2.4 Implications

According to the SEGSTAT and SEGVOL regression coefficients, power distance has the strongest explanatory power. Uncertainty avoidance, which according to *Gray* is expected to be most influential in predicting secretive accounting, on the contrary, is not significant at all. The predicted association between the **cultural** factor power distance and both segment reporting disclosure indices is negative; high power distance countries are suggested to publish less segment information. Of the three analyzed countries, France has the highest PDI value; Germany and the UK have the same PDI values. Accordingly, PDI correctly explains French companies publishing significantly less information than German and British companies. PDI fails, however, in explaining the unexpected result that German companies publish more segment information than British companies. Although country differences between Germany and the UK are only significant with respect to SEGVOL,[1346] the incapacity of the PDI country scores in explaining higher German SEGSTAT/SEGVOL values is likely to be responsible for relatively low R-squared values of the regression models. The regression and rank regression results for SEGSTAT and SEGVOL, nonetheless, suggest a strongly significant influence of power distance. The sign of the relationship between power distance and segment reporting quantity respectively secrecy is as posited before. Accordingly, the corresponding PDI hypothesis is confirmed (see Figure 4-22).

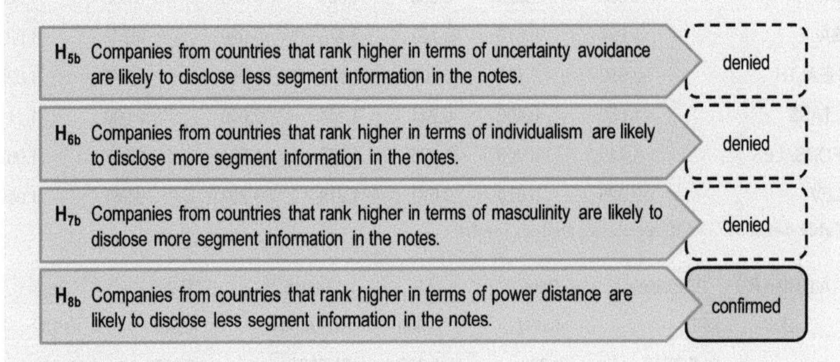

Figure 4-22: SEGSTAT and SEGVOL hypotheses test results

The second significant country factor comes from the set of **institutional** variables. The significantly positive LEGTAX result implies that companies from France and Germany (code law system / authoritative principle) report more statutory and voluntary segment information than companies from the UK (common law system / no authoritative principle). This result is surprising, on the one hand, since French companies tend to have considerably lower SEGSTAT and SEGVOL values than British companies; on the other hand, the LEGTAX indicator also explains German companies having higher SEGSTAT and SEGVOL values than British companies.[1347] Summarizing the regression results of the PDI and the LEGTAX indicator, PDI explains French companies disclosing less segment information than British and German companies and LEGTAX explains German companies disclosing more segment information than British companies.

A tentative explanation for the unexpectedly low SEGSTAT and SEGVOL values of British companies could be that British companies prefer to provide segment related infor-

[1346] See the above country based ANOVA on SEGSTAT in chapter 4.3.2.2.1.

[1347] Cf. chapter 4.3.2.2.1.

mation in the operating financial review (OFR)[1348] instead of the notes. This assumption is supported by the above ANOVA, which measures a significant country difference between Germany and the UK only for SEGVOL. British companies might tend to focus on statutory information in the notes only and provide voluntary information elsewhere. This assumption is to be interpreted carefully, however, as the German sample exceeds the British sample also in terms of SEGSTAT mean value and SEGSTAT quantile values.

From an **industrial** point of view, companies from the wholesale/retail sector are significantly associated with less statutory and voluntary segment information. Wholesale/retail companies are not as much in the focus of public attention as, for instance, companies from the pharmaceutical or defense industries. In accordance with political cost theory, these companies disclose less information than companies from high litigation industries.

The strongly significant positive relationship between **size**, measured by total assets, and SEGSTAT respectively SEGVOL is more plausible. In analogy to the strongly significant finding for NOTES, larger companies are more complex and subject to more public attention; to reduce political and agency costs, larger companies tend to publish more information to diminish information asymmetries. Another explanation could be that larger companies have larger and more competent accounting departments and, thus, more and better manpower capacity to devote to tasks like segment reporting.

The following section presents the empirical results on statutory and voluntary income tax reporting. The application of the same content analytical technique on a different topic in the notes will show whether the above described segment reporting related cognitions are supported.

4.3.2.3 Income tax reporting

As mentioned above, two disclosure indices are built to analyze income tax information in the notes. The first disclosure index measures statutory information as required by the IFRS standard only (TAXSTAT). The second disclosure index additionally measures voluntary information (TAXVOL). In analogy to the preceding chapters on segment reporting, the empirical results on TAXSTAT are presented together with the results on TAXVOL.[1349]

4.3.2.3.1 Descriptive analysis

All companies of the three country samples publish information on income tax; the TAXSTAT and TAXVOL samples therefore consist of 261 companies. Both distributions show great similarities. All TAXSTAT and TAXVOL quantiles are clearly dominated by British companies, followed by German companies and French companies at last. The maximum and minimum values in both distributions are contributed by British companies. This fact indicates a comparable larger spread of the British distribution. In fact, the British sample has the highest standard deviation, followed by Germany and France. Mean value comparison draws a picture as clear as predicted by the country distributions'

[1348] The OFR is the British management report; cf. Linsley/Shrives 2005, p. 208f.

[1349] For the single items of the income tax reporting disclosure indices cf. Appendix A, Table A 3.

quantile values. The British sample has a considerably higher mean value than the German sample, which has a higher mean value than the French sample. This country ranking confirms the posited culture based country ranking from least to most cautious accounting.

	Statutory income tax reporting				Voluntary income tax reporting			
Value (items)	Total	France	Germany	UK	Total	France	Germany	UK
N	261	88	93	80	261	88	93	80
Minimum	1.00	2.00	3.00	1.00	1.00	3.00	5.00	1.00
5% quantile	5.00	5.00	5.60	7.00	9.00	8.00	10.00	12.00
1. quartile	7.00	6.75	7.00	10.00	12.00	10.00	13.00	17.00
Median	9.00	8.00	9.00	11.00	15.00	13.00	15.00	20.00
Mean	9.27	7.86	8.88	11.28	15.94	12.89	15.22	20.15
3. quartile	11.00	9.00	10.00	13.00	19.00	15.00	17.00	24.00
95% quantile	14.00	11.00	12.40	15.05	25.00	18.65	23.00	26.00
Maximum	17.00	14.00	15.00	17.00	29.00	22.00	25.00	29.00
Standard deviation	2.72	2.05	2.23	2.74	5.00	3.48	3.66	4.94

Table 4-44: TAXSTAT and TAXVOL descriptive statistics

The below **TAXSTAT** boxplot diagrams of the three country samples indicate considerable country differences (see Figure 4-23). Although the size of the boxes is similar, the horizontal position of the boxes differs substantially; especially the British box is higher positioned. All country samples contain outliers. The German sample is characterized by one positive outlier; the British sample contains only negative outliers and the French sample contains both positive and negative outliers. Also, the French whiskers are shorter compared to the German and British sample.[1350]

ANOVA confirms the subjective impression of existing **country** difference by an exceptionally high F-value (F = 58.732; 0.000**). The non-parametric Kruskal-Wallis-Test supports the ANOVA result at the significance level of p = 0.000**. With respect to pair wise inter country differences, the Scheffé-Test indicates (strongly) significant country differences between France and Germany (p = 0.015*), France and the UK (p = 0.000**) and Germany and the UK (p = 0.000**).

[1350] The following statistical tests are performed on data that is adjusted for outliers. Cf. chapter 3.4.1.

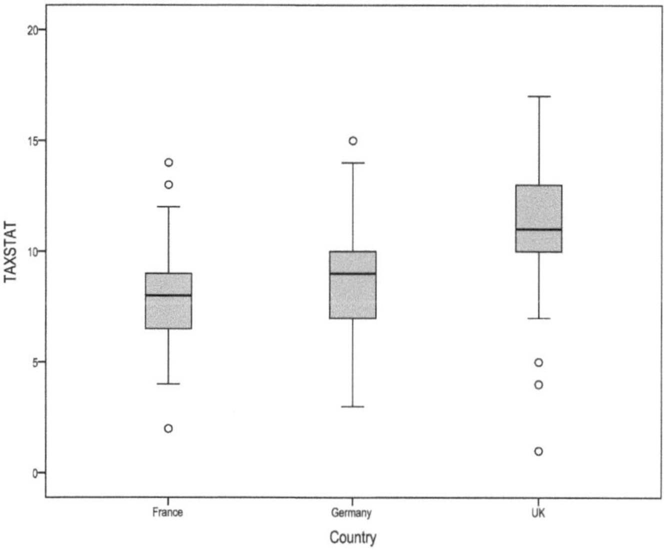

Figure 4-23: TAXSTAT boxplot diagram by country

Industry (F = 1.141; 0.334), on the other hand, is assumed to have no significant influence on income tax reporting; this result is confirmed by the non-parametric test (p = 0.293). In contrast to segment reporting, which is not affected by type of **auditor**, the T-Test on auditor indicates a strongly significant influence of (Big4) auditor on TAXSTAT (t = 6.270; p = 0.000**)[1351]. The Mann-Whitney-U-Test affirms the T-Test result at the significance level of p = 0.000**. As a consequence of ANOVA and T-Test analysis, income tax reporting is assumed to be related to both country factors and type of auditor.

The below graphical comparison of the three **TAXVOL** country samples indicates even stronger country differences (see Figure 4-24). The inclusion of voluntary income tax information appears to strengthen the effect of country. Apart from the different horizontal position of the boxes, the sizes of the boxes differ as well. The German box is considerably smaller than the French and the British box. Whereas the German sample has one positive and one negative outlier, the British sample has only negative outliers; the French sample contains no outliers at all.

[1351] Equal variances are not assumed.

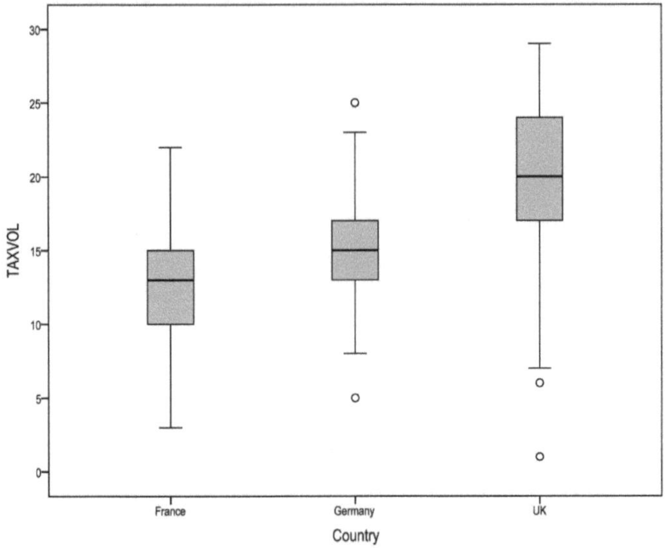

Figure 4-24: TAXVOL boxplot diagram by country

According to ANOVA, the TAXVOL **country** differences are even stronger than determined for TAXSTAT (F = 89.617; p = 0.000**). Furthermore, the Kruskal-Wallis-Test rejects the null hypothesis of equal distribution across categories of country at the significance level of p = 0.000**. With respect to multiple country comparison, the Scheffé-Test measures strongly significant country differences for all three country combinations. In analogy to the TAXSTAT ANOVA results on the context factor **industry**, ANOVA suggests no significant influence of industry on TAXVOL (F = 1.606; p = 0.114); this result is confirmed by the non-parametric test (p = 0.165). The influence of the companies' **auditor**, on the other hand, is expected to be much stronger. The T-Test mean value comparison across categories of auditor suggests a strongly significant influence of (Big4) auditor on TAXVOL (t = 5.842; 0.000**)[1352]. The non-parametric Mann-Whitney-U-Test supports the T-Test result by rejecting the null hypothesis of equal distribution at the significance level of p = 0.000**.

The TAXSTAT and TAXVOL ANOVA and T-Test results are quite consistent. Both secrecy indicators are expected to be mainly influenced by country and type of auditor. The following chapter on correlation analysis will demonstrate if the above results are supported and which other context factors could be influential in explaining statutory and voluntary income tax reporting.

[1352] Equal variances are not assumed.

4.3.2.3.2 Correlation analysis

TAXSTAT correlation analysis basically confirms the above results. Whereas all country factors and type of auditor are significantly correlated with TAXSTAT, no industry factor shows a significant correlation. The strongest significant correlation among the **cultural** variables is measured for uncertainty avoidance (r = -0.543; p = 0.000**). Companies from higher uncertainty avoidance countries are associated with less income tax reporting and higher levels of secrecy. The same association is determined for power distance, which is also significantly negatively correlated with TAXSTAT (r = -0.402; p = 0.000**). Masculinity (r = 0.402; p = 0.000**) and individualism (r = 0.361; p = 0.000**), on the other hand, are significantly positively correlated with statutory income tax information. The signs of the cultural correlation coefficients are as hypothesized: uncertainty avoidance and power distance are posited to be positively (negatively) associated with secrecy (TAXSTAT) and masculinity and individualism are posited to be negatively (positively) associated with secrecy (TAXSTAT). Strong correlations are also measured for the **institutional** variables. The institutional variable that approximates the legal respectively the tax system of the countries is significantly negatively correlated with TAXSTAT. Companies from code law countries respectively countries that apply the authoritative principle are assumed to publish less income tax information (r = -0.536; p = 0.000**). The second institutional factor financing system is not as strongly correlated to TAXSTAT. Companies from higher developed financing systems are associated with more extensive income tax reporting and less secrecy (r = 0.137; p = 0.028*).

Besides country influences, **size** is suggested to play an important role when predicting the quantity of income tax information. In analogy to the NOTES and SEGVOL results, larger companies are associated with higher TAXSTAT values. The three size variables market capitalization (r = 0.268; p = 0.000**), number of employees (r = 0.276; p = 0.000**) and total assets (r = 0.288; p = 0.000**) are significantly positively correlated with TAXSTAT. The three **internationality** factors, in contrast, show mixed correlations. Whereas foreign listing (r = -0.169; p = 0.007**) is significantly negatively correlated with TAXSTAT, SEC listing (r = 0.238; p = 0.000**) and foreign sales (r = 0.210; p = 0.001**) are significantly positively correlated with TAXSTAT. The results suggest a rather positive association between internationality and income tax reporting since the latter two positive correlation coefficients are stronger significant. As indicated by the T-Test, the type of **auditor** is strongly significantly correlated with TAXSTAT (r = 0.265; p = 0.000**). Companies audited by a Big4 audit firm are associated with higher values of TAXSTAT. Finally, **leverage** is identified as another possible influential context factor. Higher leveraged companies are strongly significantly associated with more income tax reporting (r = 0.229; p = 0.000**).

The **TAXVOL** correlation analysis results equal the above results for TAXSTAT, except for two significant correlation results regarding the utilities **industry** (r = 0.166; p = 0.007**) and the **profitability** measure return on investment (r = 0.139; p = 0.025*); both utilities companies and profitable companies are associated with higher TAXVOL values. As indicated by the country based ANOVA, TAXVOL country influences appear to be even stronger compared to TAXSTAT; the signs of the **cultural** variables' correlation coefficients are as determined for TAXSTAT. Uncertainty avoidance (r = -0.621;

p = 0.000**) and power distance (r = -0.472; p = 0.000**) are significantly negatively correlated with TAXVOL. Masculinity (r = 0.472; p = 0.000**) and individualism (r = 0.390; p = 0.000**) are significantly positively correlated with TAXVOL. In analogy to the TAXSTAT correlation results, the **institutional** variable legal/tax system (r = -0.599; p = 0.000**) is significantly negatively correlated with TAXVOL. The financing system (r = 0.151; p = 0.015*), on the other hand, is significantly positively correlated with income tax reporting.

The TAXVOL correlation results on the internal context factors size, internationality, auditor and leverage are consistent with the TAXSTAT results. The **size** indicators market capitalization (r = 0.308; p = 0.000**), number of employees (r = 0.252; p = 0.000**) and total assets (r = 0.286; p = 0.000**) are significantly positively correlated with TAXVOL. The **internationality** factors foreign listing (r = -0.204; p = 0.001**), SEC listing (r = 0.295; p = 0.000**) and foreign sales (r = 0.228; p = 0.000**), again, show inconsistent results with respect to the sign of the correlation coefficients; the former measure suggests a negative influence of internationality on statutory and voluntary income tax reporting quantity, the latter two measures imply a positive influence on TAXVOL. Analogously, companies audited by a Big4 **auditor** (r = 0.253; p = 0.000**) and companies characterized by a higher **leverage** (r = 0.212; p = 0.001**) are significantly associated with higher TAXVOL values.[1353]

The next chapter on regression analysis will show which context factors are the most appropriate predictors for TAXSTAT and TAXVOL when tested in combination with other context factors.

4.3.2.3.3 Regression analysis

The right hand side of the applied basic regression model is the same as applied before (see Formula 4.10).

Formula 4.10

$$TAXSTAT_i\ (TAXVOL_i) = \beta_1 UAI_k + \beta_2 MAS_k + \beta_3 IDV_k + \beta_4 PDI_k + \beta_l CONVAR_{i/k} + \varepsilon_i$$

where

$TAXSTAT_i$	=	*statutory income tax reporting disclosure index*
$TAXVOL_i$	=	*voluntary income tax reporting disclosure index*
UAI_k	=	*uncertainty avoidance index*
MAS_k	=	*masculinity index*
IDV_k	=	*individualism index*
PDI_k	=	*power distance index*
$CONVAR_{i/k}$	=	*country and company control variables*
β_{1-l}	=	*regression coefficients*
ε_i	=	*the companies' error term*

[1353] The TAXSTAT and TAXVOL correlation coefficients are listed in Appendix A, Table A 4.

i	=	*1,...,n (company index)*
k	=	*1,2,3 (country index)*
l	=	*5,...,17 (control variable index)*

The regression model that explains 47.7%[1354] of **TAXSTAT** variance consists of the cultural factor uncertainty avoidance, the industrial factors telecommunication and healthcare, the size indicators market capitalization, number of employees and total assets, the internationality factors SEC listing and foreign sales, type of auditor and the profitability factor return on investment. The **TAXVOL** regression model contains mainly the same variables. Only the included industries differ slightly from the TAXSTAT regression model. Instead of the healthcare industry, TAXVOL is better explained by the business equipment and the utilities industries. The described variables explain 57.9%[1355] of the total TAXVOL variance.

R	R^2	Adjusted R^2	Std. error of the estimate			Durbin-Watson	
0.705	0.497	0.477	1.926			1.962	
	Sum of squares	df	Mean square		F	Sig.	
Regression	908.621	10	90.862				
Residuals	920.136	248	3.710		24.490	0.000	
Total	1,828.757	258					
Variables	B	Std. error	Beta	t	Sig.	Tolerance	VIF
(Constant)	7.652	1.678		4.561	0.000		
UAI	-0.071	0.006	-0.547	-11.699	0.000	0.928	1.078
TEL	0.572	0.482	0.056	1.187	0.236	0.908	1.102
HEALTH	-1.000	0.508	-0.091	-1.969	0.050	0.957	1.044
LMCAP	-0.777	0.449	-0.172	-1.729	0.085	0.206	4.865
EMP	0.000	0.000	0.128	2.399	0.017	0.717	1.395
LTASS	1.199	0.391	0.301	3.069	0.002	0.210	4.753
SECLIST	0.701	0.456	0.078	1.536	0.126	0.788	1.268
FORSALES	1.922	0.419	0.219	4.590	0.000	0.891	1.122
BIG4	1.746	0.520	0.158	3.361	0.001	0.915	1.092
ROI	0.014	0.014	0.053	1.043	0.298	0.792	1.263

Table 4-45: TAXSTAT regression analysis results

The examination of the **TAXSTAT** and **TAXVOL** regression models' premises reveals no major deficiencies with respect to transferability of results, distribution and autocorrela-

[1354] This figure refers to the adjusted R^2.

[1355] This figure refers to the adjusted R^2.

tion of residuals and multi collinearity of independent variables. The F-values of 24.490** (TAXSTAT) respectively 33.271** (TAXVOL) signify that the regression results of the tested samples are transferable to the populations. Although not perfectly normal distributed, graphical analysis of the TAXSTAT and TAXVOL residuals distributions indicates nearly normal distribution. Furthermore, the Durbin-Watson coefficients imply low levels of residuals autocorrelation (TAXSTAT: DW = 1.962; TAXVOL: DW = 2.062). The multi collinearity indicators tolerance and VIF reveal acceptably low levels of multi collinearity. Only the two size variables market capitalization and total assets show increased but still acceptable multi collinearity for both TAXSTAT and TAXVOL (see Table 4-45 and Table 4-47).

As indicated by correlation analysis, **TAXSTAT** is mainly explained by the **cultural** factor uncertainty avoidance. Companies from countries that are characterized by high UAI values tend to be significantly associated with lower TAXSTAT values (β = -0.547; p = 0.000**); the strong uncertainty avoidance regression result is supported by a strongly significant rank regression result (see Table 4-46). The influence of the other cultural and **institutional** variables is not significant when uncertainty avoidance is included in the regression model.

Adjusted R^2	Variables	Beta	Sig.	Variables	Beta	Sig.
0.415	RUAI	-0.503	0.000	RLTASS	0.316	0.003
	RTEL	0.002	0.964	RSECLIST	0.032	0.537
	RHEALTH	-0.117	0.016	RFORSALES	0.166	0.001
	RLMCAP	-0.177	0.068	RBIG4	0.165	0.001
	REMP	0.122	0.071	RROI	0.051	0.358

Table 4-46: TAXSTAT rank regression analysis results

Although not significantly correlating with TAXSTAT, the healthcare **industry** (β = -0.091; p = 0.050*) is significantly negatively associated with TAXSTAT when tested in combination with other variables; the comparably weak healthcare industry result is supported by the non parametric test (see Table 4-46). As mentioned above, **size** is supposed to be an influential factor for statutory income tax reporting. In fact, the size factors number of employees (β = 0.128; p = 0.017*) and total assets (β = 0.301; p = 0.002**) are (strongly) significantly associated with TAXSTAT. Accordingly, larger companies are related to more income tax information and less secrecy. The explanatory power of the size factor total assets is questioned only by slightly higher levels of multi collinearity in combination with the other size factor market capitalization. Tolerance value and VIF, however, are still within the acceptable range; the total assets result, thus, is not to be rejected (see Table 4-45). Furthermore, the size indicator total assests is also confirmed by rank regression analysis (see Table 4-46).

Only one of the two recognized **internationality** indicators is significantly associated with TAXSTAT; companies that are characterized by higher percentages of foreign sales tend to disclose more statutory income tax information (β = 0.219; p = 0.000**). Also, the strongly significant Big4 regression result suggests a positive influence of **auditor** (β = 0.158; p = 0.001**) on the quantity of income tax information. The non-parametric test supports the regression results of both indicators (see Table 4-46).

The significant **TAXVOL** regression results very much resemble the TAXSTAT regression results, except that the TAXSTAT predictor healthcare industry is replaced by a significant regression result of the utilities industry; also, the size measure number of employees is not significantly associated with TAXVOL (see Table 4-47).

R	R^2	Adjusted R^2	Std. error of the estimate			Durbin-Watson	
0.773	0.597	0.579	3.175			2.062	
	Sum of squares	df	Mean square		F	Sig.	
Regression	3,688.350	11	335.305		33.271	0.000	
Residuals	2,489.264	247	10.078				
Total	6,177.614	258					
Variables	B	Std. error	Beta	t	Sig.	Tolerance	VIF
(Constant)	11.591	2.858		4.056	0.000		
UAI	-0.149	0.010	-0.621	-14.666	0.000	0.909	1.100
EQU	0.911	0.632	0.063	1.441	0.151	0.855	1.170
TEL	1.269	0.801	0.068	1.584	0.114	0.891	1.122
UTIL	2.033	0.986	0.087	2.061	0.040	0.905	1.105
LMCAP	-1.245	0.736	-0.150	-1.692	0.092	0.208	4.805
EMP	0.000	0.000	0.071	1.478	0.141	0.711	1.407
LTASS	2.357	0.665	0.322	3.545	0.000	0.197	5.071
SECLIST	1.457	0.756	0.088	1.927	0.055	0.781	1.281
FORSALES	3.983	0.700	0.247	5.687	0.000	0.865	1.156
BIG4	2.955	0.861	0.146	3.432	0.001	0.906	1.104
ROI	0.029	0.022	0.060	1.311	0.191	0.792	1.262

Table 4-47: TAXVOL regression analysis results

The strongest TAXVOL predictor identified by rank regression analysis is the **cultural** factor uncertainty avoidance (β = -0.621; p = 0.000**). Companies from countries that have a high UAI score are suggested to disclose less statutory and voluntary income tax information in the notes. Rank regression analysis supports this finding (see Table 4-48).

As mentioned above, the utilities **industry** (β = 0.087; p = 0.040*) is found to be significantly positively associated with TAXVOL; the significant association is confirmed by rank regression analysis. Furthermore, **size** as measured by total assets is a strongly significant predictor for TAXVOL (β = 0.322; p = 0.000**). In accordance with TAXSTAT, **internationality** is suggested to be influential with respect to TAXVOL; companies that report high percentages of foreign sales are associated with higher TAXVOL values (β = 0.247; p = 0.000**). Finally, the influence of Big4 **audit** firms (β = 0.146; p = 0.001**) on statutory and voluntary income tax information quantity is positively significant. Rank regression analysis supports the findings for size, internationality and auditor (see Table 4-48).

Adjusted R^2	Variables	Beta	Sig.	Variables	Beta	Sig.
0.493	RUAI	-0.564	0.000	RLTASS	0.292	0.004
	REQU	0.060	0.212	RSECLIST	0.055	0.265
	RTEL	0.012	0.788	RFORSALES	0.170	0.000
	RUTIL	0.102	0.029	RBIG4	0.158	0.001
	RLMCAP	-0.107	0.236	RROI	0.049	0.346
	REMP	0.076	0.233			

Table 4-48: TAXVOL rank regression analysis results

The regression analysis results on statutory and voluntary income tax information in the notes indicate that both secrecy indicators are mainly influenced by uncertainty avoidance, company size, internationality and auditor. The following chapter briefly discusses these results.

4.3.2.3.4 Implications

The above regression results strongly indicate that **culture** has an influence on national income tax reporting practices. Both TAXSTAT and TAXVOL regression models are mainly explained by the strongly significant uncertainty avoidance factor; the inclusion of voluntary information in the TAXVOL disclosure index emphasizes the cultural effect; the corresponding uncertainty avoidance regression coefficient is even stronger. The two strongly significant regression coefficients implicate that companies from high uncertainty avoidance countries are associated with less income tax reporting and more secrecy accordingly. Consequently, the prior hypothesized negative relationship between uncertainty avoidance and income tax information in the notes is confirmed. The remaining culture related hypotheses are denied; the influence of the culture factors masculinity, individualism and power distance is not significant when tested in combination with uncertainty avoidance (see Figure 4-25).

Both secrecy indicators are each significantly associated with one **industrial** variable. Whereas the healthcare industry is supposed to have a negative influence on TAXSTAT, the utilities industry is associated with higher TAXVOL values. Although confirmed by rank regression analysis, the very weak regression coefficients and the above ANOVA results cast doubt on an industry related influence. Accordingly, industrial influence on statutory and voluntary income tax reporting is rather questionable.

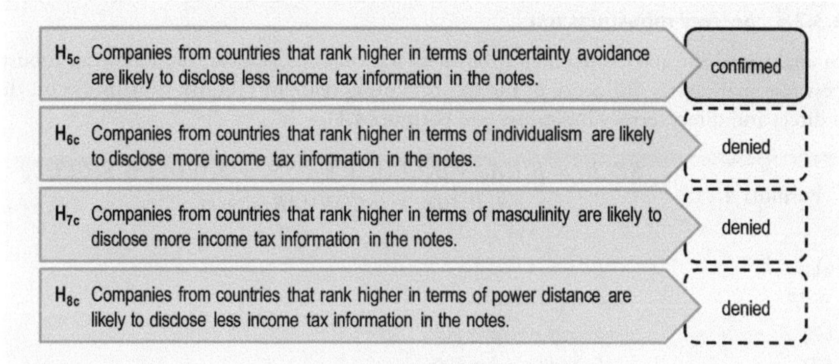

Figure 4-25: TAXSTAT and TAXVOL hypotheses test results

Size, on the other hand, is confirmed as an important context factor when it comes to predict financial accounting disclosure quantity. In analogy to the regression results for notes word count and segment reporting, size is significantly associated with more income tax disclosure. As mentioned before, increased disclosure can be interpreted as the result of a corporate information strategy to reduce political costs and agency costs.

In concordance with the above correlation analysis results, the **internationality** factor foreign sales is significantly positively associated with both TAXSTAT and TAXVOL. As outlined before, internationally oriented companies, which generate substantial parts of their turnover abroad, are likely to adapt to internationally accepted accounting procedures and disclose more (voluntary) financial information. Furthermore, substantial percentages of international operations might also lead to higher degrees of complexity of the respective companies and higher agency costs accordingly; these companies could try to lower information asymmetries and agency costs by means of increased disclosure.

In contrast to the above regression results on NOTES, SEGSTAT and SEGVOL, income tax reporting is suggested to be significantly associated with the choice of **auditor**. Companies that are audited by a Big4 auditor tend to publish more income tax information. As Big4 audit companies (1) have more reputation to loose and (2) are perceived as better litigation targets, these companies have a strong interest in their clients to publish high quality financial statements. High quality in the context of disclosure not only refers to fulfill the standards' requirements, but also to publish additional voluntary information to signal a high capital market orientation. Companies that choose to be audited by a Big4 auditor utilize the auditor's reputation and its expertise as a 'seal of quality' to signal the capital market the quality of their financial statements.

In the following chapter the presented empirical results that are based on the *Hofstede* cultural dimensions are tested for robustness by applying the more current cultural dimensions of the GLOBE study[1356].

[1356] Cf. chapter 2.2.4.1.3.

4.3.2.4 Secrecy robustness test

In analogy to the above presented robustness test on conservatism, the following robustness test analyzes the influence of the six accounting relevant GLOBE dimensions on the indirect and direct secrecy indicators (see Formula 4.1).

Formula 4.11
$$SECR_i = \beta_1 UA_k + \beta_2 GEQ_k + \beta_3 ASS_k + \beta_4 ICOL_k + \beta_5 GCOL_k + \beta_6 PD_k + \beta_l CONVAR_{i/k} + \varepsilon_i$$

where

$SECR_i$	=	*conservatism indicators*[1357]
UA_k	=	*uncertainty avoidance index*
GEQ_k	=	*gender egalitarianism index*
ASS_k	=	*assertiveness index*
$ICOL_k$	=	*institutional collectivism index*
$GCOL_k$	=	*in-group collectivism index*
PD_k	=	*power distance index*
$CONVAR_{i/k}$	=	*country and company control variables*
β_{1-l}	=	*regression coefficients*
ε_i	=	*the companies' error term*
i	=	*1,…,n (company index)*
k	=	*1,2,3 (country index)*
l	=	*7,…,20 (control variable index)*

In accordance with the *Hofstede* regression analysis, which finds the cultural factor individualism to be most influential with respect to **notes word count**, the GLOBE regression analysis identifies institutional collectivism (β = -0.214; p = 0.000**), as defined by *House et al.*, to be significantly associated with NOTES (see Table 4-49). Thus, companies from more institutionally collectivistic countries are associated with less notes disclosure and more secrecy accordingly. Although this result contradicts the *Hofstede* individualism result with respect to the sign of the posited relationship, the GLOBE results are in line with the *Hofstede-Gray* framework, which assumes a negative relationship between individualism and secrecy. Nonetheless, it is questionable whether the GLOBE dimension of institutional collectivism is comparable to the *Hofstede* dimension of individualism and whether the *Hofstede-Gray* framework is transferable to the GLOBE dimensions. As outlined by *House et al.*, the *Hofstede* individualism dimension is rather comparable to the in-group collectivism dimension, which correlates significantly negatively with individualism (r = -0.820**); the institutional collectivism dimension, on the other hand, is not significantly correlated with individualism.[1358]

[1357] SECR refers to the secrecy indicators: NOTES, SEGSTAT, SEGVOL, TAXSTAT and TAXVOL.
[1358] Cf. House et al. 2004, p. 475.

Hofstede			House et al.		
Adj. R^2	Sig. variables	β	Adj. R^2	Sig. variables	β
NOTES					
0.423	IND	-0.231**	0.423	ICOL	-0.214**
SEGSTAT					
0.160	PDI	-0.416**	0.163	UA	0.373**
SEGVOL					
0.216	PDI	-0.504**	0.214	UA	0.475**
TAXSTAT					
0.477	UAI	-0.547**	0.474	UA	0.110*
				PD	-0.535**
TAXVOL					
0.579	UAI	-0.621**	0.577	UA	0.127**
				PD	-0.611**
			* (**) represents significance at the 5% (1%) level		

Table 4-49: Secrecy robustness test results

The **segment reporting** results are neither confirmed by the GLOBE study robustness test (see Table 4-49). The *House et al.* regression results indicate that statutory and voluntary segment reporting is mainly explained by uncertainty avoidance (SEGSTAT: β = 0.373; p = 0.000**; SEGVOL: β = 0.475; p = 0.000**). The strongly significantly positive association between uncertainty avoidance and SEGSTAT respectively SEGVOL is in contrast to the power distance results of the *Hofstede* regression analyses (see Table 4-49). Furthermore, the sign of the uncertainty avoidance regression coefficient is contrary to the association posited by *Gray*.

According to the regression analysis based on the GLOBE study's dimensions, statutory and voluntary **income tax reporting** are best explained by the country factors uncertainty avoidance (TAXSTAT: β = 0.110; p = 0.024*; TAXVOL: β = 0.127; p = 0.004**) and power distance (TAXSTAT: β = -0.535; p = 0.000**; TAXVOL: β = -0.611; p = 0.000**). Whereas the sign of the uncertainty avoidance regression coefficients, in analogy to the GLOBE segment reporting results, are contrary to *Gray's* hypotheses, the significantly negative associations between power distance and TAXSTAT respectively TAXVOL are in line with the *Hofstede-Gray* framework.

The above comparison of cultural factor regression results, which are based on the *Hofstede* and *House et al.* country scores for France, Germany and the UK, indicate **conceptual differences.** Although the GLOBE results confirm the *Hofstede* results in so far that uncertainty avoidance, power distance and individualism/collectivism are assumed to be most influential with respect to the tested secrecy indicators, the GLOBE results deviate from the *Hofstede* results with respect to the particular cultural dimensions and the signs of the associations. The different results for the two sets of cultural dimensions might result from a considerable change of national culture or, as suggested by *Hofstede*, from the research design of the GLOBE study and, more specifically, from the composition of the GLOBE culture dimensions.[1359] As discussed in detail in chapter 2.2.4.1.4, the *Hofstede* study and the GLOBE study not only differ with respect to the periods of time the studies were conducted, but also with respect to the respective research approach and the development of the cultural dimensions. The substantially differing robustness test results support the notion of deviating culture concepts.

The interpretation of empirically determined national cultural differences is subjective and, accordingly, different cultural studies are difficult to compare. Nonetheless, the above robustness tests show that the measured differences in corporate conservatism and secrecy are mainly associated with cultural factors. For interpretation purposes of these differences, this study employs the *Hofstede* model being the most popular cultural approach in international financial accounting research. The NOTES, SEGSTAT/SEGVOL and TAXSTAT/TAXVOL hypotheses test results are not constrained by the above robustness test.

The following chapter summarizes and discusses the empirical findings of this study.

4.4 Summary and discussion

Chapter four presents sample characteristics and empirical results on the analyzed hypotheses. The **company sample** is described on a total and country by country basis according to the context factors size, industry, auditor, internationality, profitability and leverage. The **size** measures market capitalization, total assets and number of employees indicate that the British and French companies in the sample on average are larger than the German companies. British companies, on the other hand, tend to have a higher market capitalization than French companies and French companies tend to have more employees and total assets than British companies. The country **industry** profile characterizes the German sample by comparably more companies from the manufacturing and business equipment sector. Also, most healthcare companies come from Germany. The French sample is also dominated by companies from the manufacturing and business equipment industry and contains a considerable amount of companies from the consumer non-durables industry. The British sample includes almost as many companies from the consumer non-durables sector as the French sample. In contrast to the other two country samples, the British sample is marked by the highest number of companies from the oil and gas and utilities industry. As expected, the sample companies are mainly audited by Big4 **auditors**. The UK sample has the highest percentage of Big4 audited companies (99%), followed by the French (95%) and the German (88%) company sample. The degree of the companies' **internationality** is determined by the indicators foreign listing, SEC listing and international operations. The French company sample (99%) is characterized by the highest percentage of companies that are listed abroad (Germany: 84%; UK: 65%); the British company sample (20%) is characterized by the highest percentage of

[1359] Cf. Hofstede 2006, p. 883.

companies that are registered by the SEC (France: 7%; Germany: 4%). The German and French company samples are comparable with respect to their percentage of foreign sales to total sales; British companies dominate the two company classes of very low and very high relative foreign sales. Furthermore, as measured by ROI and profit margin, British companies tend to be more **profitable** than French and German companies. With respect to profit margin only, French companies are more profitable than German companies. Except for highly leveraged companies, country comparison regarding corporate **leverage** draws a relatively homogeneous picture of the three country samples; the sample companies that have a comparably high debt to equity ratio (>400%) are mostly British.

The second part of chapter four is dedicated to the **hypotheses tests**. The dependent variables, which are assumed to resemble conservative respectively secretive accounting practice, are described with regard to distributional characteristics and further analyzed by correlation and regression analysis to identify potential predictor variables. The following summary of regression results concerns only significant associations that are confirmed by the non-parametric rank regression analysis.

The first tested global **conservatism** indicator is market to book value (MTB). **MTB** is explained by the tested regression model by 13.8%. The main predictors are size, internationality and profitability. Cultural factors are not significantly associated with MTB. The second global conservatism indicator is negative accruals (NA). **NA** variance is only explained by 9.3%; the only significant influence factor is internationality. In analogy to MTB, culture is suggested to have no influence on NA.

The first direct conservatism indicator uses R&D capitalization practice (CAPRD) as a proxy for conservative accounting. Regression analysis demonstrates that **CAPRD**, which is explained by 29.3%, is not related to cultural influences. Instead, R&D capitalization practice is mainly affected by industry practice. Also, Big4 auditors are assumed to have a negative influence on the ratio of capitalized development costs divided by total R&D expenditures.

The first conservatism indicator, which is significantly associated with a cultural factor, is related to newly capitalized intangibles in a PPA (INT). The positive influence of uncertainty avoidance on **INT**, however, is not confirmed by rank regression analysis. The amount of newly capitalized assets relative to the total assets of the acquired company is rather influenced by the companies' degree of internationality. INT variance is explained by 16.1%.

Two conservatism indicators approximate conservative accounting by shorter depreciation periods of buildings (BUILD) and plant and machinery (PLANT). As posited, **BUILD** is negatively associated with uncertainty avoidance; this result is confirmed by the non parametric test. Accordingly, BUILD is the only conservatism indicator that supports the assumed influence of national culture on IFRS measurement practice; contrary to expected, cultural factors play no role in explaining **PLANT**. Furthermore, both BUILD and PLANT are affected by industry practice. Different industries require different depreciation periods, according to the industries' products and services. Also, size is expected to have a significantly positive influence on BUILD and PLANT depreciation periods. Internationality and profitability are only associated with BUILD. The context factors size, industry, internationality and profitability explain depreciation periods of buildings by 18.6% (official average number of years) respectively 16.3% (calculated average number of years); the context factors size and industry explain depreciation periods of plant and machinery by 47.9% respectively 24.4%.

The last conservatism indicator that measures conservative accounting practice with respect to a specific accounting issue is fair value measurement of **investment property**. Nonetheless, the empirical analysis of the company sample leads to few cases of fair value application only, which limits the robustness of statistical tests substantially. The descriptive analysis of the empirical results indicates relatively more fair value application in the UK. With regard to the influence of cultural factors, the basic empirical analysis allows for no substantiated statements.

The empirical analysis of the relationship between cultural factors and indirect and direct conservatism indicators results in the confirmation of the uncertainty avoidance BUILD sub-hypotheses and the denial of all other posited conservatism sub-hypotheses. Accordingly, the only conservatism **base hypothesis** that is confirmed is related to uncertainty avoidance (see Figure 4-26).

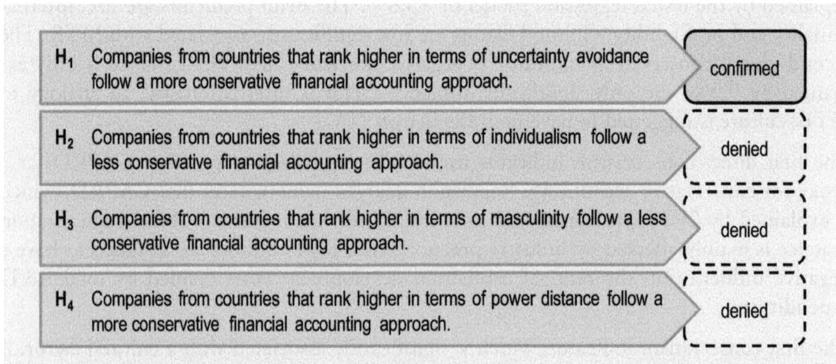

Figure 4-26: Conservatism base hypotheses test results

Nonetheless, the measured influence of national culture on the tested conservatism indicators is comparably weak. Although the *Hofstede-Gray* framework is insofar confirmed that uncertainty avoidance has the strongest influence on conservatism, only one confirmed indicator out of six tested indicators casts a certain doubt on culture related conservatism.

Cultural and institutional factors are assumed to be more influential when it comes to predict IFRS **secrecy** indicators. The amount of notes information as measured by word count (NOTES) is significantly explained by the cultural dimension of individualism; however, the measured negative association between NOTES and individualism is contrary to posited. In combination with the context factors company size and internationality **NOTES** is explained by 42.3%. The influence of internationality is related to significantly positive associations between NOTES, on the one hand, and foreign sales and SEC listing, on the other hand. Considering the latter indicator, larger values of NOTES could be related to more comprehensive disclosure requirements according to US-GAAP.

The second secrecy indicator is quantity of **segment reporting** in the notes (SEGSTAT, SEGVOL). As hypothesized above, both segment reporting secrecy indicators are significantly negatively associated with the cultural factor power distance; accordingly the power distance hypothesis is confirmed for SEGSTAT/SEGVOL. Furthermore, segment information quantity is also affected by the combined legal/tax system context factor. The segment information regression model explains 16.0% of statutory segment information and 21.6% of statutory and voluntary segment information. Besides the mentioned country factors, segment information is significantly associated with size and industry. Especially size appears to be an important predictor with respect to disclosure quantity as size also explains NOTES.

Furthermore size is significantly associated with the third tested secrecy indicator **income tax reporting** (TAXSTAT, TAXVOL). The main income tax reporting predictor, however, is uncertainty avoidance. As posited before, companies from high uncertainty avoidance countries are associated with less income tax reporting and, thus, higher levels of secrecy. Consequently, the uncertainty avoidance sub-hypothesis is confirmed with regard to income tax reporting. Moreover, the internal context factors size, industry, auditor and internationality are suggested to explain income tax disclosure quantity. The income tax regression model explains 47.7% of statutory income tax reporting and 57.9% of statutory and voluntary income tax reporting.

The two secrecy indicators that confirm the hypothesized influence of national culture are segment reporting and income tax reporting. The significant statistical associations between (1) power distance and income tax reporting and (2) uncertainty avoidance and segment reporting lead to the confirmation of the corresponding secrecy **base hypotheses** (see Figure 4-27).

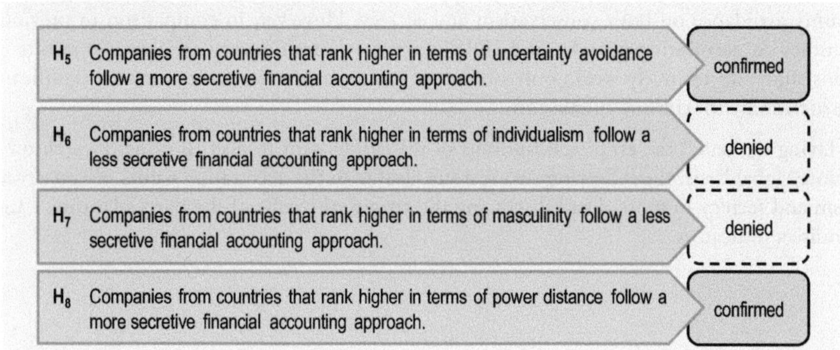

Figure 4-27: Secrecy base hypotheses test results

The cultural dimensions of the GLOBE study are employed for a **robustness test** on the *Hofstede* based hypotheses results. The GLOBE study robustness test confirms the significant influence of national culture on the conservatism indicator BUILD and the secrecy indicators NOTES, SEGSTAT/SEGVOL and TAXSTAT/TAXVOL. Although the influence of cultural variables is confirmed, the type of cultural dimension and the sign of the measured relationships differ from the *Hofstede* results. As outlined above, the different results are assumed to be due to conceptual differences between the two studies; the above confirmed hypotheses are not rejected.

Subsequent to this brief summary of empirical findings, the hypotheses test results are subjected to **discussion** in the following.

The empirical results of this study mainly confirm **prior studies** that test the cultural influence on the accounting values according to the *Hofstede-Gray* framework. This study finds cultural factors mainly associated with the accounting value of secrecy; only the conservatism indicator depreciation periods of buildings is significantly related to cultural influences. As mentioned above, prior studies on accounting practice mostly analyze the assumed association between culture and secrecy since secrecy is easier to approximate. Nonetheless, the pre-IFRS studies that investigate the *Hofstede-Gray* framework also come to significant conservatism results; especially the cultural factor uncertainty avoidance is determined as influential.[1360] IFRS application studies show mixed results.[1361] These studies mainly follow an experimental approach; the participants decide on a given accounting task and their decision is interpreted with respect to the accounting value of conservatism. These studies mainly confirm *Gray's* conservatism hypothesis.[1362] Also *Jödicke*, who analyzes financial statements with regard to overestimations of corporate provisions, finds companies from more conservative countries to overestimate their provisions.[1363] In contrast, *Tsakumis*, who conducted an experiment with US and Greek auditors, denies the tested conservatism hypothesis, while the tested secrecy hypothesis is confirmed.[1364]

Accordingly, prior studies on the accounting values of conservatism and secrecy are confirmed with respect to stronger findings for secrecy and mixed results for conservatism. Furthermore, the results of this study support the strongly significant influence of uncertainty avoidance on both conservatism and secrecy. However, in comparison to previous studies on accounting practice and IFRS practice in specific, the conservatism results of this study are relatively weak; only one of six conservatism indicators shows a significant association with cultural dimensions.

Having evaluated the empirical findings of this study with respect to prior research on a more global basis, the following two sections deal with the accounting values of conservatism and secrecy in more detail discussing the empirical results of the particular direct and indirect indicators.

1360 Cf., e.g., Salter/Niswander 1995, p. 379ff.; Lainez/Gasca 2006, p. 68ff.
1361 Cf., e.g., Schultz/Lopez 2001, p. 271ff.; Doupnik/Richter 2004, p. 1ff.
1362 Cf., e.g., Schultz/Lopez 2001, p. 271ff.; Doupnik/Richter 2004, p. 1ff.
1363 Cf. Jödicke 2009.
1364 Cf. Tsakumis 2007, p. 27ff.

Conservatism

The comparably weak conservatism results of this study may be interpreted as follows. First, the experimental **research design** of prior IFRS practice studies is explicitly constructed to discover variant degrees of conservatism and therefore may easier lead to significant results. Nonetheless, it is questionable whether the results achieved under laboratory conditions are directly transferable to reality. The influence of cultural factors like uncertainty avoidance is possibly lower for 'real life' corporate accounting decisions that are affected by corporate accounting policies or the corporate exposure to capital market pressures. The argument of research design inflicted cultural influence is weakened by another content analytical study on IFRS financial statements. The above reviewed culture study of *Jödicke* on IFRS provision estimates in France, Germany and the UK follows a non experimental research approach and finds provision measurement practice to be significantly associated with culture; however *Jödicke* does not control for institutional factors.

The latter aspect hints at an important limitation of prior IFRS practice studies; these studies mostly do not control for institutional factors.[1365] Accordingly, the significant conservatism results of prior studies might be related to the negligence of further (institutional) **context factors**, like the financing system or the legal system, that are possibly more influential than national culture.

A third explanation for the comparably weak research results on conservatism could be that the investigated accounting areas are not subject to conservatism. To mitigate the risk that conservatism as defined above has no effect on the particular conservatism indicators, this study analyzes conservatism from various **accounting perspectives.** On the one hand, the employed conservatism indicators cover (1) conservative accounting measured at global level and (2) conservative accounting regarding specific accounting issues. On the other hand, both global and specific accounting conservatism are determined by means of more than one indicator. The particular indicators are discussed in the following in more detail with respect to the accounting value they approximate.

Although ANOVA indicates that **MTB** is affected by country influences at the significance level of $p = 0.009^{**}$, none of the tested country factors leads to a significant result. Only uncertainty avoidance is included in the MTB regression model; however, the negative association between UAI and MTB is only weakly significant ($p = 0.110$) and not confirmed by rank regression analysis. One explanation for this unexpected result could be that IFRS figures are not as conservative as traditionally more prudent domestic French or German GAAP figures. And even if IFRS figures are subject to conservatism, the capital market might wrongly assume that IFRS figures, which are supposed to present the companies' economic situation fairly, are less susceptible to conservatism; a conservatism market premium would be accordingly smaller and conservatism that is not mirrored in the companies' market values is not determinable via the MTB indicator.

Alternatively, conservatism might not be reflected by relatively higher market values when these are influenced by capital market expectations that exceed the companies' future potential related to hidden reserves (conservatism). The significantly positively associated

[1365] Cf. chapter 1.5.1 respectively chapter 1.5.2.

growth and profitability indicators sales growth, ROI and profit margin support this interpretation. Also, the worldwide economic crisis might have had a biasing effect on the end of 2009 market values. An overall more prudent evaluation of companies' market values might have affected MTB as an indicator for conservatism.

Mean value comparison of the negative accruals indicator suggests that **NA** is not significantly associated with systematic country differences and no culture related association is determined. In analogy to the MTB indicator, this result can be interpreted in two ways. IFRS figures are either not subject to national conservatism patterns or conservatism is not reflected in NA. A tentative explanation for the latter suggestion could be linked to the worldwide economic crisis of 2008/2009, which might have had a considerable effect on companies' accruals. Especially increased provisions, as a consequence of the uncertain economic situation, might have had an impact on NA values. Moreover, considering that the UK as the leading capital market in the EU was more affected by the economic crisis than France and Germany, British NA values might have been lower than usual and, thus, closer to French and German NA values. As a consequence, NA country differences could be difficult to determine. Moreover, the NA value only measures conservatism of the investigated periods; prior periods' conservatism is not considered.

Contrary to the previous explanation, which assumed British companies to behave more conservatively in times of economic crisis, companies might have also made use of optimistic accounting practices to make the effects of the poor economic situation seem less grave. The NA values potential of reflecting conservative accounting would be limited. This argumentation is line with *Penman/Zhang* and *Ahmed et al.* who assume conservative companies to liquidate hidden reserves in times of declining operations.[1366]

In concordance with the two global conservatism indicators, the two capitalization indicators **CAPRD** and **INT** are not susceptible to cultural influences. Neither capitalization practices related to development costs nor capitalization practices related to intangibles in a PPA seem to be affected by national conservatism. The independence of both indicators from cultural influences could be the result of industry practice and/or the influence of the auditor. As mentioned above, the analyzed companies possess at least 5 years of IFRS experience. Accordingly, industry best-practice patterns might have been developed that prevail over other cultural influences. For example, it could be common industry practice in the pharmaceutical industry that development costs are capitalized for a new medicament when specific clinical studies, which are obligatory for all medicaments, have been successfully conducted. The significant industrial influence on CAPRD supports this argumentation. The dominance of certain industry capitalization practices could be enforced by the companies' auditor. Especially Big4 auditors might be responsible for an internationally consistent application of industry practice; as aforementioned, most of the tested companies are audited by one of the Big4 auditors; furthermore, the internal context factor auditor proved to be significantly associated with CAPRD.

The conceptual suitability of the INT indicator to measure varying degrees of accounting conservatism is supported by the empirical results. Although not confirmed by rank re-

[1366] Cf. Ahmed et al. 2002, p. 874; Penman/Zhang 2002, p. 237ff.

gression analysis, INT is significantly positively associated with uncertainty avoidance. Accordingly, higher UAI values are linked to higher INT values and, thus, assumingly higher conservatism. This finding supports the assumption that companies from countries that are characterized by high uncertainty avoidance associate the residual of the PPA, the goodwill, with more uncertainty and prefer to capitalize more intangibles instead. However, this statement is merely tentative as the regression result is not confirmed by the non-parametric test.

The two depreciation conservatism indicators only partly confirm the posited cultural influence. Whereas **BUILD** is significantly negatively associated with uncertainty avoidance, **PLANT** seems to be rather affected by the internal context factors size and industry. The strongly significantly negative association between BUILD and uncertainty avoidance is in line with the *Hofstede-Gray* framework. However, the significant difference between companies from France and Germany, on the one hand, and companies from the UK, on the other hand, could also be related to tax depreciation periods that are more influential in countries that recognize the authoritative principle. As buildings depreciation periods are much longer compared to plant and machinery, these might be stronger affected by pre-IFRS 'inherited tax burdens'. However, this argumentation is weakened by the strongly significant BUILD1 result. While BUILD2 is calculated based on the assets figures in the statement of fixed assets and, thus, might be influenced by pre-IFRS tax depreciation periods, BUILD1 is calculated based on the 'official' depreciation periods as published in the accounting policy section in the notes. It is unlikely that after at least five years of IFRS application the actual 'official' depreciation period figures are still associated with tax depreciation figures. For PLANT depreciation periods a possible influence of tax motivated depreciation figures is even more unlikely. Plant and machinery have much shorter depreciation periods compared to buildings and the influence of pre-IFRS 'inherited tax burdens' is assumingly low. Instead, the empirical findings suggest that PLANT depreciation periods are strongly influenced by industry practice that, possibly supported by Big4 auditors, is applied consistently across nations.

The investigation of **fair value** measurement of investment property led to few cases per country only, which do not allow for robust statistical tests. However, the basic analysis of the data shows that companies from the UK, which, according to its cultural profile, is expected to be the least conservative country of the three, use the fair value method relatively more often than French or German companies. Controlling for the influence of the real estate industry, which is assumed to be more experienced with respect to investment property market values and, thus, more likely to choose the fair value method, German companies apply the fair value method relatively more often than French companies. Accordingly, the culture related country ranking of Germany being more conservative than the UK and France being more conservative than Germany is supported by the empirical results on investment property fair value application. Thus, these findings, though not confirmed by regression analysis, put the comparably weak conservatism results into certain perspective.

Besides possible conceptual limitations associated with the particular conservatism indicators, the weak conservatism results of this study might be linked to the analysis of IFRS practice in general. As mentioned above, cultural differences might play only a minor role in explaining different degrees of conservatism in **IFRS** financial statements. The review of prior culturally grounded accounting studies in chapter 1.5.2 showed that the studies analyzing the *Hofstede-Gray* framework are mainly pre-IFRS studies. Furthermore, most of the culture studies that explicitly focus on IFRS practice analyze country samples that consist of European or South American countries resembling expected conservative accounting and the US resembling a rather optimistic accounting approach. Besides influences rooted in the experimental research approach,[1367] the significant conservatism results could be associated with the selection of the **US** as a sample country; US participants of the experiment, in contrast to European or South American participants, could be influenced by the comparatively optimistic US-GAAP accounting tradition.[1368]

Following the argumentation that previous culturally grounded IFRS practice studies could be affected and biased by the research respectively country sample design, the conservatism results of this study could indicate that large capital market oriented EU companies differ comparably little with regard to culture related measurement accounting decisions. This study analyses 2009 financial statements; most of the companies have at least five years of IFRS experience.[1369] The results of the study lead to the tentative interpretation that IFRS measurement practices of large capital market oriented firms assimilate over the years with growing IFRS experience. This trend is likely to be fortified by the influence of internationally operating Big4 audit firms, which follow an internationally consistent audit approach. As mentioned before, most of the sample companies are audited by Big4 auditors.

The assumption of **assimilated IFRS measurement practices** is challenged by the empirical results of *Jödicke* who analyzes corporate provisions, as published in the 2008 and 2009 financial statements, using a country sample of France, Germany and the UK.[1370] He finds cultural factors to have an influence on the degree of conservatism; notwithstanding, *Jödicke* does not control for institutional variables, which might prove to be influential.

Following the discussion of the empirical findings for the accounting value of conservatism the next section deals with the empirical results of the secrecy indicators.

Secrecy

The empirical results on the tested secrecy indicators reveal a strongly significant cultural influence. Whereas total notes disclosure is explained by the cultural dimension individualism, segment and income tax reporting quantity in the notes are explained by the cultural dimensions power distance and uncertainty avoidance. As posited, companies from high power distance countries publish less segment information and companies from high uncertainty avoidance countries publish less income tax information. Contrary to ex-

[1367] Cf. chapter 1.5.3.

[1368] Cf. Glaum 2000, p. 26.

[1369] Various capital market oriented companies applied IFRS long before it became obligatory. 30% of all Prime Standard listed German companies applied IFRS in 1999 (2003: 49%); cf. Zwirner 2010, p. 531.

[1370] Cf. Jödicke 2009.

pected, companies from high individualism countries publish less information in the notes as measured by total word count. With respect to segment and income tax information, the secrecy results of this study therewith confirm pre-IFRS studies on *Gray's* hypotheses;[1371] furthermore, this study confirms previous IFRS practice studies on secrecy.[1372]

The above results on secrecy indicate that disclosure, in comparison to measurement, is more susceptible to cultural influences. The risk that the tested secrecy indicators do not measure what they are supposed to measure is lower compared to conservatism indicators; secrecy indicators that measure information quantity are easier to interpret than conservatism indicators. Nonetheless, the tested secrecy indicators only reflect a small section of corporate disclosure.

The study shows that the cultural effects are (1) stronger and (2) as posited for income tax reporting and segment reporting compared to total notes disclosure. A tentative explanation for varying cultural effects could be related to the perceived **degree of information sensitivity**. Cultural influences might be stronger for accounting areas, which, according to corporate perception, contain more sensitive information external parties could be interested in. Whereas income tax reporting could be regarded as sensitive information with respect to the fiscal authorities, segment reporting could contain valuable information for competitors and companies might choose to follow a more restrictive information strategy. Other accounting areas that are perceived to be less important with respect to sensitivity of information could be less susceptible to cultural influences. The NOTES results support this assumption; French companies, which according to their cultural profile[1373] are expected to be the most secretive, disclose more information in the notes than German and British companies.

Although the empirical results on **NOTES** indicate that total notes disclosure as approximated by word count is significantly associated with the cultural factor individualism, the sign of the association is contrary to expected. Following the IDV country ranking and considering the assumingly negative association between IDV and secrecy, France is expected to publish less notes information than the UK and Germany is expected to publish less notes information than France. However, the empirical results suggest that French companies publish more information than German companies, which publish more information than British companies. While the difference between German and British companies according to the Scheffé-Test is not significant, French and British companies differ significantly with respect to NOTES. This constellation leads to the strongly significantly negative association with individualism.

As outlined above, a possible explanation for the unexpectedly high NOTES values for French and German companies could be related to less experience with internationally accepted financial accounting standards; British companies come from an Anglo-Saxon financial accounting background, which is conceptually closer to IFRS than the Continental European accounting approaches of France and Germany. Companies from the latter two countries could try to exceed IFRS disclosure requirements to signal the capital

1371 Cf., e.g., Chow et al. 1995, p. 29ff.; Amat et al. 1999; Lainez/Gasca 2006, p. 68ff.

1372 Cf. Doupnik/Riccio 2006, p. 237ff.; Tsakumis 2007, p. 27ff.

1373 Cf. chapter 2.2.4.7.2.

market the high 'quality' of their financial statements. Coming from a comparably 'poor' financial accounting environment, French and German companies could try to compensate for the uncertainty associated with the switch to IFRS by over-compliance of IFRS disclosure requirements.

Alternatively, British companies could tend to publish information that French and German companies include in the notes in other sections of the financial statements like the management report respectively the OFR. This statement, however, is of merely suggestive nature without empirical proof; the content analysis of the management report was not within the scope of this study. A final highly tentative explanation could be associated with the translation of French and German financial statements into English. Translating financial statements of French and German companies into English could result in longer financial statements since both languages are assumingly less efficient[1374] than English. Texts in French or German are regularly more padded than English texts and require comparably more words to say the same thing. Some of the extra text might find its way into the English translation. Analogous to the management report argumentation, this statement was not tested empirically and, thus, is to be interpreted carefully.

Considering the cautious accounting country ranking developed in chapter 2.2.4.7.2, German companies are supposed to be more secretive than British companies and French companies are supposed to be more secretive than German companies. This ranking is insofar confirmed by the **segment reporting** disclosure indices as French companies disclose significantly less segment information than German and British companies; the difference between the latter two countries turns out to be not significant. The finding of German companies disclosing as much and even more segment information in the notes might be associated to signaling strategies. As mentioned above, German companies could tend to exceed IFRS segment reporting requirements to signal the capital market a high degree of compliance. Segment reporting, in contrast to income tax reporting, might be more affected by corporate signaling strategies as segment information is assumingly more important to the capital market than income tax information. Alternatively, British companies could tend to publish segment information in the OFR and, thus, have lower disclosure scores in the notes.

The empirical results on **income tax** information confirm the cautious accounting country ranking. French companies disclose less information than German companies, which are exceeded by British companies. According to the performed Scheffé-Test, all indicated country differences are (strongly) significant. The TAXSTAT/TAXVOL disclosure indices therewith confirm the association between uncertainty avoidance and income tax reporting, which is explained by 47.7% respectively 57.9%. As mentioned above, the stronger result in comparison to segment reporting might be linked to the companies' perceived degree of uncertainty; income tax information might be considered to be more sensitive than segment information leading to more restrictive disclosure. The degree of sensitivity associated with income tax information might also be related to the national tax systems of the three countries, which are considered to be more influential in France and

[1374] Efficiency in this context refers to the number of words or sentences necessary to describe the same fact respectively the same accounting issue.

Germany. Apart from the authoritative principle linking tax and commercial accounting in France and Germany, these countries are also characterized by comparably higher marginal tax rates, which might indicate a comparably higher tax influence.[1375] Accordingly, the highest influence of corporate income tax is assumed in France (corporate tax rate of circa 34%)[1376], followed by Germany (corporate tax rate of circa 30%)[1377] and the UK (corporate tax rate of circa 28%)[1378]. The country ranking according to marginal tax rate supports the assumption of a tax related country influence. Nonetheless, the difference in marginal tax rate is not as high as to explain the significant differences measured for TAXSTAT and TAXVOL.[1379] Furthermore, tax considerations are generally expected to be of minor importance for large capital market oriented companies.[1380] This assumption is supported by prior culturally grounded research, which finds the accounting value of secrecy to be strongly associated with national culture.[1381]

The following chapter completes the study by summarizing gained cognitions, presenting possible implications, highlighting limitations and finally concluding with a brief overview of the study's perspectives for further research.

[1375] Cf. Salter/Niswander 1995, p. 386f.

[1376] French companies are subject to a corporate income tax rate of 33.33%. An additional tax for social security funding raises the legal rate by 1.1%. Cf. Biomérieux 2010, p. 131.

[1377] German companies are subject to corporate income tax and trade tax. The corporate income tax rate in Germany is 15% plus a solidarity surcharge of 5.5%. Trade tax rates differ regionally. Cf. Watrin/Rose 2009, p. 174, 234ff.; Zenthöfer/Leben 2010, p. 37, 145ff.

[1378] British companies are subject to a corporate income tax rate of 28%. Cf. Her Majesty's Revenue and Customs [HMRC] 2010.

[1379] The influence of the marginal tax rate as an indicator for the influence of the tax system has been tested for the TAXSTAT/TAXVOL regression models. When tested in combination with the cultural factor uncertainty avoidance, tax rate differences lead to no significant results.

[1380] Cf. chapter 2.3.2.1.3.

[1381] Cf. chapter 1.5.2.

5 Conclusion

This study analyzes the question whether **national cultural differences** have an impact on **IFRS practice.** The EU is identified as an ideal setting to analyze this issue since all European listed companies have to publish their group accounts in accordance with IFRS as endorsed by the EU. At the same time, the EU countries differ substantially with respect to national culture and national institutions like the legal system or the financing system. The following subchapter summarizes the theoretical and empirical findings of the study.

5.1 Main findings

As mentioned above, the European market provides some unique features as it combines high economic integration with different cultural backgrounds. The European economic convergence process also affected European financial accounting as harmonized financial accounting standards are among the main prerequisites of an integrated capital market. Although the Fourth and Seventh Directive led to more accounting harmonization in European individual and group accounting, the accounting harmonization strategy via Directives was abandoned in the 1990s by the EU; the process was too inflexible and time consuming; member states' national interests often hindered further harmonization. The enactment of the **IAS Regulation** in 2002 was the result of a different EU accounting harmonization strategy. Instead of continuing its Directive based approach or creating a separate European standard setter, the EU chose to adopt the internationally accepted IFRS as the set of rules for EU companies that had their securities admitted to trading on an EU regulated market; the endorsement process guarantees the conformity of IFRS with European accounting Directives and European interests. From 2005 respectively 2007 on, European capital market oriented companies were obliged to apply IFRS in their group accounts. EU member states may further allow IFRS for individual accounts and group accounts of non capital market oriented firms.

Despite the EU requirement to issue group accounts of capital market oriented firms in accordance with IFRS, the use of the same set of standards does not necessarily lead to consistent application of these standards. This study lists **reasons and opportunities for differing IFRS practice.** The reasons for companies to apply IFRS heterogeneously are manifold and range from the influence of national culture over internal earnings management considerations to institutional factors like the financial system. Reasons for differing IFRS application require IFRS embedded opportunities for inconsistencies, such as different translations of IFRS or gaps in IFRS. The hypotheses of this study mainly refer to the opportunity groups of (1) covert options and vague criteria in IFRS and (2) measurement estimations in IFRS.

The hypotheses that test how companies in different countries make use of IFRS opportunities are embedded in the theoretical framework of this study. **Contingency theory** serves as a meta-theoretical approach to describe the relationship between the organization as an open permeable system and its environment. Accordingly, the organization as a system and its subsystems (e.g. the accounting system) depend on the specific situation the organization is in. The multivariate personalistic open context contingency model explicitly recognizes the influence of multiple internal and external context factors and subjective discretion, which might lead to company or country specific accounting profiles. The conceptual framework spanned by contingency theory is further specified by the **societal effects approach**, which theoretically describes the relationship between companies and the national institutional environment. Following the societal effects approach, the institution company and its members are shaped by and therewith reflect the institutional parameters of their societal environment. The institutional parameters that are considered in this study are legal system, tax system, financing system, enforcement system and national GAAP system.

The cultural dimension of the companies' environment, which is the focus of this study, is theoretically underlined by **culture theory** according to *Hofstede*, who defines culture as "[...] the collective programming of the mind [...]"[1382]. *Hofstede* posits a society's collective programming respectively societal norms to be relatively stable over time, reinforced by institutional consequences like family patterns, socialization or religion. The societal norms that constitute a country's culture are multidimensional and affect all members and institutions of that country. The cultural factors identified by *Hofstede* are **uncertainty avoidance**, **individualism**, **masculinity** and **power distance.** *Gray* expects these context factors to have an influence on the accounting values 'professionalism vs. statutory control', 'uniformity vs. flexibility', '**conservatism** vs. optimism' and '**secrecy** vs. transparency'. This study focuses on the analysis of the latter two accounting values since these represent accounting **practice.** Besides cultural and institutional variables, this study also controls for the impact of internal context factors that are within the corporate sphere of influence. Sub disciplines of **institutional economics** (agency theory, political cost theory, signaling theory) and **PAT** are employed to theoretically found and predict the influence of internal context variables. The internal parameters tested in this study are size, industry, auditor, internationality, profitability and leverage.

Cultural influences on the accounting value **conservatism** are tested approximating conservative accounting practice by (1) higher market to book values, (2) lower negative accruals values, (3) lower capitalized development costs, (4) higher capitalized intangibles in PPAs, (5) shorter depreciation periods for tangible assets and (6) choosing the historical cost method instead of the fair value method for investment property evaluation. The accounting value of **secrecy**, on the other hand, is approximated by (1) lower numbers of words in the notes, (2) lower quantity of segment information in the notes and (3) lower quantity of income tax information in the notes. The latter two secrecy proxies employ disclosure indices to measure the quantity of statutory and voluntary segment and income tax disclosure.

The hypotheses on conservatism and secrecy are tested for a 261 company sample of the largest (2009 market capitalization) listed companies from **France**, **Germany** and the **UK.** These countries are selected mainly for two reasons. First, they differ substantially with respect to their cultural dimensions. Second, these countries possess the comparably largest equity capital markets in the EU, which guarantees a sufficiently large sample of publicly available financial statements in English. Moreover, these countries are comparable

[1382] Hofstede 2001, p. 9.

with respect to other external context factors like the political system, religion, country size or macroeconomic characteristics like the GDP.

The empirical analysis shows that *Hofstede's* cultural values are only significantly associated with the **conservatism indicator** depreciation periods of buildings (BUILD).[1383] Although parametric and non-parametric mean value comparison tests indicate significantly different country means for both conservatism indicators MTB and BUILD, the MTB country differences are not attributable to the tested cultural factors, as regression analysis indicates. Cultural differences are far better observable for the measured **secrecy indicators**. All three indicators show significantly different country means. The regression analyses which explain between 16.0% (SEGSTAT) and 57.9% (TAXVOL) indicate that (1) total notes disclosure, (2) segment and (3) income tax information in the notes are significantly associated with cultural factors. Whereas statutory and voluntary segment reporting is best explained by the cultural factor power distance and the institutional factor legal/tax system, statutory and voluntary income tax reporting is best explained by uncertainty avoidance. The direction of the relationships between the two disclosure index based secrecy indicators and the cultural values is as posited. Companies from high power distance countries are associated with lower segment reporting index values, as well as companies from high uncertainty avoidance countries are associated with lower income tax reporting index values. Although the more global secrecy indicator NOTES is also explained by a cultural factor, the association between NOTES and individualism is contrary to posited.

Size, industry and internationality prove to be the most influential **internal context factors** that were integrated into the conceptual framework to control for corporate characteristics. **Size** is significantly positively associated with the conservatism indicators depreciation periods of buildings (BUILD2) and plant and machinery and all three secrecy indicators. The size results for market to book value indicate a significantly negative association. **Industry**, on the other hand, seems to be most influential with respect to conservatism indicators. The amount of capitalized development costs is significantly associated with several of the tested industrial sectors. Moreover, depreciation periods of buildings respectively plant and machinery are shown to be affected by industry practice. Also, industry plays a significant role in explaining segment and income tax reporting quantity. The internal variable **auditor**, which distinguishes between Big4 auditors and other auditors, is significantly related to R&D capitalization practice and income tax reporting. With respect to the direction of auditor's influence on the two tested accounting values, the regression analyses show mixed results. Whereas Big4 auditors in the case of CAPRD are associated with lower percentages of capitalized development costs and higher degrees of conservatism, Big4 auditors in the case of income tax reporting stand for more income tax disclosures and lower degrees of secrecy accordingly.

The empirical results on the important internal context factor **internationality**, which is assumed to have a negative influence on both conservatism and secrecy, confirm only the

[1383] In analogy to the above discussion of results, the following annotations on significantly associated external and internal context factors only mention results that are confirmed to be significant by regression and rank regression analysis.

latter association. Except for a positive association with NA, the other significantly associated conservatism indicators contradict the assumption of internationally oriented companies being more conservative. In contrast, internationality indicators are positively associated with NOTES and TAXSTAT/TAXVOL and, thus, lower degrees of secrecy. Especially companies that are listed at SEC governed stock exchanges and, thus, used to reconcile their financial statements to US-GAAP are significantly related to more notes disclosure as measured by word count. The internal context factor **profitability** is significantly positively associated with the global conservatism indicator market to book value. This association is likely to be linked to higher capital market expectations related to more profitable companies and, accordingly, higher share prices and higher market capitalization. Moreover, profitability is assumed to have an influence on longer depreciation periods of buildings (BUILD1). **Leverage** as measured by debt to equity ratio shows no significant association with any of the tested conservatism and secrecy indicators. The following table gives an overview of all significant rank regression results (see Table 5-1).

		Conservatism						Secrecy		
		MTB	NA	CAPRD	INT	BUILD	PLANT	NOTES	SEG	TAX
Cultural factors	UAI					-				-
	IDV							-		
	MAS									
	PDI								-	
External context	LEGTAX								+	
	FINMCAP									
Internal context	Size	-				+[1384]	+	+	+	+
	Industry			+		-	+/-		+/-	+/-
	Auditor			-						+
	Internationality	+	+		+	-		+		+
	Profitability	+				+[1385]				
	Leverage									
+		Significantly positive association between context factor and accounting value								
-		Significantly negative association between context factor and accounting value								
+/-		Significantly positive/negative association between context factor and accounting value								

Table 5-1: Significant association matrix

The empirical findings on the significant influence of culture are tested for robustness applying the GLOBE dimensions instead of the *Hofstede* dimensions. Although the influence of national culture is confirmed by the robustness test, the GLOBE results differ

[1384] The significant association is only confirmed for BUILD2.

[1385] The significant association is only confirmed for BUILD1.

from the *Hofstede* results with respect to sign and dimension. As outlined above, the deviating interpretation of cultural differences is likely to be associated to conceptual differences between the two studies.

The following chapter addresses possible implications that result from the above described findings of this study.

5.2 Implications and contribution

The results of the study lead to various implications for accounting research and practice. First, the study contributes to **international accounting research**. Adopting the view that due to increasing harmonization future international accounting research is likely to focus on accounting practice instead of accounting rules, this study contributes to the two research streams of **culture free IFRS practice studies** and culturally grounded IFRS practice studies. The former research stream is characterized by the limitations of being rather descriptive, disregarding specific country factors, analyzing overt accounting choices only, focusing on a small number of companies per country only and lacking a conceptual framework. These limitations are addressed by this study. This study goes beyond mere description and explains IFRS practice by investigating the associations between the internal and external context of the organization and the organizational accounting decisions. The context of the organization is addressed in the conceptual framework of this study, which recognizes the influence of national culture and other institutional country factors like the financing system or the legal system. Furthermore, this study investigates the two accounting dimensions of conservatism and secrecy respectively measurement and disclosure. The only overt option analyzed is fair value measurement of investment property. The other conservatism indicators are based on covert options, vague criteria and measurement estimates; secrecy, in contrast, is approximated by word count and four disclosure indices, which measure the information quantity of segment and income tax reporting in the notes. The company samples per country vary between 80 (UK) and 93 (Germany) companies and, thus, allow for statistically robust test results.

The second relevant research stream of **culturally grounded IFRS practice studies** is also enriched both methodologically and conceptually. As mentioned above, these studies are mainly experiments analyzing IFRS practice under laboratory conditions; the participants of the experiments partially come from countries in which IFRS at the time of the experiment was not required. Furthermore, these studies are limited with respect to the internal and external context they assume to have an impact on IFRS practice. In analogy to culture free IFRS practice studies, they reveal deficiencies regarding the conceptual foundation of their analysis. These limitations are addressed in this study by investigating actual IFRS practice as published in 2009 financial statements. IFRS is required for group accounts of capital market oriented companies in the analyzed countries and the companies have at least five years of IFRS experience. In comparison to prior studies, the organizational context is amplified with respect to institutional context factors and further internal context factors; moreover, a second cultural concept is integrated to test the robustness of the empirical results based on the *Hofstede-Gray* framework. The conceptual framework establishes the theoretical relationship between internal and external context of the organization and IFRS practice.

The scientific debate related to national cultural influences on IFRS practice is enriched by this study as **measurement** indicators are mainly found to be not affected by national cultural differences. The mainly supportive conservatism results of prior studies might be associated to the experimental research design of these studies. This study investigates several conservatism indicators on global and specific measurement level and finds only support for culture related differences with regard to depreciation periods of buildings. These results suggest that IFRS measurement accounting is less susceptible to systematic country differences as expected. Moreover, this study provides further empirical evidence on the association between national cultural and IFRS **disclosure** practice. This study finds total notes disclosure, segment and income tax reporting in the notes to be strongly significantly associated with cultural differences and, thus, confirms prior research. Considering the influence of national culture, the adoption of IFRS seems to have had no or little effect on companies' disclosure practice. The quantity of disclosed information still differs considerably on an international level. Besides cultural and institutional influences on depreciation periods of buildings, notes, segment and income tax disclosure, this study finds other control variables to be significantly associated with the tested conservatism and secrecy indicators.

As outlined above, differences in measurement are mainly attributable to the **internal context factors** size, industry and internationality. Contrary to expected, the internal context factor size is related to less conservative accounting. The **industry** results are mixed with respect to industrial sector and direction of the relationship; as posited, industry is most influential with respect to capitalization of development costs and depreciation periods. Although the results for the particular conservatism indicators are not entirely consistent with regard to the sign of the association, **internationality** is suggested to rather lead to more conservative measurement. The measured effect of **profitability** is comparably small and inconsistent regarding the direction of the effect on conservatism. **Leverage** is not found to be significantly influential and **Big4** auditors are assumed to be associated with conservative capitalization of development costs only. The empirical findings are more consistent regarding the association between internal context and IFRS disclosure practice. Both **size** and **internationality** are, in accordance with agency theoretical considerations, significantly positively associated with disclosure quantity. Moreover, **Big4** auditors are positively related to income tax reporting in the notes. The **industry** results are mixed. Although significantly associated with both segment and income tax reporting quantity, the empirical findings allow for no conclusions on the disclosure practice of a certain industry in general.

The findings of this study might also be interesting for financial statement users like **analysts** or investors. The empirical results imply that national cultural or institutional differences play only a minor role in explaining IFRS measurement practice. However, depreciation periods of buildings seem to be affected by national culture. Also, the rudimentary analysis of the application of the fair value method for investment property indicated that (1) real estate companies use fair measurement more often than non real estate companies and (2) British companies use fair value measurement more often than French or German companies. Analysts and investors could integrate these conservatism related findings in their investment decisions. Moreover, internal context factors like size, industry or internationality should be considered when comparing and analyzing financial statements of large, capital market oriented EU companies. With respect to IFRS disclosure practice, analysts and investors might benefit from the knowledge of certain disclosure country profiles. Furthermore, this study showed that French and German disclosure is better in terms of information quantity than expected. Although both countries, according to their cultural profile and the relative development of their equity capital markets, are assumed to be more secretive than Anglo-Saxon countries like the UK, this study finds French companies to disclose more information in the notes than German companies, which disclose more than British companies. A tentative explanation for these findings could be that British companies disclose the information elsewhere in the financial statements. Investors and analysts might have to consider other sections like the management report for reasons of comparison.

Furthermore, the IASB as IFRS **standard setter** might benefit from this study's findings. IFRS are regularly criticized to contain too many options and too much discretion, which could allow for systematic country differences.[1386] This study analyzes various issues of **measurement** discretion and finds country differences to be of minor importance. However, the analysis of fair value application for investment property indicates that, except for companies from the real estate industry, the fair value method is rarely applied. This finding suggests that the companies tend to avoid the effort and costs associated with the complex calculation of fair values when there is no active market available. As the fair value concept is an important element of the IASB strategy of providing fairly presented, decision-useful information to the capital market, the results of this study might give reason to revise the fair value concept as it is. Apart from country differences related to fair value application or depreciation periods of buildings, IFRS measurement practice is rather influenced by internal context factors like industry or internationality. Such internal systematic differences do not conflict with the interests of the IASB since accounting options and discretion shall allow companies with different economic characteristics to fairly present their activities. The country differences found for IFRS **disclosure** practice are assumed to be of less interest to the IASB as the standards' specifications are clear in what is to be disclosed. The compliance with the IASB's specifications is rather a task for the responsible national enforcement bodies. However, the significantly positive association between firm size and disclosure quantity might indicate that smaller companies have difficulties to comply with the comprehensive IFRS disclosure requirements. This finding might be considered by the IASB in the future revision of standards that require the publication of information in the notes. It is questionable whether extensive disclosure requirements for the notes improve the quality and understandability of financial statements when the extent and the complexity of the notes prohibit the identification of relevant, decision-useful information.

[1386] Cf. Kvaal/Nobes 2010, p. 186.

The above findings also result in implications for **regulators** like the SEC, which is about to decide on the acceptance of IFRS for US domestic companies.[1387] As mentioned above, the SEC long criticized the IASB for allowing too much discretion. The conservatism results, which indicate that IFRS measurement rules are mainly applied consistently across countries could encourage the SEC to accept IFRS as equivalent to US-GAAP. The secrecy results, however, reveal that IFRS disclosure practice is characterized by substantial country differences. The significant association between the internal context factor SEC listing and total notes disclosure underlines remaining differences between IFRS and US-GAAP disclosure. As the provision of additional notes information might be related to a considerable increase in costs and effort and, accordingly, result in a possible competitive disadvantage for US domestic listed companies, the SEC might want to address the topic of notes disclosure requirements in the decision on IFRS acceptance.

The empirical findings of this study on deviating disclosure practice are better addressed to the European **enforcement** bodies than to the standard setter. As outlined above, enforcement in the EU is the responsibility of the various member states. Although European national enforcement agencies meet on a regular basis trying to coordinate their actions, so far there is no supranational European enforcement mechanism; instead, the national enforcement bodies follow different enforcement approaches and are equipped with different sovereign competencies. The study's findings on disclosure differences accentuate the importance of further harmonization of the European enforcement environment. Although European governments seem to fear the assignment of enforcement to a supranational organization they have only limited influence on, in the long run this solution is surely without alternative. The described enforcement issue might also be relevant for **auditors**; auditors are assumed to have an influence on corporate R&D capitalization practice and income tax reporting quantity. Auditors that are embedded in an international firm network could help to diminish disclosure country differences by enforcing similar disclosure concepts. The findings of this study could help (Big4) auditors to identify accounting areas that require to be further aligned on an international level.

The following section deals with limitations that might result from the research design of the study.

5.3 Limitations

This study is subject to certain methodological limitations that have to be considered when interpreting the above described results and implications. As mentioned before, neither significant correlation results nor significant regression results indicate existing **causality** between the tested dependent and independent variables. Significant correlation or regression results only imply a statistical association between the analyzed factors without indicating a factual cause and effect relationship. Such cause and effect relationships could only be determined under immensely restrictive laboratory conditions, which, especially in the complex field of business economics, seldom represent reality.

[1387] Securities and Exchange Commission [SEC] 2010c; American Institute of Certified Public Accountants [AICPA] 2010.

Although this study investigates real financial accounting phenomena by analyzing corporate financial statements as published by the companies, certain limitations exist with reference to the **transfer of results** and implications to other companies. This study tests a sample of the 110 largest listed companies of each of the French, German and British capital markets. It is questionable whether the results of this study are transferable to other countries of the European Union or to smaller and to unlisted companies. Also, banks and insurance companies were initially excluded from the sample; accordingly, the interpretation of the study's results with respect to these companies is problematic.

Furthermore, the list of external and internal **context factors**, although theoretically founded and checked for plausibility with reference to other studies, is surely not complete. This study mainly concentrates on internal context factors that are measurable and that can be extracted from financial statements respectively data banks like OSIRIS. Other internal context factors like the professional education or the IFRS experience of the accountant are not considered. The partially rather low R-squared values indicate that for some dependent variables only a small percentage of the variable's variance is explained by the employed internal and external context factors. The rest of the variance is associated with context factors not analyzed in this study or random.

As outlined above, the application of *Hofstede's* **cultural dimensions** might be regarded as a limitation to this study. Although successfully applied in numerous studies, culture theory by *Hofstede* attracted critical opinions, as well. The most common objections are that (1) culture is viewed through the eyes of the IBM corporation, (2) culture is too complex to be captured by four respectively five dimensions only and (3) the *Hofstede* data is outdated.[1388] These points of criticism were discussed in the culture theoretical chapter above.[1389] Additionally, the cultural results of this study were tested for robustness applying the cultural dimensions identified by the GLOBE study. The robustness tests confirm the *Hofstede* results with respect to a significant influence of national culture *per se*. The significant cultural dimensions and the directions of the measured significant relationships, however, mostly differ from the *Hofstede* results. Consequently, the GLOBE study robustness tests cast some doubt on the interpretation of cultural differences according to the *Hofstede-Gray* framework. Nonetheless, the deviating results are assumed to be rather attributable to the research design of the two culture studies and the interpretation of their results than to the different research periods of the two studies.[1390] As outlined above, various *Hofstede* replication studies confirm his results and show that his data is not outdated. This study therefore applied the cultural concept by *Hofstede* as it is still the most applied concept in accounting literature; more current cultural concepts so far were not able to usher in a new era of cultural thought.[1391]

Apart from limitations that are related to the selection and operationalization of the independent variables tested in this study, possible limitations might also be associated with the tested dependent variables, i.e. **conservatism** and **secrecy indicators**. Whereas secrecy

---

[1388] Cf. Williamson 2002, p. 1377; Kutschker/Schmid 2011, p. 731ff.; McSweeney 2002, p. 95.

[1389] Cf. chapter 2.2.4.4.

[1390] Cf. chapter 2.2.4.1.4.

[1391] Cf. Jödicke 2009, p. 25.

indicators are mainly limited with regard to the method of data collection,[1392] conservatism indicators might be susceptible to conceptual limitations. As outlined above, the MTB indicator might be biased by capital market expectations; to control for such effects, growth and profitability measures were integrated into the conceptual framework of this study. Furthermore, declining operations as a consequence of the worldwide economic crisis might have had a biasing effect on NA. With respect to limitations regarding the more specific conservatism indicators, CAPRD and INT might be biased by the companies' industry; industries like the automobile industry might be characterized by higher percentages of development costs compared to total R&D costs and other industries like the pharmaceutical industry might be characterized by relatively higher percentages of research costs. Differing CAPRD values would, thus, not be associated to conservatism but to industrial peculiarities. Analogously, higher percentages of newly capitalized intangibles in a PPA might be the consequence of higher importance of intangible assets in certain industries (e.g. software industry). Depending on the industrial structure of the analyzed sample countries,[1393] the companies' industry might have a biasing effect on the countries' CAPRD and INT distribution. To control for such effects, the companies' industry is considered as a context factor in this study. The corresponding empirical findings indicate that the assumed industrial influence is only supported for the CAPRD indicator.

Furthermore, the depreciation period indicators are subject to certain limitations. These indicators could be biased by asset impairments that are not reported separately, asset acquisitions during the year or historical cost values that include fully depreciated assets; also the application of tax accounting depreciation periods might have a biasing effect. To control for these limitations, this study employs a second set of depreciation indicators that is based on the 'official' useful lifetime figures as published in the notes; moreover, the influence of the tax system is controlled for by the LEGTAX context factor.

Limitations could also result from **content analysis** and the content analytical instrument disclosure index. As referred to above, content analytical procedures are susceptible to different kinds of biases. Although the content analysis is performed by one person only to avoid inter-personal differences, the subjective perception by the encoder could have a biasing effect on the data. Also, learning effects and differing concentration of the encoder must be considered as potentially biasing factors. To control for such effects, a code book was developed to guarantee the consistent application of the two disclosure indices on segment and income tax information. The content analysis was conducted by the author himself to assure maximum motivation and accuracy. Furthermore, the analysis is performed for one topic only at a time to avoid conceptual distraction.

The instrument of the **disclosure index** could be the reason for methodological limitations, as well. It is debatable whether a disclosure index measures disclosure quality or, as assumed in this study, disclosure quantity only. Higher index scores, thus, do not imply higher information quality. The corresponding regression results on segment and income tax information have to be interpreted carefully with respect to conclusions on informa-

---

[1392] Limitations regarding the method of data collection are discussed below.

[1393] The industrial structure of the country samples is described in chapter 4.2.3.

tion quality. Moreover, the quality of the disclosure index is determined by the quality of its categories. The categories for the statutory information are predetermined by the corresponding IFRS standards. The categories that capture the voluntary information, however, might be incomplete. To guarantee the integrity of the voluntary categories, the initial disclosure index contained categories for all types of information discovered in the pretest; additional categories were created when information items occurred that were not considered before.

Based on the research design and the empirical findings of this study, the following chapter gives a brief outlook on future research.

5.4 Perspectives

Although the harmonization process of international financial accounting gained momentum in the last 20 years, which leads some authors to question the academic field of international accounting research,[1394] this study shows that there is plenty of room for future research. However, the focus of international accounting research is likely to shift from research on different accounting systems to research on different **accounting practice**. The research design of this study is extendable in various ways.

First, future studies might analyze different **sample countries**. These studies might integrate non-European countries that require capital market oriented companies to apply IFRS like Australia, for instance; national IFRS modifications that lead to differences with regard to the IFRS standards as issued by the IASB needed to be taken into account.[1395] Studies focusing on the EU area, which offers the advantage of homogeneous accounting standards (IFRS as endorsed by the EU), could focus on countries that have smaller capital markets than France, Germany and the UK. Accounting practice of companies listed at less developed capital markets could tend to be more influenced by national cultural patterns. Moreover, future studies could investigate more than three countries to investigate a larger spectrum of cultural facets. As outlined in chapter 3.4.4.3, a higher number of analyzed countries offers the advantage to integrate more country variables into the regression model without raising the problem of perfect multi collinearity.

Second, it could prove to be interesting to analyze IFRS financial statements for a **number of years** and assess the development of IFRS practice over time. Researchers could test the tentative hypothesis that IFRS practice converges over the years.

Besides possible variation in sample countries and number of analyzed years, future research could develop and test **different conservatism and secrecy indicators**. Measurement and disclosure issues are far from being extensively tested for cultural and other influences. The above chapter[1396] on opportunities for IFRS differences lists further overt and covert options and room for discretion that could be analyzed with respect to systematically differing IFRS practice.

[1394] Cf. Nobes 2006, p. 233.

[1395] In contrast, financial statements in accordance with Australian IFRS are supposed to be free of translation related bias.

[1396] Cf. chapter 1.3.4.2.

Furthermore, this study, in analogy to most accounting studies, tests a **company sample** from which banks and insurance companies were previously excluded as these companies possess different economic characteristics. Future studies on IFRS application could follow a different approach and analyze financial institutions instead. Analyzing companies from the comparably less explored financial sector would surely lead to interesting insights and bear the advantage that industry must not be controlled for. On the other hand, country samples would be much smaller as there are not as many financial institutions. Alternatively, future research could focus on the investigation of smaller companies. Whereas large companies are generally widely analyzed, accounting research seldom focuses on small and medium companies. The assessment of IFRS practice of smaller companies could bear the advantage that these are less susceptible to the pressures of the national and international capital market and, accordingly, more susceptible to cultural influences.

Finally, future research could also vary with respect to **research methodology**. This study concentrates on financial information that is directly extractable from corporate financial statements. Nonetheless, especially measurement decisions are often not directly observable in published financial documents. Supplemental questionnaires could be a proper instrument to develop more sophisticated conservatism indicators that are based on unpublished information, as well. Additionally, questionnaires could be employed to inquire further internal context factors like the education or IFRS experience of the accountant. Also, an experimental research design might prove useful to investigate conservative respectively secretive accounting practice. In contrast to prior studies, these experiments should focus on actual IFRS users only to control for national (US-) GAAP related effects.

As outlined above, the academic fields of international accounting in general and international IFRS practice in specific offer a wide spectrum of research opportunities. Research in this area is of great importance to further promote the integration of the international capital market, which is one of the main premises of a prosperous world economy.

Appendix

Table A 1: SIC code industry aggregation[1397]

1 Consumer non-durables - food, tobacco, textiles, apparel, leather, toys					
0100-0999	2700-2749	3100-3199	2000-2399	2770-2799	3940-3989
2 Consumer durables - cars, TV, furniture, household appliances					
2500-2519	2590-2599	3630-3659	3710-3711	3714-3714	3716-3716
3750-3751	3792-3792	3900-3939	3990-3999		
3 Manufacturing - machinery, trucks, planes, chemicals, paper, printing					
2520-2589	2600-2699	2750-2769	2800-2829	2840-2899	3000-3099
3200-3569	3580-3621	3623-3629	3700-3709	3712-3713	3715-3715
3717-3749	3752-3791	3793-3799	3860-3899		
4 Oil, gas and coal extraction and products					
1200-1399	2900-2999				
5 Business equipment - computers, software and electronic equipment					
3570-3579	3622-3622	3660-3692	3694-3699	3810-3839	7370-7372
7373-7373	7374-7374	7375-7375	7376-7376	7377-7377	7378-7378
7379-7379	7391-7391	8730-8734			
6 Telephone and television					
4800-4899					
7 Wholesale, retail and some services (laundries, repair shops)					
5000-5999	7200-7299	7600-7699			
8 Healthcare, medical equipment, and drugs					
2830-2839	3693-3693	3840-3859	8000-8099		
9 Utilities					
4900-4949					
10 Other - mines, construction, transport, hotels, bus services, entertainment, finance					

[1397] Adopted from French/Fama 2010.

Table A 2: Segment reporting disclosure index

Item group	SV	S	Description	G	F	UK	∑
General segment information	1	1	Segment factor definition	56	41	58	155
	2	2	Segment description	68	46	52	166
	3	3	Information on segment aggregation	14	9	16	39
	4		Information on segmental changes	20	8	23	51
	5		Definition of the 'chief operating decision maker'	26	17	19	62
	6		Segment definition with reference to the internal decision processes resource allocation / performance measurement	23	30	27	80
	7		Key performance indicators named	43	19	21	83
	8		Segment definition with reference to internal control system	63	39	24	126
	9		Additional period reported	3	24	11	38
	10	4	Information on the segment reporting basis of measurement	40	25	7	72
	11	5	Information on inter segment transfer prices	63	26	31	120
Consolidation	12		Separate 'other' / 'corporate' column	49	48	56	153
	13		Separate consolidation column	62	39	31	132
Segment profit and loss	14	6	Segment profit and loss	88	83	73	244
	15		Profit and loss according to different segmentation	7	6	10	23
Segment revenues	16	7	Segment revenues	86	79	75	240
	17	8	Internal segment revenues	77	53	50	180
	18	9	External segment revenues	80	54	52	186
	19	10	Interest from investments in associates / joint ventures	40	31	29	100
	20	11	Segment interest income	27	10	12	49
	21	12	Other material segment revenues items	9	10	5	24
	22		Segment revenues according to different segmentation	78	56	52	186
	23		Segment revenues of discontinued operations	2	1	5	8
	24		Information on revenues of major clients (>10%)	32	9	19	60
Segment expenses	25	13	Segment expenses	9	15	10	34
	26	14	Segment interest expenses	31	13	18	62
	27	15	Segment depreciation / amortization	86	67	71	224
	28	16	Other material noncash items	56	48	41	145
	29	17	Segment tax expenses / income	17	13	11	41

Item group	SV	S	Description	G	F	UK	∑
	30	18	Other material expense items	19	18	11	48
	31		Segment expenses according to different segmentation	3	2	1	6
Segment assets	32	19	Segment assets	81	73	77	231
	33	20	Investments in associates / joint ventures	30	23	30	83
	34	21	Segment capital expenditure	80	59	72	211
	35		Segment asset description	19	15	20	54
	36		Segment assets according to different segmentation	68	38	46	152
	37		Detailed information on consolidated assets	23	21	48	92
Segment liabilities	38	22	Segment liabilities	60	54	61	175
	39		Segment liabilities description	12	9	15	36
	40		Segment liabilities according to different segmentation	7	2	4	13
	41		Detailed information on consolidated liabilities	15	15	38	68
Other information	42	23	Segment cash flow	9	10	0	19
	43		Number of segment employees	32	7	5	44

SV = statutory and voluntary information

S = statutory information

Table A 3: Income tax reporting disclosure index

Item group	SV	S	Description	G	F	UK	∑
Current tax information	1	1	Current tax expenses	91	86	79	256
	2		Foreign current tax expenses	43	14	49	106
	3	2	Current tax adjustments for prior years	41	11	59	111
	4	3	Information on current tax benefits from previously unrecognized tax losses / credits / temporary differences	8	4	10	22
	5	4	Unrecognized tax liabilities as a consequence of dividends	6	2	0	8
	6	5	IAS 12.52A tax consequences	0	0	0	0
	7	6	Current tax effect regarding discontinued operations	7	0	8	15
	8	7	Aggregated current tax effect on equity	5	1	29	35
	9	8	Reconciliation between accounting profit and current tax	92	84	78	254
General tax information	10		Nominal local corporate tax rate	91	84	76	251
	11		Effective local corporate tax rate	48	60	38	146
	12		Foreign average tax rate	23	4	4	31
	13		Information on additional period	4	18	10	32
	14	9	Information on changes of accounting policies / errors	3	1	0	4
	15	10	Explanation of tax rate changes	2	14	10	26
	16	11	Current tax effect on OCI	9	7	17	33
Deferred tax information	17	12	Deferred tax expenses from temporary differences	86	86	79	251
	18		Foreign deferred tax expenses	31	10	17	58
	19		Deferred tax adjustments for prior years	9	3	48	60
	20	13	Effect of deferred tax rate changes	13	10	21	44
	21	14	Information on deferred tax benefits from previously unrecognized tax losses / credits / temporary differences	12	7	14	33
	22	15	Deferred tax expenses resulting from the write down or reversal of previous write downs of assets	9	2	1	12
	23	16	Deferred tax effect regarding discontinued operations	1	1	6	8
	24	17	Deferred tax changes related to business combinations	3	9	16	28
	25	18	Amount of tax assets dependent on future taxable profits	46	9	16	71
	26	19	Amount of deferred tax assets; prior corporate losses	7	5	1	13
Deferred tax assets	27	20	Deferred tax assets	88	80	69	237
	28		Detailed amount of deferred tax assets	86	39	36	161

Item group	SV	S	Description	G	F	UK	Σ
	29	21	Profit and loss effect of deferred tax assets	7	18	25	50
	30		Exchange differences from deferred tax assets	3	11	15	29
	31		Deferred tax assets due < / > 1 year	41	23	20	84
	32		Equity effect of deferred tax assets	12	13	13	38
Deferred tax liabilities	33	22	Deferred tax liabilities	89	78	69	236
	34		Detailed amount of deferred tax liabilities	87	39	35	161
	35	23	Profit and loss effect of deferred tax liabilities	7	18	25	50
	36		Exchange differences from deferred tax liabilities	2	11	15	28
	37		Deferred tax liabilities due < / > 1 year	14	10	15	39
	38		Equity effect of deferred tax liabilities	10	13	12	35
Deferred tax assets and liabilities netted	39	24	Net deferred tax assets / liabilities	2	4	8	14
	40		Detailed net amount of deferred tax assets / liabilities	4	33	37	74
	41		Reference to deferred tax offsetting process	19	4	31	54
	42	25	Net profit and loss effect of deferred tax assets / liabilities	15	33	51	99
	43		Detailed net profit and loss effect of deferred tax assets / liabilities	3	3	44	50
	44		Net exchange differences from deferred tax assets / liabilities	8	25	38	71
	45		Detailed net exchange differences from deferred tax assets / liabilities	0	0	28	28
	46	26	Net equity effect of deferred tax assets / liabilities	37	38	54	129
	47		Detailed net equity effect of deferred tax assets / liabilities	5	4	45	54
Unrecognized deferred tax assets and liabilities	48	27	Unrecognized deferred tax assets	71	61	65	197
	49		Explanation of unrecognized deferred tax assets	21	19	40	80
	50	28	Expiry date of unrecognized deferred tax assets	37	21	45	103
	51	29	Unrecognized deferred tax liabilities related to investments	32	2	47	81
	52		Explanation of unrecognized deferred tax liabilities related to investments	25	2	44	71

SV = statutory and voluntary information

S = statutory information

Table A 4: Spearman correlation coefficients

	MTB	NA	CAPRD	INT	BUILD1	BUILD2	PLANT1	PLANT2	NOTES	SEGSTAT	SEGVOL	TAXSTAT	TAXVOL
UAI	-0.224**	-0.073	0.157	0.003	-0.240**	-0.128	-0.075	0.053	0.172**	-0.090	-0.176**	-0.543**	-0.621**
MAS	0.191**	0.082	-0.204	0.000	0.181**	0.163*	0.057	-0.048	-0.132*	0.230**	0.309**	0.402**	0.472**
IDV	0.099	-0.001	0.134	-0.003	0.150*	-0.044	0.046	-0.017	-0.107	-0.233**	-0.203**	0.361**	0.390**
PDI	-0.191**	-0.082	0.204	0.000	-0.181**	-0.163*	-0.057	0.048	0.132*	-0.230**	-0.309**	-0.402**	-0.472**
LEGTAX	-0.193**	-0.043	0.016	0.003	-0.232**	-0.050	-0.073	0.042	0.164**	0.084	0.016	-0.536**	-0.599**
FINMCAP	0.081	-0.085	0.041	0.060	0.011	-0.090	-0.028	-0.048	-0.108	-0.101	-0.071	0.137*	0.151*
CONNDUR	0.074	0.095	0.030	0.016	-0.004	0.077	-0.015	-0.008	-0.089	-0.076	-0.074	0.047	0.032
CONDUR	-0.093	0.017	0.137	0.000	0.013	0.133*	0.054	-0.002	0.083	0.009	0.037	-0.022	-0.035
MAN	-0.079	0.006	-0.306**	-0.042	-0.176**	0.115	0.100	0.141*	0.034	0.086	0.127*	0.003	-0.003
OIL	0.083	-0.062	0.112	0.000	-0.062	-0.074	0.174**	0.118	0.080	0.111	0.095	0.114	0.102
EQU	0.182**	-0.020	-0.212	0.300*	-0.037	-0.073	-0.229**	-0.108	-0.109	-0.006	-0.004	-0.058	-0.048
TEL	0.018	-0.031	0.121	-0.022	-0.053	-0.247**	-0.103	-0.055	0.081	0.040	0.044	-0.015	-0.025
SALE	-0.143*	-0.086	0.078	-0.081	0.142*	0.064	-0.218**	-0.171*	-0.015	-0.126*	-0.089	0.058	0.036
HEALTH	0.113	0.139*	0.066	-0.032	-0.043	-0.052	-0.082	-0.051	0.047	-0.042	-0.065	-0.121	-0.065
UTIL	0.062	0.066	0.255*	-0.075	0.103	0.031	0.309**	0.229**	0.119	0.020	0.061	0.078	0.166**
OTH	-0.138*	-0.070	0.136	-0.124	0.125	-0.010	0.070	-0.059	-0.082	-0.003	-0.085	-0.038	-0.073
LMCAP	0.168**	-0.036	0.132	0.006	0.025	0.038	0.166*	0.220**	0.384**	-0.003	0.090	0.268**	0.308**
EMP	-0.157*	-0.061	0.059	0.065	0.051	0.046	-0.023	0.155*	0.380**	0.056	0.141*	0.276**	0.252**
LTASS	-0.255**	-0.096	0.122	0.032	0.084	0.116	0.221**	0.341**	0.518**	0.065	0.138*	0.288**	0.286**
FORLIST	-0.120	-0.061	-0.044	-0.013	-0.151*	-0.054	-0.092	-0.008	0.157*	0.030	-0.005	-0.169**	-0.204**
SECLIST	0.126*	-0.022	-0.003	0.331**	0.025	-0.102	0.139*	0.066	0.212**	0.030	0.036	0.238**	0.295**
FORSALES	0.194**	0.113	-0.243*	0.085	-0.101	-0.131	0.005	-0.019	0.076	0.026	0.027	0.210**	0.228**
BIG4	-0.072	-0.076	-0.177	0.156	0.032	0.105	0.022	0.119	0.142*	-0.002	0.057	0.265**	0.253**
LEV	-0.013	-0.202**	0.032	0.301*	0.144*	0.115	0.119	0.144*	0.289**	0.121	0.185**	0.229**	0.212**
PROFIT	0.334**	0.107	0.117	-0.020	0.186**	-0.030	0.172*	-0.030	-0.100	-0.186**	-0.207**	-0.043	0.018
ROI	0.497**	0.145*	0.122	0.079	0.087	-0.062	0.016	-0.123	-0.118	-0.155*	-0.137*	0.076	0.139*
SALGRO	0.320**	0.158*											

* (**) represents significance at the 5% (1%) level

Bibliography

Accounting Standards Board [ASB] (1999): Statement of Principles for Financial Reporting, available at: http://www.frc.org.uk, last revised 01.03.2011.

Accounting Standards Board [ASB] (2011): About the ASB, available at: http://www.frc.org.uk, last revised 01.03.2011.

Ahmed, A. S./Billings, B. K./Morton, R. M./Stanford-Harris, M. (2002): The Role of Accounting Conservatism in Mitigating Bondholder-Shareholder Conflicts over Dividend Policy and in Reducing Debt Costs, in: The Accounting Review, 77 (4), p. 867–890.

Ahmed, A. S./Duellman, S. (2007): Accounting conservatism and board of director characteristics: An empirical analysis, in: Journal of Accounting and Economics, 43 (2-3), p. 411–437.

Aisbitt, S. (2001): Measurement of harmony of financial reporting within and between countries: the case of the Nordic countries, in: European Accounting Review, 10 (1), p. 51–72.

Aisbitt, S. (2003): Disclosure and choice of accounting policies: The case of cross–border mergers, in: Accounting Forum, 27 (1), p. 4–27.

Aisbitt, S./Nobes, C. W. (2001): The true and fair view requirement in recent national implementations, in: Accounting & Business Research, 31 (2), p. 83–90.

Akerlof, G. A. (1970): The Market for 'Lemons': Quality Uncertainty and the Market Mechanism, in: Quarterly Journal of Economics, 84 (3), p. 488–500.

Albert, H. (1984): Wissenschaftstheorie, in: Grochla, E./Wittmann, W. (eds.): Handwörterbuch der Betriebswirtschaft, Stuttgart (1984), p. 4674–4692.

Aledo, J./Garcìa-Martìnez, F./Diazaraque, J. M. M. (2009): Firm-specific factors influencing the selection of accounting options provided by the IFRS – Empirical evidence from Spanish market, Banco de España working paper series, Madrid, available at: http://ideas.repec.org, last revised 01.03.2011.

Alexander, D./Archer, S. (2000): On the Myth of "Anglo-Saxon" Financial Accounting, in: The International Journal of Accounting, 35 (4), p. 539–557.

Alexander, D./Eberhartinger, E. (2010): The European Union Endorsement Process for International Financial Reporting Standards: A Telos-Based Analysis, in: Accounting in Europe, 7 (1), p. 37–62.

Alford, A. (1993): The Relative Informativeness of Accounting Disclosures in Different Countries, in: Journal of Accounting Research, 31 (Supplement), p. 183–223.

Ali, A./Hwang, L.-S. (2000): Country-Specific Factors Related to Financial Reporting and the Value Relevance of Accounting Data, in: Journal of Accounting Research, 38 (1), p. 1–21.

Al-Laham, A. (1997): Strategieprozesse in deutschen Unternehmungen – Verlauf, Struktur und Effizienz, Wiesbaden.

Alsaeed, K. (2005): The Association Between Firm-Specific Characteristics and Disclosure: The Case of Saudi Arabia, in: Journal of American Academy of Business, 7 (1), p. 310–321.

Alvarez, M./Fink, C. (2003): Qualität der Segmentberichterstattung in Deutschland, in: KoR, 3 (4), p. 275–288.

Amat, O./Blake, J./Wraith, P./Oliveras Sobrevias, E. (1999): Dimensions of National Culture and the Accounting Environment - The Spanish Case, available at: http://ssrn.com, last revised 01.03.2011.

American Institute of Certified Public Accountants [AICPA] (1964): Professional Accounting in 25 Countries.

American Institute of Certified Public Accountants [AICPA] (1975): Professional Accounting in 30 Countries.

American Institute of Certified Public Accountants [AICPA] (2010): SEC Releases Update on IFRS Plan, available at: http://www.journalofaccountancy.com, last revised 01.03.2011.

Amir, E./Harris, T. S./Venuti, E. K. (1993): A Comparison of the Value-Relevance of U.S. versus Non-U.S. GAAP Accounting Measures Using Form 20-F Reconciliations, in: Journal of Accounting Research, 31 (3), p. 230–264.

Ampofo, A. A./Sellani, R. J. (2005): Examining the differences between United States Generally Accepted Accounting Principles (U.S. GAAP) and International Accounting Standards (IAS): implications for the harmonization of accounting standards, in: Accounting Forum, 29 (2), p. 219–231.

Anderson, D. R. (2009): Statistics for business and economics, London.

Anderson, J. C./Gerbing, D. W. (1991): Predicting the Performance of Measures in a Confirmatory Factor Analysis With a Pretest Assessment of Their Substantive Validities, in: Journal of Applied Psychology, 76 (5), p. 732–740.

Arbeitskreis "Immaterielle Werte im Rechnungswesen" der Schmalenbach-Gesellschaft für Betriebswirtschaft e.V. (2009): Immaterielle Werte im Rahmen der Purchase Price Allocation bei Unternehmenszusammenschlüssen nach IFRS - Ein Beitrag zur Best Practice, in: ZfbF, 61 (special issue).

Archambault, J. J./Archambault, M. E. (2003): A multinational test of determinants of corporate disclosure, in: The International Journal of Accounting, 38 (2), p. 173–194.

Archer, S./Delvaille, P./McLeay, S. (1995): The Measurement of Harmonisation and the Comparability of Financial Statement Items: Within-Country and Between-Country Effects, in: Accounting & Business Research, 25 (98), p. 67–80.

Armour, J./Deakin, S./Sarkar, P./Siems, M./Singh, A. (2009): Shareholder Protection and Stock Market Development: An Empirical Test of the Legal Origins Hypothesis, in: Journal of Empirical Legal Studies, 6 (2), p. 343–380.

Armstrong, C. S./Barth, M. E./Jagolinzer, A. D./Riedl, E. J. (2008): Market Reaction to the Adoption of IFRS in Europe, available at: http://ssrn.com, last revised 01.03.2011.

Arnold, D./Bernardi, R./Neidermeyer, P./Schmee, J. (2007): The Effect of Country and Culture on Perceptions of Appropriate Ethical Actions Prescribed by Codes of Conduct: A Western European Perspective among Accountants, in: Journal of Business Ethics, 70 (4), p. 327–340.

Arrow, K. J. (1991): The economics of agency, in: Pratt, J. W./Zeckhauser, R. J. (eds.): Principals and agents. The structure of business, Boston, Mass. (1991), p. 37–54.

Ashbaugh, H. (2001): Non-US Firms' Accounting Standard Choices, in: Journal of Accounting and Public Policy, 20 (2), p. 129–153.

Ashbaugh, H./Olsson, P. (2002): An Exploratory Study of the Valuation Properties of Cross-Listed Firms' IAS and U.S. GAAP Earnings and Book Values, in: The Accounting Review, 77 (1), p. 107–126.

Ashbaugh, H./Pincus, M. (2001): Domestic Accounting Standards, International Accounting Standards, and the Predictability of Earnings, in: Journal of Accounting Research, 39 (3), p. 417–434.

Assenmacher, W. (2002): Einführung in die Ökonometrie, München.

Atteslander, P. (2008): Methoden der empirischen Sozialforschung, Berlin.

Auer, K. V. (1996): Capital market reactions to earnings announcements: empirical evidence on the difference in the information content of IAS-based earnings and EC-Directives-based earnings, in: European Accounting Review, 5 (4), p. 587–623.

Auerbach, C. M. (2009): Fusionen deutscher Kreditinstitute. Erfolg und Erfolgsfaktoren am Beispiel von Sparkassen und Kreditgenossenschaften, Wiesbaden.

Austen-Smith, D./Wright, J. R. (1996): Theory and Evidence for Counteractive Lobbying, in: American Journal of Political Science, 40 (2), p. 543–564.

Autorité des Normes Comptables [ANC] (2011): Missions and organization, available at: http://www.anc.gouv.fr, last revised 01.03.2011.

Bachert, K./Kajüter, P. (2010): Fair Value Accounting and Financial Analysts' Forecast Accuracy: Empirical Evidence from Seven European Countries, Paper presented at the 33st Annual Congress of the European Accounting Association, Istanbul.

Backhaus, K./Erichson, B./Plinke, W./Weiber, R. (2011): Multivariate Analysemethoden – Eine anwendungsorientierte Einführung, Berlin.

Baetge, J. (2009): Verwendung von DCF-Kalkülen bei der Bilanzierung nach IFRS, in: WPg, 62 (1), p. 3–23.

Ball, R. (2006): International Financial Reporting Standards (IFRS): pros and cons for investors, in: Accounting & Business Research, 36 (special issue), p. 5–27.

Ball, R./Brown, P. (1968): An Empirical Evaluation of Accounting Income Numbers, in: Journal of Accounting Research, 6 (2), p. 159–178.

Ball, R./Kothari, S./Robin, A. (2000): The effect of international institutional factors on properties of accounting earnings, in: Journal of Accounting and Economics, 29 (1), p. 1–51.

Ball, R./Leuz, C. (2001): Infrastructure requirements for an economically efficient system of public financial reporting and disclosure, in: Litan, R. E./Herring, R. (eds.): Brookings-Wharton Papers on Financial Services, Washington DC (2001), p. 127–169.

Ball, R./Robin, A./Sadka, G. (2008): Is financial reporting shaped by equity markets or by debt markets? An international study of timeliness and conservatism, in: Review of Accounting Studies, 13 (2), p. 168–205.

Ball, R./Shivakumar, L. (2005): Earnings quality in UK private firms: comparative loss recognition timeliness, in: Journal of Accounting and Economics, 39 (1), p. 83–128.

Ballas, A. A./Tzovas, C. (2010): An empirical investigation of Greek firms' compliance to IFRS disclosure requirements, in: International Journal of Managerial and Financial Accounting, 2 (1), p. 40–62.

Ballwieser, W. (2001): Germany - Individual Accounts, in: Ordelheide, D./KPMG (eds.): Transnational accounting, Basingstoke (2001), p. 1217–1352.

Bankhofer, U./Vogel, J. (2008): Datenanalyse und Statistik, Wiesbaden.

Bartel, R. (1990): Charakteristik, Methodik und wissenschaftsmethodische Probleme der Wirtschaftswissenschaften, in: Wirtschaftswissenschaftliches Studium, 19 (2), p. 54–59.

Barth, D. (2009): Prognoseberichterstattung – Praxis, Determinanten und Kapitalmarktwirkungen bei deutschen börsennotierten Unternehmen, Frankfurt am Main.

Barth, K. (1953): Die Entwicklung des deutschen Bilanzrechts und der auf ihm beruhenden Bilanzauffassungen, handelsrechtlich und steuerrechtlich, Stuttgart.

Barth, M. E./Clinch, G. (1996): International Accounting Differences and Their Relation to Share Prices: Evidence from U.K., Australian, and Canadian Firms, in: Contemporary Accounting Research, 13 (1), p. 135–171.

Barth, M. E./Landsman, W. R./Lang, M. H. (2008): International Accounting Standards and Accounting Quality, in: Journal of Accounting Research, 46 (3), p. 467–498.

Bartov, E./Bodnar, G. M. (1996): Alternative Accounting Methods, Information Asymmetry and Liquidity: Theory and Evidence, in: The Accounting Review, 71 (3), p. 397–418.

Bartov, E./Goldberg, S. R./Kim, M. (2010): Comparative Value Relevance Among German, U.S. And International Accounting Standards: A German Stock Market Perspective, available at: http://papers.ssrn.com, last revised 01.03.2011.

Baskerville, R. F. (2003): Hofstede never studied culture, in: Accounting, Organizations and Society, 28 (1), p. 1–14.

Baskerville-Morley, R. F. (2005): A research note: the unfinished business of culture, in: Accounting, Organizations and Society, 30 (4), p. 389–391.

Basu, S. (1997): The conservatism principle and the asymmetric timeliness of earnings – Properties of Accounting Earnings, in: Journal of Accounting and Economics, 24 (1), p. 3–37.

Batanic, B./Reips, U. D./Bosnjak, M. (2002): Online Social Sciences, Seattle.

Bauer, T. K./Fertig, M./Schmidt, C. M. (2009): Empirische Wirtschaftsforschung – Eine Einführung, Berlin.

Baydoun, N./Willett, R. (1995): Cultural Relevance of Western Accounting Systems to Developing Countries, in: Abacus, 31 (1), p. 67–92.

Beattie, V./McInnes, B./Fearnley, S. (2004): A methodology for analysing and evaluating narratives in annual reports: a comprehensive descriptive profile and metrics for disclosure quality attributes – Corporate financial communication and voluntary disclosure, in: Accounting Forum, 28 (3), p. 205–236.

Beaver, W. H. (1968): The information content of annual earnings announcements, in: Journal of Accounting Research, 6 (3), p. 67–102.

Beaver, W. H./Ryan, S. G. (2000): Biases and Lags in Book Value and Their Effects on the Ability of the Book-to-Market Ratio to Predict Book Return on Equity, in: Journal of Accounting Research, 38 (1), p. 127–148.

Beaver, W. H./Ryan, S. G. (2005): Conditional and Unconditional Conservatism:Concepts and Modeling, in: Review of Accounting Studies, 10 (2), p. 269–309.

Beck, T./Demirgüç-Kunt, A./Levine, R. (2003): Law and finance: why does legal origin matter?, in: Journal of Comparative Economics, 31 (4), p. 653–675.

Behrens, G. (1993): Wissenschaftstheorie und Betriebswirtschaftslehre, in: Wittmann, W./Kern, W./Köhler, R./Küpper, H.-U./Wysocki, K. v. (eds.): Handbuch der Betriebswirtschaft, Stuttgart (1993), p. 4763–4772.

Belkaoui, A. (1983): Economic, political, and civil indicators and reporting and disclosure adequacy: Empirical investigation, in: Journal of Accounting and Public Policy, 2 (3), p. 207–219.

Belkaoui, A. (1985): Accounting theory, Orlando, Florida.

Berelson, B. (1971): Content analysis in communication research, New York.

Berelson, B. R. (1952): Content analysis in communication research, New York.

Berger, A. (2008): Die IFRS als prinzipienbasiertes Normenwerk – Wie viel Prinzipienorientierung ist aus Sicht einer Enforcementeinrichtung verträglich?, in: Bruns, H.-G./Herz, R. H./Neubürger, H.-J./Tweedie, D. (eds.): Globale Finanzberichterstattung. Entwicklung, Anwendung und Durchsetzung von IFRS, Stuttgart (2008), p. 489–514.

Berger, A. (2009): Herausforderungen an das externe Rechnungswesen – Zur Entwicklung und zum Stand des Enforcements in der Europäischen Union, in: Betriebswirtschaftliche Forschung und Praxis, 61 (6), p. 599–621.

Berger, A. (2010): The Development and Status of Enforcement in the European Union, in: Accounting in Europe, 7 (1), p. 15–35.

Bergström, C. F. (2005): Comitology. Delegation of Powers in the European Union and the Committee System, Oxford.

Bhimani, A. (1999): Mapping methodological frontiers in cross-national management control research, in: Accounting, Organizations and Society, 24 (5-6), p. 413–440.

Bhimani, A. (2005): International comparative management accounting, in: Garrett, I./Cooper, C. L./Argyris, C./Starbuck, W. H. (eds.): The Blackwell encyclopedia of management, Malden, Mass. (2005), p. 250–255.

Biddle, G. C./Saudagaran, S. M. (1989): The Effects of Financial Disclosure Levels on Firms' Choices among Alternative Foreign Stock Exchange Listings, in: Journal of International Financial Management & Accounting, 1 (1), p. 55–87.

Bieg, H./Bofinger, P./Küting, K./Kußmaul, H./Waschbusch, G./Weber, C. P. (2008): Die Saarbrücker Initiative gegen den Fair Value, in: Der Betrieb, 61 (47), p. 2549–2552.

Biomérieux (2010): Reference Document and Financial Annual Report 2009, available at: http://www.biomerieux.com, last revised 01.03.2011.

Boehnke, K./Dettenborn, H./Horstmann, K./Schwartz, S. (1994): Value priorities in the United Germany: Teachers and students from East and West compared, in: European Journal of Psychology of Education, 9 (3), p. 191–202.

Böhler, H. (2004): Marktforschung, Stuttgart.

Boone, J. P./Khurana, I. K./Raman, K. K. (2010): Do the Big 4 and the Second-tier firms provide audits of similar quality?, in: Journal of Accounting and Public Policy, 29 (4), p. 330–352.

Borchardt, A./Göthlich, S. E. (2009): Erkenntnissgewinnung durch Fallstudien, in: Albers, S./Klapper, D./Konradt, U./Walter, A./Wolf, J. (eds.): Methodik der empirischen Forschung, Wiesbaden (2009), p. 33–48.

Bortz, J./Döring, N. (2006): Forschungsmethoden und Evaluation: für Human- und Sozialwissenschaftler, Heidelberg.

Botosan, C. A./Harris, M. S. (2000): Motivations for a Change in Disclosure Frequency and Its Consequences: An Examination of Voluntary Quarterly Segment Disclosures, in: Journal of Accounting Research, 38 (2), p. 329–353.

Botosan, C. A./Plumlee, M. A./Xie, Y. (2004): The Role of Information Precision in Determining the Cost of Equity Capital, in: Review of Accounting Studies, 9 (2), p. 233–259.

Botosan, C. A./Stanford, M. (2005): Managers' Motives to Withhold Segment Disclosures and the Effect of SFAS No. 131 on Analysts' Information Environment, in: The Accounting Review, 80 (3), p. 751–772.

Boubakri, N./Cosset, J.-C. (1998): The Financial and Operating Performance of Newly Privatized Firms: Evidence from Developing Countries, in: The Journal of Finance, 53 (3), p. 1081–1110.

Braun, R. (2009): Die Neuregelung des Firmenwertes nach International Financial Reporting Standards, München.

Breid, V. (1995): Aussagefähigkeit agencytheoretischer Ansätze im Hinblick auf die Verhaltenssteuerung von Entscheidungsträgern, in: ZfbF, 47 (9), p. 821–854.

Brewer, P./Venaik, S. (2010): GLOBE practices and values: A case of diminishing marginal utility[quest], in: Journal of International Business Studies, 41 (8), p. 1316–1324.

Brigham, E. F./Ehrhardt, M. C. (2008): Financial management – Theory and practice, Mason, Ohio.

Brose, P. (1984): Konzeption, Varianten und Prespektiven der Kontingenztheorie, in: Journal für Betriebswirtschaft, 5 , p. 230–243.

Brosius, F. (2004): SPSS 12, Bonn.

Brown, P./Tarca, A. (2001): Politics, Processes and the Future of Australian Accounting Standards, in: Abacus, 37 (3), p. 267–296.

Brown, P./Tarca, A. (2005): A commentary on issues relating to the enforcement of International Financial Reporting Standards in the EU, in: European Accounting Review, 14 (1), p. 181–212.

Brown, P./Tarca, A. (2007): Achieving High Quality, Comparable Financial Reporting: A Review of Independent Enforcement Bodies in Australia and the United Kingdom, in: Abacus, 43 (4), p. 438–473.

Brown, W. B./Moberg, D. J. (1980): Organization theory and management – A macro approach, New York, NY.

Buchheim, R. (2009): Exposure Draft Management Commentary des IASB – Neues zum Lagebericht aus London?, in: Betriebs-Berater, 64 (32), p. 1685–1687.

Buchheim, R./Knorr, L./Schmidt, M. (2008): Anwendung der IFRS in Europa: Die Auswirkungen des neuen Endorsement-Verfahrens auf die Rechnungslegung, in: KoR, 8 (6), p. 373–379.

Buchheim, R./Gröner, S./Kühne, M. (2004): Übernahme von IAS/IFRS in Europa : Ablauf und Wirkung des Komitologieverfahrens auf die Rechnungslegung, in: Betriebs-Berater, 33 (33), p. 1783–1788.

Bundesministerium der Justiz [BMJ] (2009): Wesentliche Änderungen des Bilanzrechtsmodernisierungsgesetzes im Überblick, available at: http://www.bmj.bund.de, last revised 01.03.2011.

Burgstahler, D./Hail, L./Leuz, C. (2006): The Importance of Reporting Incentives: Earnings Management in European Private and Public Firms, in: The Accounting Review, 81 (5), p. 983–1016.

Burns, T./Stalker, G. M. (1961): The Management of Innovation, London.

Buschan, G. (1895): Vorgeschichtliche Botanik der Cultur- und Nutzpflanzen der alten Welt auf Grund prähistorischer Funde, Breslau.

Busche, H. (2000): Was ist Kultur? Erster Teil: Die vier historischen Grundbedeutungen, in: Dialektik, 10 (1), p. 69–91.

Bushman, R. M./Piotroski, J. D. (2006): Financial reporting incentives for conservative accounting: The influence of legal and political institutions – Conference Issue on Implications of Changing Financial Reporting Standards, in: Journal of Accounting and Economics, 42 (1-2), p. 107–148.

Busse von Colbe, W. (1996): The state of the art in German accounting, in: Walton, P. (ed.): Country studies in international accounting. Europe, Cheltenham (1996), p. 244–265.

Busse von Colbe, W./Pohlmann, P. (1981): Comtemporary issues in financial accounting – A European review, in: Choi, F. D. S. (ed.): Multinational accounting. A research framework for the eighties, Ann Arbor, Mich. (1981), p. 175–188.

Buzby, S. L. (1974): Selected items of information and their disclosure in annual reports, in: Accounting Review, 49 (3).

Buzby, S. L. (1975): Company Size, Listed Versus Unlisted Stocks, and the Extent of Financial Disclosure, in: Journal of Accounting Research, 13 (1), p. 16–37.

Cable, J. (1985): Capital market information and industrial performance: The role of West German banks, in: Economic Journal, 95 (377), p. 118–133.

Camfferman, K./Cooke, T. E. (2002): An Analysis of Disclosure in the Annual Reports of U.K. and Dutch Companies, in: Journal of International Accounting Research, 1 (1), p. 3–30.

Canibano, L./Mora, A. (2000): Evaluating the statistical significance of de facto accounting harmonization: a study of European global players, in: European Accounting Review, 9 (3), p. 349–369.

Carcello, J. V./Nagy, A. L. (2004): Audit Firm Tenure and Fraudulent Financial Reporting, in: Auditing, 23 (2), p. 57–71.

Carlin, T. M./Finch, N./Ford, G. (2007): An Examination of Disclosure Quality of Goodwill Impairment Testing in a Post-IFRS Environment - A Stakeholder Perspective, available at: SSRN: http://ssrn.com, last revised 01.03.2011.

Carlisle, H. M. (1973): Situational management: a contingency approch to leadership, New York.

Carmona, S./Trombetta, M. (2008): On the global acceptance of IAS/IFRS accounting standards: The logic and implications of the principles-based system – International Financial Reporting Standards, in: Journal of Accounting and Public Policy, 27 (6), p. 455–461.

Carnegie, G. D./Napier, C. J. (2002): Exploring comparative international accounting history, in: Accounting, Auditing & Accountability Journal, 15 (5), p. 689–718.

Chakrabarti, R./Gupta-Mukherjee, S./Jayaraman, N. (2008): Mars-Venus marriages: Culture and cross-border M&A, in: Journal of International Business Studies, 40 (2), p. 216–236.

Chaloner, K./Brant, R. (1988): A Bayesian approach to outlier detection and residual analysis, in: Biometrika, 75 (4), p. 651–659.

Chanchani, S./MacGregor, A. (1999): A Synthesis of Cultural Studies in Accounting, in: Journal of Accounting Literature, 18 , p. 1–30.

Chen, B./Feng, Y. (2001): Openness and trade policy in China: an industrial analysis, in: China Economic Review, 11 (4), p. 323–341.

Chen, J. J./Cheng, P. (2007): Corporate Governance and the Harmonisation of Chinese Accounting Practices with IFRS Practices, in: Corporate Governance: An International Review, 15 (2), p. 284–293.

Child, J. (1981): Culture, contingency and capitalism in the cross-national study of organizations, in: Research in Organizational Behavior, 3 (3), p. 303–356.

Chmielewicz, K. (1994): Forschungskonzeptionen der Wirtschaftswissenschaft, Stuttgart.

Choi, F. D. S. (1973): Financial Disclosure in Relation to the European Capital Market, in: International Journal of Accounting, 9 (1), p. 53–66.

Choi, F. D. S./Bavishi, V. B. (1982): Financial Accounting Standards: A Multinational Synthesis and Policy Framework, in: International Journal of Accounting, 18 (1), p. 159–183.

Choi, F. D. S./Levich, R. M. (1990): The Capital Market Effects of International Accounting Diversity, Homewood.

Choi, F. D. S./Meek, G. K. (2008): International accounting, Upper Saddle River, NJ.

Choi, F. D. S./Mueller, G. G. (1978): An introduction to multinational accounting, Englewood Cliffs, NJ.

Chow, C. W./Wong-Boren, A. (1987): Voluntary Financial Disclosure by Mexican Corporations, in: The Accounting Review, 62 (3), p. 533–541.

Chow, L. M.-y./Chau, G. K.-k./Gray, S. J. (1995): Accounting Reforms in China: Cultural Constraints on Implementation and Development, in: Accounting & Business Research, 26 (1), p. 29–49.

Christensen, H. B./Lee, E./Walker, M. (2007): Do IFRS/UK-GAAP Reconciliations Convey New Information?, available at: http://ssrn.com, last revised 01.03.2011.

Christensen, H. B./Nikolaev, V. (2010): Does Fair Value Accounting for Non-Financial Assets Pass the Market Test?, available at: http://papers.ssrn.com, last revised 01.03.2011.

Christensen, J. (2010): Conceptual frameworks of accounting from an information perspective, in: Accounting & Business Research, 40 (3), p. 287–299.

Christenson, C. (1983): The Methodology of Positive Accounting, in: The Accounting Review, 58 (1), p. 1–22.

Christopher Earley, P. (2006): Leading cultural research in the future: a matter of paradigms and taste, in: Journal of International Business Studies, 37 (6), p. 922–931.

Cieslewicz, J. (2010): Culture, Institutions, and National Accounting: Evaluating Gray's Cultural Framework, Paper presented at the 33st Annual Congress of the European Accounting Association, Istanbul.

Claessens, S./Klingebiel, D./Schmukler, S. L. (2006): Stock market development and internationalization: Do economic fundamentals spur both similarly?, in: Journal of Empirical Finance, 13 (3), p. 316–350.

Clark, G. L./Knight, E. R. W. (2009): Implications of the UK Companies Act 2006 for institutional investors and the market for corporate social responsability, in: University of Pennsylvania Journal of Business Law, 11 (2), p. 259–297.

Clements, C./Neill, J. D./Stovall, O. S. (2008): The Impact of Cultural Differences on the Convergence of International Accounting Codes of Ethics, available at: http://ssrn.com, last revised 01.03.2011.

Cohen, D. A. (2002): Financial Reporting Quality and Proprietary Costs, available at: http://archive.nyu.edu, last revised 01.03.2011.

Cohen, J. (2009): Applied multiple regression/correlation analysis for the behavioral sciences, Mahwah, NJ.

Cole, V./Branson, J./Breesch, D. (2010): The Illusion of Comparable European IFRS Financial Statements - The View of Auditors, Analysts and Other Users, available at: http://ssrn.com, last revised 01.03.2011.

Commission des Opérations de Bourse [COB] (1980): Rapport Annuel, Paris.

Committee of European Securities Regulators [CESR] (2003): Standard No. 1 on Financial Information: Enforcement of standards on financial information in Europe, available at: http://www.esma.europa.eu, last revised 01.03.2011.

Committee of European Securities Regulators [CESR] (2004a): Guidance for implementation of co-ordination of enforcement of financial information, available at: http://www.cesr-eu.org, last revised 01.03.2011.

Committee of European Securities Regulators [CESR] (2004b): Standard No. 2 on Financial Information: Coordination of enforcement activities, available at: http://www.esma.europa.eu, last revised 01.03.2011.

Committee of European Securities Regulators [CESR] (2007): CESR's review of the implementation and enforcement of IFRS in the EU, available at: http://www.standardsetter.de, last revised 01.03.2011.

Committee of European Securities Regulators [CESR] (2010): CESR in short, available at: http://www.cesr-eu.org, last revised 01.03.2011.

Companies House [CH] (2009): Northern Ireland Company Registry Integration, available at: http://www.companieshouse.gov.uk, last revised 01.03.2011.

Consultative Committee of Accountancy Bodies [CCAB] (1988): The making of accounting standards – Dearing Report, London.

Contact Committee on Accounting Directives [CCAD] (1990): The Accounting Harmonisation in the E. C: Problems of Applying the 4th Directive on the Annual Accounts of Limited Companies, Luxembourg.

Cooke, T. E. (1989): Voluntary Corporate Disclosure by Swedish Companies, in: Journal of International Financial Management & Accounting, 1 (2), p. 171–195.

Cooke, T. E. (1991): An Assessment of Voluntary Disclosure in the Annual Reports of Japanese Corporations, in: The International Journal of Accounting, 26 (3), p. 174–189.

Cooke, T. E. (1992): The impact of size, stock market listing and industry type on disclosure in the annual reports of Japanese listed corporations, in: Accounting & Business Research, 22 (87), p. 229–237.

Cooke, T. E. (1993): The Impact of Accounting Principles on Profits: The US versus Japan, in: Accounting & Business Research, 23 (92), p. 460–476.

Cooke, T. E. (1998): Regression Analysis in Accounting Disclosure Studies, in: Accounting & Business Research, 28 (3), p. 209–224.

Cooke, T. E./Wallace, R. (1995): United Kingdom - Individual Accounts, in: Ordelheide, D./KPMG (eds.): Transnational Accounting, Basingstoke (1995), p. 2627–2800.

Cooke, T. E./Wallace, R. (1990): Financial disclosure regulation and its environment: A review and further analysis, in: Journal of Accounting and Public Policy, 9 (2), p. 79–110.

Core, J. E./Guay, W. R. (2001): Stock option plans for non-executive employees, in: Journal of Financial Economics, 61 (2), p. 253–287.

Courtis, J. K. (1992): The Reliability of Perception-Based Annual Report Disclosure Studies, in: Accounting & Business Research, 23 (89), p. 31–43.

Coy, D./Dixon, K. (2004): The public accountability index: crafting a parametric disclosure index for annual reports, in: The British Accounting Review, 36 (1), p. 79–106.

Craig, R./Diga, J. (1998): Corporate Accounting Disclosure in ASEAN, in: Journal of International Financial Management & Accounting, 9 (3), p. 246–274.

Cranach, M./Frenz, H. G. (1969): Systematische Beobachtung, in: Graumann, C. F. (ed.): Handbuch der Psychologie: Sozialpsychologie (1969), p. 269–330.

Craswell, A. T./Taylor, S. L. (1992): Discretionary disclosure of reserves by oil and gas companies: an economic analysis, in: Journal of Business Finance & Accounting, 19 (2), p. 295–308.

Cray, D./Mallory, G. (1998): Making sense of managing culture, London.

Cuijpers, R./Buijink, W. (2005): Voluntary Adoption of Non-Local GAAP in the European Union: A Study of Determinants and Consequences, in: European Accounting Review, 14 (3), p. 487–524.

Dahl, S. (2004): Intercultural Research: The Current State of Knowledge, available at: http://ssrn.com, last revised 01.03.2011.

D'Arcy, A. (2001): Accounting classification and the international harmonisation debate – An empirical investigation, in: Accounting, Organizations and Society, 26 (4-5), p. 327–349.

Dargenidou, C./McLeay, S./Raonic, I. (2006): Expected earnings growth and the cost of capital: an analysis of accounting regime change in the European financial market, in: Abacus, 42 (3/4), p. 388–414.

Daske, H. (2006): Economic Benefits of Adopting IFRS or US-GAAP – Have the Expected Costs of Equity Capital Really Decreased?, in: Journal of Business Finance & Accounting, 33 (3/4), p. 329–373.

Davidson, R. A./Chrisman, H. H. (1993): Interlinguistic Comparison of International Accounting Standards: The Case of Uncertainty Expressions, in: International Journal of Accounting, 28 (1), p. 1–17.

Davison, M. L./Sharma, A. R. (1990): Parametric statistics and levels of measurement: Factorial designs and multiple regression, in: Psychological Bulletin, 107 (3), p. 394–400.

Dawo, S. (2003): Immaterielle Güter in der Rechnungslegung nach HGB, IAS/IFRS und US-GAAP, Herne.

DeAngelo, L. E. (1988): Managerial competition, information costs and corporate governance – The use of accounting performance measures in proxy contests, in: Journal of Accounting and Economics, 10 (1), p. 3–36.

Deegan, C./Unerman, J. (2006): Financial accounting theory, Maidenhead.

DeFond, M. L./Subramanyam, K. R. (1998): Auditor changes and discretionary accruals, in: Journal of Accounting and Economics, 25 (1), p. 35–67.

Delger, A./Committee of European Securities Regulators [CESR] (2008): IASCF-Foundation. IFRS Conference, Amsterdam. CESR-Fin. Current activities, available at: www.iasb.org, last revised 01.03.2011.

Deloitte Touche Tohmatsu (2009): Deloitte reports global revenue of US$ 26.1 billion for fiscal 2009, available at: http://www.deloitte.com, last revised 01.03.2011.

Deloitte Touche Tohmatsu (2010): Use of IFRSs by Jurisdiction, available at: http://www.iasplus.de, last revised 01.03.2011.

Delucchi, K. L./Bostrom, A. (2004): Methods for Analysis of Skewed Data Distributions in Psychiatric Clinical Studies: Working With Many Zero Values, in: American Journal of Psychiatry, 161 (7), p. 1159–1168.

Demaria, S./Dufour, D. (2007): First time adoption of IFRS, fair value option, conservatism – Evidences from French listed companies, Paper presented at the 30st Annual Congress of the European Accounting Association, Lisbon.

Dempsey, S. J. (1989): Predisclosure Information Search Incentives, Analyst Following, and Earnings Announcement Price Response, in: The Accounting Review, 64 (4), p. 748–757.

Den Hartog, D. N./House, R. J./Hanges, P. J./Ruiz-Quintanilla, S. A./Dorfman, P. W. (1999): Culture specific and cross-culturally generalizable implicit leadership theories: Are attributes of charismatic/transformational leadership universally endorsed?, in: The Leadership Quarterly, 10 (2), p. 219–256.

Department for Business Innovation & Skills [BIS] (2010): Evaluation of the Companies Act 2006, Executive Summary, available at: http://www.bis.gov.uk, last revised 01.03.2011.

Deutsches Rechnungslegungs Standards Committee [DRSC] (2011a): Organisation und Ziele des DRSC, available at: http://www.standardsetter.de, last revised 01.03.2011.

Deutsches Rechnungslegungs Standards Committee [DRSC] (2011b): Welchen Rechtscharakter haben Deutsche Rechnungslegungs Standards, die vom Bundesministerium der Justiz bekannt gemacht werden?, available at: http://www.standardsetter.de, last revised 01.03.2011.

Devalle, A./Onali, E./Magarini, R. (2010): Assessing the Value Relevance of Accounting Data After the Introduction of IFRS in Europe, in: Journal of International Financial Management & Accounting, 21 (2), p. 85–119.

Dewing, I. P./Russell, P. O. (2004): Regulation of UK Corporate Governance: lessons from accounting, audit and financial services, in: Corporate Governance: An International Review, 12 (1), p. 107–115.

Dhaliwal, D. S. (1981): Improving the Quality of Corporate Financial Disclosure, in: Accounting & Business Research, 10 (40), p. 385–391.

Diaconu, P. (2007): Impact of Globalization on International Accounting Harmonization, available at: http://ssrn.com, last revised 01.03.2011.

Diamond, D. W./Verrecchia, R. E. (1991): Disclosure, Liquidity, and the Cost of Capital, in: The Journal of Finance, 46 (4), p. 1325–1359.

Diekmann, A. (2007): Empirische Sozialforschung : Grundlagen, Methoden, Anwendungen, Reinbek bei Hamburg.

Dietsche, M./Fink, C. (2008): Die Qualität der Lageberichterstattung in Deutschland – Empirische Analyse der Unternehmen des HDAX, in: KoR, 8 (4), p. 250–261.

Ditting, C. (2005): Aufstellung und Prüfung des IFRS-Einzelabschlusses nach dem BilReG, in: Freidank, C.-C. (ed.): Bilanzreform und Bilanzdelikte, Wiesbaden (2005), p. 101–119.

Döllerer, G. (1983): Handelsbilanz ist gleich Steuerbilanz, in: Baetge, J. (ed.): Der Jahresabschluss im Widerstreit der Interessen, Düsseldorf (1983), p. 157–177.

Donaldson, L. (1987): Strategy and structural adjustment to regain fit and performance: in defence of contingency, in: Journal of Management Studies, 24 (1), p. 1–24.

Donaldson, L. (1996): The Normal Science of Structural Contingency Theory, in: Clegg, S./Hardy, C./Nord, W. R. (eds.): Handbook of organization studies, Thousand Oaks (1996), p. 57–77.

Donaldson, L. (2001): The contingency theory of organizations, Thousand Oaks, Calif.

Dorfman, P. W./Howell, J. P./Farmer, R. N./McGoun/E.G. (1988): Dimensions of national culture and effective leadership patterns: Hofstede revisited, in: Advances in international comparative management, 3 (1), p. 127–150.

Doupnik, T. S. (1987): Evidence of International Harmonization of Financial Reporting, in: International Journal of Accounting, 23 (1), p. 47–68.

Doupnik, T. S./Riccio, E. L. (2006): The influence of conservatism and secrecy on the interpretation of verbal probability expressions in the Anglo and Latin cultural areas, in: The International Journal of Accounting, 41 (3), p. 237–261.

Doupnik, T. S./Richter, M. (2003): Interpretation of uncertainty expressions: a cross-national study, in: Accounting, Organizations and Society, 28 (1), p. 15–36.

Doupnik, T. S./Richter, M. (2004): The Impact of Culture on the Interpretation of "In Context" Verbal Probability Expressions, in: Journal of International Accounting Research, 3 (1), p. 1–20.

Doupnik, T. S./Salter, S. B. (1993): An empirical test of a judgmental international classification of financial reporting practices, in: Journal of International Business Studies, 24 (1), p. 41–60.

Doupnik, T. S./Salter, S. B. (1995): External Environment, Culture, and Accounting Practice - A Preliminary Test of A General Model of International Accounting Development, in: The International Journal of Accounting, 30 (3), p. 189–207.

Doupnik, T. S./Tsakumis, G. T. (2004): A Critical Review of Tests of Gray's Theory of Cultural Relevance and Suggestions for Future Research, in: Journal of Accounting Literature, 23 (1), p. 1–48.

Drazin, R./van Ven, A. H. de (1985): Alternative Forms of Fit in Contingency Theory, in: Administrative Science Quarterly, 30 (4), p. 514–539.

Duke, J. C./Hunt III, H. G. (1990): An empirical examination of debt covenant restrictions and accounting-related debt proxies, in: Journal of Accounting and Economics, 12 (1-3), p. 45–63.

Dumontier, P./Raffournier, B. (1998): Why Firms Comply Voluntarily with IAS: an Empirical Analysis with Swiss Data, in: Journal of International Financial Management & Accounting, 9 (3), p. 216–245.

Dye, R. A./Sridhar, S. S. (1995): Industry-Wide Disclosure Dynamics, in: Journal of Accounting Research, 33 (1), p. 157–174.

Easley, D./O'Hara, M. (2004): Information and the Cost of Capital, in: The Journal of Finance, 59 (4), p. 1553–1583.

Eberhartinger, E. L. E. (1999): The Impact of Tax Rules on Financial Reporting in Germany, France, and the UK, in: The International Journal of Accounting, 34 (1), p. 93–119.

Eccles, T./Holt, A. (2005): Financial statements and corporate accounts: the conceptual framework, in: Property Management, 23 (5), p. 374–387.

Eckey, H.-F./Kosfeld, R./Rengers, M. (2002): Multivariate Statistik – Grundlagen, Methoden, Beispiele, Wiesbaden.

Eckey, H.-F./Kosfeld, R./Türck, M. (2008): Deskriptive Statistik – Grundlagen - Methoden - Beispiele, Wiesbaden.

Eckstein, P. P. (2008): Angewandte Statistik mit SPSS, Wiesbaden.

Eddie, I. A. (1990): Asia Pacific cultural values and accounting systems, in: Asia Pacific International Management Forum, 16 (1), p. 22–30.

Eiselt, A./Pleitner, C. (2010): Enforcement der Rechnungslegung in Deutschland, Frankreich und Großbritannien. eine vergleichende Betrachtung länderspezifischer Enforcement-Systeme, in: ZCG, 5 (6), p. 302–308.

El-Gazzar, S. M./Finn, P. M./Jacob, R. (1999): An empirical investigation of multinational firms' compliance with international accounting standards, in: The International Journal of Accounting, 34 (2), p. 239–248.

Emenyonu, E. N./Gray, S. J. (1992): EC Accounting Harmonisation: An Empirical Study of Measurement Practices in France, Germany and the UK, in: Accounting & Business Research, 23 (89), p. 49–58.

Enevoldsen, S./Oversberg, T. (2008): Importance of a European voice in international standard setting - the role of EFRAG, in: Bruns, H.-G./Herz, R. H./Neubürger, H.-J./Tweedie, D. (eds.): Globale Finanzberichterstattung. Entwicklung, Anwendung und Durchsetzung von IFRS, Stuttgart (2008), p. 89–106.

Erchinger, H./Melcher, W. (2007): Neuregelung der SEC zu IFRS-Abschlüssen von Foreign Private Issuers, in: Der Betrieb, 60 (48), p. 2635–2636.

Erchinger, H./Melcher, W. (2008): Neuerungen bei der Berichterstattung für Unternehmen, die den US-Kapitalmarkt in Anspruch nehmen, in: Der Betrieb, 61 (42), p. 2292–2295.

Erlei, M./Leschke, M./Sauerland, D. (2007): Neue Institutionenökonomik, Stuttgart.

Ernst, C./Seidler, H. (2008): Handelsrechtliche Rechnungslegung vor dem Hintergrund internationaler Entwicklungen – Weiterentwicklung und friedliche Koexistenz oder Auslaufmodell?, in: Bruns, H.-G./Herz, R. H./Neubürger, H.-J./Tweedie, D. (eds.): Globale Finanzberichterstattung. Entwicklung, Anwendung und Durchsetzung von IFRS, Stuttgart (2008), p. 107–127.

Ernst & Young (2006): IFRS – Observations on the implementation of IFRS, London.

Ernst & Young (2009): Ernst & Young reports fiscal year 2009 global revenues of US$21.4 billion, available at: http://www.ey.com, last revised 01.03.2011.

Ernstberger, J./Hitz, J.-M./Stich, M. (2011): Enforcement of Accounting Standards in Europe: Empirical Evidence for the Two-Tier Mechanism in Germany, available at: http://ssrn.com, last revised 01.03.2011.

Ernstberger, J./Stich, M./Vogler, O. (2008): Economic Consequences of the German Reforms on the Enforcement of IFRS, available at: http://ssrn.com, last revised 01.03.2011.

Esser, S. (2010): Produktorientiertes Kostenmanagement in der chemischen Industrie, Frankfurt am Main.

European Commission [EC] (1978): Fourth Council Directive 78/660/EEC of 25 July 1978 based on Article 54 (3) (g) of the Treaty on the annual accounts of certain types of companies, in: Official Journal of the European Communities (L 222), p. 11–31.

European Commission [EC] (1983): Seventh Council Directive 83/349/EEC of 13 June 1983 based on the Article 54 (3) (g) of the Treaty on consolidated accounts, in: Official Journal of the European Communities (L 193), p. 1–17.

European Commission [EC] (1984): Eighth Council Directive 84/253/EEC of 10 April 1984 based on Article 54 (3) (g) of the Treaty on the approval of persons responsible for carrying out the statutory audits of accounting documents, in: Official Journal of the European Communities (L 126), p. 20–26.

European Commission [EC] (1989): Eleventh Council Directive 89/666/EEC of 21 December 1989 concerning disclosure requirements in respect of branches opened in a Member State by certain types of company governed by the law of another State, in: Official Journal of the European Communities (L 395), p. 36–39.

European Commission [EC] (1995): Accounting harmonization: a new strategy vis-á-vis international harmonization, available at: http://ec.europa.eu, last revised 01.03.2011.

European Commission [EC] (1998): Financial services: building a framework for action, available at: http://ec.europa.eu, last revised 01.03.2011.

European Commission [EC] (1999): Examination of the conformity between International Financial Accounting Standards and the European Accounting Directives, available at: http://ec.europa.eu, last revised 01.03.2011.

European Commission [EC] (2000): EU financial reporting strategy: the way forward, available at: http://eur-lex.europa.eu, last revised 01.03.2011.

European Commission [EC] (2001): Proposal for a regulation of the European Parliament and of the Council on the application of international accounting standards, available at: http://eur-lex.europa.eu, last revised 01.03.2011.

European Commission [EC] (2002): Regulation (EC) No 1606/2002 of the European Parliament and of the Council of 19 July 2002 on the application of international accounting standards, in: Official Journal of the European Communities (L 243), p. 1–4.

European Commission [EC] (2003): Directive 2003/51/EC of the European Parliament and of the Council of 18 June 2003 amending Directives 78/660/EEC, 83/349/EEC, 86/635/EEC and 91/674/EEC on the annual and consolidated accounts of certain types of companies, banks and other financial institutions and insurance undertakings, in: Official Journal of the European Union (L 178), p. 16–22.

European Commission [EC] (2007): Treaty of Maastricht on European Union, available at: http://europa.eu, last revised 01.03.2011.

European Commission [EC] (2008): Implementation of the IAS Regulation (1606/2002) in the EU and EEA, available at: http://ec.europa.eu, last revised 01.03.2011.

European Commission [EC] (2009): Europe in figures – Eurostat yearbook 2009, available at: http://epp.eurostat.ec.europa.eu, last revised 01.03.2011.

European Commission [EC] (2010a): EU Languages and Language policy, available at: http://ec.europa.eu, last revised 01.03.2011.

European Commission [EC] (2010b): The EU at a glance – What do we do, available at: http://europa.eu, last revised 01.03.2011.

European Financial Reporting Advisory Group [EFRAG] (2009): IFRS 9 endorsement advice postponed, available at: http://www.efrag.org, last revised 01.03.2011.

European Financial Reporting Advisory Group [EFRAG] (2010a): EFRAG facts, available at: http://www.efrag.org, last revised 01.03.2011.

European Financial Reporting Advisory Group [EFRAG] (2010b): Supervisory Board and Founding Fathers, available at: http://www.efrag.org, last revised 01.03.2011.

European Free Trade Association [EFTA]: EEA Agreement, available at: http://www.efta.int, last revised 01.03.2011.

Euwema, M. C./Wendt, H./van Emmerik, H. (2007): Leadership styles and group organizational citizenship behavior across cultures, in: Journal of Organizational Behaviour, 28 (8), p. 1035–1057.

Evans, L. (2004): Language, translation and the problem of international accounting communication, in: Accounting, Auditing & Accountability Journal, 17 (2), p. 210–248.

Evans, L./Nobes, C. W. (1996): Some mysteries relating to the prudence principle in the Fourth Directive and in German and British law, in: European Accounting Review, 5 (2), p. 361–373.

Evans, L./Nobes, C. W. (1998): Harmonization of the structure of audit firms: incorporation in the UK and Germany, in: European Accounting Review, 7 (1), p. 125–148.

Evans, T. G./Taylor, M. E. (1982): "Bottom Line Compliance" with the IASC: A Comparative Analysis, in: International Journal of Accounting, 18 (1), p. 115–129.

Fahrmeir, L./Brachinger, W. (1996): Multivariate statistische Verfahren, Berlin.

Fama, E. F./Jensen, M. C. (1983): Agency Problems and Residual Claims, in: Journal of Law and Economics, 26 (2), p. 327–349.

Fan, J. P. H./Wong, T. J. (2002): Corporate ownership structure and the informativeness of accounting earnings in East Asia, in: Journal of Accounting and Economics, 33 (3), p. 401–425.

Faulkender, M./Petersen, M. A. (2006): Does the Source of Capital Affect Capital Structure?, in: The Review of Financial Studies, 19 (1), p. 45–79.

Fédération des Experts Comptables Européens [FEE] (1989): European Survey of Published Financial Statements in the Context of the Fourth EC Directive, Brussels.

Fédération des Experts Comptables Européens [FEE] (1991): FEE European survey of published accounts - European survey of published accounts, London.

Fédération des Experts Comptables Européens [FEE] (1992): 1992 FEE Analysis of European Accounting and Disclosure Practices, London.

Fédération des Experts Comptables Européens [FEE] (2000): Discussion Paper on a Financial Reporting Strategy within Europe, in: The International Journal of Accounting, 35 (2), p. 293–294.

Fédération des Experts Comptables Européens [FEE] (2001): Enforcement mechanisms in Europe: A preliminary investigation of oversight systems, available at: http://www.fee.be, last revised 01.03.2011.

Fédération des Experts Comptables Européens [FEE] (2002): Discussion Paper on Enforcement of IFRS within Europe, available at: http://www.fee.be, last revised 01.03.2011.

Feldkämper, U. (2000): Empirische Untersuchung der Segmentberichterstattung am deutschen Kapitalmarkt, in: Der Betrieb, 56 (27/28), p. 1459–1468.

Feltham, G. (1995): Valuation and Clean Surplus Accounting for Operating and Financial Activities, in: Contemporary Accounting Research, 11 (2), p. 689–732.

Fidrmuc, J. P./Jacob, M. (2009): Culture, Agency Costs and Dividends, available at: http://ssrn.com, last revised 01.03.2011.

Financial Accounting Standards Board [FASB] (2002): Norwalk Agreement, available at: http://www.fasb.org, last revised 01.03.2011.

Financial Reporting Council [FRC] (2011): About the FRC, available at: http://www.frc.org.uk, last revised 01.03.2011.

Fink, C./Ulbrich, P. (2006): Segmentberichterstattung nach ED 8 - Operating Segments, in: KoR, 6 (4), p. 233–243.

Finnerty, J. E. (1976): Insiders and Market Efficiency, in: The Journal of Finance, 31 (4), p. 1141–1148.

Firth, M. (1979): The Impact of Size, Stock Market Listing, and Auditors on Voluntary Disclosure in Corporate Annual Reports, in: Accounting & Business Research, 9 (36), p. 273–280.

Firth, M. (1980): Raising Finance and Firms' Corporate Reporting Policies, in: Abacus, 16 (2), p. 100–115.

Fischer, A./Schneider, W. (2007): Goodwill-Bilanzierung nach IFRS 3 - Impairment-Only Approach und Full Goodwill Bilanzierung, Saarbrücken.

Fischer, T. M./Kloepfer, E. (2008): Bilanzpolitisches Gestaltungspotenzial bei der Umstellung der Rechnungslegung von HGB auf IFRS — Empirische Untersuchung deutscher börsennotierter Unternehmen, in: Zeitschrift für Bebriebswirtschaft, 78 (6), p. 623–650.

Forker, J. J. (1992): Corporate Governance and Disclosure Quality, in: Accounting & Business Research, 22 (86), p. 111–124.

Förschler, D. (2009): Auswirkungen der achten EU-Richtlinie auf die interne Revision, in: Risk, Compliance & Audit, 1 (4), p. 38–43.

Fortin, A. (1996a): French accounting thought from 1970 to 1982 as reflected in the evolution of the Plan Comptable General, in: Walton, P. (ed.): Country studies in international accounting. Europe, Cheltenham (1996), p. 65–105.

Fortin, A. (1996b): The 1947 French accounting plan: origins and influences on subsequent practice, in: Walton, P. (ed.): Country studies in international accounting. Europe, Cheltenham (1996), p. 1–25.

Foster, G. (1986): Financial statement analysis, Englewood Cliffs, NJ.

Francis, J. R. (2004): What do we know about audit quality?, in: The British Accounting Review, 36 (4), p. 345–368.

Francis, J. R./Khurana, I. K./Martin, X./Pereira, R. (2008): The Role of Firm-Specific Incentives and Country Factors in Explaining Voluntary IAS Adoptions: Evidence from Private Firms, in: European Accounting Review, 17 (2), p. 331–360.

Franke, G. R./Richey, R. G. (2010): Improving Generalizations from Multi-country Comparisons in International Business Research, in: Journal of International Business Studies, 41 (8), p. 1275–1293.

Frankel, R./Lee, C. M. C. (1998): Accounting valuation, market expectation, and cross-sectional stock returns, in: Journal of Accounting and Economics, 25 (3), p. 283–319.

Franks, J./Mayer, C. (2001): Ownership and Control of German Corporations, in: The Review of Financial Studies, 14 (4), p. 943–977.

Freisleben, N./Leibfried, P. (2004): Warum IAS/IFRS-Abschlüsse nicht (miteinander) vergleichbar sind - fehlende Detailregelungen, Auswirkungen von US-GAAP und Mangel an Kontrolle, in: KoR, 4 (3), p. 101–109.

French, K. R./Fama, E. F. (2010): Detail for 10 Industry Portfolios, available at: http://mba.tuck.dartmouth.edu, last revised 01.03.2011.

Friedman, M. (1953): The methodology of positive economics, in: Friedman, M. (ed.): Essays in positive economics, Chicago (1953), p. 3–43.

Früh, W. (2001): Inhaltsanalyse – Theorie und Praxis, Konstanz.

Fülbier, R./Gassen, J./Sellhorn, T. (2008): Vorsichtige Rechnungslegung — Theoretische Erklärung und empirische Evidenz —, in: Zeitschrift für Betriebswirtschaft, 78 (12), p. 1317–1342.

Fülbier, R. U. (2004): Wissenschaftstheorie und Betriebswirtschaftslehre, in: Wirtschaftswissenschaftliches Studium, 33 (5), p. 266–271.

Gallo, J. G./Apilado, V. P./Kolari, J. W. (1996): Commercial bank mutual fund activities: Implications for bank risk and profitability, in: Journal of Banking & Finance, 20 (10), p. 1775–1791.

García, V. F./Liu, L. (1999): Macroeconomic determinants of stock market development, in: , 2 (1), p. 29–59.

Gassen, J./Sellhorn, T. (2006): Applying IFRS in Germany: Determinants and Consequences, in: Betriebswirtschaftliche Forschung und Praxis, 58 (1), p. 365–386.

Gee, M./Haller, A./Nobes, C. (2010): The Influence of Tax on IFRS Consolidated Statements: The Convergence of Germany and the UK, in: Accounting in Europe, 7 (1), p. 97–122.

Gélard, G. (2001): France - Individual Accounts, in: Ordelheide, D./KPMG (eds.): Transnational accounting, Basingstoke (2001), p. 1009–1126.

Gelderman, M. (2000): Contingency theory and moderated regression analysis : the effect of measurement level, measurement error and non-linear relations, available at: ftp://zappa.ubvu.vu.nl, last revised 01.03.2011.

Gelhausen, H. F./Hönsch, H. (2005): Das neue Enforcement-Verfahren für Jahres- und Konzernabschlüsse. Durchsetzung fehlerfreier Rechnungslegung durch die Deutsche Prüfstelle für Rechnungslegung (DPR) und die Bundesanstalt für Finanzdienstleistungsaufsicht, in: Die Aktiengesellschaft, 50 (13-14), p. 511–529.

Gernon, H. (1993): An Investigation of the Reporting of Questionable Acts in an International Setting: Discussion, in: Journal of Accounting Research, 31 (1), p. 104–110.

Gernon, H. M./Meek, G. K. (2001): Accounting – An international perspective, Boston.

Gibson, C. H. (2007): Financial reporting & analysis – Using financial accounting information, Mason, Ohio.

Ginsberg, A./Venkatraman, N. (1985): Contingency Perspectives of Organizational Strategy: A Critical Review of the Empirical Research, in: The Academy of Management Review, 10 (3), p. 421–434.

Givoly, D./Hayn, C. (2000): The changing time-series properties of earnings, cash flows and accruals: Has financial reporting become more conservative?, in: Journal of Accounting and Economics, 29 (3), p. 287–320.

Glaum, M. (2000): Bridging the GAAP: the Changing Attitude of German Managers towards Anglo-American Accounting and Accounting Harmonization, in: Journal of International Financial Management & Accounting, 11 (1), p. 23–47.

Glaum, M./Street, D. L. (2003): Compliance with the Disclosure Requirements of Germany's New Market: IAS Versus US GAAP, in: Journal of International Financial Management and Accounting, 14 (1), p. 64–100.

Glaum, M./Street, D. L./Vogel, S. (2007): Making Acquisitions Transparent – An Evaluation of M&A-Related IFRS Disclosures by European Companies in 2005, Frankfurt a.M.

Göbel, E. (2002): Neue Institutionenökonomik – Konzeption und betriebswirtschaftliche Anwendungen, Stuttgart.

Goeltz, R. K. (1991): International Accounting Harmonization: The Impossible (and Unnecessary?) Dream, in: Accounting Horizons, 5 (1), p. 85–88.

Goldsmith, C. (1995): EU members keep loopholes open as they sign onto new regulations, in: Wall Street Journal (August 15), p. 12.

Goodstein, L. D. (1981): American business values and cultural imperialism, in: Organizational Dynamics, 10 (1), p. 49–54.

Gottwald, J.-C./Paré Valérie (2004): Frankreichs Weg zur Allfinanzaufsicht? Die Autorité des Marchés Financiers, available at: http://www.chinapolitik.de, last revised 01.03.2011.

Granger, C. W. J. (1988): Some recent development in a concept of causality, in: Journal of Econometrics, 39 (1-2), p. 199–211.

Gravetter, F. J./Wallnau, L. B. (2008): Essentials of statistics for the behavioral sciences, Pacific Grove, CA.

Gray, S. J. (1980): The Impact of International Accounting Differences from a Security-Analysis Perspective: Some European Evidence, in: Journal of Accounting Research, 18 (1), p. 64–76.

Gray, S. J. (1983): International Accounting: A Review of Academic Research in the United Kingdom, in: International Journal of Accounting, 19 (1), p. 15–43.

Gray, S. J. (1988): Towards a Theory of Cultural Influence on the Development of Accounting Influence Systems Internationally, in: Abacus, 24 (1), p. 1–15.

Gray, S. J./Vint, H. M. (1995): The impact of culture on accounting disclosures: some international evidence, in: Asia Pacific Journal of Accounting, 21 , p. 33–43.

Gray, S. J./Meek, G. K./Roberts, C. B. (1995): International Capital Market Pressures and Voluntary Annual Report Disclosures by U.S. and U.K. Multinationals, in: Journal of International Financial Management & Accounting, 6 (1), p. 43–68.

Gregoire, T. G./Driver, B. L. (1987): Analysis of ordinal data to detect population differences, in: Psychological Bulletin, 101 (1), p. 159–165.

Grochla, E. (1978): Einführung in die Organisationstheorie, Stuttgart.

Grottke, M./Krammer, S. (2008): Was bringt der management approach des IFRS 8 den Jahresabschlussadressaten? - Eine kritische Analyse, in: KoR, 8 (11), p. 670–679.

Grünberger, D. (1999): Die Rechnungslegung in Frankreich, in: SWI, 9 (12), p. 543–546.

Guay, W./Verrecchia, R. (2006): Discussion of an economic framework for conservative accounting and Bushman and Piotroski (2006) – Conference Issue on Implications of Changing Financial Reporting Standards, in: Journal of Accounting and Economics, 42 (1-2), p. 149–165.

Guenther, D. A./Young, D. (2000): The association between financial accounting measures and real economic activity: a multinational study, in: Journal of Accounting and Economics, 29 (1), p. 53–72.

Hacker, B./Dobler, M. (2000): Empirische Untersuchung der Segmentpublizität in Deutschland, in: WPg, 53 (17), p. 811–819.

Hagerman, R. L./Zmijewski, M. E. (1979): Some economic determinants of accounting policy choice, in: Journal of Accounting and Economics, 1 (2), p. 141–161.

Hail, L./Leuz, C./Wysocki, P. (2010a): Global Accounting Convergence and the Potential Adoption of IFRS by the U.S. (Part I): Conceptual Underpinnings and Economic Analysis, in: Accounting Horizons, 24 (3), p. 355–394.

Hail, L./Leuz, C./Wysocki, P. (2010b): Global Accounting Convergence and the Potential Adoption of IFRS by the U.S. (Part II): Political Factors and Future Scenarios for U.S. Accounting Standards, in: Accounting Horizons, 24 (4), p. 567–588.

Hall, E. (1966): The hidden dimension – Man's use of space in public and private, New York, NY.

Hall, E./Hall, E. T. (1976): Beyond culture, New York.

Hall, E. T. (1983): The dance of life – The other dimension of time, Garden City N.Y.

Hall, E. T./Hall, M. R. (1990): Understanding cultural differences, Yarmouth, Me.

Hall, F. L. (1989): Australians in a corporate culture: the national characteristics, are they intrinsic?, Sidney.

Haller, A. (1992): The Relationship of Financial and Tax Accounting in Germany: A Major Reason for Accounting Disharmony in Europe, in: International Journal of Accounting, 27 (4), p. 310–324.

Haller, A. (1994): Positive Accounting Theory : die Erforschung der Beweggründe bilanzpolitischen Verhaltens, in: Die Betriebswirtschaft, 54 (5), p. 597–612.

Haller, A. (2002): Financial accounting developments in the European Union: past events and future prospects, in: European Accounting Review, 11 (1), p. 153–190.

Haller, A. (2010): Die Bilanzierung von Entwicklungskosten nach IFRS bei deutschen börsennotierten Unternehmen - Eine empirische Analyse, in: Der Betrieb, 63 (13), p. 681–689.

Haller, A./Eierle, B./Evans, L./Evans, E. (2001): Das britische Financial Reporting Review Panel - ein Vorbild für ein deutsches Enforcement-Gremium?, in: Betriebs-Berater, 56 (33), p. 1673–1680.

Hammann, P./Erichson, B. (2000): Marktforschung, Stuttgart.

Hardy, M. A. (2007): Regression with dummy variables, Newbury Park, Calif.

Harris, M. S./Muller, K. A. (1999): The market valuation of IAS versus US-GAAP accounting measures using Form 20-F reconciliations, in: Journal of Accounting and Economics, 26 (1-3), p. 285–312.

Harris, T. S. (1995): International Accounting Standards versus US-GAAP Reporting – Empirical evidence based on case studies, Cincinnati, Ohio.

Harrison, G. L./McKinnon, J. L. (1986): Culture and accounting change: A new perspective on corporate reporting regulation and accounting policy formulation, in: Accounting, Organizations and Society, 11 (3), p. 233–252.

Hartmann-Wendels, T. (1989): Principal-Agent-Theorie und asymmetrische Informationsverteilung, in: Zeitschrift für Bebriebswirtschaft, 59 (7), p. 714–734.

Hartmann-Wendels, T. (1992): Agency Theorie, in: Frese, E. (ed.): Handwörterbuch der Organisation, Stuttgart (1992), p. 72–79.

HassabElnaby, H. R./Mosebach, M. (2005): Culture's consequences in controlling agency costs: Egyptian evidence, in: Journal of International Accounting, Auditing and Taxation, 14 (1), p. 19–32.

Healy, P. M./Palepu, K. G. (2001): Information asymmetry, corporate disclosure, and the capital markets: A review of the empirical disclosure literature, in: Journal of Accounting and Economics, 31 (1-3), p. 405–440.

Healy, P. M./Wahlen, J. M. (1999): A Review of the Earnings Management Literature and Its Implications for Standard Setting, in: Accounting Horizons, 13 (4), p. 365–383.

Heeren, T./D'Agostino, R. (1987): Robustness of the two independent samples t-test when applied to ordinal scaled data, in: Statistics in Medicine, 6 (1), p. 79–90.

Hellriegel, D./Slocum, J. W. (1976): Organizational behavior: contingency views, St. Paul.

Helmreich, R. L./Merritt, A. C. (1998): Culture at work in aviation and medicine. National, organizational and professional influences, Aldershot.

Hendriksen, E. S. (1965): Accounting Theory, Homewook.

Henseler, J./Ringle, C. M./Sinkovics, R. R. (2009): The use of partial least squares path modeling in international marketing, in: Sinkovics, R. R. (ed.): New challenges to international marketing, London (2009), p. 277–320.

Her Majesty's Revenue and Customs [HMRC] (2006): International Accounting Standards - the UK tax implications, available at: http://www.hmrc.gov.uk, last revised 01.03.2011.

Her Majesty's Revenue and Customs [HMRC] (2010): Corporation Tax rates, available at: http://www.hmrc.gov.uk, last revised 01.03.2011.

Herrmann, D./Thomas, W. (1995): Harmonisation of Accounting Measurement Practices in the European Community, in: Accounting & Business Research, 25 (100), p. 253–265.

Herzig, N./Briesemeister, S. (2009): Steuerliche Konsequenzen des BilMoG - Deregulierung und Maßgeblichkeit, in: Der Betrieb, 62 (18), p. 926–931.

Heyd, R./Lutz-Ingold, M. (2005): Immaterielle Vermögenswerte und Goodwill nach IFRS, München.

Heyd, R./von Keitz, I. (eds.) (2007): IFRS-Management, München (2007).

Hirshleifer, D./Thakor, A. V. (1992): Managerial conservatism, project choice, and debt, in: Review of Financial Studies, 5 (3), p. 437–470.

Hoarau, C. (1995): International accounting harmonization – American hegemony or mutual recognition with benchmarks?, in: European Accounting Review, 4 (2), p. 217–233.

Hofstede, G. (1980a): Culture's consequences. International differences in work-related values, Beverly Hills, Calif.

Hofstede, G. (1980b): Motivation, leadership, and organization. Do American theories apply abroad?, New York.

Hofstede, G. (1982): Dimensions of national culture, in: Rath, R. (ed.): Diversity and unity in cross-cultural psychology. Selected papers from the 5th international congress of the International Association for Cross-Cultural Psychology, Lisse (1982).

Hofstede, G. (1983): The Cultural Relativity of Organizational Practices and Theories, in: Journal of International Business Studies, 14 (2), p. 75–89.

Hofstede, G. (1993): Interkulturelle Zusammenarbeit. Kulturen, Organisationen, Management, Wiesbaden.

Hofstede, G. (2001): Culture's consequences – Comparing values, behaviors, institutions, and organizations across nations, Thousand Oaks.

Hofstede, G. (2006): What Did GLOBE Really Measure? Researchers' Minds versus Respondents' Minds, in: Journal of International Business Studies, 37 (6), p. 882–896.

Hofstede, G. (2010): The GLOBE debate: Back to relevance, in: Journal of International Business Studies, 41 (8), p. 1339–1346.

Hofstede, G./McCrae, R. R. (2004): Personality and Culture Revisited: Linking Traits and Dimensions of Culture, in: Cross-Cultural Research, 38 (1), p. 52–88.

Holland, K. (1998): Accounting Policy Choice: The Relationship Between Corporate Tax Burdens and Company Size, in: Journal of Business Finance & Accounting, 25 (3-4), p. 265–288.

Holsti, O. R. (1969): Content analysis for the social sciences and humanities, Reading Mass.

Hommelhoff, P. (2001): Für ein spezifisches deutsches Durchsetzungssystem: Schaffung einer Kontrollinstanz zur Sicherstellung der internationalen Wettbewerbsfähigkeit des deutschen Enforcement-Systems, in: WPg, 54 (WPg Sonderheft 2001), p. 39–50.

Hommelhoff, P. (2005): Deutsches Enforcement im richtigen Fahrwasser?, in: Baetge, J. H.-J. (ed.): Anpassung des deutschen Bilanzrechts an internationale Standards. Bilanzrechtsreformgesetz und Bilanzkontrollgesetz, Düsseldorf (2005), p. 57–86.

Hoogendoorn, M. N. (1996): Accounting and taxation in Europe - A comparative overview, in: European Accounting Review, 5 (4), p. 783–794.

Hope, A. C. A. (1968): A Simplified Monte Carlo Significance Test Procedure, in: Journal of the Royal Statistical Society. Series B (Methodological), 30 (3), p. 582–598.

Hope, O.-K. (2003a): Disclosure Practices, Enforcement of Accounting Standards, and Analysts' Forecast Accuracy: An International Study, in: Journal of Accounting Research, 41 (2), p. 235–272.

Hope, O.-K. (2003b): Firm-level Disclosures and the Relative Roles of Culture and Legal Origin, in: Journal of International Financial Management & Accounting, 14 (3), p. 218–248.

Hope, O.-K./Jin, Y. J./Kang, T. (2006): Empirical Evidence on Jurisdictions that Adopt IFRS, available at: http://ssrn.com, last revised 01.03.2011.

Hope, O.-K./Kang, T./Thomas, W./Yoo, Y. K. (2008): Culture and auditor choice: A test of the secrecy hypothesis, in: Journal of Accounting and Public Policy, 27 (5), p. 357–373.

Hoppe, M. H. (1990): A comparative study of country elites. international differences in work-related values and learning and their implications for management training and development, Chapel Hill.

Hoppe, M. H./Bhagat, R. S. (2009): Leadership in the United States of America: The Leader as Cultural Hero, in: Chhokar, J. S. (ed.): Culture and leadership across the world. The GLOBE book of in-depth studies of 25 societies, New York (2009), p. 475–545.

Hopwood, A. G. (1994): Some reflections on 'The harmonization of accounting within the EU', in: European Accounting Review, 3 (2), p. 241–254.

Horton, J./Serafeim, G. (2007): Value Relevance of the International Financial Reporting Standards (IFRS): Investigations of the Transitional Documents for UK, Spanish, French and Italian companies, in: Institute of Chartered Accountants in England and Wales [ICAEW] (ed.): EU implementation of IFRS and the Fair Value Directive. A report for the European Commission, London (2007), p. 206–226.

Horton, J./Serafeim, G. (2010): Market reaction to and valuation of IFRS reconciliation adjustments: first evidence from the UK, in: Review of Accounting Studies, 15 (4), p. 725–751.

Hossain, M./Perera, M. H. B./Rahman, A. R. (1995): Voluntary Disclosure in the Annual Reports of New Zealand Companies, in: Journal of International Financial Management & Accounting, 6 (1), p. 69–87.

Hossain, M./Tan, L.-M./Adams, M. (1994): Voluntary disclosure in an emerging capital market: some empirical evidence from companies listed on the Kuala Lumpur stock exchange, in: International Journal of Accounting, 29 (4), p. 334–351.

House, R. J./Hanges, P. J./Javidan, M./Dorfman, P. W./Gupta, V. (2004): Culture, leadership, and organizations – The GLOBE study of 62 societies, Thousand Oaks, Calif.

Huerta, E./Salter, S. B. (2008): Knowledge Sharing Across Cultures, available at: http://ssrn.com, last revised 01.03.2011.

Huijgen, C./Lubberink, M. (2005): Earnings Conservatism, Litigation and Contracting: The Case of Cross-Listed Firms, in: Journal of Business Finance & Accounting, 32 (7-8), p. 1275–1309.

Hung, M. (2000): Accounting standards and value relevance of financial statements: An international analysis, in: Journal of Accounting and Economics, 30 (3), p. 401–420.

Hung, M./Subramanyam, K. (2007): Financial statement effects of adopting international accounting standards: the case of Germany, in: Review of Accounting Studies, 12 (4), p. 623–657.

Hüttche, T. (2009): Aus Fehlern lernen : eine Analyse von der DPR entdeckter und nicht entdeckter Fehler in der Rechnungslegung, in: IRZ, 4 (7/8), p. 325–333.

Imhoff, E. A. (1992): The relation between perceived accounting quality and economic characteristics of the firm, in: Journal of Accounting and Public Policy, 11 (2), p. 97–118.

Inchausti, A. G. (1997): The influence of company characteristics and accounting regulation on information disclosed by Spanish firms, in: European Accounting Review, 6 (1), p. 45–68.

Inglehart, R. (2004): Human beliefs and values – A cross-cultural sourcebook based on the 1999 - 2002 values surveys, México, DF.

Inglehart, R./Basañez, M./Menéndez Moreno, A. (1998): Human values and beliefs – A cross-cultural sourcebook; political, religious, sexual, and economic norms in 43 societies; findings from the 1990 - 1993 World Values Survey, Ann Arbor.

International Accounting Standards Board [IASB] (2005): History, available at: http://www.iasb.org, last revised 01.03.2011.

International Accounting Standards Board [IASB] (2009a): ED/2009/5 Fair Value Measurement, available at: http://www.ifrs.org, last revised 01.03.2011.

International Accounting Standards Board [IASB] (2009b): IASB and the IASC Foundation – Who we are and what we do, available at: http://www.iasb.org, last revised 01.03.2011.

International Accounting Standards Board [IASB] (2010a): ED/2010/7 Measurement Uncertainty Analysis Disclosure for Fair Value Measurements, available at: http://www.ifrs.org, last revised 01.03.2011.

International Accounting Standards Board [IASB] (2010b): Extractive Activities, available at: http://www.iasb.org, last revised 01.03.2011.

International Accounting Standards Board [IASB] (2010c): IASB publishes IFRS Practice Statement on Management Commentary, available at: http://www.ifrs.org, last revised 01.03.2011.

International Accounting Standards Board [IASB] (2010d): IASB work plan - projected timetable as of 19 April 2010, available at: http://www.iasb.org, last revised 01.03.2011.

International Accounting Standards Board [IASB] (2010e): IFRS Advisory Council (formerly the SAC), available at: http://www.iasb.org, last revised 01.03.2011.

International Accounting Standards Board [IASB] (2010f): Insurance Contracts, available at: http://www.iasb.org, last revised 01.03.2011.

International Accounting Standards Board [IASB] (2010g): Who we are and what we do, available at: http://www.iasb.org, last revised 01.03.2011.

International Accounting Standards Committee [IASC] (1975): Work and Purpose of the International Accounting Standards Committee, London.

International Accounting Standards Committee [IASC] (1988): Survey of the use and application of international accounting standards – 1988, London.

International Organization of Securities Commissions [IOSCO] (2000): A Resolution on IASC Standards, available at: http://www.iosco.org, last revised 01.03.2011.

Jaafar, A./McLeay, S. (2007): Country Effects and Sector Effects on the Harmonization of Accounting Policy Choice, in: Abacus, 43 (2), p. 156–189.

Jaggi, B./Low, P. Y. (2000): Impact of Culture, Market Forces, and Legal System on Financial Disclosures, in: The International Journal of Accounting, 35 (4), p. 495–519.

Jeanjean, T./Stolowy, H. (2008): Do accounting standards matter? An exploratory analysis of earnings management before and after IFRS adoption – International Financial Reporting Standards, in: Journal of Accounting and Public Policy, 27 (6), p. 480–494.

Jenner, T. (2001): Zur Verwendung des Kontingenzansatzes in der betriebswirtschaftlichen Forschung, in: Das Wirtschaftsstudium, 30 (1), p. 79–84.

Jensen, M. C./Meckling, W. H. (1976): Theory of the firm: Managerial behavior, agency costs and ownership structure, in: Journal of Financial Economics, 3 (4), p. 305–360.

Jödicke, D. (2009): Einfluss kultureller Unterschiede auf die Anwendung internationaler Rechnungslegungsregeln – Eine theoretische und empirische Untersuchung zur Anwendung der IFRS in Deutschland, Frankreich und UK, Hamburg.

Johnson, J. P./Lenartowicz, T. (1998): Culture, freedom and economic growth: Do cultural values explain economic growth?, in: Journal of World Business, 33 (4), p. 332–356.

Jones, M. L. (2007): Hofstede - Culturally questionable?, Paper presented at the Oxford Business & Economics Conference, Oxford, available at: http://ro.uow.edu.au, last revised 01.03.2011.

Jost, P.-J. (2001): Die Prinzipal-Agenten-Theorie im Unternehmenskontext, in: Jost, P.-J. (ed.): Die Prinzipal-Agenten-Theorie in der Betriebswirtschaftslehre, Stuttgart (2001).

Jupe, R. E. (1999): Enforcing compliance with accounting standards: The role of the Financial Reporting Review Panel in the UK regulatory framework, in: Journal of Financial Regulation and Compliance, 7 (4), p. 323–330.

Kajüter, P./Guttmeier, M. (2009): Der Exposure Draft des IASB zum Management Commentary – Kritische Analyse und Vergleich mit DRS 15, in: Der Betrieb, 62 (44), p. 2333–2339.

Kajüter, P. (2000): Proaktives Kostenmanagement – Konzeption und Realprofile, Wiesbaden.

Kajüter, P./Bachert, K./Blaesing, D. (2010): Ergänzung des IFRS Abschlusses um einen Managementbericht, in: KoR, 10 (4), p. 183–190.

Kajüter, P./Barth, D. (2007): Segmentberichterstattung nach IFRS 8 - Übernahme des Management Approach, in: Betriebs-Berater, 62 (8), p. 428–433.

Kaplan, A./Goldsen, J. M. (1965): The reliability of content analysis categories, in: Lasswell, H. D. (ed.): Language of politics: studies in quantitative semantics, Cambridge (1965), p. 83–112.

Kassarjian, H. H. (1977): Content Analysis in Consumer Research, in: The Journal of Consumer Research, 4 (1), p. 8–18.

Kast, F. E./Rosenzweig, J. E. (1973): Contingency views of organization and management, Chicago.

Kaya, M. (2009): Verfahren der Datenerhebung, in: Albers, S./Klapper, D./Konradt, U./Walter, A./Wolf, J. (eds.): Methodik der empirischen Forschung, Wiesbaden (2009), p. 49–64.

Kern, M. (1979): Klassische Erkenntnistheorien und moderne Wissenschaftslehre, in: Raffée, H./Abel, B. (eds.): Wissenschaftstheoretische Grundfragen der Wirtschaftswissenschaften, München (1979), p. 11–27.

Keynes, J. N. (1891): The scope and method of political economy, London.

Khurana, I. K./Raman, K. K. (2004): Litigation Risk and the Financial Reporting Credibility of Big 4 versus Non-Big 4 Audits: Evidence from Anglo-American Countries, in: The Accounting Review, 79 (2), p. 473–495.

Kiener, S. (1990): Die Principal-Agent-Theorie aus informationsökonomischer Sicht, Heidelberg.

Kieser, A./Kubicek, H. (1978): Organisationstheorien, Stuttgart.

Kieser, A./Walgenbach, P./Kieser-Walgenbach (2010): Organisation, Stuttgart.

Kim, B./Jung, K. (2007): The Influence of Tax Costs on Accounting Conservatism, available at: SSRN: http://ssrn.com, last revised 01.03.2011.

Kinney, W. R. (1986): Empirical Accounting Research Design for Ph. D. Students, in: The Accounting Review, 61 (2), p. 338–350.

Kirca, A. H./Cavusgil, S. T./Hult, G. T. M. (2009): The effects of national culture on market orientation: Conceptual framework and research propositions, in: International Business Review, 18 (2), p. 111–119.

Kirkman, B. L./Lowe, K. B./Gibson, C. B. (2006): A Quarter Century of "Culture's Consequences": A Review of Empirical Research Incorporating Hofstede's Cultural Values Framework, in: Journal of International Business Studies, 37 (3), p. 285–320.

Kirsch, H. (2007): Segmentbezogene Jahresabschlussanalyse nach IFRS 8, in: PiR, 3 (1), p. 61–67.

Kleinbaum, D. G. (2008): Applied regression analysis and other multivariable methods, Belmont, Calif.

Kluckhohn, C. (1951): The study of culture, in: Lerner, D./Lasswell, H. D. (eds.): The policy sciences: recent developments in scope and method, Stanford (1951).

Kluckhohn, F. R./Strodtbeck, F. L. (1961): Variations in value orientations, Evanston.

Knorr, E. M./Ng, R. T. (1997): A Unified Notion of Outliers: Properties and Computation, in: Heckerman, D. M. H./Pregibon, D./Uthurusamy, R. (eds.): Proceedings of the Third International Conference on Knowledge Discovery and Data Mining, Menlo Park, Calif. (1997), p. 219–222.

Knorr, L. (2004): Gewährleistung der Einhaltung internationaler Rechnungslegungsstandards: Zum Referentenentwurf des Bilanzkontrollgesetzes in seinem internationalen Umfeld, in: KoR, 4 (3), p. 85–89.

Kolbe, R. H./Burnett, M. S. (1991): Content-Analysis Research: An Examination of Applications with Directives for Improving Research Reliability and Objectivity, in: The Journal of Consumer Research, 18 (2), p. 243–250.

Königsgruber, R. (2008): IASB und FASB zwischen Autonomie und Eingebunden-Sein, in: IRZ, 3 (5), p. 245–549.

Kornmeier, M. (2007): Wissenschaftstheorie und wissenschaftliches Arbeiten – Eine Einführung für Wirtschaftswissenschaftler, Heidelberg.

Kothari, S. (2000): The role of financial reporting in reducing financial risks, in: Rosengren, E. S./Jordan, J. S. (eds.): Conference Series 44: Building an Infrastructure for Financial Stability, Boston (2000), p. 89–102.

KPMG (2007): Audit Committee Quarterly. II/2007, available at: http://www.audit-commitee-institute.com, last revised 01.03.2011.

KPMG (2009): KPMG Reports 2009 Revenues of US $20.1 Billion, available at: http://www.kpmg.com, last revised 01.03.2011.

KPMG (2010): International Financial Reporting Standards (IFRS), available at: http://www.kpmg.com, last revised 01.03.2011.

KPMG/von Keitz, I. (2006a): The Application of IFRS: Choices in Practice, London.

KPMG/von Keitz, I. (2006b): The application of IFRS: Disclosures in practice – International Financial Reporting Standards, Bodmin, Cornwall.

Kraayenhof, J. (1960): International Challenges for Accounting, in: Journal of Accountancy, 55 (1), p. 34–38.

Kräkel, M. (2007): Organisation und Management, Tübingen.

Krippendorff, K. (2004): Content analysis – An introduction to its methodology, London.

Kroeber, A. L./Kluckhohn, C./Untereiner, W. (1952): Culture: a critical review of concepts and definitions, New York.

Kromrey, H. (2006): Empirische Sozialforschung – Modelle und Methoden der standardisierten Datenerhebung und Datenauswertung, Stuttgart.

Kubicek, H. (1975): Empirische Organisationsforschung – Konzeption und Methodik, Stuttgart.

Kubicek, H. (1977): Heuristische Bezugsrahmen und heuristisch angelegtes Forschungsdesign als Elemente einer Konstruktionsstrategie empirischer Forschung, in: Köhler, R. (ed.): Empirische und handlungstheoretische Forschungskonzeptionen in der Betriebswirtschaftslehre. Bericht über die Tagung in Aachen, März 1976, Stuttgart (1977), p. 3–36.

Kübler, F. (1995): Vorsichtsprinzip versus Kapitalmarktinformation, in: Förschle, G./Budde, W. D. (eds.): Rechenschaftslegung im Wandel. Festschrift für Wolfgang Dieter Budde, München (1995), p. 361–375.

Kuhn, T. S./Neurath, O./Dewey, J. (1970): The structure of scientific revolutions, Chicago.

Kuhner, C. (2008): Die Zielsetzung von IFRS, US-GAAP und HGB und deren Konsequenzen für die Abbildung von Unternehmenskäufen, in: Ballwieser, W./Beyer, S./Zelger, H. (eds.): Unternehmenskauf nach IFRS und US-GAAP. Purchase Price Allocation, Goodwill und Impairment-Test, Stuttgart (2008), p. 1–34.

Küting, K. (2009): Grundlagen der fair value-Bewertung – Zugleich: Aufstieg und Fall einer als überlegen propagierten Bewertungskonzeption, in: StuB, 11 (22), p. 829–835.

Küting, K./Hayn, S. (1995): Wesentliche Unterschiede der Rechnungslegung in Großbritannien und Deutschland, in: Zeitschrift für Unternehmens- und Gesellschaftsrecht, 24 (1), p. 417–422.

Küting, K./Zwirner, C./Reuter, M. (2007): Zur Bedeutung der Fair Value-Bewertung in der deutschen Bilanzierungspraxis - Empirische Analyse von IFRS-Konzernabschlüssen, in: DStR, 45 (11), p. 500–506.

Kutschker, M./Schmid, S. (2011): Internationales Management, München.

Kvaal, E./Nobes, C. W. (2008): Measuring international differences in IFRS policy choice, Paper presented at the 31st Annual Congress of the European Accounting Association, Rotterdam.

Kvaal, E./Nobes, C. W. (2010): International differences in IFRS policy choice: a research note, in: Accounting & Business Research, 40 (2), p. 173–187.

Kwok, W. C. C./Sharp, D. (2005): Power and international accounting standard setting - Evidence from segment reporting and intangible assets projects, in: Accounting, Auditing & Accountability Journal, 18 (1), p. 74–99.

La Porta, R. A. (1997): Legal Determinants of External Finance, in: Journal of Finance, 52 (3), p. 1131–1150.

Lafferty, M./Cairns, D. (1980): Financial times – World survey of annual reports 1980, London.

Lafferty, M./Cairns, D./Carty, J. (1979): 1979 Financial Times survey of 100 major European companies' reports & accounts / by Michael Lafferty with David Cairns and James Carty, London.

Lainez, J. A./Gasca, M. (2006): Obstacles to the harmonization process in the European Union: the influence of culture, in: International journal of accounting, auditing and performance evaluation, 3 (1), p. 68–97.

Lamb, M. (1996): The relationship between accounting and taxation - The United Kingdom, in: European Accounting Review, 5 (1), p. 933–950.

Lamb, M./Nobes, C. W./Roberts, A. (1998): International Variations in the Connections Between Tax and Financial Reporting, in: Accounting & Business Research, 28 (3), p. 173–188.

Lambert, R. A./Leuz, C./Verrecchia, R. E. (2008): Information Asymmetry, Information Precision, and the Cost of Capital, available at: http://papers.ssrn.com, last revised 01.03.2011.

Lamfalussy, A. (2001): Final report of the The Committee of Wise Men on the regulation of European securities markets, available at: http://www.docstoc.com, last revised 01.03.2011.

Lane, C. (1989): Management and labour in Europe – The industrial enterprise in Germany, Britain and France, Aldershot.

Lane, C. (1995): Industry and society in Europe: stability and change in Britain, Germany, and France, Brookfiend, Vt.

Lang, M. H./Lundholm, R. (1993): Cross-Sectional Determinants of Analyst Ratings of Corporate Disclosures, in: Journal of Accounting Research, 31 (2), p. 246–271.

Lara, J. M. G./Osma, B. G./Penalva, F. (2009a): The Economic Determinants of Conditional Conservatism, in: Journal of Business Finance & Accounting, 36 (3-4), p. 336–372.

Lara, J. M. G./Garcia Osma, B./Penalva, F. (2009b): Accounting Conservatism and Corporate Governance, in: Review of Accounting Studies, 14 (1), p. 161–201.

Laughlin, R. (2007): Critical reflections on research approaches, accounting regulation and the regulation of accounting, in: The British Accounting Review, 39 (4), p. 271–289.

Laux, H. (2006): Unternehmensrechnung, Anreiz und Kontrolle – Die Messung, Zurechnung und Steuerung des Erfolges als Grundprobleme der Betriebswirtschaftslehre, Berlin, Heidelberg.

Lawrence, P. R./Lorsch, J. W. (1969): Organization and Environment, Homewood.

Lee, T. A. (1974): Accounting for and Disclosure of Business Combinations, in: Journal of Business Finance & Accounting, 1 (1), p. 1–21.

Leffson, U. (1987): Die Grundsätze ordnungsmäßiger Buchführung, Düsseldorf.

Lehn, K./Makhija, A. K. (1997): EVA, Accounting Profits, and CEO Turnover: an empirical examination, 1985–1994, in: Journal of Applied Corporate Finance, 10 (2), p. 90–97.

Leland, H. E. (1992): Insider Trading: Should It Be Prohibited?, in: The Journal of Political Economy, 100 (4), p. 859–887.

Leuz, C. (2003): IAS versus U.S. GAAP: Information Asymmetry-Based Evidence from Germany's New Market, in: Journal of Accounting Research, 41 (3), p. 445–472.

Leuz, C./Verrecchia, R. E. (2000): The Economic Consequences of Increased Disclosure, in: Journal of Accounting Research, 38 , p. 91–124.

Levine, R. (2002): Bank-Based or Market-Based Financial Systems: Which Is Better?, in: Journal of Financial Intermediation, 11 (4), p. 398–428.

Levine, R./Zervos, S. (1996): Stock Market Development and Long-Run Growth, in: The World Bank Economic Review, 10 (2), p. 323–339.

Lewis, C. M./Hunter, J./Harriss, J. (1995): The new institutional economics and third world development, Routledge.

Liebowitz, S. J. (1982): What Do Census Price-Cost Margins Measure?, in: Journal of Law and Economics, 25 (2), p. 231–246.

Lingnau, V. (1995): Kritischer Rationalismus und Betriebswirtschaftslehre, in: Wirtschaftswissenschaftliches Studium, 24 (3), p. 124–129.

Linsley, P. M./Shrives, P. J. (2005): Transparency and the disclosure of risk information in the banking sector, in: Journal of Financial Regulation & Compliance, 13 (3), p. 205–214.

Liouville, J./Schmidt, G. (1996): Gibt es eine ideale Methode für die international vergleichende Managementforschung? Folgerungen aus einer empirischen Studie, in: Engelhard, J. (ed.): Strategische Führung internationaler Unternehmen. Paradoxien, Strategien und Erfahrungen, Wiesbaden (1996), p. 257–271.

Lisch, R./Kriz, J. (1978): Grundlagen und Modelle der Inhaltsanalyse – Bestandsaufnahme und Kritik, Reinbek bei Hamburg.

Littlechild, S. C./Crew, M./Parker, D. (2008): Regulation of British Telecommunications' Profitability, in: Crew, M. A./Parker, D. (eds.): Developments in the economics of privatization and regulation, Cheltenham (2008), p. 357–399.

Littleton, A. C. (1962): Accounting Theory : continuity and change, Englewood Cliffs, New Jersey.

Litz, H. P. (2000): Multivariate statistische Methoden und ihre Anwendung in den Wirtschafts- und Sozialwissenschaften, München.

Löffler, H./Rohatschek, R. (eds.) (2007): Internationale und nationale Rechnungslegung am Wendepunkt, Wien (2007).

Loitz, R./Weber, T. (2008): Herausforderungen bei der Anhangerstellung nach IFRS - eine empirische Untersuchung, in: Der Betrieb, 61 (40), p. 2149–2155.

Loughran, T./Ritter, J. R. (1997): The Operating Performance of Firms Conducting Seasoned Equity Offerings, in: The Journal of Finance, 52 (5), p. 1823–1850.

Lowe, E. A./Puxty, A. G./Laughlin, R. C. (1983): Simple theories for complex processes: Accounting policy and the market for myopia, in: Journal of Accounting and Public Policy, 2 (1), p. 19–42.

Lowe, S. (1996): Hermes revisited: A replication of Hofstede's study in Hong Kong and the UK, in: Asia Pacific Business Review, 2 (3), p. 101–119.

MacArthur, J. B. (1996): An Investigation into the influence of Cultural Factors in the International Lobbying of the International Accounting Standards Committee – The Case of E32, Comparability of Financial Statements, in: International Journal of Accounting, 31 (2), p. 213–238.

Macve, R. (2010): Conceptual frameworks of accounting: some brief reflections on theory and practice, in: Accounting & Business Research, 40 (3), p. 303–308.

Maher, M. W./Tiessen, P./Colson, R./Broman, A. J. (1992): Competition and Audit Fees, in: The Accounting Review, 67 (1), p. 199–211.

Malone, D./Fries, C./Jones, T. (1993): An Empirical Investigation of the Extent of Corporate Financial Disclosure in the Oil and Gas Industry, in: Journal of Accounting, Auditing & Finance, 8 (3), p. 249–273.

Marston, C. L./Shrives, P. J. (1991): The use of disclosure indices in accounting research: a review article, in: British Accounting Review, 23 (1), p. 195–210.

Martinez-Diaz, L. (2005): Strategic experts and improvising regulators: explaining the IASC's rise to global influence, 1973-2001, in: Business and Politics, 7 (3), p. 1–26.

Maseland, R./van Hoorn, A. (2010): Values and marginal preferences in international business, in: Journal of International Business Studies, 41 (8), p. 1325–1329.

Mason, A. K. (1981): The Evolution of International Accounting Standards, in: Choi, F. D. S. (ed.): Multinational accounting. A research framework for the eighties, Ann Arbor, Mich. (1981), p. 155–170.

Maurice, M. (1979): For a study of the "societal effect": Universality and specificity in organization research, in: Lammers, C. J. (ed.): Organizations alike and unlike. International and interinstitutional studies in the sociology of organizations, London (1979), p. 42–60.

Maurice, M./Sorge, A./Warner, M. (1980): Societal Differences in Organizing Manufacturing Units: A Comparison of France, West Germany, and Great Britain, in: Organization Studies, 1 (1), p. 59–86.

Maury, B./Pajuste, A. (2005): Multiple large shareholders and firm value, in: Journal of Banking & Finance, 29 (7), p. 1813–1834.

Mayring, P. (2003): Qualitative Inhaltsanalyse – Grundlagen und Techniken, Weinheim.

Mazey, S./Richardson, J. (1993): Lobbying in the European Community, Oxford.

McGrath, R. G./MacMillan, I. C./Scheinberg, S. (1992): Elitists, risk-takers, and rugged individualists? An exploratory analysis of cultural differences between entrepreneurs and non-entrepreneurs, in: Journal of Business Venturing, 7 (2), p. 115–135.

McKinnon, J. L./Dalimunthe, L. (1993): Voluntary Disclosure of Segment Information by Australian Diversified Companies, in: Accounting & Finance, 33 (1), p. 33–50.

McKinnon, S. M./Janell, P. (1984): The International Accounting Standards Committee: A Performance Evaluation, in: International Journal of Accounting, 19 (2), p. 19–35.

McSweeney, B. (2002): Hofstede's Model of National Cultural Differences and their Consequences: A Triumph of Faith - a Failure of Analysis, in: Human Relations, 55 (1), p. 89–118.

Meek, G. K./Gray, S. J. (1989): Globalization of Stock Markets and Foreign Listing Requirements: Voluntary Disclosures by Continental European Companies Listed on the London Stock Exchange, in: Journal of International Business Studies, 20 (2), p. 315–336.

Meek, G. K./Roberts, C. B./Gray, S. J. (1995): Factors influencing voluntary annual report disclosures by U.S., U.K. and continental European multinational corporations, in: Journal of International Business Studies, 26 (3), p. 555–572.

Meek, G. K./Saudagaran, S. M. (1990): A survey of research on financial reporting in a transnational context, in: Journal of Accounting Literature, 9 (1), p. 145–182.

Melcher, W./Schaier, S. (2009): Zur Umsetzung der HGB-Modernisierung durch das BilMoG: Einführung und Überblick, in: Der Betrieb, 62 (23), p. 4–9.

Merten, K. (1995): Inhaltsanalyse. Einführung in Theorie, Methode und Praxis, Opladen.

Meyer, C./Stiglingh, M./Venter, E. (2006): The extent of compliance with income tax presentation and disclosure requirements in the financial statements of companies in south Africa, in: Kantarelis, D. (ed.): 2006 Business & Economics Society International Conference (2006), p. 83–95.

Meyer, C. (2005): Bilanzrechtsreformgesetz (BilReG) und Bilanzkontrollgesetz (BilKoG) - Die Änderungen im Überblick, in: Deutsches Steuerrecht, 43 (1), p. 41.

Meyer, C./Weiss, S. (2010): IFRS 8 Operating Segments – Eine Untersuchung der erstmaligen Anwendung in der Schweiz, in: Der Schweizer Treuhänder, 84 (12), p. 848–855.

Meyer, H. (2008): Aktuelle Fragen des Enforcement in Deutschland: Aufgaben der Deutschen Prüfstelle für Rechnungslegung, in: Horváth, P. (ed.): Mehr Verantwortung für den Controller, Stuttgart (2008), p. 59–73.

Meyer, H. (2010): Aktuelle Entwicklungen des Enforcement in Deutschland, in: IRZ, 5 (4), p. 153–158.

Meyer, H./Naumann, K.-P. (2009): Interview - Enforcement der Rechnungslegung - aktuelle Entwicklungen, in: WPg, 62 (16), p. 807–811.

Meyer, J. W./Rowan, B. (1977): Institutionalized Organizations: Formal Structure as Myth and Ceremony, in: The American Journal of Sociology, 83 (2), p. 340–363.

Milne, M. J./Adler, R. W. (1999): Exploring the reliability of social and environmental disclosures content analysis, in: Accounting, Auditing & Accountability Journal, 12 (2), p. 237–256.

Möller, H. P./Hüfner, B. (2002): Empirische Forschung, in: Küpper, H.-U. (ed.): Handwörterbuch Unternehmensrechnung und Controlling, Stuttgart (2002), p. 351–359.

Moosa, I. A. (2002): Foreign direct investment – Theory, evidence and practice, Basingstoke, Hampshire.

Mosler, K./Schmid, F. (2006): Beschreibende Statistik und Wirtschaftsstatistik, Berlin.

Mouck, T. (1992): The Rhetoric of Science and the Rhetoric of Revolt in the "Story" of Positive Accounting Theory, in: Accounting, Auditing & Accountability Journal, 5 (4), p. 35–56.

Mouritzen, P. E./Svara, J. H. (2002): Leadership at the apex. Politicians and administrators in Western local governments, Pittsburgh.

Moxter, A. (1985): Bilanzrechtsprechung, Tübingen.

Mueller, G. G. (1967): International Accounting, New York.

Mueller, G. G. (2003): Harmonization efforts in the European Union, in: Choi, F. D. S. (ed.): International finance and accounting handbook, Hoboken, NJ (2003), p. 11.1-11.33.

Müller, S./Gelbrich, K. (2004): Interkulturelles Marketing, München.

Müller, S./Reinke, J. (2010): Überwachung durch die Deutsche Prüfstelle für Rechnungslegung (DPR) und die vom Enforcementverfahren ausgehende Präventionsfunktion – Empirische Analyse der Entwicklung anhand der Angaben zu IAS 36 für die Jahre 2005 bis 2009, in: IRZ, 5 (11), p. 505–510.

Müller, W. (1988): Die Grundsätze ordnungsmäßiger Bilanzierung und ihre Kodifizierung nach neuem Bilanzrecht, in: Mellwig, W. (ed.): Einzelabschluß und Konzernabschluß, Wiesbaden (1988), p. 3–26.

Müller-Böling, D. (1992): Methodik der empirischen Organisationsforschung, in: Frese, E. (ed.): Handwörterbuch der Organisation, Stuttgart (1992), p. 1492–1506.

Murphy, A. B. (1999): Firm Characteristics of Swiss Companies that Utilize International Accounting Standards, in: The International Journal of Accounting, 34 (1), p. 121–131.

Myers, S. C. (1977): Determinants of corporate borrowing, in: Journal of Financial Economics, 5 (2), p. 147–175.

N.U. (1611): The King James Version: Gen.11:1-9, available at: http://www.biblegateway.com, last revised 01.03.2011.

Nair, R. D./Frank, W. G. (1980): The Impact of Disclosure and Measurement Practices on International Accounting Classifications, in: The Accounting Review, 55 (3), p. 426–450.

Nair, R. D./Frank, W. G. (1981): The Harmonization of International Accounting Standards, 1973-1979, in: International Journal of Accounting, 17 (1), p. 61–79.

Naser, K./Al-Khatib, K./Karbhari, Y. (1993): Empirical evidence on the depth of corporate information disclosure in developing countries: the case of Jordan, in: International Journal of Commerce and Management, 12 (3/4), p. 122–155.

Naumann, K.-P. (2000): Financial reporting enforcement mechanisms as an element of corporate governance in Germany and reflections on their further development, in: European Accounting Review, 9 (4), p. 655–672.

Newman, P./Sansing, R. (1993): Disclosure Policies with Multiple Users, in: Journal of Accounting Research, 31 (1), p. 92–112.

Niehus, R. J. (2005): Die IFRS auf Deutsch – Fehler und Unzulänglichkeiten der Übersetzung, in: Der Betrieb, 58 (46), p. 2477–2483.

Nikolaev, V. (2010): Debt Covenants and Accounting Conservatism, in: Journal of Accounting Research, 48 (1), p. 51–89.

Nobes, C./Roberts, A. (2000): Towards a Unifying Model of Systems of Law, Corporate Financing, Accounting and Corporate Governance, in: Australian Accounting Review, 10 (20), p. 26–34.

Nobes, C./Schwenke, H. R. (2006): Modelling the Links between Tax and Financial Reporting: A Longitudinal Examination of Norway over 30 Years up to IFRS Adoption, in: European Accounting Review, 15 (1), p. 63–87.

Nobes, C. W. (1983): A judgmental international classification of financial reporting practices, in: Journal of Business Finance & Accounting, 10 (1), p. 1–19.

Nobes, C. W. (1995): Corporate financing and its effects on accounting differences, in: Discussion papers in accounting, finance and banking, 43 (Series D).

Nobes, C. W. (1998): Towards a General Model of the Reasons for International Differences in Financial Reporting, in: Abacus, 34 (2), p. 162–187.

Nobes, C. W. (2006): The survival of international differences under IFRS: towards a research agenda, in: Accounting & Business Research, 36 (3), p. 233–245.

Nobes, C. W./Parker, R. H. (2008): Comparative international accounting, Harlow.

Noravesh, I./Dilami, Z. D./Bazaz, M. S. (2007): The impact of culture on accounting - does Gray's model apply to Iran?, in: Review of accounting and finance, 6 (3), p. 254–272.

NYSE Euronext (2009): Rules for the CAC 40 index, available at: http://www.euronext.com, last revised 01.03.2011.

NYSE Euronext (2010): NYSE Euronext Corporate Timeline, available at: http://www.nyse.com, last revised 01.03.2011.

Obermaier, R. (2009): Fair Value-Bewertung nach IFRS auf der Basis von Barwertkalkülen – Ermittlung und Wirkungen kapitalmarktorientierter Basiszinssätze, in: KoR, 9 (10), p. 545–554.

O'Connell, V./Sullivan, K. (2008): The Impact of Mandatory Conversion to IFRS on the Net Income of FTSEurofirst 80 Firms, in: Journal of Applied Research in Accounting and Finance, 3 (2), p. 17–26.

O'Hara, M. (2003): Presidential Address: Liquidity and Price Discovery, in: The Journal of Finance, 58 (4), p. 1335–1354.

Ohlson, J. A./Zhang, X.-J. (1998): Accrual Accounting and Equity Valuation, in: Journal of Accounting Research, 36 (1), p. 85–111.

Online Etymology Dictionary (2010): Babel, available at: http://www.etymonline.com, last revised 01.03.2011.

Online Etymology Dictionary (2011): Culture, available at: http://www.etymonline.com, last revised 01.03.2011.

Ordelheide, D. (1994): Notwendigkeiten und Probleme der Weiterentwicklung der EG-Bilanzrichtlinien und des deutschen Konzernabschlussrechts, in: Baetge, J. (ed.): Die deutsche Rechnungslegung vor dem Hintergrund internationaler Entwicklungen, Düsseldorf (1994), p. 11–40.

Ordelheide, D. (2001): Germany - Group Accounts, in: Ordelheide, D./KPMG (eds.): Transnational accounting, Basingstoke (2001), p. 1353–1450.

Ordelheide, D./KPMG (eds.) (1995): Transnational Accounting, Basingstoke (1995).

Organisation for Economic Co-operation and Development [OECD] (1980): Accounting practices in OECD member countries, Paris.

Otley, D. T. (1980): The contingency theory of management accounting: Achievement and prognosis, in: Accounting, Organizations and Society, 5 (4), p. 413–428.

Pacter, P./Colson, R. H. (2003): Convergence IFRS and U.S. GAAP, in: CPA Journal, 73 (3), p. 67.

Parker, R. H. (2001): Accounting in Europe – European languages of accounting, in: European Accounting Review, 10 (1), p. 133–147.

Paul, S. R./Zhang, X. (2010): Testing for normality in linear regression models, in: Journal of Statistical Computation and Simulation, 80 (10), p. 1101–1113.

Pellens, B./Fülbier, R. U./Gassen, J./Sellhorn, T. (2008): Internationale Rechnungslegung, Stuttgart.

Pellens, B./Jödicke, D./Jödicke, R. (2007): Anwendbarkeit nicht freigegebener IFRS innerhalb der EU, in: Betriebs-Berater, 62 (46), p. 2503-2407.

Pellens, B./Sellhorn, T./Strzyz, A. (2008): The role of conservatism in decision-useful financial reporting, in: Bruns, H.-G./Herz, R. H./Neubürger, H.-J./Tweedie, D. (eds.): Globale Finanzberichterstattung. Entwicklung, Anwendung und Durchsetzung von IFRS, Stuttgart (2008), p. 167–193.

Peltzman, S. (1976): Toward a More General Theory of Regulation, in: Journal of Law and Economics, 19 (2), p. 211–240.

Penman, S. H./Zhang, X.-J. (2002): Accounting Conservatism, the Quality of Earnings, and Stock Returns, in: The Accounting Review, 77 (2), p. 237–264.

Perera, H./Most, K. S. (1994): Culture and International Accounting: Some Thoughts on Research Issues and Prospects, in: Advances in international accounting, 7 (1), p. 267–285.

Perotti, E. C./van Oijen, P. (2001): Privatization, political risk and stock market development in emerging economies, in: Journal of International Money and Finance, 20 (1), p. 43–69.

Peterson, M. F./Castro, S. L. (2006): Measurement metrics at aggregate levels of analysis: Implications for organization culture research and the GLOBE project – Special section: Cross-Cultural Leadership, in: The Leadership Quarterly, 17 (5), p. 506–521.

Petite, M. (1984): The conditions for consolidation under the 7th Company Law Directive, in: Common Market Law Review, 9 (21), p. 81–121.

Pfaff, D./Zweifel, P. (1998): Die Principal-Agent Theorie - Ein fruchtbarer Beitrag der Wirtschaftstheorie zur Praxis, in: Wirtschaftswissenschaftliches Studium, 27 (4), p. 184–190.

Picot, A. (1991): Ökonomische Theorien der Organisation: ein Überblick über neuere Ansätze und deren betriebswirtschaftliches Anwendungspotential, in: Ordelheide, D./Rudolph, B./Büsselmann, E. (eds.): Betriebswirtschaftslehre und ökonomische Theorie, Stuttgart (1991), p. 143–170.

Piot, C./Dumontier, P./Janin, R. (2010): IFRS Consequences on Accounting Conservatism Within Europe, available at: http://ssrn.com, last revised 01.03.2011.

Pöller, R. (2007a): Explizite Wahlrechte und Ermessensspielräume (faktische Wahlrechte) nach IFRS - Teil 1: Sachanlagevermögen und als Finanzinvestitionen gehaltene Immobilien, in: Bilanzbuchhalter und Controller, 31 (1), p. 1–6.

Pöller, R. (2007b): Explizite Wahlrechte und Ermessensspielräume (faktische Wahlrechte) nach IFRS ; Teil 2: immaterielle Vermögenswerte, in: Bilanzbuchhalter und Controller, 31 (6), p. 172–177.

Pöller, R. (2008): Explizite Wahlrechte und Ermessensspielräume (faktische Wahlrechte) nach IFRS, Teil 3 : langfristige finanzielle Vermögenswerte, in: Bilanzbuchhalter und Controller, 32 (5), p. 118–121.

Pope, P. F./Rees, W. P. (1992): International Differences in GAAP and the Pricing of Earnings, in: Journal of International Financial Management & Accounting, 4 (3), p. 190–219.

Popper, K. R. (1994): Logik der Forschung, Tübingen.

Pourjali, H./Meek, G. K. (1995): Accounting and culture: the case of Iran, in: Research in Accounting in Emerging Economies, 3 (1), p. 3–17.

Price Waterhouse (1973): Accounting Principles and Reporting Practices: A Survey in 38 Countries, London.

Price Waterhouse (1976): A survey in 46 countries. Accounting principles and reporting practices, London.

Price Waterhouse (1979): International Survey of Accounting Principles and Reporting Practices, London.

PricewaterhouseCoopers (2009): PricewaterhouseCoopers post FY2009 global revenues of US$26.2 billion, available at: http://www.pwc.com, last revised 01.03.2011.

PricewaterhouseCoopers Österreich (2008): IFRS aktuell. Neues aus der internationalen Rechnungslegung, available at: http://www.pwc.com, last revised 01.03.2011.

Qiang, X. (2007): The Effects of Contracting, Litigation, Regulation, and Tax Costs on Conditional and Unconditional Conservatism: Cross-Sectional Evidence at the Firm Level, in: The Accounting Review, 82 (3), p. 759–796.

Radebaugh, L. H./Gebhardt, G./Gray, S. J. (1995): Foreign Stock Exchange Listings: A Case Study of Daimler-Benz, in: Journal of International Financial Management & Accounting, 6 (2), p. 158–192.

Radebaugh, L. H. (1975): Environmental Factors Influencing the Development of Accounting Objectives, Standards, and Practices in Peru, in: International Journal of Accounting, 11 (1), p. 39–56.

Radebaugh, L. H./Gray, S. J./Black, E. L. (2006): International accounting and multinational enterprises, Hoboken, NJ.

Raffée, H. (1974): Grundprobleme der Betriebswirtschaftslehre, Göttingen.

Raffée, H. (1993): Gegenstand, Methoden und Konzepte der Betriebswirtschaftslehre, in: Bitz, M./Domsch, M./Ewert, R./Wagner, F. W. (eds.): Vahlens Kompendium der Betriebswirtschaftslehre, München (1993), p. 1–46.

Raffée, H./Abel, B. (1979): Aufgaben und aktuelle Tendenzen der Wissenschaftstheorie in den Wirtschaftswissenschaften, in: Raffée, H./Abel, B. (eds.): Wissenschaftstheoretische Grundfragen der Wirtschaftswissenschaften, München (1979), p. 1–10.

Raffournier, B. (1995): The determinants of voluntary financial disclosure by Swiss listed companies, in: European Accounting Review, 4 (2), p. 261–280.

Rahman, A./Perera, H./Ganesh, S. (2002): Accounting Practice Harmony, Accounting Regulation and Firm Characteristics, in: Abacus, 38 (1), p. 46–77.

Rahman, A./Yammeesri, J./Perera, H. (2010): Financial reporting quality in international settings: A comparative study of the USA, Japan, Thailand, France and Germany, in: The International Journal of Accounting, 45 (1), p. 1–34.

Rees, L./Elgers, P. (1997): The Market's Valuation of Nonreported Accounting Measures: Retrospective Reconciliations of Non-U.S. and U.S. GAAP, in: Journal of Accounting Research, 35 (1), p. 115–127.

Reichelstein, S. (2000): Providing Managerial Incentives: Cash Flows versus Accrual Accounting, in: Journal of Accounting Research, 38 (2), p. 243–269.

Revsine, L./Collins, D. W./Johnson, W. B. (2005): Financial reporting and analysis, Upper Saddle River, NJ.

Richard, J. (2001): France - Group Accounts, in: Ordelheide, D./KPMG (eds.): Transnational accounting, Basingstoke (2001), p. 1127–1216.

Richard, J. (2005): Système comptable français et normes IFRS, Paris.

Richter, F. (2010): Segmentberichterstattung nach IFRS – Eine Fallstudie zur praktischen Umsetzung, in: IRZ, 5 (11), p. 511–518.

Richter, R./Bindseil, U. (1995): Neue Institutionenökonomik, in: Wirtschaftswissenschaftliches Studium, 24 (3), p. 132–140.

Richter, R./Furubotn, E. G./Streissler, M. (2003): Neue Institutionenökonomik – Eine Einführung und kritische Würdigung, Tübingen.

Riesenhuber, F. (2009): Großzahlige empirische Forschung, in: Albers, S./Klapper, D./Konradt, U./Walter, A./Wolf, J. (eds.): Methodik der empirischen Forschung, Wiesbaden (2009), p. 1–16.

Roberts, C. B./Salter, S. B. (1999): Attitudes towards Uniform Accounting: Cultural or Economic Phenomena?, in: Journal of International Financial Management & Accounting, 10 (2), p. 121–142.

Roberts, C. B./Weetman, P./Gordon, P. (2008): International corporate reporting – A comparative approach, Harlow.

Roberts, J./Scapens, R. (1985): Accounting systems and systems of accountability - understanding accounting practices in their organisational contexts, in: Accounting, Organizations and Society, 10 (4), p. 443–456.

Roberts, R. W. (1992): Determinants of corporate social responsibility disclosure: An application of stakeholder theory, in: Accounting, Organizations and Society, 17 (6), p. 595–612.

Rogler, S. (2009a): Segmentberichterstattung nach IFRS 8 im Fokus von Bilanzpolitik und Bilanzanalyse (Teil 1), in: KoR, 9 (9), p. 500–505.

Rogler, S. (2009b): Segmentberichterstattung nach IFRS 8 im Fokus von Bilanzpolitik und Bilanzanalyse (Teil 2), in: Zeitschrift für kapitalmarktorientierte Rechnungslegung, 9 (10), p. 576–583.

Ross, S. A. (1973): The Economic Theory of Agency: The Principal's Problem, in: American Economic Review, 63 (2), p. 134–139.

Rössler, P. (2005): Inhaltsanalyse, Konstanz.

Ruekert, R. W./Walker, O. C./Roering, K. J. (1985): The Organization of Marketing Activities: A Contingency Theory of Structure and Performance, in: The Journal of Marketing, 49 (1), p. 13–25.

Russel, R. (2008): UK Companies Act 2006 - the next implementation phase, available at: http://www.mallesons.com, last revised 01.03.2011.

Ryan, T. P. (2009): Modern regression methods, Hoboken, NJ.

Salter, S. B./Niswander, F. (1995): Cultural influence on the development of accounting systems internationally – A test of Gray's (1988) Theory, in: Journal of International Business Studies, 26 (2), p. 379–397.

Salvatore, D./Reagle, D. P. (2002): Schaum's outline of theory and problems of statistics and econometrics, New York.

Samuels, J. M./Oliga, J. C. (1982): Accounting Standards in Developing Countries, in: International Journal of Accounting, 18 (1), p. 69–88.

Samuels, J. M./Piper, A. G. (1985): International accounting – A survey, London.

Sanio, J. (2008): Das deutsche Enforcementsystem – Erfahrungen und Perspektiven für die Zukunft, in: Bruns, H.-G./Herz, R. H./Neubürger, H.-J./Tweedie, D. (eds.): Globale Finanzberichterstattung. Entwicklung, Anwendung und Durchsetzung von IFRS, Stuttgart (2008), p. 515–528.

Saudagaran, S. M./Biddle, G. C. (1992): Financial Disclosure Levels and Foreign Stock Exchange Listing Decisions, in: Journal of International Financial Management & Accounting, 4 (2), p. 106–148.

Saudagaran, S. M./Diga, J. G. (1999): Evaluation of the Contingency-Based Approach in Comparative International Accounting - A Case for Alternative Research Paradigms, in: Journal of Accounting Literature, 18 (1), p. 57–95.

Saudagaran, S. M./Meek, G. K. (1997): A Review of Research on the Relationship between International Capital Markets and Financial Reporting by Multinational Firms, in: Journal of Accounting Literature, 16 (1), p. 127–159.

Saville, D. J. (1990): Multiple Comparison Procedures: The Practical Solution, in: The American Statistician, 44 (2), p. 174–180.

Scheid, J. C./Walton, P. (1992): European Financial Reporting: France, London.

Schendera, C. F. G. (2007): Datenqualität mit SPSS, München.

Schipper, K. (1981): Discussion of Voluntary Corporate Disclosure: The Case of Interim Reporting, in: Journal of Accounting Research, 19 (1), p. 85–88.

Schipper, K. (2005): The introduction of International Accounting Standards in Europe: Implications for international convergence, in: European Accounting Review, 14 (1), p. 101–126.

Schleicher, T./Tahoun, A./Walker, M. (2010): IFRS adoption in Europe and investment-cash flow sensitivity: Outsider versus insider economies, in: The International Journal of Accounting, 45 (2), p. 143–168.

Schmid, S. (1996): Multikulturalität in der internationalen Unternehmung – Konzepte, Reflexionen, Implikationen, Wiesbaden.

Schmid, S./Kotulla, T. (2010): Die GLOBE-Studie - Kultur und erfolgreiches Leadership in Zeiten der Globalisierung, in: Wirtschaftswissenschaftliches Studium, 39 (2), p. 61–69.

Schnell, R./Hill, P. B./Esser, E. (2005): Methoden der empirischen Sozialforschung, München.

Schreyögg, G. (1980): Contingency and Choice in Organization Theory, in: Organization Studies (Walter de Gruyter GmbH & Co. KG.), 1 (4), p. 305–326.

Schroeder, R. G./Clark, M. W./Cathey, J. M. (2008): Financial accounting theory and analysis – Text readings and cases, Hoboken, NJ.

Schüle, A. (2006): Die Bilanzierung immaterieller Vermögenswerte einschließlich des Goodwills im Rahmen von Unternehmenserwerben gemäß IFRS 3 und IDW RS HFA 16 - Unter besonderer Berücksichtigung der Phase II des IASB-Projekts 'Business Combinations', Hamburg.

Schultz, J. J./Lopez, T. J. (2001): The impact of national influence on accounting estimates – Implications for international accounting standard-setters, in: International Journal of Accounting, 36 (3), p. 271–290.

Schultze, W./Kafadar, K./Thierke, S. (2008): Die Kaufpreisallokation bei Unternehmenszusammenschlüssen nach IFRS 3 (a. F.) und IFRS 3 (rev. 2008) - Eine kritische Analyse ausgewählter Aspekte, in: Deutsches Steuerrecht, 46 (28), p. 1348–1354.

Schwartz, S. H. (1994): Beyond Individualism/Collectivism: New Dimensions of Values, in: Kim, U./Triandis, H. C./Kagitcibasi, C./Choi, S. C./Yoon, G. (eds.): Individualism and collectivism. Theory, method, and applications, Thousand Oaks, Calif (1994), p. 85–122.

Schweikart, J. A. (1985): Contingency Theory as a Framework for Research in International Accounting, in: International Journal of Accounting, 21 (1), p. 89–99.

Scott, W. R. (2006): Financial accounting theory, Toronto.

Securities and Exchange Commission [SEC] : Release NO. 33-8879: Acceptance From Foreign Private Issuers of Financial Statements Prepared In Accordance With International Financial Reporting Standards Without Reconciliation To U.S. GAAP, available at: http://www.sec.gov/rules/final/2007/33-8879.pdf, last revised 01.03.2011.

Securities and Exchange Commission [SEC] (2000): SEC Concept Release: International Accounting Standards, available at: http://www.sec.gov, last revised 01.03.2011.

Securities and Exchange Commission [SEC] (2005): Chairman Donaldson Meets with EU Internal Market Commissioner McCreevy, available at: http://www.sec.gov, last revised 01.03.2011.

Securities and Exchange Commission [SEC] (2007): Acceptance from foreign private issuers of financial statements prepared in accordance with International Financial Reporting Standards without reconciliation to U.S. GAAP, available at: http://www.sec.gov, last revised 01.03.2011.

Securities and Exchange Commission [SEC] (2008a): Division of Corporation Finance: Standard Industrial Classification (SIC) Code List, available at: http://www.sec.gov, last revised 01.03.2011.

Securities and Exchange Commission [SEC] (2008b): The Investor's Advocate: How the SEC Protects Investors, Maintains Market Integrity, and Facilitates Capital Formation, available at: http://www.sec.gov, last revised 01.03.2011.

Securities and Exchange Commission [SEC] (2010a): Commission Statement in Support of Convergence and Global Accounting Standards, available at: http://www.sec.gov, last revised 01.03.2011.

Securities and Exchange Commission [SEC] (2010b): Search the Next-Generation EDGAR System, available at: http://www.sec.gov, last revised 01.03.2011.

Securities and Exchange Commission [SEC] (2010c): Work Plan for the Consideration of Incorporating International Financial Reporting Standards into the Financial Reporting System for U.S. Issuers: Progress Report October 29, 2010, available at: http://www.sec.gov, last revised 01.03.2011.

Sellhorn, T./Gornik-Tomaszewski, S. (2006): Implications of the 'IAS Regulation' for Research into the International Differences in Accounting Systems, in: Accounting in Europe, 3 (1), p. 187–217.

Shalev, R. (2009): The Information Content of Business Combination Disclosure Level, in: The Accounting Review, 84 (1), p. 239–270.

Siegel, S. (1956): Nonparametric statistics for the behavioral sciences, New York.

Siegel, S. (1957): Nonparametric Statistics, in: The American Statistician, 11 (3), p. 13–19.

Siegfried, J. (1975): Determinants of Antitrust Activity, in: Journal of Law and Economics, 18 (2), p. 559–581.

Silverstein, C./Brin, S./Motwani, R./Ullman, J. (2000): Scalable Techniques for Mining Causal Structures, in: Data Mining and Knowledge Discovery, 4 (2), p. 163–192.

Simmonds, A./Azières, O. (1989): Accounting for Europe : success by 2000 AD?, London.

Simunic, D. A./Stein, M. T. (1996): The Impact of Litigation Risk on Audit Pricing: A Review of the Economics and the Evidence, in: Auditing, 15 (2), p. 119–134.

Singhvi, S. S./Desai, H. B. (1971): An empirical analysis of the quality of corporate financial disclosure, in: The Accounting Review, 46 (1), p. 129–138.

Singleton, W. R./Globerman, S. (2002): The changing nature of financial disclosure in Japan, in: The International Journal of Accounting, 37 (1), p. 95–111.

Sivakumar, K./Nakata, C. (2001): The Stampede toward Hofstede's Framework: Avoiding the Sample Design Pit in Cross-Cultural Research, in: Journal of International Business Studies, 32 (3), p. 555–574.

Sivitanides, P./Southard, J./Torto, R. G./Wheaton, W. C. (2001): The determinants of appraisal-based capitalization rates, in: Real Estate Finance, 18 (2), p. 27–38.

Slovic, P./Fleissner, D./Bauman, W. S. (1972): Analyzing the Use of Information in Investment Decision Making: A Methodological Proposal, in: The Journal of Business, 45 (2), p. 283–301.

Smith, M. (2011): Research methods in accounting, Los Angeles.

Smith, M./Taffler, R. J. (2000): The chairman's statement - A content analysis of discretionary narrative disclosures, in: Accounting, Auditing & Accountability Journal, 13 (5), p. 624–646.

Smith, P. B./Peterson, M. F./Schwartz, S. H. (2002): Cultural Values, Sources of Guidance, and their Relevance to Managerial Behavior, in: Journal of Cross-Cultural Psychology, 33 (2), p. 188–208.

Solo, R. A. (1991): The philosophy of science, and economics, Armonk, NY.

Sondergaard, M. (1994): Research Note: Hofstede's Consequences: A Study of Reviews, Citations and Replications, in: Organization Studies (Walter de Gruyter GmbH & Co. KG.), 15 (3), p. 447–456.

Sorge, A./Maurice, M. (1993): The societal effect in the strategies of French and West German machine tool manufacturers, in: Kogut, B. (ed.): Country competitiveness. Technology and the organizing of work, New York (1993), p. 57–90.

Sorge, A./Warner, M. (1986): Comparative factory organisation – An Anglo-German comparison of manufacturing, management, and manpower, Aldershot, Hants, England, Brookfield, Vt., USA.

Spence, M. (1973): Job Market Signaling, in: Quarterly Journal of Economics, 83 (3), p. 355–374.

Spence, M. (2002): Signaling in Retrospect and the Informational Structure of Markets, in: The American Economic Review, 92 (3), p. 434–459.

Spremann, K. (1987): Agency theory and risk sharing, in: Bamberg, G./Ballwieser, W. (eds.): Agency theory, information, and incentives, Berlin (1987), p. 3–38.

Spremann, K. (1991): Asymmetrische Information, in: Zeitschrift für Bebriebswirtschaft, 60 (5/6), p. 561–586.

St. Pierre, K./Anderson, J. A. (1984): An Analysis of the Factors Associated with Lawsuits Against Public Accountants, in: Accounting Review, 59 (2), p. 242–263.

Staehle, W. H./Conrad, P. (2009): Management. Eine verhaltenswissenschaftliche Perspektive, München.

Steinmann, H./Scherer, A. G. (2000): Wissenschaftstheorie, in: Corsten, H. (ed.): Lexikon der Betriebswirtschaftslehre, München (2000), p. 1056–1063.

Sterling, R. R. (1967): Conservatism: The Fundamental Principle of Valuation in Traditional Accounting, in: Abacus, 3 (2), p. 109–132.

Sterling, R. R. (1990): Positive Accounting: An Assessment, in: Abacus, 26 (2), p. 97–135.

Sterling, T. D. (1959): Publication Decisions and Their Possible Effects on Inferences Drawn from Tests of Significance--Or Vice Versa, in: Journal of the American Statistical Association, 54 (285), p. 30–34.

Stevens, S. S. (1946): On the Theory of Scales of Measurement, in: Science, 103 (2684), p. 677–680.

Stickel-Wolf, C./Wolf, J. (2005): Wissenschaftliches Arbeiten und Lerntechniken, Wiesbaden.

Stigler, G. J. (1971): The Theory of Economic Regulation, in: The Bell Journal of Economics and Management Science, 2 (1), p. 3–21.

Stiglitz, J. E. (1975): The Theory of "Screening", Education, and the Distribution of Income, in: The American Economic Review, 65 (3), p. 283–300.

Stilling, P./Norton, R./Hopkins, L. (1984): Financial Times World accounting survey 1984: an analysis of major international companies annual reports and accounts, and digest of their results, London.

Stinchcombe, A. L. (1959): Bureaucratic and Craft Administration of Production: A Comparative Study, in: Administrative Science Quarterly, 4 (2), p. 168–187.

Stolowy, H./Haller, A./Klockhaus, V. (2001): Accounting for Brands in France and Germany Compared With IAS 38 (Intangible Assets): An Illustration of the Difficulty of International Harmonization, in: International Journal of Accounting, 36 (2), p. 147–168.

Street, D. L./Bryant, S. M. (2000): Disclosure level and compliance with IASs: a comparison of companies with and without US listings and filings, in: The International Journal of Accounting, 35 (3), p. 305–329.

Street, D. L./Gray, S. J. (2001): Observance of international accounting standards – Factors explaining non-compliance, London.

Street, D. L./Gray, S. J./Bryant, S. M. (1999): Acceptance and Observance of International Accounting Standards: An Empirical Study of Companies Claiming to Comply with IASs, in: International Journal of Accounting, 34 (1), p. 11–38.

Subramaniam, N. (2006): Agency theory and accounting research: an overview of some conceptual and empirical issues, in: Hoque, Z. (ed.): Methodological issues in accounting research. Theories, methods and issues, London (2006), p. 55–81.

Sudarwan, M./Fogarty, T. J. (1996): Culture and Accounting in Indonesia: An Empirical Examination, in: International Journal of Accounting, 31 (4), p. 463–482.

Sunder, S. (1997): Theory of accounting and control, Cincinnati, Ohio.

Szabo, E./Brodbeck, F. C./Den Hartog, D. N./Reber, G./Weibler, J./Wunderer, R. (2002): The Germanic Europe cluster: where employees have a voice, in: Journal of World Business, 37 (1), p. 55–68.

Tabachnick, B. G./Fidell, L. S. (2007): Using multivariate statistics, Boston, Mass.

Tanski, J. S. (2004): Bilanzpolitische Spielräume in den IFRS, in: Deutsches Steuerrecht, 42 (43), p. 1843–1847.

Taras, V./Steel, P./Kirkman, B. L. (2010): Negative practice-value correlations in the GLOBE data: Unexpected findings, questionnaire limitations and research directions, in: Journal of International Business Studies, 41 (8), p. 1330–1338.

Tarca, A. (2004): International Convergence of Accounting Practices: Choosing between IAS and US GAAP, in: Journal of International Financial Management & Accounting, 15 (1), p. 60–91.

Tarca, A./Moy, M./Morris, R. D. (2005): An Investigation of the Relationship Between Use of International Accounting Standards and Source of Company Finance in Germany, available at: http://ssrn.com, last revised 01.03.2011.

Tay, J. S. W./Parker, R. H. (1990): Measuring International Harmonization and Standardization, in: Abacus, 26 (1), p. 71–88.

Taylor, M. E./Evans, T. G./Joy, A. C. (1986): The Impact of IASC Accounting Standards on Comparability and Consistency of International Accounting Reporting Practices, in: International Journal of Accounting, 22 (1), p. 1–10.

Taylor, P. A. (1995): United Kingdom - Group Accounts, in: Ordelheide, D./KPMG (eds.): Transnational Accounting, Basingstoke (1995), p. 2801–2956.

Thomas, A. P. (1986): The contingency theory of corporate reporting: Some empirical evidence, in: Accounting, Organizations and Society, 11 (3), p. 253–270.

Thomas, A. P. (1991): Towards a Contingency Theory of Corporate Financial, in: Accounting, Auditing & Accountability Journal, 4 (4), p. 40–57.

Thorell, P./Whittington, G. (1994): The harmonization of accounting within the EU, in: European Accounting Review, 3 (2), p. 215–240.

Tinker, A. M./Merino, B. D./Neimark, M. D. (1982): The normative origins of positive theories: Ideology and accounting thought, in: Accounting, Organizations and Society, 7 (2), p. 167–200.

Toutenburg, H./Schomaker, M./Wißmann, M. (2006): Arbeitsbuch zur deskriptiven und induktiven Statistik, Berlin.

Trompenaars, A. (1993): Riding the waves of culture – Understanding cultural diversity in business, London.

Tsakumis, G. T. (2007): The influence of culture on accountants' application of financial reporting rules, in: Abacus, 43 (1), p. 27–48.

Tunc, A. (1982): A French Lawyer Looks at American Corporation Law and Securities Regulation, in: University of Pennsylvania Law Review, 130 (4), p. 757–774.

Tung, R. L./Verbeke, A. (2010): Beyond Hofstede and GLOBE: Improving the quality of cross-cultural research, in: Journal of International Business Studies, 41 (8), p. 1259–1274.

Udy, S. H., JR. (1959): "Bureaucracy" and "Rationality" in Weber's Organization Theory: An Empirical Study, in: American Sociological Review, 24 (6), p. 791–795.

Uhde, M. (1999): Harmonisierung der Rechnungslegung nach den Vorschriften des IASC? – Anwendung im internationalen Vergleich, München.

Ulrich, B. (1993): Kontingenztheorie und autopoietische Systemtheorie der Organisation: ein evaluativer Vergleich zweier organisationstheoretischer Ansätze unter besonderer Berücksichtigung der Organisations-Umwelt-Beziehung.

Ulrich, P./Hill, W. (1976a): Wissenschaftstheoretische Grundlagen der Betriebswirtschaftslehre (Teil I), in: Wirtschaftswissenschaftliches Studium, 5 (7), p. 304–309.

Ulrich, P./Hill, W. (1976b): Wissenschaftstheoretische Grundlagen der Betriebswirtschaftslehre (Teil II), in: Wirtschaftswissenschaftliches Studium, 5 (8), p. 345–350.

Unerman, J. (2000): Methodological issues - Reflections on quantification in corporate social reporting content analysis, in: Accounting, Auditing & Accountability Journal, 13 (5), p. 667–680.

Utz, D./Hoheisel, M. (2010): Wegfall der umgekehrten Maßgeblichkeit durch das BilMoG - die Bilanzierung von § 6b-Rücklagen (Aufzeichnungspflichten), in: Zeitschrift für Bilanzierung, Rechnungswesen und Controlling, 34 (7), p. 322–325.

van der Meulen, S./Gaeremynck, A./Willekens, M. (2007): Attribute differences between U.S. GAAP and IFRS earnings: An exploratory study, in: The International Journal of Accounting, 42 (2), p. 123–142.

van der Tas, L. G. (1988): Measuring Harmonisation of Financial Reporting Practice, in: Accounting & Business Research, 18 (70), p. 157–169.

van der Tas, L. G. (1992): Evidence of EC financial reporting practice harmonization, in: European Accounting Review, 1 (1), p. 69–104.

van Horne, J. C./Wachowicz, J. M. (2005): Fundamentals of financial management, Harlow.

van Hulle, K. (1997): The true and fair view override in the European Accounting Directives, in: European Accounting Review, 6 (4), p. 711–720.

van Hulle, K. (2004): From Accounting Directives to International Accounting Standards, in: Leuz, C./Pfaff, D./Hopwood, A. G. (eds.): The economics and politics of accounting. International perspectives on research trends, policy, and practice, Oxford (2004), p. 349–375.

van Hulle, K. (2008): IFRS as accounting standards for Europe, in: Bruns, H.-G./Herz, R. H./Neubürger, H.-J./Tweedie, D. (eds.): Globale Finanzberichterstattung. Entwicklung, Anwendung und Durchsetzung von IFRS, Stuttgart (2008), p. 71–87.

van Nimwegen, T. (2002): Global banking, global values: The in-house reception of the corporate values of ABN Amro, Delft.

van Tendeloo, B./Vanstraelen, A. (2005): Earnings management under German GAAP versus IFRS, in: European Accounting Review, 14 (1), p. 155–180.

Velleman, P. F./Leland Wilkinson (1993): Nominal, Ordinal, Interval, and Ratio Typologies Are Misleading, in: The American Statistician, 47 (1), p. 65–72.

Venaik, S./Brewer, P. (2010): Avoiding uncertainty in Hofstede and GLOBE, in: Journal of International Business Studies, 41 (8), p. 1294–1315.

Verrecchia, R. E. (1983): Discretionary disclosure, in: Journal of Accounting and Economics, 5 (1), p. 179–194.

von Keitz, I. (2005): Praxis der IASB-Rechnungslegung – Best practice von 100 IFRS-Anwendern, Stuttgart.

von Keitz, I. (2007): Einheitliche oder länderspezifische Auslegung der IFRS?, in: Kirsch, H.-J./Thiele, S. (Eds.), Rechnungslegung und Wirtschaftsprüfung, Düsseldorf, p. 321-357.

von Keitz, I./Stolle, I. (2008): Fehlerfeststellung, -veröffentlichung und -korrektur im Rahmen des deutschen Enforcement – Anforderungen, Herausforderungen und Analyse der praktischen Umsetzung, in: KoR, 8 (4), p. 213–226.

Wagenhofer, A. (2005): Internationale Rechnungslegungsstandards - IAS/IFRS, Frankfurt a.M.

Wagner, F. W. (1990): Tax balance sheet, in: Grochla, E./Gaugler, E. (eds.): Handbook of German business management, Stuttgart (1990), p. 2334–2340.

Wallace, R./Gernon, H. (1991): Frameworks for International Comparative Financial Accounting, in: Journal of Accounting Literature, 10 (1), p. 209–264.

Wallace, R./Naser, K. (1995): Firm-specific determinants of the comprehensiveness of mandatory disclosure in the corporate annual reports of firms listed on the stock exchange in Hong Kong, in: Journal of Accounting and Public Policy, 14 (4), p. 311–368.

Wallace, R./Naser, K./Mora, A. (1994): The relationship between the comprehensiveness of corporate annual reports and firm characteristics in Spain, in: Accounting & Business Research, 25 (97), p. 41–53.

Walsh, P./Craig, R./Clarke, F. (1991): 'Big Bath Accounting' Using Extraordinary Items Adjustments: Australian Empirical Evidence, in: Journal of Business Finance & Accounting, 18 (2), p. 173–189.

Walton, P. (1992): Harmonization of Accounting in France and Britain: Some Evidence, in: Abacus, 28 (2), p. 187–199.

Walton, P. (1993): Introduction: the true and fair view in British accounting, in: European Accounting Review, 2 (1), p. 49–58.

Wang, J. (1993): A Model of Intertemporal Asset Prices Under Asymmetric Information, in: The Review of Economic Studies, 60 (2), p. 249–282.

Wang, K./O, S./Claiborne, M. C. (2008): Determinants and consequences of voluntary disclosure in an emerging market: Evidence from China, in: Journal of International Accounting, Auditing and Taxation, 17 (1), p. 14–30.

Wang, R. Z./Ó Hogartaigh, C./van Zijl, T. (2009): Measures of Accounting Conservatism: A Construct Validity Perspective, in: Journal of Accounting Literature, 28 (1), p. 165–203.

Wasserhess, J. (2006): IFRS 3 Business Combinations - Kaufpreisallokation und immaterielle Vermögenswerte, Saarbrücken.

Watrin, C./Hoehne, F./Lammert, J. (2009): IAS 27. Konzern- und separate Einzelabschlüsse nach IFRS (Consolidated and Separate Financial Statements), in: Hennrichs, J./Kleindiek, D./Watrin, C. (eds.): Münchner Kommentar zum Bilanzrecht, München (2009).

Watrin, C./Rose, G. (2009): Ertragsteuern – Einkommensteuer, Körperschaftsteuer, Gewerbesteuer, Berlin.

Watrin, C./Strohm, C. (2006a): Principles-Based Accounting Standards - Paradigmenwechsel der US-Rechnungslegung?, in: KoR, 6 (2), p. 123–127.

Watrin, C./Strohm, C. (2006b): The Joint Business Combinations Project – IFRS 3 and the Project's Impact on Convergence with U.S. GAAP, in: CPA Journal , p. 22–25.

Watts, R. L. (1995): Nature and origins of positive research in accounting, in: Jones, S./Romano, C./Ratnatunga, J. (eds.): Accounting Theory : a contemporary review, Sydney; London (1995), p. 295–353.

Watts, R. L. (2003a): Conservatism in Accounting Part I: Explanations and Implications, in: Accounting Horizons, 17 (3), p. 207–221.

Watts, R. L. (2003b): Conservatism in Accounting Part II: Evidence and Research Opportunities, in: Accounting Horizons, 17 (4), p. 287–301.

Watts, R. L./Zimmerman, J. L. (1978): Towards a Positive Theory of the Determination of Accounting Standards, in: The Accounting Review, 53 (1), p. 112–134.

Watts, R. L./Zimmerman, J. L. (1979): The Demand for and Supply of Accounting Theories: The Market for Excuses, in: The Accounting Review, 54 (2), p. 273–305.

Watts, R. L./Zimmerman, J. L. (1983): Agency problems, auditing, and the theory of the firm: some evidence, in: Journal of Law and Economics, 26 (3), p. 613–633.

Watts, R. L./Zimmerman, J. L. (1986): Positive accounting theory, Englewood Cliffs, New Jersey.

Watts, R. L./Zimmerman, J. L. (1990): Positive Accounting Theory: A Ten Year Perspective, in: The Accounting Review, 65 (1), p. 131–156.

Weetman, P./Jones, E. A. E./Adams, C. A./Gray, S. J. (1998): Profit Measurement and UK Accounting Standards: A Case of Increasing Disharmony in Relation to US GAAP and IASs, in: Accounting & Business Research, 28 (3), p. 189–208.

Weetman, P./Gray, S. J. (1990): International Financial Analysis and Comparative Corporate Performance: The Impact of UK versus US Accounting Principles on Earnings, in: Journal of International Financial Management & Accounting, 2 (2-3), p. 111–130.

Weirich, T. R./Avery, C. G./Anderson, H. R. (1971): International Accounting: Varying definitions, in: International Journal of Accounting, 7 (1), p. 79–88.

Weizsäcker, C. F. v. (2006): The structur of physics, Dordrecht.

Welch, D. E./Welch, L. S. (2008): The importance of language in international knowledge transfer, in: Management International Review, 48 (3), p. 339–360.

Wendlandt, K. (2008): Einfluss der IFRS auf die Entwicklung der DRS und deren praktische Anwendung, in: Bruns, H.-G./Herz, R. H./Neubürger, H.-J./Tweedie, D. (eds.): Globale Finanzberichterstattung. Entwicklung, Anwendung und Durchsetzung von IFRS, Stuttgart (2008), p. 445–469.

Wenger, E. (1988): Die Beziehung zwischen Agent und Prinzipal als Baustein einer ökonomischen Theorie der Organisation, in: Wirtschaftswissenschaftliches Studium, 17 (10), p. 506–514.

Westfall, P. H. (1986): Asymptotic Normality of the Anova Estimates of Components of Variance in the Nonnormal, Unbalanced Hierarchal Mixed Model, in: The Annals of Statistics, 14 (4), p. 1572–1582.

Westwood, R. G./Everett, J. E. (1987): Culture's consequences: A methodology for comparative management studies in Southeast Asia?, in: Asia Pacific Journal of Management, 4 (3), p. 187–202.

Whittington, G. (1986): Financial Accounting Theory: an Overview, in: British Accounting Review, 18 (2), p. 4–41.

Whittington, G. (1987): Positive Accounting: A Review Article, in: Accounting & Business Research, 17 (68), p. 327–336.

Whittington, G. (2005): The adoption of International Accounting Standards in the European Union, in: European Accounting Review, 14 (1), p. 127–153.

Wiggins, B. C. (2000): Detecting and Dealing with Outliers in Univariate and Multivariate Contexts, Paper presented at the Annual Meeting of the Mid-South Educational Research Association, Bowling Green.

Williams, E. J. (1959): The Comparison of Regression Variables, in: Journal of the Royal Statistical Society, 21 (2), p. 396–399.

Williamson, D. (2002): Forward from a Critique of Hofstede's Model of National Culture, in: Human Relations, 55 (11), p. 1373–1395.

Wilmshurst, T. D./Frost, G. R. (2000): Corporate environmental reporting: A test of legitimacy theory, in: Accounting, Auditing & Accountability Journal, 13 (1), p. 10–26.

Wolberg, J. (2006): Data analysis using the method of least squares – Extracting the most information from experiments, Berlin.

Wolf, J. (2005): Organisation, Management, Unternehmensführung : Theorien und Kritik, Wiesbaden.

Wollnik, M. (1977): Die explorative Verwendung systematischen Erfahrungswissens – Plädoyer für einen aufgeklärten Empirismus in der Betriebswirtschaftslehre, in: Köhler, R. (ed.): Empirische und handlungstheoretische Forschungskonzeptionen in der Betriebswirtschaftslehre. Bericht über die Tagung in Aachen, März 1976, Stuttgart (1977), p. 37–64.

Wolz, M./Oldewurtel, C. (2011): Einfache und kostengünstige Rechnungslegung durch Übernahme internationaler Konzepte im Rahmen des BilMoG?, in: KoR, 12 (1), p. 41–48.

Woodward, J. (1958): Management and Technology, London.

Woodward, J. (1965): Industrial Organization: Theory and Practice, Oxford.

Wooldridge, J. M. (2009): Introductory econometrics – A modern approach, Mason, Ohio.

World Databank (2010): World Development Indicators (WDI) & Global Development Finance (GDF), available at: http://databank.worldbank.org, last revised 01.03.2011.

World Federation of Exchanges [WFE] (2009): Annual report and statistics 2008, available at: http://www.world-exchanges.org, last revised 01.03.2011.

Wulf, I. (2008): Bilanzierung immaterieller Vermögenswerte nach IFRS - Ansatz, Bewertung, Goodwill Bilanzierung, Berlin.

Wüstemann, J./Kierzek, S. (2006): Das europäische Harmonisierungsprogramm zur Rechnungslegung: Endorsement und Enforcement von IFRS, in: Betriebs-Berater, 61 (Special 4), p. 14–22.

Xiao, J. (2004): Political Influence and Coexistence of a Uniform Accounting System and Accounting Standards: Recent Developments in China, in: Abacus, 40 (2), p. 193–218.

Yeh, R. (1989): On Hofstede's Treatment of Chinese and Japanese Values, in: Asia Pacific Journal of Management, 6 (1), p. 149–160.

Yeh, R.-S./Lawrence, J. J. (1995): Individualism and confucian dynamism: a note on Hofstede's cultural root to economic growth, in: Journal of International Business Studies, 26 (3), p. 655–669.

Yin, R. K. (2009): Case Study Research, Thousand Oaks, Calif.

Zarzeski, M. T. (1996): Spontaneous harmonization effects of culture and market forces on accounting disclosure practices, in: Accounting Horizons, 10 (1), p. 18–37.

Zeff, S. A. (2003): U.S. GAAP Confronts the IASB: Roles of the SEC and the European Commission, in: North Carolina Journal of International Law and Commercial Regulation, 28 (4), p. 879–892.

Zeghal, D./Ahmed, S. A. (1990): Comparison of Social Responsibility Information Disclosure Media Used by Canadian Firms, in: Accounting, Auditing & Accountability Journal, 3 (1), p. 38–53.

Zeimes, M./Kühne, M. (2004): Die neue Bilanzierung von Übernahmen, in: Frankfurter Allgemeine Zeitung (April 5), p. 20.

Zellner, A. (1975): Bayesian Analysis of Regression Error Terms, in: Journal of the American Statistical Association, 70 (349), p. 138–144.

Zenthöfer, W./Leben, G. (2010): Körperschaftsteuer, Gewerbesteuer, Stuttgart.

Zhang, J. (2008): The contracting benefits of accounting conservatism to lenders and borrowers, in: Journal of Accounting and Economics, 45 (1), p. 27–54.

Zhang, X.-J. (2000): Conservative accounting and equity valuation, in: Journal of Accounting and Economics, 29 (1), p. 125–149.

Zimmermann, J. (2003): Das deutsche Enforcement-Modell des Bilanzkontrollgesetzes: Ausgestaltung und Implikationen für Rechnungslegung und Abschlussprüfung, in: StuB, 7 (8), p. 353–360.

Zmijewski, M. E./Hagerman, R. L. (1981): An income strategy approach to the positive theory of accounting standard setting/choice, in: Journal of Accounting and Economics, 3 (2), p. 129–149.

Zülch, H. (2005a): Das deutsche Enforcement-Modell des Bilanzkontrollgesetzes: Ausgestaltung und Implikationen für Rechnungslegung und Abschlussprüfung, in: StuB, 7 (1), p. 1–9.

Zülch, H. (2005b): Die Deutsche Prüfstelle für Rechnungslegung DPR e.V.: Organisation und Prüfverfahren, in: StuB, 7 (13), p. 565–570.

Zülch, H./Burghardt, S. (2007): Die deutsche Prüfstelle für Rechnungslegung DPR e.V.: Bestandsaufnahme nach knapp zwei Jahren Tätigkeit, in: StuB, 9 (10), p. 369–375.

Zülch, H./Burghardt, S. (2008): Akzeptanz der IFRS am amerikanischen Kapitalmarkt, in: PiR, 4 (3), p. 98–99.

Zünd, A. (1992): Controlling und Revision der internationalen Unternehmenstätigkeit, in: Kumar, B. (ed.): Handbuch der internationalen Unternehmenstätigkeit, München (1992), p. 913–930.

Zwirner, C. (2010): Kapitalmarktorientierung im Jahr 2010, in: Zeitschrift für kapitalmarktorientierte Rechnungslegung, 10 (11), p. 529–531.

Zysman, J. (1983): Governments, markets, and growth: financial systems and the politics of industrial change, Ithaca, NY.

Münsteraner Schriften zur Internationalen Unternehmensrechnung

Herausgegeben von Peter Kajüter

Band 1 Daniela Barth: Prognoseberichterstattung. Praxis, Determinanten und Kapitalmarktwirkungen bei deutschen börsennotierten Unternehmen. 2009.

Band 2 Tobias Dickmann: Controllingintegration nach M&A-Transaktionen. Eine empirische Analyse. 2010.

Band 3 Simon Esser: Produktorientiertes Kostenmanagement in der chemischen Industrie. Eine empirische Analyse. 2011.

Band 4 Christian Reisloh: Influence of National Culture on IFRS Practice. An Empirical Study in France, Germany and the United Kingdom. 2011.

www.peterlang.de

Stefan Veith

The EU Emission Trading Scheme

Aspects of Statehood, Regulation and Accounting

Frankfurt am Main, Berlin, Bern, Bruxelles, New York, Oxford, Wien, 2010.
XX, 203 pp., num. tab. and graph.
European University Studies. Series 5: Economics and Management. Vol. 3363
ISBN 978-3-631-60315-4 · pb. € 45,80*

The emission trading scheme is the most recent instrument of the EU environmental policy. Its underlying mechanisms and economic consequences are yet less straightforward than policymakers initially had expected: As this study shows, the regulation probably yields unintended distributional effects and imposes additional risk on the regulated companies. Consequently, meaningful accounting for emission rights is not only a necessity for regulators and customers, who need transparency, but also for investors on capital markets, who bear the additional regulatory risk. This study empirically assesses the usefulness of various accounting alternatives and provides evidence that cost and fair value approaches dominate the widely used mixed models.

Content: Transformation of Environmental and Energy Policies in the EU · Mapping Emission Rights to Financial Accounting and Performance Reporting · Pricing Effects of Emission Right Returns · Interacting Economic Effects of Energy and Allowance Markets · Relative Usefulness of Accounting Treatments for Emission Rights